THE UNIVERSITY OF CHICAGO
ORIENTAL INSTITUTE PUBLICATIONS
VOLUME XC

THE UNIVERSITY OF CHICAGO
ORIENTAL INSTITUTE PUBLICATIONS
VOLUME XC

PTOLEMAIS
CITY OF THE LIBYAN PENTAPOLIS

BY CARL H. KRAELING

WITH CONTRIBUTIONS BY D. M. BRINKERHOFF, R. G. GOODCHILD,

J. E. KNUDSTAD, L. MOWRY, AND G. R. H. WRIGHT

THE UNIVERSITY OF CHICAGO PRESS · CHICAGO · ILLINOIS

Library of Congress Catalog Card Number: 62–9742

THE UNIVERSITY OF CHICAGO PRESS, CHICAGO 37

The University of Toronto Press, Toronto 5, Canada

All rights reserved by The University of Chicago. Published 1962
Composed and printed by J.J.AUGUSTIN, Glückstadt, Germany

PREFACE

THE Oriental Institute excavations in the Province of Cyrenaica that forms part of the modern Kingdom of Libya were the result of a combination of factors. One factor was my personal desire to explore a site which would contribute to our knowledge of the urban development of the eastern Mediterranean in Hellenistic and Roman times and where field work could be undertaken during the brief part of the year when I could absent myself from Chicago without neglecting my administrative responsibilities as Director of the Institute. This desire responded to my earlier association with the excavation of Gerasa in Transjordan and of Dura-Europos on the middle Euphrates and to my intention not to let administrative duties throttle completely my devotion to research. Another factor was a letter of August 25, 1952, from the Honorable Henry S. Villard to his former Harvard roommate and classmate, Mr. Hermon Dunlap Smith of Chicago, inquiring whether the University of Chicago might care to avail itself of opportunities for archeological work just opening up in the newly created Kingdom of Libya, where he was then serving as U. S. Minister and to which he was subsequently accredited as the first U. S. Ambassador. To take advantage of such an opportunity offered the possibility of providing gainful employment to a local labor force and thus of assisting, however modestly, in the economic advancement of a new state and a free people.

The letter from Mr. Villard was duly brought to my attention by Mr. Smith as a Trustee of the University of Chicago and a member of the Visiting Committee of the Oriental Institute. In the spring of 1953 I was able, in connection with the discharge of regular duties elsewhere in the Orient, to make a brief survey of the antiquities sites of Cyrenaica and Tripolitania, which Mr. Villard and the members of his staff graciously facilitated with all the means at their disposal. The result of my visit was an application to the Department of Antiquities of Cyrenaica for permission to make a sounding at the site of Ptolemais, a city founded by the Greek kings of Egypt, the remains of which lie buried beside and under the modern village of Tolmeita on the shore of the Mediterranean some 100 kilometers east of Benghazi and where Italian archeologists had done important work during the years 1935–42. The purpose of our sounding, made during the period May 19–June 7, 1954, with Mr. Naim Makhouly of the Department of Antiquities in charge, was to test the potentialities of the site, the available labor supply, and the living conditions. When the test proved successful, I applied for permission to undertake three seasons of work of not less than three months each, these covering, as it developed, the spring of 1956, 1957, and 1958 respectively.

During all four periods of residence and work at Ptolemais I had as my associate Dr. Charles F. Nims, of the Oriental Institute's Epigraphic Survey staff at Luxor, Egypt, who also compiled the bulk of the excellent photographic record of the site and of our excavations. For the three major campaigns of 1956, 1957, and 1958 I was fortunately able to obtain as field architect Mr. G. R. H. Wright, formerly connected with the British School at Ankara. In each of these three years we had also a field assistant, in 1956 Professor Lucetta Mowry of Wellesley College, in 1957 Miss Joan Farwell of Chicago, and in 1958 Mr. James Knudstad, newly appointed junior field architect of the Oriental Institute. Mrs. Kraeling, Mrs. Nims, and Mrs. Wright performed important services for the expedition, assisting with photography and recording as required and administering the whole complicated business of communications, transport, provisioning, and housekeeping. Masaud Bil'id, chief of the Department of Antiquities guards at the site, acted as foreman of the labor force throughout. Dr. Richard Goodchild, Comtroller of Antiquities for Cyrenaica, always a welcome visitor, came frequently to inspect and further our efforts.

v

The Oriental Institute expedition to Ptolemais excavated three buildings, a villa of the Roman period, a public building with attached bath and dwelling on the Street of the Monuments, and the City Bath of the Byzantine period. The third chapter of this report gives a full account of these structures, and the fourth chapter presents a systematic treatment of the finds made in the course of the excavations. But, since my purpose was to make a contribution to the knowledge of the urban development of the eastern Mediterranean, we extended our interest to the exploration of the site as a whole. The results of this study are embodied in the descriptive second chapter of this report and in the sketch of the history of Ptolemais, so far as it is known to date, that forms the first chapter. My effort to make the general description as complete as possible by incorporating information and some few drawings published in widely scattered contexts by our Italian predecessors at the site is done in grateful recognition of their efforts to record and conserve the monuments and with the thought of making their contribution more immediately accessible.

When we began our work in Libya, Cyrenaica was still recovering from the ravages of World War II and the bureaus of the federal and provincial governments were just establishing themselves. Yet, in the midst of their preoccupation with much more important matters, the representatives of the Libyan Government and of the foreign governments accredited to Libya gave unsparing attention to our needs and full assistance to the achievement of our objectives. Our warmest thanks are due to His Excellency the Nazir of Education of Cyrenaica, to his efficient representative, Mr. G. Kajian, in the office of the Nazirate, and to Dr. Richard Goodchild, the Comtroller of Antiquities. And we should not fail to record our gratitude to Dr. Aneizi, Director of the Libyan National Bank, and to the Chief Accountant of the Provincial Government of Cyrenaica, whose staff disbursed the wage payments made to our laborers. The kindness we received extended from the administrative headquarters at Benghazi to the postmaster at el-Merj, who handled our mail and telegrams, and the *mudir* of Tolmeita, the *shawish* of the local constabulary, the "medico" of the local dispensary, and the members of our staff of workmen. To all of them we are sincerely grateful.

Among the representatives of foreign governments we are grateful to the diplomatic and consular officials of the U. S. Government under Ambassador Villard and his successors Ambassadors Tappin and Jones. On the British side it is pleasant to record here our thanks to Sir Alec Kirkbride, an old-time aquaintance from Jordan, and to Ambassador Graham. Above all we are indebted, for very practical reasons, to Sir Arthur Dean, General Manager of the Libyan Public Development and Stabilization Agency, who supplied our transport needs and provided a Diesel engine for the Decauville railway at the site, and to his helpful representative at Benghazi, Mr. J. Higgins.

On the scholarly side it is only proper that we should first thank our Italian predecessors, especially Professor Giacomo Caputo, for permission to reproduce from their publications the drawings that appear here as Figures 2, 8, 15, 21, 22, 26, 39, and 40. Next it seems proper to mention those who contributed to this report. Among them we have Richard Goodchild, who gave us his account of the excavation of the "Odeon" undertaken by the Department of Antiquities, supplied the plan and section made by his assistant Abdulhamid Abdussaid, and, in commenting on such parts of this text as could be sent to him before his departure for Kenya, gave us the benefit of his accurate and thorough knowledge of the monuments and history of Cyrenaica. We should also mention Margareta Bieber, who interrupted her own work to give us a first analysis of the sculptures of Ptolemais, and Dericksen M. Brinkerhoff, who produced the sculpture inventory in its fully developed form and contributed also the essay on the significance of the material. To these names should be added those of Lucetta Mowry, who worked with me as Research Associate during the summer of 1959 on the preparation of this report and gave special attention to the study of the mosaics, and G. R. H. Wright and James E. Knudstad, who supplemented their work at the drafting table with written accounts of particular structures and a general consideration of architectural form in the buildings excavated. Colleagues and friends at many institutions, whose names do not appear in the Table of Contents, were always available for consultation and assistance. Among them I mention gratefully Dr. Watson Boyes of the Oriental Institute and Professors A. R. Bellinger and T. V. Buttrey, Jr., of Yale, who helped me with matters numismatic, Professors C. B. Welles of Yale, A. D. Nock of Harvard, and

Miss Joyce Reynolds of Oxford, who gave me their advice on certain inscriptions and the history of the city, and Professors K. Weitzmann of Princeton, G. H. Forsyth, Jr., of Ann Arbor, F. E. Brown of Yale, and J. B. Ward Perkins of the British School at Rome. Mrs. Elizabeth Hauser, Editorial Secretary of the Oriental Institute, who edits all Institute manuscripts with scholarly care and sees them through the press, also belongs in this context. Mrs. Emily Chandler, of the Administrative Offices of the Institute, turned my complicated manuscript into an intelligible typescript.

In this connection I would wish to express my thanks also to Mrs. Claire Swift-Marwitz, patroness of the University of Chicago, member of the Oriental Institute, and personal friend, for a gift to the Institute which, with her consent, was used to help defray the cost of this publication.

The passage of half a century of time and the added strength that frequent sojourns in foreign lands give to the sense of solidarity with one's own countrymen make it seem appropriate to dedicate this volume to the memory of the first American archeological expedition to Cyrenaica (1910–11), of whose members Herbert Fletcher De Cou lies buried at Cyrene, the victim of a disaffected tribesman's bullet.

Carl H. Kraeling

Chicago

*On the termination
of my Directorship
of the Oriental Institute*

June 30, 1960

TABLE OF CONTENTS

LIST OF ILLUSTRATIONS

PLATES

xi

PLANS

TEXT FIGURES

LIST OF ABBREVIATIONS

ADAI	Deutsches archäologisches Institut. Archäologischer Anzeiger. Beiblatt zum Jahrbuch (Berlin, 1889——).
AJA	American journal of archaeology (Baltimore etc., 1885——).
Barth, *Wanderungen*	Barth, Heinrich. Wanderungen durch die Küstenländer des mittelländischen Meeres in den Jahren 1845–47. I. Wanderungen durch das punische und kyrenäische Küstenland (Berlin 1849).
BCH	Bulletin de correspondance hellénique (Paris, 1877——).
Beechey, *Proceedings*	Beechey, Captain F. W., and Beechey, H. W. Proceedings of the expedition to explore the northern coast of Africa, from Tripoly eastward, in MDCCCXXI and MDCCCXXII (London, 1828).
BMC, *Cyrenaica*	British Museum. Catalogue of the Greek coins of Cyrenaica, by E. S. G. Robinson (London, 1927).
Brunn-Bruckmann's *Denkmäler*	Brunn, Heinrich von, *et al.* Denkmäler griechischer und römischer Sculpturen (München, 1888–1947).
BSRAA	Société royale d'archéologie d'Alexandrie. Bulletin (Alexandrie, 1898——).
CAH	Cambridge ancient history (Cambridge, 1923–39).
Caputo, "Protezione"	Caputo, Giacomo. La protezione dei monumenti de Tolemaide negli anni 1935–1942. Quaderni di archeologia della Libia III (1954) 33–66.
CC	Catalogue général des antiquités égyptiennes du Musée du Caire (Le Caire etc., 1901——).
CIG	Boeckh, August (ed.). Corpus inscriptionum Graecarum (4 vols.; Berolini, 1828–77).
EA	Arndt, Paul, *et al.* Photographische Einzelaufnahmen antiker Sculpturen ... mit Text (München, 1893——).
IGRR	Inscriptiones Graecae ad res Romanas pertinentes auctoritate et impensis inscriptionum litterarum humaniorum collectae et editae (Paris, 1901–27).
ILN	The illustrated London news (London, 1842——).
JDAI	Deutsches archäologisches Institut. Jahrbuch (Berlin, 1887——). Ergänzungshefte (Berlin, 1888——).
JHS	The journal of Hellenic studies (London, 1880——).
JRS	Journal of Roman studies (London, 1911——).
MAMA	Monumenta Asiae Minoris antiqua (London, 1928–56).
MDAIA	Deutsches archäologisches Institut. Athenische Abteilung. Mitteilungen (Athen etc., 1876——).
MDAIR	Deutsches archäologisches Institut. Römische Abteilung. Mitteilungen (Roma, 1886——). Ergänzungshefte (München, 1931——).
MP	Académie des inscriptions et belles-lettres. Commission de la Fondation Piot. Monuments et mémoires (Paris, 1894——).
OLZ	Orientalistische Literaturzeitung (Berlin, 1898–1908; Leipzig, 1909—).

PBSR	British School at Rome. Papers (London, 1902———).
QDAP	The Quarterly of the Department of Antiquities in Palestine (Jerusalem, 1931–50)
RAL	Accademia nazionale dei Lincei. Classe di scienze morali, storichi e filologiche. Rendiconti. Serie ottava (Roma, 1946———).
R.-E.	Paulys Real-Encyclopädie der classischen Altertumswissenschaft . . . hrsg. von G. Wissowa (Stuttgart, 1894———).
REG	Revue des études grecques (Paris, 1881———).
Sammlung Ernst von Sieglin	Sieglin, Ernst von (ed.). Die griechisch-ägyptische Sammlung Ernst von Sieglin (Expedition Ernst von Sieglin. Ausgrabungen in Alexandria II). I. Malerei und Plastik. Teil A, bearbeitet von Rudolf Pagenstecher † (Leipzig, 1923). Teil B, bearbeitet von Carl Watzinger (Leipzig, 1927). III. Die Gefäße in Stein und Ton, Knochenschnitzereien, von Rudolf Pagenstecher (Leipzig, 1913).
SEG	Hondius, J. J. E. (ed.). Supplementum epigraphicum Graecum (Lugduni Batavorum, 1923———).
TAPA	American Philological Association. Transactions (Hartford, Philadelphia, etc., 1869/70———).

THE HISTORY OF THE CITY

Iᴛ is still much too early to write a well balanced and comprehensive history of the Ptolemais with which this volume deals. The literary evidence is meager and needs to be supplemented by a thorough knowledge of the archeological remains, most of which lie buried beneath the surface of fields regularly subject to cultivation. Yet, in a report on the Oriental Institute's excavations at the site, accompanied as they were by a study of the city plan, of the standing monuments, and of the earlier work of the Italian archeologists, some attempt should be made to sketch that history in preliminary fashion, if only to suggest proper contexts for the several items of information now available.

In order properly to organize this information it is useful to have some knowledge of the physical geography of the site and the region, for the nature of the land mass was clearly one of the factors in the colonial development of the area by the Greeks and in a sense of the success of that development. More important, however, is a knowledge of the history of the other cities of the Libyan Pentapolis, because Ptolemais was in fact a refoundation of the earlier inland city of Barca, which in turn was a schismatic offshoot of Cyrene, and because the fortunes of the Cyrenaican cities were linked closely together.

Scholarly discussions of the history of Cyrene and Cyrenaica are by no means plentiful. A. H. M. Jones and R. G. Goodchild have each given accurate if brief accounts of the entire subject, but for the Greek period as it is known from the literary references the work of Thrige is still the best compendium of information, while for the Roman period we now have the careful and detailed study of Romanelli in which, as in the work of Goodchild, the available archeological evidence is put to use.[1] Those wishing to study the archeological evidence at second hand have still to fall back upon widely scattered reports and monographs, but most of the epigraphic material is fortunately quite readily accessible, as is also the information provided by the coins.[2] Without the full use of this material it would be impossible to attempt to reconstruct the hitherto unexplored history of Ptolemais, and, indeed, there is no guarantee that in a first attempt the special subject can be seen in its proper perspective, with the major emphases correctly distributed.

GENERAL BACKGROUND

What attracted the Greek colonists to Cyrenaica in the first half of the seventh century B.C. and made possible its subsequent urban development is a combination of factors, including ultimately the physical geography of the region. Here for a distance of some 270 kilometers, between the Gulf of Sirte on the west and the Gulf of Bomba on the east, the otherwise relatively flat coast of North Africa is interrupted by a mountainous region known today as the Jebel Akhdar, the "Green Mountain" (see Fig. 1 for sketch map).[3]

[1] See A. H. M. Jones, *Cities of the Eastern Roman Provinces* (1937); R. G. Goodchild, *Cyrene and Apollonia: An Historical Guide* (London, 1959); J. P. Thrige, *Res Cyrenensium* (1828; re-issued by S. Ferri, Rome, 1940); P. Romanelli, *La Cirenaica romana (96 a. C. – 642 d. C.)* (Verbania, 1943).

[2] For the inscriptions see G. Oliverio, *Documenti antichi dell'Africa italiana* I 1 (1932), I 2 (1933), II 1 (1933), and II 2 (1938); the material is now incorporated in *SEG* IX (1944). For the coins see BMC, *Cyrenaica*.

[3] An accurate historical map is now available in Goodchild, *Tabula Imperii Romani: Cyrene* (Oxford, 1954).

The jebel develops in a series of escarpments, which in early geological times may have been three in number but which, since the last interglacial period with its heavy precipitation, have been reduced to two and have at the same time been cleft by deeply worn systems of wadies.[4] The jebel is set back behind a coastal plain along its western half, but its eastern half rises directly from the Mediterranean. The coastal plain, some 50 kilometers deep at the extreme western end of the jebel in the Sirtic region and some 25 kilometers deep behind Euesperides-Berenice (modern Benghazi), narrows progressively eastward.[5] It is reduced to a depth of some 6 kilometers at the site of ancient Tauchira-Arsinoë (modern Tocra) and is finally pinched out completely some 15 kilometers east of Ptolemais (modern Tolmeita). Seen from the coastal plain, the first escarpment of the jebel has the appearance of a line of hills, owing to the erosion that has carved successive wadies in its northern face. Actually it forms a solid terrace that extends inland for a maximum of about 40 kilometers and whose height is between 250 and 300 meters above sea level. The second escarpment, beginning at the west in the latitude of Euesperides and thus considerably shorter than the first, moves continually northward in its easterly course, coming ever closer to the edge of the first escarpment, so that in the vicinity of ancient Cyrene (modern Shahat) the two escarpments are only a kilometer or so apart. The highest point of the second escarpment is slightly more than 800 meters above sea level. Of the cities of the ancient Pentapolis, Apollonia-Sozusa (modern Marsa Suza), Ptolemais, Tauchira, and Euesperides are located in the coastal plain, while Barca (modern el-Merj) is on the first step of the jebel and Cyrene on the second.

What makes the physical geography suitable for the colonial development of the region is its effect upon the weather. It is not so much that the altitude of the inland plateau provides an escape from the heat of the typical North African summer but rather that the jebel, by its very existence,

causes the cool damp northeast winds from the Mediterranean to deposit here their moisture. The rains, falling between November and February (see p. 68, n. 71), have encouraged the growth of vegetation, which, through the millenniums, has created a soil that is often highly productive. Extending inland from the coast for a distance of some 40 kilometers, the zone of maximum precipitation has a typically Mediterranean character so far as its flora are concerned. Tall conifers still grow naturally in some of its deeper wadies, and extensive sections are entirely wooded, albeit with high shrubs and small trees. Behind this zone of genuine agricultural potential lies a zone of approximately equal depth that has sufficient ground water for occasional good wells and sufficient precipitation for occasional dry farming and excellent grazing. Sloping generally southward, the Libyan plateau ends on a line close to the 29th parallel of latitude in an escarpment at the foot of which lies a series of oases that offer the possibility of inland communication between the Nile Valley and the Sirtic region.[6]

Having such natural advantages the Cyrenaican region was indeed suitable for exploitation by colonists from the Greek city-states, and the colony established at Cyrene by Thera was, like its later dependencies and rivals, soon producing a notable prosperity for its citizens from both agriculture and animal husbandry.

The insistence of the Delphic Oracle upon the foundation of Cyrene, as told by Herodotus, the eloquence of Pindar's references to Libya and to the wealth of its royal house, the victories won by its representatives in chariot races and athletic contests in Greece, together with the imposing ruins of Cyrene itself, reflect the reputation and the prosperity which the earliest Greek settlements attained in capitalizing upon the productive capacity of the country.[7] They provide at the same

---

[4] On the geological history of the region see now S.B.M. McBurney and R. W. Hey, *Prehistory and Pleistocene Geology in Cyrenaican Libya* (1955).

[5] In the present volume the spellings of ancient place names follow those of Goodchild in *Tabula Imperii Romani: Cyrene*, even though in accordance with the most ancient tradition "Barce" would be preferable to "Barca" and "Teuchira" or "Teucheira" to "Tauchira."

[6] See the important passage in Herodotus iv. 181–85 and its recent discussion by Rhys Carpenter, "A trans-Saharan caravan route in Herodotus," *AJA* LX (1956) 231–42. It may be noted that Pliny *Natural History* v. 5 also divides Cyrenaica into three horizontal belts—one fertile and wooded, one good for agriculture only, and one in which only *lasari* (silphium) grows.

[7] The standard epithets μηλοτρόφος and πολύμηλος applied to Cyrenaica appear for the first time in the words of the Delphic Oracle as rendered by Herodotus iv. 155 and by Pindar *Pythian Ode* 9.6 respectively. Pindar *Pythian Odes* 4–5 celebrate victories in chariot races by

time an impression of the augury under which ambitious foundations such as that of Ptolemais were undertaken in the centuries that followed. But, if we are to understand not only the bright but also the tragic aspects of Ptolemais' history, we need to introduce a corrective element into the vision of hope and splendor with which that history probably began. This element is to be found in the problem of the relations with the native population that the Greek efforts to colonize and exploit the region necessarily raised.

What has been said above about the physical geography of Cyrenaica and the productive capacity of the several zones into which it divides itself from north to south implies that for a native population optimum conditions prevail when it has free access to and use of the coastal plain, the two escarpments of the Jebel Akhdar, and the arid interior. These conditions prevailed in the second millennium B.C. when the Libyan tribes

provided a mighty threat to Egypt.[8] The country was able to absorb without difficulty a single colonial settlement such as that at Cyrene in the first phase of its history. But, when mass immigration from the Peloponnese and the Greek islands followed and more colonies and cities were established, difficulties with the native population were bound to develop. The cities absorbed for their own use the zone of maximum economic potential, forcing the natives back upon the semi-arid grazing lands and the arid interior. For all its high promise and early achievement, the colonial development of Cyrenaica in the Greek and Roman periods was therefore fraught with the growing danger of conflict with the native population. For Ptolemais this danger was as much a part of the initial augury of its foundation as for any other city of the Pentapolis. The only difference is that we happen to have for Ptolemais a more vivid account of the agony of the inevitable conflict.[9]

THE EARLIEST SETTLEMENT AT THE SITE OF PTOLEMAIS

The spot in the coastal plain later occupied by Ptolemais was apparently settled first by people from Barca, a city some 25 kilometers to the south on the first escarpment of the Jebel Akhdar, founded in the middle of the sixth century B.C. by a schismatic element of the population of Cyrene. The involved early history of Barca need not concern us here.[10] It is important to note, however,

that Barca soon flourished in spite of tensions between it and Cyrene, that, having friendly relations with the natives, it soon developed a territory of its own, known as Barcaia, with dependent settlements such as Tauchira in the coastal plain to the northwest, and that it engaged in the silphium traffic alongside Cyrene.[11] For its various products, including no doubt grain from

---

the king of Cyrene. Panathenaic amphorae of which the latest is dated 321/320 B.C. have been found in Cyrenaica, three at Tauchira and ten at Euesperides. See E. Breccia, *Iscrizioni greche e latine* ("Catalogue général des antiquités égyptiennes du Musée d'Alexandrie, Nos. 1–568" [Le Caire, 1911]) pp. xviii–xx.

[8] The period is that of Seti I, Merneptah, and Ramses III, whose wars against the Libyans are recounted in their inscriptions; see e.g. W. F. Edgerton and J. A. Wilson, *Historical Records of Ramses III: The Texts in Medinet Habu Volumes I and II* ("Studies in Ancient Oriental Civilization," No. 12 [Chicago, 1936]). See also O. Bates, *The Eastern Libyans* (1914) pp. 210–28. The fact that Libya has no tells, and indeed no Bronze Age urban settlements, indicates that the economy was that of a population moving freely between the several zones of the region.

[9] The analogy between the difficulties encountered by the Greek colonists in antiquity and those encountered by the Italians during the years 1911–32 is interesting. On the Italo-Senussi war see E. E. Evans-Pritchard, *The Sanusi of Cyrenaica* (1949). The analogy is further developed in my article "Now and then in Libya,"

Journal of the American Oriental Society LXXX (1960) 104–11.

[10] For this history, derived largely from Herodotus iv. 160.–67 and 200–205, see W. Tomaschek in *R.-E., s.v.* "Barke," and P. Smith in the *Dictionary of Greek and Roman Geography* (1856).

[11] Herodotus was the first to use the term "Barcaia." The *Periplus* of pseudo-Scylax indicates that at the end of the fourth century the territory extended as far as Euesperides (see C. Mueller, *Geographi Graeci Minores* [1882] pp. 83–84). Ptolemy (*Geography* iv. 4. 6) applies the term "Barcitae" to the nonurban people of the region eastward of Euesperides. When Tauchira is first mentioned, it is spoken of as a "city of Barcaia" (Herodotus iv. 171). It is much more logical to assume that Tauchira was settled by the people of Barca to exploit the resources of the coastal plain than to follow the scholiast to Pindar (*Pythian Ode* 4. 26) and make it a foundation of Cyrene. Having no harbor, Tauchira was not easily accessible from Cyrene. Trade in silphium as a factor in Barca's economy is reflected in the fact that when the coinage of the city begins (*ca.* 525 B.C.) the silphium plant is represented on the issues (see BMC, *Cyrenaica*, p. clxvi).

the fertile Barca plain, the inland city needed an export outlet. Along its entire coast line the Barcaian territory offered natural facilities for the creation of such an outlet at only one point, namely at the site where Ptolemais was subsequently built, a site equally accessible from Barca and Tauchira. It is likely therefore that the site of Ptolemais was occupied and developed as soon as Barca entered upon its commercial enterprise, that is, as early as the last quarter of the sixth century B.C., when also the Barcan coinage began.

What the settlement at the site of Ptolemais was like in those early days we have at present no way of knowing. It consisted, no doubt, of a small company of people who loaded and unloaded such vessels as put in there and who contributed to their own support by farming the relatively fertile stretch of the coastal plain in the immediate vicinity. In all probability the harbor facilities were quite primitive and the installations for the storage of goods in transit little more than a heterogeneous collection of roomlike shelters owned by the Barcan producers and shippers. Someone representing the Barcan royal house and controlling the incoming and outgoing shipments may have been in residence as the head of the port. Throughout all this earliest period of its history, however, the settlement at the site of Ptolemais remained nameless, for this is how we find it at the end of the fourth century B.C.

How the changing fortunes of Barca in the fifth and fourth centuries B.C. affected the life of the coastal settlement we cannot know. What Herodotus tells about the siege of Barca by the Persians and about the exile of its people sounds more ominous than perhaps it actually was. The city,

including its defenses, seems to have remained intact and much of the population may have been spared also. The real change was that the anti-Battid elements of the population were removed and that a pro-Battid faction was placed in a position of authority through Pheretime, the mother of the murdered Arcesilaus III.[12] The result of all this, therefore, was not that the commercial enterprise of Barca came to a halt but that more of the income from it now accrued to the ruling house of Cyrene. Indeed this seems to be implied by Pindar when, in describing the opulence of Arcesilaus IV, he calls him "king of mighty cities" (*Pythian Ode* 5. 15). As to what happened to Barca when the Battid dynasty came to an end at Cyrene with Arcesilaus IV, we are ill informed. The Cyrenaican "alliance coins" from the latter half of the fifth century suggest not only that Barca returned to independence but also that it exercised a certain degree of leadership among the Greek cities of the region.[13] At the end of the fourth century, when pseudo-Scylax divides Cyrenaica into two regions, that of the Cyrenaioi and that of the Barcaioi, the settlement at the site of Ptolemais may have been regarded as the harbor of the second most important city of the entire area. Even at this time, however, it still lacked a name, for pseudo-Scylax merely refers to it as the "harbor at Barca," quite as he speaks of the settlement at the site of later Apollonia merely as the "harbor of Cyrene."[14] Even though the coastal settlement at the site may thus have grown materially after the sixth century, the founding of Ptolemais belongs to the Hellenistic period and must be understood in connection with the developments of that period.

THE FOUNDING OF THE CITY

The period that began with Alexander the Great and that saw Greek civilization enter upon its world mission wrought great changes in the political, social, economic, and cultural life of the ancient world generally and therefore obviously also in the circumstances and distribution of its urban establishments. The sources place a good deal of emphasis upon the colonialism of the period, and, however much the picture they give us may need to be revised so far as the identity of the founders and the purposes of the new foundations

are concerned, the fact remains that for vast areas of the ancient world the period marks the beginning

[12] See in general Jones, *Cities of the Eastern Roman Provinces*, pp. 353–54.

[13] On the "alliance coins" see BMC, *Cyrenaica*, pp. xliv–xlvi. The important fact is that on certain of the joint issues the name of Barca precedes that of Cyrene. Further indications of Barca's regained independence can be found in the statements of late authors such as Polyaenus *Strategika* vii. 28 (ed. E. Wölfflin [1887] pp. 340–41) that Barca adopted a democratic form of government at this time.

[14] See *Periplus* (Mueller, *op. cit.* p. 84).

of a new phase in its urbanization and its settlement patterns.[15] Less well known are details concerning the status of the cities, old and new, and their relations to the new monarchies that grew from the empire of Alexander. While the "liberation of the cities" and the preservation of the "freedom of the Greeks" were widely proclaimed and avowed by the rival dynasts and while apparently no definitive formula regulating the position of the cities in the new kingdoms was ever developed, it is also true that the cities ceased henceforth to be, each in its own sphere, prime movers in the major political developments of the period. A new comprehensive setting had been created into which the cities were absorbed or with which they had to come to terms by aligning themselves with one or another of the dynasties that had divided the world among them. Even so it is to be noted that on the economic side, in spite of heavy levies imposed upon them by the warring Diadochoi, many of the cities were in the early Hellenistic period raised to unexpected, if temporary, heights of prosperity as new markets were opened and new resources became available for exploitation.[16]

Against this general background it seems only natural that in the Hellenistic period new cities should have been founded in Cyrenaica. Equally natural are two further propositions. The first is that any city founded in Cyrenaica would be Ptolemaic in origin, for it was to the Ptolemies that the region between Egypt and the Gulf of Sirte fell in 322/321 B.C.[17] The second is that any city founded in Cyrenaica would in all probability be established on the seacoast, where harbor facilities were available, rather than inland, for the new order of things required new emporia that would help tie together the several parts of the vast commercial empire that the Greek rulers of Egypt were developing in the eastern Mediterranean.[18] How the new order of things affected conditions in Cyrenaica is reflected in the growing importance of the "harbor of Cyrene," the later Apollonia, which now began to mint coins and which was at the same time the base for overseas operations such as those of Thibron against Cyrene.[19]

As for the coastal settlement at the site of Ptolemais, which pseudo-Scylax knew as the "harbor at Barca," it is not mentioned in the events of the late fourth century recorded by Diodorus and Arrian. That it was unaffected by those events is quite unlikely, the only question being how to understand the changes by which it became the city of Ptolemais. Attention is sometimes called in this connection to the fact that both Pliny (*Natural History* v. 5) and Strabo (*Geography* xvii. 3. 20) speak of Ptolemais as having formerly been called Barca, from which it could be inferred that the inland city was transferred to the seacoast and re-established as a "New Barca."[20] The Oriental Institute expedition's study of the plan and the defenses of Ptolemais (see p. 38–41 and 51–60) has revealed in both a degree of excellence and ambitiousness that suggests a royal foundation, and if Ptolemais was a royal foundation then certainly it was one that from the outset had a dynastic name. Whether new settlers were brought in from the outside by the founder is unknown. In the new order of things the older inland city was absorbed into the new, perhaps by the application of the typical procedure of the *synoikismos*, becoming henceforth a deme of the

[15] On Hellenistic colonialism see M. I. Rostovtzeff, *The Social & Economic History of the Hellenistic World* (1941) I 130–58. As to the founders and the purposes of the foundations, see especially V. Tscherikower, "Die hellenistischen Städtegründungen von Alexander dem Großen bis auf die Römerzeit," *Philologus* Supplementband XIX 1 (1927), and A. H. M. Jones, *The Greek City* (1940) pp. 1–26.

[16] On the political status of the cities in the new kingdoms see A. Heuss, *Stadt und Herrscher des Hellenismus in ihren staats- und völkerrechtlichen Beziehungen* (*Klio* Beiheft XXXIX [1937]); E. Bikermann, *Institutions des Séleucides* (1938); V. Ehrenberg, *Der Staat der Griechen* II (1958) 44–55 and review by C. B. Welles in *Classical Philology* LV (1960) 136–40. For the economic circumstances of the cities see Rostovtzeff, *op. cit.* pp. 153–56, 158–87.

[17] The date is implied in Diodorus' account (*History* xviii. 21. 9) of the Thibron episode. On the earlier boundaries of Cyrenaica see Jones, *Cities of the Eastern Roman Provinces*, p. 486, n. 14; for the later period see

P. Romanelli, "Il confine orientale della provincia romana di Cirene," *Pontificia accademia romana di archeologia, Rendiconti*, Ser. III, XVI (1940) 215–23.

[18] On the commercial and economic empire of the Ptolemies see Rostovtzeff in *CAH* VII (1928) 130–36.

[19] On the new mint at Apollonia, whose issues use the crab as a symbol, see BMC, *Cyrenaica*, pp. cxv, cxcviii–cxcix. The story of how the adventurer Thibron tried, by interfering in a party conflict in Cyrene, to possess himself of Cyrenaica before it became part of the Ptolemaic sphere of influence is recounted in full by Diodorus xviii. 19–21.

[20] See e.g. Thrige, *op. cit.* pp. 138–39.

younger city.[21] Citizens of Barca with the proper property qualifications naturally became citizens of Ptolemais in the process, and, while the older inland settlement continued to exist, its name disappeared.

The question arises as to which of the early Ptolemies may have been the founder of the new city in Cyrenaica that bore his name. The fact that Ptolemy I Soter gave a new constitution to Cyrene is irrelevant because it does not involve a new foundation.[22] Most of the period of Ophellas' administration of the region for Ptolemy I is an unlikely context because Ptolemy did not style himself "king" until 305 B.C. and would scarely have founded a city with a dynastic name until after that date. Hence during the reign of Ptolemy I only the early years of Magas' administration of the area deserve consideration and even these scarcely recommend themselves, for Soter was not noted as the founder of many cities, at least not outside Egypt. Precedence has undoubtedly to be given to Ptolemy II Philadelphus (283–246 B.C.) and Ptolemy III Euergetes I (246–221 B.C.).[23] A case can be made for Ptolemy II from an inscription found at Ptolemais in which the city honors an Arsinoë who seems to have been Arsinoë II and who died in 270/269 B.C.[24] But the argument is not absolutely cogent, for "the city" mentioned in the inscription could have been Barca honoring the queen by a dedication erected at its "harbor" precisely because it would most readily be seen there by officials and merchants coming from Egypt. Moreover, due allowance must be made for Magas' "revolt" early in the reign of Ptolemy II, for the creation of the pentapolitan league that seems to represent a period after the death of Magas in which the cities were relatively independent, and for the re-establishment of Ptolemaic suzerainty over the region in the years that followed.[25] The optimum date for the founding of Ptolemais would therefore appear to be the beginning of the reign of Ptolemy III, when by his marriage to Berenice II, the daughter of Magas, Cyrenaica was reunited with Egypt and an occasion for conferring special favors upon the land of her birth was thus provided.[26] A necessary corollary of this conclusion would be that Ptolemais after its foundation replaced the charter member Barca in the league of the Pentapolis.[27]

THE HELLENISTIC PERIOD (322–96 B.C.)

In the Hellenistic period the cities and settlements of Cyrenaica came into the orbit of and under some form of control from Ptolemaic Egypt. The several changes in the nature of the relationship to Egypt suggest a subdivision of the period into three parts, even though at the present state of

[21] On the *synoikismos* as an instrument of dynastic policy in the Hellenistic period see W. W. Tarn and M. I. Rostovtzeff in *CAH* VII 81, 180 and Heuss, *op. cit.* pp. 99–103.

[22] For the text of the new constitution see *SEG* IX 1–4, No. 1. Its date is in dispute, but most scholars prefer a date in the reign of Ptolemy I (so e.g. F. Heichelheim, "Zum Verfassungsdiagramma von Kyrene," *Klio* XXI [1927] 175–82). Jones, *Cities of the Eastern Roman Provinces*, p. 359, however, associates it with the period of Ptolemy III.

[23] On the second and third Ptolemies as founders of cities see J. Beloch, *Griechische Geschichte* IV 1 (1925) pp. 260–62, 283–84, and Hans Volkmann in *R.-E.*, *s.v.* "Ptolemaios."

[24] For the text, its reconstruction, and its probable date see Oliverio, *Documenti antichi* I 1, pp. 68–69, No. 3, and *SEG* IX 70, No. 357.

[25] The whole complicated history of the period so far as it concerns Cyrenaica is variously reconstructed from the scattered sources by the several interpreters. See Thrige, *op. cit.* pp. 223–31; BMC, *Cyrenaica*, pp. xvi–xvii; E. Bevan, *A History of Egypt under the Ptolemaic Dynasty* (1927) pp. 373–75; Jones, *Cities of the Eastern Roman Provinces*, pp. 358–59; Tarn in *CAH* VII 704, 712–13; Geyer in *R.-E.*, *s.v.* "Magas"; Volkmann in *R.-E.*, *s.v.* "Ptolemaios."

[26] See Justin *History* xxvi. 3 and Volkmann in *R.-E.*, *s.v.* "Ptolemaios." The favors were presumably not limited to Ptolemais but included also the refounding of Euesperides as Berenice and the application of the name Arsinoë to Tauchira in honor of the mother of Ptolemy III. See also BMC, *Cyrenaica*, p. xvi.

[27] The creation of the league, about which little else is known, is reflected in the coinage of Cyrenaica in the κοινόν issues, some of which are overstruck on pieces of Magas (see BMC, *Cyrenaica*, pp. cxxxiv–cxxxvii). The first literary reference to the Libyan Pentapolis is in Pliny *Natural History* v. 5, where the cities making up the league are Berenice, Arsinoë, Ptolemais, Apollonia, and Cyrene.

our knowledge it is not clear what those changes may have involved. During the first part of the period, that is, from 322 to 258/257 or 251/250 B.C., while Ptolemais was still the "harbor at Barca," Cyrenaica was administered for the kings of Egypt by a resident governor, first Ophellas and then Magas, who was apparently relatively autonomous in his sphere or at least used his relative independence to exercise more than the constitutional rights of the strategos set forth in the *diagramma* of Cyrene.[28] In the second part of the period, from 247/246 to 162 B.C., that is, after the "revolt" of Magas and beginning with the acts of benevolence of Ptolemy III that included the foundation of Ptolemais, the entire region was firmly and directly integrated in the Ptolemaic kingdom and administered presumably by an extension of the bureaucratic machine that functioned so effectively in Egypt proper and that found it possible to keep in continuous adjustment to each other royal prerogatives and civic laws.[29] During the third part of the period, from 162 to 96 B.C., Cyrenaica was, save for an interlude of 30 years, something of an independent kingdom ruled by a resident monarch who was by descent a member of the Ptolemaic family, first Ptolemy "the younger," the brother of Ptolemy VI Philometor, and later Ptolemy Apion, the illegitimate son of Ptolemy "the younger"[30].

How Ptolemais fared during the Hellenistic period is a question to which, at the present state of our knowledge, it is difficult to formulate an adequate answer. The literary sources are silent with respect to it, the epigraphic material is as yet meager, and excavation can scarcely be said to have done more than give an inkling of its structures. Archeologically speaking, a fuller knowledge of the city's harbor installations (see pp. 48–51) and of its agora (see p. 116) would do most to remedy the situation, for it was clearly in these two areas that the early life of the city had its foci. Yet some inferences about Hellenistic Ptolemais

can be drawn, partly from a general knowledge of the period and partly from the scanty archeological evidence for this and the succeeding phases of its history.

That Ptolemais was organized as a typical Greek city is obvious. As ἡ πόλις it honored Ptolemy VI Philometor with a statue.[31] Acts of its βουλή were recorded as late at the Antonine period,[32] and the existence of στρατηγοί and ἐφήβαρχοι can be documented for even later times (see p. 210, Inscription 5). The precise nature of its constitution is unknown, but the probability is that it paralleled that of Cyrene as modified in the *diagramma* mentioned above.[33] This means that citizenship was limited and had a property qualification but could also be conferred by the soveriegn, presumably in connection with property grants. It means also that certain controls were exercised over the city's actions by magistrates appointed by and responsible to the monarch. No doubt the amount of control varied during the Hellenistic period, but it is not evident when it may have been strictest. Clearly the crown administered carefully the region as a whole, claiming as γῆ βασιλική what it had not granted to the cities as γῆ πολιτική. A specific example of a well developed piece of royal property in the immediate vicinity of Ptolemais will concern us below.

As a member of the league of the Pentapolis Ptolemais had certain constitutional and administrative features in common with the other cities of the region and can be assumed to have granted reciprocity of rights and privileges to citizens of those cities, while being protected from and exposed to encroachments of monarchic authority equally with them.[34]

So far as the economic, social, and cultural aspects of the life of Hellenistic Ptolemais are concerned, we are again dependent largely upon inference. That, so long as Egypt's overseas empire held together and its commercial enterprise dominated the scene in the eastern Mediterranean, the

[28] On the Ptolemaic constitution see n. 22.

[29] On the administration of Ptolemaic Egypt and its outlying "provinces" see Rostovtzeff in *CAH* VII, chap. iv.

[30] On the circumstances that led to the creation of the separate Ptolemaic kingdom of Cyrenaica see W. Otto, *Zur Geschichte der Zeit des 6. Ptolemäers* (Bayerische Akademie der Wissenschaften, philosophisch-historische Abteilung, "Abhandlungen," Neue Folge XI [1934]). In the interval between the two rulers Cyrenaica probably returned to its earlier status as a "province" of Egypt.

[31] Oliverio, *Documenti antichi* I 1, pp. 42–45, No. 2, and *SEG* IX 70, No. 358.

[32] See *SEG* IX 72, No. 368.

[33] For discussion of its provisions see Rostovtzeff in *CAH* VII 127 and Jones, *The Greek City*, pp. 104, 159.

[34] On the function of such leagues as devices for the standardization of administrative procedure in the relations between "free" cities and monarchies see Rostovtzeff, *Social & Economic History of the Hellenistic World* I 154.

enterprise and the population of the new foundation grew is implied in the ambitiousness and actual development of its city plan. The one thing we can know about the population is that it included the property-owners of the Barca plain who chose to participate actively in the administration of the city and to avail themselves of its economic advantages. These were the κτηματικοί, to use the language of Diodorus in his description of Cyrene. As at Apollonia, in Diodorus' account (*History* xviii. 19. 5, 20. 2) of the Thibron episode, the population included also, as the next most important element, the merchants (ἔμποροι), who handled the traffic in goods, whether for export or import. In this group there may well have been resident representatives of firms that operated out of important Mediterranean commercial centers such as Rhodes.[35] To these elements we must add the greatly increased number of native workers employed in the transport of goods, in warehousing, and in the loading and unloading of cargo as well as various types of transients—sailors, sea captains, and mercantile passengers traveling from port to port. A special and highly important, if numerically small, group was constituted by the representatives of the Egyptian government. This must have included a small military guard and its chief officer, the representative of the king in the civil administration (perhaps a στρατηγός), the chief Egyptian fiscal and tax official (perhaps an οἰκονόμος), and such assistants as played a part in the administration of the royal estates.

In the case of Cyrene a good deal can be inferred about the city's cultural life from its relations with Athens, which during the fourth century brought philosophy and learning to flower on the Libyan plateau and in the third century supplied Alexandria with Cyrenaican scholars, scientists, and men of letters. Something can also be known from the Egyptian papyri about Cyrenaicans who, having served in the Ptolemaic armies, were eventually settled in Egypt, particularly in the Fayyum.[36] That Ptolemais played a role similar to that of Cyrene in such matters cannot be demonstrated and is inherently quite unlikely, partly

because Cyrene's contribution to Egyptian life and culture belongs to the early Hellenistic period and largely because Ptolemais was and probably remained primarily a mercantile city, one of the many that served to keep produce and manufactured goods moving, but not one that was ever distinguished as a cultural center or a military base.

What Ptolemais could and did supply to world trade was what Cyrenaica as a whole had to offer. The range was not wide, but the quantity was on occasion amazing.[37] Ptolemais had the grain and fruits of the adjacent coastal region and those of the rich Barca plain to distribute. It had good access, if not better than did Cyrene, to the silphium-bearing region and was surrounded by areas usable for grazing and for the production of olive oil and honey. In addition it had accessible in the deep wadies of the Jebel Akhdar supplies of timber and of wood such as acacia, which Egypt was buying as far away as Syria.

As to monuments and materials of the Hellenistic period found at Ptolemais, the range of evidence is still meager but now somewhat broader than it was at an earlier stage in the study of the site. The oldest pieces are a funerary stele with a metrical inscription recording the unfortunate lot of a woman of Euesperides who died there so far from her home,[38] the dedication to Arsinoë II (see p. 6), and the dedication to Ptolemy VI (see p. 7).[39] The dedication to Arsinoë II was in all probability intenoed to demonstrate that Barca participated in the cult of the queen that was instituted in

[35] On firms with overseas representatives in other ports and on Rhodes as the intermediary for Mediterranean trade see *ibid.* pp. 226–28.

[36] See especially F. Heichelheim, *Die auswärtige Bevölkerung im Ptolemäerreich* (*Klio* Beiheft XVIII [1925]) pp. 43–46, 93–94.

[37] The best indication of the productive potential of Cyrenaica is its shipment of 800,000 medimni of grain to the Greek cities during the famine of the years 330–326 B.C. (see Oliverio, *Documenti antichi* II 1, pp. 7–94; *SEG* IX 4–5, No. 2). On the products of Cyrenaica generally see Rostovtzeff, *Social & Economic History of the Hellenistic World* I 333 and III 1398.

[38] The funerary stele of Arata, wife of Kallikrates (see Oliverio, *Documenti antichi* II 2, pp. 257–58, No. 537, and *SEG* IX 71, No. 362), was taken to el-Merj after World War II for safe-keeping and is reported by Oliverio as being in the museum there, but it has since been returned to the museum at Tolmeita. The text is assigned by the editor of *SEG* to the fourth century B.C. on paleographical grounds, which are, however, still insecure in Cyrenaica (see below p. 208). It is obvious that whatever forced the couple from Euesperides to reside at the "harbor at Barca," it was from their point of view a sorry fate to which to be consigned.

[39] Both dedicatory inscriptions were reused in the construction of the Square of the Cisterns in Roman times (see p. 70).

270 B.C. and that became a state cult after Arsinoë's death in the next year.[40] That eventually there was erected at Ptolemais an altar or even a temple for the cult of the Egyptian ruler is to be expected.[41] With the period of the foundation of Ptolemais we can now confidently associate its city plan (see pp. 38–41) and its girdle of fortifications (see pp. 51–62). The much mutilated remains of a small temple which was cleared by the Department of Antiquities in 1955 (see p. 90) can also be attributed to the Hellenistic period. Since it is difficult to visualize a Hellenistic city without a theater, inclusion of the Upper Theater (Building 28 on Plan XXII) among the buildings of the earliest period may deserve consideration. But so little remains of the structure (see pp. 93–94) that the hypothesis cannot be verified. The only other edifice among those known at present that gives promise of belonging to the Hellenistic period is Building 26, which may have been the main shrine of the Hellenistic city (see p. 116).

Some mention must be made in this connection of three Egyptian sculptures discovered in the "Palazzo delle Colonne," the best known and probably the most elaborate of the private houses at Ptolemais.[42] These are a granite statuette of Amenmose son of Pendjarti, a green basalt statuette of Harpocrates, king's general and scribe, and the base of a green basalt statuette of the general Ps..., probably Psammetichus.[43] From a study of the first two and from his reading of their hieroglyphic inscriptions Alan Rowe[44] has inferred that there was an Egyptian colony at the site of

Ptolemais "probably in the time of Ptolemy III (or II), but perhaps even earlier," and that a military garrison was stationed there, commanded by Harpocrates, who erected there a temple dedicated to Osiris and also repaired an earlier temple sacred to the same god. The name of the colony was Ḥut-Isert, meaning "House of the Tamarisk Grove," a name appropriate to the importance which the cult of Osiris had there. The three statuettes were studied by G. Botti[45] with quite different results and have been re-examined by Charles Nims of the Oriental Institute staff. Nims is inclined to agree with E. Otto, who reviewed Rowe's article, that the statuette of Harpocrates is Saite in date, and he believes that the statuette of Psammetichus is probably Saite also. He points out further that evidence long since collected by Sayyid Labib Habachi, formerly chief inspector of the Egyptian Department of Antiquities at Luxor, shows that Amenmose son of Pendjarti belonged to the period of Ramses II and was buried at Thebes.[46] All that the sculptures can tell us about Ptolemais is, therefore, that they were brought from Egypt, presumably in the Hellenistic period, by someone who may have been devoted to the cult of Osiris. As such they are not unimportant, for they attest the presence in the city of persons, especially officials, from Egypt and confirm what is said below (pp. 177–80) about the survival there of the Egyptianizing tradition in the sculptures of the later periods.

Outside the city to the west there exists one further monument which it is reasonable to associate with the Hellenistic period of Ptolemais. This is the massive Tower Tomb that forms a landmark for all visitors to the site (see pp. 113–15). Apparently as much a commemorative as a funerary structure, it is of such scope and pretensions compared with other tombs in Cyrenaica as

[40] In the text as reconstructed by Oliverio she is styled Βασίλισσα Ἀρσινόη Θεὰ Φιλάδελφος ἡ Πτολεμαίου καὶ βερενίκης Θεῶν Σωτήρων. On the importance of the cult of Arsinoë II see Bevan, *History of Egypt under the Ptolemaic Dynasty*, pp. 129–30, and W. Otto, *Priester und Tempel im hellenistischen Ägypten* II (1908) 274.

[41] The discovery by the Oriental Institute expedition of a life-size statue identified as that of Cleopatra I (see pp. 188–90) is not without relevance to this probability. The Director of Antiquities of Cyrenaica, Dr. R. G. Goodchild, indicates the discovery of a second statue of a Ptolemaic queen in 1960.

[42] Published by Gennaro Pesce under the title *Il "Palazzo delle Colonne" in Tolemaide di Cirenaica* ("Monografie di archeologia libica" II [Roma, 1950]), it has become a *Musterbeispiel* of domestic architecture in the "Alexandrine" manner. See also pp. 85–87 below.

[43] *Ibid.* Figs. 77–78, 85–87, and 79–81 respectively.

[44] "A history of ancient Cyrenaica," *Supplément aux Annales du Service des antiquités de l'Egypte* XII (1948) esp. pp. 13, 62–76.

[45] See Pesce, *op. cit.* pp. 70–75.

[46] For Otto's review see *Bibliotheca orientalis* VIII (1951) 28–29. Three other statuettes of the Amenmose in question are known to exist, of which the one at Cairo connects him with the period of Ramses II. It seems quite unnecessary in the present context to discuss the different interpretations of the hieroglyphic inscriptions or to belabor the point that the Turah limestone said to have been used in the temple that Amenmose built is an Egyptian limestone. Rowe's interpretation is not made more acceptable by its use in M. Stracmans, "A propos de deux étendards ptolémaïques," *La nouvelle Clio* V (1953) 163–71.

to require some special *raison d'être*. That any merchant prince of the period to which the tower can belong architecturally would have had the same inclination to monumentalize his family tomb as those who later built the tower tombs at Palmyra and Dura-Europos may well be doubted. Otherwise we might expect to find remains of similar structures elsewhere in Cyrenaica. As for governors and other officials, beginning with the Roman period they would certainly not have expected to have their remains interred so far from home. In all probability we are, therefore, thrown back upon the period and the roster of the resident dynasts such as Magas became and such as Ptolemy "the brother" and Ptolemy Apion were.

To associate the monument with someone like Ptolemy "the brother" might seem to be yielding to fanciful local tradition were it not for one additional consideration. This is the fact that the area immediately outside and to the west of Ptolemais was part of the *ager regius* which the Romans inherited from Ptolemy "the brother" upon the death of Ptolemy Apion. A stele testifies to the recapture of the property by the Romans in the period of Vespasian (see p. 113). How large this section of the royal estates may have been is not known. If, as the inscription says, it was a *hortus*, it is reasonable to assume that it included the spring some 3 kilometers west of the city (see p. 68), though it may, of course, also have included more of the fertile coastal plain and some part of the forested ridges of the Jebel Akhdar.[47] During the period between its administration by the agents of the king and its recapture under Vespasian the property is known to have been exploited by other parties, in part apparently by a great quarrying operation that left the tower standing on an isolated cube of the native rock. In its original setting the tower stood on the crest of an unbroken ridge in the coastal plain, looking out over the sea, and thus very appropriately in

a "garden."[48] In any case the existence of a portion of the royal estates near Ptolemais may have been of no small importance for the economic life of the city in the Hellenistic period.

No doubt the founding of Ptolemais was attended by high hopes. The location was in most respects excellent; the plan of the city had been developed with care; its defenses were adequate; the markets of the eastern Mediterranean were open so long as the Egyptian fleet "ruled the waves"; the technology and administrative supervision needed to increase local production were available, as was the royal favor that could supply them. In the first century of the city's history some measure of the promise attending its foundation was undoubtedly fulfilled. By the time of Ptolemy VI, however, when the local Cyrenaican dynasty was established, conditions had begun to change radically. Egypt was losing her position as the dominant power of the eastern Mediterranean and was torn by internal dissensions that reduced greatly her economic potential. Delos was replacing Rhodes as the crossroads emporium of the eastern Mediterranean, and Roman *negotiatores* were already in the field supplying the markets of Greece and the Aegean with Roman products.[49] At Cyrene lands that had been under cultivation were abandoned or under threat of forfeit, requiring the issuance of royal decrees to get them back into production.[50] Under the circumstances the fortunes of Ptolemais must be thought to have declined in the late Hellenistic period.

---

[47] It was evidently different in character from the sacred precincts at Cyrene known as the Πτολεμαιεῖον, which Rostovtzeff has discussed (*The Social and Economic History of the Roman Empire* [2d ed.; Oxford, 1957] II 681, n. 64) and which upon recapture may have become a public park.

[48] The interior shows that the structure was intended to serve also as a tomb, but towers serving other purposes are familiar as parts of country estates for instance in Attica (see J. H. Young, "Studies in South Attica," *Hesperia* XXV [1956] 122–46). The fact that the structure bears no inscription might be taken to imply that it had been built for Ptolemy "the brother," who, having ruled Cyrenaica, unexpectedly succeeded to the throne of Egypt upon the death of his brother Ptolemy VI Philometor and died there.

[49] On the Roman merchants see J. Hatzfeld, *Les trafiquants italiens dans l'Orient hellénique* (1919).

[50] For the relevant inscriptions from Cyrene see Oliverio, *Documenti antichi* II 2, pp. 259–65, No. 538, and *SEG* IX 8–9, No. 5. For the history of the period see Rostovtzeff, *Social & Economic History of the Hellenistic World* II 870–914, and for the interpretation of the inscriptions from Cyrene see *ibid.* pp. 914–17.

THE ROMAN PERIOD (96 B.C.–A.D. 395)

When Ptolemy Apion, the second and last of the autonomous Hellenistic kings of Cyrenaica, died in 96 B.C., the country passed into the hands of the Roman people in accordance with his will, a counterpart no doubt of that of his father.[51] As excavation at the site proceeds the Roman period will come to be particularly well known, for it was clearly the most important in the entire life of the city. At present, however, there are many gaps in our knowledge of it, which can be bridged only by inferences based largely upon general observations. All that can be said about the years from 96 to 31 B.C., for instance, is, on the one hand, that they were apparently years of confusion and, on the other hand, that they may have provided unusual opportunities for self-advancement to those who knew how to capitalize upon existing conditions.

When Rome by the action of Ptolemy Apion inherited Cyrenaica it still had many vicissitudes to pass through before the *Pax Augusta* could dawn. By the bitter experience of the Social War it had still to clarify its understanding of who, in return for services rendered, had a right to be included in the Roman People. It had subsequently, through the Mithridatic Wars, to work out the implications of its intervention in Greece and of the earlier benefaction that made it the heir of Attalus III. It had finally to pass through the period of the Civil War and the struggle among the Triumvirs. There was little opportunity, therefore, for it to concern itself with the strategically unimportant part of the Mediterranean world that was Cyrenaica. Still conservatively inclined as regards the multiplication of provinces, the Senate apparently responded to the situation created by Ptolemy Apion's death in guarded fashion. It accepted the γῆ Βασιλική and declared the cities with their γῆ πολιτική to be free, thus giving over to them the administration of local and regional affairs.[52] The action had the effect of relieving the cities and the

producers of monopoly goods from the φόροι that had been payable to the crown, but it left them and the league of the Pentapolis with a host of administrative problems with which they were not prepared nor organized to cope. The result was an anarchy of which we catch only occasional glimpses. One is contained in the story about a certain Aretaphila who enlisted the aid of a Libyan tribal chief Anabus to rid Cyrene of the tyrannical son of a tyrant Nikocrates.[53] Another is provided by the report that Lucullus, chancing to visit Cyrene while searching for ships to help Sulla, found the city in confusion due to successive tyrannies and wars.[54] The fact that, according to Plutarch, he was entreated on this occasion to draft laws for the people may reflect the embarrassment as to administrative procedure in which the cities found themselves and out of which the internal strife may have arisen. Similarly, the fact that Lucullus in his search for transport went first to Cyrenaica may indicate that he had reason to expect to find idle bottoms there and that export trade was still languishing.[55]

Conditions did not necessarily improve materially after 74 B.C., when Cyrenaica was recognized as a province, nor after 67 B.C., when it may for the first time have been joined with Crete for administrative purposes.[56] To be sure, the presence of the governors meant that a person in authority was available to regulate the affairs of the cities, but their efforts were not always successful and with them the process of tax collecting was

---

[51] For the text of his father's will, displayed at Cyrene, see Oliverio, *op. cit.* Vol. I 1, pp. 11–84, No. 1, and *SEG* IX 10–11, No. 7. The Romans were named beneficiaries on a contingent basis, namely in case the king died without issue.

[52] See especially Livy *Epitomes* 70. For the history of Cyrenaica in the Roman and Byzantine periods it is possible to make use of the excellent work of Romanelli, *La Cirenaica romana*, pp. 39–65.

[53] Plutarch *Moralia*: *On the Bravery of Women* 19 (dated in Mithridatic times).

[54] Plutarch *Lucullus* 2. 3–4.

[55] His search apparently had good results, though we are told that he lost most of the ships he had hired in Cyrenaica before they reached Alexandria because of an attack by pirates (*Lucullus* 2. 5).

[56] The earliest governors had the competence and rank merely of quaestors. Only after 27 B.C., when Cyrenaica was made a senatorial province, did it have a regular *legatus pro praetore*. For the establishment and administration of the province of Cyrenaica see J. Marquardt, *Römische Staatsverwaltung* I (2d ed.; Leipzig, 1881) 457–64. On the reluctance of the republican Senate to increase the number of the provinces see *CAH* IX (1932) 437–43. Romanelli, *La Cirenaica romana*, pp. 47–65, gives the names of the earliest among the Roman governors of Cyrenaica and discusses the question of the early union of Crete and Cyrenaica.

resumed, which was certainly not particularly welcome. One matter that clearly must have provoked discord was the attempt of the governors to recapture for the Roman people the alienated royal estates. Particulars are lacking, but we do hear from Cicero that the attempt was abandoned.[57] Another source of continued confusion was that in the struggle among the Triumvirs the basic arrangement for the administration of the province was modified and finally set aside, first by the assignment of Cyrenaica to Cassius in 44 B.C. and next by the action of Antony, who, having come into control of Cyrenaica, eventually declared it the private estate of his daughter Cleopatra Selene, thereby intending no doubt to restore the conditions existing in the days of Ptolemy "the brother" and Ptolemy Apion. No less disturbing was the appearance of Roman troops in the area, whose billeting and supply must have imposed severe burdens upon the cities, first in the period after Pompey's death, when Cato the Younger assembled there the remnants of Pompey's following, and again in the years before Actium, when Antony stationed four legions there to offset the threat of a flanking movement against him from provincial Africa.

Yet in the midst of all this upheaval the foundations for a new, more stable era were being laid and new opportunities were developing for escape from the stagnation into which the affairs of the region had fallen toward the end of the Hellenistic period. Important presuppositions of the change were Pompey's campaigns in the eastern Mediterranean and the Roman occupation of Crete, which finally put an end to the threat of piracy. From this time on the sea was again open to shipping for the regular export of goods. In addition, the provisioning and transport of the large forces which the Civil War deployed eastward must have provided unusual opportunities for gain to those who had produce to sell and ships for hire.

So far as Ptolemais itself is concerned, the evidence for its involvement in these developments is still meager but not for that reason uninstructive. One interesting fact revealed by the epigraphic material is the presence there of persons bearing the *nomen gentile* of the Julii and the Antonii.[58]

The same types of names occur elsewhere in Cyrenaica, at Cyrene and Tauchira, and for that matter also in other eastern provinces of the Empire, for instance in Asia.[59] The appearance of these names can, of course, have various connotations, but prime among them certainly are the immigration of freedmen, for whatever purposes, directly from Italy and the award of Roman citizenship to Greek residents of Cyrenaica in connection with economic, administrative, or military services performed there in the pre-Actian and post-Actian periods.[60]

Another interesting fact relating to the history of Ptolemais during the period under discussion has developed from the study of the provincial bronze coinage of Cyrenaica that began with the issues of a certain P. Licinius and continued sporadically until the reign of Tiberius.[61] Among the coins assigned to the period is a single piece struck, it would seem, at Ptolemais itself. It has on the obverse the head of a Tyche wearing a turreted crown with the inscription ΠΤΟΛΕΜΑΙ[Σ] and on the reverse a crocodile with the legend ΚΡΑΣ[ΣΥΣ].[62] The Crassus in question is presumably P. Canidius Crassus, who is known to have been closely associated with Cleopatra. This fact, together with the appearance of the crocodile on the reverse, is taken to imply that the issue represents the period when Cyrenaica was administered by Antony for Cleopatra Selene. The interest in the coin in the present context is by no means limited to the discovery of a late imperial version of the head of the Tyche of Ptolemais (Pl. XXXVII *A* and p. 203, No. 61). It necessarily

---

[57] *Oration on the Agrarian Law* 2. 51.

[58] The persons in question are a Gaius Julius Stephanus and Flavius Antonius, son of Sulla (see Oliverio, *op. cit.* Vol. II 2, pp. 244, No. 486, and 243, No. 482; *SEG* IX 72, No. 369, and 71, No. 361).

[59] Familiar at Cyrene is the Marcus Antonius Caskellius who constructed the rock-cut basin outside the Fountain of Apollo. Among the names inscribed on the curtain walls of Tauchira the Julii are particularly numerous. Presumably members of the local Roman garrison, the Flavius Julius, Sestius Julius, G. Julius Pakulius, G. Julius Secundus, and G. Julius Maker who appear there belong to the period between 22 and 11 B.C. See Oliverio, *op. cit.* Vol. II 2, pp. 183–88, Nos. 225–26, 235, 248–49; *SEG* IX 81–82, Nos. 487–88, 497, 508–9.

[60] On the interpretation of the significance of Antonii in Asia at this time see Rostovtzeff, *Social & Economic History of the Hellenistic World* II 1007.

[61] See in general BMC, *Cyrenaica*, pp. ccii–ccxxviii, and Romanelli, *La Cirenaica romana*, pp. 55–58.

[62] The coin, which is in Vienna and was first published by Svoronos, is reproduced in BMC, *Cyrenaica*, Pl. XLII 10, and discussed on pp. ccxxi–ccxxii; see also Romanelli, *op. cit.* p. 57.

extends to the implications that the small change in circulation needed to be replaced or increased, that a mint was set up at Ptolemais to help supply it, and that someone in the city had the benefit of the gain that moneyers supplying bronze coins enjoyed in particular measure.

If the first sixty years of Roman rule saw Cyrenaica moving slowly but surely out of the dead water into which it had drifted in the late Hellenistic period and through a maze of confusing cross currents, the next century and a half, from Augustus through Trajan, saw it being carried along swiftly on the high tide of Roman imperial prosperity. Symbolic of the turn of affairs was the adoption of the Actian era for reckoning time. The region was now firmly joined with Crete as a single Senatorial province administered by a proconsul, accredited as the highest representative of the Roman government. The stabilization of Roman political life, the establishment of a strong centralized internal administration with adequate checks and controls, the development and maintenance of a standing army distributed among the provinces, the promotion of urbanization as a matter of imperial policy, the enlargement of the Italian market for overseas goods, the availability of Roman capital seeking investment, the movement to the provinces of retired veterans, members of the mercantile class, and freedmen representing the estates and enterprises of the emperor and the Roman aristocracy—this combination of factors provided the solid basis for the improvement of conditions in the provinces, for the increase there of both production and industry, and for the rise of a local freeborn middle class.[63]

That the period was not without its difficulties for the cities of Cyrenaica is to be expected. Two problems which confronted them at the outset are matters of record. The first was an uprising of the native tribes that must have had its hearth in the oases along the southern and eastern frontiers of the province. It was quelled by P. Sulpicius Quirinius in what is known as the Marmaritic War during the very first years of our era and may have constituted a threat largely in the east, where its termination was celebrated at Cyrene.[64] The second,

more pervasive, problem was presented by the tendency of the citizens of the Greek cities to feel that they were now on an unequal footing with the residents of Cyrenaica who had or had acquired Roman citizenship. They found themselves discriminated against in the administration of justice in civil and criminal cases, in the settlement of disputes over impounded assets, and in the refusal of Roman citizens to bear with them the burdens of local taxation. It can be taken for granted that Roman entrepreneurs and immigrants resident in Cyrenaica came there largely to exploit the country and tended to take advantage of its "provincials" whenever possible by clubbing together, by using the Roman administrative officials to their advantage, and by claiming exemptions for themselves and thus provided at least a partial justification for the local complaints. But these were given speedy consideration at Rome and adjudicated by Augustus in a series of edicts of which copies were on public display at Cyrene and no doubt elsewhere.[65] The edicts restored to the citizens of the Greek cities equal representation at law, gave them the right of appeal to the Senate in cases of impounded assets, and required Roman residents to pay local taxes.

Ultimately involved in the questions at issue was the disposition of the royal estates of Ptolemy Apion, of which one parcel was, as we have seen (p. 10), located in the immediate vicinity of Ptolemais. Much of the property had long since been taken over by the cities or their citizens, with or without the connivance of Roman administrative officials, and was either claimed by them as their own or being used for public or private gain. Thus either Ptolemais itself or some enterprising dealer in building materials was in early imperial times developing the area around the Tower Tomb as a great quarry (see p. 115). Efforts made in the days of Cicero to reassert title and to sell the lands to those using them, or to others, had naturally failed. Roman fiscal officials of the early imperial period in working over the property registers and the tax lists must repeatedly have found themselves

---

[63] On the period in general see Rostovtzeff, *Social and Economic History of the Roman Empire* (2d ed.) I 37–105.

[64] See in general Romanelli, *op. cit.* pp. 76–80; for the pertinent inscription at Cyrene see Oliverio, *op. cit.* Vol. II 1, pp. 100–102, No. 67, and *SEG* IX 29, No. 63.

[65] For the text of the edicts see Oliverio in *Notiziario archeologico* IV (1927) 13–67 and *SEG* IX 11–16, No. 8. For discussion see especially J. Stroux and L. Wenger, *Die Augustus-Inschrift auf dem Marktplatz von Kyrene* (Bayerische Akademie der Wissenschaften, philosophisch-philologische und historische Klasse, "Abhandlungen" XXXIV, No. 2 [1928]). Romanelli, *op. cit.* pp. 80–87, has a brief discussion and a full bibliography.

challenging rights of possession and usufruct. Finally, in the days of Claudius the praetor L. Acilius Strabo was sent to Cyrenaica to investigate and to adjudicate the whole matter. There followed a period of bitter wrangling which extended into the reigns of Nero and Vespasian and which involved executive orders to proceed with the sequestration, protests to the Senate by the people of Cyrenaica, senatorial investigations of previous actions, requests to the administrative branches of the government for information and final executive decisions, the implications of which are not always clear.[66] A parcel near Qasr Taurguni was recaptured in the days of Nero, and parcels at Cyrene and Ptolemais were recaptured in the early years of Vespasian.[67] The holdings must have been extensive and their recapture might have affected adversely the local economy, but the entire episode was handled in accordance with the right of appeal to the Senate guaranteed by the edicts of Augustus and, coming in a period of relatively high prosperity, it apparently had no long-term ill effects.[68]

The participation of Ptolemais in the prosperity of the early Roman Empire is reflected by its structural development during this period. In part the new building enterprises may well have represented a public works program undertaken with the use of government funds, but in part it was civic and individual. One element of the public works program was the improvement and building of roads, including a new highway leading westward from Cyrene (see p. 34). Begun in the reign of Claudius with repairs to the stretch from Cyrene to Balagrae, it was eventually extended across the Wadi Quf, leading via Cenopolis and Callis directly to Ptolemais, which it may have entered via the old stone bridge that is still preserved across the Wadi Zawana. The fact that in the days of Trajan connections between coastal and inland cities, such as that between Apollonia and Cyrene,

were receiving attention might indicate that at some time the old track connecting Ptolemais with the Barca plain was also improved. At Cyrene the program included the rebuilding of the walls of the Acropolis, an undertaking completed by Q. Lucianus Proculus in the reign of Augustus. We have no knowledge at present of any similar undertaking at Ptolemais, but it is notable that at both Ptolemais and Tauchira inscriptions recording the names of soldiers who guarded the walls and gates began to appear in the very first years of the Actian era.[69] The regular manning of the walls, notable in itself, may well have been associated with repairs to the defenses, already over two centuries old. At Cyrene, finally, the building program included new care for the system of water supply, more particularly the development of the *Aqua Augusta* by the legate Vestalis, probably in the reign of Augustus.[70] Ptolemais apparently had a counterpart in the Square of the Cisterns (see pp. 62–67), which on structural and architectural grounds is to be assigned to early imperial Roman times.[71]

At Ptolemais, as at Cyrene, the century and a half that began with Augustus must have been marked by new civic building enterprises the cost of which was defrayed either by the municipality or by certain of its wealthier citizens. Among the unexcavated public buildings at the site the Hippodrome (Building 27 on Plan XXII), provided it was not Hellenistic, and the Amphitheater (Building 1) could well belong to this period (see pp. 95–96). Once a public water-supply system was available, the construction of a public bath would not have been long delayed, perhaps on the site and well below the level of the Byzantine

---

[66] The chief problem is to reconcile the statement in Tacitus *Annals* xiv. 18 with the Cyrenaican inscriptions. For discussions, with bibliography, see Oliverio, *Documenti antichi* II 1, pp. 128–33, and Romanelli, *op. cit.* pp. 97–103.

[67] For the texts, in addition to Oliverio, *Documenti antichi* II 1, pp. 128–33, see *SEG* IX 66–67, No. 352, 47, Nos. 165–66, 70–71, Nos. 360–61.

[68] An unpublished inscription of Ptolemais (Romanelli, *op. cit.* p. 102, n. 3) suggests that in the reign of Domitian (A.D. 88–89) a further parcel of land that had once been city property and had been similarly alienated by private individuals was restored to the municipality.

[69] For the rebuilding of the walls of Cyrene see Oliverio, *Documenti antichi* I 2, p. 181, No. 54. For the inscriptions on the curtains of the walls of Tauchira see *ibid.* Vol. II 2, pp. 167–95, Nos. 142–286, and *SEG* IX 76–85, Nos. 419–556; the earliest text belongs to year 2 of the Actian era (i. e., 29 B.C.). For the analogous texts on the Tauchira Gate of Ptolemais see Oliverio, *op. cit.* Vol. II 2, pp. 247–49, Nos. 494–507, and *SEG* IX 73–74, Nos. 378–90; the earliest text here belongs to year 1 of the Actian era.

[70] See Goodchild, *Cyrene and Apollonia*, p. 65. The work at the Fountain of Apollo was done under private local auspices.

[71] A fragmentary Latin inscription referring to the water conduit and control system may, of course, apply to a repair, unless the text was originally bilingual (see Oliverio, *Documenti antichi* II 2, p. 251, No. 508).

City Bath.[72] Fountains or water basins such as are found along the Street of the Monuments (see pp. 79, 81) would presumably have been added as a matter of course. The only public building of the period known from excavation is on the Street of the Monuments on the site of the administrative headquarters of the Byzantine governor Paul (Building 8 on Plan XXII). Of the Roman building, however, little more than a partial ground plan could be recovered (see p. 140 and Fig. 52), and its function was not evident. That the building enterprises of the period were extensive is indicated by the size of the quarries that were developed in the area west of the city (see p. 108).

Private building enterprise also was stimulated at this time at Ptolemais. The area outside the city wall must have seen the addition of many free-standing funerary monuments of the temple and tholos types to those already aligned along the highways leading eastward and westward (see p. 109). Loculus tombs were cut into the sides of older quarries, as indicated by the Tomb of the Kartilioi from the years immediately preceding the beginning of our era (see pp. 113–15). Within the city, we now have two important private dwellings, namely the "Palazzo" excavated by the Italian archeologists and the Villa cleared by the Oriental Institute expedition. Belonging apparently to the century between Caesar and Vespasian these two buildings are of the highest importance for the knowledge of life at Ptolemais in the early imperial period. Their size and elegance reflect the wealth and the high standard of living enjoyed by the citizens of Ptolemais. These people lived surprisingly well and knew how to surround themselves with comforts and amenities comparable to the best that could be found anywhere at the same time. The structures themselves, representing a development of the "peristyle house" of the eastern Mediterranean, reveal not only the continued dominance of the Greek cultural tradition but also the successful solution of the problem of adapting its traditional architectural forms to the mercantilism of the Hellenistic and Roman periods. In the "Palazzo" the needs of the owner as the head of a household and as a man of affairs

were provided for by the addition of a second oecus, whereas in the Villa a self-contained residential apartment was added (see pp. 87–88). Allowing for different degrees of elegance, we see that the two buildings use a vocabulary of architectural form, a "structural" type of wall painting, and a repertory of dominantly geometric mosaic paving and *opus sectile* that represents a *koiné* unaffected by the extravagancies illustrated in contemporaneous Campanian wall decoration. The chief difference between the two dwellings is that between the confined vertical development of the "Palazzo" and the more expansive horizontal deployment of the Villa. In this particular the association of the Villa is with the country estates of Tripolitania and North Africa (see p. 85). That this association or the appearance of a cippus dedicated to the "august gods" reflects a westward reorientation of the city's cultural life the growing sculpture inventory from the site must inevitably call into question. The nonveristic naturalism of the portrait head of an elderly lady (p. 192, No. 3, and Pl. XL) found in the ruins of the Public Building on the Street of the Monuments is perhaps the best example available of the type of work admired locally and the best indication of the provenience of artists commissioned privately for such work.

For the economic and social life of Cyrenaica in general and of Ptolemais in particular the public, civic, and private building enterprises of the early Roman imperial period were undoubtedly of great importance. They required the presence of and gave employment to corps of workers in stone and metal, in plastering, painting, and mosaic, increased the importation of metal, marble, and household equipment, and gave architects and sculptors the opportunity to display their talents. The enterprises necessarily imply the increase in production and export that provided the wealth put to use in them. During the years under consideration the presence of Roman army units in the country, the recruitment of soldiers, and the settlement of discharged veterans must also have begun to affect local conditions. Several units of the Roman army can be known from the adjective *Cyrenaica* in their names to have seen service in the area, but the period and the length of their stay there is for the most part unknown.[73] The only two

---

[72] The importance and size of this building (No. 15 on Plan XXII) precluded investigation below its floors to verify the suggestion that it was set atop a bath of the Roman period (see pp. 174–75).

[73] Such are a *cohors Cyrenaica* stationed in Germany after A.D. 74, the *cohors I Lusitanorum Cyrenaica* stationed in Moesia after A.D. 99, the *cohors II Hispanorum scutata*

units which at this time seem to have played important parts in the life of the province are a detachment of Syrians stationed at Agedabia, near the eastern frontier (probably a part of the *cohors I Apamenorum*), and the *legio III Cyrenaica*, both of which may have served in the Marmaritic War.[74] Their importance lies in the stabilization of the country's southern, eastern, and western frontiers, which in turn formed the basis for the beginning of its development in depth.

As to the soldiers used to man the defenses of the cities, such as Tauchira and Ptolemais, they were probably auxiliary units brought in from other parts of the Mediterranean. Among the soldiers who inscribed their names on the walls of Tauchira there was a Domitius from Oeia, suggesting that the contingent used there came from Tripolitania.[75] The names on the Tauchira Gate at Ptolemais are all Greek, suggesting that its contingent came from the central or eastern Mediterranean. The counterpart of the importation of auxiliary troops into Cyrenaica for the garrisoning of its cities was, of course, the recruitment of soldiers locally for use in other parts of the

Empire. That this was being actively pursued during the period in question is shown by the statement of Tacitus (*Annals* xiv. 18) to the effect that in A.D. 60 a certain Pedius Blaesus was expelled from the Senate for having falsified the military levy in Cyrenaica by venality and favoritism. There exist *tituli militares* from several parts of the Empire mentioning men in military service who are said to be from a Ptolemais, but it is impossible to tell which of the several cities of that name may be in question save in a list from Numidia which includes the names of a good many men recruited from Cyrenaica and Syria.[76] Since in this list soldiers from the Palestinian Ptolemais-Acce, which Claudius raised to the rank of a colony, are properly said to be from Cl(audia) Ptolemais, those designated as coming merely from Ptolemais should be among the soldiers recruited in Cyrenaica and hence from our Ptolemais. As to veterans retired upon the land in Cyrenaica, the epigraphic material is meager. To the one veteran who is known to have retired at Cyrene, his native city, after thirty years of service in the *legio III Adiutrix*, a tombstone at Ptolemais can add a veteran of uncertain and perhaps later date, a certain Q. Aemilius Valens, *veteranus cohortis III ex honesta missione*.[77]

What the productive economy of Cyrenaica and its cities was based on in this period of obvious prosperity is only partly clear. Silphium was a rarity in the area, and the market for it was being supplied from more remote regions.[78] Timber may still have been exported to Egypt but was not needed in the west, and trade in exotic wild animals for the *venationes* and the zoos followed the lines of communication that ran southward from the province of Africa to the equatorial regions.[79]

Cyrenaica, and the *legio III Cyrenaica*. Romanelli, *La Cirenaica romana*, pp. 192–94, has brought together the scattered epigraphic material documenting the presence of individual soldiers of some of these units in Cyrenaica.

[74] For the inscriptions recording the presence of the Syrians at Agedabia see *SEG* IX 100–102, Nos. 775, 776, 778, 782, 794. For the suggestion that they represented an element of the *cohors I Apamenorum* see F. Cumont in *Syria* VIII (1927) 84; in the second century this cohort was stationed in Egypt. For the history of the *legio III Cyrenaica* see W. Kubitschek in *R.-E.*, *s. v.* "legio." The participation of this legion in the Marmaritic War is not documented but should be conjectured as S. Ferri has conjectured the participation of the Syrians of Agedabia (see *Rivista della Tripolitania* II [1925–26] 362–86). In the later years of Augustus and during the reign of Tiberius the legion was stationed in the Thebaid, the best location for a force with competence and experience in desert fighting to control the oases running westward from this area along the 29th parallel. On these oases and their importance for Cyrenaica and for the origin of the disturbance called the Marmaritic War see pp. 2 and 13 above. On the legion in Egypt see P. M. Meyer, *Das Heerwesen der Ptolemäer und Römer in Ägypten* (1900) pp. 158–69. The fact that the legion was later moved to Bosra, to police the arid frontier zone of the newly created province of Arabia, shows that it had had experience in desert warfare.

[75] See Oliverio, *Documenti antichi* II 2, p. 182, No. 216, dated 13 B.C.; *SEG* IX 80, No. 480. But Oliverio's reading is questioned by Miss Joyce Reynolds, who is re-editing the inscriptions of Cyrenaica, as I learn from her directly.

[76] For the list see *Corpus inscriptionum Latinarum* VIII, No. 18084, and R. Cagnat, *L'Armée romaine d'Afrique et l'occupation militaire de l'Afrique sous les Empereurs* (Paris, 1913) I 288–291. The Ptolemaeans of H. Dessau, *Inscriptiones Latinae selectae* (1892–1916) No. 897, who may have been in Italy but were not in military service, are properly styled *Ptolemaici Cyrenenses*; for interpretation of the designation see Rostovtzeff, *Social and Economic History of the Roman Empire* (2d ed.) II 681, n. 64.

[77] So rendered by Oliverio, *Documenti antichi* II 2, p. 257, No. 535.

[78] Pliny *Natural History* xix. 15.

[79] The ostrich, which could be found along the whole of the desert frontier of northern Africa, was still being hunted in and exported from Cyrenaica in Byzantine

Pliny mentions certain flowers, plants, and rare woods the Cyrenaican species of which were deemed particularly desirable and useful,[80] but these scarcely played a large part in the economy. The breeding of horses apparently continued until late times, but strains from other parts of the world were now clearly competing with the local variety in the hippodrome and in the army.[81] It would therefore seem necessary to assume that the basis of Cyrenaican prosperity in the period of the early Roman Empire was its participation in the grain and olive-oil trade, particularly the former. The measure of that prosperity is, on the one hand, the extent to which and the care with which the arable lands were put to use and, on the other hand, the growing dependence of Italy and Greece upon outside supplies, precisely of grain.[82]

The one hundred and fifty years of peace and stability that began for Cyrenaica with Actium were brought to an end in A.D. 115–16 by the great Jewish uprising. Loss of life among the non-Jewish elements of the population is said to have been very great, and the damage done to public buildings, particularly temples, at Cyrene was so extensive as to have left ruins that were never removed in antiquity and are still visible today. Large armed forces had to be dispatched from other parts of the Empire to deliver the city from the hands of the insurrectionists, and the work of repairing the damage, taken in hand by Hadrian and involving not only the reconstruction of some of the public buildings but also the introduction of new settlers and the founding of a new city, Hadrianopolis, west of Tauchira, was long drawn out.[83] It would be interesting to know to what extent Ptolemais was affected by these developments.

That there were Jews in all the seaport cities of Cyrenaica at this time seems obvious, but the

evidence available currently suggests that they were more numerous and more prominent at Tauchira and Berenice than at Ptolemais.[84] Yet from Ptolemais we now have available at least one Jewish coin, from the period of the Maccabean Revolt (see p. 268), and perhaps the name of a Jewish lady on the Tomb of the Kartilioi (see p. 215, Inscription 51). The only other evidence that may possibly have bearing on the Jewish uprising is the fact that among coins found at Ptolemais there are no less than seven silver denarii of Trajan and of an issue that is generally connected with the mint of Caesarea in Cappadocia (see pp. 268–69). These could represent soldier pay brought in by military units from overseas that helped quell the uprising and might indicate that one detachment was stationed for a while at Ptolemais. That the entire episode represented a setback for Cyrenaica is clear, but it may be that under the circumstances obtaining at the time much of the wealth and enterprise of the country had already begun to move from the inland cities to those along the coast, so that the length of time which it took for Cyrene to recover is to be taken as the measure of Cyrene's declining importance rather than as the measure of the damage done to the fortunes of the province as a whole or to such cities as Ptolemais and Apollonia in particular.[85]

The period that began with the Antonines and extended to the reign of Diocletian is something of a mystery as far as the history of Ptolemais is concerned. In part this is because of the paucity of evidence, in respect to which the situation is not much different elsewhere in the region; in part, however, it is because of the difficulty of interpreting correctly under these circumstances the one body of material now being brought to our attention, namely the sculptures found at the site.

---

times, as we learn from Synesius (see *The Letters of Synesius of Cyrene*, translated into English with introduction and notes by Augustine FitzGerald [London, 1926] p. 227, No. 134).

[80] Cyrenaican roses from which a scented balm was made (*Natural History* xxi. 10), a wild saffron (*crocus*; *ibid.* xxi. 17), Christ's thorn (*paliurus*; *ibid.* xiii, 33), and a citrus tree (*arbor citri*; *ibid.* xiii. 30).

[81] See Strabo *Geography* xvii. 3. 21 and cf. Pliny *Natural History* viii. 64–67 and Synesius *Letters*, No. 40.

[82] See Rostovtzeff, *Social and Economic History of the Roman Empire* (2d ed.) I 67 and 91–101.

[83] See in general Romanelli, *La Cirenaica romana*, pp. 109–20.

[84] A goodly number of Hebrew funerary inscriptions from Tauchira have now been published by John Gray in *Cyrenaican Expedition of the University of Manchester, 1952* (1956) pp. 43–56. For Berenice see J. and G. Roux, "Un décret du politeuma des Juifs de Bérénikè en Cyrénaïque au Musée Lapidaire de Carpentras," *REG* LXII (1949) 281–96; the inscription, belonging to the period between 30 B.C. and A.D. 100, honors a certain Decimus Valerius Dionysius for having decorated with pictures the walls of the local amphitheater.

[85] In this connection we may note inscriptions assigned to the early Roman imperial period in which Ptolemais honors a citizen and strategos of Cyrene (*SEG* IX 70, No. 359) and Tauchira honors a certain Masyces the Ptolemaean (*SEG* IX 76, No. 417).

The history of the Roman Empire during the period in question is too well known to require extensive comment here. Beginning with the Empire riding along majestically on the tide of an inherited prosperity that was just coming to its fullest flood and ending with the efforts of a succession of soldier-emperors to stem a fast-flowing ebb and keep the ship of state afloat, the period saw crucial changes in the structure of the Empire and in the social and economic life of its vast domain. From the disaster, the disillusionment, and the internal conflict of the third century Rome emerged with a military leadership that saw the Quirites lose the last vestiges of their authority, that relied increasingly for its support upon the cultivation of the lower classes, and that financed its expenditures by currency devaluation and the growth of the imposts levied upon the cities through their *decemprimi*. Time was running out for the urban middle class which the early Empire had brought to such wealth and prominence and for the role of the city as the medium for the expression of man's economic, political, and cultural potential at the hands of a privileged class.[86]

Cyrenaica escaped the horrors of the wars that ravaged Syria and the northern provinces of the Empire and also, it would seem, the bitter struggle between the legions and the Senate that marked the rise of the military monarchy. But it was not unaffected by the social and economic changes resulting from the crisis. At best, as Romanelli has so aptly said, it became "una provincia lontana, priva di interesse e di valore," returning thus in some sense to the status it had toward the end of the Hellenistic period.[87] That this was for the cities of Cyrenaica by no means a happy state is evident. The real question, however, is not how ill the province fared in the years following the accession of Maximinus but to what extent it may have participated in the end of the Empire's prosperity under the Antonines and the Severi. At Cyrene a certain amount of building was still going on, especially in connection with the work of repairing the damage done in the Jewish revolt. At Ptolemais the only building known at present that appears to belong to this period is the "Odeon"

(see pp. 89–93). By contrast the Public Building on the Street of the Monuments had apparently already fallen into disrepair and the Villa was rapidly approaching a similar state (see p. 138).

Necessarily striking to anyone familiar with the archeological remains of the Antonine period in Syria and other eastern provinces and with those of the Severan period in the province of Africa is the absence in Cyrenaica generally and at Ptolemais in particular of evidence for the ostentatious and often grandiose construction to which these periods gave rise elsewhere. It may be that we still know too little about the sites to pass judgment, but by analogy with other parts of the Empire we might properly expect to find here and there jumbles of massive structural elements representing Antonine or Severan monuments. Either, then, the Byzantines looted earlier buildings with particular thoroughness, or Ptolemais never had the equivalent of the structural programs that elsewhere are reminders of Antonine and Severan optimism. The only pieces of typical Antonine proportions presently exposed at Ptolemais are two massive Corinthian capitals (e.g. Pl. XX *B*) that can be seen just eastward of the Headquarters of the Dux (Building 23 on Plan XXII). From the following period there is today only an inscription (p. 212, No. 15) reused in the Byzantine development of the Public Building on the Street of the Monuments, recording a dedication to the Emperor Septimius Severus.[88]

Under these circumstances it is surprising that the bulk of the statuary brought to light at the site of Ptolemais should be assigned by those who have studied it to the second and third centuries of our era. The material in question ranges from statues of Athena (p. 204, No. 64), Artemis Colonna (p. 206, No, 68), Harpocrates (p. 205, No. 66), Herakles (p. 196, No. 12), the Tyche of Ptolemais (p. 203, No. 61), and a group of dancing maenads (see p. 193, No. 5) to a figure of Aeschines type which may represent a local magistrate (p. 195, No. 10), a sarcophagus and its lid (p. 206, Nos. 69–70), and a stele of the gladiator Hippomedes (p. 207, No. 71). It is important to note in this connection that several of these pieces are made

---

[86] See in general Rostovtzeff, *Social and Economic History of the Roman Empire* (2d ed.) I 353–501, and in *CAH* XII (1939) chaps. i–vii.

[87] See Romanelli, *La Cirenaica romana*, pp. 123–31.

[88] In the excavations conducted by the Department of Antiquities at the site of the modest *triconchos* that is Building 16 on Plan XXII an inscription recording the presence of a *vexillatio* of the *III Augusta* was found, which will be published elsewhere. The excavation of the *triconchos* has not been completed.

of Greek marble, that of Herakles bearing the name of its Athenian sculptor, and that there is reason to regard not only the stele but also such works as an Asklepios head (p. 191, No. 2) and other pieces as products of Libyan ateliers. All this suggests on the part of the donors an opulence and a civic pride for which there was no counterpart in the structural development of the city during the same period. Is this seeming contradiction sheer accident, or was the wealth of the citizens not sufficient to extend beyond such ornament, or did the citizens, as Greeks, shun ostentation and prefer to beautify the city rather than to magnify it? The answer remains in doubt.

So far as the use and development of the land is concerned, it is clear from such guides as the *Antonine Itinerary* that the interior of the province was being more thoroughly charted and more and more easily traveled than ever before.[89] In part the development of the interior corresponds to the intensity of settlement and production, which in turn had some bearing on the economic life of the cities. In part it corresponds to growing control by administrative and tax officials over the persons and resources of the region. A particularly important witness to this development is provided by a papyrus whose obverse records part of a property register of a portion of Marmarica based upon a revision made in A.D. 188–89.[90] Based on a cadastral survey, it illustrates the care taken even in remote and relatively unproductive areas to make available a detailed record of the land units, their character, their products, and their improvements.[91] The power that the possession of such documents gave to an increasingly tax-hungry state is obvious. As to the settlers in the interior, it is probable that in Cyrenaica, as in neighboring Tripolitania, the period under consideration saw the establishment of a half-military, half-peasant type of colonist who eked out a meager existence even in the best years.[92] It is

thus by no means surprising that in the reign of Claudius II the native tribes of the interior became restive once again, as more and more of the grazing lands were being occupied by settlers.[93] The situation had not yet become crucial and in this instance apparently was disturbing particularly in the eastern part of the province, but it was destined to become increasingly worse. For the standing army, meanwhile, more and more reliance was being placed upon local levies, but provincialization made it less effective as time went on and the establishment of the *numeri* on the land does not seem to have added greatly to the defensive strength.[94]

If sculptures found at Ptolemais give us some grounds for believing that a measure of prosperity was maintained there during the Antonine and Severan periods, there is also evidence to show that in the succeeding critical years its fortunes suffered a radical decline. The Villa ceased to be maintained after the reign of Gordian III. The Public Building on the Street of the Monuments was in ruins. Sections of the city wall apparently had fallen into disrepair, and there is reason to suppose that the Square of the Cisterns ceased to supply an adequate flow of water (see p. 70).

The last hundred years of Roman rule in Cyrenaica, extending from Diocletian to Theodosius, were ushered in by changes that may for a time have seemed to make up for the recession of the immediate past, but actually their beneficial effects were short-lived and by the end of the fourth century, or at least by the middle of the fifth, the city entered into a further decline from which it never fully recovered.

In the background of these developments, of course, was the heroic effort of Diocletian to reverse the tide that since the middle of the third century had been running so strongly against the Empire. His peaceful settlement with the Sasa-

---

[89] See K. Miller, *Itineraria Romana* (1916).

[90] See M. Norsa and G. Vitelli, *Il Papirio Vaticano Greco 11* ("Studi e testi" LIII [Città del Vaticano, 1931]). The Marmarica was apparently transferred from Cyrenaica to the province of Egypt between the time of Pliny and that of Ptolemy the Geographer.

[91] See Romanelli, *op. cit.* pp. 123–131.

[92] For Tripolitania see R. G. Goodchild and J. B. Ward Perkins, "The *Limes Tripolitanus* in the light of recent discoveries," *JRS* XXXIX (1949) 81–95, and D. Oates, "The Tripolitanian Gebel," *PBSR* XXI (1953) 81–117.

For similar developments on the northern frontier of the Empire see Rostovtzeff, *Social and Economic History of the Roman Empire* (2d ed.) II 724–25, n. 51.

[93] See Oliverio, *Monumenti antichi* II 1, pp. 102–3, No. 68; *SEG* IX 16, No. 9.

[94] On the provincialization of the Roman army see Rostovtzeff, *op. cit.* pp. 126–29, 404, and A. Alföldi in *CAH* XII 208–13. On the *numeri* see H. T. Rowell in *R.-E.*, s. v. "numerus," and in general G. J. Cheesman, *The Auxilia of the Roman Army* (Oxford, 1914). Possibly a fragmentary inscription (p. 210, No. 134) found in the fill above the Roman Villa at Ptolemais and reading merely [. . .] X Num[. . .] refers to a *numerus*.

nians, his successful campaigns against the Alamanni and the Sarmatians on the Danube, and his quick disposal of an Arab invasion of Syria and of a revolt in middle Egypt checked the erosion on the frontiers and the internal threat to imperial authority. In the administrative reforms that accompanied these military actions Cyrenaica was separated from Crete and divided into two provinces, Libya Pentapolis (or Upper Libya) and Dry Libya (or Lower Libya), which along with the several provinces into which Egypt was divided became a part of the *dioecesis Orientis*. This signalized a return to an eastward orientation in the life of the region, a change that remained effective until the Italian occupation of 1913. Equally important was the fundamental division between the military and the civil administration of the provinces, in consequence of which the defense of Cyrenaica was placed in the hands of a *dux Aegypti et Thebaidos, utrarumque Libyarum*, whose headquarters were in Egypt, while the civil affairs of each of the two Libyas were in charge normally of a *praeses*.[95]

For Ptolemais the most important aspect of the changes was that under Diocletian it became the capital city of the province of Libya Pentapolis. In part the new role assigned to Ptolemais may reflect continued decline in the importance of Cyrene (see p. 17).[96] In part, however, it was only a corollary of the division of Cyrenaica into two provinces and their assignment to the *dioecesis Orientis*. The policy decision that placed them under the *comes Orientis* may well have suggested that the *praesides* of the provinces be accessible from Egypt by ship, and the establishment of the administrative headquarters of Dry Libya at Paraetonium would have called for the adminstration of Libya Pentapolis from a coastal city farther west than Apollonia. Only later, when Ptolemais was seen to be too exposed to the raids of tribes from the interior, was the metropolis of Libya Pentapolis shifted to the less exposed Apollonia.

What its new status meant to Ptolemais cannot

yet be determined fully, but it can be legitimately inferred that the city had henceforth a residence for the civil governor, that its population was swelled by the presence of an administrative bureaucracy, and that it became as never before a focal point for communications with the entire region. Such factors clearly should have brought more life and activity to the city. Some indications of the changes seem to be provided by monuments at the site. One such may well be the repair of the city wall, especially in the neighborhood of the Tauchira Gate (see pp. 61–62). A second is the construction of a large reservoir (Building 12 on Plan XXII) to replace or to supplement the Square of the Cisterns (see p. 70). Still a third is the transformation of the "Odeon" into a building for the showing of water spectacles (see p. 92). A Latin inscription pieced together by Goodchild indicates, finally, that between A.D. 311 and 313 the Triumphal Arch at the western end of the excavated portion of the Street of the Monuments (see pp. 75–78) was erected in honor of Constantine and Licinius.[97] The erection of the arch was no doubt in response to some favor shown to the city by the Emperors, but what remission or exemption or other favor may be involved is unknown. Since its emplacement must have been carefully considered, it is natural to suppose that the Street of the Monuments already had or was in this connection given some particular importance of which we are not yet aware. This assumption is not without bearing upon the fact that the effects of a rehabilitation program in the reign of Valens and Valentinian are visible there (see p. 80). All we can say about the street at the beginning of the fourth century, however, is that the gap left at the sourthern end of the insula adjacent to the Triumphal Arch by the destruction of the Public Building (No. 8 on Plan XXII) was closed presumably by nothing more impressive than a row of shops (see p. 159).[98]

Of Ptolemais' new relation to its environment there are also sundry indications. It was now the hub of communications with the entire province of Libya Pentapolis, a factor that may have some

[95] See in general Romanelli, *op. cit.* pp. 135–41, and Oliverio, *Documenti antichi* II 2, pp. 146–53.

[96] The familiar statement of Ammianus Marcellinus (*History* xxii. 16. 4) about Cyrene, *urbs antiqua sed deserta*, should be understood to apply primarily to the reduction in the size of the population. Ptolemais is second among the cities of Cyrenaica as listed by Ammianus and first in the list of the *Expositio totius mundi et gentium* 62 (see A. Riese, *Geographi Latini Minores* [1878] p. 123).

[97] Advance information concerning the inscription was kindly communicated to me by Goodchild. He has now published it in *Quaderni di archeologia della Libia* IV (1961) 83–95.

[98] The shops at the northern end of the insula containing the now abandoned Roman Villa were still in operation and were beginning to absorb some of the adjacent rooms of the dwelling (see p. 135).

relation to the increase in the number of towns and stopping places that appear in the *Itineraria* along the road eastward from the city.[99] A milestone on the coastal road leading westward to Tauchira suggests that the road was repaired or rebuilt in the period of the Tetrarchy, if the inscription has been properly recorded.[100] With this period it may be appropriate to associate also a line of forts or fortified farms between Ptolemais and Tauchira (see pp. 105–7). These have necessarily to be understood in connection with the special studies that have in recent years been devoted to isolated fortresses and fortlike structures particularly in Tripolitania and Cyrenaica. That individual forts of a type somewhat different from those of the later periods were constructed at important points along the frontier of Cyrenaica in the first century of the Roman Empire is clearly indicated by Goodchild's investigation of ancient Boreum and Qasr el-Heneia.[101] Such forts and the larger *castella* that were scattered among the villages that surrounded the larger cities in the province of Africa, serving as refuges for the rural population in times of necessity, were the forerunners of a second group, which belongs to the period beginning with Alexander Severus. It is said to have been part of Alexander's policy for the settlement of captured lands by the *limitanei* and for the defense of the Empire to erect chains of fortified establishments in strategic areas, particularly along the roads into and along the frontiers of the northern and southern provinces.[102] Corresponding chains of forts and fortresses have been established by the explorations of Goodchild in Cyrenaica.[103] Their function was, clearly, to provide mobile defense forces with bases and supply depots, on the one hand, and with advance posts, on the other. Difference in size among the several types of establishments creates ambiguity as to what may properly be called a "fort" and what might more appropriately be called a "fortified farm." This ambiguity applies directly to the interpretation of the structures along the road between Ptolemais and Tauchira. In size and plan these correspond to the smaller of Goodchild's "forts" and to the first of his three types of "fortified farms."[104] In Tripolitania these are assigned to the early part of the third century of our era. Whether the structures between Ptolemais and Tauchira are "forts" or "fortified farms" is, of course, an academic question. We speak of them as "forts" because the relative excellence of their masonry suggests government rather than private enterprise, because they appear to have had watchtowers extending above the level of the second floor, corresponding in this respect to advance posts between established bases and supply depots, and because along the same road there are remains of less closely knit constructions to which the designation "farms" seems more applicable. A somewhat later date is here assigned to the "forts" because of analogies between their masonry and that of the Headquarters of the Dux at Ptolemais, which very likely belongs in the early fifth century (see pp. 102–3).

For all its importance as the focal point for the administrative life of the Pentapolis, Ptolemais can scarcely be said to have flourished greatly during the late Roman period. Times had changed too markedly, affecting the status and function of the urban establishments and reducing the economic competence of their citizens. The duties and costs of magistracies were required of those enrolled among the *curiales*, tax apportionment and collection rested upon the shoulders of the *decemprimi*, the repair of public buildings was a part of the common "liturgy," and properties that had once belonged to the cities and from which they had drawn income were appropriated or made less productive.[105] Copies of Diocletian's Price Edict,

---

[99] Especially on the *Tabula Peutingeriana*, which seems to be based upon the fourth-century work of Castorius.

[100] See Oliverio, *Monumenti antichi* II 2, p. 246, No. 492, and *SEG* IX 75, No. 413. For the larger context see Goodchild, "Roman milestones in Cyrenaica," *PBSR* XVIII (1950) 83–91.

[101] See "Boreum of Cyrenaica," *JRS* XLI (1951) 11–16, and "Libyan forts in south-west Cyrenaica," *Antiquity* XXV (1951) 130–41.

[102] *Scriptores historiae Augustae: Alexander Severus* lviii. 2. On the emporia of Thrace and the *castella* of Upper Germany and Africa see Rostovtzeff, *Social and Economic History of the Roman Empire* (2d ed.) I 425–30, II 723–26.

[103] See "The Roman and Byzantine *Limes* in Cyrenaica," *JRS* XLIII (1953) 65–76, and "The *Limes Tripolitanus* II," *JRS* XL (1950) 30–38.

[104] See *JRS* XL 30–38 and the *castellum* at Henscir Suffit published by R. Bartoccini in *Africa italiana* II (1928/29) 106–10.

[105] For the general picture see E. Stein, *Geschichte des spätrömischen Reiches. I. Vom römischen zum byzantinischen Staate* (1928) pp. 65–75, and Jones, *The Greek City*, chaps. ix, xii. Constantius' appropriation of city property, an action rescinded by Julian, was upheld by Valens with the modification, however, that one-third of the income was to be payable to the cities.

representing an attempt to combat rising costs resulting from currency changes, were exhibited publicly at Ptolemais as at other cities of the Pentapolis, but the effort had no long-term effect and the slabs upon which the edict was inscribed were eventually put to other uses.[106] For those who still had some means at their disposal the alternatives developing from these conditions were to enter the services of the imperial government or to retire to country estates, where life could be on a relatively self-sufficient basis, and thus to pass on to others the responsibilities of civic life. Save as an instrument of imperial control, the life of the Greek cities was gradually coming to an end.

Special circumstances seem to have conspired to make the lot of the cities of Cyrenaica still more difficult. In A.D. 365 there occurred a violent earthquake that wrought great havoc at Cyrene.[107] With this earthquake should probably be associated damage to certain buildings at Ptolemais, such as the collapse of the entire south section of the peristyle of the Square of the Cisterns (see p. 66) and the weakening of the structure of the "Odeon,"

which led to the introduction of heavy masonry piers into the ambulacrum (see p. 91). In Building 6 (see p. 100), which may have been a church, the semidome of the apse threatened to collapse, so that heavy retaining walls had to be built against the side walls in the area of greatest thrust. The most extensive damage, however, apparently occurred along the Street of the Monuments in the area of the double insula (see p. 41), where important buildings of the early Roman period must have stood (see n. 119). In cases of disaster it was customary for cities to call upon their emperors for help, and at Ptolemais such help apparently was forthcoming in the reign of Valens and Valentinian. This is suggested by an architrave inscription honoring them (see p. 80). Other inscriptions honor Gratian[108] and Arcadius and Honorius (see p. 80). This series of inscriptions suggests a large-scale rehabilitation project, perhaps on the basis of some earlier plan for the development of the thoroughfare. One feature of this rehabilitation was the construction of the City Bath (see pp. 160–75).

THE BYZANTINE PERIOD (A.D. 395–643)

At the threshold of the last period in the history of Ptolemais as an outpost and instrument of ancient Mediterranean civilization stands the only individual who ever lived there whom we can know as a person, none other than its Bishop Synesius. Thus it seems appropriate here to review briefly what is known about the beginnings of the Church in Cyrenaica. They are, of course, obscure. Irenaeus says that there were Christians in Libya in his day (*ca.* A.D. 180), but the earliest specific information comes from the period of Dionysius, bishop of Alexandria (*ca.* A.D. 246–65). Eusebius reports in one context that a doctrinal dispute which had developed at Ptolemais of the Pentapolis was referred to Dionysius and in another quotes from a letter which Dionysius wrote to a certain

Basilides, "bishop of the parishes in the Pentapolis."[109] The dispute turned about a form of modalistic monarchianism that is associated with the name of a certain Sabellius, whom later tradition identifies as a presbyter of the church at Ptolemais.[110] Swayed in he third century by modalism, Ptolemais seems to have turned in the fourth to Arianism, for its Bishop Secundus was among those banished by the Nicene Council as supporters of Arius, the ant -Homoousian presbyter of Alexandria. Since this same council in its Canon vi made the traditional responsibility of the archbishops of Alexandria for the metropolitan bishops of Cyrenaica a matter of record, Athanasius appointed as bishop of Cyrenaica resident at Ptolemais one Siderius of the parish church of Palaebisca under whom, as under his successors up to and including Synesius, trinitarian orthodoxy

---

[106] See G. Caputo and R. G. Goodchild, "Diocletian's Price-Edict at Ptolemais (Cyrenaica)," *JRS* XLV (1955) 106–15, and p. 215 below (Inscription 47) for new fragments of the text. On the currency situation see Rostovtzeff, *Social and Economic History of the Roman Empire* (2d ed.) I 516, and in *CAH* XII 338.

[107] See especially Goodchild, *Cyrene and Apollonia*, p. 25.

[108] Fragment of text on plastered block reused in Public Building (see p. 212, No. 17).

[109] See Irenaeus *Against the Heresies* i. 10 and Eusebius *Church History* vii. 6, 26. 3.

[110] Epiphanius *Panarion*, Heresy 62.

was firmly established as the proper doctrinal statement of the faith.[111]

In Synesius Cyrenaica had more than an orthodox ecclesiastic. Born of Greek parents about A.D. 370 at Cyrene and, like his father, a citizen of that city, he is the last known representative of the tradition of Greek culture, learning, and devotion to civic virtues that had long flourished there. The excellent training in Greek letters that he must have acquired in his earliest years was supplemented by a period of study at Alexandria, which brought him under the lasting spell of the Neoplatonic philosopher Hypatia. Resolved to devote himself henceforth to the contemplative life, he made a pilgrimage to Athens, the hearth of so much of ancient Greek learning, was deeply disappointed in what he found there, and retired to the peaceful surroundings of a country estate south of Cyrene, which the family, in keeping with the times, had acquired in order to preserve something of its fortune and dignity. From the quiet of the farm he was on two occasions called away, first, shortly before A.D. 400 when his city, Cyrene, asked him to undertake an embassy to Arcadius at Constantinople, which it took him three years to discharge successfully, and, second, about A.D. 410 when Ptolemais asked him, a nonchurchman, to accept appointment as its bishop and hence as metropolitan of the Pentapolis, to which office he devoted the last five years of his life. Fortunately Synesius enjoyed putting his thoughts on paper and left in his letters, treatises, sermons, addresses, and hymns a treasure house of information about the intellectual, the political, and the social and economic life of his times.[112] His letters are

particularly worthy of attention in the present context.

On the political side the conditions and events cast in sharpest relief by the writings and activities of Synesius were the incompetence and self-aggrandizement of the highest administrative and military officials and the outbreak of a new conflict between the settled population and the native tribes of the interior. To protest against the injustice of the civil governors and to plead for integrity of administration was the purpose of Synesius' embassy to the court at Constantinople, but it was also, together with a similar indictment of the military commanders, a feature of his efforts to help defend the country against the tribesmen from the desert. About the former we hear particularly in the oration *de regno* which he prepared in connection with his audience with Arcadius. The latter is a common theme of his letters, from which we learn that Cyrenaica had recently been given its own military governor, a *dux* or comes, the new arrangement having apparently come into force in connection with the separation of Egypt from the *dioecesis Orientis*.[113] Synesius gives penetrating pictures of a series of these governors—Cerealis, Gennadius, Andronicus, Anysius, Innocentius, and Marcellinus—describing every second one as a coward or as a man who robbed those he was supposed to protect.[114] It appears, however, that the military commander had as yet no fixed residence in the province but

[111] See in general A. von Harnack, *Die Mission und Ausbreitung des Christentums* (3d. ed.; 1915) II 180–81, and G. Grützmacher, *Synesius von Kyrene* (Leipzig, 1913) pp. 8, 152. Synesius says in his *Letters*, No. 67, that Athanasius tried by this appointment to keep alive the tiny spark of orthodox faith still remaining at Ptolemais. By the time of the Nicene Council there were bishops also at Berenice, Tauchira, and Barca. The only other doctrinal problem of which we hear that it was discussed in Cyrenaica is that of Anhomoianism as preached by Eunomius, against the followers of whom Synesius warns the elders of the churches in his *Letters*, No. 5.

[112] Synesius' *Opera quae extant omnia* are accessible in Migne, *Patrologia Graeca* LXVI. In addition to *The Letters of Synesius of Cyrene*, A. FitzGerald has translated *The Essays and Hymns of Synesius* (2 vols.; London, 1930). On Synesius' writings in general see *Wilhelm von Christs Geschichte der griechischen Litteratur* II 2 (1924) pp. 1397–

1401. For a few of the many excellent discussions of his life and works see H. Druon, *Oeuvres de Synésius, Évêque de Ptolemais, dans la Cyrénaïque au commencement du Ve siècle* (Paris, 1878); O. Seeck, "Studien zu Synesius," *Philologus* LII (1893) 442–83; Grützmacher, *Synesius von Kyrene* (1913); J. C. Pando, *The Life and Times of Synesius of Cyrene as Revealed in His Works* (Washington D. C., 1940), and C. Lacombrade, *Synésios de Cyrène, Hellène et Chrétien* (Paris, 1951).

[113] On this development of A.D. 383 in Egypt see M. Gelzer, *Studien zur byzantinischen Verwaltung Ägyptens* (Diss.; Leipzig, 1909) p. 7. Synesius (*Letters*, No. 95) pleads for the restoration of the earlier system in which, as indicated above (p. 20), the defense of Cyrenaica was administered from Egypt by a *dux Aegypti et Thebaidos, utrarumque Libyarum*. It is not clear whether in the new arrangement both Libyas were entrusted to one *dux* or whether there was already a single *dux* for each of them.

[114] Ammianus' account of the efforts of the city of Leptis in neighboring Tripolitania to obtain a hearing for its charges against the military governor of Africa in the days of Valentinian I suggests that Synesius is not exaggerating (see Ammianus *History* xxvii. 9, xxviii. 6).

made his headquarters now in one city and now in another. As to the soldiers under his command, it would seem that the local levies were useless and that the *limitanei* never played any effective part in the defense of the areas in which they were settled. The only troops for which Synesius had any praise was a detachment of forty Unnigardae and a Dalmatian cohort stationed at Ptolemais.[115]

Why the colonial development of Cyrenaica should have led to armed conflicts with the native tribes has been indicated above (p. 3). The settlement of the country in depth in the fourth century was one of the factors that led to the renewal of such conflicts in Synesius' day and is the measure of the intensity of the struggle, which had now become in a very real sense a struggle for survival. The hostilities, taking the form of raids from the interior by bands of Austuriani or Ausuriani and Maceti or Makai, seem to have been concentrated in several periods, at least two of which are clearly distinguishable and may have covered a total of seven years.[116] One set of raids, providing a severe threat to Cyrene, occurred while Synesius was still (or again) residing at his country estate south of the city. Another set occurred when he was bishop of Ptolemais and is notable because of its threat to the metropolis of the province.[117] The number of the raiders does not in any instance seem to have been large, but by pillage, arson, quick forays from cover, and continuous brigandage along the highways they spread terror and destruction across the countryside. The outlying farms of the settlers were put to the torch, their inhabitants slain, the farm animals butchered or led away, and the crops destroyed. The country estates of the wealthy suffered no less, and small towns were occupied by the raiders at least for short periods.[118] The cities themselves were threatened, but whether they were ever directly attacked or even occupied is uncertain and may have depended upon the condition of their defenses. When his own country estate was ravaged Synesius in deep despair could

well write "all is lost, all is destroyed" (*Letters*, No. 69), considering the importance which the property had for him economically and as a philosopher. But, being a patriot as well as a philosopher, he collected a body of "irregulars" to fight the raiders and himself did sentinel duty somewhere in the countryside between two widely separated watchtowers (*Letters*, No. 130). Later, when he was bishop of Ptolemais, he remarked that on more than one occasion during a single month he had himself "rushed to the ramparts" to help beat off a threatened attack (*Letters*, No. 89).

An interesting question arises in this connection concerning the status of the defenses of Ptolemais. It grows out of finds made in the Byzantine City Bath, to which is attributed an inscription honoring Arcadius and Honorius (see p. 81).[119] Many large stones bearing precisely such inscriptions as appear on the towers of the Tauchira Gate at Ptolemais and on the curtains of the city walls of Tauchira itself were reused in the construction of the bath (see pp. 212–14, Nos. 20–35, 39–40, 42–46). It is natural to infer that they actually came from the city wall and that in the period after the earthquake and before the episcopate of Synesius the wall, being in part at least in a ruinous condition, was beginning to serve as a quarry for the city's rehabilitation program. The problem is how to reconcile this inference with Synesius' statement that he mounted the *chemin de ronde* (ἔπαλξις) of the city's defenses. There are, of course, several possible solutions. One is to assume that at this early date a decision had already been made to shorten the perimeter of the defenses and that the stones came from an abandoned section of the wall.[120] Another is to assume that in the period of the earlier raids, which may have affected particularly the plateau, hasty efforts were made to restore with mud brick the ruinous and looted

---

[115] *Letters*, Nos. 78 and 87.

[116] The seven-year figure is given in Synesius *Catastasis*.

[117] Romanelli, *La Cirenaica romana*, p. 140, n. 1, argues for three sets of raids: the first preceding Synesius' embassy to Constantinople and therefore occurring in *ca.* A.D. 395, the second from A.D. 405 to 409, while Synesius was at Cyrene, and the third from A.D. 410 to 413, while Synesius was bishop of Ptolemais. See also *ibid.* pp. 145–63.

[118] Synesius *Letters*, No. 125.

[119] The construction of the bath was apparently part of the rehabilitation of the Street of the Monuments (see p. 174) and presupposes improvement of the water-supply system of the city by construction of a large reservoir (Building 12 on Plan XXII). The construction in the frigidarium of the bath of a platform which may have been used as a bema (see p. 166), suggesting that public meetings were held there, reflects a not unimportant side light on the extent to which other public buildings may have been damaged by the earthquake of A.D. 365 and left in ruins.

[120] Goodchild, *Cyrene and Apollonia*, p. 27, finds evidence of such shortening, presumably in the fifth century, though it is not clear what the evidence may be.

portions of the wall. Actually, it would seem that the threatened attacks that provoked Synesius' heroic acts never materialized and that Marcellinus, the last of the generals mentioned by Synesius, was able to deliver the city from the fear of their immediate recurrence.[121]

On the social and economic side the contemporary scene is also brightly illumined in the writings of Synesius. Cyrene had become insensible to philosophy (*Letters*, No. 139), the civic duties of a *curialis* were a burden rather than a privelege (*Letters*, No. 100), and reliance on "rhetoric" alone guided those who tried to deliver the cities from their misfortunes (*Letters*, No. 103). In fact, city life was dominated no longer by the citizen magistrates but rather by a small circle of high officials—the military governor, the civil governor, and the bishop of the local parish. Among them there was a bitter rivalry and an almost traditional hostility, illustrated by the episode in which Andronicus posted notices on the church doors of Ptolemais denying to the churches the right of asylum and in which Synesius in turn excommunicated Andronicus (*Letters*, No. 58). Both parties naturally appealed to higher officials at Constantinople in this as in all other matters of local importance. To escape from civic reponsibilities and from continuous wrangling with the bureaucracy was therefore the chosen way to preserve some measure of peace and self-esteem. No wonder, then, that we find Synesius describing in such glowing terms the amenities of another social context, that of the country estate, where he lived with simple people, enjoyed the pleasures of hunting and caring for his livestock, and rejoiced in the quality of his produce, which he considered better than the imports that the city people wanted (*Letters*, No. 148).[122] No wonder, also, that the insecurity of the open countryside and the damage done to it by the tribal raiders affected him and his social stratum so severely. Yet it is important to remember that in every emergency Synesius was found ready to forego his own advantages and place himself at the disposal of the cities of Cyrenaica. Civic virtue and civic loyalty were dying but were not yet entirely dead.

As regards production and commerce, conditions had not changed materially by Synesius' day, though apparently more was produced for local consumption than for export.[123] Honey, oil, and wine were still being exported, as was a certain amount of silphium, which was now being cultivated in private gardens, however, rather than being collected in the open range.[124] His own wealth, Synesius confesses, and that of most of his neighbors, lay in cattle, herds of camels, and horses, but goats and sheep were also among the animals on his farm, and we find him sending a horse to a Greek friend as a gift.[125] Ptolemais was still an important port, for in writing from Cyrene to his brother, who lived nearby, he used on one occasion the metaphorical expression "what are the exports from Ptolemais" when asking for the latest news from there (*Letters*, No. 109). In the period of the tribal raids, and for some reason quite unknown to us, shipping was interrupted there, with cargoes continuing to lie on the docks, local shipowners refusing to send vessels into the Aegean, and Syrian ships passing by without stopping.[126] Particularly interesting in this connection is a statement in *Letters*, No. 134:

> We caught ostriches in the days when peace allowed us the pleasure of hunting, but we have not been able to send them to sea owing to the enemies' armaments, nor could we put upon our ships any part of the goods lying on the wharves. There is only a cargo of wine and as to olive oil, by your noble head, they have not succeeded in embarking a single measure, so far as I know.

Once we pass from the lifetime of Synesius the history of Ptolemais loses the graphic detail provided by his writings, but the general course of developments can be followed with the help of the archeological materials. There was apparently a period of recuperation and stabilization, as suggested by the provisions which seem to have been made for the operations of the top civil and military officials.

From the time of the reorganization of the Empire by Diocletian Cyrenaica had a separate civil governor, and it must be assumed that he resided at Ptolemais, though his place of residence

---

[121] Synesius, *Letters*, No. 62.

[122] What Synesius describes is shown in pictorial mosaics in the country villas of Tripolitania (see P. Romanelli, "La vita agricole attraverso le rappresentazioni figurate," *Africa italiana* III [1930] 53–75).

[123] Among the *Letters*, No. 148 is important in this connection because it shows that Synesius was on the defensive with regard to the excellence of the local products.

[124] See *Letters*, Nos. 134, 148, and 106.

[125] See *Letters*, Nos. 130 and 40.

[126] *Letters*, Nos. 134 and 148.

during the fourth century is unknown. The excavation of the Public Building (No. 8 on Plan XXII) on the Street of the Monuments (see (pp. 140–60) revealed that a suite of offices was constructed on the site by a certain Paul. That he must have been one of the civil governors of the province seems obvious, the only problem being the period of his incumbency. In one of the walls which he built there is a reused stone bearing part of a monumental inscription honoring Gratian (p. 212, No. 17). Unless there was some occasion for Gratian's having fallen into disfavor locally, the reuse of this stone would militate against Paul's having held office in the late fourth or early fifth century.[127] In his own inscription (p. 211, No. 14) Paul, who held the rank of *consularis*, applies to himself the Greek equivalent of the title *magnificentissimus*. His rank was not typical for civil governors of Cyrenaica during the fourth century, and the title *magnificentissimus* was not normally applied to governors until the days of Justinian. But by that time Ptolemais had ceased to be the metropolis of Libya Pentapolis (see p. 27), and it is therefore suggested that Paul may have had claim to his rank and title by virtue of earlier, higher appointments elsewhere (see p. 211) and that as civil governor of this region he may belong to the first half of the fifth century of our era.

If in the period of recuperation and stabilization that followed the disturbed days of Synesius the affairs of the civil government can be said to have been provided for by new construction at Ptolemais, the same can be said still more appropriately for the affairs of the military government. In the period of the conflict with the Austuriani Libya Pentapolis (or perhaps the two Libyas together) had a military governor independent of the *praefectus* (*augustalis*) of Egypt (see p. 23).[128] At that time, however, he had as yet no fixed headquarters but resided sometimes at Cyrene, sometimes at Tauchira, and sometimes at Ptolemais.[129] Sometime in the early fifth century he too was provided for at Ptolemais, namely by the erection of a large fortress (Building 23 on Plan XXII) on the Street of the Monuments on the façade of which the Edict of Anastasius (see p. 101) regulating the affairs of the *dux* and the *ducani* was subsequently inscribed. Its great size, the solidity of its construction, and the provisions in its bailey for residential quarters justify the application to it of the designation Headquarters of the Dux (see pp. 101–3). Associated with it in type and probably also in time are two other large buildings (Nos. 4 and 24 on Plan XXII).

These three structures represent a massive and expensive building enterprise that must have involved government subsidy even though labor may have been provided by the city as part of its *munera*.[130] Their character is that of forts such as are found elsewhere in Cyrenaica at Qasr Beni-Gdem and Qasr el-Shahden.[131] The fact that fortresses such as Buildings 4, 23, and 24 were erected inside the pomerium of Ptolemais implies a change in the policy or pattern of its defense. This change involved the final abandonment of the old system of perimeter defense and provides the necessary explanation for the almost complete disappearance of the stonework of the old city wall. It substituted zone defense by means of separately defensible forts, similar to those of the open countryside, in the construction of which were used blocks from the city wall. In the now "open" city, life presumably went on much as before, save that more reliance was obviously placed upon the resident *dux* and his forces. In the course of time small square buildings analogous to the *castella* of the open countryside began to dot the urban scene (Buildings 3, 17–20, 22, and 25 on Plan XXII).

---

[127] The failure of harvest in A.D. 383 in Egypt and Africa was taken there as a sign of divine disfavor toward the Emperor (see *R.-E., s. v.* "Gratianus").

[128] That each of the two Libyas had its own military governor by A.D. 470 is indicated by the decree of Leo (*Codex Justinianus* xii. 59).

[129] In the *Letters* of Synesius, Cerealis seems to be residing at Cyrene (Nos. 144, 146), Anysius at Tauchira (No. 94), and Andronicus at Ptolemais (No. 58).

[130] See Stein, *Geschichte des spätromanischen Reiches* I 24, and Jones, *The Greek City*, pp. 256–58, for services required of cities by the government at this time.

[131] For Qasr Beni-Gdem and Qasr el-Shahden see Goodchild in *JRS* XLIII 70–72. He assigns the latter to the fifth century. The structural features common to both and to the Headquarters of the Dux at Ptolemais are well dressed ashlar masonry, the use of string courses at regular intervals, and walls with separate inner and outer facings (*ibid.* Pl. VI–VII). These same characteristics make it desirable to associate more closely in date the earlier of the "forts" along the coastal road between Ptolemais and Tauchira (especially Fort 2; see Pl. XVII *A* below). The type of building that served the *dux* of Libya Pentapolis at Ptolemais may be contrasted with the earlier "Palace of the *Dux Ripae*" at Dura-Europos (see *The Excavations at Dura-Europos: Preliminary Report of the Ninth Season of Work*, Part III [New Haven, 1952] pp. 1–96, Figs. 7–8).

These repeated in miniature the theme of the great fortress that is the Headquarters of the Dux (see pp. 101–3).

To the construction work of the fifth century by which provision was made for dignifying its major officials it is necessary to add the magnificent Fortress Church (Building 2 on Plan XXII), excavated and partially reconstructed by the Italian archeologists. In the absence of epigraphic evidence there was at first some hesitation about dating it, but the recent work of Goodchild and Perkins on the churches of Tripolitania and Cyrenaica has provided the comparative material that makes a date in the middle of the fifth century entirely appropriate (see pp. 99–100). Its presumably modest baptistery and its location far from the business and residential center of the city indicate clearly that it was not a parish or diocesan church, and its small lateral entrance suggests that it was associated at the north with unexcavated subsidiary buildings and that it served a special clerical or monastic group (see p. 100). Sharing with the secular buildings of the same period the heavy fortress-like construction, it clearly reflects the insecurity of the days of Synesius and the changed pattern of civic defense.

The massive structures whose imposing ruins still dominate the scene testify that the half-century following the period of the tribal raids was for Ptolemais a time of recovery and stabilization. The city must still have been well populated, must have recouped some of its economic and commercial losses, and apparently was looked to by the imperial government as still the most appropriate site for the administrative and military headquarters of the province. Sometime between the middle and the end of the fifth century, perhaps just before or during the early years of the reign of Anastasius, all this changed. The administrative and military headquarters of Libya Pentapolis were shifted to Apollonia-Sozusa, which henceforth served as the metropolis of the province.[132] Precisely why this change was made is not known. Perhaps a period of anxiety over new incursions by tribal groups from the interior made it desirable to seek for the metropolis the least exposed location.[133] Perhaps a periodic shift in storm tracks had sanded up the harbor and made access from the sea difficult. Whatever the cause, the effect was catastrophic.

With the removal of the metropolitan headquarters to Apollonia, Ptolemais went into a rapid decline. What it lost in the way of further development can be read in the remains of the ornate churches of sixth-century Apollonia, for which there is no counterpart at Ptolemais. What it lost immediately was, of course, the entire corps of the higher administrative, military, and religious officials and their immediate retinue, which comprised in the Byzantine state of things the wealthiest and most important element of its population. At the same time it ceased to be the center of communications for the entire province. This undoubtedly made an enormous difference in its social and economic life and in the amount of help that it could obtain from the imperial government for the maintenance and improvement of its structures and services. It also meant for those who remained a change in attitude toward the already difficult problems of civic life. A particularly disastrous effect of the changes was that the city water-supply system was permitted to fall into disrepair. About this Procopius (*De aedeficiis* vi. 2) has the following to say:

> In Libya there is a city by the name of Ptolemais, in olden times prosperous and populous, but as time went on it was reduced to a few people because of water scarcity. For the greater majority of the population, driven by thirst, had moved from there long since, wherever they could.

What else can be known about the history of Ptolemais in the years between the beginning of the reign of Anastasius and the reign of Justinian is meager. Because of the state of the city water-supply system the City Bath was no longer usable. Its caldarium fell into ruins, and from the peristyle court of its frigidarium all but a few broken

---

[132] The position assigned to Apollonia-Sozusa at the head of the list of the cities of Cyrenaica in the *Synecdemus* of Hierocles and in George of Cyprus' *Description of the Roman World* reflects the change. Both lists are conveniently available in Jones, *Cities of the Eastern Roman Provinces*, p. 540. For recent comment on the material, particularly upon the sources from which the lists are drawn, see E. Honigmann, *Le Synekdèmos d'Hiéroklès* (1939) pp. 3–6. Romanelli, *La Cirenaica romana*, pp. 172–73, is inclined to date the change after the reign of

Justinian. Goodchild assigns it to the reign of Anastasius (see *Cyrene and Apollonia*, p. 80, and *JRS* XLIII 74, n. 36). Honigmann's analysis of the sources of Hierocles makes it necessary to keep the entire period down to A.D. 460 open for the change.

[133] Romanelli (*op. cit.* p. 170) and Bates (*Eastern Libyans*, p. 238) quote from secondary sources evidence for an incursion in A.D. 491.

columns were removed for use elsewhere, perhaps even in another city. To make up for the loss, it would seem, the small bathing establishment of the Public Building on the Street of the Monuments was made accessible from the street and hence available for public use (see p. 159). The establishment was a very modest one, and there are indications that finally water had to be brought in on the backs of animals quartered in what had been the governor's stables and fed by hand into the plunge and the tubs. Seen in this light, the last phase of the Public Building stands in sharp contrast to the scope of the original construction and provides a sad commentary on the ability of the early sixth-century community to keep alive the inherited traditions of the "good life." What individual members of the community could do for themselves in this period of acute water shortage is best indicated, perhaps, by small fortress-like houses (Buildings 14 and 21 on Plan XXII) in which the entire first floor was given over to vaulted cisterns; the well built vaults still remain standing, while the inclosing structures have disappeared (see p. 73). They reflect the need for dwellings that were both defensible units and provided with an independent water supply.

For evidence of what the imperial and provincial government was able to do for the city we are dependent upon the Edict of Anastasius (*ca.* A.D. 501), inscribed on the façade of the Headquarters of the Dux (see p. 101).[134] What the edict, with its province-wide application, implies for Ptolemais is limited to the information that can be gleaned between the lines about the type of soldiers normally used to garrison the cities, about their efforts to obtain financial benefits for themselves by various means including barter, about the use of the *castra* or *castella* for residential purposes by nonmilitary personnel, about the restrictions placed upon travelers wishing to enter the areas controlled by the "barbarians," and about the conditions under which members of the Makai tribe could enter the region of the Pentapolis.[135] None of this information is very reassuring and the last items are particularly revealing, for while it is clear that the limes was the line along which the *cordon sanitaire*

between the Pentapolis and the "barbarians" was to be drawn, the actual zone of separation probably was much closer at hand and lessened materially the depth of the area upon which cities like Ptolemais could draw for their commercial enterprise.

That Ptolemais complained bitterly to the *praeses* of the province about its destitution may be taken for granted, but nothing seems to have been done for it until the public works program of Justinian was launched. In Libya this program seems to have applied largely to the fortification and refortification of the frontier and of the cities particularly exposed to threats from the Sirtic area (Berenice and Tauchira). At Ptolemais no attention was paid to the fortifications, nor were any churches built under royal auspices. Instead, the water-supply system was rehabilitated.[136] The grant is known to have applied to the restoration of the aqueduct leading from a reservoir in the Wadi Habbun, some 20 kilometers east of the city. It may, of course, have applied also to the repair of the reservoir, and at the city end it apparently involved the construction of a new water-storage basin (Building 11 on Plan XXII). The new basin (see p. 71) was not impressive as compared to the two earlier reservoirs (Buildings 10 and 12) between which it was built, but the revived system apparently functioned and could conceivably have been kept in working order for some time.

Procopius closes his remarks about what Justinian did for Ptolemais by saying that thus the Emperor "gave back to the city the former guise of its well-being." That the city fathers hoped for a return of the better days is quite likely. They put the City Bath back into operation on a reduced basis, transforming the erstwhile tepidarium into a caldarium and the apodyteria into a tepidarium (see p. 174). At this point they may have felt that the "good life" could begin again. That it ever did is questionable. The coin yield from the city continues into the reign of Heraclius, but in other respects the history of Ptolemais in the later sixth and early seventh centuries is still a blank. Within two years after the death of Heraclius the life of the Greek city that was Ptolemais was brought to an end by the Arab conquest of Cyrenaica under Amr ibn el-ʿAsi.[137]

---

[134] See in general Romanelli, *La Cirenaica romana*, pp. 195–98.

[135] Because of the discovery of another copy of the edict at Apollonia it is impossible to infer from the Ptolemais copy that the military headquarters of the province were still at the latter city.

[136] Procopius *De aedificiis* vi. 2.

[137] On the disturbed conditions in Cyrenaica following the reign of Justinian and the subsequent administrative union of Cyrenaica and Tripolitania see Romanelli, *La Cirenaica romana*, pp. 173–75.

LATER DEVELOPMENTS

With the Arab conquest of Cyrenaica in A.D. 643 the history of the settlement that had been Ptolemais becomes disjointed and obscure. Undoubtedly there were whole centuries in which nothing of any consequence happened. Fortunately it is not necessary for the purposes of this report to try to construct a connected narrative. In the later history of the site, however, three periods yield information of such practical importance for the archeological study of its remains that at least a brief word of comment is in order here, if only to provide access to the essential bibliography. The first period is that of late 'Abbasid and early Fatimid times, the second that from the eighteenth century to World War I, and the third that of the years 1935–42. The first brings us information concerning the continued use of the site as a seaport, the second furnishes reports of early European visitors to the site, and the third marks the beginning of excavation and conservation of antiquities.

What happened to the people of Ptolemais when Barca—which now reappears upon the scene—submitted to Amr ibn el-'Asi is not known. We should assume that they were included among those from whom tribute was demanded, but, since the surrender was not preceded by a bitter armed conflict, life at Ptolemais as elsewhere presumably went on somewhat as before for those who did not choose to move to parts of the world still belonging to the Byzantine Empire.[138] Indeed, there is excellent evidence to show that in the seventh to the eleventh centuries the region of Barca was highly productive and very prosperous.[139] The really significant feature of the new situation was the further emphasis upon the connections with the east and the west as the determinants of the area's economic, social, and administrative life. Much of the produce of the Cyrenaican jebel must have moved along the great overland route that now linked Egypt with Cyrenaica, el-Qayrawan, and the Maghreb. But there was enough so that some went by sea, and for the ample produce of Barca the convenient port was naturally the medieval Tolometa (or Tolomieta). Thus the site of ancient Ptolemais returned to the role it had played at the beginning, that of being the "harbor at Barca." Its services in this capacity seem to have extended even beyond the bitter years that saw the Beni Hilal of the Nejd let loose upon the jebel, plunging into ruin what remained of the ancient cities and destroying the foundations of the area's prosperity.[140]

From the twelfth and the fourteenth century respectively there are two brief descriptions of medieval Tolometa that provide information about its role, its population, and some of its structures. The first is that of Idrisi, who says that it was a populous city, that it was inclosed by a ring of stone walls, and that ships from Alexandria came there to exchange cotton for local produce.[141] The second is that of Abu el-Fida, who says that there was a community of Jews at the place, numbering about two hundred souls, who paid tribute to the Arabs and served as intermediaries in the trade between the Arabs and the ships that came in from overseas. The ships, we are told, landed immediately in front of or near a chateau occupied by the Jews, and this chateau is described as having the form of a large tower.[142] Both descriptions are naturally of importance for the study of the fortifications of the city (see p. 51). How long the Jewish community, recruited no doubt from the mercantile families of Alexandria, survived at the site is not known, but more information may come to light from the unpublished

---

[138] For details on the Islamic conquest of Cyrenaica see especially Ibn 'Abd el-Ḥakam, whose account is available in a French translation by A. Gateau, *La Conquête de l'Afrique du Nord et de l'Espagne* ("Bibliothèque arab-française" II [Alger, 1947]) esp. pp. 35–37. For other comment see L. Caetani, *Annali dell'Islam* IV (1911) 532–36.

[139] See especially el-Bakri, whose account is available in a French translation by Mac Guckin de Slane, *Description de l'Afrique septentrionale par El-Bekri* (rev. ed.; Alger, 1913) esp. pp. 14–15.

[140] On the history of the period see in general G. Marçais, *Les Arabes en Berbérie du XIᵉ au XIVᵉ siècle* (1913). On the effect of the invasion of the Beni Hilal upon Cyrenaica see Goodchild, *Cyrene and Apollonia*, pp. 30–31.

[141] See the French translation by P. A. Jaubert, *Géographie d'Edrisi* (1836) I, esp. p. 295.

[142] See the French translation by J. Reinaud, *Géographie d'Aboulféda* II (Paris, 1883) première partie, p. 204

correspondence that forms part of the Cairo Genizah archives and that is said to contain documents bearing upon the associations of Egyptian Jews with those along the coast of North Africa.

The barren Cyrenaican jebel, with its ruthless brigands that Leo Africanus described so vividly,[143] did not begin to come to the attention of Western readers in firsthand accounts written in their own languages until the eighteenth century. It is unnecessary to consider here all the early European travelers who visited the region, but it is not unimportant to comment briefly upon those who visited the site of Ptolemais and gave significant descriptions of its remains.

The credit for having been the first Europeans to reach the site goes apparently to James Bruce (between 1768 and 1773), Paolo della Cella (before 1817), and Father Pacifique of Monte Cassino (1819).[144] Enticing as the earliest descriptions are, they cannot compare with the accounts of the next visitors. Too much praise cannot be bestowed upon the Beechey brothers, who as the result of their visits in 1821 and 1822 not only provided the first really informative and always highly accurate account of the antiquities at the site but also prepared a plan of the city (reproduced below as Fig. 4) that is still most useful archeologically.[145] Not a little is to be gained by the modern archeologist also from a careful study of the reports of Pacho, who during his visit (1824–26) gave attention for the first time to the inscriptions at the site, of Barth, who between 1845 and 1847 gave particular attention to the fortifications and harbor installations, and of Hamilton (1852), who severely and justly criticized the French Consul

M. Vattier de Bourville for the violence of the procedure by which in 1848 he removed from the façade of the Headquarters of the Dux the text of the Edict of Anastasius for shipment to France.[146] Among the nineteenth-century travelers there remain only Smith and Porcher, whose important contributions to the knowledge of Cyrene tend to eclipse their valuable comment on the Square of the Cisterns at Ptolemais as they saw it in 1860–61, and Rohlfs (1868–69), who described the aqueduct, the "Odeon," the Amphitheater, and what has turned out to be the "Palazzo."[147] Little more is to be gained from the later reports until we come to the years just before and just after the Italian occupation of the coastal ports of Cyrenaica from Derna to Tripoli (including modern Tolmeita[148]) in September of 1911. From these years the accounts of the visits of Halbherr, Norton, the leader of the ill-fated American expedition to Cyrene, Robinson, Checchi, and Ghislanzoni all deserve scrutiny.[149]

After World War I, since Turkey had ceded Libya to Italy by the Treaty of Lausanne (1912)

[143] Leo's *De totius Africae descriptione libri IX* (Antwerp, 1556) is available in the French translation of J. Temporal, *De l'Afrique, contenant la description de ce pays par Léon l'Africain* ... II (1830) esp. pp. 92–93.

[144] James Bruce, *Travels to Discover the Source of the Nile, 1768–1773* I (1790) xliii; Paolo della Cella, *Viaggio di Tripoli di Barbaria alle frontiere occidentali d'Egitto* (1817) pp. 198–99; Père Pacifique de Monte Cassino, "Rélation succincte de la Pentapole Libyque," translated by M. Delaporte, *Recueil de voyages et de mémoires publié par la Société de géographie* II (Paris, 1825) 30. The description of Paolo della Cella is so casual that one wonders whether he was reporting from hearsay rather then from personal observation.

[145] See Captain F. W. Beechey and H. W. Beechey, *Proceedings of the Expedition to Explore the Northern Coast of Africa from Tripoly Eastward* (1828).

[146] See J. R. Pacho, *Rélation d'un voyage dans la Marmarique, la Cyrénaique et les oasis d'Audjelah et de Maradeh* (1829) pp. 174–82, 397–403; Heinrich Barth, *Wanderungen durch die Küstenländer des mittelländischen Meeres in den Jahren 1845–47* I (1849) 396–403; James Hamilton, *Wanderings in North Africa* (1856) pp. 138–45. The Vattier de Bourville incident is reflected in a series of brief communications in *Révue archéologique*, namely "Lettre de M. Vattier de Bourville a M. Letronne sur les premiers résultats de son voyage a Cyrène," Vol. V (1848) 150–54; Letronne, "Quelques notes sur la lettre de M. de Bourville, relative a l'exploration de la Cyrénaique," *ibid.* pp. 279–81; "Lettre de M. Vattier de Bourville a M. Lenormant, sur les antiquités de la Cyrénaique," Vol. VI (1849) 56–58.

[147] See R. M. Smith and E. A. Porcher, *History of Recent Discoveries at Cyrene Made during an Expedition to the Cyrenaic in 1860–1861* (1864) pp. 65–67; G. Rohlfs, *Von Tripoli nach Alexandrien* (1871) pp. 156–65.

[148] This spelling (instead of Tolmeta or medieval Tolomieta) reflects the adoption by the local population of the Italian long *e*.

[149] See S. Aurigemma, "Federico Halbherr e la Missione archeologica italiana in Cirenaica e in Tripolitania," *Africa italiana* III (1930) 242–43; G. Oliverio, "Federico Halbherr in Cirenaica," *Africa italiana* IV (1931) 229–89; R. Norton, "From Bengazi to Cyrene," *Bulletin of the Archaeological Institute of America* II (1910/1911) 57–67, esp. p. 64; D. M. Robinson, "Inscriptions from the Cyrenaica," *AJA* XVII (1913) 185–87; S. Checchi, *Attraverso la Cirenaica* (1912) pp. 107–18; E. Ghislanzoni, "Notizie archeologiche sulla Cirenaica," *Notiziario archeologico* I (1915) 114–54.

and since with the death of Omar Mukhtar in 1932 local resistance to Italy's domination ceased, it became possible for Italian archeologists to begin excavations at the site of Ptolemais in connection with their government's colonial development of the region.[150] The excavations and the important conservation work that accompanied them were conducted from 1935 to 1942 under the able supervision of Professor Giacomo Caputo in his capacity as Superintendent of Antiquities of Cyrenaica. Other operations had been under way at Cyrene since 1925. Of the work done by Caputo, his engineers, his architects, and his archeologists, especially E. Paribeni and G. Pesce, the members of the Oriental Institute expedition can speak only in the highest terms and gladly voice the gratitude which they and all scholars owe to the Italian mission that contributed so much to our knowledge of the site and to the preservation of its monuments.[151]

From their enterprise the Italian archeologists had naturally to exempt the area inside the strong defensive wall which the Italian garrison of the earlier and more difficult days had erected around its beach-head—constructed of stones borrowed largely from the ancient buildings in the vicinity— and the pillboxes that were its outposts.[152] Clearances and soundings, so far as they are indicated by traces still visible on the surface, were made along the western perimeter wall of the

ancient city and particularly at the Tauchira Gate, in the Amphitheater (Building 1 on Plan XXII), in the "Odeon" (Building 9), in the presumed temple complex (Building 26), and in the Upper Theater (Building 28) at the extreme southern end of the site. Full-fledged excavations were undertaken in the so-called "Via Monumentale," for which we use here the designation Street of the Monuments, and, in combination with careful reconstruction work, at the "Mausoleum" (here called Tower Tomb) outside the city to the west, at the "Forum" (here called Square of the Cisterns, Building 10), at the "Christian Basilica" (here called Fortress Church, Building 2), and at the "Palazzo delle Colonne" (Building 13). Summary reports on most of the actual excavations and the reconstruction work were prepared by Professor Caputo himself, to which should be added his articles that provide a general orientation upon the site and its monuments and special studies devoted to the Triumphal Arch, the Fortress Church, and certain of the more important sculptures.[153] Among the publications of his associates, those of Gennaro Pesce on the "Palazzo" and on other sculptures from the excavations deserve particular mention.[154] All these, and other contributions mentioned below, were carefully consulted in the course of the work of the Oriental Institute expedition and in the preparation of the present report. That the work of Oliverio on the inscriptions has been invaluable

---

[150] It is interesting to note that as early as 1888 the German Ambassador at Constantinople had proposed resettlement of a community of Dobruja Germans at the site of ancient Ptolemais (see G. Hildebrand, *Die Grundzüge der Landesnatur von Barka als Gebiet europäischer Siedelung* [Diss.; Marburg, 1902] pp. 67–76) and that just prior to the outbreak of the Italo-Turkish War of 1911–12 Halbherr had planned to undertake archeological work at the site on a large scale jointly with G. de Sanctis (see Oliverio in *Africa italiana* IV 229–89).

[151] The Italian archeologists had naturally to begin by training a staff of local workmen and equipping them for the actual digging. It is a pleasure to record here that a few of the men trained by our Italian colleagues were still available for service in the American excavations, that we were able to use what remained of the Decauville railroad, and that we followed the excellent Italian precedent of dumping earth and surface debris outside the inhabited area of the ancient city near the seacoast, at the east.

[152] The course of the wall is indicated on Plan XXII. It inclosed the older Arab settlement near the harbor and, to the east of it, the Italian barracks, courthouse, church, and school, now virtually all in ruins.

[153] Among the summary reports on the excavations the most important publication, with excellent photographs and some drawings, is Caputo's "La protezione dei monumenti de Tolemaide negli anni 1935–1942," *Quaderni di archeologia della Libia* III (1954) 33–66. On the excavation of the Street of the Monuments there exists a holograph communication of Caputo to which access was kindly supplied by the Department of Antiquities of Cyrenaica, which preserves it in its files at Shahat. Among Caputo's articles that provide a general orientation upon the site the most important is "Tolemaide," *Enciclopedia italiana* XXIII (1937) 976, with good bibliography. Among his special studies see "Arco trionfale in Cirenaica," *Atti del Terzo Congresso de studi coloniali* IV (Firenze, 1937) 133–37; "Una basilica cristiana in Tolemaide," *Comunicazioni presentate al Convegno nazionale di storia dell' architettura 1938* (Roma, 1940) pp. 159–62; *Lo scultore del grande bassorilievo con la Danza delle Menadi in Tolmaide di Cirenaica* ("Monografie di archeologia libica" I [Roma, 1948]).

[154] See his *Il "Palazzo delle Colonne" in Tolemaide di Cirenaica* and "Statue scoperte in Tolemaide," *Bulletin de la Société royale d'archéologie d'Alexandrie* XXXIV (1941) 40–47.

will already have become evident. Lacking in the published records of the Italian excavations are only the description of archeological details such as the interior appointments in the nave of the Fortress Church and an account of minor finds such as coins, bronzes, and pottery. Some of the findings of the later excavations will help to fill gaps left in the picture at these points.

World War II, which brought the Italian excavations to a premature end, did no damage to the antiquities site, though the guardian in charge of the magazine (museum) where the movable finds from the excavations had been stored reports that some of the more readily portable sculptures were stolen by marauding soldiers. How, when at the close of the war the Italians were forced to leave Cyrenaica, the Oriental Institute became for a limited period involved in the further excavation of the site is told in the Preface.

THE SITE, ITS ORGANIZATION, AND ITS MONUMENTS

LOCATION AND CONNECTING ROADS

THE site of ancient Ptolemais no doubt recommended itself to its earliest Greek settlers and to those who ultimately founded the city there for a variety of reasons. Three we can safely infer at this remove from the events. The first is a promontory that projects several hundred meters into the sea, with which are associated at the east two rocky outcrops forming small islands. Even in their natural state these would have provided the rudiments of shelter for ships on easterly, westerly, and southerly courses, the only such shelter between Euesperides-Berenice to the west and Apollonia-Sozusa to the east. The second is the location of the site almost directly north of Barca, giving the most direct outlet from and access to the older, inland settlement and to the highly productive area surrounding it. The third is the amenity and the advantages which certain features of the physical geography of the coastal plain impart to precisely this spot (see pp. 1–2).

At the site of Ptolemais the coastal plain is neither so wide as it is at Euesperides-Berenice nor so undulating as it is at Tauchira and Apollonia-Sozusa. Underlaid with a solid stratum of hard limestone, it rises gradually and quite evenly (Pl. I A), reaching an elevation of approximately 70 meters above sea level on a line about 1.5 kilometers inland (see Plan XXII). At this line it meets a trilobed spur of the Jebel Akhdar, whose crown has a height of 276 meters, that is, only slightly less than the average height of the first step of the inland plateau (Pl. I B). The recesses that mold the spur into three lobes are shallow and have gentle contours, but at either end of the spur the jebel is deeply cleft, by the Wadi Zawana at the east and the Wadi Hambish at the west. Their stream beds, dry save in the rainy season, cut furrows into the coastal plain on their way to the sea, providing natural eastern and western boundaries for the site and enhancing its defensive potentialities (see pp. 51–62).[1] At Ptolemais the moderate width of the plain, which is gradually pinched out completely by the spurs of the jebel, its steady gentle rise, and the symmetry in the arrangement of both the adjacent hills and the valleys impart to the site qualities that impressed early visitors such as the Beecheys[2] and would not have been wasted upon city planners of antiquity. Among the features that the ancients would have appreciated are the sure footing for buildings, the excellent opportunities for drainage, the relative degree of protection against the torrid *ghibli* winds from the Sahara, and the tendency of the cooling inshore breezes to counteract the heat of summer, usually before midday.

Ptolemais was by no means so isolated in antiquity as it was during the Italian occupation and the early years of modern Libya's autonomy (Fig. 1). But the pattern of the roads connecting it with other parts of Cyrenaica as well as the amount and the nature of the traffic upon them changed during the several periods of the region's political history.

If what has been said above (pp. 3–4) about the early use of the site by the merchants of Barca is correct, there must have been a well worn track leading from the Barca plain down through the narrow wadies between the spurs of the Jebel Akhdar to the coast as early at least as the late

---

[1] The bed of the Wadi Zawana is moderately wide and as much as 9.50 m. deep, while that of the Wadi Hambish is relatively narrow and only *ca.* 3 m. deep save at its extreme northern end.

[2] "There is no place on the coast of Northern Africa, between Ptolemeta and Tripoly, which can at all be compared ..., Lebda alone excepted" (Beechey, *Proceedings*, p. 361).

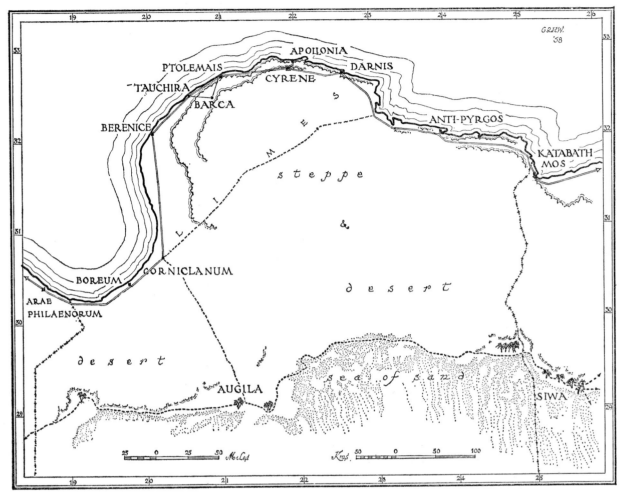

Fig. 1.—Sketch Map of Ancient Cyrenaica. *G. R. H. Wright*

sixth century B.C. The existence of a track from Barca down to the coastal city of Tauchira is suggested by Herodotus' reference to Tauchira as a city of Barcaia.[3] For the second half of the third century B.C., when the city of Ptolemais was being built, the existence of an important connection westward along the coastal plain to Tauchira is indicated by the monumentality of Ptolemais' own Tauchira Gate (see pp. 58–60). A triangle of well established tracks was, therefore, the earliest system of connections between Ptolemais and its environs, while those who ventured to travel overland to Cyrene may well have followed the general line of the present "south road" from Barca via Marawa and Slonta to Cyrene.

Early in the period of Roman occupation, apparently during the reign of Claudius, the pattern

and the nature of the connecting roads must have begun to change. Barca faded into the background as a communications center, and direct connections between Ptolemais and Cyrene were being developed, if not already established, as indicated by the discovery just west of Cyrene of three milestones, one dated by an inscription of Claudius (A.D. 45/46).[4] The milestones belong to the road leading westward from Cyrene to ancient Balagrae, near the modern Zauia Beda, and it is fair to assume as Goodchild does that this stretch formed part of the artery Balacris–Cenopolis–Callis–Ptolemaide that appears later on the *Tabula Peutingeriana*.[5] Though its course has not been followed west of modern Messa, it is clear that the road must have descended from the inland plateau to reach the coast west of the deep cleft formed by the

---

[3] Herodotus iv. 171: πόλις τῆς Βαρκαίας, which should mean a city situated within the territory belonging to Barca.

[4] See Goodchild in *PBSR* XVIII 84–85.

[5] K. Miller, *Die Peutingersche Tafel* (1916) Segmenta VIII and IX.

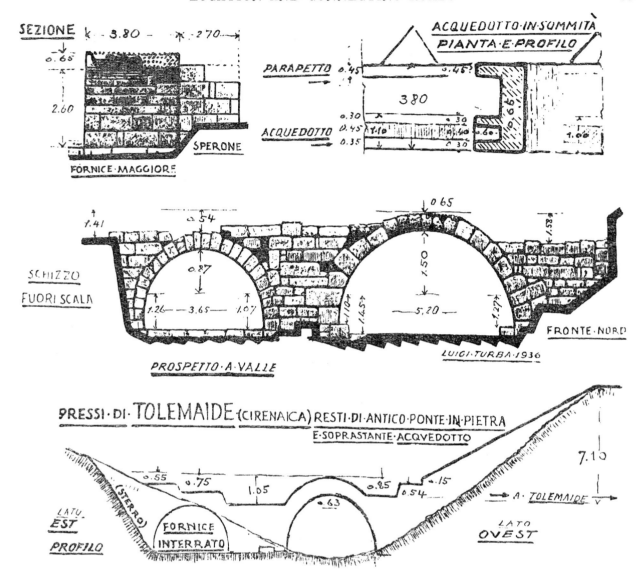

Fig. 2.—Bridge and Aqueduct Crossing Wadi Zawana. After Luigi Turba in Caputo, "Protezione," Fig. 45

Wadi Quf, continuing in general proximity to the coast westward to Ptolemais. The location of the intervening towns is unknown. The text of the inscribed milestone mentioned above says that Claudius "restored" or, perhaps better, "improved" (*restituit*) the road, certainly implying the application of the well known Roman engineering skill, whether for the first or the second time to all or part of the road.[6]

That, whatever may be true about the earlier history of the stretch Cyrene–Balagrae, a planned thoroughfare leading eastward from Ptolemais played a part in the life of the city in the Roman period is suggested by the combination of two facts. The first is the appearance in the *Geography* of

Ptolemy (iv. 4. 3), and here for the first time, of a settlement called Ausigda, which Goodchild places on the coast some 45 kilometers east of Ptolemais.[7] The second is a bridge over the Wadi Zawana at Ptolemais which seems to the present writer of typically Roman construction (Fig. 2 and Pl. I *C*).[8]

[6] See Goodchild in *PBSR* XVIII 89.

[7] See map in Goodchild, *Tabula Imperii Romani: Cyrene*.

[8] I would incline to differ at this point with the distinguished Professor Caputo, who assigns the structure to the period of Justinian, since it also carried the aqueduct repaired by Justinian (see pp. 72–73 below), while remarking on the preservation or the repristination of the old Roman engineering skill at so late a date ("Protezione," p. 62). It should be clear from the emplacement of its trough that the reconstruction of the aqueduct and the construction of the bridge can be considered separately. While it is entirely possible that some parts of the

There exist at Ptolemais today remains of at least the abutments of two other bridges, crossing the shallower Wadi Hambish opposite the Barca Gate and opposite the Tauchira Gate, and the always careful Beecheys report that they saw remains of a second bridge across the Wadi Zawana, near the seacoast and presumably south of the track that crosses the bed of the wadi today and continues past the east quarries (see Fig. 4).[9] In locations where there are only periodic flash floods, rather than deep perennial streams, the existence of such masonry bridges may well be taken to represent the provisions made to cope with the needs of wheeled traffic. This is, of course, exactly what the engineered roads of the Roman period provided for and encouraged. It seems legitimate, therefore, to combine the pieces of information available at Cyrene and at Ptolemais and to suggest that in the early imperial period an engineered road was created between the two cities, joining, of course, with the coastal road leading westward from Ptolemais to Tauchira and beyond. By the time of Ptolemy the geographer (second century) it could well have led to the formation of the settlement called Ausigda and by the time of the *Tabula Peutingeriana* to the growth of the additional villages listed there. If so, the picture that emerges must be thought to imply a steady increase in the use of the thoroughfare and the need of providing for its maintenance and improvement. An intermediate phase of this development is attested by the milestone at the end of the first mile on the road to Tauchira just west of Ptolemais, and if the few dim traces of its inscription have been properly read it should apply to the period of the Tetrarchy (see p. 21). The fact that as the result of the reforms of Diocletian Ptolemais became the capital of Libya Pentapolis and thus the center of communications for the entire province would explain the repair of the coastal stretch westward at this time.

Important as the east-west highway through Ptolemais may have been in the Roman period, its development naturally did not interrupt connections with the interior. The *Antonine Itinerary* gives some impressions about these inland connections in Roman times in reporting (twice in succession) a road Ptolemais–Semeros–Lasamices–Cyrene.[10] This Goodchild plausibly connects with the modern "south road," suggesting the identification of ancient Semeros with modern Marawa.[11] One would expect to find Barca in the list of towns on this road, and the reason for its absence is not clear. It may be, of course, that in the later Roman period the southbound traffic preferred a track leading up to the plateau via the Wadi Habbun, some 20 kilometers east of the city. But in Hellenistic and early Roman times a road certainly ran directly to Barca. The only questions are whether the earlier road southward from Ptolemais was ever developed by Roman engineers and precisely where it may have run. On the first question evidence is lacking, and on the second there are conflicting opinions, particularly among the modern inhabitants of the area. For the seminomadic inhabitants of the area and their relatives among the townspeople of modern Tolmeita there are as many ways of ascending the Jebel Akhdar as there are wadies entering the plain, and all are used. No doubt the situation in antiquity was comparable. Inhabitants of modern Tolmeita like to point to the gentle slope leading upward between the easternmost and middle lobes of the spur of the jebel, directly south of Ptolemais, as the location of the ancient road to Barca, where traces of scarping can be seen (see Fig. 4 for location). Even though the scarping is not too evident, there may well have been a laid-out road ascending this recess in antiquity. But examination of the southern defenses of the city has shown that such a road could have led only to the plateau of the spur and to its acropolis fort, beyond which progress had been made impossible by those who organized the defenses (see pp. 54–56). Exploration of the Wadi

---

bridge were rebuilt in Byzantine times, the structure of at least the large arch and of the buttress protecting the central pier seems distinctly Roman. Compare for instance the bridge across the Wadi Zedi near Jemerrin in Syria, studied and drawn by H. C. Butler and assigned by him to the mid-second century after Christ (*Publications of the Princeton University Archaeological Expeditions to Syria, in 1904–5 and 1909* II A 5 [1915] pp. 300 and 304, Figs. 272–73), and the bridges at el-Kantara and Gastal in provincial Africa (S. Gsell, *Monuments antiques de l'Algérie* II [1901] pp. 7 and 9, Pls. 73–74).

[9] Beechey, *Proceedings*, p. 379.

[10] O. Cuntz, *Itineraria Romana* I (1929) pp. 9–10. The distances between the settlements are 32, 26, and 25 Roman miles respectively. The date of the *Antonine Itinerary* is, of course, debated, but some of its elements and in particular what it says about Cyrenaica can properly be associated with the period before Diocletian.

[11] See *PBSR* XVIII 91, n. 16, and map in Goodchild, *Tabula Imperii Romani: Cyrene*.

Zawana, to the east, indicates that its bed is too narrow and that its sides are too steep to provide for the regular and easy movement of beasts of burden, not to speak of wheeled traffic.[12] On the other hand, the Wadi Hambish, to the west, offers relatively open going and should in our judgment be taken as the valley through which the main track or road descended from the Barca plain in antiquity.[13] Several facts about Ptolemais and the organization of its defenses point in this direction. The first is the existence of remains of lookout or guard towers on the hilltops on *both* sides of the Wadi Hambish precisely where its course can best be seen. The second is the emplacement of a special gate (here called the Barca Gate) at exactly the point most suited to receive traffic from the wadi (see p. 57). The third is the existence outside the city at the very mouth of the wadi of a group of buildings that can be construed as a military or police post (see p. 105). There are no comparable features in the vicinity of the mouth of the Wadi Zawana.

Exploration of the higher part of the Wadi Hambish has not yielded positive traces of scarping and grading that might show whether the ancient track had been improved for the use of wheeled traffic, and further examination particularly of the southerly of the two branches of the wadi is needed. It may be noted in this connection, however, that the paved roadway through the Barca Gate is more deeply rutted by wagon wheels than that of any of the other known gates (Pl. V *C*).

The changing internal conditions in Cyrenaica during the late fourth and the fifth century may have reduced still further the importance of Ptolemais' connections with the interior. What we learn from Synesius about the persistent raids of the Austuriani and from the Edict of Anastasius about the restrictions placed upon contacts with the natives suggests that the interior became less and less accessible as time went on (see pp. 24 and 28). This condition may be reflected in the fact that at some time in the history of Ptolemais while its perimeter defenses were still being maintained the Barca Gate was walled up (see p. 62). This could not have been done much later than the end of the fourth century of our era. Traffic from that time onward must have been largely along the coastal plain and in zones protected by forts on the Jebel Akhdar.[14]

After the Islamic conquest the picture changed radically. Travelers not using coastal vessels normally followed the upland road that went from Derna via el-Merj to Benghazi. Only a few of the medieval geographers, therefore, say anything about Ptolemais. By contrast, Barca returned to prominence and the site of Ptolemais reverted to its original status as the "harbor at Barca." The road to the south again became the most important line of communication for the coastal city.

THE CITY PLAN

In discussions of ancient Greek, Italic, and Roman city planning, a subject that has received no little attention especially since 1924, the cities of Cyrenaica have played almost no part.[15] This is not surprising considering the lack of adequate information about them but is all the more regrettable because the period they cover is one of such strategic importance for the general development and because the differences between the plans of the earlier and the later foundations in this area can be discussed without consideration of the vexatious questions of Etruscan origins and Italic and Greek interdependence. Even today the record of city planning in Cyrenaica is by no means complete. The plans of Barca and Berenice are

[12] The description of the wadi by the Beecheys, who explored it rather carefully (*Proceedings*, p. 359), reflects its glenlike character and may suggest something of its condition in antiquity.

[13] This was the route by which the Beecheys traveled from Ptolemais to Barca in 1821 (*ibid.* p. 387).

[14] On these forts see Goodchild in *JRS* XLIII 65–76. The picture is slightly enlarged below (pp. 105–7), with emphasis on the importance of the coastal stretch Tauchira–Ptolemais and hence indirectly supporting what is conjectural here about the east-west road.

[15] Comprehensive treatments of the subject include particularly the following: F. Haverfield, *Ancient Town-Planning* (Oxford, 1913); G. Cultrera, "Architettura ippodamea," R. Accademia nazionale dei Lincei, *Memorie* XVII (1923) 357–603; A. von Gerkan, *Griechische Städteanlagen* (Berlin, 1924); Fabricius and K. Lehmann-Hartleben in *R.-E., s. v.* "Städtebau" (1929); R. Martin, *L'Urbanisme dans la Grèce antique* (Paris, 1956); F. Castagnoli, *Ippodamo di Mileto e l'urbanistica a pianta ortogonale* (Rome, 1956).

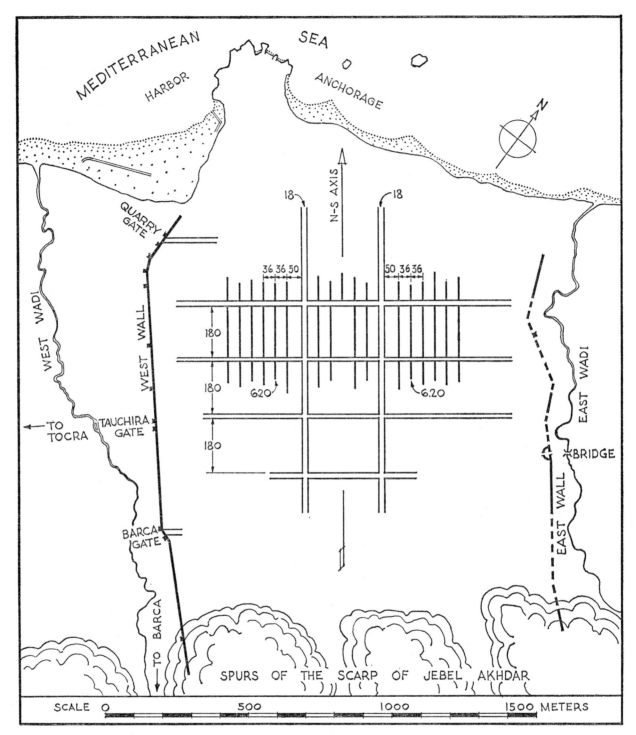

Fig. 3.—Schematic Plan of Ptolemais. *G. R. H. Wright* and *R. C. Haines*

still and will in all probability continue to be unknown, and those of the other sites are known only in part. But enough information is now available concerning Cyrene, Euesperides, Tauchira, and Ptolemais to afford an opportunity for at least a preliminary appraisal of the evidence. In the present context this subject has, of course, to be approached with the city plan of Ptolemais in the forefront of attention.

The city plan of Ptolemais presented herewith (Plan XXII) is based on a survey made for the Oriental Institute expedition by G. R. H. Wright.[16]

[16] Of the plans previously published that of the Beecheys (reproduced here as Fig. 4) is important but gives no clue

Wright had of necessity to rely heavily, though not exclusively, on surface observation, and the plan is therefore both incomplete and subject to future correction. But the outlines of the street grid can be seen clearly from the adjacent spurs of the Jebel Akhdar and are indicated on the ground by remains of building lines and patterns of crop planting. Here, as at so many other antiquities sites, cultivation tends to limit itself to the insulae, leaving the area of the streets, where the soil is shallower, to grow up to weeds. How clearly the growth and withering of the weeds (particularly thistles) outlines the course of the streets at Ptolemais can be seen for example on Plate I *D*, where a stretch of the decumanus leading westward toward the Tauchira Gate is delineated by them.

The salient features of the plan of Ptolemais can readily be discerned from Figure 3, which sets out in schematic fashion what is recorded on Plan XXII. The street grid, excellently adapted to the gentle slope of the coastal plain, is dominated by two cardines running north and south and by at least five decumani intersecting the cardines approximately at right angles. The grid is basically unrelated to the circuit walls and, save at the northwest, to their gates—a typical feature of Hellenistic town planning.[17] Some of the factors that went into the planning of the grid are readily recognizable. One is the distinction between major thoroughfares, which run both east-west and north-south, and minor streets, which run only north-south. The standard width of the cardines among the major thoroughfares it has not been possible to establish, but they seem to reach a maximum width of 18 meters. The decumani seem to have a basic core that is 8.80 m. wide, but the typical width of the Street of the Monuments, including the adjacent porticoes, is 14.80 m. (see Plan VII). The minor streets are typically 6.20 m. wide. The

emplacement of the decumani was based in part on a simple mathematical proposition, namely that the individual insulae were to be 180 meters long. The only questions that arise in this connection concern the number of decumani and the point from which they were counted off. There are good reasons for not increasing the number of decumani at the south above that shown in Figure 3.[18] But it is quite possible that at the north one additional major east-west thoroughfare existed, running along the southern edge of the modern village of Tolmeita, roughly parallel to the coast and well inside the coastal defense wall (see Fig. 4 for approximate position). This possibility is suggested not only by the availability of space for another row of insulae 180 meters long, but more especially by the necessity of providing for communication between the interior of the city and the harbor outside its circuit wall (see pp. 49–50). It is, of course, possible that the nameless settlement that served as the "harbor at Barca" as early as the sixth century B.C. and that must have had its focus in this general vicinity (see p. 4) was incorporated unchanged into the ambitious grid of the later period. If so, the city grid would have been laid around the old harbor town and would presumably have had no more than the five decumani indicated in Figure 3. As to the point from which the decumani were counted off, the fact that the street leading eastward on the line of the Quarry Gate is in precisely the right position to allow an interval of 180 meters between it and the next decumanus to the south is suggestive. Here and here alone, so far as our present knowledge of the site goes, there is a relation between a city gate and the street grid. Conceivably, then, this was the point from which the emplacement of the decumani was calculated. In a city whose harbor was its *raison d'etre*, this seems only natural. It would be important to know in this connection whether the agora was located in this area (see p. 116).

The emplacement of the cardines was determined by considerations which do not include reference to a specific monument or section of the city. People naturally used the western cardo to reach the important Building 26 (see Plan XXII), perhaps

to the street grid. The one used by Oliverio in *Africa italiana* IV 254 is a washed-out version of the Beechey plan. The one that appears with Caputo's article in *Enciclopedia italiana* XXIII is useless; the one he presents in his "Protezione," Fig. 2, places in their proper relationship the Street of the Monuments and eight other known features of the site but gives no indication of the street grid.

[17] See A. von Gerkan, *op. cit.* pp. 128–29, and Martin, *op. cit.* pp. 120–21. The opposite tendency in Italic city planning is properly emphasized by J. B. Ward Perkins, "Early Roman towns in Italy," *Town Planning Review* XXVI (1955–56) 127–54, esp. pp. 144–49.

[18] The reasons include (1) absence of positive indications on the ground, (2) the rapid rise of the level of the coastal plain in this area toward the spurs of the jebel, and (3) the location of the city's great water-storage reservoirs northward of the southernmost observable decumanus.

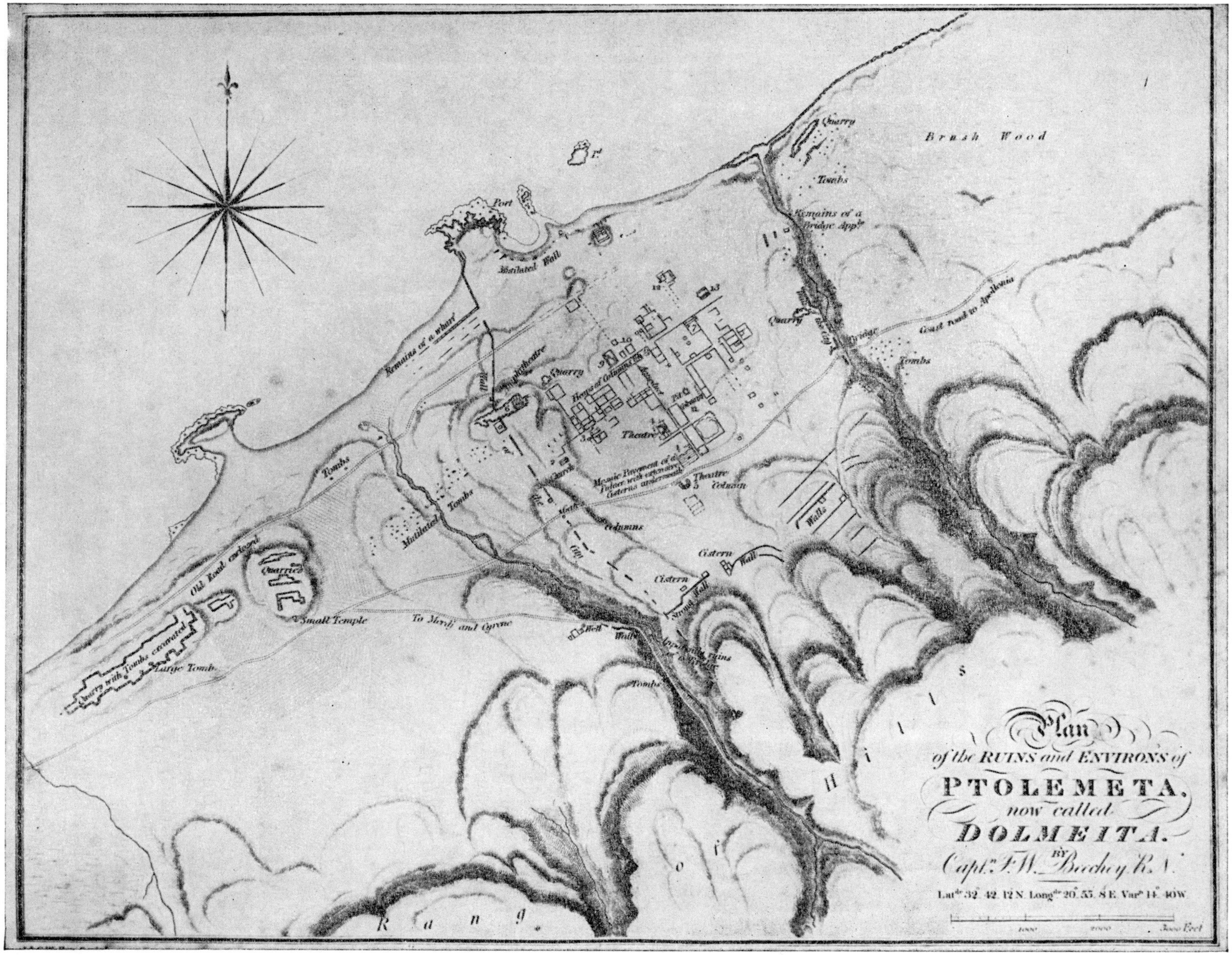

Fig. 4.—Plan of Ptolemais Showing Remains Visible in 1822. After *F.W. Beechey*

the city's major temple, as they used the eastern cardo to reach the Hippodrome (Building 27) and the Upper Theater (Building 28). But the cardines were not oriented upon these structures any more than they were oriented upon an agora or an acropolis. Wherever the agora of Ptolemais may have been, it was not between the two cardines at the north. The very fact that the city had two cardines rules out the use of a cardo as the axis of the street grid. Indeed, the planners evidently used as an axis not a major thoroughfare but a theoretical north-south line approximately halfway between the natural eastern and western boundaries of the site and thus halfway between the eastern and western city walls. The line of this axis coincides with the course of a minor north-south street (see Fig. 3). The cardines were so placed as to allow for the creation of three insulae (each 36 m. wide) on either side of the line.

Two further aspects of the planning can readily be discerned from Figure 3. The planners departed from the standard dimensions of 36 × 180 meters for insulae at three points. West of the western cardo and east of the eastern cardo insulae were established that were 50 meters rather than 36 meters wide. There have as yet been no excavations in any of these insulae, but the extra width was presumably provided so that the buildings to be erected in them could be set to face the cardines and the heart of the city and still have adequate room for development in depth. The second departure from the standard is south of the Street of the Monuments, where the present condition of the site indicates an insula of double width (72 × 180 m.). This double insula should on general principles contain some of the major structures of the civic organism, but all we know about it at present is that its northwest corner was occupied by the City Bath in the Byzantine period (see pp. 160–75). Because the building level had been raised here by about 1.20 m. in the rehabilitation of the thoroughfare in the late fourth century, it was impossible to determine whether the double insula was a product of the rehabilitation or of the original city plan. Only additional excavation farther to the south can provide the needed information. There are, however, no indications of building lines at the appropriate intervals in the entire terrain south of the double insula, and the fact that early European travelers noted remains of an aqueduct leading north from the Square of the Cisterns (see

p. 71) suggests that the area was not subdivided into insulae of regular size. Indeed, the provision along the outer sides of the cardines for insulae 50 meters wide would, if our suggestion about their purpose is correct, imply the existence of a central area toward which the buildings occupying these insulae might be oriented. Whether in the centuries of its structural development the city justified the hopes of those who planned it and used the special features of its plan in accordance with their suggested purposes is, of course, quite another matter.

The street grid of Ptolemais, so far as we know it today, is thus an excellent example of the vision and technical competence of ancient city planners. It is well adapted to the site, has regularity, and is composed of homogeneous elements. Regularity is saved from the monotony of sheer repetition by the introduction of variety so disposed as to add an element of symmetry. Finally, the regular features and the variations (but *not* the major thoroughfares) seem to emphasize a focal area which provides a unifying element for the entirety. Obviously a plan of this character was the work of a skilled architect whose services were obtained or provided for the development of the site. The plan is therefore also the most eloquent testimony we have at present that the city was "founded," with all that this term implies. The foundation, as suggested above (p. 6), belongs to the second half of the third century B.C., that is, to the early years of the reign of Ptolemy III Euergetes I. The importance of the city plan as a creation of this period must be considered in connection with a comparative study of other city plans in Cyrenaica and elsewhere and in the light of the contemporary discussion of the development of ancient town planning generally in the several periods of Greek and Roman cultural history.

The plan of Cyrene, the oldest and most important of the Greek cities of Cyrenaica, is gradually becoming clearer, thanks to the recent work of Goodchild, as can be seen from his sketch that is reproduced here as Figure 5.[19] The grid, so far as it is known, consists of three cardines along the major, northwest-southeast, axis and one decumanus on the northeast-southwest axis. Simple in

[19] See Goodchild, *Cyrene and Apollonia*, pp. 37–39. See also the plan offered by Derek Buttle in *Cyrenaican Expedition of the University of Manchester, 1952*, Fig. XIII. Both plans are based on Italian drawings.

character, it is so naturally adapted to the uneven contours of the site as to be almost inevitable. The central cardo follows the valley between the two hills along whose summits the other two cardines run, and the decumanus connects the three cardines at approximately the point where the valley can first be crossed at a grade feasible for wheeled traffic. All four major thoroughfares served as approaches to areas of basic importance for the life of the city. The central cardo leads to the great Terrace of Apollo with its Fountain, the southerly cardo through the area chosen for the city's public buildings to the Acropolis, the decumanus and the northerly cardo to the Temple of Zeus (*V* on Fig. 5) and the later Hippodrome (*U*).

in Sicily at Selinus, and in the Greek sphere at Olbia on the Black Sea as early as the late sixth century B.C. and that survived into the period of Roman colonialism, for instance at Cosa.[20]

The only region in which subdivision of the areas blocked out by the major thoroughfares can currently be followed at Cyrene is south of the southerly cardo, between the Roman theater and the so-called Prytaneum. Here a series of insulae are occupied by private houses. The houses are Roman and Byzantine and the earliest of them tend to overrun the street lines, but the insulae are by that very token older. It is important to note that the insulae do not meet the cardo at right angles, having been accommodated no doubt

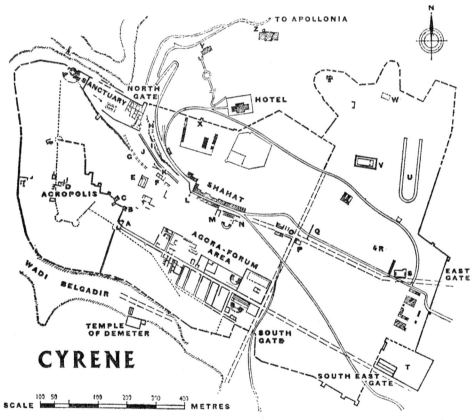

Fig. 5.—GENERAL PLAN OF CYRENE. After R. G. Goodchild, *Cyrene and Apollonia* (opp. p. 37)

Even though many of the buildings in these focal areas are preserved in the form given to them in the Roman period, the grid itself is by no means late. On the contrary, its basic characteristics of intersecting major thoroughfares adapted to the lay of the land and serving as approaches to focal areas represent a type that was developed independently in Italy, for example at Marzabotto,

[20] For the general description of the type see F. E Brown, "Cosa I," *Memoirs of the American Academy in Rome* XX (1951) 107. For Olbia see A. Schulten in *R.-E.* Marzabotto and Selinus appear in virtually all the comprehensive works on ancient city planning listed in n. 15 above (e.g. Castagnoli, *Ippodamo*, pp. 1–2, 50–52). The resemblance between the plan of Selinus and that of Cyrene was pointed out as early as 1913 (Haverfield, *op. cit.* p. 35). Perkins (*op. cit.* p. 130, n. 2) has strong reservations about an early date for the plan of Selinus.

to the existing building lines of public buildings in the Agora area.[21] Thus a grid was developed in this area without reference to an abstract geometrical scheme but quite as naturally as the system of major thoroughfares. Standing at the crossing of the decumanus and the southerly cardo and looking southwest over the planted fields beyond the Wadi Belgadir, one can readily see indications of subsequently developed sections of the city determined in accordance with a regular geometric pattern of the *per strigas* type that was developed first in the fifth century B.C., that was maintained for many centuries throughout the ancient world, and that is known from many examples in Greece (e.g. at Olynthos), in Italy (e.g. at Naples and Herculaneum), and in the Near East in Hellenistic times (e.g. at Laodicea).[22]

Euesperides, founded apparently as a dependency of Cyrene at the end of the sixth century, is known in part at least from work undertaken there by C. N. Johns in 1952. What the excavations showed about the city plan is indicated in Figure 6, which is based on information supplied through the kindness of R. Hamilton of the Ashmolean Museum.[23] Worthy of particular notice in connection with any appraisal of the plan for historical and comparative purposes is the fact that nothing is known of the gently sloping hill forming the northern and most prominent part of the site, since it became a cemetery during the period of the Italian occupation of Benghazi. If the hill was an important focal area of the site, the cardines must have connected it with the important focal area of the docks that lined the shore of a narrow channel running in from the Mediterranean past

the city to the lagoon that served as an anchorage.[24] Johns suggests that the connection was made via an agora which he places hypothetically between two known sections of the city grid, directly inside a supposed gate opening on the harbor. So interpreted, the plan of Euesperides is, like that of Cyrene, functional in its major elements, and, while rectangular insulae do emerge, the resultant grid is anything but an artificial geometrically determined unit.[25] The so-called "Hippodamian" pattern was either not yet normative when Euesperides was developed or was not considered important by those who founded the city. The dependence of Euesperides upon Cyrene as a foundation of the latter suggests the first alternative and links their plans in both time and place.

For Tauchira the only plan currently available is that of the Beecheys, made in 1821 but quite satisfactory for modern use, as Figure 7 and a careful examination of the site itself show. Known to Herodotus and a foundation either of Cyrene or, more likely, of Barca (see p. 3, n. 11), Tauchira had no harbor and must have served primarily for the exploitation of the fertile well watered easterly end of the coastal plain, which is pinched out by the encroaching Jebel Akhdar (see p. 2). Eventually it became an important stopping place on the coastal road and a defensive stronghold against raiders from the jebel. The organization of the city grid with its emphasis upon east-west thoroughfares reflects the city's lateral connections. The most clearly defined of these thoroughfares (*ca.* 5.30 m. wide) runs straight from the eastern gate to the western gate at the base of a low ridge between it and the coast. In their present form these gates represent the work of refortification carried on in Byzantine times, but there is no reason to believe that their position or that of the decumanus connecting them was ever shifted.[26]

---

[21] The insulae are approximately 78 m. long, and sample measurements kindly supplied by Goodchild give widths of 34.25, 34.40, and 34.90 m.

[22] For Olynthos see D. M. Robinson and J. W. Graham, *Excavations at Olynthos. VIII. The Hellenic House* (Baltimore, 1958) pp. 29–38; for the many Italian examples see Castagnoli's *Ippodamo*, pp. 21–50, and his more recent "La pianta di Metaponto," *RAL* XIV (1959) 49–55; for Laodicea see J. Sauvaget, "Le plan de Laodicée- sur-Mer," *Bulletin d'études orientales* IV (1935) 11–114.

[23] The excavation report has not yet appeared. A more schematic though slightly more enlightening plan, coupled with an air photo, has been published by Johns' successor as Comtroller of Antiquities in Cyrenaica (see Goodchild, "Euesperides—a devastated city site," *Antiquity* XXVI [1952] 208–12) and in this form has passed into Castagnoli, *Ippodamo*, p. 20.

[24] The lagoon is the modern salt marsh Sebkha Ain el-Selmani. For these details see Goodchild in *Antiquity* XXVI 208–12

[25] Castagnoli, *Ippodamo* p. 20, records insulae measuring 35×100 m. in the northern section of the grid and 44×80 and 130 m. in the southern section.

[26] Tauchira's girdle of fortifications is commonly attributed to Justinian on the strength of the statement of Procopius *De aedificiis* vii. 2. 4–5. But the matter may not be quite so simple and is of some concern in connection with the fortifications of Ptolemais (see p. 61 below). Procopius tells about Justinian's efforts in behalf of several cities of Cyrenaica. He speaks of the fact that Boreion, at the western end of Upper Libya, had had no

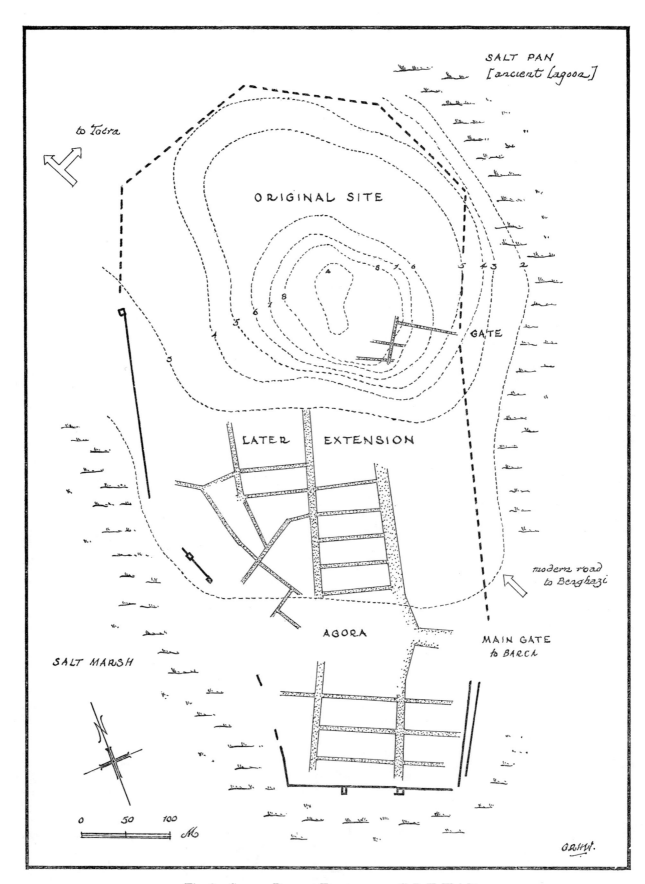

SALT PAN
[ancient lagoon]

to Tocra

ORIGINAL SITE

GATE

LATER EXTENSION

modern road
to Benghazi

SALT MARSH

AGORA

MAIN GATE
to BARCA

N

0   50   100

M

G.R.H.W.

Fig. 6.—Sketch Plan of Euesperides. *G. R. H. Wright*

44

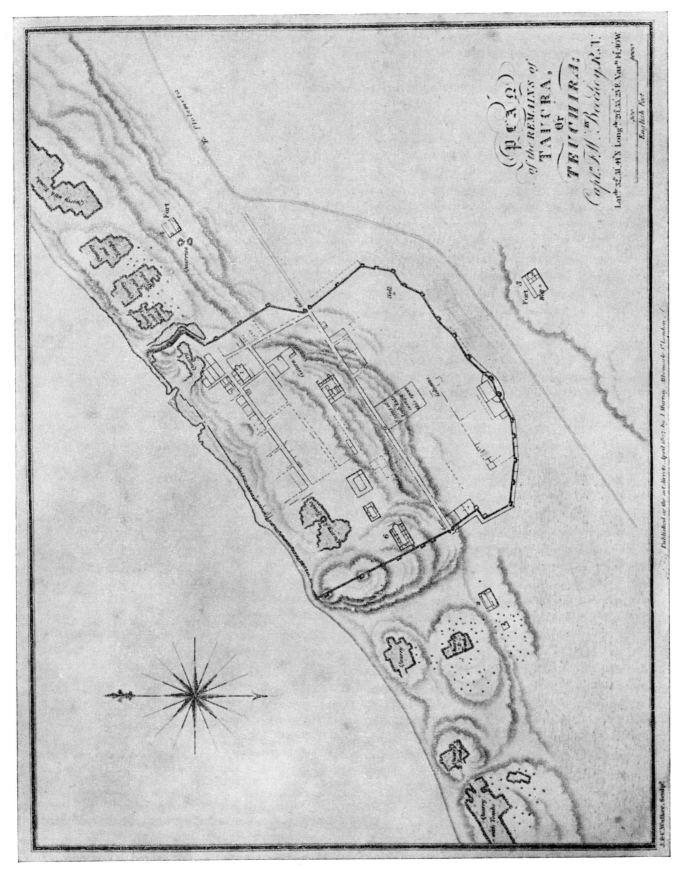

PLAN
of the REMAINS of
TAUCRA,
Or
TEUCHIRA:
Capt. F. W. Beechey R.N.
Lat. 32.31.40 N Long. 20.33.25 E Var. 11. 30 W

English Feet

Fig. 7.—PLAN OF TAUCHIRA. After *F. W. Beechey*

South of this decumanus are well watered gardens in which only scant remains of ancient structures other than the circuit wall are visible. It is probable that in antiquity also the more prominent part of the city lay between this decumanus and the coast. Visible in that area are a second decumanus of similar width, running along the top of the low ridge on which the city was built, and a lesser street, perhaps only an alley, between the two decumani. North-south streets subdivide the region between the northern decumanus and the alley and between the alley and the southern decumanus into insulae, relatively clear examples of which can be seen in the neighborhood of the single building excavated by the Italian archeologists. Between the northern decumanus and the alley an insula about 83 meters long and 39.50 m. wide could be established and between the alley and the southern decumanus an insula about 71 meters long and 38 meters wide. Insulae existed also between the northerly decumanus and the coast, but their northern limits were not clearly definable. Two major north-south streets seem to have existed, the more westerly one (*ca.* 3.70m. wide) running on irregularly to the south gate (not shown on Fig. 7). In general, however, the north-south members of the grid are not at all prominent in comparison with the decumani, and no major crossing of what could be called a cardo and either of the decumani can be established at present. Nor do the existing minor north-south streets normally enter the two sides of the decu-

mani at corresponding points. The insulae, therefore, do not fall into parallel rows and the *per strigas* effect is absent.

All this suggests that here once again in Cyrenaica the regularity of the so-called Hippodamian grid is absent. But so also is the intersection of major axial thoroughfares, although this feature is present at Cyrene and Ptolemais. If our knowledge of pre-Hippodamian city plans were limited to the *incrocio stradale* of Marzabotto, Selinus, and Olbia, the arrangement at Tauchira might indeed be puzzling. But the element of adjustment to circumstance such as is elsewhere exhibited in adaptation to the lay of the land and the fact of application to practical purpose and focal areas provide an explanation. The dominance of the east-west thoroughfares at Tauchira corresponds, as we have seen, to the city's lateral connections, and the southern decumanus, leading from one gate at the east straight to another at the west, is an excellent example of functional arrangement. The northern decumanus and the slightly diagonal north-south street just inside the east city wall lead in the direction of the medieval castle that should mark the site of an ancient acropolis, the decumanus following a geographical feature—the crown of the ridge on which the city was built—and the north-south street leading from the area of the presumed acropolis to the eastern gate, through which the southern decumanus leaves the city. If the north-south streets are neither prominent nor continuous, this may well indicate adaptation to circumstances, for it is clear that, being so close to the coast, the city was exposed to the full force of the gales driving in from the northeast and the northwest. Wide north-south thoroughfares and insulae in parallel files would have exposed the interior of the city in much greater measure to the sweep of the winds. It was functionally in order in this location to avoid such exposure and to arrange the insulae irregularly.[27] Thus the street grid of Tauchira does in a sense correspond with those of Cyrene and Euesperides and reflect the custom followed generally before the geometric regularity of the Hippodamian period became a factor. Indeed, the plan of Apollonia, still largely unknown, may prove to have several features in common with that of Tauchira because of its comparable seaside location.

---

walls and that Justinian supplied them (vii. 2. 11). As regards the walls of Berenice he tells us that Justinian rebuilt them from their foundations, ἐκ θεμελίων ἀνῳκοδομήσατο (vii. 2. 5). As to Tauchira, Justinian inclosed the city with a strong defense, τὴν πόλιν ἐρύματι ἐτειχίσατο ἐχυρωτάτῳ (vii. 2. 4). This expression might apply to the construction (scarcely to the repair) of a girdle of walls but equally well to the creation of the breastwork outside the walls which Oliverio has noted (*Documenti antichi* II 2, p. 166). The expression also appears in and may well be borrowed from Thucydides i. 11.1, where it applies to the breastwork erected about their camp by the Greeks in their operations against Troy. Tauchira must have had walls at the end of the fourth century B.C. if Diodorus Siculus (xviii. 20. 6) was accurate in saying that Thibron besieged it (the verb used being ἐκπολιορκέω). Inscriptions carved on the curtain walls in great numbers and recorded by Oliverio range from year 2 of the Actian era to the reign of Domitian (see p. 14, n. 69, above). This is not to deny that the particularly well preserved western gate at Tauchira is late. Indeed with its solid triangular towers set on square bases it is strange as a work of the period of Justinian and may even be later.

[27] The importance of this type of consideration in ancient city planning is emphasized by Vitruvius *De architectura* i. 6.

Thus it would seem that the plan of Ptolemais is fundamentally different from those of the other cities of Cyrenaica that are at least partially known today. True, it shares with them the distinction between major thoroughfares and lesser streets, but its thoroughfares are not functionally oriented and the insulae that subdivide the areas bounded by cardines and decumani are arranged with geometric precision. By virtue of these features the plan of Ptolemais is necessarily much later than those of the neighboring cities. Its significance as an example of later city planning in Cyrenaica is suggested by its relation to later developments in the eastern Mediterranean generally.

Our understanding of the history of city planning in the Greek and Roman world would be greatly increased if we knew exactly what Hippodamos of Miletus did or did not contribute to the development in the fifth century B.C. On this point opinions are still sharply divided and probably will continue to be so.[28] Among cities whose plans are attributed to him only the Piraeus and the Greek colony of Thurium in southern Italy can safely be regarded as his work, and neither of the two is at present well known. That the basic concept of a geometrically determined grid of corresponding insulae (which is loosely spoken of as "Hippodamian") was his contribution seems unlikely in view of what is known about Miletus and about the frequent appearance of the *per strigas* organization in fifth-century Italy.[29] This type of grid is suddenly present on the scene simultaneously in the eastern Mediterranean and in the Italian west and continues to be a feature of city planning until the period of the Roman Empire.[30] The plan

of Ptolemais is in part at least a debtor to and a product of this development.

In the period that began with the conquests of Alexander the so-called Hippodamian grid found a new sphere of usefulness and expression in the lands conquered by the Macedonians and maintained as elements of the rival kingdoms of the Diadochoi. It provided the pattern for the settlements created as military and commercial outposts along far-flung lines of communications and in established spheres of interest. Whatever is true of the number and the character of the settlements established by Alexander himself, it was clearly the house of Seleucus that carried off the palm as the outstanding instrument of urbanization among the rival dynasties.[31] The excavation of Dura-Europos and the search in modern urban contexts for surviving remains of ancient Laodicea, Aleppo, Apamaea, and Damascus have given us a fairly clear picture of the plans of several Seleucid foundations.[32] In all of them the element of geometric symmetry and correspondence in the size and arrangement of the insulae is the dominant feature. The distinction between major and minor thoroughfares survives from the pre-Hippodamian period of city planning but with nothing like the emphasis visible in the more familiar sixth-century examples and in Cyrenaica.[33] Brown in his discussion of the agora at Dura calls attention to the differences between the city plan of Dura and those of the earlier planned cities of the Greek Mediterranean—Miletus, Priene, and Olynthos—and to the general homogeneity of the plans of the known

[28] The earlier opinions on the importance of Hippodamos are reflected in A. von Gerkan, *op. cit.* esp. pp. 42–61, and Cultrera, *op. cit.* esp. pp. 361–77, where also the literary tradition is fully presented. More recent discussions tend to limit Hippodamos' contribution. See especially Castagnoli, *Ippodamo*, pp. 61–65; Martin, *op. cit.* pp. 16–17; Perkins, *op. cit.* pp. 130, 144.

[29] Even A. von Gerkan was able to salvage Hippodamos' relation to the rebuilding of Miletus only by pushing back the date of his birth (*op. cit.* pp. 43–46). On the relevant examples of geometrically determined fifth-century grids in Italy and Sicily, whether as adjuncts to older establishments or as earmarks of new foundations, at Agrigentum, Naples, Pompeii, Paestum, and elsewhere, see Castagnoli, *Ippodamo*, pp. 21–44. Metapontum falls into line with these as Castagnoli has shown in *RAL* XIV 49–50.

[30] To uphold the Greek origin of this type of grid we must with Axel Boëthius speak of the rapid and immediate

adoption of Greek innovations in Italy. See his "Die hellenisierte italische Stadt der römischen Republik," *Opuscula Atheniensia* I ("Skrifter utgivna av Svenska Institutet i Athen," 4°, II [Lund, 1953]) 172–86, esp. p. 178.

[31] See particularly Tscherikower, "Die hellenistischen Städtegründungen von Alexander dem Großen bis auf die Römerzeit," *Philologus* Supplementband XIX 1.

[32] On the plan of Dura-Europos see especially the comment of F. E. Brown in *The Excavations at Dura-Europos: Preliminary Report of the Ninth Season of Work*, Part I (1944) pp. 23–26. On Laodicea see Sauvaget, *op. cit.*, where also some information about the plans of the other cities is available

[33] At Dura-Europos evidence points to a maximum width of 12.67 m. for "Main Street," of 8.45 m. for Street H, the most impotant cross street, and of 6.33 m. for all the other streets. The insulae measured 70.40 × 35.20 m., a standard proportion of 2:1. Measurements of street widths are not available for Laodicea, but insulae are calculated by Sauvaget at 112 × 57 m., which reflects the 2:1 ratio.

Seleucid foundations. He speaks in this connection of a uniform and standardized Seleucid planning system, which he very properly regards as the natural outcome of what was very literally a "mass production" of cities.[34]

It becomes highly desirable in the light of the developments in the Seleucid sphere to have an insight into Ptolemaic city planning. This is more difficult to come by partly because the Ptolemies were less active in urbanization and partly because their most readily accessible foundations, such as Ptolemais-Acce and Philadelphia, are irretrievably lost. Ptolemais in Cyrenaica offers the first clear-cut example of Ptolemaic city planning. For the comparison of Seleucid and Ptolemaic city planning, which now becomes possible for the first time, several features of the grid of Ptolemais are of importance. The first is, of course, the fact that geometric and mathematical factors entered into its preparation. Thus both Seleucids and Ptolemies were debtors in their planning to the developments of the fifth century B.C. But over against this we must put, in the second place, the absence of any indication of "mass production" by the Ptolemies, the importance and elaborate development of a framework of major thoroughfares at Ptolemais, the provision made in advance for variety in the size of the insulae, and the creation of a unifying focus at the center of the plan. Seen in relation to the earlier history of city planning, the plan of Ptolemais would seem to be a highly successful combination of the older axial system of organization and the fifth-century grid of geometrically arranged insulae. Seen in relation to the contemporary developments in the Seleucid realm, it shows greater pliability, diversification without sacrifice of symmetry, and in general a more imaginative and creative approach to the problem of city planning.

Finally, as to Hippodamos, it seems inherently likely that he did not invent either the standardized grid or the earlier axial type of city plan. What is said by Diodorus about the plan of Thurium, which Hippodamos did produce, has been interpreted recently by Castagnoli as referring to a combination of a system of axial thoroughfares and a grid.[35] If, indeed, Hippodamos' claim to fame is that he was the first to combine successfully the older axial type of city plan and the geometric grid of corresponding insulae, it may well be that the plan of Ptolemais in Cyrenaica provides a better (if somewhat modified) example of the Hippodamian pattern than do the colonial and Greek cities of Italy.

THE HARBOR AND THE ANCHORAGE

Ptolemais was in all probability founded to supply a link in the chain of seaports by which the earlier Greek kings of Egypt sought to exploit and administer to their advantage the economic life of the eastern Mediterranean. For the several services it was expected to perform, in giving access to products of the interior and in providing an intermediate station on the commercial route to the west, its harbor was essential.

Except for a few shallow lagoons and half submerged rocks, the coast line of Cyrenaica between Euesperides (Benghazi) and Apollonia (Marsa Suza) is devoid of unusual physical features save precisely at the site of Ptolemais. Here the continuous series of long shallow indentations by which the coastal plain and the encroaching Jebel Akhdar trace their course northeastward is interrupted by a promontory (see Plan XXII). The promontory is a mass of rock that broadens as it projects from the shore, instead of narrowing to a point. It rises from a level of only a meter or so above the water at the southwest to a height of about 10 meters above the water at the east and north and is covered today with beach grass and a thin layer of blown sand. Its northern face has been deeply eroded and indented by the action of wind and water, the porous rock cut into fantastic shapes.

At the east the promontory creates a shallow bay that is protected by two small offshore islands,

---

[34] *The Excavations at Dura-Europos: Preliminary Report of the Ninth Season of Work*, Part I, p. 26.

[35] Diodorus (*History* xii. 10. 7) says that the city was divided lengthwise by four thoroughfares (πλατείαι) and breadthwise by three, each having a proper name. He then goes on to say that because the στενωποί were filled with houses, the city gave the impression of being well constructed. The question at issue is whether the στενωποί were inclosed by the πλατείαι or whether they were themselves subdivided. Castagnoli (*Ippodamo*, pp. 20–21) adopts the second alternative.

but the bay at the west was much deeper because of an indentation in the shore line (see Fig. 3). Today this indentation is completely sanded up (see Pl. II *A*), and the depth of the beach thus formed is only gradually reduced as the shore line advances westward. The west bay is therefore now only about half as deep as it was in antiquity.

The smaller of the two islands is today only an eroded rocky ledge that rises a meter or so above mean water level at its northern end. The southern portion of the rocky shelf extends landward a goodly distance at or just below water level. In some years, in accordance with changes in the wind and the movement of the sea sand, it is connected with the mainland by a sand spit. In other years small boats pass freely in a channel that is all of 2 meters deep. We saw it both ways. The Beecheys' map (Fig. 4) indicates that the sand spit was in evidence at the time of their visit. The larger island is a longish mass of rock (see Pl. III *B*) rising rather sharply from the bed of the sea and not eroded by the action of the water. Between the promontory and the smaller island, between the two islands, and between the larger island and the coast there are channels sufficiently deep to afford passage for fishing boats. The boats of the Cretan fishing fleet that still put in here during the spring season each year use the channel between the promontory and the smaller island if the sea is calm and the channel between the larger island and the shore in all kinds of weather. In fair weather they run lightly ashore on the beach; in stormy weather they anchor in the shelter of the larger island. The mother ships, being of deeper draft, invariably anchor in the bay west of the promontory.

Affording protection against the prevailing and often stormy winds from the northeast, the promontory and its islands thus provide the physical essentials for an anchorage at the east and a harbor at the west. How these were developed in ancient times only an archeological examination can reveal. What can thus be learned will be limited by the changes that more than two thousand years of exposure have wrought in the outlines of the promontory and the islands and in the man-made harbor installations. It will also be affected by the gradual settling of the coast line along most of the eastern Mediterranean, a settling which amounted at Apollonia to as much as 3 meters. What can be said in the absence of such an examination is even

more limited, comprising only a record of such traces of the ancient installations as have been observed at various times and some suggestions about the interpretation of the evidence.

Since the exploration of ancient Carthage, and particularly since more importance has been attached to the study of the social and economic aspects of the history of the ancient world, the harbors of the eastern Mediterranean have received increasing attention.[36] From this has come a clearer understanding of the standard features of harbor installations developed as a result of the advancing technological knowledge of the Hellenistic and Roman periods and of the infinite variety in their adaptation to the physical geography of the individual sites. The harbors of ancient Cyrenaica, like those of Palestine, are relatively unknown, but recent work at Apollonia will shortly remedy this situation at the most important point.[37] The installations at Ptolemais apparently never rivaled those at Apollonia in either scope or elaborateness, but they should by no means be neglected, even though our knowledge of them is still relatively meager.

To understand the nature of the harbor installations at Ptolemais it is important to realize that the west city wall, now traceable only to a point some distance south of the paved road leading to the modern town, originally continued, after a slight change in direction, northward to the west side of the promontory (see pp. 52–53, Fig. 4). Hence the harbor lay outside the confines of the city proper, as was the case in so many seaports of the ancient world, separating the transient "strangers" from the "citizens" and providing a *zone franche* for transshipment, exchange, and unloading of goods.[38] Plate II *B* shows the remains of several solidly built walls entering into or emerging from the ridge of sand, boulders, and latter-day masonry

[36] See especially K. Lehmann-Hartleben, *Die antiken Hafenanlagen des Mittelmeeres* (*Klio* Beiheft XIV [1923]) and in *R.-E.*, *s. v.* "Städtebau." Information comes also from the French exploration of the harbor of Tyre (A. Poidebard, *Un grand port disparu, Tyr* ("Bibliothèque archéologique et historique" XXIX [Paris, 1939]) and the American exploration of Seleucia Pieria.

[37] A preliminary sketch plan of the installations at Apollonia will be found in Goodchild, *Cyrene and Apollonia*, opp. p. 81.

[38] See A. von Gerkan, *Griechische Städteanlagen*, p. 114, and Lehmann-Hartleben, *Die antiken Hafenanlagen*, pp. 29–41.

that today forms and follows the west side of the promontory at the edge of the modern town of Tolmeita. No one of them is part of a sea wall nor, in all probability, of the city wall. Rather they seem to represent elements of structures built on or behind a continuous quay that must have run along the east side of the bay outside the city wall. Stones possibly belonging to such a quay lie in the sand in the foreground.

Along the south side of the bay, at a good distance from the present shore line, the top of a long thick wall running westward can at certain times and seasons be seen projecting slightly from the sand (see Plan XXII). This wall was noted also by the Beecheys in 1821–22 and by Barth in 1845–47, together with certain supplementary features not visible more recently, whether because of changes in wind and weather that have increased the coverage of sand or because of looting.[39] The Beecheys testify that "the remains of the Naustathmos ... begin from the (west city) wall, following the line of the beach towards the mouth of the western ravine (the brook bed issuing from the Wadi Hambish), and ... protected from the sea by a breakwater of about fourteen feet in thickness." From this both they and Barth observed other walls projecting at intervals. These were, of course, the piers that inclosed rectangular slips.[40] Those that Barth saw he describes specifically as projecting toward the sea, that is, northward. The Beecheys' use of the term "breakwater," if strictly applied, would suggest that the piers extended from it in a southerly direction. Conceivably there was once an inner basin with piers and slips on either side. Barth also noted light fortifications south of these installations, paralleling and perhaps protecting the road leading to the site, but they have disappeared and whether they were older than the medieval period it would be difficult to say.

It is thus clear that the bay west of the promontory was indeed the harbor of ancient Ptolemais and that typical facilities for the loading and unloading of merchandise were amply supplied. In the light of what is known about harbor installations elsewhere, we would expect to find a jetty projecting westward from the end or the side of

the promontory, partly closing the bay for the protection of ships, but of such a construction there are currently no traces. Instead we find on the west side of the promontory, near its outer end, two wide sloping channels that have been cut into the rock by human hands and extend out into the water (see Pl. III A). It is tempting to regard them as ship pens, but their antiquity and their purpose cannot be established.

In the area east of the promontory the ancient defenses of the city seem to have continued along the shore (see p. 53), separating the anchorage from the town quite as the harbor at the west was separated from it. In both areas gates must have been provided to facilitate and control communication with the city (see p. 56). No installations in the area east of the promontory are visible today along the coast line, which has, of course, receded over the centuries under the pounding of the surf. On the larger of the two islands, however, there are extensive indications of quarrying (Pl. III C) which require explanation. It is possible that the quarry provided blocks for a structure on the island itself, but no traces of a structure exist there today.[41] Underwater explorations between the east tip of the island and the coast revealed the remains of a row of large untrimmed blocks (Pl. III D), apparently remnants of a short breakwater that projected from the island and protected the anchorage against the northeast winds. Since it would have been difficult to transport across the open channel the stones for a breakwater based on the

---

[39] See Beechey, *Proceedings*, pp. 377–78, and Barth, *Wanderungen*, pp. 400–401.

[40] The always precise Beecheys give the width of the piers as 7 feet and that of the slips as 30–40 feet.

[41] The suggestion that a lighthouse once stood on the island was originally made by Pacho (*Rélation d'un voyage dans ... la Cyrénaique ...*, p. 178) and repeated recently by Oliverio (*Documenti antichi* II 2, p. 255). It rests on the combination of two facts, namely (1) that Synesius (*Letters*, No. 4) mentions a φάριος Μύρμηξ in telling of his journey from Alexandria to Cyrenaica and (2) that Ptolemy (*Geography* IV. 4. 8) mentions an island called Myrmex in describing the coastal region of Cyrenaica. That the reference in Ptolemy is to the island off Ptolemais is possible, but ancient authors have associated it with Ausigda, a town east of Ptolemais (see p. 35 above). The Pharios Myrmex of Synesius, however, must have been in the region of the Nile Delta, since Synesius mentions it at the beginning of his narrative of the journey from Alexandria westward and says that the ship's running-aground in the harbor behind the island was a bad augury for an even worse voyage. The Beecheys (*Proceedings*, p. 378) more wisely say that if Ptolemais had a lighthouse it must have stood on the promontory, where, of course, it could have been more readily serviced and where a modern lighthouse stands today.

island, it seems logical to suppose that they were quarried on the island itself.[42] Representations of ancient harbors suggest in addition to walls separating them from the city proper the existence of strong defensive forts.[43] In the periods during which the commercial emporia of the Mediterranean littoral were exposed to or practiced piracy, as the case might be, such fortifications were often very necessary. The Beecheys[44] speak of "strong forts" at either end of the section of the city wall inclosing the anchorage and show on their plan (Fig. 4), near the coast, a square building that may be the more easterly of the two. This may well be the medieval "chateau des Juifs" mentioned by Abu el-Fida (see p. 29), but little of it remains visible today.

That the harbor was a busy one in Hellenistic times and again during the two centuries when Ptolemais was the metropolis of the Roman province of Libya Pentapolis is quite likely. Its natural features do not compare favorably with those of either Apollonia or Euesperides-Berenice, and if modern conditions are any criterion it must at all times have had periods in which its facilities were clogged with shifting masses of sea sand. Its present condition, while not necessarily typical or permanent, shows what changes in winds and storm tracks could have wrought in earlier centuries. Perhaps a succession of years marked by inroads of sea sand was one of the factors that led to the transfer of the provincial metropolis to Apollonia. Certainly in the medieval period, if we have correctly interpreted Abu el-Fida, the anchorage rather than the harbor was being used for the loading and unloading of merchandise, the ships being lightly run ashore to be serviced, as they are at the present time.

THE PERIMETER DEFENSES

Seen across the centuries the defenses at the site of Ptolemais provide an interesting example of changes made to protect the inhabitants under a variety of circumstances and in keeping with changing economic and political conditions. The latest fortifications are those erected by the Italian military during the Italo-Senussi war of 1911–32, when modern Tolmeita was as yet only a beachhead to be held against armed raiders from the interior. These consist of a perimeter wall inclosing only a fraction of the area of the ancient city (see Plan XXII and Pl. II *A*) and a number of outlying blockhouses and coastal forts used to mount guns, all constructed largely of materials taken from ancient buildings.

The Italian wall of the present century, already in a ruinous condition, would scarcely deserve mention in this context, save as an obstruction on the antiquities site, did it not offer analogies in its emplacement, character, and function to earlier defensive installations on the site. As to emplacement and character, the Italian wall may well illustrate a phase in the medieval history of the settlement described by the geographer Idrisi. Writing in the middle of the twelfth century Idrisi said that the Tolomietha of his day, serving as a commercial emporium for the overseas trade particularly with Alexandria, was a "place très forte, ceinte de murailles en pierre."[45] Where the circuit wall of the medieval town ran is currently unknown, but that it did not inclose all of the site of the ancient city is clear. As to function, the Italian wall, and for that matter the medieval wall also, illustrates a feature of the ancient system of defense, namely emphasis upon the protection of the inhabitants against raids from the uplands of the interior.

The fortifications of ancient Ptolemais were much more extensive and were organized in accordance with the Hellenistic stage in the development of a pattern whose beginnings in the eastern Mediterranean go back to the sixth century B.C.

---

[42] Barth, *Wanderungen*, p. 400, says that the anchorage had a breakwater here, but whether on the basis of observation or inference is not clear. The same applies to the statement of Smith and Porcher, *History of Recent Discoveries at Cyrene*, p. 67, that the promontory and the island were at one time connected by an "artificial pier." This statement is the more dubious because the narrow channel at this point is very deep. Pacho's description (*op. cit.* p. 178) of the marble and porphyry blocks visible in the water of the anchorage seems quite fanciful.

[43] See e. g. Rostovtzeff, "Die hellenistisch-römische Architekturlandschaft," *MDAIR* XXVI (1911) 1–160.

[44] *Proceedings*, p. 378.

[45] Jaubert, *Géographie d'Edrisi* I 295.

Much of what we know about them we owe to the Italian archeologists, who laid bare the cradle of a good part of the west wall in the coastal plain and published a sketch plan of one gate (Fig. 8). The Oriental Institute expedition was able to supplement the Italian work in some measure and to re-examine the cleared section of the wall at crucial

and gates are left above present ground level and at least one early European traveler believed that the ancient city lacked defensive walls.[46]

WALLS

Approximately a kilometer of the cradle of the western wall was laid bare by the Italian arche-

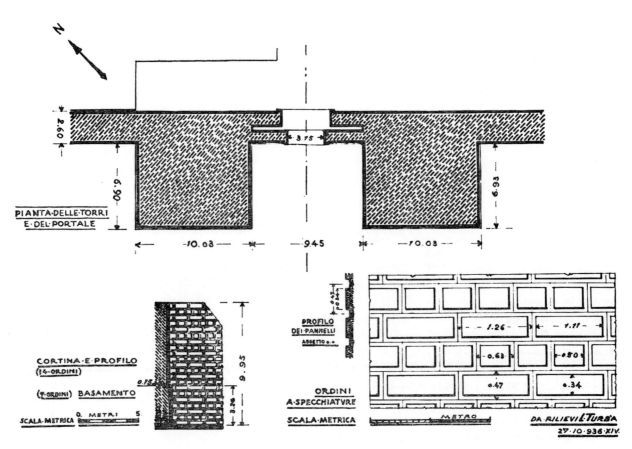

Fig. 8.—PLAN OF TAUCHIRA GATE OF PTOLEMAIS. After Luigi Turbo in Caputo, "Protezione," Fig. 23

points. This first written account of the fortifications provides part of the over-all description of the ancient city and its monuments rather than a detailed comparative study of the defenses. As a matter of fact, the defenses of ancient Ptolemais seen in their entirety are by no means unusual and offer little that is not already well known from other sites. Perhaps the most unusual thing about them is that they were apparently razed by the inhabitants of the city in later antiquity in the course of a historical development that led to the substitution of a system of zone defense for the system of perimeter defense (see pp. 26–27, 100–104). Because of this development few traces of the walls

ologists. It runs in virtually a straight line from the foot of the spur of the Jebel Akhdar that forms the east side of the Wadi Hambish northward down the gently sloping coastal plain to a great quarry (see Plan XXII). Here it is roughly parallel to the cardines, but its course was a by-product of adaptation to the natural contours of the land rather than the result of efforts to co-ordinate city planning and city defense, for it follows the crest of a slight rise to the east of the deep narrow gully cut

[46] So Père Pacifique de Monte Cassino in *Receuil de voyages et de mémoires publié par la Société de géographie* II (1825) 30.

in the plain by the waters that run down from the Wadi Hambish in the rainy season. North of the quarry the wall angles sharply toward the promontory. Here its course has been laid bare almost to the modern road connecting Tolmeita and el-Merj. At this point its course is lost in the sea sand through which the road was laid, no doubt because its stones were used in the creation of the Italian defenses nearby. The Beecheys show a second angle in the course of the wall in this area (see Fig. 4), no doubt with good authority, since they actually saw the wall preserved here to a height of some 12–13 feet.[47] This angle would have brought the wall against the west side of the promontory at a very narrow angle. Plate II *B* shows a series of walls emerging at such angles from the west face of the promontory, but they seem to belong to the medieval development of the harbor area rather than to the ancient. The only other places where the wall is interrupted is at the quarry. There we must assume its razing was accompanied or followed by an extension westward of the quarry itself, so that originally the wall continued at ground level just beyond the end of the quarry or on a narrow footing of the native limestone shelf left for it by quarrymen working on either side of its established line. Fallen sections of this footing are to be seen in the quarry.

The construction of this whole stretch of the west wall as revealed by the clearances is quite homogeneous and basically very simple (see Pl. II *C* and Plans II–III). Two parallel rows of heavy rectangular blocks form its inner and outer faces and are connected at irregular intervals by blocks of lesser strength that divide the interior into compartments. Even at the base course, which is all that is preserved, some of the transverse members are bonded into the facings as headers, and no doubt such occasional bonding continued upward to whatever height stone was used in the construction. The compartments were presumably filled with earth, field stones, and chips to give solidity to the core. This type of construction is typical of early Greek and especially of Hellen-

istic defensive walls, as numerous parallels show.[48] In view of what the Beecheys tell us about the walls in the harbor area it seems likely that there at least the city wall must have been faced with stone to the very parapet and *chemin de ronde*. That it consisted elsewhere of a stone and rubble socle surmounted by mud brick plastered to protect it from the weather is by no means impossible.[49] The typical thickness of the curtains in the exposed area is 2.60 m., which we may assume was standard throughout. At this thickness they can scarcely have been more than 5 to 7 meters high.

Very little can be added about the east wall of the city. It occupied a corresponding position, overlooking the much deeper and wider trough formed by the waters issuing from the Wadi Zawana, but its course was less rectilinear than that of the west wall, though the precipitousness of the descent into the stream bed may have caused the displacement of residual elements of the base course over the centuries. In any event nothing like the straight lines of cradling exposed at the west by the Italians is visible at the east today. The sections of the east wall whose course could be followed by stones visible on the surface are indicated on Plan XXII.

[47] "The remains of the wall between the quarry and the sea are very conspicuous and decided; they run down quite to the water's edge, and are here about eight feet in thickness, and, in some parts, as much as twelve and thirteen feet in height. Without these (to the westward) ... are the remains of the Naustathmos ..." (Beechey, *Proceedings*, p. 377).

[48] Good examples are provided by Herakleia (F. Krischen, *Die Befestigungen von Herakleia am Latmos* [Staatliche Museen zu Berlin, *Milet* III 2 (1922)]) and by the later walls of Pompeii (Krischen, *Die Stadtmauern von Pompeji* [1941] pp. 9–13). On the ἔμπλεκτον type of wall construction generally see Vitruvius *De architectura* ii. 8. 7.

[49] Bricks were used in the upper sections of pre-Hellenistic walls for instance at Mantinaea (see G. Fougères, *Mantinée et l'Arcadie orientale* [1898] p. 145 and Fig. 22). In the Hellenistic period city walls faced with stone to the very top were more typical, and climatic conditions at Ptolemais would lead one to believe that the same type of construction was used here throughout the city wall. What gives pause is, first, that mud-brick walls on a stone socle were commonly used at Ptolemais in early Roman private houses (see pp. 119 and 216 below), and, second, that nowhere, to the best of our knowledge, has the razing of the city wall left more than a base course *in situ*. One would think that the razing of a city wall built to its crown with stone facing would have supplied Byzantine builders with such a mass of material that at some points piles of debris would reveal standing remains several courses high. That a stone socle would in any case have been several courses high and that in areas of special importance (such as the harbor area) the wall would have been faced with stone to the very top is, of course, to be taken for granted.

Whether the wall observable at either side of the site in the coastal plain was continued at the north, along the coast, is not clear. Parallel examples in other coastal cities of the eastern Mediterranean and North Africa would suggest that it was, for danger in the Hellenistic period at least threatened from the sea almost as much as from the interior. Today no remains of a coastal wall are visible at Ptolemais, but, exposed as such a wall would necessarily have been both to the surf raised by northeast storms and to looting for building purposes at all times, the absence of visible remains is scarcely a criterion. The European traveler Barth, who visited the site in 1845–47, records a continuous line of defensive walls along the coast from at least the middle of the north side of the city to the harbor at the west but suggests that they were of medieval construction.[50] Perhaps he was right. The Beecheys make no such restriction in their comment, which is still more interesting. After describing the harbor west of the promontory they go on to speak of what we designate as the "anchorage" east of the promontory and state that "remains of a wall running round the small port within the town . . . , and which we may call the eastern harbour, are still visible; and a strong fort yet remains on either side of it, at the eastern and western extremity of the wall, which appears often to have been the case." They also speak of the "remains of a bridge which was formerly thrown across the ravine, running down to the wall of this port."[51] The interpretation of the "bridge" offered below (p. 57), if correct, indicates that the coastal wall, in its original form, was not medieval but ancient.

The city wall of Ptolemais was strengthened by the addition of towers between stretches of curtain, but such towers are by no means as frequent as one might expect. At the east remains of only a single tower are visible on the surface, but of course there must have been more. At the west towers flank each of the three gates (see below), and Italian clearances fixed the location of three more at intervals of about 45 meters. The southernmost of these overlooks the edge of the vast quarry at the point where the city wall coming down the plain from the south now disappears at the quarry face. Tests along the outer face of the wall have revealed remains, unexcavated, of two other towers at intervals of 195 and 130 meters southward from the quarry tower, the more southerly one being about 100 meters north of the Tauchira Gate (see Plan XXII). The length of the intervals suggests that other towers may exist but have remained unnoticed.

The towers themselves are known only from their first courses, which naturally do not give a clear picture of the interior arrangement. Examples of their ground plans will be found on Plans II and III. Apparently they were of elementary construction. Some were platforms filled solidly with rubble; others had interior chambers and possibly (wooden) staircases. The towers were either set against the outer face of the wall or, more commonly, bonded into it, at least at the base course. The interrelation of wall and tower is unusual in one case, where the exterior facing of the wall continues diagonally through the interior of the tower (see Plan II). The dimensions of the square towers vary from 9 to 19 meters on a side. Not all the towers, however, were square. Those flanking the Barca Gate were rectangles, the one at the aouth being about 12.70 m. wide and projecting sbout 9 meters from the face of the wall.

The Defenses on the Jebel Akhdar

To have protected the city only at the north and in the coastal plain at the east and west would have left it extremely vulnerable, especially in view of the threat from the native tribes of the upland interior that became more and more serious as time went on. It has frequently, if not generally, been assumed that at the south the city wall followed an unknown line at the foot of the spurs of the jebel. The Beecheys clearly had this impression,[52] but it is not clear whether it was based on inference or on observation such as that of Barth, who states positively that the walls could be followed at the west to the foot of the jebel, then eastward, where there were inner and outer walls (of which the latter served in his judgment to deflect the rain water from the jebel toward the Wadi Hambish!), and then northward along the side of the Wadi

[50] See Barth, *Wanderungen*, p. 400: "Mein erster gang . . . führte mich an's Meer hinab etwa in der Mitte der Breite der Stadt, und gleich hier fand ich die Berichte der Arabischen Geographen bestätigt; das ganze Ufer entlang zeigte sich entschieden mittelalterliches Gemauer daß mich nach Westen begleitete an die für solche Stadt allerdings kleine Hafenbucht."

[51] Beechey, *Proceedings*, pp. 377–78.

[52] *Ibid.*

Zawana to the sea.[53] This statement is not easy to assess. Short stretches of terrace walls serving agricultural purposes are visible along the base of the jebel here and there, but there is nothing that can be regarded as part of a city wall. The early travelers may have mistaken the terrace walls for remains of the city wall, or what they saw may now be completely buried under the soil that washes down each year from the jebel. Certainly, if a wall is buried here, the process of erosion would have been completed long before the nineteenth century and certainly, also, there is something of a conflict between the existence of a perimeter wall at the foot of the jebel and the use of its slope as a source of supply for the great reservoir (Building 12 on Plan XXII) just below it (see pp. 71–72). To resolve the problem the Oriental Institute expedition made a fuller investigation of the adjacent slopes of the jebel and discovered a continuation of the defensive system that included these slopes (Plan I).

The natural contours of the terrain in this area have one feature of great importance for the deployment of a defensive system. The three lobes of the jebel directly south of the city join at the top to form a triangular plateau whose base, at the north, is parallel to the coast line and whose apex is connected with the rest of the jebel only by a single sharp spine with deeply declivitous slopes. Those who planned the defenses of Ptolemais continued its walls southward and upward along the edges of the Wadi Hambish at the west and the Wadi Zawana at the east to the level of this plateau and then along the converging sides of the triangle to its apex. In so doing they naturally made the best possible use of the spurs and shoulders of the mountain, running the wall along those that provided the most commanding positions and the most continuous line of ascent. On the slopes the course of the wall is therefore irregular. On the plateau it runs at the very edge of an escarpment (3–5 m. high) that represents the outer face of the limestone layer forming the top of the mountain. Emplacements of exterior watchtowers and outlines of guardhouses set into protected depressions inside the wall were noticeable at irregular intervals.

The installations at the apex of the triangle are particularly interesting. A twofold provision was

made here to protect the city against ready invasion from the uplands of the interior. A deep fosse was cut through the sharp spine that connects the plateau with the further rise of the jebel to the south, and an acropolis fort with towers at the most strategic points (Fig. 9) was constructed within the apex. The masses of fallen stonework are here more extensive than elsewhere on the plateau; rectangular towers and what may be bastions emerge, but without excavation details must remain obscure. The presence of at least one cistern for collecting rain water from the triangular surface of the acropolis fort could be verified. What shelter was provided for guards or garrison is unknown.

The construction of the fortifications on the jebel differs markedly from that used in the coastal plain, and its nature is such that the walls could well have escaped attention, particularly at the very beginning of the ascent at the west. Here for a distance of several hundred meters from the point where the ashlar masonry cradle stops, 100 meters or so south of the Barca Gate, the wall today consists of large irregular and crudely quarried limestone blocks set in two parallel rows with a third row ranged on top of and between them (Pl. IV *A*). The barrier thus created is solid enough and well over a meter high in spots, but what its superstructure may have been is no longer apparent. This type of construction stops where, as the ascent continues, the limestone ceases to present a hard solid surface and becomes flaky. From here on the wall is composed of large chips and blocks, quarried in the immediate vicinity and carefully arranged with flat faces toward the exterior but without any attempt at coursing. At the top of the plateau the tendency of the uppermost limestone layer to break naturally into quadratic units was particularly favorable to the work of the builders.

Commonly the extant remains of the wall are scarcely more than 20–30 cm. high, so that they had to be searched for in the underbrush (Pl. IV *B*). But once they were identified and a direction was established, they could readily be followed. In general a width of 2.00–2.60 m. was maintained. The towers, save at a few important points, were apparently only raised platforms that provided lookout possibilities. The absence along the course of the wall of large masses of loose stone debris that could represent displaced upper elements was something of a puzzle. The stones may have cas-

[53] Barth, *Wanderungen*, p. 401. Perhaps Smith and Porcher (*History of Recent Discoveries at Cyrene*, p. 65) should be supposed to take the same position when they speak of the city as being square.

caded down the declivitous sides of the jebel, or here again we may have an indication of the possible use of mud brick set on a stone socle. Naturally a wall even of breastwork height would have sufficed at most points. In any case it should be clear that in spite of a diversity of construction the defenses of Ptolemais represent a single unified plan.

of this port (the anchorage)." Of such an arched structure no remains are now visible. The eastern face of the promontory where it joins the mainland rises some 5 meters above the beach, and, while there is no occasion for the emplacement here of an actual bridge, we can understand what the Beecheys noted by using the analogy of an unpublished structure still partially preserved at

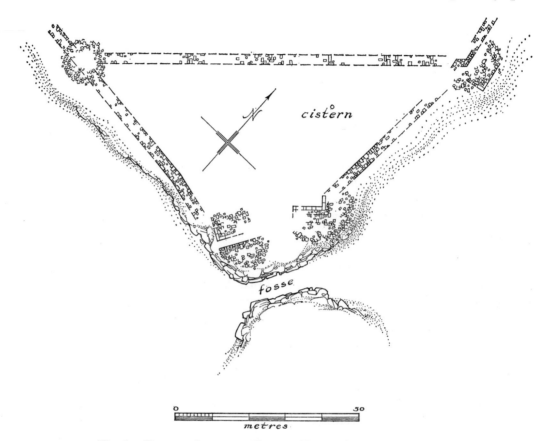

Fig. 9.—PLAN OF ACROPOLIS FORT OF PTOLEMAIS. *J. E. Knudstad*

GATES

Ptolemais probably had seven gates. At the north there must have been a gate providing access to the harbor on the west side of the promontory, if our suggestion as to the probable location of the agora has merit (see p. 116). Since the bay east of the promontory was used as an anchorage and since the city wall presumably continued eastward along the coast, cutting across or surrounding the isthmus, it is probable that there was also a gate leading down to the waterfront at the anchorage. Mention has already been made (p. 54) of the Beecheys' report about the remains of a "bridge thrown across the ravine, running down to the wall

Apollonia. That structure is a water gate through which connection was established between a road running at a relatively high level above the shore and a mole extending outward to the ancient harbor.[54] The road sloped sharply down to the mole, passed through a gateway set between flanking towers, and issued into a semicircular court or *piazzetta*. Plate V *D* shows the inclined roadway coming down to the level of the mole between inclosing walls at the left, and one-half of the semicircle inclosing the *piazzetta* is at the right. Of the other half only the outline of the curving trench cut in the native limestone to receive the

[54] The structure is No. 11 on Goodchild's sketch plan of Apollonia (*Cyrene and Apollonia*, opp. p. 81).

masonry remains. Our suggestion is that at Ptolemais such an inclined roadway contained between retaining walls led down from the naturally high level of the land mass to the beach through a gateway at the southeastern terminus of the promontory and that the gateway was placed below the wall, close to shore level. The wall, then, would have been continued over the gateway, its arched support (the "bridge") inclosing the gateway at the top.

At the east Ptolemais probably had two gates, only one of which can be located with any assurance. The existence of a second is suggested by the fact that the Beecheys saw remains of two bridges when they traced the city wall running parallel to the "eastern ravine,"[55] that is, the deep trough through which the waters of the Wadi Zawana reach the sea. Where there were bridges there must also have been gateways giving access to the roads which the bridges carried across the stream bed. The more southerly of the two bridges is still preserved (see p. 35, Pl. I C, and Plan XXII). The more northerly bridge must have been close to the track which today runs eastward from the city along the coast. The assumption that this track was also an ancient roadway is verified by the existence along its course of a quarry that eventually became a burial ground in ancient times.

While no traces of the eastern gates are known to exist, the position of one can be determined with reference to the more southerly bridge. The banks of the Wadi Zawana are here very steep, and much of the superstructure of the gateway may long since have fallen into it to be washed down toward the seacoast. What remains of the city wall opposite the bridge suggests that the portal of the gateway was at the back of a semicircular court or *piazzetta* flanked by the projecting ends of the curtain walls (see Plan XXII). The type is found in Cyrenaica at Apollonia (see above) and elsewhere in North Africa, for instance at Tipasa.[56] The structure at Ptolemais may originally have had a certain charm. Its graceful features would have been in keeping with the glenlike character of the adjacent Wadi Zawana.

The western side of the city, at all times more important for overland communications with the rest of Cyrenaica, was provided with three gates,

all of which are known. The southernmost, which connected with the road to Barca (see p. 33) and which we call the Barca Gate, and the northernmost, referred to here as the Quarry Gate because it connects with a track leading along the shore to the great quarries west of the city, are known only from their foundations. These had been cleared by the Italian archeologists, and only the removal of small surface deposits and supplementary inquiries into the location of the adjacent towers were required to produce the plans provided in this report. The most important gate, in the middle of the west wall, through which the coastal road from Tauchira entered the city and which is therefore referred to here as the Tauchira Gate, still exists in a somewhat ruinous condition. It has been noted by almost all European travelers and was cleared in part by the Italian archeologists.

The Barca Gate and the Quarry Gate illustrate two different solutions of the same architectural problem, that of accommodating a gate to a road approaching the city wall obliquely. At the Barca Gate (Plan II) the wall itself was deflected for a stretch of 35 meters (see Fig. 3) in such a way that the gateway faced the incoming road at right angles. Of the superstructure of the gate nothing remains. The paved roadway through the gate is still in position (Pl. V C) and shows that the passageway was 3.80 m. wide. Its heavy paving blocks, deeply rutted by wheeled vehicles, show the sockets in which the gateposts turned and the lock-bar holes. Towers flanked the gateway asymetrically. The south tower, cleared by the Italian archeologists, projected about 9 meters from the face of the wall and was about 12.70 m. wide. Presumably it was hollow and permitted the mounting of wooden staircases that provided access to the platform at the top. Located only about 1.80 m. from the roadway of the gate, it would have screened the entrance effectively. The north tower was not excavated, but a section of its southerly face was located (see Plan II). It shows that the tower was so placed as to protect and screen the point where the wall was deflected so that the gate could have the proper relation to the incoming road. Eventually the gateway was blocked by the addition of a new curtain piece running diagonally between the two flanking towers. When the gateway was blocked the perimeter defense of the city was therefore still being maintained.

At the Quarry Gate (Plan III) the city wall

[55] Beechey, *Proceedings*, p. 379.

[56] See P.-M. Duval, *Cherchel et Tipasa* ("Bibliothèque archéologieque et historique" XLIII [Paris, 1946]) Fig. 3.

was not deflected from its established direction to accommodate the gate to the angle of the incoming road, but it was stepped back for a short distance. In one corner of the rectangular bay thus formed the gateway was somewhat awkwardly set into the wall (Pl. V *A*). In the paving of its roadway (*ca.* 3.50 m. wide) the holes that received the lock bars of its door leaves are clearly visible. Heavy stones set into the roadway at either side served as doorstops. Just south of the bay a drain was cut into the base course of the wall to carry off rain water, presumably from a small plaza inside. Heavy and perhaps solid towers flanked the gateway; the north tower projected 6.40 m. from the curtain wall and was 9.60 m. wide (Pl. V *B*).

The Quarry Gate and the Barca Gate are interesting chiefly as examples of road engineering[57] and doubtlessly were devoid of important decorative features. By contrast the Tauchira Gate was a very regular and quite elegant piece of construction, in accord with its dignity as the main gateway to the city. Cleared of incumbering masses of fallen masonry by the Italian archeologists, it has received less attention than it deserves as a monument and less than is required to solve the problems it presents. Only clearance of the interior chambers and a study of the details of construction can provide the answers to questions at issue. In our judgment a fuller study will show that radical changes were made in the structure at some point in its history.

Seen from without, the Tauchira Gate (Plan IV) consists of two massive rectangular towers set out from the line of the curtain walls and flanking an exterior bay or court about 9.50 m. wide (Pl. VI *A*). The rear wall of this court, aligned with the curtains, contains the single portal (3.20 m. wide). The towers are 10.05 m. wide and project 6.85 and 6.97 m. from the line of the curtain walls. The portal wall has the same thickness as the curtain walls generally (2.60 m.).

Each tower has a socle seven courses high, above which the walls are set back 20 cm. On three sides the walls are constructed of carefully cut blocks, closely joined at all four edges. The surfaces are

smooth, weathered to a rich tan, like the *mezze* limestone of Syria and Palestine, and have been only lightly pitted in the course of time (Pl. VII *A*). The stones are laid in alternate courses of headers and stretchers, with square blocks of intermediate length used at the corners in the header courses. The typical stretcher is 1.26 m. long; headers vary from 50 to 63 cm.; corner stones in the header courses measure about 91 cm. On the front faces of the towers, the stretcher courses contain 8 blocks, the header courses 13 blocks between corner pieces. On the sides facing the court the stretcher courses contain 5 blocks in addition to the head of the stretcher from the front face, the header courses 9 blocks in addition to the square corner block. The courses are about 46 cm. high throughout. These dimensions apply to the socles, to which observation was limited in the absence of scaffolding. Each stone has a marginal drafting 5 cm. wide and deep enough to permit the boss to project about 1.5 cm. from the drafted surface. The joins of alternate courses are in approximately vertical rows, and there are no visible signs of departure from the horizontal in the lines of the courses. The regularity and good preservation of the masonry provide not only an indication of the excellence of the workmanship but also a criterion for distinguishing between earlier and later elements of the structure as we know it. On the socles there are masons' marks and brief commemorative inscriptions consisting typically of a year number and the name of a person. Oliverio interprets the inscriptions as recording the names of soldiers assigned to guard duty at the gate and along the wall (see p. 16). Plate VI *A* shows, set against the south tower, the stele recording the recapture by the Romans of a *hortus* forming part of the royal estates of the Ptolemaic kings of Cyrenaica (see p. 10).

Above the socles the outer walls of the towers are preserved today to a maximum height of fourteen additional courses (Pl. VI *A*). On the interior face of the stones of the fourteenth course are visible holes that received the ends of beams which supported the platforms at the top of the towers. Above the fourteenth course we can safely conjecture a crown of several courses, and it is logical to suppose that it projected to the line of the socle. Such projection would have been possible because the fourteenth course is a stretcher course and the first course of the crown would therefore have been a header course.

---

[57] The identical problem was solved with much greater nicety for instance in the North Gate at Gerasa of the Syrian Decapolis and in the triple gateway of the main thoroughfare at Palmyra; see C. H. Kraeling, *Gerasa: City of the Decapolis* (New Haven, 1938) Plan XVII, and T. Wiegand, *Palmyra* (Berlin, 1932) Pl. 11.

Seen from inside the city, the Tauchira Gate as it exists today presents a glaring contrast to its outer elegance (Pl. VII *B–C*). Here the stones were laid quite as they came from the quarries and without interchange of header and stretcher courses. The lack of bonding in these walls would, of course, have been appropriate if they were set against the curtain walls or if they formed dividing walls within the towers. On this inner, east side the structural remains of the gate consist of three elements (see Plan IV). The first and most westerly element consists of the walls of undressed stones just described. They rise at one point to a height of fifteen courses above the socle and are pierced at two levels by openings (*ca.* 1.34 m. wide) that represent corbeled doorways (see Plan IV, section). The upper openings are each six courses high; those at ground level are seven courses high in the south tower and eight courses high in the north tower. The second element, set directly against the first, consists of solid masonry walls (2.00 m. thick) built of carefully squared and fitted blocks, laid in courses of different height from those of the towers. These walls continue the line of the curtains of the city wall, which they apparently join at either end of the gate, albeit not in the same way at the north as at the south. Today they rise no higher than the doorways opening into the towers at ground level, where the wall behind the north tower contains an opening from which was managed a horizontal lock bar that helped to hold the door leaves shut. Behind the south tower the solid wall is less well preserved. Between the two towers this solid continuation of the curtains contains the portal of the gateway. It here achieves the thickness of the curtains (2.60 m.) by virtue of its dressed outer face. It must be assumed that it once reached the height of the upper doorways in the towers, that it was arched across the portal, inclosing it at the top, and that its *chemin de ronde*, providing for continuous movement of the defenders, was used to control the exterior court and to give access through the upper doorways to the platforms at the top of the towers. The third structural element consists of platforms (*ca.* 4.00 × 12.00 m.), framed with undressed blocks and filled with rubble, placed behind the towers. One would assume that staircases once mounted upon them led to the top of the solid walls set against the towers.

All this makes a simple sensible picture, and undoubtedly the defenses of the city in the area

of the Tauchira Gate were organized in this fashion at one time. Several structural peculiarities strongly suggest, however, that the gate as we know it represents a secondary development. Perhaps the least important among them are the eastward projection into the zone of the circuit wall of individual stones belonging to the masonry of the towers and the offset along the entire east side of both towers at the top of the socles (see Pl. VII *B*). Offsets exist at the same height within the towers and were used, presumably, to carry wooden platforms. Another peculiarity is the fact that the solid continuation of the curtains is reduced to a width of 2 meters at the rear of the towers, just where one would suppose that provision for movement on the *chemin de ronde* would have been supplied most lavishly. It should be noted in this connection that the assumption of their concealment by the solid continuation of the curtain walls is not a sufficient explanation of the coarse, undressed masonry of the east faces of the towers. If we make the natural assumption that the top of the continuation of the curtains was at the level of the upper doorways, the upper parts of the tower walls would have been exposed to view from within the city. Furthermore, where the outer facings of the curtains joined the towers at the southern and northern extremities of the gate (see Pls. VI *B* and VII *D*), the coursing does not correspond to the projections in alternate courses which the builders of the gate carefully supplied for the bonding of the curtains into the towers. And it is clear that a number of the projections have been chiseled away.

The most serious problem arises in connection with the wall that contained the portal of the gateway. South of the gateway it can be seen from the outside to be properly bonded into the structure of the tower. It is carefully footed, and its facing pilaster is mounted on an especially heavy block (Pl. VIII *A*). North of the gateway it is not bonded to the adjacent tower and is poorly footed in comparison (Pl. VI *C*). Finally, the passageway through the gate was not of sufficient depth to protect the door leaves when they were open. All these peculiarities, in addition to the glaring contrast between the undressed stones used at the east and the outer elegance at the west, suggest that the gate as we know it is the result of partial rebuilding.

A guess concerning the supposed earlier form of the gate can be hazarded on the basis of Hellenistic and Roman gate construction generally and in consideration of the purposes of the existing arrangement. The solid masonry behind the towers continues the line of the curtain walls, so that the existing arrangement has the advantage of unifying wall and gate defense and providing for defenders directly above the portal. If the gate was remodeled to achieve this advantage, it would be natural to assume that originally it interrupted the curtain walls, which would then have abutted its sides rather than its corners. The towers would then originally have been about a third longer, the eastward extension (now destroyed) of each tower housing a stair well that was separated from the western part (existing) by an interior wall which is now exposed and which served in the remodeling as the facing to which the solid extension of the curtains was applied. Towers of such additional length would have provided between them a vaulted passageway of sufficient depth to accommodate two successive sets of door leaves. Such elongated gate towers are familiar from the excavations at Dura-Europos, and passageways with inner and outer sets of door leaves, permitting raiding parties to sally from and return to the city without exposing its interior, were still being built in early Roman imperial times.[58] The change from such an earlier type of gate to that now visible could be said to have involved the substitution of a defensive for an offensive strategy. Naturally, only additional clearances could verify this hypothesis.

DATING

To establish firmly the date of Ptolemais' perimeter defenses would require a full knowledge of all incidental findings made in the course of the Italian excavations, further clearances in search of additional detail, and a comparative study of the system and its several elements. In this first descriptive treatment of the visible remains only a general appraisal is possible.

From the description given above it should be clear that we are dealing here with a defense system, that is, with a comprehensive scheme developed as a unit on the basis of a careful study

of the potentialities of the site, the network of the city's communications, and the dignity to which the city aspired. It is of the same order, in other words, as the city plan in the scope and character of the conception that underlies it and should in plan at least be of the same vintage and hence a product of the third century B.C. That the plan of the defenses is not tied in all respects to the plan of the street grid provides no argument against this inference, since a measure of disjunction in this respect was typical of Hellenistic city planning.[59] That all parts of the system at Ptolemais as we know them were executed at the same time—in the third century B.C.—does not follow from the general inference about the plan as a whole.

The actual remains as described above are in accord with the suggestion of a Hellenistic origin for the system in a number of particulars. The ambitiousness of the scheme, the incorporation of the Jebel Akhdar in the system of defense, and the creation on the jebel of an acropolis fort all recall the patterns that developed throughout the Greek world beginning in the sixth century B.C. and that continued to be in vogue until the economic decline of the late second century B.C.[60] Two close parallels to the organization of the defenses at Ptolemais are to be found at Alea in Arcadia (Fig. 10) and Priene. As to the details of construction, mention has already been made of the common use of a cradle with rubble fill in Greek walls and of the early use of a stone socle with mud-brick superstructure (see p. 53). The examples of Herakleia and Pompeii cited in this connection could, of course, be multiplied greatly.[61] What is known about the stonework of the curtain walls at Ptolemais from the base course that survives in the coastal plain (see Pl. II *C*) suggests isodomic ashlar construction of the type that became particularly popular, with varieties of dressing, beginning in the fourth century B.C.[62] The marginal drafting of the masonry in the Tauchira Gate goes back to the same general period.[63] How many courses high the

---

[58] For the Main Gate at Dura-Europos see *The Excavations at Dura-Europos: Preliminary Report of the Seventh and Eighth Seasons of Work* (1939) Fig. 1 and for the later period see M. H. Kähler, "Die römischen Torburgen der frühen Kaiserzeit," *JDAI* LVII (1942) 1–104, esp. pp. 4–5.

[59] See A. von Gerkan, *Griechische Städteanlagen*, pp. 27 and 111, and Martin, *L'Urbanisme dans la Grèce antique*, p. 175.

[60] See in general A. von Gerkan, *Griechische Städteanlagen*, pp. 17–28, and Martin, *op. cit.* pp. 31–32, 189–203.

[61] See e.g. A. von Gerkan, *Die Stadtmauern* (Staatliche Museen zu Berlin, *Milet* II 3 [1935]) p. 13 and *passim*.

[62] See R. L. Scranton, *Greek Walls* (1941) pp. 99–136 and "List of Walls" on pp. 175–83.

[63] *Ibid.* p. 179.

stonework of the typical curtains may have been at Ptolemais is difficult to say. If the height of the socles of the Tauchira Gate is any criterion, the stonework of the curtains may be supposed to have been seven courses high. As regards towers

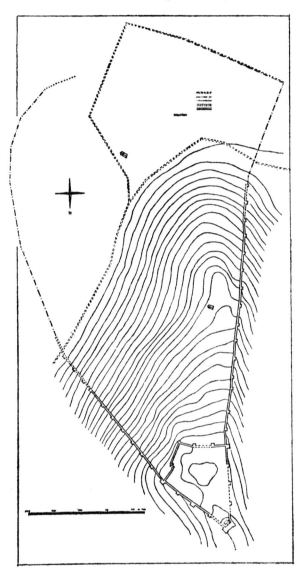

Fig. 10.—PLAN OF FORTIFICATIONS AT ALEA. After Roland Martin, *L'Urbanisme dans la Grèce antique*, Fig. 35

and gates, square and rectangular towers incorporated in or applied to the exterior of the wall are among the regular features of early systems of defense, as compared with the semicircular and the still later round-headed towers.[64] The Barca

[64] Typically, of course, towers were set into walls between stretches of curtain, but early examples of towers applied to the exterior of walls exist e.g. at Mantinaea (see Fougères, *Mantinée et l'Arcadie orientale*, Fig. 23).

Gate and the Quarry Gate offer little opportunity for comparative study, since so little of them remains. An early analogy to the east gate at Ptolemais, the one with the semicircular court set between projecting ends of the curtain walls (see p. 57), is Gate A at Mantinaea.[65] And if our suggestion as to an earlier form of the Tauchira Gate is correct, there can be little doubt that its antecedents also were at least as early as the Hellenistic period.[66]

In addition to this general orientation, certain particulars are available for the dating and history of the perimeter defenses of Ptolemais. First, there are the inscriptions on the towers of the Tauchira Gate (see p. 58). The interpretation of the date formula "year 1" or "year 12" in these and similar texts from the City Bath at Ptolemais and from the curtain walls of the city of Tauchira is discussed on page 209, where the reasons are given for concluding that the formula is to be understood as using the Actian era. The inscriptions on the Tauchira Gate at Ptolemais begin chronologically with "year 1" and thus document the existence of the gate in 31/30 B.C. However, an inscribed block (Pl. LII *A*) reused upside down as a transverse member in the base course of the curtain wall a short distance north of the Tauchira Gate may seem to provide evidence contrary to the general assumption that the system of defense is a product of the Hellenistic period, for the block bears the well carved monumental inscription T. FLAVIUS AU[. . .]. Since the inscription must be early Roman imperial, the block can scarcely have found its way into the cradling of the city wall prior to the second century of our era at the very earliest! The reuse of this block is not easy to explain. It should be noted in this connection that in the cradling of the city wall south of the Tauchira Gate, as it was left by the Italian archeologists, there are visible, reused as cross members, elements of domestic and funerary architecture.[67] While none of these pieces provides

[65] *Ibid.* Fig. 27.

[66] To what can be learned in general from Kähler, *op. cit.* reference may be added here e.g. to the later form of the Sacred Gate at Miletus (see A. von Gerkan, *Die Stadtmauern*, Fig. 10–11) and to the Main Gate at Dura-Europos.

[67] The following were noted: (1) a frieze block carved in the Doric order; (2) an unfluted column drum; (3) a molded architrave block with two fasciae, a fillet, and a *cyma reversa*; (4) a pier with attached Ionic colonnette and projecting tongue such as was found in the Villa of

a specific date, their presence in the cradling implies that an important initial period in the life of the city had already passed and that a second period of growth and development was under way when they were appropriated for use in the wall. All these particulars would constitute a strong argument for assigning the city defenses to a late date were it not for the supposed change in the Tauchira Gate, the change that presumably saw its eastern end demolished and the curtains of the city wall extended across the entire area behind it. Such changes could have involved also the rebuilding of the adjacent stretches of curtain wall. If so, the incorporation of the inscribed block in the curtain to the north and of the architectural elements in the curtain to the south testifies not to the date of the original construction of the defenses but to a period of rebuilding. One might associate their use and the changes at the gate with the third century of our era.

Two other particulars have chronological implications. The diagonal wall with which the Barca Gate was closed to further use (see p. 57) clearly represents a period when the system of perimeter defense was still being maintained but when connections with Barca were no longer as important as they had been at the beginning of the city's

history. From the changes in the city's system of communications, beginning with the construction of a direct road eastward to Cyrene (see p. 34), it would seem that the Barca Gate could have been closed some time after the first century of our era, presumably much later but not after the end of the fourth century.

A separate section (pp. 100–104) describes the forts and blockhouses constructed inside the city of Ptolemais that betoken the development of a pattern of zone defense which ultimately replaced the earlier system of perimeter defense. This development we are inclined to associate in the main with the first half of the fifth century of our era, but the looting of the city's curtain walls may have begun much earlier. Presumably from the fifth century on new Byzantine structures erected at the site were built largely of stones taken from the perimeter defenses. Otherwise it would be difficult to account for the disappearance of so much of the walls themselves, of the superstructure of the Quarry Gate and the Barca Gate, and of the eastern gates. That a large part of the towers of the Tauchira Gate survived the raids of Byzantine looters is a final testimony to the excellence of their construction, which made it difficult to dislodge the individual blocks without damaging them.

THE SQUARE OF THE CISTERNS

By J. E. Knudstad

The extant remains of the Square of the Cisterns (Building 10 on Plan XXII), covering an area of about 65.85 by 70.60 m., represent a complex consisting of an extensive system of vaulted cisterns arranged within a square to support an architecturally graced platform (Plans V–VI). The structure was approached from the north (Pl. IX *A*), where there was a street or plaza. Elements of what appear to be two detached but related decorative features erected at street level flank the frontage of the square north of its corners. The ascent to the platform is axial, two forward stairways leading from the street to an intermediate terrace. The terrace extends the full width of the

frontage and has centered upon it a podium rising above the level of the great paved platform. Upon the podium stand two Ionic columns of a monument originally featuring six (Pl. XX *C*). Access from the terrace to the podium was achieved by means of two stairways inserted into it and rising from its forward corners. Also at terrace level and of a length equaling the width of the podium is a rectangular pool that may have sported a fountain. These features intrude into the rectangular area occupied by the cisterns. Hence the platform supported by the cisterns incloses this southern projection of the terrace on three sides. The cisterns themselves are contained within the area of the pavement, and the outer limits of the square are defined by heavy masonry walls built in part of blocks with drafted margins of Hellenistic style. It seems certain that the square was framed on the

---

the Roman period and in the "Palazzo" (see p. 128 and Plan XIV 14); (5) the stone door of a tomb; (6) what seems to be either part of an altar or an altar-like part of a funerary monument.

east, south, and west by a Doric peristyle. The site abounds with sufficient remains of the order for such a lengthy colonnade, and the existing borders of the paved area prove visibly to be a stylobate. Construction of the cisterns necessitated excavation of the seaward-sloping plain to a depth which allowed the finished platform to be placed at the southern grade level so that water directed through surface channels and aqueducts could enter the cisterns properly at the top of the vaults (see p. 72). The cisterns, essentially completely preserved, are arranged in three rectangular blocks consisting of parallel series of vaulted chambers interconnected via passages through their walls.

The Vaulted Cisterns

The central block of cisterns is the smallest of the three blocks and is composed of nine short chambers constructed perpendicularly to the square's approximately north-south axis of symmetry. These chambers measure almost 19 meters in length and average 3 meters in width (Pl. IX *B*). The volume of the fourth chamber from the north is considerably reduced by an entrance stairway at its east end and by the brick and rubble casing of a well shaft that divides it in two (see Plan VI). The well shaft (1.00 × 3.50 m.) at present is filled with debris to 11.50 m. below its opening at the surface of the square, so that its depth is unknown. Flanking the central block and the unchambered area under the podium and pool are the two larger cistern blocks, which fill the remaining two-thirds of the square. Each of these side blocks contains four long chambers paralleling the north-south axis and averaging 52 meters in length by 3.50 m. in width. The easternmost chamber of the eight contains an entrance stairway as well as an open water-intake trough at its south end. This trough and a smaller opening at the top of the adjacent chamber's south wall are the only observable devices for directing water into the system. Construction is uniform throughout the three blocks of cisterns, except that the heavily incased well shaft is in part of brick and the use of brick extends into the upper walls of the chamber which contains it. A heavy accumulation of debris prohibited examination of the lower features of every chamber, but one totally excavated chamber in the central block revealed a flat heavily plastered floor sealed and waterproofed along the bases of the walls with

a rounded step or two of plaster. The walls are of squared heavy stone blocks, those separating pairs of chambers being 90 cm. thick. The walls rise 2.50 m. from the known floor level. Stones protruding in the top courses may have been so placed in order to support centering during the construction of the vaulting. All walls between chambers are pierced by passageways of a roughly standard size (2.00 m. high by 70 cm. wide) but of irregular and apparently random spacing. The entrances to the passageways are corbeled and capped with lintel stones.[68] Several passageways in the east block appear to have been partially or fully blocked with stones and then plastered over after completion of the chamber system.

The rubble vaulting springs directly from the stone walls of the chambers on a base slightly thinner than the walls. Rubble is used also in the vault closures at the end walls. The vaults, semicircular in section and rising 4.50 m. above the floor, were formed over wooden centering planks placed horizontally, as their impressions on the vault surfaces show. The interiors of the chambers are completely sealed with plaster; its thickness and stratification suggests several extensive replasterings. The rubble is composed of lime mortar and a mixed aggregate of field stones and pulverized bricks. The stones, flat and palm-sized, are placed horizontally to the inner surface of the vault except in the uppermost part, where they are wedged in vertically. At random intervals there are openings (average diameter, 50 cm.) in the top of the vault in each chamber to give light and access. Addition of rubble fill between vaults and a leveling layer of stones and mortar above the fill prepared the resulting raised platform for its pavement of large white tesserae in 3-cm. rows.[69]

From all surface indications the vaulting does not abut the stylobate wall ringing the platform on the east, south, and west. Instead there exists an inner inclosure of heavy masonry that contains the rubble mass, with earth-filled gaps roughly 3 meters wide between it and the east and west stylobate foundations. Adjoining the outer northeast corner of this masonry inclosure and the east stylobate foundation is a small supplementary

---

[68] Corbeling was used at Ptolemais in the Tauchira Gate, the Tower Tomb, and the Byzantine City Bath and therefore has no relevance for dating.

[69] On the openings and the mosaics see Caputo, "Protezione," pp. 52–53.

chamber (2.00 × 14.00 m.), walled and vaulted with rubble, that was apparently secondary and has no visible connection with the cisterns. The stylobate foundation forming its east end has a duct cut through it for introducing water. A doorway, obviously intrusive in character, cuts into the north side of this chamber, linking it with a small inclosure in the northeast corner of the square. The use of overturned and stacked column drums for the wall that was added to form this inclosure points to Byzantine origin. A smaller but similar construction exists in the northwest corner of the square.

The Podium

To judge by the extant remains, the podium was the focal point of the architectural whole. The elevation which the platform gains because of the decidedly northward slope of the coastal plain and the forward position of the podium in the square give the columnar feature mounted upon it a commanding height above the northern approach from the city. As indicated above, the podium is centered on an intermediate terrace that is served by two central stairways rising from the street level. The podium consists of two roughly square stone inclosures, the smaller and higher one fitting within the three sides of the larger one that flanks it and backs it to form a finished exterior of dressed stone complete with molded base. The dressed exterior may be a facing or retaining wall that was set around a core built up of rubble and fill. The whole structure is approximately 13 meters square and rises about a meter and a half above the terrace. The stairways rising from its forward corners, between the two inclosures, indicate that the podium was originally finished at the top as a paved dais, although no paving is preserved.

The inner stone inclosure serves essentially as a high foundation for a three-sided columnar feature of the Ionic order, while its forward (northern) side forms the front of the podium. Two angle columns still stand on the stylobate that is supported by the inner inclosure. The base of a third of the four columns that stood in line is *in situ* next to the west angle column (Pl. XX *C*). The use of angle columns and evidence that the stylobate continued northward from the two standing columns indicate that at least one column existed forward of each standing column in the original arrangement.

Fifteen drums, each 47 cm. high, plus base and capital give the columns a height equal to eight times the lower diameter (1.00 m.) and a good Ionic ratio. A 2-cm. drafting of the margins of each drum replaces vertical fluting. Even the lower margin of the first drum is drafted, and, in place of the proper apophyge there, a simple fillet is found on the base. The base, consisting in order downward from this fillet of a scotia, a torus, a scotia, and a torus, is of unusual profile. The angle capitals, although heavily eroded, exhibit the undersized appearance characteristic of late Hellenistic work and its Roman echo. This effect is produced mainly by the hyperflattened and protruding echinus, resulting in a monumental equivalent of the capitals in the peristyle of the Villa (see p. 218). Immediately below the echinus and separated from it by a thin molding is a narrow band of residual fluting deeply inset from the face of the otherwise unfluted shaft. This interesting feature can also be seen on the heavy Doric double-engaged angle pier (see p. 116) rising from an unexcavated structure (No. 26 on Plan XXII) immediately to the south of the Square of the Cisterns. An entablature surmounting the six columns must be assumed, but no evidence remains.

Behind the podium and abutting the carved molding of its outer facing in a definitely intrusive manner is a rectangular pool with heavy stone base and fragmentary molded rim. Over half of the rim is made up of miscellaneous unmatched stones, but fragments of plaster waterproofing on them and on the area inclosed confirm their use as the frame of a basin. In the center of the basin there is an incomplete arrangement of stones that may be the foundations of a decorative element. To the west of the podium and pool there is a partially excavated and fragmentary open drain that slopes to the north. Its exact function is uncertain, however, since its two extremities are unknown.

The Peristyle

The unbroken stylobate along the east, south, and west sides of the Square of the Cisterns provides the border for the paved platform (60 × 66 m.) and comprises a single row of blocks 30 cm. high and 1.00 meter wide with approximate lengths of 1.22 m. at the south and 1.15 m. at the east and west. These dressed stones are centered on the

ORDER OF THE PERISTYLE

Fig. 11.—MAIN ORDER OF SQUARE OF THE CISTERNS. *J. E. Knudstad*

header course of a roughly faced foundation wall about 1.30 m. thick. On the east and west the stylobate is preserved well toward the northern limit of the square, but the treatment at the northeast and northwest corners is unknown. Seven meters east of the east stylobate and paralleling it for half the length of the square the remains of a wall of drafted masonry (65 cm. thick) are preserved to a height slightly above that of the stylobate. It was not only a retaining wall between the square and a lower grade level to the east but also in its upward continuation, we assume, was part of an outer wall that inclosed the square on the east, south, and west. On this assumption rests the inference that the Square of the Cisterns had roofed porticoes on three sides. The outer inclosing wall was preserved only at the east because there it served as a retaining wall of the adjacent Byzantine reservoir that is Building 11 on Plan XXII (see p. 71).

The southeast angle pier with one of its two engaged Doric half-columns is the sole standing fragment of the peristyle (Pl. VIII *B*). Intercolumniations vary to match the stone lengths in the stylobate. Column emplacements on every other stone produce spacings of 2.45 m. for the south row and average spacings of 2.30 m. for the east and west rows. The east emplacements are represented merely by less weathered circular areas on alternating stones, but on the south and west 5-cm. dowel holes and diagonally cut square holes (10 cm. on a side), respectively, appear on every other stone. Parallel indentations in the mosaic paving of the platform along the south stylobate indicate that the south portion of the peristyle fell inward as a whole, perhaps in the earthquake of A.D. 365 (see p. 70). Depressions from the impact of the entablature are not noticeable, but indentations perpendicular to the stylobate coincide exactly with all of the column emplacements. No paving remains along the east and west stylobates to reveal similar indentations.

A Doric order of fairly canonical form but so proportioned in detail as to suggest a late origin adorned the peristyle (Fig. 11). Eleven drums plus capital rose from the stylobate approximately 5.40 m. to give a ratio of just under seven times the lower diameter of 81 cm. The diameter diminishes with an entasis to 68 cm. The usual twenty flutes were maintained on the drums, which average 46 cm. in height, but necking grooves are absent. The echinus on the otherwise well pro-

portioned capital is so lacking in curvature as to suggest Roman workmanship. The entablature likewise is reconstructed from remains found in abundance on the site. The three elements, maintaining typically Doric lines, are disposed on separate blocks, with lengths determined by the intercolumniations. Both the frieze blocks and the architrave blocks equal the intercoluminations in length, but the cornice blocks are only half as long. Regulae and surmounting triglyphs are centered over columns and spaced two at the third points between. Hence the architrave joints split regulae over columns, and the frieze blocks, cut to the left margin of every third triglyph, are positioned to overlap these joints. Important to note on the frieze blocks are the canted molding on their reverse sides and the squarely cut terminals to the triglyph bevels. The glyphs terminate at a horizontal face which is cut in perpendicularly to the triglyph face, rather than curved, a distinct mark of Roman work. Additional details of the frieze blocks are a shallow taenia broken by the triglyphs and recesses (6 × 23 cm.) above the canted molding on the reverse sides, cut to receive roof beams. The cornice, presenting two mutules for each triglyph, is cut to the left of every third mutule. A 13-cm. gutter in the sloping top of the cornice was, at undetermined intervals, drained by tapered troughs cut through to the fascia. Some form of decorative spouts centered on the respective cornice blocks protruded at these points. The whole of the entablature as reconstructed rises 1.35 m. above the abacus, and selected elements of it still exhibit layers and colors of paint. The complete exterior of columns and entablature was finished in plaster.

The one standing element of the peristyle, the southeast angle pier (Fig. 12), exhibits only one of its two engaged half-columns. The drums of the half-column to the west are integral with the blocks of the pier, whereas the missing drums of the half-column to the north were cut separately and set into shallow troughs in the pier. Recesses 5 cm. deep were cut into every other pier block to receive the projections that bonded the alternate half-drums. The four faces of the square pier have an entasis matching that of the order, and two small bands of molding returning into the capitals from the outer corners adorn the top. Recesses 7–12 cm. deep were cut at about mid-height into the outer, east and south, faces of the pier to receive five plaques, three on the east face and two on the south face. The missing plaques are judged to have been tall and rectangular with the exception of one which had a gabled crown.

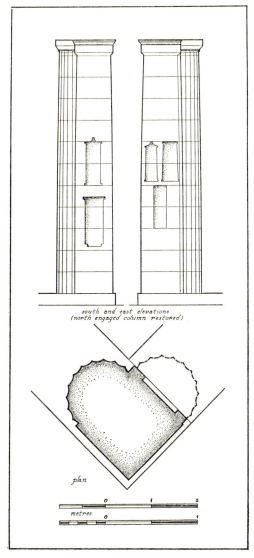

south and east elevations
(north engaged column restored)

plan

metres

Fig. 12.—Southeast Angle Pier of Peristyle of Square of the Cisterns. *J. E. Knudstad*

The Flanking Feature

To the east of the axial approach and presumably detached from the square are the low massive foundation and the stylobate of some manner of monumental feature set at street level (see Plan V). With U-shape recalling that of the columnar feature on the podium this stylobate in its existing form opens westward toward the approach. A similar arrangement of heavy stones in a corresponding position to the west is as yet unexcavated but suggests that the feature at the east was one of

two that flanked the northern approach to the square. One large column base is *in situ* on one of two remaining plinth blocks, which in turn rest on the equally fragmentary stylobate. The stylobate is supported by a heavier stone course placed directly on a foundation constructed of reused column bases, capitals, and other architectural fragments. Nearby were found drums, bases, and capitals of a monumental Corinthian order belonging to the feature. The size and layout of the stylobate suggest that four such columns completed the affair. Within the stylobate cut stones are arranged presumably to support a podium or impost, perhaps for a piece of statuary.

The shafts of the columns were composed of seventeen unfluted drums and had a lower diameter of 1.09 m. and an upper diameter of 94 cm. A short drum and two toruses separated by a scotia formed the base. Acanthus leaves on the capital, arranged in two registers of eight each, cling closely to the bell for most of their length but curl out strongly at the tips. Angle volutes springing from cauliculi just above the leaves of the upper register rest on the tips of these leaves. Central spirals, also springing from the cauliculi, support a centered spray cluster well forward and detached from each face of the abacus. The total height of the capital is 1.07 m. Important to note is a fragment of a voussoir lying with the column elements and being of their same grand scale. A portion of it shows an elaborate use of classic motifs arranged in concentric bands.

Also present about the Corinthian feature are sufficient fragments to illustrate completely a much smaller-scaled and quite simplified order plus the profile of a similarly scaled entablature. The architrave and frieze of this entablature are combined on blocks 46 cm. high, surmounted by cornice blocks 26 cm. high. Two fasciae and a projecting molding above complete the architrave. The frieze is a continuous register of vertical acanthus leaves. A band of dentils forms the base of the cornice, and its soffit is broken into alternating modillions and lacunae, each ornamented with a finely cut acanthus leaf. The column fragments are of an unfluted and possibly late Doric order with simply molded base attached. The lower diameter of the column is 56 cm. Although no support can be gained from the extant remains, it is simplest to suppose that these smaller-scaled pieces belonged to the flanking feature in whatever form it may have stood.

5*

WATER SUPPLY AND STORAGE

For cities not located in the immediate vicinity of adequate perennial sources of drinking water provision for its supply and storage forms an important factor in both the planning and the administration of their communal life. The installations at ancient Ptolemais provide an unusually good example of how such cities sought to cope with this problem and are worthy of careful attention on that account.

Of all the ancient cities of Cyrenaica, Cyrene was the only one fortunate enough to have a copious and readily accessible spring, and the tribute paid to it in the story of Apollo and the Nymph and in the cult of the god reflect the sense of special privilege and gratitude which the city felt in its possession. Ancient Ptolemais had nothing comparable to boast of or to rely upon. A natural spring does exist almost at the very edge of the coastal plain some 3 kilometers west of the city. It is now associated with the tomb of Sidi Abdullah, which stands nearby, and in the period of Italian colonization was protected by a fortress in the ruins of which the basin inclosing it is located. It still provides the best drinking water in the area and during the last season of our excavations was being piped to the modern village of Tolmeita. The Italian fortifications, however, were only the successors of more ancient ones, for James Hamilton, who visited the site in 1852, mentions the spring as the third and last on the road from el-Merj to Tolmeita and says that it was located in the ruins of a "fortalice."[70] Water could have been and probably was transported from the spring in small quantities to Ptolemais in antiquity, quite as during more recent times, but the founding fathers justifiably located the city at a distance from the spring to take full advantage of the harbor facilities and the greater defensive potentialities of the site chosen. Obviously the spring could not supply the entire needs of such a city as they planned in any case.

In common with the other cities of Cyrenaica Ptolemais could count on the physical geography of the region to supply in some measure what the absence of strong perennial springs denied, for the bold rise of the Jebel Akhdar causes the northeast winds to precipitate their moisture in the form of rain. Records covering the past twenty years show an annual rainfall average of 350 mm. at Ptolemais between November and February.[71] Much of the rain water runs off immediately through the deep wadies unless it is artificially held, but enough penetrates the soil and finds its way to natural underground catch basins to permit dry farming and the digging of the wells that provide for the watering of flocks, for human consumption, and for small-plot irrigation agriculture. Such wells exist and are in use today inside the city limits of ancient Ptolemais, very possibly in continuation from its earliest days. They are relatively shallow and tend to become exhausted in the summer months.

Water for individual houses and families in ancient Ptolemais, as in its modern successor, was provided in part by cisterns in appropriate places about the premises. Such cisterns were carefully built and maintained where they provided a first and most readily accessible source of supply. A good example of a cistern of the Roman period, typical as to both shape and dimensions, came to light in the Public Building on the Street of the Monuments (see Fig. 54). In the Villa of the Roman period there were four cisterns so placed as to catch a maximum amount of rain water from the roofs of the several chambers and porticoes and to make it readily available in the areas of maximum use—the living quarters, dining rooms, and bath. All were carefully constructed of a very hard mixture of mortar and crushed bricks and bedded in a surrounding layer of fist-size stones.

In more pretentious establishments the cistern as an immediate source of water supply was supplemented by the driven well. An excellent example

---

[70] Hamilton, *Wanderings in North Africa*, p. 139. Ghislanzoni associates it with "una toretta d'osservatione d'età romana o bizantina" (*Notiziario archeologico* I 117).

[71] A rainfall map of Cyrenaica, kindly prepared by Dr. Lamar E. Fort of the Libyan USOM in co-operation with the Meteorological Office of the Libyan Nazirate of Communications, gives the following picture as concerning the major ancient sites: average annual rainfall in millimeters at Agedabia (Corniclanum) 129, Benghazi (Euesperides-Berenice) 266, Tocra (Tauchira) 311, Tolmeita (Ptolemais) 350, el-Merj (Barca) 485, Marsa Suza (Apollonia) 403, Shahat (Cyrene) 596, Tobruk 146. Special thanks are due to the persons and agencies that provided this information.

of such a well came to light in the Roman Villa (see p. 136). When the inverted column base which plugged its mouth was removed a test showed that the well was quite free of refuse and contained about 5 meters of water. The shaft had an interior diameter of about a meter and was no less than 21 meters deep. To cut such a shaft through the stratified limestone underlying the sloping coastal plain with the tools available in antiquity was a difficult not to say dangerous undertaking. Recesses cut in opposite sides of the shaft at half-meter intervals for hand- and footholds provided the precarious means of descent into and ascent from the well. Such wells undoubtedly were expensive and therefore limited to the houses of men of means and to civic establishments. Two driven wells, one even larger and deeper than that of the Villa, exist on the premises of the "Palazzo." Another forms part of the installations of the Square of the Cisterns (see p. 63). Still another, carefully framed several meters down from the top with a masonry shaft some 2 meters square, is visible today a few meters west of the fortress that is Building 24 on Plan XXII. The excavation of the City Bath revealed a similar masonry shaft under the floor of Room 14, with hand- and footholds that identified it as the frame of still another well shaft (see p. 172). Masonry frames are necessary where solid rock lies some distance below the natural ground level. An event in the recent history of the well near Building 24 points up an engineering feature that is important if the result desired—a good supply of drinkable water—is to be accomplished. The event in question is the reported attempt of the Italian settlers to put this well to use. The pump installed at the well, it was reported, produced water in quantity, but it proved to be saline and undrinkable. The well, which has a total depth of 21 meters, like that of the Villa, was dug at a site only about 17 meters above mean sea level.[72] Seepage from the sea through the porous limestone undoubtedly accounts for the salinity of the water, even though the well is half a kilometer inland from the coast. In the Villa, on the other hand, where the shaft went down almost to but not below sea level, the water was sweet.[73] The proper procedures had

obviously been followed here to insure an outcome appropriate to the investment. In the "Palazzo," one well (21 m. deep) is said to yield drinkable water and the other (reputedly 50 m. deep) is said to yield water quite as salty as that of the sea.

In a city of the size and pretensions of Ptolemais, provision for a steady and sufficient water supply could, of course, not be limited to shallow wells draining natural catch basins in the folds of the limestone underlying the coastal plain and to such cisterns and wells as individual enterprise and means might create in the several domestic and civic establishments. Some effort on the part of the city was called for to provide for the needs of the community as a whole. The nature of this effort is excellently illustrated at Ptolemais by the structures identified as Buildings 10, 11, and 12 on Plan XXII. These represent three large storage reservoirs, of which the one farthest to the west, the Square of the Cisterns (see pp. 62–67), was partly cleared and restored by the Italian archeologists.[74] The tall standing columns on its northern side (Pl. *IX A*) have caught the eyes of travelers since the days of James Bruce (1768) and of the Beecheys (1821–22) and have given rise to a succession of theories about the structure that vary in proportion as the columnar feature or the open plaza into which the columns were set was emphasized. Bruce thought of the columnar feature as part of a temple.[75] The Beecheys regarded the platform over the cistern as part of the court of a palace.[76] More recent interpreters have spoken of the structure as the "agora" or the "forum" of the city.[77]

The structure had a long and complicated history, some elements of which can be read from the surviving remains, as Caputo and after him Knudstad have done. One important element of this history is the fall of the entire south section of the peri-

---

[72] Ground level at the neighboring Headquarters of the Dux (Building 23) is 17.65 m. above datum (sea level).

[73] Floor level in the adjacent Room 5 of the Villa is 21.11 m. above sea level.

[74] An account of the important work done here by the Italians is given in Caputo, "Protezione," pp. 51–53 and Figs. 28–36, which include a partial sketch plan (Fig. 33) and a model (Fig. 36).

[75] *Travels to Discover the Source of the Nile* I xliii.

[76] Beechey, *Proceedings*, pp. 357–58. While only two columns of the columnar feature are standing today, the early travelers saw three. Pacho's account from the years 1824–26 is published with an etching showing them (see his *Relation d'un voyage dans ... la Cyrénaïque ...*, p. 179 and n. 2). There is a local tradition at the modern village of Tolmeita about the fall of the third column.

[77] So for example Oliverio, *Documenti antichi* I 1, p. 42, and Caputo, "Protezione," p. 53.

style, which left indentations upon the mosaic paving. Since Caputo with his usual good judgment assigns this paving to the fourth century and associates the fall with an earthquake, it is possible to think of the fall as another consequence of the earthquake that in A.D. 365 did such damage at Cyrene.[78] But the condition of the vaulted storage chambers is such that they must have been kept in working order or restored to working order in the Byzantine period. The early travelers speak of finding water in them on occasion.[79]

For the dating of the monument early in the Roman period the architectural analysis of Knudstad (pp. 62–67) provides a solid basis. An identical lower limit can be inferred from the reuse in the columnar feature of blocks with inscriptions of the Hellenistic period, the important dedicatory texts honoring Arsinoë II and Ptolemy VI (see p. 8). The Roman dating follows also from the brickwork in the well shaft and the vaulted chamber containing it (see p. 63). It is not at all impossible, however, that the entire system of vaulted chambers and decorative features was in Roman times set into a large open basin that served the same general purpose in the Hellenistic period. This possibility is suggested by the earth-filled gaps (3 m. wide) between the masonry that incloses the vaulted chambers and the walls supporting the stylobate on the east and west (see p. 63). The gaps may have been required to allow for the incline of the inclosing wall of an earlier open reservoir. Naturally the value of this suggestion needs to be tested by further excavation. As they stand, the chambers of the Square of the Cisterns would have been able to store roughly 1,850,000 gallons of water—a goodly supply, but one that eventually became inadequate, as two other reservoirs nearby indicate.

Buildings 11 and 12 are both merely large open-air basins and are at present so filled with earth and debris that they lack definition for photographic purposes and can be known only from the surface remains of their rubble and cement inclosing walls (Pl. X *A–B*). Of the two, Building 12 must be the next after the Square of the Cisterns in sequence of construction. There are no tangible clues to its

actual date, but one might properly think of the period beginning with Diocletian, when Ptolemais became the administrative headquarters of the province, as one of particular civic growth that might require provision for large additional water supply. Presumably the only real rival to this period would be that of the Severi, if Cyrenaica shared even in small measure the attention given to Tripolitania at that time (see pp. 18–19).

The reservoir that is Building 12 is a rectangle whose outer dimensions are 118 meters from east to west and 126 meters from north to south (Fig. 13).

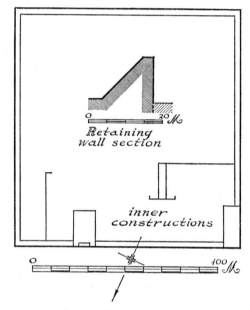

Fig. 13.—Sketch Plan of Open Reservoir (Building 12). *J. E. Knudstad*

Its frame, a solid mass of mortar mixed with hand-sized field and beach stones, was 3 meters thick at the top. We must naturally assume that the inner face of this retaining mass was beveled, running inward at an angle of perhaps 45°. At the west, where the side of the reservoir is exposed, can be seen the remains of a facing wall one stone thick applied to the rubble mass. The facing wall was carefully constructed of marginally drafted stones similar to those used in the outer wall to the east of the Square of the Cisterns (see p. 66). The height to which the rubble mass was carried from present surface level on the west side could be estimated at 12 meters. If we assume that at the opposite side and to the south the ground was excavated to the same depth when the reservoir was fashioned and that the floor was at that level and remained con-

[78] See Caputo, "Protezione," p. 51, and Goodchild, *Cyrene and Apollonia*, p. 58.

[79] Smith and Porcher, *History of Recent Discoveries at Cyrene*, p. 66, mention goats drinking from pools of water in the vaulted chambers, and Checchi, *Attraverso la Cirenaica*, p. 116, says there was "good clear water" there.

stant throughout the inclosed basin, the reservoir could have held approximately 26 million gallons of water. Truly this represents a heroic effort to provide for the welfare of the city.

Like the Square of the Cisterns, Building 12 was supplied with decorative features. One of these at least was an integral element of the construction. It is at the northwest corner of the inclosing rectangle and has an over-all length of about 22 meters and a width of about 9 meters (see Fig. 13). Here the retaining wall reached its maximum height above ground level, so that the corner permitted a monumental development, the nature of which is still largely conjectural. Visible on the surface at the level of the top of the reservoir are large sections of broken rubble walls and vaulting, the inner faces of which are composed of small rectangular cut stones instead of the usual fist-size field stones. The effect is that of a coarse *opus reticulatum*. One would infer that the feature in question was a long vaulted cavelike room, rather carefully finished on the interior. A formal entrance at the north was flanked by piers that once supported columns presumably carrying an architrave with surmounting pediment. The remains of this portico are probably imbedded in the debris in front of the doorway. Perhaps this feature, with its formal façade, was intended to simulate a cavern such as that connected with the fountain at Cyrene and was dedicated to the Nymph Cyrene. The shrine would have been accessible from the decumanus running along the northern face of the reservoir. Two-thirds of the way from the northwest corner of the reservoir a flight of stairs leads up from the street to the top of the retaining wall. Whether this feature was marked by a colonnaded portico is not known.

The interior of the reservoir shows lines of masonry whose purpose and date cannot be determined without excavation (see Fig. 13). Some of them may represent building enterprises of a period when the basin had lost its original function and had been permitted to fill up. Some of them may represent subdivisions of the basin intended to assist in the purification of the water. A rectangle outlined immediately to the south of the stairs leading up from the decumanus may belong to a decorative feature whose superstructure is buried in the fill of the reservoir.

Between the Square of the Cisterns and the reservoir just described there eventually came to be built a second open-air reservoir (Building 11). It was much smaller than either of its neighbors, measuring about 52.50 m. from east to west and about 37.50 m. from north to south. Its east and west walls were set against the neighboring structures and could therefore be built with a thickness of only a single row of blocks. At the north and south heavy masses of rubble were needed to retain the water, and these were faced at the north by two rows of blocks with fill between them and at the south by three rows, the innermost being set upon the rubble mass that forms the actual basin. A test pit, apparently sunk by the Italian archeologists, had penetrated to and laid bare a small part of the floor near the center of the reservoir. A small clearance here revealed that it is composed of cement mixed with crushed brick and laid on a carefully constructed bedding of small stones. No attempt was made to estimate the cubic content of this reservoir. It should belong to the Byzantine period.

How the water was brought to these reservoirs for storage and distributed from them is only partially known. The position chosen for them, between the two cardines and at a level higher than most of the residential and all of the civic and commercial sections of the city, indicates that distribution by piping was intended. Excavation of the area directly north of them would presumably reveal parts of a distributing system leading at least to the City Bath (pp. 160–75) and probably also to the fountains (pp. 79–81) at street intersections along the Street of the Monuments. Among the early travelers the always most observant Beecheys noted remains of an aqueduct leading northward from the Square of the Cisterns "through the centre of the town" and incorporated it on their plan (Fig. 4).[80] Its remains have meanwhile disappeared. If it was a surface installation it may represent a late phase of the distributing system, connected perhaps with the building of the City Bath at the end of the fourth century of our era, rather than an earlier or original system of underground stone conduits.

From the position of the reservoirs it is possible to draw inferences concerning the system by which they were supplied. One obvious inference is that they were intended to store rain water that fell in

[80] Beechey, *Proceedings* p. 362. See also Rohlfs, *Von Tripolis nach Alexandrien* (1871) p. 161, who connects the aqueduct with the City Bath.

the wintry season on the long slopes of the Jebel Akhdar to the south. An average annual precipitation of 350 mm. over the whole of the drainage area to the south would if properly channeled have provided no small quantity of water for storage. That such channeling was a part of the arrangement is likely even though no traces are currently distinctly visible. In spite of the fact that various early travelers noted walls at the foot of the jebel and interpreted them as part of the city's perimeter defenses, the city's girdle of walls did not run on this line but went up to the top of the jebel (see pp. 54–56). The travelers may have seen merely field walls or terrace walls such as are still in evidence here and there in the area, but the Beecheys speak specifically of "remains of stone conductors leading into these cisterns from the mountains at the back of the town," and, even if they refer only to simple field walls channeling the run-off diagonally into the area of the reservoirs, their statement deserves attention.[81] What gives the highest measure of probability to the supposition that rain water from the adjacent slopes of the jebel was collected by the reservoirs is the fact that the entire potential drainage area between the Wadi Hambish to the west and the Wadi Zawana to the east is completely devoid of tombs and burial caves. This undoubtedly reflects careful observance of a municipal ordinance, intelligible among other reasons if the slopes were used for drainage.[82]

Of the arrangements for the entrance of water into the reservoirs we have currently only two indications. In the southwest corner of the smaller open-air reservoir (Building 11) there is a small rectangular inclosure into which an intake pipe comes from the south. A similar installation exists in the adjacent southeast corner of the Square of the Cisterns, where an intake channel leads to a trough in the south end of the easternmost vaulted chamber (see Plan V and p. 63). It may well be that these were settling basins, intended to hold back sediment brought with the water, but it is also possible that water could be dipped up directly from them,

at least when the level in the reservoirs was comparatively low. Both were relatively accessible, the trough in the Square of the Cistern being located in the immediate vicinity of a staircase leading down into the vaulted chambers. However this may be, it should be clear that these installations were not connected with the run-off of rain water from the jebel. They could not have handled the quantity. Conceivably, then, the huge open-air reservoir (Building 12), now completely filled with sediment, received rain water directly from the jebel. The other two must have received water in much smaller quantities, presumably mainly from an aqueduct.

That Ptolemais had an aqueduct is known from literary sources and from archeological evidence. The Italian archeologists found a section of a stone trough that formed part of an aqueduct when they examined the bridge leading eastward from the city over the Wadi Zawana (see pp. 35–57) and properly concluded that the aqueduct crossed the brook bed of the wadi on top of the bridge (see Fig. 2). Remains of the aqueduct were spotted by early travelers and can still be followed along the coastal plain eastward of Ptolemais.[83] They lead necessarily to the Wadi Habbun, some 20 kilometers east of the city, where the contours of the jebel permitted the development of a large catch-basin reservoir, remains of which are said still to be visible. The construction of those sections of the aqueduct preserved within an hour's walking distance east of the city is by no means impressive. An open channel constructed of cement and crushed brick and contained between rows of untrimmed field stones meanders along the hillside very little above ground level, following the natural contours of the coastal plain.[84] The channel is typically not more than 30 cm. wide. At the bridge the trough in which it ran was 45 cm. wide and 60 cm. high.[85]

---

[81] See Beechey, *Proceedings*, p. 363.

[82] This did not preclude the erection or presence of other types of structures in the area. Most of these structures seem to have been elementary (small garden houses for example), but the one designated Building 26 on Plan XXII was apparently a large and ancient temple complex (see p. 116).

[83] Smith and Porcher, *op. cit.* p. 65. Ghislanzoni (*Notiziario archeologico* I 129) followed it for a distance of 8 km.

[84] A photograph of a section of it will be found in Oliverio, *Documenti antichi* II 2, Pl. XLIX = Pl. C, Fig. 86. The legend "Cyrene 357" is misleading. See the text (p. 250) for verification of the attribution.

[85] The stone representing this trough could not be found and is perhaps no longer there. There may be something of a problem about the passage of the aqueduct over the bridge, since the levels of the aqueduct where its probable course could be followed immediately east and west of the bridge are slightly higher than that assigned to the stone trough on the bridge. It is unlikely that water

That this aqueduct could have conducted water to the reservoirs that are Buildings 10 and 11 is physically possible, the top of the bridge being 34.70 m. above sea level and the southwest corner of the paved surface of the Square of the Cisterns being 30.25 m. above sea level. That it actually did so cannot be demonstrated without further excavation, but among the early travelers Smith and Porcher[86] say that "within the walls the aqueduct led in the direction of a series of enormous reservoirs near the center of the city." It is important to note in this connection a block with part of an inscription, seen by Oliverio, that was reused in a wall eastward of the Square of the Cisterns.[87] Portions of the two lines of text read [... *a*]*edificandas et ...* / [...]*t valvas et hydr*[*agogium ...*] and refer clearly to a water conduit and control system. Since the block was reused eastward of the Square of the Cisterns, it would demonstrate that probably the aqueduct ran through this area toward it. The fact that the text is in Latin suggests that it commemorated a construction or repair of the late Roman period, unless the inscription was bilingual.

We have, then, a fairly clear picture of the water-supply system as developed by the city of Ptolemais for public use during the course of several centuries. The first stage in the development, so far as it is known to us, is represented by the Square of the Cisterns, which belongs presumably to the early Roman imperial period. It implies an aqueduct, which may or may not be the one that can now be followed east of the city. The second stage is represented by the ambitious reservoir that is Building 12, which served essentially to hold rain water that ran off the Jebel Akhdar and which may belong to the end of the third century of our era, when Ptolemais became the capital city of Libya Pentapolis. Then came the reservoir that is Building 11, which may belong to the period of Arcadius and Honorius, to whom the City Bath is attributed. It implies either that the aqueduct was

still working or that it had been restored to serviceability.[88] In the fifth century the water-supply system was in disrepair (see p. 27), and the largest reservoir (Building 12) may already have been filled with sediment. The aqueduct was repaired by Justinian, and, if their extant condition is any criterion, so were the vaulted chambers of the Square of the Cisterns, to which the water was presumably brought by the aqueduct.

Finally, there is evidence of individual provision for water supply represented by a type of installation other than the small cisterns and driven wells that we find in houses of the Roman period. At various places within the city limits of Ptolemais large vaults may be seen standing high above ground level. A good example is Building 14 (Pl. X *C*). These structures are commonly and, we believe, properly referred to as "cisterns," but how they may have functioned is somewhat difficult to understand. Some help is afforded by Building 21, where a similar large vaulted chamber is visible and the crown of the vault is well above ground level. But here there are still to be seen inclosing lines of masonry which suggest that the vaulted chamber formed at least a large part of the ground floor of a house whose outer shell and entire upper floor, built around and over the vaulted chamber, have been removed by looters. If so, Buildings 14 and 21 represent a blockhouse type of city dwelling, whose inhabitants lived for protection in the upper floor and collected all the water they could get in one large vaulted chamber below in order to be as independent as possible of outside supply and thus to be able to withstand a long siege if necessary.[89] Thus we have all the earmarks of the kind of dwelling and the kind of provision for water supply that would have been appropriate to the difficult fifth century in the history of Ptolemais' effort to cope with the water-supply problem. It may have been equally appropriate in the successive centuries as well, in spite of the assistance provided by Justinian.

---

could have been contained by the trough, in spite of a dip, with the help of the flat capstone suggested in the drawing of Turba (see Caputo, "Protezione," Fig. 46). Rather the trough must be supposed to have been set atop a parapet at the side of the roadway over the bridge.

[86] *Op. cit.* p. 65. The remarks of Pacho, *Rélation d'un voyage dans ... la Cyrénaique ...*, p. 181) to the same effect are too general to have evidential value.

[87] Oliverio, *Monumenti antichi* II 2, p. 251, No. 32.

[88] The statements about a shortage of water supply in Synesius *Homily* 2 cannot be applied specifically to Ptolemais (see Pando, *Life and Times of Synesius*, p. 5).

[89] An Italian fortress close to the sea shore, near the eastern end of the area inclosed by the Italian perimeter wall, is set upon a building with the same sort of vaulted substructure. It does not appear on Plan XXII.

THE STREET OF THE MONUMENTS

By G. R. H. Wright *and* C. H. Kraeling

The streets of Ptolemais were basically of two different kinds, major thoroughfares with a maximum width of 18 meters and a minimum core of 8.80 m. and minor streets with a typical width of 6.20 m. (see p. 39 and Fig. 3). No one of them has been excavated completely or even mapped by soundings along its entire course, but a sampling of each type has been made.

A sample of a minor street was provided in connection with the excavation of the Villa (Building 5 on Plan XXII), where the street along the east side of the building was cleared to its full width for a distance of some 54 meters. The removal of the debris produced no unusual results. The street was about 6.30 m. wide between house walls and well paved throughout with heavy blocks laid in no regular pattern. There were no raised sidewalks. A drain for surface water, constructed of heavy blocks and providing a channel about 60 cm. wide and high, ran down the center of the street under the paving (Fig. 14). It was only partly clogged with

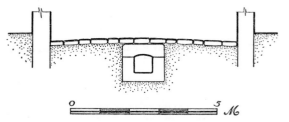

Fig. 14.—Section of Street East of Villa, Showing Drain. *J. E. Knudstad*

fine sand. Since no openings to feed surface water into the drain were observed along the sides nor in the center of the street, presumably openings to drain the streets themselves were located primarily at their intersections.[90] However, an intake channel did lead from the interior of the house to the south of the Villa eastward under the pavement of the street to the drain. This must have carried off surplus rain water from the court of the house and

perhaps also water from its bath. The beginning of a drainage system for the peristyle court of the Villa was observed at the fourth intercolumniation (counting from west) of the north portico and, in spite of the looting of the walls along the east side of the building, a section of its bedding and a few stones of its side walls came to light under the north end of the east portico. The connection with the street drain was not followed up, but apparently such installations were typical of the organization of the city's over-all drainage system. Along the east side of the street there was a solid line of house walls interrupted occasionally by doorways. These did not obstruct or reduce the width of the roadway, save for the interposition of a single step down from a threshold which lay a course above street level.

The sample of a major thoroughfare was provided by the Italian excavation of a stretch of some 250 meters along one of the decumani, the street referred to in the Italian reports as the "Via Trionfale" and the "Via Monumentale" and spoken of in this report throughout as the "Street of the Monuments" (Plan VII).[91] The attention of the Italian archeologists was attracted to the site by a jumble of ruins first noted by the Beecheys and described by them as containing "heaps of columns."[92] The Italian archeologists exposed the stretch of the thoroughfare that lies between the two cardines, and in 1957–58 the Department of Antiquities of Cyrenaica cleared another insula and a half eastward in the direction of the Headquarters of the Dux (Building 23 on Plan XXII).

These clearances revealed that, local infringements aside, the Street of the Monuments was main-

---

[90] During heavy rains sizable streams of water probably accumulated between intersections, as suggested by a row of stones outside the main doorway to the Villa that may have been added to prevent water from draining into the vestibule (see p. 120).

[91] No detailed report on the Italian excavations is available, but Professor Caputo's holograph communication on the Street of the Monuments, preserved in the files of the Department of Antiquities of Cyrenaica at Shahat, has been studied with care. A plan of the street by R. Rinaldis at greatly reduced scale appears in Caputo, "Protezione," Fig. 2. The plan of G. R. H. Wright provided here as Plan VII is based on a resurvey of the thoroughfare.

[92] So Caputo in his holograph communication, where he refers to the Beecheys' plan of Ptolemais (reproduced above as Fig. 4).

tained throughout the life of the city on the line assigned to it in the original plan of the third century B.C. and that it was kept at a relatively constant level until it was choked by the fall of the porticoes that turned it into a heap of columns.[93] This relatively unusual state of affairs may be the result in part of a single episode in the history of the thoroughfare, namely a rehabilitation program that began in the fourth century of our era, but in part it would seem to reflect also a general maintenance standard higher than that of cities less conscious of their Greek inheritance. How early this particular part of the street was actually graded, paved, and laid out on the lines provided in the city plan is not possible to say at present.[94] But the basic organization of the several elements of the thoroughfare seems not to have been changed radically during the entire period of its history.

Fundamentally the Street of the Monuments in this part of its course comprises five elements (Plan VII). There was in the first place a central carriageway 4 meters wide, in which wheel ruts are clearly visible. This was flanked on either side by slightly raised footpaths or sidewalks about 2.40 m. wide. The footpaths had the stylobates of colonnaded porticoes as their outer limits. The depth of these porticoes as excavated varies from insula to insula and from 3.00 to 5.90 m., no doubt because of changes in the building frontages from age to age. The section of the Street of the Monuments between the two cardines is emphasized by

a commanding monument at each extremity—at the west by the Triumphal Arch and at the east by the Tetrapylon. Scattered in the debris or found *in situ* particularly along the sides of the double insula in the center were architectural members, installations, sculptures, and inscriptions bearing upon the history of the street. Lines of masonry and masses of rubble along the frontages of the several insulae show that the entire stretch was built up, but to date only two of the buildings have been excavated, namely the Public Building (No. 8 on Plan XXII) and the City Bath (No. 15). A detailed report on these excavations is given below (pp. 140–75), while here we offer a general description of the monuments revealed by the earlier work in the area.

Of the Triumphal Arch only the four podia and parts of the socles of the piers resting upon them are preserved *in situ* (Pl. XI *A*). The podia are set out only about 50 cm. from the western frontage of the cardo. The east-west emplacement of the arch was therefore such as to offer a minimum of obstruction to the north-south traffic and a maximum of exposure to those viewing it from the east (see Plan VII). The north-south emplacement, which involved setting the outer podia beyond the building lines of the Street of the Monuments, was such as to bring the outer archways into line with the porticoes along the sides of the street. For anyone moving along the street by the carriageway or through the porticoes there were thus pleasing vistas upon and through the arch, clearly an intentional feature of the planning.

The outer socles are imperfectly preserved, but the inner pair clearly gives the typical dimensions of 1.87 × 1.87 m. The central archway was of course wider than those at the sides (4.50 m. as compared with *ca.* 2.50 m.), and the line of the spring of the arches must have been something of the order of 6 meters above pavement level.

There is available a published plan of the Triumphal Arch, with an elevation involving a reconstruction of the superstructure, made by Luigi Turba in 1936 (Fig. 15). Both Turba in the terminology applied to his elevation and Caputo in his text[95] indicate the hypothetical nature of certain features of the reconstruction, for example the over-all height of the monument. We therefore attempted to check the fallen remains, so far as

---

[93] Caputo in his holograph communication notes that soundings made underneath the extant paving revealed sherds of coarse ribbed and combed ware belonging to the period from the fourth to the sixth century of our era but interprets their presence as resulting from repairs made to offset deep wear and gaps. Evidence of such repairs can, indeed, be seen in front of the Public Building (No. 8 on Plan XXII), and re-examination of the thoroughfare justified Caputo's judgment that the presence of late sherds under the pavement has only local significance. Actually, the street presents a relatively homogeneous surface and maintains its own level remarkably well throughout. The excavations at the site of the Public Building showed that the levels of its Roman phase were identical with the level of the adjacent roadway. Immediately below a wall of the Roman phase lay virgin soil in which were imbedded sherds of Attic ware of the fourth century B.C. (see p. 156 below).

[94] Caputo in his holograph communication suggests that the Corinthian-Ionic frames of two fountains on the south side of the double insula (see p. 79 below) should be attributed to the late Hellenistic period. This we are inclined to doubt.

[95] See Caputo, "Arco trionfale in Cirenaica," *Atti del Terzo Congresso di Studi Coloniali* IV 133–37.

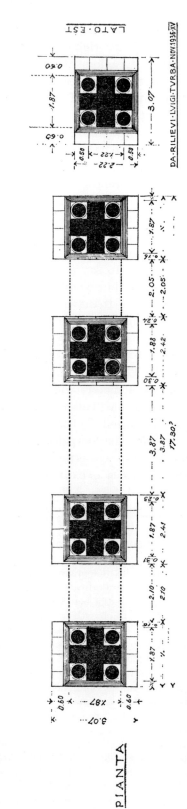

Fig. 15.—Plan and Reconstruction of Triumphal Arch. After Luigi Turba in Caputo, "Arco trionfale in Cirenaica," Fig. 1

76

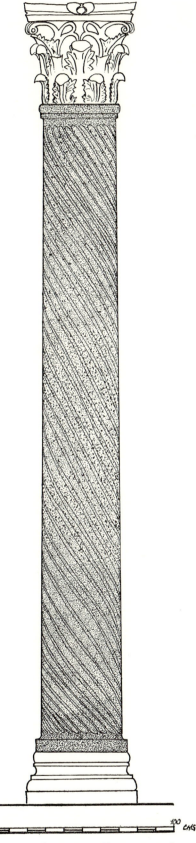

Fig. 16.—COLUMN OF TRIUMPHAL ARCH.
G. R. H. Wright

they were still available, and particularly to examine the moldings and render them to scale (Plan VIII). For the piers Turba suggests a combination of four spirally fluted blue marble Corinthian columns, each with white marble base and capital, and a central core having in plan the form of a Greek cross. The stone of which the columns are cut is identified by the Italian archeologists as "marmo nero del Tenaro." The columns are still there to see, so that the order can readily be reconstructed (Fig. 16 and Plan VIII 3–4), and the marks of their emplacement are clearly visible. As for a core in the form of a Greek cross, the only alternative would be a smaller square pier occupying only the center of the podium and obviously giving less solidity to the structure.

The rest of the reconstruction is sensible so far as the superimposition of the several members is concerned. The preserved fragments of cornices and string courses lend themselves to the kind of distribution suggested, with a cornice to crown the order (Plan VIII 7), a second serving as impost for the arches (Plan VIII 10), a string course for the main story (Plan VIII 6) and a cornice to crown it (Plan VIII 8). It is proper to postulate for the monument an attic sufficiently high to contain and set off a lengthy inscription in two lines—there being inscribed blocks with (Plan VIII 5) and without a taenia at the top—and to inclose it within base molding and crowning cornice (Plan VIII 2 and 9). The molded members measured but not drawn by Turba were readily identifiable, with allowance for slight variations in the excellence of the workmanship, save in one instance. The exception is the crowning cornice of the main story, to which Turba seems to give a rise of 42 cm. broken into two registers of 17 and 15 cm. (*sic*). An error seems to have crept in at this point, and the heavy cornice (Plan VIII 8) with a rise of 46 cm. no doubt should occupy the position. The evidence for the string course in the main story (Plan VIII 6) is tenuous and may be provided by some small weathered fragments. An interesting feature that is not apparent from Turba's drawing is that the voussoirs, while all bearing the same archivolt molding, have two distinct dimensions to the die, namely 18 and 13 cm., which presumably reflect a difference between one face of the arch and the other.[96]

[96] There is a vague reference by Caputo (*ibid.* p. 135) to remains of animal decoration, which it was not possible to check.

Fig. 17.—CIPPI ON STREET OF THE MONUMENTS. *G. R. H. Wright*

Caputo has pointed to the relative scarcity of this type of structure in North Africa and to the importance of the arch of Annuna-Thibilis in Algeria as a parallel. Perhaps the closest parallel is the triumphal arch in the Forum of Theodosius at Constantinople, for which there is literary testimony and remains of which were found in the course of British excavations in 1928.[97] Here again we have square podia, each supporting four columns. The differences are in size, in the type of column, in the absence of an attic, and in the doubling of the number of podia, a necessary corollary of the monumental proportions of the

structure. At Ptolemais it seems proper to associate the unpublished fragmentary inscription of the attic[98] with the late fourth or early fifth century of our era. But it cannot be taken to imply the date of the structure, as Caputo has already indicated. A long unpublished Latin inscription cut on a series of marble slabs that were found in the excavations must originally have been fixed across the face of the Triumphal Arch. The text is a dedication of the Constantinian period, as we are informed by Goodchild. The arch must therefore be of the early fourth century. Whether the attic inscription refers to an event in the history of the arch (such as repair, rededication, erection of statues of emperors atop the monument) or to an event in the history of the Street of the Monuments is unknown.

[97] *Scriptores originum Constantinopolitarum*, ed. Th. Preger (1901) p. 175, ch. 47, and S. Casson and D. Talbot Rice, *Second Report upon the Excavations Carried Out in and near the Hippodrome of Constantinople in 1928 on Behalf of the British Academy* (London, 1929) pp. 36–40, Fig. 47. This was a much more monumental structure (43 m. long, 25 m. high) and supported statues of Arcadius and Honorius.

[98] The letters are shallow, tall, and thin, like those of an inscription honoring Arcadius and Honorius found on the Street of the Monuments farther to the east (Oliverio, *Documenti antichi* II 2, Fig. 91 *a*).

Leaving the Triumphal Arch and continuing along the Street of the Monuments, we note first a square fountain set against the corner of the insula across the cardo at the south (see Plan VII). Its curb rises only about 40 cm. above pavement level and consists of plain unmolded blocks. It cannot lay claim to elegance and manifestly is a late installation, but it raises the interesting question as to how it and other installations along the decumanus were supplied with water. With the fountain it may be proper to join mention of several cippi that stand along the north side of the decumanus, at the corner across from the fountain and in front of the entrance to the Public Building in the adjacent insula (Fig. 17; see also Pl. XXVIII B). They are no doubt of different date, but being uninscribed their function remains undetermined. Cippi also flank the entrance to the Villa (see p. 120).

Along the first pair of insulae no footpath or sidewalk was noted in the Street of the Monuments, the blocks ending at the east with indications of piers both in the decumanus itself and in the cross street. They suggest light archways carried over the cross streets and projecting for unknown reasons into the footpath areas of the decumanus. These are clearly features of the Byzantine development, as their association with the Byzantine east exterior wall of the Public Building indicates.

Of the buildings which fronted on the Street of the Monuments in the second pair of insulae nothing is known, and of the street itself nothing noteworthy is to be reported save that here the footpaths are clearly visible together with the emplacements of the columns on the stylobates of the porticoes. With the next insulae we enter the section of the Street of the Monuments where important changes were made in the late Roman and Byzantine periods. The most noticeable changes are a setback in the frontage line of the buildings to the south, which had the effect of increasing the depth of the porticoes to 5.90 m. (Fig. 18), and the construction of a broad raised porch in front of them that extended the full width of the double insula (see Pl. X D).[99] The porch had a height of about 1.20 m. above street level, corresponding in

this particular and in general to the one built by the governor Paul along the west cardo (see p. 141). It is a question of no small importance whether in the construction of the raised porch along the south side of the Street of the Monuments the southward extension of one of the cross streets was abandoned or whether the double insula was an original part of the city plan (see p. 41).

Of the structures that fronted on this raised porch only two are known at present, the Byzantine City Bath in the northwest corner of the double insula and a heavy apsidal hall, partially cleared by the Italian archeologists, which Caputo associates with Caracalla.[100] Access to these buildings was provided by several stairways leading up from the streets to the level of the raised porch (see Fig. 18), but they were not all of the same date nor type of construction. A stairway set into the cross street at the northwest corner of the double insula and constructed of large building stones laid without thought of formal design (see Pl. XXXII D) is no doubt the latest. A rectangle of masonry projecting into the Street of the Monuments just around the corner (see Plan XX) seems to represent the first step of a similar staircase. Earlier and more clearly representing the plan for the construction of the porch are two staircases leading up from the Street of the Monuments, one on the north-south axis of the double insula directly opposite the cross street running north on this axis and the other in front of the apsidal hall. Both interrupt the footpath, the latter with two flights of steps mounting from east and west to a projecting landing and the other with a single flight of steps mounting from the north directly to the porch. Even though both staircases in their present form are probably secondary features, as Caputo has observed, the one on the axis of the double insula would seem to provide a formal central feature of the porch, placed as it is between two fountains that are built into the outer wall of the porch and contained within molded Corinthian-Ionic frames which give them the shape of *kathedrai* (see Plan XX). Water was conducted to these fountains by a channel running out from the City Bath under the paving of the porch.

---

[99] A setback in the building line is noticeable in this same area at the north also, but indications of a raised porch are not so evident. Caputo and Goodchild (*JRS* XLV 106) state that on each side of the street a raised porch continued along the fronts of four pairs of insulae or a total distance of at least 160 m.

[100] So Caputo in his holograph communication. The association is made on the strength of a fragmentary Latin inscription which Caputo reads "(M. Aur. Antonin)us Aug(ustus) Piu(s)." Spirally fluted blue marble columns marked the entrance to this hall, which appears in Fig. 18.

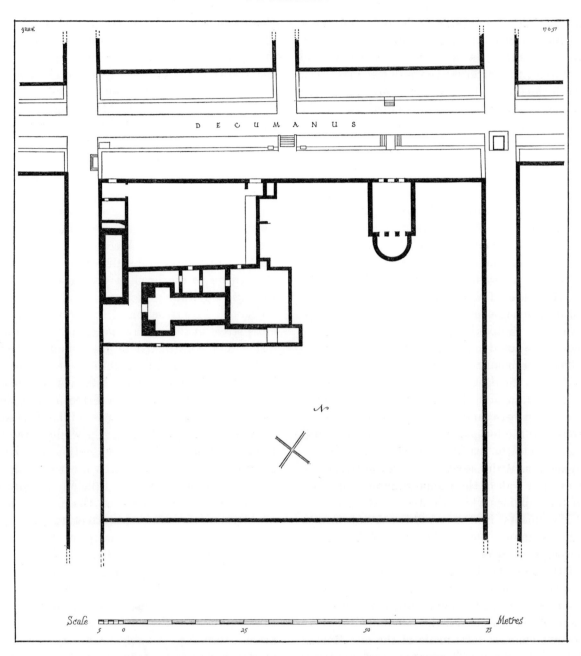

Fig. 18.—Sketch Plan of Double Insula. *G. R. H. Wright*

The outer wall of the porch bore the columns of the porticoes that decorated the façades of the buildings that fronted on the porch. The monolithic shafts of these columns had fallen in confusion to produce the "heaps of columns" noted by the Beecheys. Opposite the City Bath the columns were of granite, and farther to the east they were of blue and light green marble, unfluted. This difference suggested, of course, the existence of separate buildings behind the unified porch. In and among the fallen columns there were visible even before the Italian excavations inscribed architrave blocks which belong to two different buildings. One inscription honors Valentinian and his colleagues (A.D. 367–75),[101] the other Arcadius and Honorius (A.D. 395–408).[102] On the strength of the observation that in falling the architrave of a building on the south side of the Street of the Monuments would have landed on the north side,

[101] Oliverio, *Documenti antichi* II 2, p. 252, No. 512; *SEG* IX 71, No. 364.

[102] Oliverio, *op. cit.* p. 252, No. 513; *SEG* IX 71, No. 365.

and vice versa, the inscription honoring Arcadius and Honorius (see Pl. LIV *A–B*) is ascribed to the City Bath portico, though it was found on the north side of the street, and that honoring Valentinian is ascribed to an unknown building on the north side of the street, though it was found on the south side.[103] The implication is that the later years of the fourth century saw a considerable increment of civic building activity in this area and that the present aspect of the remains dates from approximately that time.

The porch was shown by the excavations to have been paved on two successive occasions. The lower and hence earlier pavement was of marble slabs of varied size and color. Among these was a fragment, reused upside down, bearing part of the Latin text of Diocletian's Price Edict (Pl. LV *A*).[104] It has been suggested that the marble paving is contemporary with the construction of the porch, that the porch itself belongs to the period of Valentinian, and that its upper paving of small sandstone blocks belongs to the period of Arcadius and Honorius.[105] However, what is known about the date of the Triumphal Arch suggests that the plan for the rehabilitation of the Street of the Monuments, with which the construction of the porch is associated, may at least have been formulated in the first half of the fourth century. In any event, the reuse here of the marble slab bearing the text of the Price Edict suggests that in the late third century of our era there stood in this general vicinity an important public building on which the edict was mounted for all to see and from which it was removed when it had lost its validity.

To a still earlier period in the life of the Street of the Monuments belong two marble statues which probably stood on two inscribed pedestals found with them. The statues at present are set against the outer wall of the porch in front of the City Bath (Pl. L *B–C*) and in Byzantine times either occupied this same position or stood on the porch between columns of its porticoes. The pedestals are in honor of Claudia Eupomane (by M. Antonius Flavianus, presumably her husband) and Marcus Aurelius Flavianus (by Valeria Marciane, his mother) and hence, like the two statues that must

originally have stood upon them, point to the Antonine period or to the reign of Caracalla at the latest (see pp. 203–4, Nos. 62–63).[106] To the same general period belong fragments of a relief representing the dance of the maenads, found here by the Italian archeologists.[107] The fact that the missing section of the relief was reused in the City Bath (see p. 165) would seem to indicate that the other fragments may have been not in their original location but on the way to a limekiln installed in the bath. Yet the probability is that they had been transported from not too distant a location and therefore that a public building of some importance stood in this general vicinity in the second century of our era.

Of the further course of the Street of the Monuments eastward only two details need to be mentioned. The first is a public fountain at the intersection east of the double insula. This is a more elaborate basin than that on the west cardo (see p. 79) and occupies most of the width of the cross street south of the intersection (see Fig. 18 and Plan VII). Its date would be difficult to determine. At the next intersection the Street of the Monuments crosses the east cardo, and this intersection is marked by the Tetrapylon.

Plan IX shows the intersection more clearly than a photograph could, outlining the unobtrusive, indeed tenuous, evidence that something was once mounted here. So far as the setting is concerned, the picture is only slightly obscured by late constructions intrusive upon the east footpath of the cardo at the south and upon the same footpath and part of the roadway at the north. Once these encroachments, occasioned by the efforts of squatters to live among the ruins, are discounted, there emerges an open piazza (14.80 × 18.20 m.) created by the meeting of the two major thoroughfares. In the paving here there are noticeable four areas about 4.50 m. square, so set as to be quartered by extensions of the lines on which the curbs of the cardo's footpaths and the porticoes of the decumanus ran. They left ample space (*ca.* 4.00 m.) for wheeled

---

[103] So Caputo in his holograph communication.

[104] See Caputo and Goodchild in *JRS* XLV 106–7, Pl. XXXVII 2.

[105] *Ibid.* p. 107.

[106] On Pl. X *D* the pedestals and statues can be seen standing approximately where they were found. The inscriptions on the pedestals appear in Oliverio, *Documenti antichi* II 2, pp. 252–53, Nos. 515–16, and *SEG* IX 72, Nos. 367–68. Oliverio reads "Claudia Euporiane."

[107] See Caputo, *Lo scultore del grande bassorilievo con la Danza delle Menadi*. On the place of discovery see pp. 5–6. Caputo (pp. 23–24) dates the relief a century earlier than Brinkerhoff does (see p. 193 below).

3.52
0.24 5
G.R.H.W.
'58

Fig. 20.—Profile of the Order of the Tetrapylon. *G. R. H. Wright*

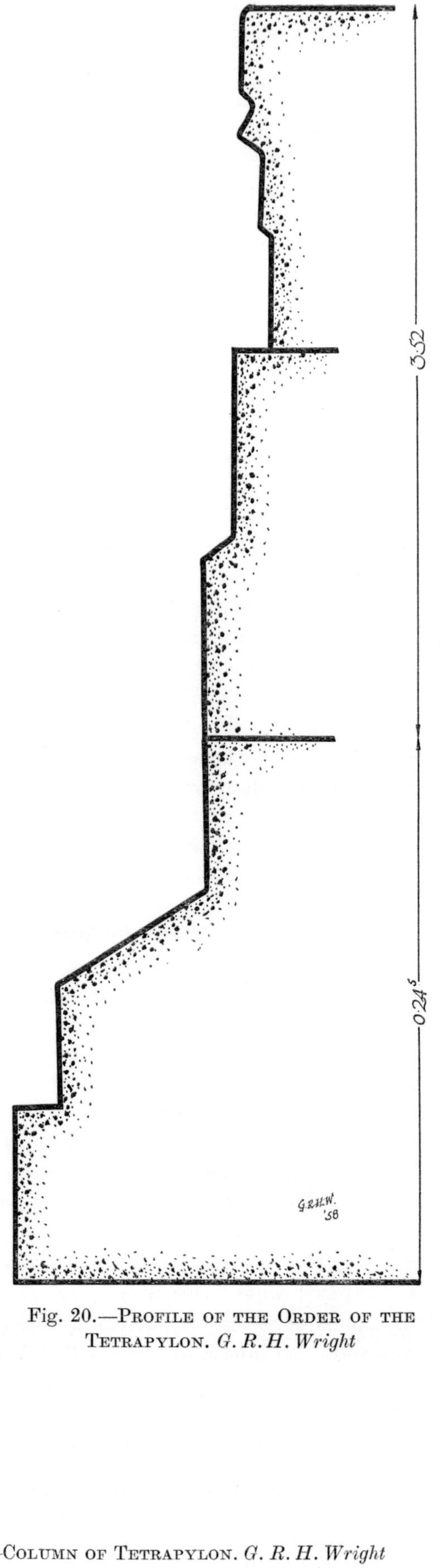

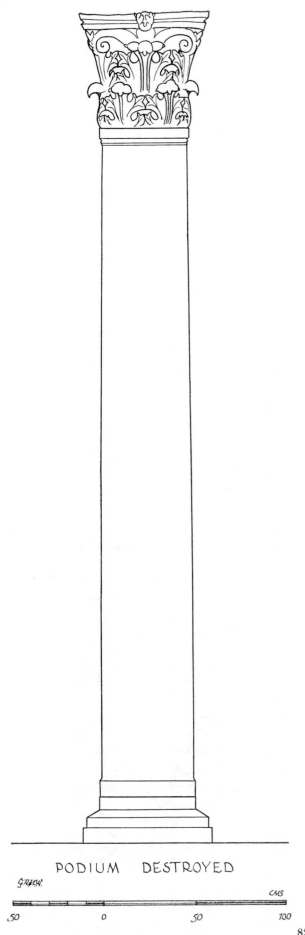

PODIUM DESTROYED
G.R.H.W.
CMS
50
0
50
100

Fig. 19.—Column of Tetrapylon. *G. R. H. Wright*

traffic along either thoroughfare and only partially obstructed pedestrian traffic along the footpaths. They are not set off by the foundations of solid podia nor are they incumbered with successive courses of masonry rising above pavement level, save at the southwest. Here remains of a second course exist, made up, however, of reused large entablature blocks including a fragment of a triglyph frieze. Otherwise (and predominantly) the four areas are marked only by organization in particular or diverse ways of precisely such stones as also make up the paving of the roadways and footpaths. Lying loose and broken in the piazza were found considerable remains of four monolithic white marble columns with Corinthian capitals. The total height of the order is 4.36 m. (Fig. 19). The stiff formality of the capital and the equally stiff angular fillets of the base (Fig. 20) are unmistakably Byzantine.[108] It is, of course, tempting to assume that the columns stood one each on four masonry piers in the piazza, representing thus a late Byzantine counterpart of the tetrapylons with which the Roman architects of the Antonine period loved to decorate street intersections, as for instance at Gerasa, Palmyra, and Philippopolis.[109] But, though this may indeed have been the case, it is difficult to visualize podia sufficiently solid to support the weight of these columns footed and constructed of materials such as mark the four areas set out in the street intersection. Moreover, the period to which structural procedures and materials of such poor quality would have to be assigned would scarcely seem likely to have indulged

in a purely decorative enterprise. Yet something clearly stood here, and perhaps the simplest assumption is that the four areas now set off by paving stones and reused architectural members did at one time provide for the emplacement of heavy properly footed podia that were later completely removed. Such a structure one would certainly wish to connect with the second century of our era, generally speaking. As to what happened later, one can assume either that the areas once occupied by the podia of the Tetrapylon were so paved that the outlines of the original installation were not obscured or that low masonry masses were assembled here in late Roman or Byzantine times to simulate the older construction. In the case of the latter assumption, the construction of such masses would remain something of an enigma.

From this intersection the Department of Antiquities has been continuing the clearance of the Street of the Monuments eastward in the direction of the Headquarters of the Dux (Building 23 on Plan XXII). The discoveries made thus far are of no great moment save perhaps for elements of a small *triconchos* which have come to light at the northeast corner of the same street intersection and to which Goodchild is inclined tentatively to assign the white marble columns found in the piazza.[110] The further excavation of the street will, however, continue to be watched with interest because even the structures and embellishments already known provide important insights into many periods of the history of the city.

DWELLINGS: THE "PALAZZO" AND THE VILLA OF THE ROMAN PERIOD

It would by no means be surprising if, when its excavation has ultimately been completed, Ptolemais should turn out to have been proportionately much more residential in character than might be expected of a city of its size. At the present stage in our knowledge of the site this possibility is suggested on the one hand by the fact that areas

burdened with a heavy overlay of architectural debris from ruined public buildings are relatively few and on the other hand by the fact that remains of rubble vaulting from small private baths are distributed so widely. From the areas inside its walls that could have been developed residentially, we must necessarily exclude a sizable portion of the northwest sector of the city, where some of the more ancient quarries lay (see p. 108) and where

[108] Goodchild compares them to similar capitals and bases of a sixth-century church recently excavated at Apollonia.

[109] See Kraeling, *Gerasa*, pp. 103–15 and Plan XII; Wiegand, *Palmyra*, pp. 24–25, Figs. 23–25; H. C. Butler, *Architecture and Other Arts* (New York, 1903) p. 393 and Fig. 130. In general see now also Martin, *L'Urbanisme dans la Grèce antique*, pp. 177–83.

[110] So in a recent private communication suggesting that the *triconchos* may be a church. The structure is not to be confused with another *triconchos* (Building 16 on Plan XXII), farther to the north, partly cleared by the Department of Antiquities.

6*

the native rock, used by the inhabitants of modern Tolmeita to dry and thresh their grain, presents to view a continuous unworked surface. This area extends westward from the Amphitheater (Building 1 on Plan XXII) to the adjacent small quarry and northward to the Italian city wall. We must probably exclude also the area south of the great reservoirs (Buildings 10–12) because this was presumably the city's watershed (see p. 72). Along the shore, and particularly near the harbor (under the modern town), the structures of the ancient city were no doubt just such a confusion of warehouses, shops, taverns, and accommodations for port officials, sailors, and stevedores as the excavations of M. Montet have revealed in the portside area of Apollonia.[111] Elsewhere, save in the apparently limited areas occupied by public buildings, we may properly imagine that the site was residentially developed, typically with two, three, or even four establishments to the insula.[112]

In what has hitherto become known about private houses in Cyrenaica through the medium of publication, Ptolemais has played a dominant role thanks to the important work of Pesce on the "Palazzo delle Colonne" (Building 13 on Plan XXII).[113] That the "Palazzo" will continue to dominate the scene so far as the domestic architecture of Cyrenaica in the early Roman period is concerned is entirely possible.[114] Perhaps, however, its very elegance and the fact that it had to be seen in isolation, without benefit of comparative material, have tended to warp the perspective upon the nature and development of house types in Cyrenaica and have made the building seem somewhat older than it is. Perhaps, too, the term *palazzo* is unfortunate, corresponding more to modern and post-Renaissance usage than to that of antiquity.[115] But certain at least of the short-

comings that may have been inherent in the early treatment can be readily overcome with the help of the new comparative material now in hand and without detracting in the least from the importance of Pesce's contribution.

Of private dwellings now known at Ptolemais in addition to the "Palazzo," we have the Villa of the Roman period (see pp. 119–39) and part at least of the residence attached to the Public Building on the Street of the Monuments (see pp. 153–54). The inferences that can be drawn about the dates of these newly excavated structures from the study of their coins, mosaics, wall decoration, inscriptions, and architecture are given below, but their importance for the knowledge of domestic architecture at Ptolemais it seems appropriate to discuss in the present context. By including here also occasional references to the House of Jason Magnus at Cyrene[116] we can extend somewhat the scope of the inferences to be drawn.

About the residential buildings that we know thus far at Ptolemais and Cyrene two things can be said with assurance, namely that no one of them shows influence of the Campanian atrium house and that all of them are examples of the peristyle house (Pl. XI *B*). They represent, thus, the flat-roofed type of structure, featuring an oecus opening on a courtyard set out with colonnaded porticoes, that seems to have developed first in the southeastern Mediterranean, that began rivaling the more northerly megaron house in the fifth century B.C., that became the dominant type throughout the Aegean area in the Hellenistic era and was eventually combined with the atrium house in Italy in the last century of the Roman Republic.[117]

---

[111] The results of these excavations have not yet been published.

[112] Even the "Palazzo" did not occupy an entire insula, and the block in which the Villa of the Roman period stood was presumably occupied by two additional houses. In insulae that were 50 m. wide (rather than the typical 36 m.) the number of houses could have been even greater.

[113] *Il "Palazzo delle Colonne" in Tolemaide di Cirenaica* (1950).

[114] Cyrene, of course, offers the better prospects for the Greek period and Apollonia for the Byzantine period.

[115] On the use of the word *palatium* generally see now the interesting study of Ziegler in *R.-E.* The designation "Palazzo" is retained in the present report for purposes of identification.

[116] There is now reason to look forward to its publication, but the only data currently available in print are a brief description by Goodchild, *Cyrene and Apollonia*, pp. 43–44, with sketch plan, and Derek Buttle's plan of the architectural remains of Cyrene in *Cyrenaican Expedition of the University of Manchester, 1952*, Fig. XIII. To judge by its mosaics the House of Jason Magnus is later than the Villa at Ptolemais and belongs perhaps to the Flavian period (see p. 000 below).

[117] On the general development see e.g. W. B. Dinsmoor, *The Architecture of Ancient Greece* (1950) pp. 322–26, D. S. Robertson, *Handbook of Greek and Roman Architecture* (1954; reprint of 2d ed. of 1940) pp. 297–314, and especially D. M. Robinson in *R.-E.* Supplementband VII (1940) *s.v.* "Haus," where many examples of the peristyle house are listed from Olynthos, Priene, Rhodes, Delos, Pergamum, etc.

In its simplest form the peristyle house of Cyrenaica is exhibited in the dwelling attached to the Public Building on the Street of the Monuments at Ptolemais, even though this dwelling is only imperfectly known. At the center lies a roughly square open courtyard, presumably developed as a garden, with colonnaded porticoes on all four sides. The house is entered through a passageway giving upon the south portico. In an axial position off the south side of the courtyard is located the largest chamber in the excavated (southern) part of the dwelling, a rectangular hall (Rooms 27–28 on Fig. 51) whose entrance could be closed in part or in whole by movable doors (see particularly Plan XVI and p. 154). This is the oecus, described by Vitruvius (*De architectura* vi. 3. 8–10) as being typical of the Greek house and as being used by the women and also for large dinner parties. In Cyrenaica, so far as we can tell today, special provision was made for the women in other parts of the house and the oecus was thus left free for use by the master, corresponding perhaps to the diwan of the Oriental type of house.[118] In Cyrenaica also, so far as we can tell at present, the preferred position for the oecus was at the south of the peristyle court, undoubtedly for climatic reasons, while in the Aegean area, for similar reasons, it was at the north.[119]

All the ancient private houses that we know of today in Libya, namely those at Ptolemais, the House of Jason Magnus at Cyrene, and a villa near Homs in Tripolitania on which Renato Bartoccini has reported briefly,[120] belong to this general type, though some show important modifications. What this means for the history of domestic architecture

in Cyrenaica is as yet impossible to say. Clearly none of the examples are earlier than the late Hellenistic and Republican Roman periods, and they permit no inferences concerning the house types of early Hellenistic and Greek times. Since the peristyle house was so well adapted to the warmer climate of Cyrenaica, it must have been an immediate favorite at least in the coastal cities as soon as the type became known, and for a city like Ptolemais, whose *floruit* began in the Hellenistic period, it may well have been the dominant type from the outset.

As variations upon the theme of the peristyle house the "Palazzo" at Ptolemais and the Villa of the Roman period have certain features in common and certain features which illustrate developments tending in opposite directions. Common to both is the presence at the north end of the establishment of shops and private bathing facilities.[121] In the "Palazzo" the baths are very elaborate (see Pl. XI *C*) and according to their excavator are in their final form a product of the first or second Christian century.[122] In the Villa the bathing facilities are elementary by contrast, providing merely a caldarium (Room 1), with its necessary furnace room (Room 24), and a room off the east portico where movable tubs for cold ablutions may have stood (Room 20). Whatever may be true about the time and place of the invention of the *suspensura*, the installation of facilities for steam and hot- or cold-water baths in private houses was a common practice not only in Pompeii but at least as early as the first century B.C. in the Near East also.[123] In this connection it is important to keep in mind what Josephus (*Antiquities* xv. 53–56) reports about Herod's drowning of Aristobulus, the brother of Mariamne, in the pool of his villa at Jericho and to note the presence of plunges and a caldarium in the building excavated at Jericho that is in all probability that very villa.[124]

[118] On the Oriental type see e.g. *Excavations at Dura Europos: Preliminary Report of the Fifth Season of Work* (1934) esp. pp. 31–34 and Pl. VI.

[119] For analogous peristyle houses and the arrangement of their rooms in other parts of the eastern Mediterranean compare House A next to the Agora at Pergamum (W. Dörpfeld, "Die Arbeiten zu Pergamon, 1902–1903," *MDAIA* XXIX [1904] 116–200, Pl. VII); Houses XXII and XXXIII at Priene (T. Wiegand and H. Schrader, *Priene* [1904] pp. 285–328); the House of the Masques at Delos (*Exploration archéologique de Délos*. XIV. *Les mosaïques de la Maison des Masques*, by J. Chamonard [1933] Pl. I and pp. 26–32); Houses A 3 and A 5 at Olynthos (Robinson and Graham, *Excavations at Olynthos* VIII, Pl. 89, pp. 73–75).

[120] See "Rinvenimenti vari di interesse archeologico in Tripolitania (1920–1925)," *Africa italiana* I (1927/28) 226–32. The house has two oeci on the south side of the peristyle court.

[121] For the "Palazzo" see Pesce, *Il "Palazzo delle Colonne,"* Pl. XII, Rooms 50–62 (shops) and Rooms 29–47 (baths); for the Villa see Fig. 43 below, Rooms I–IV (shops) and Rooms 1, 20, 24 (bath).

[122] Pesce, *op. cit.* p. 107.

[123] See Johannes Overbeck, *Pompeji* (4th ed.; Leipzig, 1884) Houses 10 (M. Caesius Blandus), 22 (Casa del Laberinto), 23 (Casa del Fauno), 24 (Casa del Centenario), etc. For Boscoreale see Robertson, *Handbook of Greek and Roman Architecture*, pp. 310–11.

[124] See J. A. Pritchard, *The Excavation at Herodian Jericho, 1951* ("The Annual of the American Schools of Oriental Research" XXXII–XXXIII [New Haven, 1958]) Pls. 63 and 66 (Rooms 9, 15, 19).

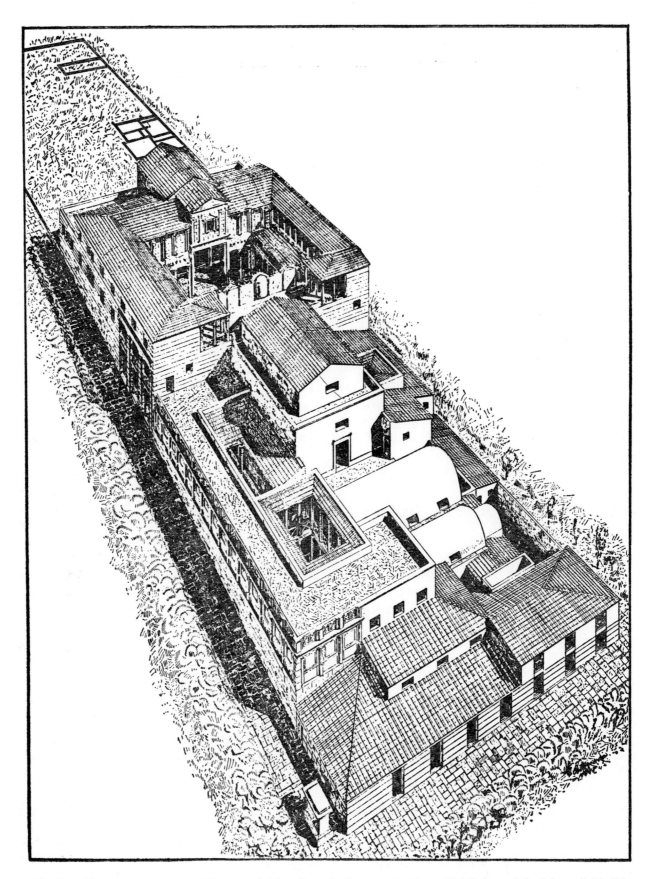

Fig. 21.—RECONSTRUCTION OF "PALAZZO." After Carmelo Catanuso in Pesce, *Il "Palazzo delle Colonne,"* Pl. IX

86

Other aspects of the development of the peristyle house as we see them reflected at Ptolemais can be illustrated by the differences between the "Palazzo" and the Villa of the Roman period. Perhaps the most fundamental differences are not those of relative elegance and the arrangement of corresponding elements but rather those reflected in the treatment of the mass. In the case of the "Palazzo" the structure was developed vertically, its mass building up to a great height (Fig. 21). In part this treatment resulted from the natural lay of the land, whose slope required a lofty substructure to hold the living quarters at the level of the peristyle. But this is by no means the entire story, as the relative heights of the columns and ceilings and the existence of a floor above courtyard level indicate.[125] The "Palazzo" is a peristyle house that was apparently adapted to the circumstances of a crowded metropolis (in which connection one thinks naturally of Alexandria), where building lots were limited and where vertical development not only provided for the inclusion of all the facilities desired but also had the advantage of providing better ventilation and escape from street noises. It is interesting and not unimportant for the understanding of the cultural history of Ptolemais to find such a house in the city.

By contrast the mass of the Villa is distributed horizontally. The peristyle court occupies an unusually large part of the lot as compared with the chambers (see Fig. 43), in spite of the existence of a second story in the area behind the south portico (see pp. 127–28). Indeed, one has the impression that the Villa was a structure basically appropriate to the expansiveness of a rural setting, which was crowded into a city block with a resultant imbalance on the east side, where there was room for a portico but not for a series of chambers.[126]

It is not surprising, therefore, that the parallels for the curving colonnade of its south portico are to be found in the façades of country villas shown in the architectural landscapes of Pompeian wall decoration.[127]

In the arrangement of their basic structural elements the "Palazzo" and the Villa are also instructive, showing two different solutions to the problem of providing for the public and the private affairs of the owner. In the "Palazzo" we have at the south of the peristyle court the typical oecus (Room 11 on Fig. 22) and across the court at the north a still larger rectangular hall (Room 19) set out with columns and paved with marble and mosaics. The latter is not a second peristyle court but a second oecus, as Pesce has correctly seen.[128] The two oeci, at opposite ends of the peristyle, provided separate facilities for the two facets of the life of the owner, and we can imagine one oecus with its adjacent chambers serving the family and the other serving the business visitors and guests, quite in accordance with what Vitruvius says about the requirements of men of affairs. It may be noted incidentally that colonnades appear in such formal oeci not only in the great palaces at Rome (e.g. the *domus Domitiana*) but also in earlier and more modest villas such as that of Herod the Great at Jericho.[129]

The Villa at Ptolemais illustrates a different way of separating family and public life within the confines of the peristyle house. Holding themselves to the horizontal organization of space, the builders set into the southwest corner of the structure a suite of rooms (Rooms 9–14 on Fig. 43), self-contained and well organized, that provided everything needed for the private life of the owner. If the suite was connected via a stairway in Room 13a (see p. 131) with what were probably the women's quarters in the second story above Rooms 15–17

---

[125] The existence of an upper story has been doubted by A. von Gerkan (*Gnomon* XXIII [1951] 337–40). As in his discussion of the date of the building, his position on this point seems extreme. In our judgment the question is not so much whether there was an upper story, but how one arranges the architectural elements that probably belonged to it.

[126] The rural villa of the Roman period, traditionally known from what Horace and Pliny the Younger have written about their country retreats, has in recent years become increasingly familiar from archeological research. Two types are properly distinguished by Robertson, *op. cit.* pp. 310–11. Of the simple more functional type examples have come to light for instance at Boscoreale (*ibid.* Fig. 131), outside Homs in Tripolitania (see Bartoc-

cini in *Africa italiana* I 226–32), and at Uthina (see P. Gauckler, "Le domaine des Laberii à Uthina," *MP* III [1896] 177–229). The great imperial villas, from those of Tiberius on Capri and Hadrian at Tivoli to the villa of Maximanius Herculius at Piazza Armerina, provide the most monumental examples of residential architecture expansively developed, but they really form a type of their own.

[127] See e.g. Rostovtzeff, "Die hellenistisch-römische Architekturlandschaft," *MDAIR* XXVI, Pls. VI 2 and VII 2, pp. 90 and 76.

[128] *Il "Palazzo delle Colonne,"* p. 46.

[129] See Pritchard, *op. cit.* Pl. 66 (Room 33).

it provided also for the life of his family. Basically the suite is nothing more than a small peristyle house within a large house of the same type. A small peristyle court with a hypethral water basin (Room 11) was the center of communications. On its axis was an oecus or a diwan (Room 12) connected with a private dining room (Room 14) on one side and a bedroom (Room 10) on the other. Even though at the south of Rooms 13, 13*a*, and 14 the villa lacks its own exterior wall (see pp. 131–32), it would appear that the suite is an integral part of the house as planned, making all the more interesting the architect's solution of his problem.

As regards the rest of the establishment, the Villa at Ptolemais is a combination of traditional features and modifications not necessarily connected with the emplacement of the residential suite in the southwest corner of the premises. The bathing facilities, as we have seen, are rudimentary for the Roman period. The area along the west portico provided two dining rooms, presumably a summer and a winter dining room (Rooms 5 and 6), for entertaining guests. The separate provisions made here for the convivial aspects of hospitality were undoubtedly connected with the handling of the oecus (Room 16), which lies quite properly on

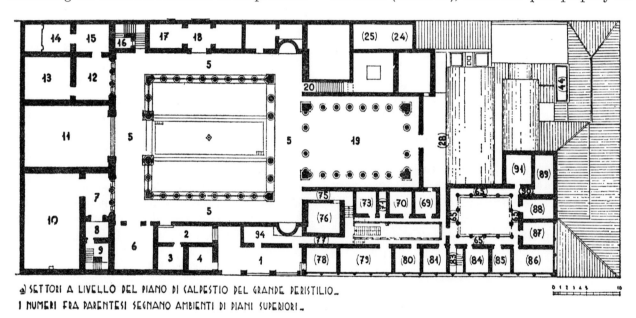

Fig. 22.—PLAN OF "PALAZZO." After Carmelo Catanuso in Pesce, *Il "Palazzo delle Colonne,"* Pl. XI

Clearly, then, advances were being made in Cyrenaica along various lines in the development of the peristyle house to adapt it to the mercantile and civic life of the Mediterranean world in the Hellenistic and Roman periods. Of these advances what we know today about the houses at Ptolemais is perhaps more interesting and significant than what at present is known from Cyrene, where the simpler and probably intrinsically older method of joining adjacent premises and thereby doubling facilities is illustrated by the House of Jason Magnus.[130]

the axis of the peristyle court, behind the south portico. It is a relatively small and distinctly inclosed chamber, flanked by two smaller chambers (Rooms 15 and 17) that originally were connected only with it. The existence of analogous groups of two and three rooms of relatively equal size along one side of the court of peristyle houses for instance at Olynthos suggests at first glance that the arrangement in the Villa at Ptolemais is a survival from the period when the oecus was not yet fully differentiated in form from the other rooms.[131]

[130] For similar houses with double courtyards see the enlarged House XXXIII at Priene and the House of the Masques at Delos. Plans of both are conveniently accessible in Robinson's article in *R.-E.* Supplementband VII, *s.v.* "Haus," cols. 266, Fig. 10, and 275, Fig. 14.

[131] See e.g. the House of the Comedian and House A xi 9 at Olynthos (Robinson and Graham, *op. cit.* Pls. 87 and 102 respectively). Similarly inclosed and relatively undifferentiated are the rooms on the two sides of the peristyle court of the villa near Homs in Tripolitania, among which one or another must have served as the oecus (see Bartoccini in *Africa italiana* I, plan on p. 226).

But the actual explanation probably is quite different and hangs together with the fact that the peristyle is of the Rhodian type, the greater height of the south colonnade allowing for the development above Rooms 15–17 of a second story. For the support of such a superstructure it was necessary to keep the rooms at courtyard level low and small and their walls as heavy and continuous as possible, with heavy trim. It was probably to compensate for the less expansive character of the Villa's oecus that a large extra dining room (Room 6) was provided behind the west portico. Rooms 15–17 can therefore properly be said to have fulfilled the demands which the business and social affairs of the owner created and to have served as a combination of oecus and guest rooms, like the rooms at the south end of the "Palazzo."

As regards the internal appointments and furnishings of the houses at Ptolemais little can be said at present. Some were undoubtedly more lavish than others, but the degree of lavishness seems to reflect the economic competence and the official status of the owners rather than the date of the establishments. Mosaic pavements and *opus sectile* in marble were regular parts of the picture, as was bright wall decoration (see pp. 237–51 and 225–36). The "Palazzo" counted among its ornaments interesting pieces of marble sculpture, and such may

also have adorned the Villa, though none that could definitely be assigned to it came to light in the excavations. Furniture, draperies, and utensils —all readily movable—were naturally among the first things to disappear. But, all things considered, the life of those citizens of Ptolemais who lived in its villas must originally have been both cultivated and comfortable. How long this state of affairs remained typical for the city is difficult to say. No doubt in the fourth and even in the fifth century men like Bishop Synesius and Paul the *consularis* lived in reasonably well appointed traditional establishments. But when the incursions of the nomadic peoples became more frequent and more devastating, the open peristyle house probably became less desirable as a habitation and its movable effects were subject to constant reduction by looting. At this time, it may be, there developed a different type of dwelling, a tower or blockhouse type that was more readily defensible and that had a vaulted cistern on the lower floor (see p. 73). Those who did not have the means to build such new structures lived as squatters in the ruins of the older peristyle houses (see p. 122), taking refuge from raids in the city's internal fortresses and finding themselves each time more impoverished by the looting of the possessions they could not hide or remove.

THE "ODEON" AND RELATED STRUCTURES

By R. G. Goodchild *and* C. H. Kraeling

The building which may conveniently be termed the "Odeon" (Building 9 on Plan XXII)—if not with accuracy, at least to distinguish it from the two other theaters of Ptolemais—was first identified in 1822 when the brothers Frederick and Henry Beechey planned the ruins of the city. It seemed then to be "too much ruined, and too much encumbered" to be surveyed with any precision,[132] and it therefore appears only schematically on the Beecheys' plan of Ptolemais (Fig. 4).

In 1935, when Professor Giacomo Caputo, then directing the Italian antiquities service in Cyrenaica, began the first systematic excavations at Tolmeita, the "Odeon" was included among the monuments to be explored. It was completely

cleared along its outer frontages, while exploratory trenches were cut through the rubble that filled the interior down to the level of the orchestra floor. This work was sufficient to reveal the general plan of the "Odeon" but not to elucidate its full character and structural development.[133] In later years the interior soundings silted up and bushes began to grow over the unexcavated areas.

In 1955 the Department of Antiquities, with funds provided by the Libyan Public Development and Stabilization Agency, undertook the complete

---

[132] Beechey, *Proceedings*, p. 380.

[133] A description with sketch plan appears in Caputo "Note sugli edifici teatrali della Cirenaica," *Anthemon: Scritti in onore di Carlo Anti* (1954) pp. 10–12 and Fig. 1, and with amplification in Caputo, *Il Teatro di Sabratha e l'architettura teatrale africana* ("Monografie di archeologia libica" VI [Roma, 1959]) pp. 65–69 and Pl. 93.

clearance of the interior of the "Odeon."[134] The work, which was completed in a single campaign, was directed by the writer (R.G.G.) and supervised by Messrs. Naim Makhouly and Abdulhamid Abdussaid. The latter carried out a survey on which the accompanying plan and section are based (Plans X–XI).

The following description of the "Odeon" must be considered as provisional pending a fuller investigation of the earlier features concealed by the theatrical installations of the latest age. The latter are of very considerable interest, and it seemed prudent not to be overhasty in demolishing them, even though such caution may leave certain questions unanswered.

The "Odeon" lies on the east side of the west cardo of the city, which ran past the Square of the Cisterns (Building 10) and down to the anchorage east of the promontory (see Plan XXII). Although this street has yet to be fully excavated, its line is clear from surface indications, and it would seem that the back wall of the stage was separated from the street only by a single portico, of imposing elevation, which formed the western and principal façade of the "Odeon." The northern side of the "Odeon" seems to have opened onto a street or piazza, but a series of widely spaced fluted columns which run parallel to the north wall appears too distant from the "Odeon" to have any direct structural relationship.

On the east side the "Odeon" is not completely freestanding. A small hall (L on Plan X) occupied the northeast corner of the site, opening onto the piazza, but it is not yet fully excavated and its function cannot be guessed. Farther to the south on the east side, a well and some late walls indicate that other more humble buildings backed up against the "Odeon." On the south, and apparently antedating the "Odeon," are the much mutilated remains of a temple with a raised podium. The pronaos (M) has been stripped down to its footings, as have both side walls. There remains, however, part of the stone-slab paving of the rear of the cella, together with the bottom course of what was presumably a broad basement (N) for cult statues

built up against the back wall. A large Corinthian capital of Hellenistic type lying within the ruins is the only indication of the temple's adornment.

It is clear that the builders of the "Odeon" utilized the back wall of the temple, building eastward from it to form the southeast "staircase corner." There are, however, no surviving traces of any direct communication between temple and "Odeon," and it would be rash to suppose that the former was a "theater-temple" of the type recently studied by Hanson.[135]

Three principal phases in the structural history of the "Odeon" (Pl. XII) are apparent. The "First Odeon" differed principally from its successors in the arrangements of its orchestra, stage, and parodoi. The parodoi led into the orchestra, not onto the stage as subsequently. Evidence for this original layout exists at several points: (1) the straight joints visible in the inner wall of the *ambulacrum* at points A and B on Plan X; (2) the actual remains of early parodoi at C and D; (3) the footings of the original prolongations of the stage wall at E and F; (4) changes in the masonry of the orchestra parapet at G and H, indicating a westward enlargement of the orchestra. Of the back wall of the stage (or *scaenae frons*) of this phase nothing seems to survive above ground. Indeed, the possibility must be borne in mind that our so-called "First Odeon" represents only a preliminary stage of the construction that was modified or left incompleted when it was decided to give the building a more unorthodox layout. Future excavation alone can perhaps decide this point.

The "Second Odeon" is substantially the building we see today, with the principal lateral entrances leading directly onto the stage. The stage was, however, of timber, with the customary crypt (hyposcenium) underneath it. The slots cut to carry the beams that supported the stage floor can still be seen on both the inner face of the *pulpitum* and the outer face of the *scaenae frons* footings. The *scaenae frons*, of which only the lower part has survived, was pierced by three doorways, while two stairways cut in the thickness of the wall gave access to upper galleries. The façade toward the stage was revetted with marble slabs, as is shown by small holes for bronze cramps. No columns or other architectural members indicative of a conventional decoration of this back wall can be

[134] I must here record the Department's deep gratitude to Sir Arthur Dean, General Manager of the L.P.D.S.A., for his Agency's generous grants to the antiquities of Cyrenaica during the years 1955–59. The administrative buildings and equipment of the archeological *chantier* of Ptolemais, ravaged by the Second World War, have thereby been restored. (R.G.G.)

[135] J. A. Hanson, *Roman Theater-Temples* (Princeton, 1959).

identified; but the building was probably stripped of all usable marble in late antiquity.

The orchestra (11.40 m. in diameter) was separated from the *cavea* by a continuous parapet 1.25 m. high and was only accessible by two flights of steps leading down from the stage, one in each corner. The floor of the orchestra was paved with marble slabs, all of which have disappeared, leaving only their impress on the concrete bedding. The face of the *pulpitum* toward the orchestra was decorated with five niches, the central one being rectangular and the two flanking pairs semicircular.

The *cavea* rose steeply from the orchestra parapet, but only six tiers of seats have survived wholly or in part. They bear traces of five radial stairways, two of which are against the paradoi. It is clear, despite assertions to the contrary, that the *cavea* had a *maenianum* which rested on the vault of the semicircular *ambulacrum* and that there were therefore probably as many as fifteen rows of seats.[136]

Access to the *maenianum* was provided by the two staircases which formed the northeast and southeast corners of the "Odeon's" rectangle and were originally entered only from the *ambulacrum*. The southern doorway (*J*) still survives intact, together with the bottom of its connected staircase. The northern doorway (*K*), however, was blocked at some secondary period and a new staircase was inserted, rising from the piazza outside rather than from the *ambulacrum*.

Structurally the "Third Odeon" represents only a minor modification of the "Second Odeon," but functionally it was entirely different. The orchestra was made watertight by plaster renderings with large quarter-round moldings at all angles where leakage might be expected. Water was brought into this improvised tank by means of a channel (*O*) coming down the roadside from the south and entering the theater through the southernmost doorway in the *scaenae frons*. In the center of the *cavea*, immediately above the parapet, a small rectangular "box" or tribune (*P*) was constructed. Fallen columns within it seem to indicate an architectural treatment of its front, but their emplacement is not certain. Around the entire edge of the orchestra, now converted to a tank, was erected a light balustrade of wood or metal, of which only the setting holes survive. Along the stage side this balustrade followed the outline of

the niches, which had by this time been stripped of their cornices. It also ran down the outer edges of the twin stairways leading into the orchestra-tank. The hyposcenium was now filled in and paved over.

Other features of the "Third Odeon" include intrusive piers and supporting arches (*Q*) within the *ambulacrum*, whose vault was by this time evidently in precarious condition. The character of its fill suggested that the *ambulacrum* may have later been deliberately filled with soil. On the west, or street side, the colonnade, previously reinforced by the conversion of two columns into rectangular piers, was now completely blocked up with walling and pierced by two doorways, whose sills remain.

In considering the general character of the "Odeon" and the significance of the changes that we have noted we cannot fail to take account of the small theater of Philippopolis in Syria, remarkable for its state of preservation, for the detail in which it has recently been published,[137] and for its points of similarity to the "Odeon."

Externally the "Odeon" might seem to have little in common with the theater of Philippopolis, where the semicircular curve of the *cavea* represents a main external wall and where the *ambulacrum*— as in most Roman theaters—was pierced with doorways leading from the exterior. Since the ground level permitted it, the architect of the Philippopolis theater was able to create a high-level *ambulacrum* with only a small ascent from it to the *praecinctio*.

At Ptolemais, on a relatively flat site where the axis of the theater had for topographical reasons to be at right angles to the slope of the ground, this system could not be adopted. There was no necessity for the outer wall of the *ambulacrum* to limit the whole building, and therefore it was possible to add the two "staircase corners," which in fact made the building virtually rectangular. The proximity on the west of a major street (which seems not to have been the case at Philippopolis) made it expedient to give a more monumental treatment to the postscenium.

Once we enter these two small theaters, however, the points of similarity are striking. Both have an austere rectilinear *scaenae frons* pierced by three doorways, and both lack the stage-side "saloni" or "foyers" characteristic of the larger theaters of

---

[136] See Caputo, *Il teatro di Sabratha*, p. 67: "La cavea è costituita da un solo meniano di sette gradini."

[137] P. Coupel and E. Frézouls, *Le théâtre de Philippopolis en Arabie* ("Bibliothèque archéologique et historique" LXIII [Paris, 1956]).

the Roman Empire. What is most striking is that, although the Philippopolis theater has the normal passages leading into its orchestra, they run only from the *ambulacrum* and not from the exterior of the building. At Philippopolis, as at Ptolemais, the principle passages from the exterior lead directly onto the stage.

We have already seen that the "First Odeon" had—or was intended to have—passages leading into its orchestra and that these were either modified or perhaps never completed. But it seems clear that they led only from the *ambulacrum* as at Philippopolis. In the plan of the "Second Odeon" the architect went even farther than his Syrian colleague and left the orchestra completely isolated. Caputo, observing this fact, claimed "a new architectural arrangement, which would be incompatible with the ends of musical and scenic performance but not with those of a place of assembly."[138] He therefore proposed that the "Odeon" at Ptolemais should be interpreted as a *bouleutereion*.

Whether or not the premises are correct, Caputo's argument is attractive, more especially with reference to the Cyrenaican cities where there seem to have been so many "theaters" (four at Cyrene, three at Ptolemais). However, a grave objection to the hypothesis will arise when we consider the function of the "Third Odeon," and I may say in advance that I am, reluctantly, inclined to reject the *bouleutereion* theory.

What, then, was the precise character of the performances that took place in the "Second Odeon"? Despite the high parapet around the orchestra, the possibility of animal fights must be discounted. It would be too difficult to maneuver any self-respecting beasts down the twin staircases that form the only access to the orchestra![139] The timber stage and its underlying crypt suggest that normal stage representations took place. Perhaps certain types of performances requiring close attention (jugglers, acrobats, and the like) overflowed occasionally into the orchestra.[140] Serious

gladiatorial combat is hardly likely to have taken place in so restricted a space.

In the case of "Third Odeon," however, there can be little doubt as to the nature of the performances. The conversion of the orchestra into a tank cannot easily be explained merely in terms of water storage. The erection of a light balustrade around the tank would hardly have been necessary for so functional a purpose. Moreover, a "box" for some important personage was centrally placed in the *cavea*.

During the excavation of the "Odeon" I was at first inclined to regard the watertight orchestra as a late cistern, but during a visit in 1957 Professor A. H. M. Jones suggested that it might have been used for the late Roman water spectacles which have sometimes been associated with the notorious pagan "Maiumas" festivals. This suggestion was reinforced, a year later, when Dr. Gustavo Traversari visited Ptolemais and was immediately convinced that the late arrangements of the "Odeon" were designed for the water spectacles which he has studied extensively.[141] While Caputo is right in emphasizing the danger of interpreting late water tanks in theaters as necessarily connected with aquatic spectacles, I am convinced that in the case of the "Odeon" at Ptolemais Traversari's arguments are proved beyond any reasonable doubt.

Traversari rejects any specific association between theatrical water spectacles and the little-known "Maiumas" rites. He shows that the former were merely a manifestation of Roman taste which became increasingly popular in the later period of the Empire. As early as the time of Martial (*Epig.* xxv) there is reference to a representation of Hero and Leander performed in water, while by the time of the early Fathers of the Church such spectacles had become a scandal. St. John Chrysostom (*In Matthaeum*, Homily 7) fulminated against those citizens who flocked to the theater "to see naked women swimming."

The prominent if small "box" centrally placed in the *cavea* of the "Third Odeon" at Ptolemais was presumably for the accommodation of the highest local authority—no doubt the *praeses* of Libya Pentapolis, whose headquarters were in Ptolemais after the reign of Diocletian and for at least the

---

[138] Caputo, *Il teatro di Sabratha*, p. 67.

[139] Cf. E. Dyggve, "Le théâtre mixte du Bas-Empire d'après le théâtre de Stobi," *Revue archéologique*, 1958, I 137–57 and II 20–39. Complete excavation of the theater at Stobi is greatly to be desired.

[140] Synesius (*Calvitii encomium* 13) describes a bald-headed acrobat whose main virtue was the thickness of his skull. A performance of this type might well have taken place in the orchestra rather than on the stage.

[141] Traversari, "Tetimimo e Colimbétra," *Dioniso* XIII (1950) 18–35 and XV (1952) 3–12. A comprehensive monograph on the whole subject by the same author is now in preparation.

first part of the fifth century of our era. The blocking of the portico or postscenium was perhaps intended to provide changing rooms for the ladies who performed in the spectacles. The spectacles must certainly, at Ptolemais as elsewhere in the Roman world, have met with severe criticism from the leaders of the Church, and the "Odeon" had probably been closed down even before Synesius became bishop. Synesius has many harsh things to say about the governor Andronicus, but enthusiasm for bathing belles is not included in the long catalogue of his faults nor does Synesius refer to aquatic spectacles in any way.[142]

While, therefore, we may assume that the active life of the "Odeon" ended before about A.D. 400, it is more difficult to determine the date of its initial construction. No relevant inscriptions have been found, and only future stratigraphic soundings might perhaps solve this problem. A Roman date is, however, certain, and the somewhat characterless, if competent, type of masonry employed would suggest a date in the second or early third century of our era. Two statues found within the "Odeon" were donated to the city by a certain M. Ulpius Cominius, and one of them (p. 204, No. 64) is tentatively dated by Caputo to the second century.[143]

It would be useful, certainly, to establish the precise date of the construction of the "Odeon"— more especially in view of its points of similarity to the theater of Philippopolis. The publishers of the latter monument claim that it "does not correspond rigorously to any known type" and argue, with perhaps excessive eloquence, that it was a manifestation of a particular historical circumstance— the elevation to municipal dignity of a small village which had had the good fortune to produce an emperor, Philip the Arab (A.D. 244–49).[144] In the light of the arrangements of the "Odeon" their conclusions perhaps need reconsideration. A comprehensive survey is required of those smaller theaters of the Roman Empire which, by very virtue of their restricted dimensions, are most likely to have broken away from the stereotyped

tradition set by the great buildings that are so much better known to archeologists. Although Caputo's attractive proposal of a theater-*bouleutereion* may not be valid in the case of the "Odeon" of Ptolemais, on other sites and in other monuments it will probably find confirmation.[145] It seems unlikely that a pre-existing *bouleutereion* would have been given over to public spectacles soon after Ptolemais became the provincial capital.

To make our general description of the monuments of Ptolemais as complete as possible it seems proper to add to what Goodchild has reported above about the clearance of the "Odeon" by the Department of Antiquities of Cyrenaica a few words concerning the four other structures of the same general category that are known to exist at Ptolemais. Two are theaters, one is a hippodrome, and one is an amphitheater. Though there have been partial clearances by the Italian archeologists in two of these buildings, none has been excavated.

The larger of the two theaters, which we speak of as the Upper Theater (Building 28 on Plan XXII), is set into a natural recess in the central lobe of the Jebel Akhdar that may, of course, have been further shaped by hand (Fig. 23). The setting is such as would have appealed to architects familiar with the Greek tradition and such as was used at Athens (Theater of Dionysos), Epidamus, and Priene, to mention only examples that are familiar to all. The Italian archeologists cleared the brush from a narrow strip of the section occupied by the *cavea*, exposing the cuttings made in the stratified limestone to receive the seats. Apparently they also made soundings in the area of the orchestra and the *scaena*, the effects of all of which are shown on our photograph (Pl. XIII A). To judge by surface indications the orchestra had a diameter of about 36 meters and the *cavea* an upper circumference of ± 156 meters. The gradient of the ascending rows of seats was extremely steep. The seats themselves have been systematically looted, as has most of the rest of the building, but from the cuttings it is possible to infer that each row provided a space

[142] See Pando, *The Life and Times of Synesius*, pp. 101–5.

[143] *RAL* IX (1954) 458–66. The second statue is represented only by the inscribed base, on which survive two pairs of feet suggestive of a statue of Dionysos and a satyr. An inscribed block recording another dedication by the same donor was found in 1960, reused upside down in the reconstruction of the stage.

[144] Coupel and Frézouls, *op. cit.* pp. 120–28.

[145] The use in the Greek world of theaters or theater-like buildings as places of political assembly is attested as late as the fourth century of our era by Ausonius (*Ludus septem sapientum* xiii. 2). Three of the four theaters at Cyrene have now been excavated, but a definitive analysis of their dates and functions must await the excavation of the fourth—the so-called "Odeon" lying immediately west of the Caesareum.

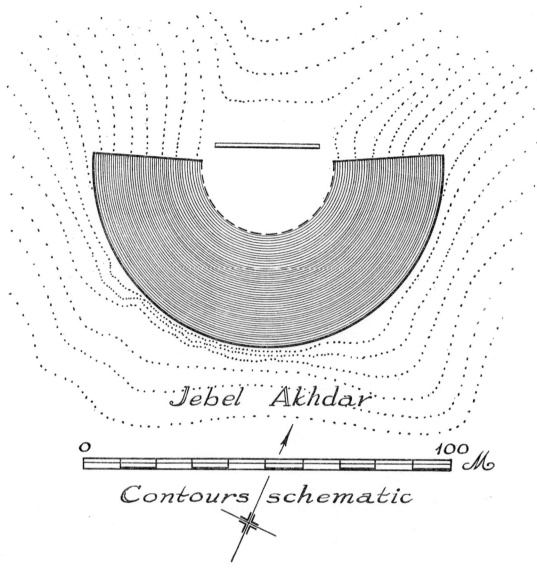

Fig. 23.—Sᴋᴇᴛᴄʜ Pʟᴀɴ ᴏғ Uᴘᴘᴇʀ Tʜᴇᴀᴛᴇʀ (Bᴜɪʟᴅɪɴɢ 28). *J.E.Knudstad*

of about 60 cm. for seating and for the feet of the spectators in the next higher row. The height to which the surface of the recess in the jebel was molded to receive the seats allows at a normal rise per tier for about 50 rows. There is no indication that either the *cavea* or the orchestra formed more than half of a circle. Since there was no opportunity for the construction of *ambulacra* leading to the *cavea* from behind and underneath the seats, all spectator movement must have been through the orchestra. As in the "Odeon" there must therefore have been major entrances, from the north, leading to the orchestra and *cavea* through or at the sides of the *scaena*. The foundations of the southern face of the *pulpitum* are still visible in part and

seem to indicate that the *scaena* was not more than 25–28 meters long.

The systematic looting of the Upper Theater may reflect the disturbed internal conditions of the province in late Roman times, for clearly, after the city's perimeter defenses had been abandoned (see pp. 24–26), the audience would have been in an exposed position had raiders swooped down from the jebel during a performance. Other provision for the type of entertainment offered in the Upper Theater would therefore have been required, especially after the "Odeon" was adapted to the presentation of water spectacles (see above). It is not surprising, then, that a third theater exists at Ptolemais (Building 7 on Plan XXII), a block south of the "Odeon" on the opposite side of the west cardo. We speak of it as the Byzantine Theater. Like most of the buildings of relatively late date, such as the forts, its ruins lie exposed on the surface (Pl. XIII *B*) instead of being deeply buried and its stonework is coarse, with only the simplest dressing. What can be seen on the surface (Fig. 24) indicates a simple semicircular *cavea* (ca. 72 m. in diameter) set around an orchestra 28 meters in diameter. It is estimated that there were about 36 rows of seats, each row being 60 cm. wide. All details about *ambulacra*, parodoi, *pulpitum*, and *scaenae frons* are lacking.

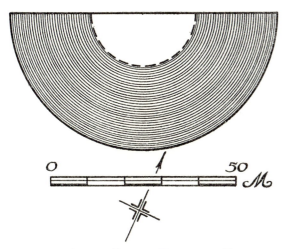

Fig. 24.—Sketch Plan of Byzantine Theater (Building 7). *J. E. Knudstad*

Even less is known about the Hippodrome (Building 27 on Plan XXII), which lies at the foot of the central lobe of the jebel. Approach to it from the city must have been via the two cardines and up a sharply rising roadway now buried under a deep deposit of earth washed down from the jebel. The same road had, no doubt, originally provided access also to the Upper Theater. All that is visible at the site of the Hippodrome today is a flat terrace, normally planted to wheat (Pl. XIII *C*), whose eastern end has the typical curve of a hippodrome track. The terrace is supported at the north by a jumble of stones that presumably represents what remains of the foundations that supported the northern bank of seats. At the south, whence it was less convenient to carry off stones, there is a much higher jumble of stones. Here, presumably, only the dressed stones of the seats and the podium wall were removed. There is no visible trace at the west of the *carceres* and no

trace in the planted field of a spina. It is possible, under the circumstances, to consider the Hippodrome an illusion, but the outline seen from the Upper Theater is convincing and the importance of horse breeding in Cyrenaica in remote antiquity and the renown of Battid chariot races which Pindar celebrated in the Greek period imply the appropriateness of such a structure at Ptolemais.[146]

The Amphitheater (Building 1 on Plan XXII) is relatively well preserved (Pl. XIII *D*), partly because it was set into the eastern end of what may have the earliest of the quarries developed at the site (see p. 108). Exploration of the building by the Italian archeologists resulted in the discovery of a painting representing a *venator* and a mythological figure executed upon the wall of the *ambulacrum*.[147] It is badly faded but has been provided with a protective covering, thanks to Professor Caputo's careful work. Figure 25 gives a sketch of those elements of the Amphitheater that could be observed without excavation. The structure was typically elliptical, with an arena measuring 47 meters on the major, east-west, axis and 44 meters on the minor, north-south, axis. Inside the high podium wall, of which 12 courses representing a height of 3.40 m. are visible, a parapet wall 1.80 m. thick is set into the arena at a distance of 2.65 m. from the face of the podium. Its function, no doubt, was to provide a barrier protecting the spectators from such wild animals as might seek to escape from the arena via the *cavea* when the Amphitheater was being used for *venationes*. The seats for the spectators, rising in rows from the top of the podium wall, covered an area at least 18.50 m. wide which, with an average row width of 60 cm., would have provided for a minimum of 30 rows and a seating capacity of about 7,000 persons. Only the rubble fill on which the seats were bedded remains in place, the dressed stone seats having long since been looted. At the east the *cavea* is interrupted by the walls of a passageway leading into the arena. The passageway is wide enough to accommodate the cages in which wild animals were transported

[146] The available information is collected by Thrige, *Res Cyrenensium*, pp. 402–5.

[147] See Caputo, "Protezione," p. 62 and Fig. 48. Oliverio, *Documenti antichi* II 2, pp. 246–47, tells how the Italian artillerymen encamped in the Amphitheater during the first days of the occupation of the site found certain capitals there (*ibid*. Pl. XCIV 77–78) and, nearby, we judge in a rock-cut tomb, wall paintings of the funerary-banquet type (*ibid*. Pl. XCVII 81).

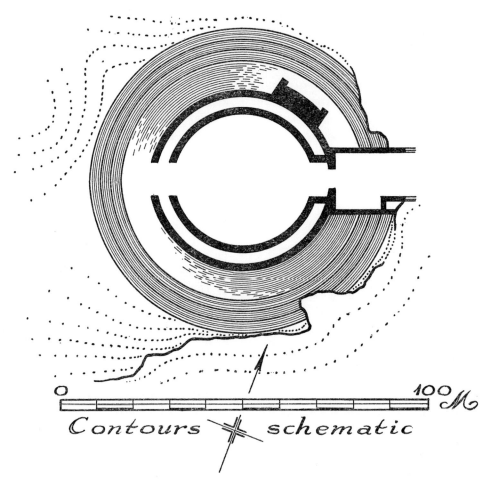

Fig. 25.—Sketch Plan of Amphitheater (Building 1). *J. E. Knudstad*

for use at the *venationes* and no doubt had special provisions for their release into the arena without danger to the handlers. Above the passageway, which must have been covered or vaulted, one can imagine a decorative feature or a loge for high provincial officials, unless the platform set into the northeastern section of the *cavea* provided for the latter. The arrangements at the western end of the main axis for entrance into and exit from the arena are not clear at present.

The importance of Africa as a source of supply for the animals used in the *venationes* at Rome is well known. It is not strange that animal hunts should have been a feature of popular entertainment also in Africa itself, as is well indicated by the remains of amphitheaters at both Sabratha and Leptis.[148] More enlightening, however, are the representations of both animal hunts and gladiatorial combats in the mosaics of the justly famous villa of Dar Buc Amméra.[149] The Amphitheater at Ptolemais was used also for gladiatorial combat, as two stelae (e.g. Pl. *L D*) that were found just outside the city and that commemorate gladiators who fought there testify (see p. 207, No. 71). At present there is no sure way of dating the structure, but it may be noted that lamps with scenes of gladiatorial combat, belonging to the second century of our era, were found at Ptolemais (Pls. LXII *D*, upper right, and LXIII *B*, upper right) and that there is epigraphic evidence for the existence of an amphitheater at Berenice at least as early as the first century of our era.[150]

---

[148] See S. Aurigemma, "Notizie archeologiche sulla Tripolitania," *Notiziario archeologico* I 55 and Fig. 18, and *I mosaici di Zliten* ("Africa Italiana: Collezione di monografie a cura del Ministero delle Colonie" II [Roma-Milano, 1926]) pp. 148–49, n. 4.

[149] Aurigemma, *I mosaici di Zliten*, pp. 180–97, Figs. 111a–25.

[150] See J. and G. Roux in *REG* LXII 281–96.

CHURCHES

Churches were prominent features of the urban scene in Cyrenaica as in other parts of the Mediterranean world in Byzantine times. It is only natural to expect that Ptolemais was quite as well endowed with ecclesiastical structures as the other cities of Libya Pentapolis, Tripolitania, and North Africa, especially since it had so long an involvement in the development of Christian doctrine and had at least at certain intervals, as in the case of Synesius, so effective a clerical leadership (see pp. 22–23). To date, however, this expectation can be said to have been fulfilled only in scant measure. At Ptolemais, in contrast to Cyrene and more particularly to the coastal cities Tauchira and Apollonia, remains of ancient church buildings are not now obvious surface features. Nor were they in the days of the early European travelers. It is of course possible that such buildings were looted more systematically at Ptolemais than elsewhere in medieval times or that they are deeply buried. But the more likely explanation is that because of the sharp decline in Ptolemais' fortunes at the end of the fifth century, due to the removal of the provincial capital to Apollonia, it did not enjoy in the sixth century the harvest of donations and pious foundations whose outward manifestations are the expansive, internally resplendent churches that one associates naturally with the period of Justinian.

As things stand, Ptolemais boasts of but one structure that can with certainty be identified as a church, namely Building 2 on Plan XXII. The apse, projecting from a deep deposit of heavy debris, attracted the attention of European travelers as early as the days of the Beecheys, Rohlfs being the first to infer that it belonged to a church.[151] The excavation and partial reconstruction of the building under the supervision of Professor Caputo have given to the site a monument that compensates in excellence and importance for what is lacking in numbers.[152]

Caputo's plan (Fig. 26) shows a massive rectangle (35.40 × 21.90 m.), within which is contained a basilica complete with narthex, nave and side

aisles, inscribed apse, baptistery(?), and diaconicon. The word "contained" is used advisedly, for the church has one dominant feature that sets it apart from the other known churches of Cyrenaica. This is the massive quadratic solidity of its exterior, which gives little hint of the organization of its interior, whose ponderous austerity and simplicity contrast so sharply with the bright elegance of the mosaic-paved and marble-sheathed columnar basilicas of other sites. On this account it merits the name "Fortress Church," which is assigned to it in this report.

Entrance into the Fortress Church is not through the narthex but only through a small doorway in its northern lateral wall, which led directly into the north aisle. The opening that today exists into the stairwell in the southwest corner of the building was apparently not a means of ingress in antiquity but a by-product of the partial disintegration of the structure. The interior is so divided that the nave has almost three times the width of each of the aisles. Nave and aisles are separated by heavy rectangular piers that rest on solid stylobates and rise 3.20 m. to an unadorned fillet at the spring line of the arches spanning the intercolumniations. The piers are well preserved, as are sections of the roofs of the aisles, which show that they were spanned by particularly fine rib vaulting (Pl. XIV A). From the arcades the walls of the nave rise unadorned to a height of 7.70 m., where there is a simple cornice that continues unbroken around the apse at the eastern end. The cornice marks the spring of the semidome over the apse and perhaps also the bases of upper arcades through which galleries over the aisles opened upon the nave. How the nave was roofed Caputo does not venture to say, but parallels (see below) suggests that it too had a rib vault.

The narthex, at the western end of the building, was completely inclosed and divided on the lines of the piers into three chambers accessible from nave and aisles. The chamber in the southwest corner provided the well for a stone staircase mounting, as Caputo suggests, to galleries over the aisles. It could also have led to a simple square corner tower such as was common in forts and blockhouses. The function of the other chambers of the narthex is unknown. Particular interest at-

---

[151] Rohlfs, *Von Tripoli nach Alexandrien,* p. 157.

[152] See Caputo, "Protezione," pp. 53–58, and "Una basilica cristiana in Tolemaide," *Comunicazioni presentate al III Convegno nazionale di storia dell'architettura 1938,* pp. 159–62.

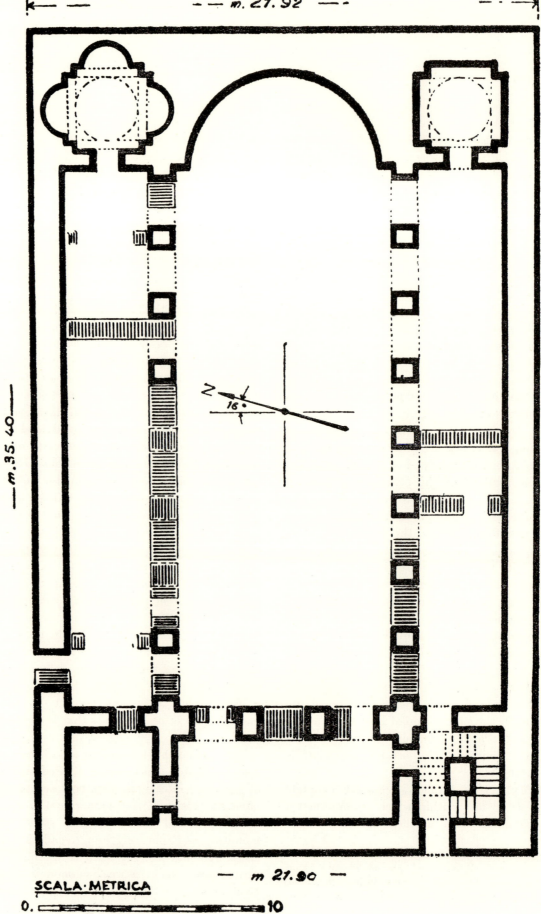

Fig. 26.—Plan of Fortress Church (Building 2). After Giacomo Caputo,
"Una basilica cristiana in Tolemaide," Fig. 1

taches necessarily to the two chambers at the eastern ends of the aisles which, together with the apse, are inscribed in the rectangular east end of the building. They recall, thus, the prothesis and the diaconicon of the churches that were a feature of northern Syria in the fourth and early fifth centuries of our era and the chambers at the ends of aisles in North African churches with inscribed apses.[153] However, the chambers in this instance do not open on the apse and differ from one another in construction. That at the south is square and has simple corner piers from which transition is made to a superimposed dome. That at the north is a square within a trefoil of niches or apses, each finished at the top with a semidome. From the arches spanning these niches pendentives lead over to the dome that finished the chamber at the top. Caputo has already called attention to the historical importance of the appearance here in a basilical structure of a full-blown example of the "central" or "domical" type of church construction.[154]

About the internal arrangements in apse and nave precise information is lacking. The floor is missing, along with any structural installations that may have been set upon it, but the fact that it was removed and the absence of random *tesserae* suggest that it consisted of well cut stone slabs.[155] If the lack of dressing on the stones of the two lowest courses of the apse wall is any criterion, floor level in this area must have coincided with that in the nave, which in turn coincided with that of the stylobates supporting the piers. There are no indications where the altar may have been placed and whether there was a synthronus. If the line of holes in the wall of the apse at the level of the fillet crowning the piers represents the emplacement of poles supporting a baldachino, the existence of a synthronus would be likely. Lines of foundations in the nave suggest that the chancel projected into it in the form of a rectangle, but there seem to be no comparable foundations for an ambo.

In the absence of inscriptions Caputo wisely hesitated to assign a date to the Fortress Church, pointing instead to two possible periods for its construction, that at the end of the fourth and the beginning of the fifth century, the one marked by the episcopate of Synesius, and that of Justinian early in the sixth century. But further study of the history of Ptolemais has clarified the perspective in which the structure must be seen, and, more important, the work of Goodchild and Perkins on the churches of Tripolitania and Cyrenaica has provided the comparative material needed for a proper attribution.[156] From the comparative material it would appear that fundamentally the Fortress Church of Ptolemais represents a type which had already become established in the coastal regions of Tripolitania by the beginning of the fifth century of our era and had taken on a more fortress-like character in the interior of the province of Africa even in the period preceding the Vandal invasion. Its connection with exposed frontier establishments seems to have enhanced its massivity while reducing its size. Perhaps the closest parallel for the Ptolemais structure is the church associated with the Qasr el-Suq el-Oti in Tripolitania, a heavily built basilica with inclosed narthex, arcades resting on piers, rib vaulting in aisles and nave, and rectangular east end that incloses apse and side chambers.[157] It must have been built well before the Vandal invasion. The one particular in which the Fortress Church of Ptolemais shows a real advance over its closest regional counterpart is in the use of the "central" type of construction in the chamber north of the apse. Domes on pendentives were, of course, not new in the fifth century, but what the appearance of this type of construction in so small a chamber

[153] For Syria see in general H. W. Beyer, *Der syrische Kirchenbau* (1925), and for North Africa see P. Gauckler, *Basiliques chrétiennes de Tunisie* (1913) esp. Pls. 2 (Qasr el-Hamar), 13 (Haidra), and 14 (Haidra, church near the Triumphal Arch).

[154] Caputo, "Protezione," p. 56.

[155] Romanelli, *La Cirenaica romana*, Fig. 30 (opp. p. 145) shows the remains of foundations below floor level (as revealed by the excavations). The installation is not so clearly visible today.

[156] See Perkins and Goodchild, "The Christian antiquities of Tripolitania," *Archaeologia* CXV (1953) 1–82; Perkins, "Christian antiquities of the Cyrenaican Pentapolis," *Bulletin de la Société d'archéologie copte* IX (1943) 123–39, and "The Christian antiquities of Libya since 1938," *Actes du Ve Congrès international d'archéologie chrétienne* ("Studi di antichità cristiana" XXII [Rome and Paris, 1957]) pp. 159–62.

[157] See Perkins and Goodchild, *op. cit.* pp. 54–56, Fig. 30, Pl. XXIV. That the masonry above the level of the arcades is the product largely of a period of reconstruction that presumably followed the Vandal invasion is suggested partly by the nature of the masonry itself and partly by the handling of the ribs, which, as at Ptolemais, should stand out from and lend support to the vaulting of nave and aisles.

means as regards the date or the function of the room and the building would be difficult to guess in the absence of additional examples in the same region.

That the Fortress Church of Ptolemais is not the one at which Synesius officiated is likely on several counts. For one thing, its location in the southwest quarter of the city, remote from the presumed areas of densest population, was quite unsuitable for a parish or diocesan church. For another, Synesius tells us (*Letters*, No. 66) that he was accustomed to pass through the city's agora on the way from his residence to the church where he officiated, and it seems quite improbable that by "agora" he meant the Square of the Cisterns. Finally, the building does not have the proper installations, for instance for baptism. Though there is nothing beneath floor level to indicate it, the chamber north of the apse may be the baptistery. But for a parish or diocesan church such provision is not adequate, as the churches at Apollonia and elsewhere clearly indicate. The location of the Fortress Church and the fact that ingress was solely through a small doorway in a side wall suggest that it was associated with unexcavated subsidiary structures lying immediately to the north of it and served the purposes primarily of a special clerical or monastic group. Only further excavation could, of course, indicate whether this suggestion has merit. If so, the church could be the foundation of a pious donor, for it is well known that in Byzantine times wealthy families "adopted" one or another institution or monastery for the exercise of their benevolence.

As to the monumentality and fortress-like character of the building, it should be said that the closest parallels on the Tripolitanian Jebel are much smaller. But the question of size is largely a question of location, as larger examples of the same type of church in the coastal area of Tripolitania indicate. What is important is the preservation in an urban context of the fortress-like character of the structures on the Tripolitanian Jebel. The explanation is, in all probability, that the construction looks back upon the time when the city was threatened by tribal raids from the interior and belongs to the period in which the city's system of perimeter defense was being abandoned. It can therefore well belong to approximately the middle of the fifth century of our era (see in general pp. 26–27).

That other churches must have existed at Ptolemais in antiquity, probably even before the period of the Nicene Council (see p. 22), is obvious. No doubt they are hidden under rubble and dirt and will some day emerge. It appeared for a time that the *triconchos* which the Department of Antiquities cleared in part in 1956–57 (Building 16 on Plan XXII) might be a church. But the absence of internal installations of the type commonly found in churches casts doubt on this possibility. At present the structure most likely to prove to be a church is Building 6, directly north of the Roman Villa. The semidome of an apse projects above the ground at the end of a rectangular structure that was set into an open court (Pl. XIV *B*). It is not oriented in accordance with the tradition that the apse should be toward the east, but exceptions to this tradition exist, and the building was maintained for a long period, as the buttressing applied to its outer walls to maintain them against the thrust of the semidome indicates. The fact that a pilgrim flask from the sanctuary of St. Menas in Egypt was found in a shop of the Villa across the street to the south (see p. 135) may have some bearing upon the prospects which the building presents for tracing further the history of church architecture at Ptolemais.

FORTS AND BLOCKHOUSES

Ptolemais, as noted above (p. 62), eventually abandoned the elaborate system of perimeter defense with which it had been provided in the Hellenistic period. This represents a turning point in the architectural history of the city. The visible tokens of the change are the forts and blockhouses that form so prominent and so austere a feature of the antiquities site today and that have their counterparts outside the city limits. Not a single one of these structures, either inside or outside the city, has been excavated, so that such knowledge as we can have of them is necessarily very general. Moreover, in order to understand the origin and function of these installations we need ultimately to interpret them in the light of the general military strategy and defense procedures of the late Roman and Byzantine empires. But in an over-all description of ancient Ptolemais some account of this particular group of structures must be given. For most of them the basic form at least was determined by a survey of their standing walls, which is recorded in the sketch plans of Mr. G. R. H. Wright that are presented here. The presentation of this material will supplement the important work that has been done, largely in the same manner, by Goodchild on monuments of similar character spread across the length and breadth of Cyrenaica and Tripolitania and forming the elements of their limes defense.[158]

Outstanding in their potential importance for the later internal defense of Ptolemais are three large structures, Buildings 23, 24, and 4 on Plan XXII. Two lie in the eastern part of the city, and one is in the western part. Building 23 is without doubt the earliest among them, the most carefully constructed, and the most perspicuous as to plan and arrangement (Fig. 27). Because the inscription[159] removed from its façade by Vattier de Bourville in 1848 (see p. 30) records the Edict of Anastasius to the *dux*, regulating the affairs of his subordinates, we speak of the building as the Headquarters of the Dux. Located on the Street of the Monuments east of the east cardo, it occupies the northern half of an insula, encroaching on the minor north-south street at the east and on the footpath of the major thoroughfare, as late Roman and Byzantine buildings frequently did. Its outer walls are of excellent ashlar construction, though the courses are not of uniform height (Pl. XV *A–B*). Typically they are 1.80 m. thick and consist of inner and outer shells, constructed of blocks 60 cm. thick, with a rubble core of equal thickness between. String courses (30 cm. high) of stones laid flat as headers bond the shells and the core together. At story height the string courses project from the face of the building as at Qasr Beni-Gdem and elsewhere.[160] A close study of the masonry would be rewarding, for there are also orthostat courses, particularly in the second story wall on the west

side of the building (Pl. XV *B*), whose particular purpose is not clear.

The heavy towering structure, almost 45 meters wide and well over 75 meters long, had two arched doorways set in its façade at the north and a small postern gate capped with a pointed arch in its long western side. A projection at the east apparently closed off the city street, and an irregularity in the east wall is of unexplained origin

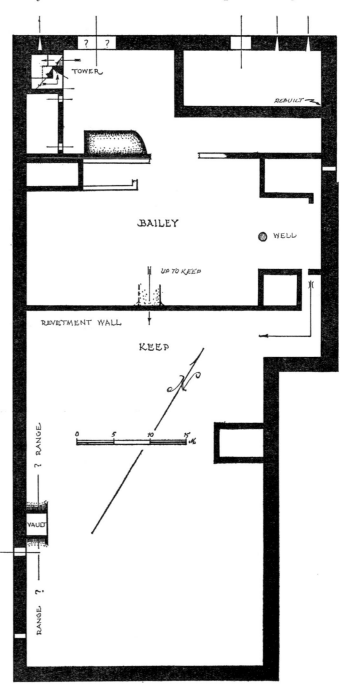

Fig. 27.—Sketch Plan of Headquarters of the Dux (Building 23). *G. R. H. Wright*

[158] See particularly Goodchild and Perkins, "The *Limes Tripolitanus* in the light of recent discoveries," *JRS* XXXIX 81–95; Goodchild, "The *Limes Tripolitanus* II," *JRS* XL 30–38; *idem*, "The Roman and Byzantine *Limes* in Cyrenaica," *JRS* XLIII 65–76; Oates, "The Tripolitanian Gebel," *PBSR* XXI 81–117.

[159] Oliverio, *Documenti antichi* II 2, pp. 135–63, No. 140; *SEG* IX 68–70, No. 356.

[160] See Goodchild in *JRS* XLIII, Pl. XI 3.

and purpose. The interior of the building is clogged with a mass of debris reaching as high as the top of the first story (Pl. XV *C*), but certain structural details are visible. Most important is a wall dividing the northern from the southern part of the building and suggesting a distinction between them such as that between "bailey" and "keep" in medieval castles. Both parts of the building were set around large central courts. To the west of the northwest

remains of vaults along the west wall near the postern gate indicate. At the east they were apparently of greater depth than at the west.

The structure is, like Qasr Beni-Gdem near the Wadi Quf, of massive proportions and may well have inspired the inhabitants of the city with a sense of security and confidence. In times of raids by border tribes it no doubt provided refuge for large numbers of local inhabitants, their live-

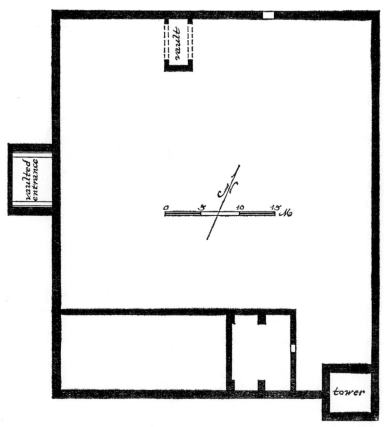

Fig. 28.—Sketch Plan of East Fortress (Building 24). *G. R. H. Wright*

gate, in the northwest corner of the bailey, something approximating the base of a tower inclosing a narrow staircase is visible, alongside which the arches of a room supporting a second floor can be seen. Inside the northeast gate heavy walls provide the support for second floor chambers with slitted window openings. Farther south on the east side of the bailey a large conical depression in the debris suggests the location of a well that was presumably kept in use long after the disintegration of the building. The keep, where the fill is even higher, provides almost no opportunity for observation of the original arrangement. The rooms were arranged in at least two ascending tiers, as

stock, and their possessions. We might be able to determine the date of the structure if the blocks bearing the Edict of Anastasius had been left in position, so that some judgment might be formulated about the relation between the text and the stonework. The photographs of the blocks suggest that they were merely part of the normal fabric of the wall and received the inscription only incidentally.[161] If so, the inscription provides only a *terminus ante quem* for the building. In the absence of such exact knowledge as would result from excavation of the structure, we can say only that it must have been built before the provincial capital

[161] See Oliverio, *op. cit.* Vol. II 2, Pls. LII–LVI.

was moved to Apollonia and that it reflects conditions created by the abandonment of the city's perimeter defenses. A date in the first half of the fifth century is therefore quite likely (see p. 26).

Buildings 24 and 4 are of coarser construction but imposing in size and built of even heavier blocks. The former, here called the East Fortress, is on the north side of the Street of the Monuments, a block to the east of the Headquarters of the Dux, and is roughly square in plan (Fig. 28). It covers an area measuring approximately 45 meters in each direction and must therefore intrude upon and block the minor north-south street at the

a square tower, also a typical feature of fortress construction, are visible.

Building 4, the West Fortress, belongs to the same general period, as is shown by the character of its masonry (Pl. XVI *A*). Located a block west of the Roman Villa (Building 5), it is all of 52 meters wide, though only about 36 meters deep (Fig. 29), and necessarily blocks two minor north-south streets while projecting northward into the decumanus. Save for incidental shops occupying the north end of the Roman Villa and the apsidal building (No. 6) across the decumanus that may have been a church, the area must have been a

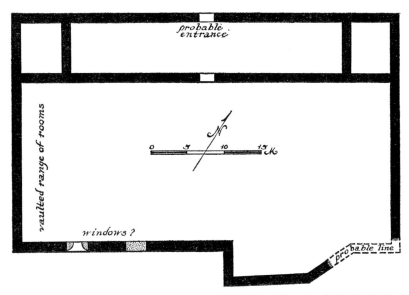

Fig. 29.—Sketch Plan of West Fortress (Building 4). *G. R. H. Wright*

west. Entrance was obtained through a small arched doorway at the north, which may have been only the postern pate, and through a gate tower at the west. The interior, clogged with fallen blocks and briars (Pl. XV *D*), shows the typical development consisting of rooms set around an open court. Heavy stone arches, some still intact, others represented by jumbles of fallen voussoirs, ranged on two sides of the court provided support for the walls and floors of second-story rooms and bays for storage at ground level. The construction is typical of blockhouses and fortresses throughout Cyrenaica and Tripolitania, as Goodchild has observed.[162] At the southeast corner the remains of

jumble of ruins when the West Fortress was erected, to allow for such intrusion upon the arteries of communication. Masses of masonry projecting northward from the face of the structure suggest corner towers, between which the main door or doors must have been located. Of the interior arrangement nothing can at present be said, but the heavy fill reaches what must have been the top of the ground floor and suggests that the structure was two stories high. It would be strange in a building of this size if there had not been a central court. Behind the building ground level slopes away sharply to the southwest because of a pocket or fault in the limestone underlying

[162] "In structures of this type, which are extremely common throughout the Cyrenaican plateau, the heavy voussoirs of the arches have survived better than the rubble-built interior partition walls; and it is no exagger-

ation to say that seemingly isolated arches protruding from fallen masses of stone are the most prominent features of ancient sites in Cyrenaica" (*JRS* XLIII 69).

the sloping plain.[163] This may account for the building's lack of depth and for the puzzling irregularity of its southern wall. That it was actually a fort cannot currently be demonstrated. In the later centuries of the history of Ptolemais all new construction took on a fortress-like character, owing to the hazardous circumstances of life in the cities. But that in times of raids by tribesmen from the interior it served as a place of refuge for the local population can scarcely be doubted.

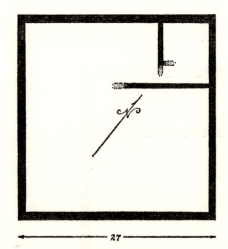

Fig. 30.—Sketch Plan of Building 19.
G. R. H. Wright

Leaving these large buildings that must, to justify their construction in a period of such financial stringency, have played some part in the efforts of the Empire to maintain the security of the provinces, we come to a group of smaller structures that seem to belong to the same general period (Buildings 3, 17–20, 22, and 25 on Plan XXII). All seven of these buildings have two things in common with the large forts. First, in contrast to buildings of even the late Roman period, they are represented by masonry and rubble masses rising high above the general level to which the rest of the antiquities site has been reduced (Pl. XVI *B–C*) and, second, their masonry shows the same general characteristics of relatively rough and coarse construction as the large forts. They must, therefore, be of Byzantine vintage.

With the exception of Building 18, they have the quadratic form typical of the blockhouses and forts that Goodchild has described and illustrated in his discussion of the Cyrenaican limes. Two of

them, Buildings 19 and 20 (Figs. 30–31), show something of a similar interior arrangement, with rooms grouped around a courtyard and the height of the surviving masonry indicating two stories. In both cases the existence of at least one corner tower is possible. It seems entirely justifiable, therefore, to speak of these buildings as small forts or blockhouses and to consider them part of the over-all picture of the changed urban landscape, implying the maintenance of some form of defensive potential. Whether they were built under private or public auspices and whether they were forts, blockhouses, or fortified dwellings it is, of course, impos-

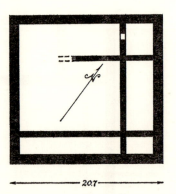

Fig. 31.—Sketch Plan of Building 20.
G. R. H. Wright

sible to tell. But the settlement of soldiers on the land and what we learn from the Edict of Anastasius about the accommodation of civilians in the military *castra* suggest that the lines were becoming more and more fluid in the Byzantine period between public and private establishments offering safety in times of trouble.[164]

Building 18 (Fig. 32) should perhaps be placed apart. The rubble mound in which it is inclosed is quite as prominent on the landscape as are the others of the group (Pl. XVI *B*), but several of its structural features are unusual. Its masonry seems closer in quality to that of the Headquarters of the Dux, and it appears to have been set on a podium that raised it above the level of the thoroughfares at the intersection of which it was placed. At the north it had an unexpectedly large entrance, and in its rubble-filled interior the top of at least one apsidal construction is visible. What to make of these features is difficult to say under the circumstances. Perhaps the building served

---

[163] An even deeper break exists emmediately to the northwest of the "Palazzo" (Building 13).

[164] See Oliverio, *op. cit.* Vol. II 2, § X 11:40–44.

some purpose other than that of residence and defense.

In view of the importance of the work done by Goodchild on the forts and blockhouses forming part of the limes defense of Cyrenaica generally, the Oriental Institute expedition examined a series of structures outside the perimeter walls of Ptolemais, particularly along the abandoned coastal road to Tauchira, which had not been incorporated in Goodchild's study but which belong in the same context and bear upon the general questions of the status and survival of Ptolemais in the later periods of its history.

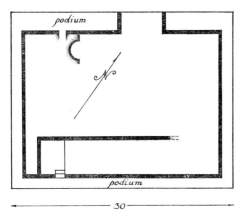

Fig. 32.—Sketch Plan of Building 18.
G. R. H. Wright

Immediately outside the city to the west, opposite the Barca Gate and across the deep cut made by the waters emerging from the Wadi Hambish was a group of buildings that may or may not be relevant. They cover a relatively large area and are represented by a jumble of blocks that are hard to record photographically (Pl. XVI *D*). Their interrelationship is not readily apparent. The masonry suggests that they are Byzantine, and one of the buildings (as seen on Plan XXII) has the typical shape of a small fort or blockhouse. Perhaps this was only a late fortified farm, but perhaps the group of buildings represents a *castrum*, the camp of a military guard placed here to control the road leading to Barca and the interior. A fort and observation post is located at the top of the spur of the Jebel Akhdar directly behind this group of buildings and thus to the west of the Wadi Hambish. It can be seen clearly from the plateau, on the spur east of the wadi, that was inclosed by the city's perimeter wall.

Along the old track leading down the coastal plain from Ptolemais to Tauchira (a distance of *ca.* 35 km.) eleven structures were located. Seven can be called forts or blockhouses, and four are more properly called farms. They were logged at the following distances from the gateway of modern Tolmeita.

0.0 km. Tolmeita Gateway.

7.7 km. Fort 1, at the seaside, near a large dune.

12.5 km. Fort 2, south of the road, near the third wadi beyond Tolmeita. Near the mouth of the wadi and a little to the east is a Roman farm building. A quarry lies 1 km. east of the wadi.

14.0 km. Roman farm, north of the road.

14.5 km. Forts 3*A* and 3*B*, at the seaside, near a modern Italian building. Other buildings exist west of these.

17.5 km. Ruins of indeterminate nature, probably Roman, at the seaside.

24.5 km. Fort 4, at the seaside. A quarry exists $1/2$ km. to the east.

27.5 km. Fort 5, north of the road.

31.0 km. Fort 6, south of the road.

32.5 km. Roman farm near a ruinous Italian building.

35.5 km. Modern Tocra.

Of the four ancient farms it was difficult to obtain an accurate impression because of the loosely knit character of their remains. Commonly there is a scattering of properly quarried but undressed blocks set in rows like fence posts at irregular intervals. Of the dwellings connected with the areas marked by these orthostats there are few traces save for what may be stone socles or incidental structural members. In no case does there seem to be enough masonry to permit one to speak of a "fortified" farm.[165] The foregoing list certainly does not include all such farms along the 35-kilometer stretch but gives only those immediately visible from the ancient track. A thorough search along the coastal plain might well increase the number tenfold, for it is clear that the plain was fertile and worthy of cultivation.

The seven buildings listed as forts are represented by tall rubble heaps, and where wall faces can be seen in the midst of the rubble there are indications of good ashlar construction (Pl. XVII). It was possible to produce sketch plans of Forts 2, 3*A*, 4, 5, and 6.

[165] The type of structure encountered here is more like that recorded and drawn by Oates, *op. cit.* Fig. 12, and called "a peasant hut" (p. 107) in contradistinction to a fortified farm such as is represented by his Fig. 11.

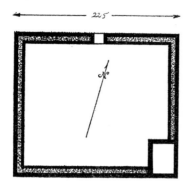

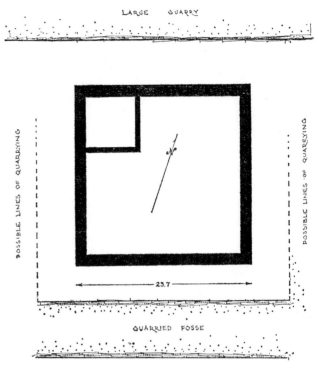

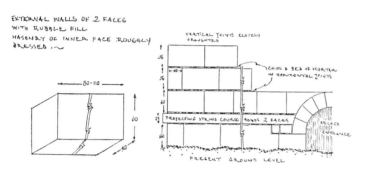

Fig. 33.—Sketch Plan of Fort 2 on Tauchira Road.
G. R. H. Wright

Fig. 34.—Sketch Plan of Fort 3A on Tauchira Road.
G. R. H. Wright

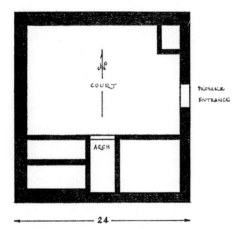

Fig. 35.—Sketch Plan of Fort 4 on
Tauchira Road. *G. R. H. Wright*

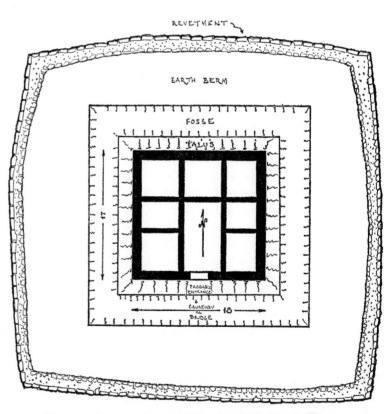

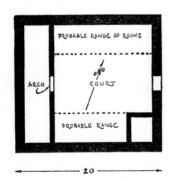

Fig. 36.—Sketch Plan of Fort 5 on
Tauchira Road. *G. R. H. Wright*

Fig. 37.—Sketch Plan of Fort 6 on Tauchira Road.
G. R. H. Wright

The walls of Fort 2 (Fig. 33) consist of outer shells and a rubble core. This fort showed a string course of stones laid flat at approximately the level of the second-story floor and an arched doorway (Pl. XVII *A*), both of which are features of the Headquarters of the Dux at Ptolemais itself. It also had the typical corner tower, as did Forts 3 *A*, 4, and 5 (Figs. 34–36). This was used no doubt by the guard who was supposed to alert the countryside at the appearance of a raiding party coming from the Jebel Akhdar onto the plain. The interior arrangements were most clearly visible in Forts 4, 5, and 6, where there were two superimposed tiers of rooms, usually arranged, however, on only two sides of the central court. Arches supported the floors of the second-story rooms, providing at ground level bays that must have been used to store produce and to house farm animals. Forts 3*A* and 6 differed from the others in that they were supplied with outworks. Fort 3*A* (Fig. 34), situated at the south of a large quarry, had a quarried fosse on the opposite side and perhaps on each of the other two sides also. Fort 6 (Fig. 37), the most elaborate of all, was inclosed by a well cut fosse, beyond which could be seen the remains of a counterscarp with a stone revetment. Similar outworks have been noted by Goodchild along the limes. That they represent a defensive development more advanced than that of Fort 2 seems likely, but at present it is impossible to gauge the length of the period intervening.

The number and solidity of the forts along the Ptolemais–Tauchira road suggest that they testify not so much to private wealth as to the effort of the Byzantine Empire to protect the agricultural population of the region and to safeguard communications along the important east-west highway. That the system did not work so well as it might have no doubt resulted from a combination of factors including the adroitness of the raiders from the upland and the obvious tendency of the populace, as represented even by men of Synesius' stature, to become panicky. The injunctions of Anastasius in his decree to the "most noble" (γενναιότατοι) soldiers—presumably the soldiers assigned to such forts—to attend zealously to their guard duty and not to engage in business on the side may well reflect still a third factor, namely a general listlessness of the defenders.[166]

Goodchild and Perkins in their study of the limes of Tripolitania have associated with the period of Septimius Severus the beginning of the new system by which the permanent installations including forts and settlements of *limitanei*, instead of military expeditions undertaken from remote bases, were used to pacify the frontier.[167] Lacking such epigraphic evidence as Tripolitania provided on this score, we cannot fix with equal certainly the period for the beginning of the use of such forts and blockhouses in Cyrenaica. It may well be that similar constructions on the Jebel Akhdar and in the interior belong to the first half of the third century of our era. The beginnings of the series along the coastal road between Ptolemais and Tauchira might preferably be associated with the period of Diocletian and his successors, because Ptolemais' rise to the status of provincial capital made the road so much more important. But the architectural affinities between the best of the forts along the road and the Headquarters of the Dux at Ptolemais itself suggest that some of the work is even later.

QUARRIES AND TOMBS

The existence of large quarries in the coastal plain immediately outside and even inside their perimeter walls is a common and somewhat surprising feature of the seaside cities of Cyrenaica. No doubt there were good practical reasons for preferring the limestone of the coastal plain to that of the adjacent spurs of the Jebel Akhdar. It was certainly more accessible, in terms of both transport and the opportunity for continuous vertical cutting. It may also have been less fissured than the layers that represent later geological formations and that form the successive escarpments of the jebel. Perhaps, too, the fundamentally utilitarian purpose of these coastal settlements as outlets for and dependencies of the inland colonies precluded consideration of the esthetic factors that might have suggested restrictions on the location of quarries. Above all, it is obvious that in all cases some uncontrolled quarrying preceded the rise of

---

[166] See Oliverio, *op. cit.* Vol. II 2, p. 145, §§ XI–XII 11:46–53.

[167] *JRS* XXXIX 82.

the settlements to civic status and that in the Byzantine period such building as was still going on was done with the use of the sources of supply closest at hand, whether by quarrying or by the looting of standing structures.

At Ptolemais four main areas supplied building stone in antiquity.[168] Three are shown on the Beecheys' plan of the city (Fig. 4). The easternmost is atop the ridge on the farther side of the Wadi Zawana. It is small and narrow and much shallower than those to the west. Presumably it was not used until the more northerly of the two bridges seen by the Beecheys had been thrown across the wadi, making the transport of its products less laborious, or perhaps it was used in connection with the construction of that bridge and of the city gate to which it must have given access (see p. 57).

The second quarry area is that which today cuts through the western city wall just south of the Quarry Gate (see Plan XXII). This is perhaps both the oldest and the most recent of the ancient sources of supply. It recommends itself as the oldest because it is closest to the presumed site of the harbor settlement created here in the sixth century B.C. by Barca and because of the likelihood that permission for its development and use would not have been given after the foundation of the city. Indeed, the emplacement of the Amphitheater (see p. 95) in its eastern end shows that in Roman times it was already out of use. Sometime later the same good limestone layer was attacked outside the city wall, and eventually, after the maintenance of the wall had been given up, quarrying was resumed, leaving the gaping void now visible in the cradle of the wall. The fact that the abandonment of the wall was a feature of the Byzantine period is what suggests that this quarry, potentially the oldest, was also among the ones last used in the history of the city.

The third quarry area lies a good kilometer west of the city, across the channel carved by the waters from the Wadi Hambish. It includes one large quarry and several smaller cuttings. All are relatively deep, so that full advantage was taken of an excellent limestone layer, as the often unbroken vertical faces clearly indicate. The smaller cuttings are near and in the sides of a slight eminence in the coastal plain (see Pl. XIX *B*). The Beecheys' plan (Fig. 4) places these smaller quarries on top of the eminence, exaggerating the contour lines. The cuttings at the top are largely the dromoi of chamber tombs. The large quarry is over half a kilometer long, and its depth can be estimated in part at least from the massive cubes of solid rock left standing at various points in its chip-strewn interior (see Pl. XIX *A*).

The fourth of the quarries of Ptolemais lies a good kilometer farther west, beyond the spring associated with the tomb of Sidi Abdullah (see p. 68) and out of reach of the Beecheys' plan. It exploited the resources of a long low eminence that rises between the Tauchira road and the coast and would be easily missed except in a systematic exploration of the region. For all its unobtrusiveness, it is clearly the second largest of all the workings.

It is natural and proper for several reasons, as we shall see, to associate Ptolemais' funerary monuments with this general description of its quarries. A city of such size and wealth as Ptolemais necessarily had a large and imposing array of tombs, but today they are not so well known as the tombs of Cyrene because those among them that were erected as freestanding buildings rather than carved in the rock were more readily accessible and have long since been removed by looters, stone by stone. Actually, of course, the types of tombs at Ptolemais were, like their locations, varied. The Oriental Institute expedition made no systematic effort to study or explore them. Their inscriptions had already been reported by and large by Oliverio.[169] Here, therefore, only a general description of the monuments and their locations is presented, along with the plan of a single loculus tomb.

While tombs must at one time have existed in large numbers to the east and west of the city, ancient burial inside the area defined by the city wall is so negligible on surface observation as to be virtually and no doubt not accidentally absent. The only indications encountered in the excavations were a large earthenware dish turned upside down over a few skeletal remains, found almost at surface level in the deep deposit over the north end of

---

[168] For the small supplementary quarry on one of the offshore islands and its possible use see p. 50.

[169] *Op. cit.* Vol. II 2, pp. 243–45, Nos. 483–91, and 253–54, Nos. 520–24; *SEG* IX 72, Nos. 369–77, and 74, Nos. 395–99.

the site of the Roman Villa, and some human bones stuffed into the flue at the north end of the lime-kiln in the courtyard of the Public Building on the Street of the Monuments. Tomblike recesses in the quarry that contains the Amphitheater could be either Byzantine or medieval, and the sarcophagi and remains of burials that dot the western slope of the stream bed emerging from the Wadi Zawana are in uncertain relation to the course of the city wall at the top of the slope. We have suggested that the absence of tombs and burial caves on the slopes of the Jebel Akhdar is to be understood in part in connection with the jebel's service as a watershed for the largest of the city reservoirs (see p. 72). However this may be, it is clear that, while burial chambers are found carved into the de-clivitous sides of the wadies that debouch into the plain to the east and west of the city, most burials were in the plain itself and that of the two sections of the plain the one west of the city was the one more highly regarded and more extensively used. The importance of this area can be understood in terms of Ptolemais' relation to western Cyrenaica (see p. 34).

What the burial customs were during the earliest centuries of settlement on the site of Ptolemais we do not at present know. Perhaps the oldest of the known funerary monuments from the site is the stele with the metrical inscription honoring Arata the wife of a certain Kallikrates. She was a native of Euesperides but had dutifully spent most of her life with her husband far from her kith and kin. Where at Ptolemais the stele may have stood and whether her body was interred are not known. The use of the commemorative stele, which with its molded pediment and the mythological allusions of its text recalls the traditions of the Greek home-land, suggests that perhaps the older custom of cremation had been followed. This would be equally possible whether the monument belongs to the fourth or to the third century B.C. (see p. 8, n. 38). Whether the lament over her remove from her home at Euesperides implies that the site of Ptolemais was during Arata's lifetime there still a remote and undeveloped settlement is equally hard to say. In any event, inhumation soon became an established custom at Ptolemais as the multi-tude and the variety of its tombs indicate.

Of the several types of inhumation tombs, the simplest and perhaps the oldest is the cist grave. It consists of a plain rectangular trough of appropriate length and depth carved in the surface of the rock and covered with three or four flat stones (Pl. XVIII *A*). Cist graves are common at many sites and were used during many centuries, but the fact that some examples of the Hellenistic period contain burials of wealthy persons suggests that in the earlier periods their use was more common and less a mark of economic incapacity than at later times.[170] Their ready accessibility has subjected them to thorough looting. Commonly they are in groups intended, no doubt, for members of the same family. At Ptolemais, in the burial area east of the city, one group of two adjacent graves was explored for the expedition by G. R. H. Wright. It was located within a temple-tomb precinct, as frag-ments of Ionic capitals scattered about the site indicated. Bedrock here was about 1.30 m. below the surface, so that the sides of the graves had to be built up with ashlar blocks (60 × 40 × 35 cm.), a procedure quite as common as straight quarrying. At the bottom smaller stones were used to key the construction into the native rock. The graves were of identical size (2.25 × 0.70 m. on the interior) and were set side by side so that one long wall was common to both. Each was sealed at the top by four flat capstones, but these had at one time been lifted, for the graves contained only vestigial remains of burials and a few sherds of coarse pottery.

More prominent, if not more numerous, were the tombs erected as freestanding buildings at Ptole-mais. They have long since disappeared as features of the landscape because they provided such ex-cellent and accessible supplies of building material. Destruction of such tombs preceded the visits of the early European travelers, who noted chiefly what remained of their contents, that is, the sar-

[170] In Cyrenaica the early use of cist graves has been noted at Tauchira by G. R. H. Wright, who worked there in 1944–45, but there is no published report of his work. For comment on the Tauchira material see G. Dennis, "On recent excavations in the Greek cemeteries of the Cyrenaica," *Transactions of the Royal Society of Literature*, Second Series, IX (1867) 135–82, and R. D. Barnett, "Tombs at Tocra," *JHS* LXV (1945) 105–6. The Greek inscriptions are given by Oliverio, *op. cit.* Vol. II 2, pp. 198–236, and the Hebrew by Gray in *Cyrenaican Expedition of the University of Manchester, 1952*, pp. 43–56. For simple cist graves of the Hellenistic period that have yielded rich treasures of gold and jewelry see H. Seyrig, "Antiquités syriennes," *Syria* XXIX (1952) 204–50 and XXX (1953) 12–24.

cophagi (see below).[171] Visible on the surface today are occasional fragments of architectural members and, above all, the scarping of the native rock undertaken to provide the proper bedding for the structures. The combination of the two is sometimes quite revealing, and it is clear that free-standing funerary monuments once stood in files and in some depth along the main roads leading eastward and westward from the city and on eminences adjacent to them. The actually recognizable types include the rectangular temple tomb, the cylindrical tholos structure, and the tomb in the form of an altar.[172] Some of these must have been elaborate structures, for there are occasional indications of architecturally decorated courts and inclosures in which they had been set.

In the larger and more pretentious temple tombs burial was in sarcophagi, which were seen by the European travelers east and west of the city. Some of the simpler and undecorated sarcophagi are still to be seen lying near the sites where they had originally been placed on the hillsides that flank the Wadi Zawana near the southeastern city gate. The more important pieces, found for the most part west of the city at the mouth of the Wadi Hambish, are now in the local museum.[173] Among the more interesting are fragments of a sarcophagus (Pl. LI B) decorated with scenes of battling Greeks and Amazons (see p. 206, No. 69) and of another with *putti* holding garlands. The three lids which are preserved in part or whole (e.g. Pl. LI A) are carved with representations of husband and wife reclining on a bolster (see p. 206, No. 70). With these sculptured funerary remains it seems proper to

mention also three stelae, two with representations of the gladiators Hippomedes (Pl. L D and p. 207, No. 71) and Hermes and one with the representation of a soldier, even though they were presumably not connected with funerary structures and are later in date.[174]

Destined by their very character to be better preserved and hence more prominent today at the site of Ptolemais are the chamber tombs hewn in the solid rock. They range from shallow caves large enough to contain only a single burial (with cist or *arcosolium* graves) to large caverns originally well planned for the use of a single family, though subsequently subject to all kinds of intrusive burials (Pl. XVIII C–D). Examples of the former can be seen especially on the slopes of the Jebel Akhdar. Examples of the latter are in evidence everywhere east and west of the city and can be divided into three groups. One group, particularly evident on and near the eminence in the third quarry area described above, approximately a kilometer west of Ptolemais, has underground chambers reached by an inclined dromos carved in the solid rock. The second group, with chambers hewn directly in the walls of ancient quarries, are currently the most evident and are being and have been for many centuries used as dwellings and stables (Pl. XIX B). The third group has chambers cut into three sides of a courtyard especially carved in the sloping rock of the coastal plain. These establishments have all the earmarks of planned enterprise, whether on the part of individual selling facilities to households or on the part of groups of households. There are several of these east of the city.

The early European traveler Pacho, who visited Cyrenaica shortly after the Beecheys and who compared the funerary installations at Cyrene and Ptolemais, remarked on the absence at Ptolemais of carved tomb façades that simulate those of Doric temples.[175] The observation is indeed valid, but conceivably it has no other meaning than that the chamber tombs, being less prominently located at Ptolemais, were not intended for external display. Doorframes were occasionally carved in the living rock to inclose the tomb openings with their heavy stone doors, and the faces of the adjacent

---

[171] See Beechey, *Proceedings*, p. 360, and Barth, *Wanderungen*, p. 398. Apparently the only European traveler to mention the tombs themselves is Halbherr, who in 1910 noted that the road leading to the Tauchira Gate was flanked by "suburban structures among which was a kind of temple" (see Aurigemma in *Africa italiana* III 242–43).

[172] For the tombs at Cyrene and their general classification see J. Cassels, "The cemeteries of Cyrene," *PBSR* XXIII (1955) 1–43, and the reports of Alan Rowe in *Cyrenaican Expedition of the University of Manchester, 1952*, pp. 4–26, and *Cyrenaican Expeditions of the University of Manchester, 1955, 1956, 1957* (1959) pp. 1–12.

[173] On the provenience of three of the pieces see Oliverio, *op. cit.* Vol. II, 2, p. 246. For the Ptolemais sarcophagus fragments generally see Ghislanzoni in *Notiziario archeologico* I 117–22 and especially A. L. Pietrogrande "Sarcofagi decorati della Cirenaica," *Africa italiana* III 108–13. They are assigned by Pietrogrande to the second and third centuries of our era.

[174] On the discovery of these stelae near the Amphitheater and for an illustration of the stele devoted to the unnamed soldier see Oliverio, *op. cit.* Vol. II 2, p. 247 and Pl. XCV 79.

[175] Pacho, *Rélation d'un voyage dans ... la Cyrénaique ...*, p. 179.

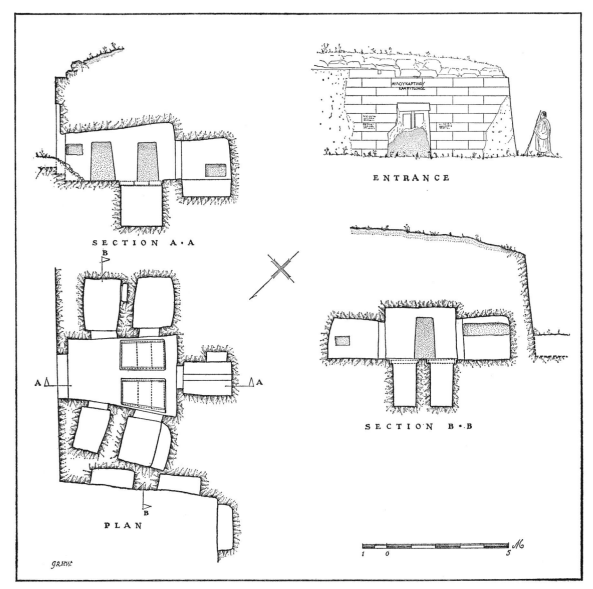

Fig. 38.—Plan and Sections of Tomb of the Kartilioi. *G. R. H. Wright*

quarry walls were in several instances incised with horizontal lines to simulate drafted masonry, but otherwise the façades are relatively plain. Two details of outward embellishment must, however, be noted. The first is the carving of small square or rectangular recesses above or at the sides of the entrance to receive either funeral offerings or less than life-size heads representing the head of the family to which the tomb belonged.[176] The second

[176] A large collection of such heads exists in the sculpture museum at Cyrene, where such recesses are common (see Cassels, *op. cit.* p. 4). Commercially produced, of course, like the Palmyrene funerary busts, they deserve study, none the less, as sources for our knowledge of the repertoire of types that formed the stock in trade of the ateliers of the lesser sculptors.

is the use of a gabled frame to set off and contain commemorative inscriptions (see Pl. XVIII *B*). Not all tomb inscriptions are so framed, but the frame, whatever it represents, is sufficiently common to be worthy of note. One obvious suggestion, of course, is that it represents a gabled sarcophagus, perhaps of the wooden type familiar from Egypt.

The Oriental Institute expedition concerned itself with but a single example of a chamber tomb, that of the family of the Kartilioi (Fig. 38). It was hewn in the vertical west face of one of the small quarries west of the city and north of the coastal road. The quarry face was dressed by incised lines to give the impression of ashlar construction. In-

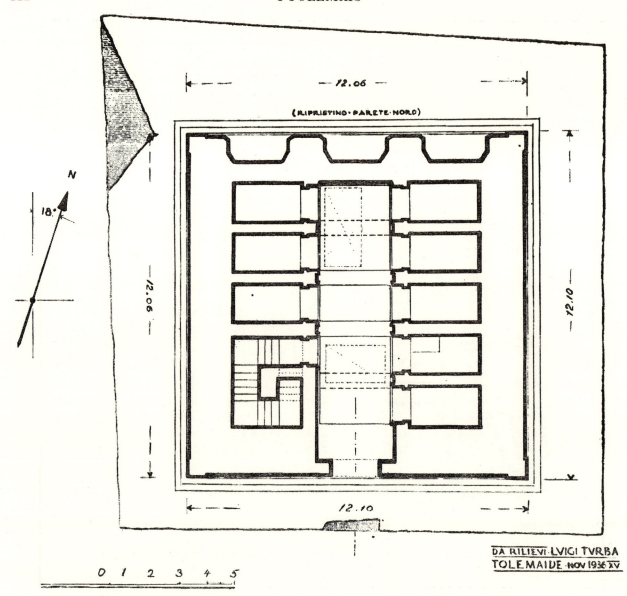

Fig. 39.—Plan of Tower Tomb. After Luigi Turba in Caputo, "Protezione," Fig. 18

scriptions above and at either side of the door record the names of the owner and members of his family buried within. These suggest that the tomb was in use during the years immediately preceding the beginning of our era.[177] A simple molded door-frame and a paneled door were carved in the native rock. It would be interesting to know the details of this feature more fully, but unfortunately tomb

robbers have broken away the lower part. The noticeable batter of the jambs and the fact that at least the upper part of the door was not functional but merely representational, being carved in and remaining part of the native rock, recall Egyptian parallels, particularly the false doors used in the interiors of tombs. The lower part of the door must either have been functional, of the swinging stone variety, or else it was built up of masonry and covered with plaster that was molded to represent the lower ends of the leaves. From the violence done to the doorway it would appear more probable that the latter method was used.[178]

[177] See p. 215, Nos. 48–51. It is probable, though not absolutely certain, that year numbers at the beginning of such texts, accompanied by indication of month and day, represent the date of demise and that year numbers at the end refer to the length of life. If so, the Kartilia Petronia of Inscription 49 died on the 27th of Choiak in the year 15, the era being probably that of Actium (see p. 209).

[178] On the use of similar false doors and half-doors at Cyrene see Cassels, *loc. cit.*

Inside, the tomb consisted of a quadrilateral chamber, wider at the back than at the front, from which large roughly rectangular bays or loculi extended in three directions. The tomb was clearly intended for inhumation burial, the bodies being deposited on the floors of the loculi. Rectangular recesses, small and large, carved in the walls of some of the loculi were intended to receive either funeral offerings or infant burials. Deep cists in the floor of the central chamber, each covered with three slabs, and a smaller cist in the loculus at the back of the chamber contained either supplementary or intrusive burials, or they served as the repositories for remains from earlier use of the loculi. The walls and the roof of the tomb are much decayed, but it is obvious that the original cutting was irregular and rough. Some few fragments of worked stone found in the interior in the upper layers of the fill suggest that there were once some interior appointments.

In this general survey of burial installations in the immediate vicinity of Ptolemais we come finally to the great Tower Tomb west of the city that has at all times been an outstanding landmark and that represents a distinct type (Pl. XIX). Carefully studied and preserved by the Italian archeologists,[179] whose plan and section are reproduced here as Figures 39 and 40, the Tower Tomb in this context invites not further study of its structural details but only a general consideration of its type and of the question as to how it came to be erected in this vicinity and at its own precise spot, along with the chronological inferences to be drawn therefrom.

A massive structure 12 meters square and still preserved to a height of 14 meters, the Tower Tomb of Ptolemais is located high on a cube of solid rock standing free in the city's largest quarry. Two similar cubes exist in the quarry farther to the west. Connected by both its architectural embellishment and its general type with such freestanding commemorative monuments as the Lion Tomb of Cnidus and the Hermel Monument of Syria, the structure was none the less created for multiple burial as were the tower tombs of Palmyra and the upper Euphrates.[180] A date in the Hellenistic period is

appropriate to the forms of its architectural decor and the excellence of its ashlar construction. Analogies to the construction of the Tauchira Gate at Ptolemais, which is probably of Hellenistic origin (see pp. 60-62), are visible at many points.

As to the construction of such a monument at Ptolemais and its emplacement on a cube of solid rock in a vast quarry, local tradition, fanciful as always, speaks of the tower as the "Tomb of Pharaoh," and with no greater reliability than when it applies the title "Qasr Fir'aun" to the only freestanding temple structure at Petra. Two European travelers, Paolo della Cella and Pacho, ventured such an opinion, suggesting that the tower was erected by Ptolemy VIII (Physcon) after he had been given title to Cyrenaica in the dispute with his older brother.[181] Lacking support in fact, their suggestion has nothing to distinguish it from local tradition save that it is more sophisticated. But the tower remains a unique monument in Cyrenaica, and one fact hitherto disregarded strongly implies that such suggestions should be not too lightly dismissed. The fact in question is the existence in the area immediately west of Ptolemais of part of the royal estate belonging to the ruling family of Hellenistic Cyrenaica. This property was so important that the question of title to it became something of a *cause célèbre* between the Romans and the people of Cyrenaica, provoking accusations before the Senate, investigations, and imperial decisions (see p. 10). The parcel at Ptolemais was sufficiently important to cause the erection of the stele, now standing outside the Tauchira Gate (see Pl. VI *A*), on which is recorded the fact that the *hortus* (being part of the *ager regius* willed by Ptolemy Apion to Rome) had been restored to the

---

[179] See Caputo, "Protezione," pp. 43-49.

[180] On the Hermel Monument and its probable commemorative (rather than funerary) function see P. Perdrizet, "Le Monument de Hermel," *Syria* XIX (1938) 47-71. For the tower tombs of Palmyra see Wiegand,

Palmyra, pp. 45-84, and for those of Dura-Europos see *The Excavations at Dura-Europos: Preliminary Report of the Ninth Season of Work*, Part II (1946) pp. 140-50. A careful analysis of the Palmyrene material, showing the evolution of the local type, is available in E. Will, "La tour funéraire de Palmyre," *Syria* XXVI (1949) 87-116, and an examination of tower-like structures generally in the Mediterranean basin and the Near East is offered by the same author under the title "La tour funéraire de la Syrie et les monuments apparentés," *Syria* XXVI 258-312. It develops from this study that the tower tomb combines a monumental commemorative structure originally set over a tomb in some cases and an instrument of multiple burial in which the burials were at one time accessible from the exterior.

[181] See Pacho, *op. cit.* p. 180.

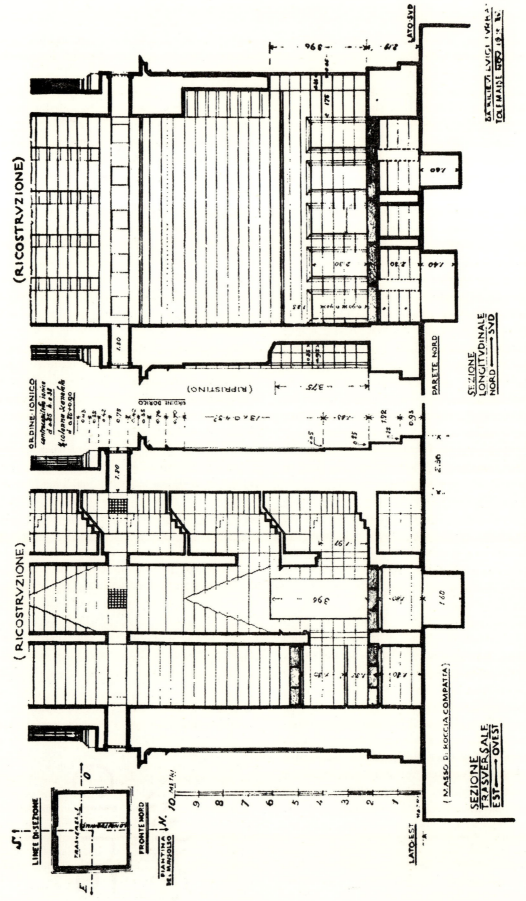

Fig. 40.—Sectional Elevation of Tower Tomb. After Luigi Turba in Caputo, "Protezione," Fig. 20

Romans in A.D. 72.[182] It is by no means unlikely that the local parcel included a sizable portion of the coastal plain and some part of the wooded Jebel Akhdar, nor is it at all impossible that, after diverse vicissitudes, it had come to Ptolemy Apion as the result of private investments made there as far back as Ptolemy VI, Magas, or even the Battids of Barca. Since the Tower Tomb of Ptolemais can well be thought to have stood in a royal garden, the suggestion of royal origin is worthy of consideration. In the absense of an inscription the identity of the person who erected it cannot be determined. The fact that the quarry may have contained originally two or three such funerary towers (to judge by the number of natural cubes left standing in it) suggests a relatively late date, perhaps the second century B.C.

If the Tower Tomb stood in what was originally a royal garden, in all probability it did not stand as now in a quarry. This inference provides an interesting outlook upon the order in which the quarries of Ptolemais came into being and thus indirectly also upon the development of its cemeteries. The wrangle with the Roman officials over the royal estate involved the appropriation of the property by members of the local community, if not by the community itself, during the period between 96 B.C. and A.D. 72. It is only logical to suppose that at least the largest of the city's quarries, the one that now encompasses the Tower Tomb, represents this period in which the property was being exploited for personal and civic gain. The quarry would thus have supplied building material for the construction work of the early Roman imperial period, and its use for burial purposes may have begun at about the same time or slightly later. The great quarry farther to the west may represent the structural period of the Severi or perhaps that which began with Diocletian. Because of its remove from the city, it was never used for funerary purposes. That the existence of the royal estate would not at any time have precluded sepulture in freestanding tombs erected along the highway running through it may be taken for granted. But tombs set back from the highway in the fields or on the eminences visible at a distance from the highway may well be no older than the early Roman period. Future excavation and study of the necropolis of Ptolemais will serve to clarify these and other details bearing upon the history of its development.

SOME GAPS IN OUR KNOWLEDGE OF THE SITE

How poorly we are at present still informed about Ptolemais is illustrated by the attempt made above to set down what is known of its history. Long periods of time still remain complete or virtual blanks, particularly the Hellenistic period and the period of the Antonine emperors. Our interest here, however, attaches not so much to the specific periods as to the types of monuments and materials that one would look for and expect to find at such a site. Although much has yet to be done by further excavation, we do at least have samplings of the types of structures discussed above and of the categories of objects presented in chapter iv. But there are categories of monuments of which we have as yet no direct knowledge, and two recommend themselves for brief discussion.

Ptolemais, as we have seen, was founded for the very specific purpose of serving as a commercial emporium by means of which the products of the coastal plain and the interior could be brought together and sent overseas for gain and by means of which foreign products could be imported. It is to be expected therefore that business affairs and their administration would have been amply provided for structurally in the development of the site. This is all the more probable because of the importance of the agora and all that it implies in the physical development of the Greek city, of which Ptolemais is an example.

At present we have some information about the outer configuration of the city, including its road connections, its harbor, its defenses, and about the circumstances surrounding the private lives of its inhabitants—their dwellings, their public and private baths, the *objects d'art* with which they surrounded themselves. But the center of their business life, and of the civic life that went with it, is still completely unknown. What is needed above all is the discovery and excavation of the agora of Ptolemais and its surrounding buildings. Since the

[182] For the text see Oliverio, *op. cit.* Vol. II 1, pp. 132–33, No. 138; *SEG* IX 70–71, No. 360.

time of the early European travelers it has become traditional to speak of the open colonnaded square that was created above the vaulted cisterns (Building 10 on Plan XXII) as the "forum" of Ptolemais. Whether Ptolemais or any other Greek city ever had a forum is questionable, but certainly the structure which we call the Square of the Cisterns was neither properly located nor equipped to handle either the commercial or the administrative business of the city. For this, future excavators will have to look elsewhere at the site.

As to the probable location of the agora, two general requirements can be formulated that might be of help to archeologists. The first is that the agora, as the center of the city's commercial life, should be near the harbor and one of the city's gates. The second is that it should be accessible from at least one, more probably from two, of the city's major thoroughfares. On both these scores it seems likely that the agora was located west of the west cardo and north of the decumanus that presumably served to determine the emplacement of the system of east-west thoroughfares, the one connecting with the Quarry Gate (see Fig. 3 and Plan XXII). In this area, immediately outside and to the south of the Italian wall, there exists today a relatively level piece of land, sometimes used as a playing field, that may mark the location of the open square that would have formed a necessary part of the agora. Along the southern side of this field the ground rises rather sharply, perhaps because the natural rise is supplemented by remains of structures concealed under dirt that has been washed down from the upper slopes of the site. It is here that the remains of some of the city's public buildings—its basilica or its *bouleutereion* and one or another of its small temples—can be looked for. At the north, in all likelihood, traces of such structures as shops and porticoes will be faint. They may well be under, or have been incorporated in, the Italian defensive wall.

The second of the two gaps in our knowledge of ancient Ptolemais to which attention is directed here is the absence of any concrete information about its pagan shrines. What this means will be evident to anyone who compares Ptolemais and Cyrene in this particular. Of course Ptolemais did not have the overtones that were lent to Cyrene by the foundation legends of Apollo and the Nymph Cyrene and the instructions of the Delphic Oracle. But of course it must have had important temples,

and, except for the small Hellenistic temple adjoining the "Odeon" (see p. 90), no temples have as yet been excavated or even located with any degree of certainty. Future excavators will do well in this connection to concern themselves with the area south of the residential section of the city and south of the city's reservoirs (Buildings 10, 11, and 12), where on Plan XXII the location of Building 26 is indicated by a right angle which represents a monumental double-engaged corner pier (Fig. 41) of a portico surrounding a large courtyard. Here may well have stood one of the earliest and most important of the city's shrines, for south of the area of the courtyard, at a higher level and hence presumably on a separate terrace, were drums and capitals of a large Doric structure probably exposed by the Italian archeologists (Pl. XX *A*). The dimensions of the capital (Fig. 42) suggest some relation in type to the Temple of Zeus at Cyrene. East of the Headquarters of the Dux (Building 23) two large Corinthian capitals are exposed to view (e.g. Pl. XX *B*). These are of the kind that one might readily associate with a temple of the Antonine period.

While it is clear that only further excavation will improve our knowledge of the pagan shrines at Ptolemais, some hints as to the potentialities may be gained from its inscriptions and sculptures. Of the long list of the deities attested elsewhere in Cyrenaica[183] none have as yet appeared in the inscriptions of Ptolemais, but we do have suggestions concerning ruler cults. A block reused in the Square of the Cisterns preserves two-thirds of a dedicatory inscription commemorating Queen Arsinoë II (see p. 6), daughter of Ptolemy I and Berenice I. This inscription, coupled with the discovery in the City Bath of a statue of Cleopatra I (see pp. 188–90), suggests that there may well have been somewhere in the city a shrine to the "brother and sister gods" that was eventually devoted also to their successors. The only other pertinent inscription (p. 209, No. 1) is a dedication to the "august gods" on a cippus (perhaps an altar) standing at the entrance to the Villa of the Roman period. This suggests that the Roman imperial household, the natural successor of the Ptolemies as the recipient of divine honors, also was eventually represented by an established priesthood and sanctuary.

[183] For such a list see L. Vitali, *Fonti per la storia della religione Cyrenaica* (Padua Università, "Publicazione della Facoltà di lettere e filosofia" I [1932]).

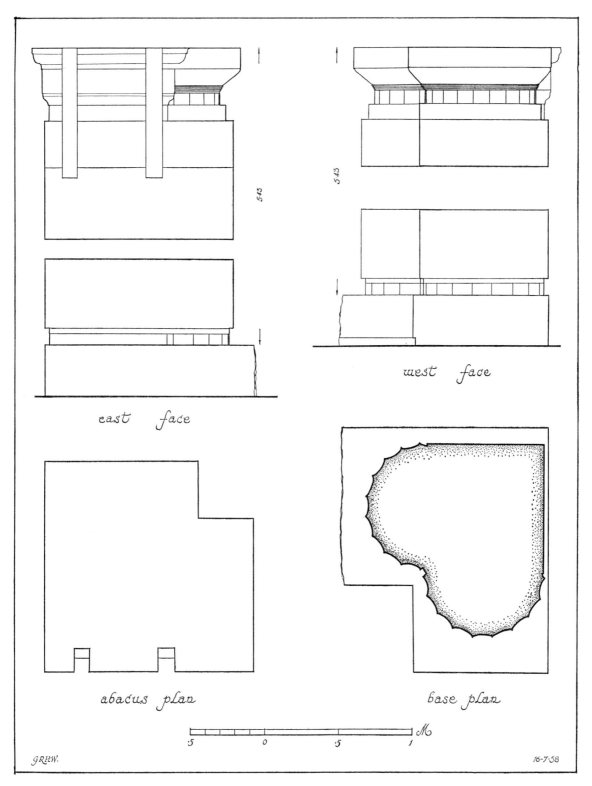

east face

west face

abacus plan

base plan

GRHW.

16-7-58

Fig. 41.—Angle Pier of Portico of Building 26. *J.E. Knudstad*

How far it is possible to judge from sculptures found at Ptolemais as to other cults provided with

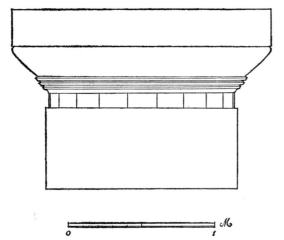

Fig. 42.—MOLDINGS OF DORIC CAPITAL OF BUILDING 26.
G. R. H. Wright

temples is difficult to say. Alan Rowe has inferred from Egyptian statuettes found in the "Palazzo," more particularly from his reading of their hieroglyphic inscriptions, the existence at Ptolemais of two temples of Osiris (see p. 9). His interpretation, however, has not been followed, and, while on general grounds it may be probable that a temple of Isis and Osiris existed at the site, no convincing evidence can be said to have been produced as yet. Statues such as those of Herakles, Asklepios, Athena, Dionysos, and Artemis, found at the site, could originally have stood in public buildings other than temples, as is certainly true of statues of Muses and of the Three Graces. The only piece that suggests a special structural context is the head of the Tyche of Ptolemais (p. 203, No. 61), which should have formed part of an over life-size image placed in the city's *tychaion*.

III

BUILDINGS EXCAVATED BY THE ORIENTAL INSTITUTE

A VILLA OF THE EARLY ROMAN EMPIRE

OF the three areas in which the Oriental Institute expedition conducted excavations at the site of Ptolemais one was in the western part of the city, where the building uncovered is identified as No. 5 on Plan XXII. The structure was completely cleared and was without doubt a private dwelling. To the east, north, and west it was bounded by paved streets, which fixed its width at 36 meters, the width of a typical city block. From the street to the north it extended southward a distance of 54.20 m. to another dwelling that occupied part or all of the remainder of the insula. Given a standard length of 180 meters for the insulae, the Villa can be said to have occupied slightly less than one-third of a city block.

The existence of a residential building at this site was revealed by parallel rows of column shafts projecting about 30–50 cm. above the surface in the midst of a wheat field, their arrangement suggesting a peristyle court. Excavation verified the inference, but the fill was much deeper than expected, ranging from 1.50 m. at the north to 2.70 m. over the central and southern parts of the area. The fact that surface level sloped away gently not only toward the north but beyond the site also toward the south indicated that the fill was in part artificial, the result of earth from adjacent areas having been dumped upon the remains of the building.

Save at its several entrances, the building was originally inclosed on the street sides by solid walls built to a certain height at least of well dressed, squared, and fitted limestone blocks with typical dimensions of 120 × 16 × 45 cm. The blocks were properly set in courses with an average height of 60 cm. The outside walls were therefore 45 cm. thick, save at foundation level, where blocks 55 cm. thick were used to provide a base course. Elements of the outside walls were found *in situ* only at the southeast and northwest corners, never more than two courses high, but the wider base course could be followed along most of the street to the east and sporadically at the north and west.

The robbing of the exterior walls and, as excavation showed, of about half of the column drums and most of the entablature blocks of the peristyle, together with most of the capitals and the jambs and lintels of doorframes throughout the structure, represents an episode in the history of the building that came during the period that saw the heavy fill deposited upon the site. That episode was preceded by the occupation of rooms along the south and north ends of the building by squatters (see pp. 138–39).

One structural feature in the southern part of the Villa deserves early mention. Here the inner walls had stone footings leveled off at an average height of 50–60 cm. above floor level. As excavation progressed from north to south remains of walls came to light whose height ranged up to the full depth of the fill (2.70 m.), and their upper parts were constructed of mud bricks coated on the interior with plaster (Pl. XXIII C). Indeed, the southern exterior wall of the building, where it paralled the exterior wall of the next house to the south (see Plan XII), was also made of mud brick above a meter-high stone footing.[1] Thus it may follow that the other exterior walls had only a socle of well dressed stone, the upper portion being of mud-brick construction. Doorframes, porticoes, and the frames of windows giving on the interior from the second story were naturally of stone.

---

[1] The bricks were *ca.* 6 cm. high and normally squared to the thickness of the wall, hence typically *ca.* 40 cm. on a side. The walls inclosing the south portico, which were thicker (*ca.* 65 cm.), were built of bricks *ca.* 32.5 cm. square, laid two rows deep.

The use of mud brick in a house of the architectural pretensions of the Villa at first seems surprising. But it may be more indicative of a historical period or of a regional practice than of an economic level or of a contradiction between pretense and competence. The use of mud bricks rather than baked bricks is sometimes scouted as a possibility even of Roman structural procedure, especially in connection with the famous dictum that Augustus found Rome a city of brick and left it a city of marble.[2] But whatever the proper understanding of the change at Rome may be, the use of mud brick in North Africa, has been demonstrated at Leptis Magna[3] and is reported also from Johns' excavations at the site of ancient Euesperides near Benghazi. That in North Africa, and especially in Cyrenaica, it reflects the influence of building methods used commonly farther toward the east, especially in Egypt, seems quite likely.

In plan the Roman Villa at Ptolemais (Pl. XXII *A*) consists of chambers placed around three sides of a court that has porticoes at all four sides (Plan XII). The long sides of the court are parallel to the north-south axis of the building, but the court, which was presumably developed as a garden, was placed about 4 meters east of that axis. The residential chambers are along the western and southern sides of the property. At the north end room was made for a row of shops or tabernae opening only on the adjacent street. Near these were service quarters and the essential elements of a bath. The east portico fronted on the adjacent street .The colonnade of the south portico was curved, describing a segment of a circle.

At the south the division between the Villa and the adjoining house was clearly marked by two readily distinguishable walls running parallel to each other for a distance of about 22 meters beginning at the street on the east side of the property. The Villa's south wall stopped at the southwest corner of Room 15. From this point westward, a

[2] See T. Ashby, *The Architecture of Ancient Rome* (1927) p. 27.

[3] See R. G. Goodchild and J. B. Ward Perkins, "The Roman and Byzantine defences of Lepcis Magna," *PBSR* XXI 72, n. 54. There is every reason to suppose that excavation would reveal the use of the material also at Tocra (ancient Tauchira) in Cyrenaica and hence at most of the ancient sites on the coast of Libya. Whether this type of construction was suited to and would have withstood the rigors of the climate at Cyrene, on the upper level of the Cyrenaican plateau, remains undetermined.

distance of about 13 meters, the rooms of the Villa were built against the adjacent dwelling, which was, therefore, earlier than the Villa. In all respects, however, the Villa as revealed by the excavations was a complete, well organized establishment, suited to the high standards of good living current among the better placed of North African society in the Roman period.

From the outside three doorways gave access to the interior of the Villa (Fig. 43). One from the street to the north led through Room 21 to the service area. A second led from the street to the west through Room 8 to the kitchen (Room 7) and was thus presumably for the use of tradesmen. The main doorway was located near the southeast corner of the building, giving off the street to the east. In the street itself this doorway was flanked by two large cippi (Pl. XXI *A*), the more southerly of which is broken off diagonally while the more northerly (Plan XIV 12) is virtually complete. On the latter at eye-level in a zone set off by fillets is a well carved Greek inscription (p. 209, No. 1).

From the street, through the main doorway (2.15 m. wide), two steps led down into the vestibule (Room 18), a room 8.60 m. long and 5.10 m. wide. The steps were deeply worn and had at some time been scarred with a sharp tool to give a better foothold. The threshold became the first step because of the emplacement before the doorway of a row of blocks that ran to the outer edges of the two flanking cippi and provided the foundation for the square plinths on which the cippi were set. To the right and left of the doorway, between it and the plinths, smaller roughly squared stones may be remains of the paving of the street, which has been robbed out elsewhere, or of a step added at a late date, because of the rise of the street level, to prevent rain water from draining into the vestibule. Of the trim of the door only two short vertical blocks remained *in situ*, one on either end of the threshold. The second step, made of three stones, had large square door sockets let in at either end. The total drop from the row of stones outside the doorway to the floor of the vestibule must have been approximately 50 cm. The paving of the vestibule, presumably of marble slabs, had been removed, but floor level was indicated by a plinth in the center of the room on which rested a rather slender column that provided support for the beams of the ceiling and by the level of the doorways in the north and west

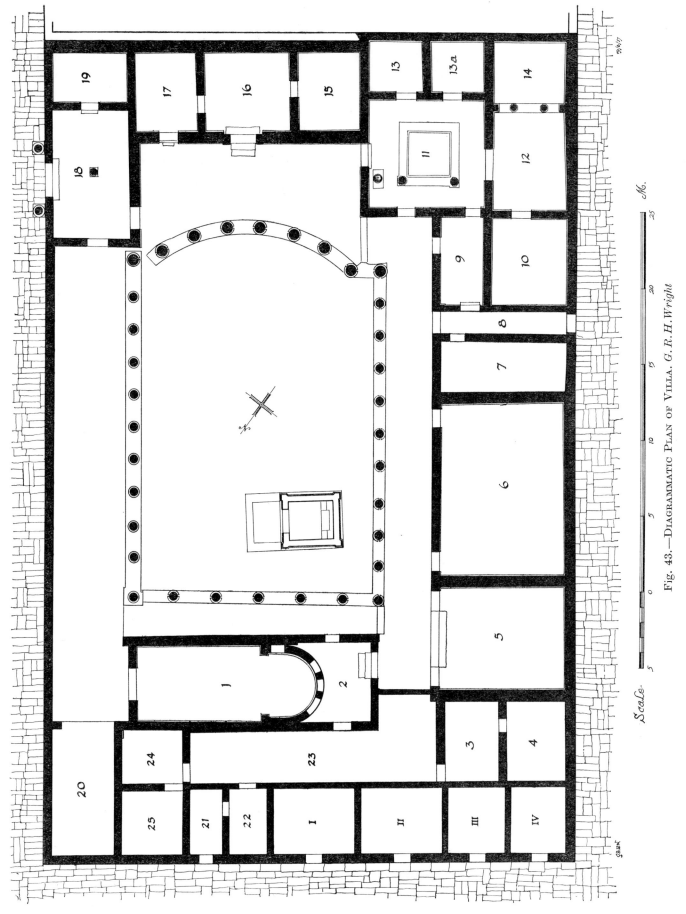

Fig. 43.—Diagrammatic Plan of Villa. *G.R.H.Wright*

Scale.

121

walls of the chamber. The west doorway (*ca.* 1.50 m. wide) had been blocked. The blocking is to be associated with the use of the room by squatters, for the bottom of the fill yielded ashes, broken cooking pots, and other refuse.

Use of the area by squatters extended in all probability to Room 19, immediately south of the vestibule in the extreme southeast corner of the Villa. The wall between it and the vestibule, though robbed out to its lowest courses, fixed the dimensions of the room at 5.19 × 3.80 m. A stepping stone set against the north face gave the general position of the doorway. Fragments of unpainted plaster on the stone footings of the walls of Room 19 and the fact that its only connection was with the vestibule indicate that it was the lodgement of

Fig. 44.—FRAME OF DOORWAY BETWEEN VESTIBULE (Room 18) AND EAST PORTICO OF VILLA. *G. R. H. Wright*

the *ostiarius*, the guardian of the door of the house. In the period of the squatters it served no doubt as the inner room of a two-room dwelling of which Room 18 was the outer and general purpose room and hence also the kitchen.

From the vestibule (Room 18) access was provided through doorways in its west and north walls to the south and east porticoes. The west doorway was set near the northern end of the wall, so as to prevent passersby on the street from looking into the south portico and thus to insure the privacy of the living quarters adjoining it at the other (west) end. The north doorway also was off-center, being about 60 cm. closer to the west than to the east wall of the vestibule. It constituted the formal entrance to the peristyle court, to judge by the excellence of its trim. This was almost completely preserved by good fortune, fixing the width of the doorway at 1.42 m. and its height at 2.50 m. (Fig. 44). It consisted of two monolithic jambs found standing (Pl. XXI *B*) and a finely carved lintel that came to light in the fill nearby (Pl. XXVI

A and Fig. 45). Its interesting decorative features are discussed below (pp. 220–21).

The four porticoes that surrounded the court, an area 15.55 m. wide and up to 23.60 m. long, were of unequal size and had other differentiating features. The east portico (Pl. XXI *C*) was the longest and of medium width, measuring about 4.90 m. from the interior face of the stylobate to the east wall of the house and running north-south for a distance of 41.30 m. The north-south dimension includes the area in front of Room 1, for no trace was found of even the footing of an east-west wall that might have inclosed this area at the south. Closely matching the east portico in length, but a good bit narrower (3.10 m.), was the west portico (Pl. XXIII *A*). Its length (presumably 31.10 m.) was difficult to determine accurately because of the looting of its terminal wall at the north. The position of that wall on Plan XII is based on the assumption that it must have continued from the north wall of Room 5. The fact that the border of the mosaic

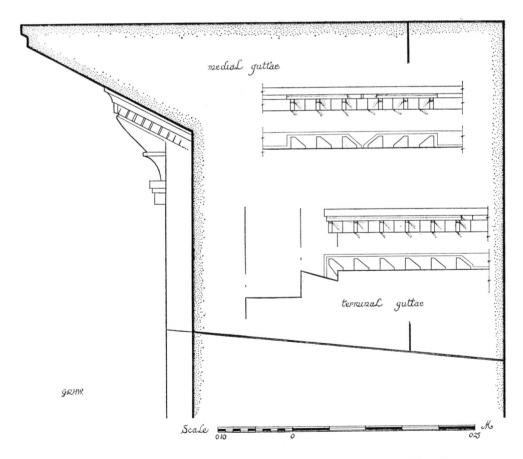

Fig. 45.—Section of Lintel of Doorway between Vestibule and East Portico of Villa. *G.R.H. Wright*

paving of the portico returned, leaving a normal terminal zone of plain white tesserae 60 cm. wide beyond it to the north, indicates that the missing wall cannot well have been located elsewhere. Still narrower and much shorter was the north portico, which was 15.90 m. long, about 2.08 m. wide at the west end, and somewhat wider at the east. The beginning of a drainage system to carry surplus rain water from the court was observed at the fourth intercolumniation (counting from west), and, in spite of the looting of the walls along the east side of the building, a section of its bedding and a few stones of its side walls came to light under the north end of the east portico. Slightly shorter (15.25 m.) and much wider, finally, was the south portico (Pl. XXIII *B*), which had widths of 7.70 and 7.90 m. at the ends and 4.70 m. at the top of the curve of the colonnade.

A 10-cm. step led down from the west portico to the north portico, and probably there was a similar step where the north portico joined the east portico or in the east portico itself in front of Room 1. All four porticoes may originally have been paved with mosaics. Those of the north, west, and south porticoes were found intact save for gaps due to hard wear (see pp. 238–40). The area of the east portico had apparently been churned up in connection with the looting of the exterior wall and the east colonnade, for all traces of the floor had disappeared. Kitchen refuse of all kinds was found here and in the adjacent sections of the court in the lowest levels of the fill.

The peristyle was of the type called Rhodian by Vitruvius, in which the columns of one of the four sides are taller and therefore also proportionately larger in girth than those of the other three. In the present instance the columns of the south portico were larger, the extra height no doubt being planned to provide for a second story over the rooms behind the portico (see pp. 127–28). The south colonnade was distinguished from the others also by being set out on the line of an arc, giving the court a southern terminus similar in shape to a shallow exedra.

The order of the peristyle it was possible to establish with assurance from the bases and lower column shafts, found standing to a maximum height of about 3 meters around the entire court except at the southeast corner and the east end of the north portico (Pl. XXII *A*), and from a capital and pieces of the entablature found lying in the fill.[4] It combined unfluted Ionic columns with an entablature containing a Doric frieze (Fig. 46). At the north, east, and west the columns are calculated to have been about 4.20 m. high (see p. 218) and at the south about 5 meters high, with portico ceiling heights of about 5 and 6 meters respectively (see p. 220). On the north, east, and west the column bases and capitals were slotted to receive poles holding awnings to shade the porticoes (see Pl. XXIII *A*). At the south an awning was unnecessary. Bases, drums, and presumably capitals were plastered and painted, enough traces of color surviving to permit a hypothetical reconstruction of the scheme of decoration (see p. 225). A detailed description of the order, based on a careful study of its characteristic features, is given on pages 217–20. Here it will suffice, therefore, to point out the irregularities in the way it was mounted.

The columns were set on a stylobate of heavy stone blocks that were squared but not particularly well trimmed. Along the east portico the blocks were laid with their heads toward the exterior wall of the building. Along the north and west porticoes the direction was reversed, so that the long sides paralleled the exterior walls. At the southwest corner the stylobate makes a 90-degree turn and at the second column of the south colonnade begins the arc that gave the south portico its special character. At the southeast corner the end of the arc was left hanging, so to speak, and there is a gap in the stylobate (see Fig. 43 and Pl. XXII *A*). Indeed, the position of the easternmost column in the arc was such that the architrave connecting it with the corner column could not have formed a right angle with the corresponding member of the east portico. At the northeast corner the terminal column was mounted on a specially squared over-size block, while elsewhere only the change in the direction in which the typical blocks were laid marked the corner.

It is tempting to suppose that these irregularities reflect different periods in the architectural development of the site, but no positive evidence to

---

[4] It is obvious that the great mass of the blocks used in the entablature, most of the capitals, and the upper parts of the column shafts were removed from the premises for use elsewhere, perhaps when the adjacent West Fortress (Building 4 on Plan XXII) was erected in Byzantine times. The preservation *in situ* of the lower column drums and bases suggests that the site was already covered with a heavy layer of fill when the looting of the architectural elements occurred.

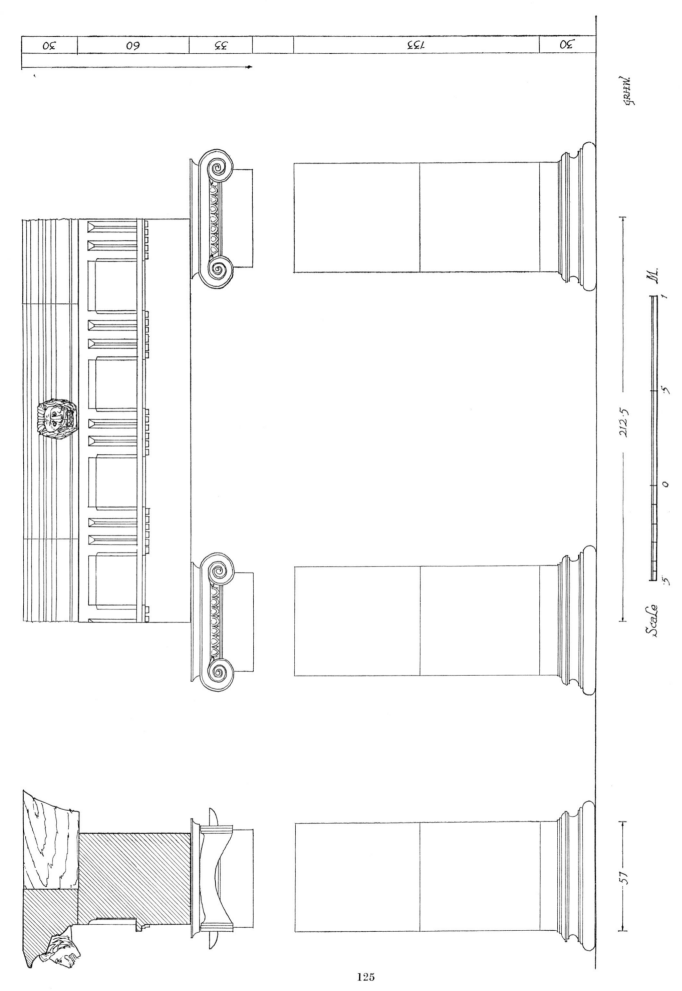

Fig. 46.—Order of the Peristyle of Villa. *G. R. H. Wright*

Scale

135

support such a hypothesis came to light. In part the irregularities may therefore merely illustrate provincial building standards, but in part they may reflect an attempt to deal practically with problems of drainage (at the southeast corner of the peristyle) and footing (at the southwest corner). In part, finally, they may represent the use of materials from various sources, whether taken from other buildings or, as seems more likely, supplied by various stone masons or from various quarries.

The stylobate was set out with thirty-four columns. The spacing of the columns was erratic, and the only explanation that can be offered is that the intercolumniations were determined by the lengths of the architrave blocks available. The interaxial distances vary from 2.00 to 2.90 m. in the north, east, and west colonnades, with 2.15–2.17 m. being the most frequent intervals. The larger columns of the south colonnade were spaced fairly uniformly, the interaxial distances being 2.31–2.34 m. The base and the lower portion of the shaft were normally cut in the same block, the height of the blocks varying from 24 to 43 cm., with about 30 cm. as the norm. The upper sections of the shafts were in two extreme instances 0.94 m. and 1.465 m. high, but the typical height was about 1.20 m. The sections were scored medially so that each represented two drums about 60 cm. high (Plan XIV 4–5). Only one capital was found (Pl. XXVI *D* and Plan XIV 3), but portions particularly of volutes of other capitals of a similar character appeared in the debris. Of the 34 blocks that originally spanned the inter-columniations and contained both architrave and frieze only three were preserved (e.g. Pl. XXVI *B*), two from the north end of the west colonnade (e.g. Plan XIV 1) and one from the south end of the east colonnade (Plan XIV 2). The variation in interaxial distances made it possible to determine precisely which intercolumniations the blocks fitted. Two complete cornice blocks (e.g. Pl. XXVI *C*) were recovered and substantial parts of several others, mostly from the vicinity of the east colonnade. They seem to have been approximately half as long as the architrave-frieze blocks. That the standard features of architrave and frieze varied in their execution (see p. 219) is less surprising than that the blocks containing them vary in height, those from the west colonnade measuring 54.6 cm. in height and the one from the east colonnade 60.5 cm. Whether the difference involved adjust-

ment to columns of different heights on opposite sides of the court, or making-do with blocks supplied by indifferent quarrymen, or even reuse of earlier material is impossible to say.

There also came to light in the fill a number of cornice blocks whose relation to the building is obscure. They fall naturally into two groups, functional and decorative (see p. 222). The functional blocks (Plan XIV 9) may have belonged to the *epikranitis* of the rear wall of the south portico or to the entablature of the upper story behind the south portico. Some of the decorative blocks (Plan XIV 7–8) are clearly of a late date and should perhaps be assigned to a separate structural feature within the peristyle court (see p. 225), which was presumably developed as a garden. This feature, irregularly placed near the northwest corner of the court, was a freestanding structure (4.00 × 3.70 m.) rising from a well molded base with offsets at the four corners (Pl. XXII *B*). Only the base course is preserved and it had been cut away in the middle at the east. Within the structure a row of heavy blocks along the west wall sets off an area (2.40 × 1.95 m.) that was cemented, plastered, and painted in imitation of mottled yellow marble and that must represent a water basin or a shallow pool. We may therefore imagine that the inner row of blocks was the foundation for an architectural adornment in which was centered a semicircular niche topped by a conch and used to set off a small statue, such as one of the fountain figures (Pl. XLIX *C*) that are now in the Tolmeita Museum (see p. 205, No. 67) or the boy with a water jar of which a fragment (Pl. XLVIII *A*) was found in the Villa (p. 200, No. 35). The building may well have been something in the nature of a *naiskos*, such as is similarly placed in the central courtyard of the House of Jason Magnus at Cyrene. Before the *naiskos* in the Villa an area 3.75 m. wide and 2.45 m. deep is set off by roughly dressed heavy stones, secondary in their emplacement to the construction of the *naiskos* proper. Perhaps they represent the stylobate of a portico eventually added to the structure.

Behind the south portico a group of three chambers (Rooms 15, 16, 17) was erected as a separate structural unit of uniform construction. At the north they have a continuous stone footing of excellent quality and extra thickness (70 cm.), which is matched at the rear (south) by the exterior wall of the house (*ca.* 75 cm. thick). The party walls of the chambers and the terminal walls at the east and west were about 45–50 cm. thick. This suite must have served a special purpose, presumably in connection with the business and social affairs of the owner, and Room 16 is interpreted as the oecus of the Villa (see p. 88).

Though of equal depth (5.25 m.) these chambers differ in width, the middle one (Room 16) being the largest (5.35 m. wide), that at the west the next largest (4.80 m. wide), and that at the east the smallest (4.30 m. wide). But all three were commodious and elegantly decorated (see pp. 226–28). The fact that every trace of their flooring had disappeared suggests that it consisted of marble slabs that were removed in the period of looting.

The entrance to the suite was through a formal doorway (2.14 m. wide) in the north wall of Room 16. The molded bases and lower sections of the jambs were found *in situ* (Pl. XXIII *B*). The doorway was placed slightly off-center in the wall, perhaps to provide a more pleasing prospect, for it faces an intercolumniation. Two steps led up from the south portico to the sill, and one step led down from the sill to the floor of the chamber, its ends inclosing the normal doorpost holes.

Room 15, at the west, opened only off Room 16 through a doorway 1.10 m. wide. Its west wall had been broken apart, especially at the north end. The large stone that ran to the northwest corner of the room was found lying inside the room, and in this corner there was above and even below floor level a rather sizable collection of ashes. Presumably these finds are connected with a late phase in the history of the house immediately to the south, from whose Room *A* (see Plan XII) a rough flight of two steps was contrived leading down into the premises of the Villa. The Villa at that time was obviously already in ruins and subject to looting. Probably the area at the foot of the crude stairway was used by squatters for domestic purposes in connection with their occupation of portions of the dwelling to the south. In any event, a short section of the southern end of the west wall of Room 15 testifies to its original thickness and construction.

Room 17, at the east, was originally entered only from Room 16, but the connecting doorway was eventually blocked. A single large stone at the bottom provided a footing for the mud brick with which the rest of the opening was sealed. The open-

ing had the same width (1.10 m.) as that between Rooms 15 and 16. The north wall of Room 17 had been broken to provide a new means of access from the south portico. The new doorway was about 1.30 m. wide. A small stone block set before it provided a makeshift step between the floor of the portico and the sill contrived in the stone socle of the wall. The wall decoration of this room was the most elegant of all three of the rooms. From this decoration, preserved to a height of about 1.62 m., it was possible to infer that the height of the chamber could not have been less than 3 meters nor much more than 3.75 m.[5]

A number of factors suggest that there was a second story over Rooms 15, 16, and 17. The fact that the south portico was higher than the other three porticoes has already been mentioned. With its ceiling at a height of about 6 meters there was sufficient room for a second story, and it is difficult to believe that with such modest dimensions (5.25 × 4.30–5.35 m.) the three rooms at ground level would have merited or received a ceiling set at the height of the portico ceiling. Furthermore, the north and south walls of the three-room suite were of exceptional thickness, and, while the exceptional thickness of the north wall might be thought appropriate to the height to which it had to be built to receive the beams of the portico roof, the extra thickness of the south wall is best interpreted as necessary to carry an upper story. It should be noted in this connection that this three-room suite was in a limited sense a separate structural unit. The south exterior wall of the Villa, being also the south wall of the suite, was not only thicker than the other exterior walls (75 cm. as compared with 45 cm.) but stopped at the west end of Room 15 (see p. 131), turning north at this point and thus inclosing the suite on the west. Three additional tokens of a second story over

---

[5] The minimum figure is arrived at on the basis of the wall decoration of Room 16 (see p. 228). If we allow for the completion of the paneling at the top by the return of its framing elements, the painted section of the walls was *ca.* 1.75 m. high. Above this there was probably a molding, for which 25 cm. can be allowed, and above this, in turn, a blank zone comparable to the plinth at the bottom, for which any figure up to 1.00 m. would be entirely appropriate. The approximate maximum figure is derived from the presumed proportions of the doorway between Room 16 and the south portico, which was 2.14 m. wide and would have been 3.75 m. high if its proportions were identical with those of the doorway between Room 18 and the east portico (see p. 123).

Rooms 15, 16, and 17 came to light. The first was the discovery at the south end of the west portico of pieces of two stone piers carved on the front with attached Ionic colonnettes and provided at the back with projecting tongues (Plan XIV 14). The tongues indicate that the piers were meant to be set into a wall and thus suggest that they belong to the decor, perhaps to the window frames, of an upper story.[6] The second token is the character and structural history of the adjacent Rooms 13*a* and 13, which are best explained on the assumption that respectively they housed the stairway and provided the landing by which a second story was reached (see p. 131). The third token is the fact that the fill was deeper over Rooms 15, 16, and 17 than it was at any other part of the site and contained whole sections of mud-brick walls still cohering but manifestly displaced from above. Being still quite solid, these sections would appear to have fallen not as the result of gradual disintegration due to exposure but rather as the result of violent removal of the beams of an upper story.

The group of rooms occupying the sheltered southwest corner of the Villa (Rooms 9–14) formed the residential suite of the owner. Well developed and appointed, the apartment was accessible through doorways in the terminal walls of the west and south porticoes. These gave on a small peristyle court (Room 11) measuring 8.15 m. from east to west and 7.20 m. from north to south (Pls. XXIII *D* and XXIV *A*). In the middle of this court was a shallow plastered water basin (2.80 m. square and 30 cm. deep) framed by heavy stones molded at the interior with an appropriate cavetto between fillets. The rim stones provided the emplacement at the four corners for octagonal plinths on which were mounted columns with Ionic bases (see Plan XIV 11 and p. 221). The columns supported the compluviate roof that left the pool open to the sky. The rain water drained from the roof into the pool, whence it was conducted by a drain to a cistern some 5 meters deep and about 1.20 m. in diameter located just inside the east entrance to the court. At some period, presumably

[6] A similar example of this type of pier (1.90 m. high) is preserved in the Tolmeita Museum. The excavation of the Public Building yielded another incomplete example (Plan XVIII 1). Pesce (*Il "Palazzo della Colonne,"* Pl. V) shows similar features in the southern face of the upper order of the Grand Peristyle of the "Palazzo," using stones found in the excavations, albeit with Corinthian colonnettes.

during the regular use of the Villa, channels were cut into the rim of the basin and into the sills of the doorways to the north and east to drain rain water from the south and west porticoes into the basin. The mouth of the cistern was covered by a heavy perforated stone slab supporting a simply modeled puteal 55 cm. high and 57 cm. in diameter (Fig. 47) through which water could be drawn up for domestic use or to replenish the contents of the pool when its drain was closed.

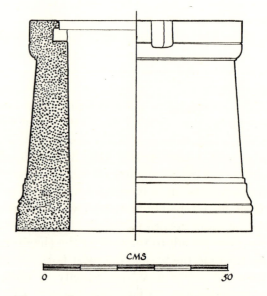

CMS

0   50

Fig. 47.—Section of Puteal in Room 11 of Villa. *G. R. H. Wright*

Columns and inclosing walls of the court were plastered and simply painted and the floor was paved with becoming mosaics (see pp. 228 and 241). The court originally had four doorways in addition to those in the terminal walls of the west and south porticoes, two to the south, one to the north, and one toward the west. The doorway to the north, giving on Room 9, was found blocked up. The court had been plastered several times, and the plastering over this opening was continuous in its later stages. Hence the change was made during the life of the Villa. All doorways into and out of the court had sockets for doorposts. The west doorway led into the oecus or, better, the diwan of the suite (Room 12), a room 6.55 m. wide and 5.05 m. deep, whose west wall was the outer wall of the house. Here the wall decoration was more elaborate (pp. 228–30), and the arrangement of the mosaic floor patterns suggested the emplacement of a couch or cushioned

Fig. 48.—Reconstruction of Colonnaded Entrance to Room 14 of Villa. *G. R. H. Wright*

seats along the west wall, facing the doorway and the court (see pp. 241–42).

Adjoining the diwan at the north was Room 10 (5.30 × 5.50 m.), elegantly decorated (see p. 230) and accessible only from the diwan through a doorway 1.28 m. wide (Pl. XXIV *C*). This was in all probability the bedroom of the apartment. Its paving consisted only of mortar mixed with a copious supply of pebbles, which would suggest that the floor was normally covered with mats or rugs.

South of the diwan, at the extreme southwest corner of the Villa, the suite included a dining room (Room 14), particularly elegant in its appoint-

ments. It was one step up from the diwan, the step being the stylobate of a colonnaded entrance that left the entire north side of the room open (Fig. 48). The bases of the columns (see Plan XIV 10) and terminal piers were found *in situ*. One voussoir of the central archway (Pl. XXVII *C* and Fig. 49) and an entablature block (Pl. XXVII *A*) from one of the trabeated lateral passages came to light in the fill nearby. On the well carved decor of the voussoir clear indications of the bright colors applied to the colonnade were still preserved (see pp. 222 and 226).

In its final form Room 14 measured 4 meters from north to south, counting from the inner

9

(south) face of the stylobate, and about 4.80 m. from east to west. But the east wall had at one time been reinforced to the extent of about 20 cm., so that the original east-west dimension was closer to 5 meters. A suggestion concerning the occasion for the reinforcement is offered below in connection with the discussion of the adjacent Room 13*a*. Plaster and paint could be seen to have been applied to the east wall twice before and twice after its reinforcement. On the south wall remains

walled up. In the original construction there was also a doorway (1.30 m. wide) providing access from Room 9 northward to the corridor (Room 8) leading to the kitchen of the Villa (Room 7) and to a door in the west exterior wall (see Fig. 43). This second doorway likewise had been blocked up. The location of Room 9, a scant 3 meters wide and some 5.90 m. long, suggests that it was intended for the use of servants. The fact that the east half of the room, set off by a row of stones, was paved,

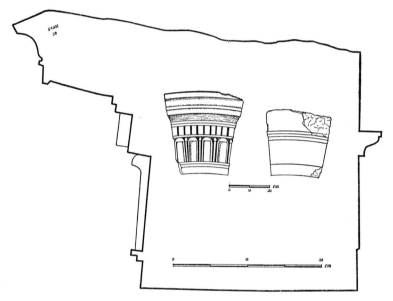

Fig. 49.—Voussoir from Colonnaded Entrance to Room 14 of Villa.
G. R. H. Wright

of four layers of painted plaster, one directly on top of another, came to light. After its reinforcement the east wall covered a strip of the plain border of the floor mosaic, whose organization and emblema clearly indicate the purpose which the room served (see pp. 242–44).

The rooms to the north and south of the court (Room 11), namely Rooms 9, 13, and 13*a*, had none of the elegance visible in the rest of the apartment. Their floors were devoid of mosaic paving, and the plaster still adhering to the footings of their walls was bare of all indications of colored decoration. They therefore were either service quarters or purely utilitarian as to function.

Room 9, to the north of the court, was connected with the west portico by a doorway 1.10 m. wide, but this had been cut through the stone footing of the portico wall and was therefore secondary. In all likelihood it was introduced when the doorway connecting Room 9 directly with the court was

like the bedroom of the apartment (Room 10), with mortar and pebbles suggests that the domestics who were in immediate service to the owner of the Villa slept here. They could thus be summoned at all times by the occupants of the apartment.

The two rooms at the south of the court (Rooms 13 and 13*a*) were of about the same size (3.50 × 3.35 m. and 3.80 × *ca.* 3.45 m. respectively), the construction of their north, east, and west walls corresponding to that used throughout the rest of the Villa. These walls, therefore, were about 50 cm. thick and were all properly footed on a socle of squared stones. The east wall of Room 13, which was simultaneously the west wall of Room 15, had been broken apart, and elements of its socle had been displaced (see p. 127). Both rooms had been plastered, but the surface of the plaster was rough and showed no traces of paint. Extra layers of plaster inside the core of the wall between Rooms 13*a* and 14 showed that it had been reinforced to the extent of 30 cm. toward the interior of Room 13a quite as it had been reinforced toward the interior of Room 14. This structural peculiarity requires some explanation, and it is suggested that Room 13a served as the well of a wooden staircase whose beams by their thrust had caused the west wall of the room to buckle, thus requiring its reinforcement. If Room 13a served as a stairwell, the roof of Room 13 could have provided the landing from which the second story over Rooms 15, 16, and 17 was entered. At court level Room 13 could have served any number of useful household purposes.

Rooms 13, 13a, and 14 were not inclosed at the south by the Villa's own exterior wall, the one delimiting Rooms 15, 16, 17, and 19 at the south. This wall, as we have seen, stopped at the west end of Room 15, where it turned north to inclose the suite giving on the south portico. Instead, Rooms 13, 13a, and 14 were inclosed at the south by a wall beginning at the street on the east side of the Villa and continuing in a straight line about 10 cm. behind the south wall of Rooms 15, 16, 17, and 19 to the street on the west side of the Villa. This second wall was the north wall of the next dwelling to the south. Since Rooms 13, 13a, and 14 were built directly against the exterior wall of another establishment, the latter would necessarily be earlier than the Villa.

The wall in question began at the street to the east with a typical low socle of heavy well laid stones supporting a mud-brick superstructure. Where its northern face was exposed behind Rooms 13a and 14 (see Pls. XXIII D and XXIV A) the stone socle rose to a height of slightly more than 2 meters above the floor level of Room 14 and consisted of three elements. The lowest element was an uneven layer of uncut stones. The second was of squared but uncoursed stones so laid as to give a level footing for the third element, the socle proper, which consisted of heavy squared blocks laid horizontally, vertically on their long sides, and vertically on their ends. Slablike blocks preserved at the top of the wall behind Room 14 (see Pl. XXIII D) suggest that the socle is here preserved to its full height. In the Villa similar slabs were found crowning the socle of the east wall of Room 9, for example, and can be seen on Plate XXIV C below cornice blocks placed upon them by the expedition for storage and display. The relative heights of the two lower elements of the

wall behind Rooms 13, 13a and 14 vary, the lowest element becoming increasingly higher toward the west end of the wall. Behind Room 13 the masonry of this wall had been disturbed, and a flight of two steps led down from it into Room 13 (see Pl. XXIV A), as mentioned above (p. 127). Excavations were therefore extended into the area south of the wall, to ascertain whether some organic relation might have existed or have been developed between it and the Villa. Parts of two rooms (A and B) were exposed here (Fig. 50), both with remains of

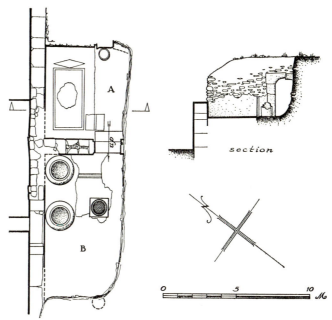

Fig. 50.—EXCAVATION PLAN OF ROOMS A AND B OF DWELLING ADJOINING VILLA AT SOUTH. *J. E. Knudstad*

mosaic paving (see p. 248). The base and lower drums of a corner column were still standing in their original position in Room B. The second element of the shaft bears an inscription (p. 209, No. 2) that had been covered with plaster. The inscription faces the open (west) interior of the room. Circular gaps in the paving of Room B suggested the emplacement of large vessels (see Pl. XXIV B). A step leads down from Room B to Room A, where remains of a plastered pier and a plastered arch came to light at the eastern limit of the excavation, but their meaning remains obscure (see Fig. 50, sectional elevation).

Several points were established by this supplementary clearance. Most important is the fact that the end of the north-south wall between Rooms A and B is immediately south of the center of the Villa's Room 13, so that there was no space here for a passageway providing an organic connection between the two parts of the insula. The steps leading up from Room 13 to the adjoining premises must have been contrived after the walls of the latter had been breached, in the period of the squatters. A Byzantine water jar standing on a deposit of debris about 20 cm. above the floor level of Room *A* (see Pl. XXIV *B*) gave indication of this period in the use of the premises. Indeed, the steps from Room 13 were contrived with the help of stones taken from the socle of the breached exterior wall. The supplementary clearance also revealed that in the area behind Room 13 the floor level in the adjoining house was almost 2 meters higher than that of the Villa. The difference in level must have been proportionately greater in the area behind Room 14. The change in level was, of course, due to the natural inclination of the ground northward and westward. The builder of the house in the center of the insula, in order to maintain his own floor level, had necessarily to raise it above surface level at the north end of his establishment and to make allowance also for the possibility that anyone building on the premises subsequently occupied by the Villa might, in order to maintain floor level there, begin on a plane well below ground level. This would explain the extra depth given to the foundations of the wall behind Rooms 13, 13*a* and 14 and would suggest why the builders of the Villa did not continue its own exterior wall west of Room 15. They had an existing solid masonry wall against which to abut the party walls of Rooms 13, 13*a*, and 14. These rooms were the more spacious because they extended to the very limits of the Villa property. The fact that the mosaics of Rooms *A* and *B* were roughly of the same period as those of the Villa suggests that the house to the south is not much earlier than the Villa. Thus it was unnecessary to dig below floor level in Rooms *A* and *B* to ascertain whether at an earlier date the relation between Room 13 and the adjacent area was any different.

The rooms along the west portico (Rooms 5–8), even though they include two of the most elegant chambers of the entire Villa, can be dealt with more succinctly, since they pose no archeological problems. Room 8 (*ca.* 8.50 × 1 27 m.) was only a corridor leading to a doorway that communicated with the street to the west (see Fig. 43). The doorway has disappeared along with all but the footing of the exterior west wall from the southwest corner

of Room 14 to Room 6. A step at the east end of the corridor led down to the west portico. As we have seen, the doorway connecting the corridor with Room 9 was found blocked up. Still open was the doorway (originally 1.10 m. wide but subsequently reduced to *ca.* 65 cm.) connecting it with Room 7. No pavement and no traces of plastering were found in the corridor.

Room 7 (*ca.* 8.50 × 3.17 m.) was unadorned and served as the kitchen of the Villa, as shown by the installations along its north wall (see Pl. XXIV *D*), which had undergone long usage and repair. A rectangle of stones 2.15 m. long and projecting 1.30 m. from the face of the wall probably supported a slab that formed either a table or, if the slab was perforated, a stand for wine amphorae. Alongside it to the west was an area paved with mortar mixed with crushed brick. It was 1.30 m. long and projected from the wall up to about 1.65 m. at the outermost limit of the arc which its southern side described. This area had been covered with additional layers of mortar and crushed brick on several occasions. Its purpose was revealed by the installation alongside it to the west. Here there was another area paved with layers of mortar and crushed brick, but the paving had a trough 60 cm. wide at the base of the wall. Across this trough were set at regular intervals stones (*ca.* 20 cm. high) that projected from the wall about 1.20 m. Three such stones found in position at intervals of 70 cm. The arrangement suggests an open range with fire troughs over which meat could be roasted. The ends of the spits or grills would have rested on the stones set across the fire troughs. The paved area between this installation and the "table" could then be interpreted as the chopping block on which the carcass of the animal was laid to be cut into pieces for roasting. In the later history of the building a similarly paved area was provided at the west end of the room in front of the "range." A stone hollowed out at the top to serve as a mortar was found in the debris nearby, as were a number of jawbones which upon examination proved to be of domestic pigs.

The installations in the kitchen as interpreted above suggest provisions for feeding large groups of diners, and that such groups were on occasion entertained on the premises is clearly indicated by Room 6 (see Pl. XXIV *D*), the largest of all the chambers of the Villa (11.45 × *ca.* 8.50 m.). Two doorways led into it from the west portico, one at either end of the room and each 1.15 m. wide. The composition of its pavement of mosaics and *opus sectile* showed beyond doubt that the room served as a public banquet hall (see pp. 244–45). Quantities of painted plaster from its walls were found in the fill, but the walls were not preserved to a sufficient height to give an idea of the scheme of decoration.

That the next chamber to the north (Room 5) was also a dining room was obvious from the organization and nature of its mosaic pavement, the most elegant in the Villa (see pp. 245–46). The room (6.90 m. × 8.60 m.) was entered from the west portico through a doorway (3.90 m. wide) with folding leaves, whose sockets and lock-bar holes were carved in a step leading down from the level of the portico. The width of the doorway and the position of the room suggest that it served as a summer dining room on formal occasions. That Room 5 continued in use even after the Villa as a whole was abandoned and the looting of its structural elements had begun is indicated by a heavy layer of mortar on its walls, under which elements of the original decoration are preserved (see p. 231). The purpose of this mortar coating remains obscure. Continued use of the room is suggested also by the emplacement of crude rim stones above and around the mouth of an underground cistern (see Pl. LX *A*) whose cover had once been imbedded in the mosaic pavement, as the arrangement of its border indicates (see Fig. 70). Connected with the continued use of the room is no doubt also the perforation of one of the stones in the north wall, near its eastern end and approximately at floor level. Perhaps the area of Room 5 was taken over by one of the adjacent shops as they expanded (see p. 135) and used henceforth as a terrace for collecting rain water in winter and for serving simple meals in summer.

Along the north portico and presumably also in the northeast corner of the Villa were situated the elements of its bath, an installation of modest proportions. Best preserved is the steam room or caldarium (Room 1), which was entered from the northward extension of the east portico through a well framed doorway 2.05 m. wide (see Fig. 43). It was a rectangular chamber (5.00 m. × 8.35 m.) with a stilted apse (4.25 m. in diameter) at its western end (Pl. XXV *A*). Elements of rubble representing the base of the semidome of the apse were found in place at the top of the apse wall. The fact that this wall was preserved to a height

of 2.40 m. above floor level made it possible to observe here a type of wall construction not otherwise evident. Whereas in the large rectangular part of the caldarium the walls had only the socle built of well dressed blocks laid in courses, the construction of the apse involved also the erection of masonry piers set on the socle. The piers were joined together at the top by a single course of masonry and the spaces between them were filled with masses of rubble laid in mortar (see Pl. XXV *A*). Some of the rubble masses were found *in situ*, and one came to light high in the fill slightly to the south. The removal of some of the masses gives the impression that the room had window-like openings, which would, of course, be out of the question in a caldarium. This type of wall construction may have been somewhat unusual but can readily be explained as a corollary, wherever optimum wall strength was desired or required, to the use of mud brick above stone footings elsewhere in the Villa. Moreover, the use of rubble filling reduced the amount of work required of skilled stonecutters.

Heating flues from the furnaces, in Room 24 (see p. 135), came up in channels set into the east wall of the caldarium on either side of its doorway. The main supply of heated air entered under the floor, which was set on piers of round tiles in normal hypocaust fashion. The *suspensura* extended along the sides of the room, leaving a solid masonry pier (2 m. square) in the middle, and continued to the very end of the apse. Outside the caldarium, at the end of the apse at floor level, was found the position of the flue by which the heated air left the hypocaust and by which the draft bringing it from the furnaces was established. In its course toward the exhaust flue the heated air passed the upper part of a cistern (*ca.* 7.00 m. deep) that was basically related to the caldarium, as indicated by the borders of the mosaic paving (see p. 247). It no doubt had a simple circular cover seated in a squared slab set flush with the paving and must have supplied the needs of the bathers. Whence it derived its supply of water remains obscure.

In the period during which the Villa was being looted and occupied here and there by squatters, the caldarium saw both use and abuse. The emblema adorning the mosaics in the area of the solidly footed central section of the room was removed (see p. 247). The cistern was supplied with a raised wellhead of crudely cut stones, and at the south side of the apse an oven was constructed of tiles taken from the *suspensura*. The solidity of its construction and lumps of slag with rounded bottoms found in the fill over the north end of the peristyle court and its porticoes suggest that the oven was used to melt metal looted from the Villa and its vicinity. The floor of the hypocaust was broken almost everywhere except in the apse, owing no doubt to the weight of the fill above it. It had subsided irregularly save over the central pier where the emblema had been removed. The north wall of the room had a 3-meter gap in it, created no doubt to permit access to the cistern and oven in later times.

The caldarium is but one of the rooms of a typical bath. Though a private bathing establishment could not be expected to provide all the installations familiar from the large public baths, at least a room for ablutions with cold water after the use of the steam room must have been available. This room, the frigidarium, should be located in proximity to the caldarium. In spite of careful search we found no chamber with traces of a built-in plunge or pool in the Villa, perhaps because of the looting of the whole northeast portion of the building but more likely because simpler installations served the same purpose. These could have been the traditional large cauldrons or basins from which water was dipped by hand or freestanding movable tubs. Baked-clay tubs have been found, for example at Thera, whose shape is duplicated in stone in the Ritual Baths at Cyrene.[7]

The only room of the Villa which seems properly placed to provide for such cold ablutions is the poorly preserved Room 20 (8.30 × 4.20 m.) at the extreme northeast corner of the buiding. The northeast corner of the room is fixed by the foundations of the exterior wall of the Villa at the corner of the insula and its western limit by a spur of the wall that divided it from Room 24. At its south end, by good fortune, where a stone sill marks the northern end of the east portico, a section of its mosaic paving (*ca.* 1.30 m. long) was preserved. The fact that, as in the caldarium, the mosaic design was executed with tesserae of more than two colors and contained fields proper for the development of emblemata suggests that the

room had a special purpose and hence was part of the bath (see p. 247). Indeed, the design of the mosaics was such as to have permitted the emplacement of movable tubs. The drain of which traces were found at the north end of the east portico may have continued under Room 20 to carry off water from there as well as from the court.

The rest of the northern part of the Villa was devoted to service quarters and a row of four shops. The rooms were at lower levels here as a result of the single plane in which everything south of the caldarium had been kept by the architect (see Plan XIII). Construction was commonly either rudely simple or downright shoddy, largely because the original walls had been pulled about and replaced by jerry-built successors in the course of centuries of reuse (Pl. XXV *C*). Occupation of the premises apparently continued in this area long after the Villa proper had been abandoned, with the shopkeepers absorbing into their establishments serviceable areas and rooms behind their shops.

The service entrance to the Villa we have assumed was through Room 21 (2.15 m. × 4.30 m.), which is to be understood as either a vestibule or an areaway that may well have been open to the sky. Its boundaries are fixed on all four sides. The east wall is of solid construction and continues the line of the west wall of Room 24, which begins at the caldarium (Room 1) though only the base course remains at this point. The south wall also is built of heavy stones, one of them cut with an offset. Because of its position at the east end of the wall we regard it as reused rather than as an indication of a doorway. The west wall is of lighter construction, though a full 60 cm. thick, and was in the subsequent reuse of the area continued over the exterior wall of the Villa into the street to the north. Near its southern end two heavy stones set vertically mark the position of a doorway (80 cm. wide) giving on Room 22 (see Fig. 43). The top of a cistern, over 6 meters deep and later covered by a large stone with a curved face, lies almost directly in front of this doorway. It is this that suggests that the area was not roofed but collected the water from the adjacent roofs.

The existence of Room 22 is largely conjectural. All we have to go on is the east-west wall that begins as the north boundary of Room 24 and must originally have extended across the entire Villa, running parallel to its exterior north wall. A stub of the foundation of this wall is visible along

[7] See Wiegand and Schrader, *Priene*, p. 318 and Fig. 362; G. R. H. Wright, "Cyrene: A survey of certain rock-cut features to the south of the Sanctuary of Apollo," *JHS* LXXVII (1957) 301–10, esp. Figs. 6 and 8.

the south side of the projected room. Another basis for the conjecture is the existence of a doorway leading from the street at the north to what we designate Shop I. If we reconstruct this shop on the analogy of the adjacent Shop II, there remains sufficient space between it and Room 21 for Room 22 and for the right-angle turns in the typical means of ingress that Room 22 would supply in order to shield the interior of the Villa from the gaze of passersby. Room 22 so delineated (2.35 × 4.30 m). would have been occupied by a guard watching over the service entrance.

If the conjectured Room 22 existed, access must have been provided from it to the rooms along the north side of the caldarium (Room 1) and of the summer dining room (Room 5). Our plan (Fig. 43) shows hypothetical doorways leading to the rooms lying eastward, namely Rooms 24 and 25. Both of these rooms are clearly outlined by remains of wall foundations. Room 24 (*ca.* 3.60 m. square), the furnace room of the caldarium, contained at the south two large clay-lined furnaces (95 and 80 cm. in diameter) that curved inward at the top (Pl. XXV *B*). Tile pipes leading into them from the north provided the draft for the fires. The heated air was conducted by flues into the hypocaust under the caldarium. The flues had disappeared from Room 24, together with the upper parts of the furnaces, but sections of flues came to light in the east wall of the caldarium (see p. 133). It is only logical to suppose that Room 25 (3.60 × 4.30 m.) was functionally related to the furnace room. Definite traces of its walls remain on all sides. It may have provided quarters for the servants who tended the furnaces or storage space for the material used in firing. Some 2.15 m. west of Room 24 the footing of a north-south wall came to light, extending from the south end of the west wall of Room 21 to the break in the north wall of Room 1. But the nature of the footing and the fact that it does not parallel the other, more solid, walls in the area suggest that it represents the reuse of the area in the period during which the shops absorbed the adjacent areas of the Villa.

The existence of Shops II–IV is clearly indicated, and we have conjectured Shop I because of a doorway in the exterior north wall of the Villa (see Fig. 43). The hypothetical Shop I has the same depth (4.30 m.) as Shops II–IV and a width of about 6 meters. Shop II (5.50 m. wide) may eventually have been extended to Room 1, with

a depth of about 7.70 m., as suggested by the late wall west of Room 24 (see above). Shop III was 3.90 m. wide. In Shop IV, at the corner, the original width of about 3.90 m. was reduced to about 3.40 by the erection of a crude wall inside it along the west, when the exterior west wall of the Villa was looted (Pl. XXV *D*). Only Shop II had any installations, but their purpose is not clear. Three circular basins with maximum diameter and depth of about 60 cm., rounded at the bottom and constructed of mortar, were set into the floor, two in the southwest corner and one in the southeast corner near the south wall. The easternmost, which was also the shallowest, was set in crude mortar paving about a meter square. In addition the shop had two deep (*ca.* 75 cm.) rectangular basins (120 × 80 and 80 × 45 cm.) along the west wall, their openings flush with the probable floor. Shop IV yielded one object worthy of note, a clay pilgrim flask from the shrine of St. Menas in Egypt.[8] If the building across the street from the Villa to the north (No. 6 on Plan XXII) is a church, as has been suggested above (p. 100), the shop conveniently located with reference to it may in Christian times have sold religious goods to the faithful.

The east-west wall that separated the shops from the Villa proper (see Plan XII), like the exterior walls of the entire establishment, was built of large blocks set on a horizontally laid base course. Behind Shop IV this wall had been broken through forcibly, a crude doorway providing access to Room 4 of the Villa. The latter thus became eventually the back room of the shop. The same thing seems to have happened in the case of Shop III and Room 3, where the wall was reduced to its base course and one stone of the next higher course. If the disappearance of all but the foundations of the wall behind Shops I and II is any criterion, the latter eventually became even more possessive of the adjacent parts of the Villa. These encroachments, of course, represent the period of looting and of occupation by squatters.

As for Rooms 3 and 4, their masonry as found has in general the character of the Villa's own construction, save that after the Villa's exterior west wall was looted the owner of Shop IV rebuilt it in the manner of the day. Room 3 (5.30 × 3.50 m.) was entered through a doorway (90 cm. wide) near

[8] Cf. K. M. Kaufmann, *Die Menasstadt* I (Leipzig, 1910) Pls. 90–100.

the north end of its east wall and was connected with Room 4 by a doorway (90 cm. wide) near the south end of its west wall. At the south was a raised area paved with a mixture of mortar and pebbles, such as was found in Rooms 9 and 10. It may have provided the emplacement for pallets on which servants slept. Eventually, however, it was used as a hearth. Room 4, entered only from Room 3, had in its floor immediately in front of the doorway a rectangular basin (65 × 50 cm. and 50 cm. deep) and along its south wall four troughs (*ca.* 1.00 × 0.65–1.20 m. and *ca.* 50 cm. deep). Their function is unknown, and whether they were contemporary with the Villa or with the reuse of the room by the owner of Shop IV is impossible to say. Yet it must be presumed that Rooms 3 and 4 formed part of the service quarters of the Villa, not only because they were at a lower level than Room 5 but also because entry to them was presumably from the service area farther to the east.

Eastward of Rooms 3 and 4 sizable sections of walls had apparently been removed in their entirety, probably so that looters could remove building stones quarried from the caldarium and the rooms along the west portico. Thus it is difficult to interpret the area immediately west of the caldarium, which we designate as Room 2 (see Plan XII and Fig. 43). The area was 5.30 m. wide and measured 3.30 m. to the crown of the arc described by the apse of the caldarium. Its south wall was defined by the north portico and a portion of its west wall by the west portico. There was a door opening in each of these walls. The one to the south was found blocked up. From the one to the west two steps led down into Room 2. Beginning at the foot of these steps the floor was paved with mortar in which were set six circular storage vats lined with mortar and reinforced on the outside with small undressed stones. The vats were about 75 cm. deep and had openings about 65 cm. in diameter. They were not symmetrically distributed but were of one construction with the paving. The center vat of the eastern row had been damaged at the top by the construction or repair of the flue which exhausted the hot air from the *suspensura* of the caldarium. All six vats were filled with dirt and debris which was indistinguishable from the fill over the rest of the area.

Whether Room 2 was inclosed at the northwest as indicated on our plans is difficult to say. All

that remains along the north is what seems to be a doorsill with a step, plus two additional stones, suggesting the existence of the proposed north wall. At the west, however, the head of a driven well lies just north of the place where the north and east walls of the west portico met and where the west wall of Room 2 should continue to join the supposed north wall (see Plan XII). The well had an internal diameter of about a meter and was no less than 21 meters deep, going down therefore almost exactly to sea level. It was found plugged at the top with an inverted column base (Pl. XXVII D). It was free of all refuse and contained about 5 meters of water when it was opened. It is difficult to imagine that the creation of such a well, involving as it did great effort and expense, preceded the development of the Villa or, if it did, that the builders of the Villa would have eliminated such a precious source of water by building a wall over it. It is just as difficult to imagine that the well was driven after the Villa was abandoned. Rather, the well must either have been dug as a part of the program for the building of the Villa—and a long difficult job it must have been—or else it was driven during the occupation of the Villa and represents an expensive solution of a serious problem of water shortage. In the first instance the area which we call Room 2 cannot originally have been inclosed at the northwest, though it might have been inclosed after the abandonment of the Villa. In the second instance it might have been inclosed at the outset, then opened to the north and west, and finally inclosed again. In any event, the storage vats must have served to contain and make immediately accessible water drawn from the well.

Of the rooms at the north end of the Villa only Room 23 remains to be mentioned. As found, this dog-legged area (*ca.* 16.60 m. long and *ca.* 3.35 m. wide) was devoid of any traces of construction or flooring. Indeed, where it adjoined Room 22 and Shop I its northern limit could not be fixed save by inference. We have therefore interpreted this area in accordance with its shape as an unroofed corridor leading from the service rooms at the east (Rooms 21, 24, 25) to the service rooms at the west (Rooms 3 and 4) and to the western portion of the Villa. It may well have provided, at a level below that of the residential part of the Villa proper, means of storage as well as of communication for the service staff.

Having thus described the Villa as excavation

revealed it, we now turn to the question of date. The wall paintings provide the widest latitude for the dating of the structure. As indicated below in full detail (pp. 232–36), the system of decoration applied to the building at the outset is tectonic in origin and reflects a form of construction in which marble slabs were set upright into a given wall between narrow masonry piers. This type of construction is here imitated in plaster and paint, taking the form of a three-zone decorative system whose closest analogies are found in the wall paintings of Italy and Sicily that mark the transition to the so-called "Second Pompeian Style." Judged by its wall decoration the Villa could therefore be as old as the early part of the first century B.C., when the Second Style began to emerge. However, the upper limit for a date determined by wall decoration alone has necessarily to be left wide open, since the same system was used in successive redecorations until the abandonment of the building, presumably after the period of Gordian III as suggested by the coins.

Similar, but slightly more sharply defined, are the chronological limits that can be inferred from the character of the architectural decor used in the construction of the Villa. The Rhodian peristyle, with its unfluted Ionic columns and its entablature containing a Doric frieze, represents a *koiné* of usage typical in the eastern Mediterranean in the late Hellenistic period. However, in its application to provincial domestic architecture the upper limits of this usage cannot be fixed save in the most general terms. These terms are implied on the one hand by the development of a new architectural mode in North Africa in the Severan period and on the other hand by the substitution of the fortified dwelling for the expansive villa of the earlier and politically more stable age. While the peristyle thus allows for a relatively open time perspective upon the construction of the Villa and while the *naiskos* in the court may actually have been built or modified in the Severan period (see pp. 224–25), there are other features that point to a relatively early period. Such are the colonnaded entrance to Room 14 and the frame of the formal entrance to the peristyle court, leading from the vestibule (Room 18) to the east portico (see p. 221). The latter in particular, with the diverging moldings of its jambs, the inclination of its soffit, and the opposed bevel of its guttae, represents sophisticated illusionistic architectural drafting

and stonecutting that cannot wisely be dissociated from the period of the Second Style.

It is clear that the mosaic tradition of the Villa is firmly rooted in a phase of mosaic development in which geometric design still played the major role and was supplemented only by simple and occasional emblemata (see pp. 256–63). It is also clear, however, that the repertoire of design had grown since the days of the pebble mosaics and that color effects had begun to play a part. But there was still no real attempt to create the element of depth perspective nor a tendency to play with color and mass in such a way as to create designs that could be read differently from different angles. More particularly, the repertory of design contains as important and frequently used items forms, such as the four-pointed star, which elsewhere were discontinued in the second century of our era and does not contain forms, such as the acanthus rinceau, which became prominent in that century. From the point of view of the handling of the emblemata also, for instance those representing the Four Seasons, a date in the first century of our era seems most appropriate to the body of the mosaic material.

The coin yield of the Villa is significant for dating in several particulars. A well attested series of Roman imperial issues that continues without a significant break from Trajan through Gordian III testifies to the main *floruit* of the building (see p. 265). For its construction, however, a smaller group of coins, from strategic locations, has greater evidential value. This group contains several small Ptolemaic bronzes, suggesting that when the Villa was built Ptolemaic bronze was still in common use for the "small change" that was always in greatest immediate demand. The appearance of single pieces of Tiberius and Domitian(?) as the earliest Roman issues to be associated with the Ptolemaic bronzes would seem to reflect the currency situation of the first century of our era, more particularly that preceding the reign of Trajan and following the reign of Tiberius (see pp. 266–67).

Sculptures, pottery, and other movable finds provide no testimony that bears upon the date of the Villa. But there is another approach to the question of date, namely the relation between the Villa and the house adjacent to it at the south. Excavation made it clear that Rooms 14, 13*a*, and 13 of the Villa were built directly against the northern exterior wall of the adjacent house, proving that the Villa was later in construction than its neighbor. The partial clearance of two rooms of the adjacent building yielded a column stub still in its original position upon which was inscribed a text with the date formula "year 15" (p. 209, No. 2). Since the era is that of Actium, the date of the inscription is 17/16 B.C., which is necessarily a *terminus ante quem* for the construction of the house in which it was found. The Villa, therefore, was necessarily built later than 17/16 B.C.

The only text that can be associated directly with the Villa itself is inscribed upon a cippus which stands outside the doorway leading from the street into the vestibule (Room 18). The text is interpreted as honoring the Roman imperial family (the οἶκος), its closest datable parallels coming from Asia Minor and belonging to the period of Nero (see p. 209, No. 1).

On the basis of the several types of evidence available it seems quite certain that the Villa represents the early Roman Empire. A date in the first century of our era appears thoroughly reasonable, and the third quarter of the century would seem most likely to satisfy the demands of all categories of information. But the possibility of construction in the second quarter should not on that account be ruled out entirely.

We turn now, finally, to consideration of the subsequent fortunes of the Villa. During its *floruit*, fixed by the coins as extending through the reign of Gordian III, the building was maintained with some care. Evidence is provided not only by the repeated replastering and redecoration of the two public dining rooms (Rooms 5 and 6) and the private residential suite (especially Rooms 10, 12, and 14) but also by the strengthening of the wall between Rooms 13a and 14, by the relocation of the doorway to Room 9 (which certainly made the room less drafty and more livable for the servants who used it), and by the channels cut to drain rain water from the south and west porticoes into the basin in Room 11.

Why regular occupancy of the Villa should have ceased in the third century, as the coins suggest, is of course unknown. There was, as the mosaics of the west portico and Room 11 show, a period during which no attempt was made to counter the effects of continuous usage. But, except for what can be inferred from the economic plight of the Empire in general and from the disturbances caused by tribal raids from the interior, there is nothing

with which we can, at the present state of our knowledge of the history of the city and of the Villa itself, associate so specific an event. There are no indications, in the architectural decor at least, of an earthquake. For whatever reason, the Villa was no longer a well kept private residence in the period that began with Diocletian, when Ptolemais became the metropolis of Libya Pentapolis. This does not mean that the four shops along its northern end were abandoned nor that all residence within its confines ended when the Villa ceased to be maintained as a single private dwelling.

The period of maintenance was followed by a twilight period in which the property was simultaneously subject to disintegration and looting on the one hand and to partial occupation by squatters or low-rental tenants on the other. The process of looting and disintegration apparently began with the lifting of marble paving and mosaic emblemata and with the removal of valuable roof timbers. The looting of the timbers in particular was an essential preliminary to the disintegration of the mud-brick walls whose substance now began to form an ever-deepening deposit over much of the site. At the southern end the removal not only of the roof beams but of the floor joists of the second story may have caused entire sections of the walls of the upper rooms to slither down into Rooms 15, 16, and 17, where they were found with rows of bricks still cohering. From the area thus being covered with a heavy sticky deposit of disintegrating mud brick we need to exempt the entire northern end of the site, Rooms 18, 19, and 13 at the south, and for a while at least the east portico.

What was going on in these portions of the site varied according to circumstances. At the north the picture is particularly clear. Here occupation continued, the shops expanding and using the adjacent chambers as back rooms. The rough curb stones set about the cistern heads in Rooms 1 and 5 and the "plug" set into the head of the driven well at the western limit of the area of Room 2 show that the facilities for storing and obtaining water continued to be guarded, drainage being now in all probability from the roofs of the enlarged shops. The association of Room 5 with one or another of the shops, whether as a summer dining terrace or for the airing and drying of materials processed in the troughs of Room 4, is indicated by the heavy mortar coating applied to its walls and by the circular aperture cut through a stone of its north wall approximately at floor level, through which surplus rain water could be conducted to cisterns and tubs in the area of the shops. The shops continued in use well into the Byzantine period, as copious fragments of ribbed pottery and the pilgrim flask from the shrine of St. Menas indicate. It should not be supposed, of course, that the reused rooms of the Villa were kept in any sort of repair. The crude curb stones set around the cistern heads in Rooms 1 and 5 suggest that the floors were already covered with an equally thick deposit of earth. The oven built in Room 1 suggests a smelting establishment, whose slag was found in the lower part of the fill over the north end of the court and in its porticoes. The deep fill in which the shops and adjacent parts of the Villa were finally buried late in the Byzantine period consisted of loose earth and stones, not of the thick sticky mass representing disintegrated mud bricks.

At the south end of the Villa, deposits of ashes in Room 18 testify to its use by squatters sometime during the twilight period and also no doubt to the use of Room 19. Room 13 was at this time connected with the adjacent dwelling to the south, itself also in ruins.

About the east portico we know only that after the removal of its paving the area served as a dump for domestic refuse of all kinds—broken pottery, random animal bones, scrap metal, etc. Whether this came from the squatters or from the shops or both or from the outside is impossible to say.

This intermediate period of disintegration and elementary looting paired with partial usage by shopkeepers, smelters, and squatters led into the final period in the history of the Villa, when it served as a quarry. Heavy building materials were now sought after, and virtually all the cornice and architrave blocks and column capitals together with the better part of the column drums, the door trim, and most of the dressed-stone footing of the exterior walls were removed from the site. Clearly this was a major enterprise, whether it transpired all at one time or extended over generations. Clearly, also, the enterprise represented a period when construction requiring heavy masonry blocks was still or again going on. It seems logical

to associate it with the period of the Byzantine emperors from Arcadius to Anastasius, when Ptolemais saw a great deal of monumental, if crude, construction. Indeed, it may well be that much of the architectural decor of the Villa was used in the Byzantine fort in the insula to the west (Building 4 on Plan XXII) or in the revetment around the apse of the building across the street to the north (Building 6). It may be noted in this connection that the west exterior wall of the Villa was removed save behind Rooms 5 and 6, providing convenient gaps for the removal of heavy architectural members to the site next door. The members were not refashioned for other use on the premises of the Villa, for no deposits of stonecutters' chips appeared in the fill. The elements that escaped the wholesale looting of the architectural decor were the doorframe between the east portico and Room 18, where squatters were in occupation, incidental architrave and cornice blocks, one capital, and the bases and lower shafts of most of the columns. The fact that the bases and lower column shafts were found standing *in situ* shows how deep was the fill over some parts of the site when the looting of the rest of the decor occurred.

The explanation of the depth of the fill is to be found in the fact that prior to, during, and after the period of looting the site served as a dumping ground for refuse of various types and proveniences. Some of the material found in the fill seems to represent discarded elements of the furnishings of other buildings of the Roman period. Such are fragments of sculpture (see pp. 198–202) and inscriptions (pp. 209–10, Nos. 3–13), bits of carved bone and metal (pp. 271–72). Other material found in the fill, such as the Ptolemaic bronze coins (see p. 264), the head of a Tanagra figurine, and tiny scraps of Greek pottery, can be supposed to have come to the site of the Villa with earth dumped there when excavations were made preparatory perhaps to the erection of new Byzantine structures on older sites. Thus the main fabric of the Villa disappeared from view completely, with only the remains of a few column shafts projecting some 20 cm. above the surface in a wheat field to suggest its existence.

A PUBLIC BUILDING ON THE STREET OF THE MONUMENTS

The site that is designated as the locus of Building 8 on Plan **XXII** recommended itself for excavation for a variety of reasons. Located at the western end of the section of the Street of the Monuments that was cleared by the Italian archeologists, it extended the full width of an insula on the north side of the street (see p. 74 and Plan VII). Its position in the immediate shadow of the Triumphal Arch that gave to the adjacent street intersection particular notability and to the series of insulae running eastward a specially formal character suggested that the site was not unimportant. Moreover, there were certain recognizable architectural features in and around the fill covering the site (Pl. XXVIII *A*). At its south end, along the Street of the Monuments, the Italian archeologists had cleared the remains of a colonnaded portico and exposed a crude but heavy flight of steps leading from the portico northward together with part of what looked like, and in fact proved to be, a spacious anteroom or vestibule (Pl. XXVIII *B*). North of this, at a higher level, the tops of solid walls could be followed in the fill, outlining three sides of a rectangle and implying the presence of a well proportioned structure, perhaps a public building. Finally, the site seemed to have boundaries, for some 50 meters north of the Street of the Monuments the surface dipped sharply to the main east-west line of the Italian-laid Decauville railroad tracks, suggesting that the building ended here at a point convenient for the removal of its debris.

Excavation proved that many of these indications were deceptive and yielded a much more complicated pattern than had been anticipated. The rectangle of walls in the heart of the area, instead of inclosing the interior of a building, inclosed an open area (Room 8) around which rooms were set. Moreover, the rooms to the south and west were puzzling as to their purpose and those to the east had undergone important reorientation. It was only as clearance was extended northward to the very edge of the railroad tracks (where the complex of structures did *not* end) that the pieces of the puzzle began to fall into place, so that it was possible to differentiate the successive steps in the architectural history of the site and to interpret the relationship of the several parts of its structures.

Unfortunately the particular purpose which the earliest known building on the site served remains uncertain. That it was connected with the life of the community, being in some sense a public building, is, however, probable.

The field plan of the excavations (Plan XVI) shows all the structural elements of the site in their respective positions. From east to west they cover 37.50 m., a meter and a half more than the width of a typical insula. This maximum extension came in the Byzantine period, when builders generally abandoned the limits of the insulae fixed by the city planners and encroached on the adjacent streets. The remains excavated stretch a distance of 46 meters from the Street of the Monuments at the south to the railroad tracks at the north. A simplified rendering of the field plan is provided in Figure 51 for easier identification of the rooms according to the numbers assigned to them.

The structural elements revealed by the excavations do not all belong to the same period, as is clearly indicated not only by differences in wall construction and obvious signs of rebuilding but also by a study of the plan from the point of view of circulation and of the sections (Plan XVII) from the point of view of levels. In the structural history of the site two major periods have been distinguished, a Roman and a Byzantine. Between the two was an intermediate period of partial reuse and disuse, when the Roman complex was severely looted. The superimposed Byzantine structures themselves underwent changes and give clear indications of declining attention to maintenance and of increasing use of crude means of keeping things going. But these changes are not of sufficient importance or coherence to suggest or permit a formal distinction of subphases in the history of the Byzantine buildings. A hypothetical reconstruction of the plan of the Roman building, clearly distinguishing what is actually known from what is inferred, is given in Figure 52. The Byzantine use of the site is represented by two plans (Figs. 53 and 55), because in this period there were two relatively independent establishments. Where Roman walls are represented as following the same lines as Byzantine walls, careful analysis of the standing remains in respect to footing, character of masonry, and bonding has justified the reprenta-tion.

The building of the Roman period, so far as it can be known without complete removal of the Byzantine remains, was connected with a residence at the north by a well marked doorway. The lock-bar emplacements were on the south side of the doorway, so that the public building could be shut against the inhabitants of the dwelling but the dwelling could not be shut against the users of the public building.

In Byzantine times, after the spoliation of the Roman building, the site was redeveloped and set out with two adjoining but not organically related structures. Along the east side of the block, the bathing facilities of the Roman period were re-organized, provided with a separate entrance from the street, and thus transformed into a public bath (see Fig. 55). Along the south and west there was contrived about 1.50 m. above the level of the Roman building a series of chambers that pre-sumably served official purposes. From these chambers new means of access were afforded to the residence at the north, indicating that the official for whose use the chambers were constructed had his residence there (see Fig. 53).

So far as building lines are concerned, the Italian excavations showed that at the south the stylobate of the portico along the Street of the Monuments and the exterior walls of both the Roman and Byzantine structures adhered closely to the requirements of the city plan that was originally normative for the structures along the south side of the street. Along the east and west sides of the insula this was not true. At the east an exterior wall that parallels the exterior west wall breaks off after a northward run of about 27 meters (see Plan XVI). But the distance between the outer faces of these walls is over a meter in excess of the width of 36 meters established for the typical insulae by the city plan and rigidly observed else-where, for instance by the builders of the Roman Villa. Furthermore, just inside the east wall there is part of another exterior wall, which would seem to indicate the building line of the Roman period. Its construction justifies this assumption as far north as the southeast corner of Room 19, where it loses both its solidity and its rectilinear character, testifying to the rebuilding and reorganization of the facilities in this area as we shall see. Since, however, this earlier east wall runs on a line about

36.50 m. from the outer face of the exterior wall at the west, which in character and relationship is clearly Byzantine, it seems likely, first, that in Byzantine times the width of the insula was in-creased by slight intrusions on the streets at *both* sides and, secondly, therefore, that the probable course of the Roman exterior wall at the west was also just inside the Byzantine wall. Because of the solidity of the Byzantine wall it was impractical to verify the latter conjecture, which is adopted, nonetheless, in the hypothetical plan of the Roman structure (Fig. 52).

Room 1, at the west, was a porch or walk (7.90 m. × *ca.* 30 m.), raised about a meter above the level of the adjacent street by a solid retaining wall and supported at the east by the high wall inclosing Rooms 8 and 29 (see Plan XVI). It is doubtful that Room 1 was inclosed at the west or roofed, since the debris incumbering it could be seen to represent only the overturned west wall of Room 8. The porch was, however, well paved with heavy slabs, some of which were so laid as to pro-duce patterns. In a patterned group that ran in a straight north-south line in the middle of the porch there was found *in situ* a stone (Pl. LIII *B*) bearing a Greek inscription (pp. 211–12, No. 14). The inscription tells us that a certain Paul, a man of consular rank bearing the honorific title μεγαλο-πρεπέστατος, had happily brought about this work of construction. He is otherwise unknown, and his date cannot be fixed with any accuracy, but it is he with whom we should associate at least part of the Byzantine phase of the Public Building.

What Paul built (Fig. 53) can be seen from the relation of the porch to the remains at the north and the south. At the north the porch was brought to an abrupt end by the eastward return of its retaining wall at a point which just barely allowed for access to the south portico (Room 26) of the attached dwelling. That the spur projecting west-ward from Room 26 (see Plan XVI) was actually the return of the retaining wall was verified by examination of the fill immediately north and south of it. To the south, that is, under the porch, the fill was carefully constructed of heavy stones laid flat to give solidity to a mass of sand and rubble set around them. To the north, there was only debris with stones and architectural members lying in the kind of confusion typical of fallen masonry. At the south the porch led at even level to a large stone-paved room (Room 2) ap-

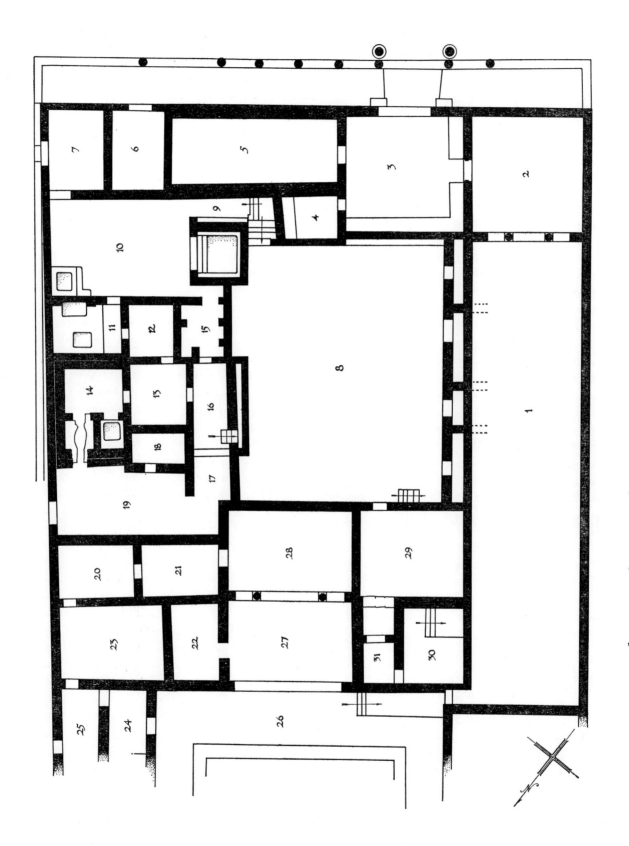

Fig. 51.—Diagrammatic Plan of Public Building. *G. R. H. Wright*

142

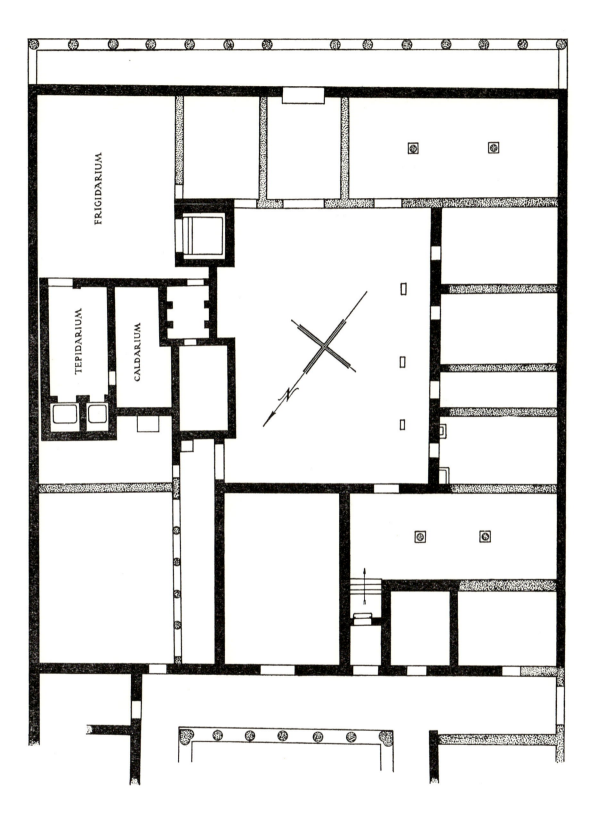

FRIGIDARIUM

TEPIDARIUM

CALDARIUM

Fig. 52.—Hypothetical Reconstruction of Earliest Phase of Public Building. *G. R. H. Wright*

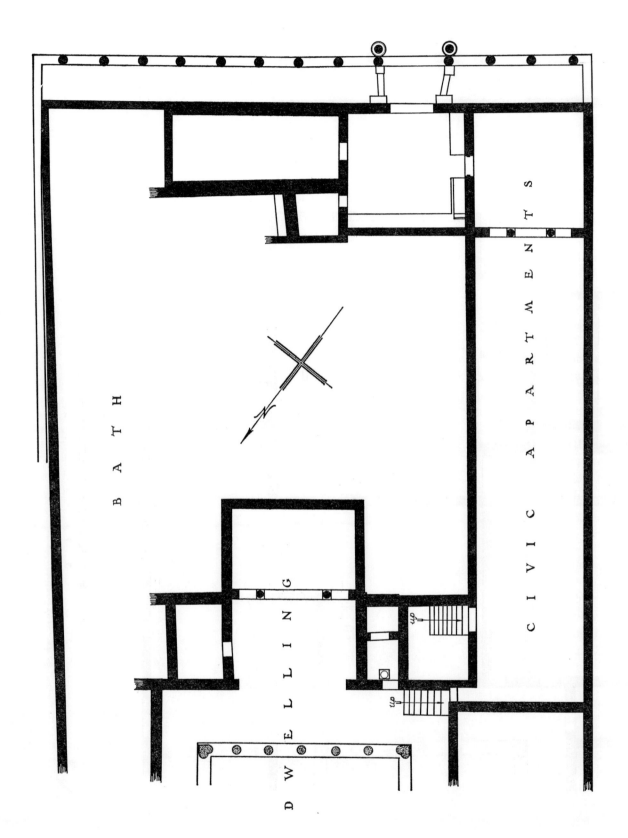

Fig. 53.—Plan of Public Building as Rebuilt by Paul. *G. R. H. Wright*

144

proximately 7.50 m. square through a colonnaded entrance. The plinths of the two columns were found in position at distances of 2 meters from each other and from the walls at either side. The existence of the colonnade indicates, of course, that Room 2 was roofed. In the debris on the floor were found not only many blocks of its inclosing walls but also the impost block from the top of one of the vanished columns. It was cut from a stone bearing an inscription of the period of Septimius Severus (p. 212, No. 15), and the beveling at the top to both left and right (Pl. LIII *C*) indicated that the entrance was arched. The floor of the chamber gave no indication of its original appointments. A single coin of the period of Justinian came to light in the fill.

Room 2 was also accessible in Paul's reorganization from a room of almost equal size (Room 3) to the east (Pl. XXVIII *C*). The trim of the doorway between the two rooms was borrowed from elsewhere, perhaps from the Roman building on the site. Reuse was indicated not only by the nature of the moldings but also by the emplacement of the lock-bar holes. The doorway had been blocked in late Byzantine times, when presumably Room 3 served as a shop or dwelling, with the help of a cornice block (Plan XVIII 6). Room 3 was in fact the vestibule or anteroom of Room 2, for it was through Room 3 that Room 2 was reached from the Street of the Monuments. A staircase constructed of heavy paving stones taken from the street led up from the portico to a wide doorway in the south wall of Room 3 (Pl. XXVIII *B*). Sill and trim had been removed by looters, but the block with the doorpost socket was preserved at the east. A pedestal with attached column base (Plan XVIII 5) found in Room 3 suggested that a column stood in the middle of the room to provide support for the ceiling beams, as did the column in the vestibule of the Villa (see p. 120). Other installations in Room 3 included stone benches along the north and west walls. The bench north of the doorway leading to Room 2 had an inclined headrest at its northern end (Pl. XXVIII *C*). These installations suggest that Room 3 was used by those who were waiting their turn to be received in audience in Room 2 and that a servant or guard slept there at night.

Room 3 provided access to two other rooms, but both doorways were found blocked up. Room 4 was a small interior room (*ca.* 2.00 × 2.50 m.) that could have served only for storage and yielded nothing of note except a coin of Honorius. Room 5 was a long well proportioned chamber (11.20 × *ca.* 4.00–4.20 m.) running parallel to the Street of the Monuments. Its north and south walls had an inner facing of relatively small stones carefully laid in courses with rubble filling behind them (see Pl. XXVIII *D* and Plan XVI). The walls against which the facing was set could not, however, be assigned to the Roman period and must therefore represent the intermediate building period (see p. 149). Exploratory excavations in the southwest corner of Room 5 revealed some 52 cm. below the floor traces of another floor and the inner face of a wall inclosing it. This wall parallels the street at the south and suggests either that the building line in Roman times was slightly farther to the south than it was in the intermediate period and in Byzantine times or, more probably, that the Roman wall was thicker than the later wall. Excavation below the floor in Room 4 revealed at a level only about 8 cm. higher than the early wall in Room 5 the interior face of a parallel wall running on the general line of the east-west bench in Room 3 and hence in front of the line of the north wall of Room 3 (see Plan XVI). It was bedded on a foundation course and typically offset; only its face could be exposed. These walls found below Byzantine floor levels in Rooms 4 and 5 we have associated with the Roman structure because of the correspondence between their levels and those of clearly identifiable remains of the Roman period exposed in Room 8 to the north (see p. 146). In the hypothetical plan of the Roman building (Fig. 52) the earlier wall in Room 5 marks not only the course of the building's exterior south wall but also the position of a symmetrically placed doorway opening through the portico onto the street about 20 cm. above the level of the sidewalk. The earlier wall in Room 4 marks the course of an interior wall of the Roman building (see p. 146).

While Rooms 1–5 may not represent the sum total of Paul's reconstruction, they form a single suite entirely separate from everything else in the excavated area except the dwelling to the north (see Fig. 53). We must infer, therefore, that they represent a complete functional unit. The function cannot be residential, for not only are the typical provisions for the operation of a household missing but the suite has, by way of the open porch, a natural and intentional connection with the dwelling to the north. The importance attaching to the formal vestibule (Room 3) of the suite suggests that the rooms served the administrative purposes of a high dignitary, for which Paul had the requisite rank. As the "offices" of a civil governor they were indeed appropriately located on the Street of the Monuments in the shadow of the Triumphal Arch. Room 2, while offering protection against the hot winds (*ghibli*) from the southwest and yet pleasantly open through the arcade to the cool winds from the north, would have been ideal for use in the warm months. Room 5 would have been ideal for winter use.

The excavations in Room 8 shed more light on the Roman phase in the history of the site and indirectly on the intermediate period. As noted above, Room 8 gave at the outset the impression of being the interior of the building, but actually it was at all times—though in differing dimensions—an open area around which rooms were set (see Plan XVI and Figs. 51–53, 55). The area as we found it was filled to the height of the highest walls that inclose it on parts of three sides with material whose nature revealed that except for a few centimeters at the top the fill had been purposely introduced in antiquity. But it was not all introduced at one time. The last stage of the fill is represented by a cemented platform set upon it near the southeast corner of the area, directly west of Room 15.[9] A water channel along the southern end of the platform led into what was subsequently revealed as the cold plunge at the west end of the frigidarium (Room 10) of the bath. The platform therefore presumably served as the emplacement for a tank from which water was conducted to the cold plunge. But this installation, being secondary to earlier installations serving the same purpose for the same plunge, can confidently be assigned to the very end of the Byzantine period. In Paul's day the level of the intentional fill was almost a meter lower, approximately at the level of the paved porch (Room 1). This level is indicated by the construction of the west wall of Room 8, which at porch level has a course of stones projecting as headers as much as 50 cm. (see Pl. XXIX *A* and Section *B–B* on Plan XVII). It is also suggested by a wall of the intermediate period that runs directly behind the north wall of the Byzantine vestibule (Room 3)

and that was left standing to a height of 14.35 m. above datum. Even so a few, but only a very few, of the vertical members of the doorframes of the Roman building projected above the level of Room 8 in Paul's reconstruction (see Section *A–A* on Plan XVII). If the area of Room 8 was paved in Paul's period, all traces of its paving have disappeared as a result of looting.

As excavation proceeded it developed that at the west the Roman level of Room 8 was 12.96–13.27 m. above datum. It was marked by the appearance, inside the footing of the Byzantine west wall, of a particularly well laid north-south wall with four doorways that led westward into four rooms covered by Paul's porch (Room 1). This wall and stubs of the party walls of the four rooms provided the basic clue to the reconstruction of the western half of the Roman building (see Fig. 52). The date of the north-south wall was indicated not merely by its priority to Paul's reconstruction but also by the fact that the west end of the wall of the intermediate period that runs behind the north wall of Room 3 had been set against it and the fact that fragments of black-glazed Greek pottery and burnished sigillata ware came to light on virgin soil at the bottom of the trench cut to receive it. A number of details of its construction are of particular interest. Its northern end abutted properly a wall running at right angles to it at the same level, the south wall of Room 29. In the corner thus formed west of the north-south wall were preserved two sides and the bottom of a water basin (see Plan XVI and Fig. 52), showing that the abutting walls were of the same period and that the wall between Rooms 8 and 29 was also the terminal wall of the northernmost of the four rooms west of the north-south wall. A second water basin was set against the north-south wall south of the doorway to Room 8. At its southern end the north-south Roman wall extended under the north wall of the Byzantine vestibule (Room 3). Our hypothetical plan of the Roman building suggests that it originally extended one stone farther south to meet at right angles the line of the wall spotted below the Byzantine floor level of Room 4 (see p. 145).

Three of the four rooms west of the Roman north-south wall were of about the same width, the second from the north being narrower. All four had had floors with a bedding of mortar and powdered brick, the narrower room showing doorpost sockets at either side of the doorway. It would be possible to interpret this room as another entrance to the Roman structure save for the fact that the locking mechanism was inside the room, that is, west of Room 8 in its Roman form. A vertical conduit of the type normally associated with heating was set into an aperture of the north wall of the northernmost chamber, but it was filled with fine clean sand rather than soot, suggesting that it carried water. The existence of the water basins and the conduit has important bearing, no doubt, upon the interpretation of the nature and purpose of the Roman building.

In the Roman building, then, the area of Room 8 was slightly larger to the south and slightly smaller to the west than in Byzantine times. The function of this courtyard in the Roman structure would be more evident if the significance of three orthostats could be determined. They came to light still standing on a well prepared bedding, though at slightly different levels, about 1.50 m. east of the Roman west wall of the courtyard (see Pl. XXIX A, Plan XVI, Section A–A on Plan XVII). They were each about a meter high, well squared but unmolded, and gave no evidence of structural connection with anything. There was no indication that they had ever had plaques attached to them nor that they had been revetted with marble.

Careful examination of the wall between Rooms 8 and 28 showed that its upper courses were of Byzantine construction and that its two lower courses, equal in height to the difference in level between Room 28 and the Roman phase of Room 8 (see Section A–A on Plan XVII), were of Roman construction. The lower courses were bonded through, and the stones were laid with regularly alternated joints. In the Roman structure the courtyard (Room 8) thus had a continuous north wall with only a single opening, namely a doorway leading to Room 29. This was marked by the socket holes for the doorposts let into the stone of the sill. In Room 29 (Pl. XXIX B) the bedding for the paving was preserved at approximately the level of the Roman courtyard, and the lower courses of the east wall and the western part of the north wall were found to be of Roman construction. The west wall was entirely of Byzantine construction and was not bonded to the north wall. The lower courses of the east wall were bonded to the south wall and ran somewhat inside the line of a Byzantine superstructure. The room was relatively large

(ca. 7.00 × 5.70 m.) and had imbedded in its floor a square plinth clearly intended to support a column. While the plinth was centered on the east-west axis of the room, it was only about 1.50 m. from the west wall. Since the west wall was Byzantine, being part of the support of Paul's porch (Room 1), we have in our hypothetical plan of the Roman building extended Room 29 westward into the area of the porch and suggested the emplacement of a second column base in it (see Fig. 52). A similar chamber is projected, quite arbitrarily, in the southwest corner of the Roman building.

Prior to the Byzantine reconstruction a staircase leading westward was contrived at the north end of Room 8, along a rebuilt version of the south wall of Room 29 (see Pl. XXIX B and Plan XVI). Cornice blocks (Plans XVIII 12 and XIX 11–12) were used as risers. What purpose the stairs may have served is unknown.

The work done in the Byzantine period included the construction of the new west wall of Room 29 and the rebuilding—above floor level—of the walls along the north and east sides of the room, thus permitting introduction of the fill that made the area a part of the enlarged central courtyard (Room 8). At the north the east end of the north wall, constructed of reused roughly dressed stones (Pl. XXIX B), blocked the top of a staircase. The stairs led downward between the well built walls of a passageway to a doorway that gave on a paved vestibule (Room 31) connecting with the south portico (Room 26) of the attached dwelling (see Plan XVI). This passageway was clearly one means of communication between the residence and the public building in Roman days. The lock-bar holes were on the side of the door toward the public building. The vestibule was probably hypethral, since the cover of a cistern was imbedded in its paving. Presumably there was a doorway between the south portico of the dwelling and the vestibule.

At its east end the north wall of the Roman courtyard (Room 8) stopped short of its Byzantine overlay, turning north at a doorjamb set against it on the south. In the Roman building there must therefore have been a doorway here leading into Room 17, though a corresponding second jamb did not come to light. Instead, the preserved jamb served as the abutment of a wall running southward for about 9 meters, in which column drums and bases were reused. The level of the top of this wall, as well as its construction, indicated that it was built as a part of the Byzantine reconstruction to retain the fill of the courtyard at its new level. A short staircase mounted to the top of it from the east (in Room 16). When the area east of the wall was cleared in depth an earlier wall came to light, running underneath it from the east and returning eastward after a run of 6.50 m. along a line about 1.80 m. to the west of it (see Plan XVI). This lower wall provided along its north side the emplacement for the missing second doorjamb, thus indicating that it belonged to the Roman building. It also indicated the eastern boundary of the Roman courtyard and that the Roman structure along the west side of the insula did connect with rooms on the east side as the preserved doorjamb had suggested. To allow for a change in levels it is necessary to suppose that a flight of two steps led down to the doorway from the Roman courtyard. Along the rest of the east side of the courtyard, where it adjoins Room 15 and the cold plunge at the west end of Room 10, there was no possibility of distinguishing between the Roman and the Byzantine masonry. We have therefore of necessity assumed that the walls followed the same course throughout, in spite of the resulting irregular outline of the Roman courtyard.

On the south side of the courtyard (Room 8), at its east end, a somewhat complicated situation was found to exist, consideration of which leads to the matter of the intermediate building period. Two courses of a well built wall which came to light here had received a new superstructure in the Byzantine period but had a doorway with a sill at approximately the Roman level (*ca.* 13.85 m.; see Section *B–B* on Plan XVII). This doorway had been filled up to serve as the emplacement of a staircase leading up from a corridor, Room 9 (see Plan XVI and Pl. XXIX *D*). The stairs as found lead to the level of the courtyard fill representing the very last days in the history of the site, that is, the level of the platform for the water tank that supplied the cold plunge (see p. 146). But the stairs were not all built at the same time. For Paul's period we can count on not more than the first three steps, which mount eastward in continuation of the corridor (Room 9), for their rise is sufficient to lead to the level of the fill in that period. Excavation on the south side of the courtyard where it adjoins Room 3 confirmed our

conclusion that the doorway was blocked to receive a staircase in the Byzantine period by showing that the westward section of the wall into which the doorway was let was not used by the builders of the office suite but was left standing unused behind the north wall of Room 3 to a height of 14.35 m. above datum, which was approximately the height of the fill created at the time of Paul's reconstruction. It has already been indicated (p. 146) that the west end of this wall had been set against the west wall of the Roman courtyard and that the latter wall continued under the north wall of Room 3. Thus it would seem that the wall under discussion was neither of the Byzantine period nor of the Roman period and must therefore belong to the intermediate period, of which we have four other indications. The first is a kiln near the center of the courtyard (see Plan XVI and Pl. XXIX *C*), which was set slightly higher than the Roman level and completely buried by the Byzantine fill. Undoubtedly marble looted from the Roman building and its neighbors was reduced to lime in this kiln, as indicated by the heavy deposit of lime within it. The kiln was heated with the help of a flue leading in from the north. Some elements of the upper half of the kiln were found in the pit. The walls were partly constructed of tiles taken from the bath at the east and showed the effect of hot firing. In the fill of the oven and its intake flue coins of Ptolemy VIII and the empress Faustina were found.

Another indication of the intermediate period is provided by a cistern at the extreme south end of the courtyard. It could well have been an installation of the Roman period, as the quality of the workmanship suggests. A few centimeters of its rim are broken off, but between its present top (13.55 m. above datum) and the level (13.84 m.) of the top of the Roman wall in Room 4 (see p. 145) there is ample space for the cistern to reach its full height without projecting above Roman floor level. The cistern, whose fill was devoid of all rubbish, was out of use in the Byzantine period, when the level of the courtyard was much higher. But there would have been no reason to reduce the height of the cistern when the level of the courtyard was raised. Actually the top of the cistern was chipped away, as Figure 54 shows, to provide the proper bedding for the wall that in the Byzantine reorganization was reused between Rooms 8 and 4 but *not* between Rooms 8 and 3. The cistern thus confirms the suggestion that the wall which was left standing behind the north wall of Room 3 belongs to the intermediate period.

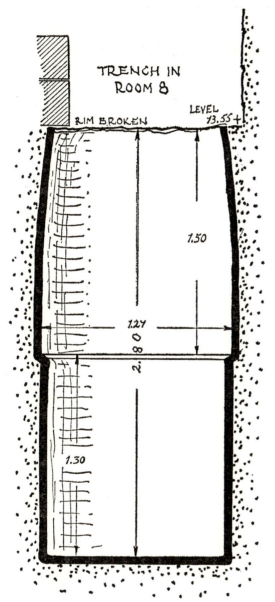

Fig. 54.—Section of Cistern in Courtyard (Room 8) of Public Building. *G. R. H. Wright*

Of the intermediate period we have further information in the north wall of Room 5, which is also the south wall of Room 9. This is one of the walls that received an inner facing in the development of the Byzantine administrative suite (see p. 145). It cannot be assigned to the Roman period, however, because of its structural character and because in Room 4, where its footing was explored, it was seen to be set on fluted Ionic column drums

that were probably taken from the portico of the Roman building.[10] Moreover, it contained doorways (at the points indicated by arrows on Plan XVI), which had been blocked up when the facing was added.[11] The number and position of the doorways suggest that they gave access to the back rooms of a row of shops located in the area of what later became Room 5 of the Byzantine office suite. Back rooms are typical of shops in all periods and have been noted in connection with the reuse of the north end of the Roman Villa (see p. 135). Soundings below the Byzantine floor level of Room 5 revealed remains of earlier north-south party walls and of shallow cemented basins and depressions for the emplacement of large storage jars—typical features of shop installations.

Finally, evidence bearing on the intermediate building period came to light in Room 6 (*ca.* 3.50 × 5.10 m.). Although it received a new rear (north) wall in the Byzantine reorganization of the bathing facilities, it was not part of the bath, as indicated by the unbroken continuity of the new wall and by benches set against its outer face. The only means of ingress to Room 6 at this time was from the portico on the Street of the Monuments at the south, and even as a one-room establishment it lends itself most readily to interpretation as a shop. This suggests that it was in the Byzantine period the last survivor of the row of shops postulated above, which included the area of Room 7 also and extended at least to the area that later became Room 3. Covering as they did the walls of the Roman level in Rooms 4 und 5, these shops must necessarily belong to the intermediate period. In replacing most of the shops with his office suite, Paul was helping to rehabilitate the frontage of an insula at an important street intersection.

The rooms along the east side of the site in both Roman and Byzantine times constituted a bathing establishment. For the Roman period we have in Figure 52 projected access to it through a room south of the cold plunge. This is entirely hypothetical and has its only justification in the fact that a connection between the courtyard and the bath was maintained on this line (through Room 9)

[10] A Doric capital (Plan XIX 4) found in the portico establishes the nature of the order used.

[11] We have interpreted the two more westerly of these three doorways as successors, at a higher level, to doorways of the Roman period in corresponding positions but farther to the north (cf. Fig. 52 with Plan XVI).

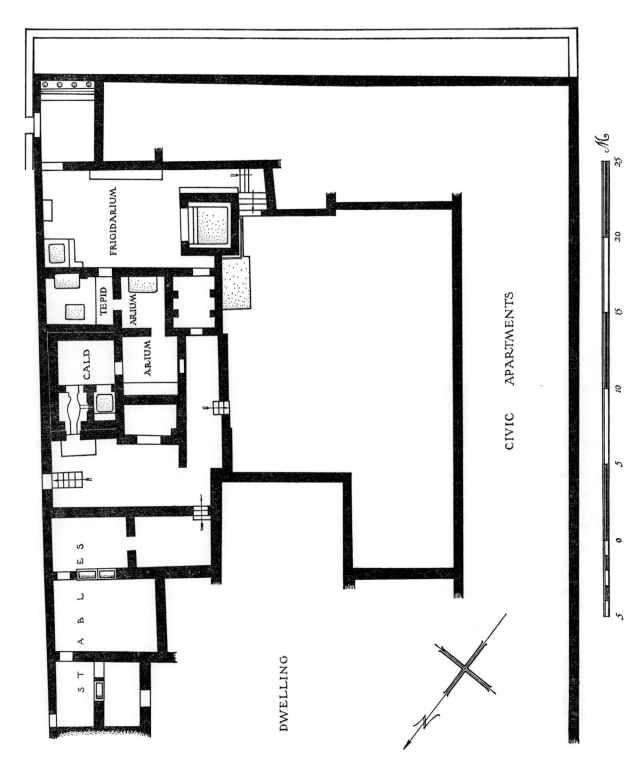

Fig. 55.—Plan of Bath of Public Building as Rebuilt for Public Use. *G. R. H. Wright*

until the last days in the history of the site. In the Byzantine period the bathing establishment took over the courtyard and was separated from the administrative suite (Fig. 55). At this time, indeed, the bath became a public facility with an entrance from the street through Room 7 (3.60 × 6.30 m.). The doorway is in the Byzantine exterior wall, and the Roman exterior wall was broken away behind it. The vestibule of the bath was also the latrine of the establishment and may be compared with the room adjoining one of the vestibules of the City Bath, a block to the east on the Street of the Monuments (see p. 162). The doorway leading into the vestibule was set at an angle to the doorway communicating with the frigidarium (Room 10) to insure a measure of privacy. The toilet facilities were along the south wall, serviced by a drain which ran out under the paving into the street.

Of the several elements of the bathing establishment the frigidarium underwent the fewest changes. In reconstructing the Roman plan we have included the area of Rooms 6 and 7 in the frigidarium (see Fig. 52), but in the Byzantine period, in spite of its reduced size (9.30 × 6.35 m.), it remained a well paved area with the cold plunge (Pl. XXX A) as a structural and decorative feature at the west. The plunge was covered with a rubble vault and received a new facing presumably in the Byzantine period. The water for the plunge was originally supplied through an opening in the north wall, accessible from a passageway leading to Room 15. It was released through a drain running eastward to a sump under the paving of the frigidarium. In the Byzantine redevelopment of the other parts of the bath additional drains ran to this sump from the east and north. The latest Byzantine usage of the site is represented by a little sitz bath added at the northeast corner of the frigidarium (Pl. XXX B) and some crude benches along its south wall. At this time water was supplied by a high tank in the courtyard outside Room 15 (see p. 146). Missing is any kind of portico in which users of the bath could enjoy shade. In the frigidarium as found there is no room for such a feature. If the room was indeed larger in the Roman period, an area shaded by a portico could have been provided at the south. A small marble Corinthian capital appropriate to columns of such a portico (Plan XVIII 9) was found in Room 10.

The caldarium, the tepidarium, and the heating system of the bath were completely reorganized,

presumably in the Byzantine period. The reorganization is most evident in the furnace area, where excavation revealed two successive heating plants. Originally Room 18 (2.00 × 3.50 m.) was the *praefurnium* area of the bath, and stoking was done through a corbeled opening in the wall between it and Room 13 (3.80 × 3.70 m.). The opening (Pl. XXXII A) had seen long use, for the limestone had been eaten away severely by the heat, but it was found blocked up. A second furnace, constructed largely of tiles and stoked from Room 19, was set into the more easterly of two alcoves connected with Room 14 (Pl. XXXII B). The wall through which the stokehole for this furnace was opened was rebuilt, apparently with an arch to eliminate pressure on the bricks of the furnace, and eventually was strengthened by a second wall built against its north face.[12] On the firebox was a place for a cauldron which received water through a duct (see Plan XVI) from a basin (see Fig. 51) constructed upon a high filling of bricks introduced into the more westerly of the alcoves of Room 14. Both alcoves as originally constructed were of excellent masonry. Our hypothetical plan of the Roman building (Fig. 52) suggests that in this period they provided the setting for warm plunges. A similar alcove with a tub was found in the tepidarium of the City Bath (see p. 168).

The change in the heating system required reorganization both of space and of the arrangements for the movement of heated air through and from the *suspensura*. When the bath was heated from Room 18, the heated air was conducted from the *suspensura* of Room 13 (Pl. XXX C) eastward through a corbeled opening especially constructed for this purpose in the north-south wall separating the area of Rooms 11 and 14 from that of Rooms 12 and 13. Where it went from there and where the escape flue that gave the draft was located have been obscured by changes in the area of Room 11. A small vertical flue in Room 11 is scarcely the original flue for the entire heating system of the bath. When the heat was supplied by the furnace in the alcove of Room 14, the heated air may have been led westward through the doorway between Rooms 13 and 14, of course through the *suspensura* and hence under the floor of the hypocaust (*ca.* 13.76 m. above datum). From here it probably was channeled to and escaped through an opening newly

[12] Room 14 measures 2.90 × 3.80 m., not counting the alcoves.

cut in the west wall of Room 13, into which the piers of the *suspensura* extend and in which remains of several vertical flues were found (see Pl. XXXII *A*). The second heating plant is clearly Byzantine, while it is tempting to associate the first with the Roman period. The only difficulty is that the wall containing its stokehole (i. e., the north wall of Room 13) does not line up with any identifiably Roman masonry and is not bonded to the north-south wall separating Rooms 13 and 14. Perhaps the original wall of the Roman period was reduced to lime dust by the heat, like its counterpart in the Byzantine furnace room, and the existing north wall of Room 13 is a replacement set on a different line.

In the area of Rooms 11 and 12 the changes were more obscure. As excavated Rooms 11 (4.55 × 3.15 m.) and 12 (2.90 × 3.35 m.) represent the Byzantine period. Entrance to them was effected by a doorway in the north wall of the frigidarium, which gave on a passageway running north along the west side of Room 11 only a few centimeters above the level of the frigidarium. The passageway ended at a secondary east-west wall set along the north side of the room and was delimited at the east by a low north-south wall. Two tubs constructed in heavy masses of rubble by the use of mortar and plaster filled the area east of the passage in awkward fashion (see Plan XVI). Remains of rubble vaulting on the surface showed how the chamber had been roofed. Room 12 was reached from the passageway by a doorway in the wall between them. A cement floor about 45 cm. above the level of the passageway showed the impression of a rectangular tub that had been imbedded in it along the south wall of the room. The water from the tub had passed under the cement bedding to the passageway, whence it ran at floor level to the sump under the paving of the frigidarium (Room 10). In the north wall of Room 12 there was a doorway leading to Room 13, but it had been blocked up.

In the Byzantine period Rooms 11 and 12 must have constituted the tepidarium of the bath, through which access was had to the caldarium (Rooms 13–14). Heated air from the furnace in the alcove at the northeast corner of Room 14 may have circulated under both Rooms 11 and 12, as the vertical flue coming up through the rubble in Room 11 suggests, but no details are evident and eventually, as the blocking of the doorway between Rooms 12 and 13 suggests, the caldarium ceased to

be used. At that time, presumably late in the Byzantine period, the water for the tubs in Rooms 11 and 12 must have been heated by other means. Extensive indications of firing along the north wall of the frigidarium (Room 10), particularly in Room 15, suggest that at the last the water was heated in the open in cauldrons and carried by hand to the tubs.

As to the organization of the rooms of the bath in Roman times, obvious indications of make-shift installations make it difficult to imagine that the pattern was identical in all respects. What we know about changes in the Byzantine period in the heating arrangements at the north suggests that equally radical changes may have occurred in the area of Rooms 11 and 12, especially since the walls separating Room 11 from Room 14 and Room 12 from Room 13 are not bonded in at either end and may well represent the Byzantine reorganization. Moreover, the east end of the wall between Rooms 12 and 13 is directly in front of the corbeled opening in the continuous north-south wall dividing Rooms 11 and 14 from Rooms 12 and 13. This opening, it will be recalled, was important for the circulation of the heated air through the *suspensura* when the bath was being heated from Room 18, that is, most likely, in Roman times. On the basis of these clues we have in Figure 52 suggested that in Roman times the area of Rooms 12 and 13 constituted a single chamber, the caldarium. For the tepidarium we have suggested a parallel chamber occupying the area of Rooms 11 and 14. In the tepidarium we have restored to their presumably original function as the emplacement for tubs the alcoves one of which in Byzantine times became the furnace room. We have placed the entrance to the tepidarium east of that to the later Room 11 because behind the sitz bath in the northeast corner of the frigidarium there are two large vertically laid blocks which could well be the lower sections of a doorframe and because the coursing clearly shows that the existing doorway to Room 11 was secondarily let into the wall. The actual organization of the Roman bath could have been determined only by the complete removal of the Byzantine installations in Rooms 11 and 12, which did not seem advisable, and we do not claim that the suggested arrangement resolves entirely the problems of circulation and escape of heated air from under the *suspensura*.

The function of two chambers (Rooms 15–16)

along the west side of the bath (Pl. XXXII *C*) is by no means clear. In their earliest form they represent the Roman establishment, since their walls are bonded to those forming the inner chambers of the bath proper. In the Byzantine redevelopment Room 16 was made narrower by a secondary west wall (see p. 148) and served as a passageway continuing northward at its own high floor level (13.49 m. above datum) through Room 17 and the western end of Room 19 to a staircase that led down from the top of the north wall of Room 19 into Room 21.[13] How Room 16 was entered in the Roman period, whether from the north alone or from both north and south, is difficult to say. A pier projecting into the southeast corner of Room 17, which determined the offset in the border of its mosaic, suggests that the course of the walls in this area in the Roman period was quite other than that now known (see p. 156). More important than Room 16 by far was Room 15 (2.80 × 3.35 m.). It had a vaulted ceiling supported on arches whose piers were found in position against the east and west walls. Patches of mosaic paving were preserved in the southeast and northwest corners. The simple quatrefoil design, typically framed, was used also in the Roman Villa at Ptolemais (see p. 251), and there can be no doubt therefore that Room 15 was part of the Roman bath. The mosaic design cleared the piers of the arches, showing that they were part of the original construction. Conceivably this room served as an apodyterium. The floor had seen much wear and was covered with a heavy deposit of ashes. A coin of Phocas found on the floor testifies to the length of time during which the premises were in use for some purpose or other.

The installations at the northern end of the site, so far as excavations have revealed them, include a stylobate along the north side of Room 26 which identifies it as a portico. On the stylobate were found, still in proper position, the bases and lower elements of engaged Ionic corner columns (see Plan XVIII 13) and of freestanding intermediate columns mostly of the Doric order (see Pl. XXXI *C*). The materials were anything but homogeneous and showed that the portico had at one time been reconstituted with the help of looted materials, but the corner columns indicated that the excavation had exposed one side of a peristyle court.

This explained the surface depression through which the Italian railway line runs and at the same time indicated that mounds of debris immediately north of the railway represent the ruined living quarters of a residence. The residential character of the northern part of the site made it possible to interpret the suite of rooms along the west and south sides of the insula (Rooms 1–5) as the offices used by the inhabitant of the dwelling and provided the much-needed perspective upon the organization and reorganization of space in the area between Rooms 8 and 26.

The south portico (3.40 × 19.40 m.) of the dwelling framed one side of a courtyard that measured 12.70 m. from east to west. The excavated portions of the walls inclosing the east and west porticoes indicated that these porticoes were 2.50 m. wide. In the south portico the bedding of the original pavement was preserved, but no traces of the paving itself came to light. A single bronze coin identifiable only as Byzantine was found in the fill. Approximately on the north-south axis of the peristyle court was a large hall (8.30 × 11.10 m.) divided into two almost equal parts (Rooms 27 and 28) by a stylobate (see Pl. XXXI *B*, Fig. 53, and Plan XVI). This hall is, of course, the oecus of the typical Greek dwelling that is discussed above (p. 85) and was used for social and dining purposes. Its importance and its appearance in what was for Cyrenaica the preferred position explain why it delimited the area of the Public Building and its courtyard (Room 8). Its west and the south walls ran on the same lines in the Byzantine and Roman periods, their lowest courses being part of the original construction. At the east the Byzantine wall ran parallel to and immediately east of the Roman wall. The width of the oecus was thus increased by about 65 cm. in the Byzantine period. The lengthening of the south wall has already been implied in connection with the discussion of the doorway between Rooms 8 and 17 (pp. 147–48). The original return of the south wall along the east side of the oecus is clearly marked by its foundation course (see Plan XVI) and by indications of chiseling that reduced the length of the block by which the first course was bonded into the south wall. This block is visible on Plate XXXI *B*. A small section of paving was preserved in the southeast corner of Room 28. It is a simple form of marble *opus segmentatum* and belongs to the

[13] The original floor level of Room 17 was *ca.* 75 cm. lower than that of the passageway.

Byzantine period, when the interior of the oecus was redone. The refurbishing included the introduction of a pair of blue marble columns with spiral fluting, the splintered elements of which were found in the oecus, one with an inscription (p. 212, No. 18) on its fillet. The square plinths on which the columns stood were found (one in position) in the oecus, but no typical white marble bases (see, however, p. 158). Instead, the fill yielded a fragment of a small ornamental arch and two Doric capitals (Plan XVIII 2–4; see also Pl. XXXI *B*, extreme left). The column seen standing in Plate XXXI *B* is not of the Byzantine order but might belong to the earlier order. It was found in the area of Room 31, the vestibule that was abandoned in the Byzantine period. The stylobate is of Roman construction, since it joins the stones of the foundation course of the Roman east wall of the oecus. Each part of the oecus had a doorway leading through the east wall. That connecting with Room 21 was found blocked up—a natural corollary of the high-level passage through Rooms 17 and 19 to Room 21 that was developed in the Byzantine period (see p. 153), when Rooms 20 and 21 were used as stables (see p. 155). The doorway to Room 22 seems to have remained open.

Along its north side the oecus was separated from the south portico of the dwelling by what was in effect a long doorsill set between projecting piers. Perhaps in Roman times the opening was shorter, but rectangular holes cut to receive vertical lock bars dot the full length of the sill and indicate that in the latest period the oecus could be opened or closed by the emplacement or removal of sectional or folding doors, depending upon the season of the year.

At its west end the south portico was incumbered by a mass of masonry oddments and displaced architectural members that formed a ramp leading up to the level of the porch constructed by Paul (Pl. XXXI *A*, *C*). The ramp blocked off Rooms 30 and 31. Indeed, its west end seems to have been built upon and with elements of the north wall of Room 31 (2.00 × 2.60 m.), which contained nothing more important than two bronze coins that proved to be illegible, a cistern head, and at the south a doorsill. As Plan XVI indicates, the stone south of the doorsill contained the sockets, and also the lock-bar holes, for the door. This room formed the vestibule for the stairs that in Roman times connected Room 29 of the Public Building

with the dwelling. It was abandoned in the Byzantine period, as indicated by the blocking of the stairs (see p. 147).

Room 30, its neighbor (4.00 × 4.80 m.), had a longer and more complicated history. The lower courses of its south and west walls are of Roman construction. Its north and west walls are buried under the ramp in the south portico of the dwelling and under Paul's porch respectively. At the southwest corner three steps of a well built staircase that leads up to the level of Paul's porch came to light (see Pl. XXXI *A*). Whether this was the first means of access from the porch to the dwelling (preceding the ramp in the south portico) is not clear but seems probable. Excavation here yielded a small engaged Ionic column (Plan XVIII 1), lying at the foot of the stairs, and three coins. The coins are issues of Justinian, Trajan, and Cyrenaica in the second century B.C. and were found in the fill, on the stairs, and on the floor respectively. In the southeast corner of the room, at the foot of the stairs, a section of the original mosaic paving was preserved (see p. 252). The mosaic indicates that the room must have been a chamber of some elegance and importance in the Roman period, opening off the south portico of the dwelling. Precisely how the connection was made is not clear.

In the Roman period the main entrance to the dwelling must have been at the west, probably on or just off the axis of the south portico. This area is suggested by the natural access provided from it to both the peristyle court and the oecus, by the presence of a displaced section of a well molded doorframe among the architectural members used to form the ramp leading upward from the south portico to Paul's porch, and by the fact that Paul's porch had its northern terminus in this vicinity. Presisely where the doorway and its vestibule were located was not possible to ascertain. In all probability Room 30 was neither the vestibule nor the porter's lodge, since its position was too far to the east and its paving too elegant. In the hypothetical plan of the Roman building (Fig. 52) we have suggested for the *ostiarius* a room west of Room 30 and have placed the doorway at the end of an extension of the south portico. This extension could, of course, have had a vestibule with an inner door to give privacy to the inhabitants. These suggestions are, naturally, entirely conjectural.

The northeast corner of the excavated area

probably saw even more drastic changes. The area comprises eight rooms (Rooms 18–25) which were shoddy in construction, confusing as to the groups of untrimmed stones found in them, and unproductive of significant objects, large or small.

Rooms 24 and 25, each approximately 2.40 m. wide and of indeterminate length, are represented by miserable lines of stones without recognizable features other than crude doorways (see Plan XVI). The walls of the Byzantine period must have been low and almost entirely of mud save for the roughest of stone footings. Those of the Roman period may well have run along generally similar lines. By good fortune the stubs of doorjambs came to light in the east wall of Room 25 just where excavation was halted by the bed of the railroad tracks. They are of coarse worksmanship but provide an important clue to circulation in the entire group of rooms. Entering Room 25 from the street, one could in the Byzantine period move through Room 24 into the south portico of the dwelling or, by turning left (southward), through Rooms 23 and 20 into Room 21, where steps led over the south wall from the high-level passage through Rooms 17 and 19 (see p. 153).

Like Rooms 24 and 25, Rooms 22 and 23 had no traces of flooring and no noteworthy features. Room 23 was the larger of the two (6.80 × 4.75 m. as against 3.00 × 4.90 m.) and may well have served as a storeroom for supplies used in Rooms 20 and 21. Room 22 seems to have been accessible only from the oecus (Rooms 27–28) of the dwelling. Whether it was roofed or not is a question because of the installation in the wall between it and Room 21. Almost identical in size, Rooms 20 and 21 were paved with heavy slabs and accessible to each other through a wide opening rather than through a framed doorway (Pl. XXXI D). A series of feed troughs cut out of building stones of normal length in the north wall of each of these rooms approximately a meter above floor level indicates that they served as stables. The regularity of the installation (see Pl. XXXI D) suggests that it may have been created in Paul's period to serve the administrative or communications system of the province. The fact that Room 21 could be reached from the frigidarium of the bath (see Fig. 55) by means of the high-level passage extending from Room 16 through Rooms 17 and 19 suggests that eventually the stables were used to house animals that carried in water for the tubs and the cold

plunge of the bath (see p. 152). Such use, of course, would not have occurred until the bath became a public institution. It will be recalled (see p. 148) that stairs mounted over the secondary west wall of Room 16 to the top of the fill in the courtyard (Room 8). Thus water could have been carried also to the tank on the platform created on that fill to supply water to the cold plunge of the frigidarium (see p. 151).

The remaining two rooms of the group, Rooms 18 and 19, gave a complicated picture. Room 18, the smaller (3.50 × 2.00 m.), originally was the *praefurnium* area of the bath and may not have been inclosed. When the furnace was moved eastward and the corbeled stokehole closed up, crude inclosing walls were erected and the room was used perhaps by those who tended the new furnace. It was warmed by the adjacent hypocaust. Room 19 (*ca.* 10.85 × 4.00 m.) may well have been open to the sky. It served, of course, as the *praefurnium* of the bath in the Byzantine period and was cluttered at what should be floor level with stubs of walls, rows of stones framing a drain, heaped-up masses of discarded building blocks, and a few architectural members including a good Corinthian capital in white marble (Plan XVIII 10). The other capitals and the base seen with it on Plate XXX D were brought here from the extreme northern end of the excavations for preservation (see p. 158). Column drums are common in the late walls along the west side of Rooms 17 and 16. A ramp constructed of oddments of building material led down into the Room 19 from the east, suggesting the existence of a late entrance from the street to these service quarters.

If Rooms 18–25 as excavation revealed them reflect the arrangements of the Byzantine period, what can be said about the area in Roman times? Was it related to the bath or to the dwelling? Or was it perhaps divided so that part belonged to the dwelling and part to the Public Building and, if so, where were the dividing lines and how was the area laid out? To these questions it would be quite impossible even to suggest any answers were it not for a few bits of information brought to light by the clearance of Room 17.

Room 17 was effectively inclosed only on three sides and at one time or another (see Figs. 51, 52, 55) formed a connecting link with the western part of the Public Building (through Room 8), with the frigidarium and the tepidarium of the bath (through

Rooms 16 and 15), and with the dwelling (through Rooms 19 and 21). In the Byzantine period circulation was only in a north-south direction, at a level of about 13.50 m., across the tops of the east-west walls that separate Rooms 16 and 17 and Rooms 19 and 21. When excavation proceeded below this level a section of mosaic paving came to light at 12.75 m. above datum. It provided an example of the pattern of squares and octagons encountered also in the Roman Villa (see p. 251). The typical border was set back at the southeast corner, maintaining the proper distance from a projecting pier (see Plan XVI). The organization of the mosaic in Room 17 was analogous to that in the north portico of the Villa, which is to say that it was set out as a "runner," with the implication that it continued northward in a straight line, perhaps to the south portico of the dwelling. It should be noted in this connection that the Byzantine rebuilding of the east wall of the oecus (Rooms 27–28) slightly to the east of the Roman wall (see p. 153) would explain the destruction of the mosaic along its course. The projected existence of a mosaic "runner" suggests, of course, a portico along the west side of the area that subsequently became Rooms 20–23. This suggestion finds confirmation in the discovery that in the immediate vicinity of Room 17 a number of drums and other structural elements of columns were reused in the walls of the Byzantine period. There is no place in the Byzantine structure where they could have fulfilled the purpose for which they were cut, and it is easier to assume that they had a structural function appropriate to their character in the Roman building than to suppose that they were brought in from the outside.

These bits of evidence taken together with the fact, noted above, that the dividing walls of Rooms 20–23 are all make-shift in construction suggest the hypothetical reconstruction of this part of the Roman building offered in Figure 52. Here we have projected for the area of Rooms 20–23 a single large open courtyard, perhaps paved, with a portico along its west side. The rooms north of this courtyard we have associated with the dwelling. The room south of it (the area of Rooms 18–19) we have interpreted as the *praefurnium* of the bath.

What has been learned from the excavations about the architectural history of the site of the Public Building is not so informative as we might wish. To draw the necessary conclusions is therefore somewhat difficult, and the results are proportionately less satisfactory. Indications of the first human occupation of the site are provided by the pottery fragments that came to light in the southwest corner of Room 8 (see p. 146). The earliest of this pottery is Attic ware of the fourth century B.C., and the latest is the ubiquitous terra sigillata ware; similar small fragments of both wares were found on the surface and in the fill in various parts of the city. At the site of the Public Building, as predominantly elsewhere at the present state of our knowledge, the sherds were not associated with a structural context. They lay on virgin soil in a trench cut to receive a wall of the earliest construction on the site. The earliest construction, therefore, followed the period to which the latest of the sherds belongs. Excavation revealed evidence of three periods in the structural development of the site. The first is that of the original building, represented by Figure 52. The second is the intermediate period, in which the original building was being looted and its inner courtyard was used as the site of a limekiln, while a row of shops was presumably developed at its southern end. The third period is that which saw the creation of a suite of offices by Paul (Fig. 53) and the transformation of the bathing facilities into a public bath (Fig. 55). The fact that Paul's reconstruction must represent early Byzantine times (see p. 159) led us to infer that the earliest building period is Roman. It is in order at this point to verify and clarify this inference in so far as the available evidence permits.

The coins found in the excavations have less to say than one might hope. The yield from the site was small. Only a portion of it could be studied in relation to find-spots and levels, and it showed merely a sketchy coverage of the general period from the first century B.C. to the seventh century of our era (see p. 267). Perhaps the only potentially significant coin was the one of the empress Faustina, found in the intake flue of the limekiln in Room 8 (see p. 148). It suggests that the kiln could have been in operation as early as the late second century of our era.[14] The building in which the lime burners were operating would on this

[14] The fact that a Ptolemaic issue also was found in the kiln does not necessarily destroy its evidential value. On the use of small Ptolemaic bronzes in Roman Cyrenaica see p. 266.

score be considerably older. Among the other movable finds from the site the most important intrinsically is the marble portrait head of an elderly lady (Pl. XL), found in the southwest corner of the courtyard (Room 8) at the level of the Roman building. Brinkerhoff dates this piece on stylistic grounds to the second half of the first century B.C. and suggests that it represents a lady of some prominence in local affairs, the wife of the representative of Roman authority or a priestess (see p. 181). The head can certainly not be used to prove that the Roman building was, as presumed for its Byzantine successor, the head-quarters of a governor. Moreover, one would scarcely regard any public building as the proper place for the exhibition of the portrait head of a lady, unless indeed she served in some important civic role such as that of a priestess. The presence of the head on the premises may therefore be but another token of the work of the lime burners, who for reasons best known to themselves set it aside instead of reducing it to lime.[15] It could therefore have come from the immediate vicinity rather than from the Public Building itself.

The structural remains of the Roman building supply at least in part the information about its approximate date that the movable finds deny. But their value is limited because so little of the actual fabric of the structure remains and its more precious surviving elements have been badly pulled about. The foundations and the lowest courses of its masonry indicate ashlar construction in which excellent materials were used and upon which good workmanship was expended. The plan was comprehensive and ambitious, and the individual rooms were spacious. The building was set at approximately the level at which the Street of the Monuments itself was developed, and its floors, largely of marble it would seem, were bedded in accordance with the best tradition. The marble, of course, disappeared into the limekiln, but some elements of mosaic paving were preserved in Rooms 15, 17, and 30, and these are of outstanding significance for dating. The size of the tesserae, the range of colors, the frames, and the designs closely match those of the Villa of the early Roman period. In the separate study of the mosaics, where the comparative material from other sites is considered, it is suggested that they are appropriate to the first

[15] On a group of marble heads set aside in the tepidarium of the City Bath see p. 170.

century of our era (see pp. 258–60). From the fact that mosaic paving was used in the attached dwelling (Room 30), in an important passageway connecting the dwelling with the Public Building (Room 17), and in the bathing establishment (Room 15) it can be inferred that all three parts of the complex represent one plan and are of the same general period.

Of the superstructure of the Public Building and attached dwelling only a few carved and molded pieces were found. With respect to them Mr. G. R. H. Wright has supplied the following statement.

The vicissitudes of the site of the Public Building were too manifold and too far-reaching in their effects to permit the survival of any coherent group of architectural elements. The fragments that came to light in the excavations are a random collection from many different periods and, indeed, in some cases cannot be shown to have been specifically associated with the known buildings. Some of the more interesting of the pieces registered are presented on Plans XVIII and XIX.

The largest number of molded architectural members was found in the northern part of the area, particularly along the south portico (Room 26) of the dwelling. Some had apparently been placed on the stylobate of the portico to provide the footing for a rough wall inclosing it toward the north. Several column bases incorporated in this walling, together with other fragments discovered nearby, would seem to represent the order of the peristyle at successive periods of its history. The only members of the peristyle *in situ* are the bases and lower shafts of the angle pilasters at the east and west corners of the stylobate. They are formed by double engaged half-columns so arranged as to give in plan a heart-shaped pattern (Plan XVIII 13). The eastern one has a plain shaft with an Ionic base, while that at the west is fluted in the Ionic fashion. The diameters of the half-columns are in both instances 60 cm., which is also the diameter of various fluted drums incorporated in the walling and of others found nearby. But these drums are fluted in the Doric manner. Manifestly to be associated with them is a Doric capital, with the upper portion of the column shaft cut in the same block, found nearby (Plan XVIII 4). The abacus and echinus of this capital are recessed for the lodgement of a curtain pole in exactly the same fashion as the base of the east angle pilaster. A small fragment of a cornice showing a mutule with guttae was found nearby. To entirely different assemblages we must assign two small Doric capitals found in Room 26 (Plan XVIII 7) and the bases of two large unfluted Ionic columns found resting on the stylobate. With the latter we should associate two fragments of volutes from Ionic capitals that came to light nearby. The capitals must have been large, for the diameter of the volutes is about 25 cm.

The engaged half-columns, heart-shaped in section, present a device familiar at Ptolemais, for instance in the "Grande Peristilio" of the "Palazzo."[16] The relation between the Ionic angle pilasters and the elements of a larger, Doric order found with them cannot be determined without extension northward of the excavations. But it is clear that at different times various elements must have been used. The smaller Doric capitals one associates quite naturally with those pleasant internal colonnades of Hellenistic and Roman private houses that represent the later "domestic Doric," so to speak, and that appear also in the "piccolo Peristilio" of the "Palazzo."[17] Where in the dwelling they may have been used is not clear, though they would have been appropriate in the suggested portico east of the oecus.

Two white marble capitals and a base go with the spirally fluted blue marble columns that were introduced in the oecus (Rooms 27–28) when it was refurbished in the Byzantine period. One of the capitals was found in Room 19 (Plan XVIII 10); the other capital and the base were taken there from the extreme northern part of the excavations for preservation, and all three elements can be seen on Plate XXX *D*. Similar columns were found along the Street of the Monuments (see p. 77) and in the City Bath (see p. 174).

Various architectural fragments found in the courtyard (Room 8) and farther south in the excavated area clearly belong to the Public Building of the Roman period because of their similarity to pieces discovered in the Roman Villa and in the "Palazzo." A sandstone Ionic base (see Pl. XXIX *B*) with traces of heavy painted plaster, found at the north end of the courtyard, has moldings like those of the various examples of this order in the Villa (cf. Plan XIV 4–5). It may have stood on the square plinth imbedded in the floor of Room 29. There are several interesting Doric capitals from the southern part of the building. One of monumental proportions with an abacus 75 cm. square has all the proper moldings excellently cut and the fluting of the attached portion of the shaft nicely done (Plan XIX 4). It was found in the portico along the Street of the Monuments and reflects, it would seem, the order used along this part of the

thoroughfare. Cornice fragments discovered at the north end of the courtyard and in the doorway between Rooms 2 and 3 (Plan XIX 7, 9–12) are in exactly the same style as those of the "Palazzo."[18] One, however, is of later origin, with the modillions emphasized by deep scoring around the margins and medially done with the help of a drill (Plan XVIII 12). Comparable examples were found in the Villa (Plan XIV 7–8). The scoring was later covered by plaster. At the site of the Public Building and at the "Palazzo" there was noticeable the phenomenon that a majority of the cornice fragments bore a terminal feature at one end. This surely must bespeak the practice of using various broken registers of ornamental *epikranitis* as an integral part of the internal decoration, as at Pompeii.[19]

Finally, there are several interesting fragments which cannot even tentatively be associated with any structural features. The small engaged Ionic column found in Room 30 (Plan XVIII 1) is carved on the face of a pier that is grooved at the back for mounting. Similar pieces supplied with projecting tongues were found in the Villa (Plan XIV 14) and at the "Palazzo" (see p. 128). We have learned to associate them with the architectural embellishment of upper stories. There are two surviving bits of what must have been a sophisticated architectural ornament. They are pieces of the entablature of an *aedicula*, the smaller one internally plastered and painted with a floral motif and the other (Plan XVIII 11) representing a considerable portion of the pediment. The latter was found at the south end of the courtyard at the Roman level. A segment of a small framed ornamental arch with false masonry scorings (Plan XVIII 2) appeared in the fill in Room 28.

The architectural elements found on the site of the Public Building permit three conclusions. The first is that at least the original structure was a building of some elegance, as indicated by the ornamental pieces. The second is that there were many close similarities between its architectural members and those of the Roman Villa and the "Palazzo," implying that the three buildings were not far removed from one another in time of construction. The third is that there was general similarity between architectural elements of the Byzantine reconstruction of the Public Building and those at the City Bath and elsewhere along the Street of the Monuments.

---

[16] See Pesce, Il *"Palazzo delle Colonne,"* Pl. XI and and p. 24: "Nei pilastri a coppie di semicolonne abbinate, queste ultime sono disposte in modo che ciascuna guarda un lato del portico, di guisa che in sezione questi pilastri assumono un singolare aspetto cuoriforme."

[17] *Ibid.* Pl. II *B* and pp. 60–62. On the house type see Robinson and Graham, *Excavations at Olynthos* VIII 142 and Fig. 5.

[18] Cf. Pesce, *op. cit.* Pl. VIII.

[19] See Hugh Plommer, *Ancient and Classical Architecture* ("Simpson's History of Architectural Development" I [London, 1956]) Figs. 81 and 83.

It might well be of some help in the dating of the Public Building if its purpose could be further defined, so that it could be studied also as a representative of a type. Part of the problem is, of course, to explain the relationship of the building proper, the bathing facilities, and the attached dwelling. It is tempting in this connection to think of the function of a magistrate such as the ephebarch, whose official duties required close association with his charges and with the scene of their activities.[20] But the structure is of such modest proportions as compared with the establishments for the training of the young known to us from large cities such as Olympia, Pergamum, Delos, Delphi, and Priene[21] and is relatively so poorly preserved that identification along such lines is quite impossible.

Having therefore to be satisfied with the general observation that the original complex belongs to the first century of our era, we can infer from the sequence of the archeological remains that it was in a ruinous condition perhaps in the second half of the second century and certainly in the third century. Whether it was torn down so that it could be replaced or whether other circumstances were responsible for its disintegration cannot be known. In any event its central courtyard was put to use by lime burners who appropriated its marble elements, and presumably the frontage along the Street of the Monuments was used for a row of shops. A precise date for this phase is also impossible to determine, but a suggestion can be offered on the strength of two relevant facts. First, the designation of Ptolemais as the capital city of the province of Libya Pentapolis under Diocletian stimulated the city's economic life, making the construction of shops entirely plausible, and, second, in the reign of Constantine and Licinius the Triumphal Arch was erected on the Street of the Monuments at the southwest corner of the insula occupied by the ruined building. A row of shops could have been erected at this time, in part at least to screen the site left vacant by the disintegration of the Public Building.

[20] An inscription honoring an ephebarch was found in the fill over the Villa (see p. 210, No. 5).

[21] See G. Fougères in C. Daremberg and Edm. Saglio, *Dictionnaire des antiquités grecques et romaines d'après les textes et les monuments* (Paris, 1873–1919) *s.v.* "Gymnasium," and E. N. Gardiner, *Greek Athletics and Sports* (1910) chap. xxii.

Eventually, in the Byzantine period, the shops were replaced by the suite of offices of the Paul who in his inscription (p. 211, No. 14) has left us the record of his work. If indeed he was the civil governor of the province, as his rank suggests, his work must belong to the period prior to the reign of Anastasius, when the metropolis of the province was removed to Apollonia (see p. 27). But a difficult question is posed by the exalted title which he applies to himself and which was not normally applicable to civil governors until a much later date. On this account and because the inscription recording the title is so clearly a part of the fabric of the new construction, it is hardly possible to associate Paul's efforts with the rehabilitation of the Street of the Monuments in the reigns of Valens and Valentinian and Arcadius and Honorius, that is, at the end of the fourth century (see p. 22). A suggestion is made below (p. 211), however, that might permit us to think of Paul's reconstruction as a continuation of the rehabilitation and as a product of the first half of the fifth century.

The archeological evidence is not sufficiently precise to permit separate consideration of the several parts of the Byzantine reconstruction program. Paul's offices were clearly connected with the adjacent dwelling, and that the dwelling was at least refurbished when the offices were built is indicated by the introduction into the oecus (Rooms 27–28) of spirally fluted blue marble columns such as were used in the Triumphal Arch and in the Byzantine City Bath. That the bathing facilities were rehabilitated at this time seems quite obvious, but it seems equally obvious that their use would have been limited to Paul and his friends. Eventually, however, the bath was opened to access from the street, becoming thus a public asset. It is tempting to associate this development with the end of the fifth and the early part of the sixth century, after the capital of the province had been shifted to Apollonia. During this period there was extreme water shortage in the city because of the interruption of the supply from the aqueduct which Justinian subsequently repaired (see p. 27). The shortage affected the City Bath, which was shut down and allowed to fall into disrepair. Conceivably prior to the rehabilitation of the City Bath, which followed Justinian's repair of the aqueduct, the bathing facilities of the Public Building were put into service for the benefit of the community. The installations by means of which water was conducted from a high-placed tank to the cold plunge in the frigidarium (Room 10) and by means of which beasts of burden housed in the stables could have carried water to that tank and to the tubs are in accord with the circum-stances of a period of water shortage and a token of how low the fortunes of the city had fallen. Thus the bathing facilities of the Public Building apparently retained their usefulness longer than any other part of the complex establishment.

THE CITY BATH OF THE BYZANTINE PERIOD

In the heart and on the axis of the city grid as we know it today Ptolemais had in late Roman and Byzantine times and probably also from the outset an insula of double width on the south side of the Street of the Monuments (see Fig. 3). The importance attaching to the double insula by virtue both of its position and of the findings made by the Italian archeologists along its northern frontage (see pp. 79–81) suggested that exca-vation should seek to penetrate into its interior so far as time and circumstances would permit. Work was therefore undertaken in a rectangular area at its northwest corner (see Fig. 18). This area was delimited at the north and west by intersecting streets and at the south and east by the tops of walls visible on the surface amid shrubs and debris (Pl. XXXIII *A*) and measured about 41.65 m. from east to west and about 32.40 m. from north to south. Clearances had to be made along the eastern and western sides of the rectangle to provide access to the interior for the removal of debris. The excavations laid bare what had been anticipated, namely a bath, but one of such dignity and size that it deserves to be called the City Bath (Building 15 on Plan XXII). It belongs essentially to the Byzantine period, but its im-portance for this period ruled out systematic inquiry below its floor levels to ascertain what may have stood on the site in Roman times. Light may eventually be shed on this point indirectly by examination of the remaining three-quarters of the double insula, which certainly also contained public buildings of note, but the chances are that the Byzantine structure merely replaced at a higher level a Roman building of the same function and the same general plan. Indeed, it may be that some elements of the Byzantine City Bath carry through from the Roman period (see pp. 174–75).

Excavation had to contend with the higher building level that was established along the Street of the Monuments when the building line was set back and a porch (5.90 m. deep) was constructed 1.20 m. above street level (see p. 79). This provided an obstacle to the entrance of Decauville railroad tracks, and an effort was therefore made to gain access to the interior by clearing the cross street along the west side of the bath (Pl. XXXII *D*). The effort was abandoned when the west exterior wall of the building proved to be solid and un-broken, but the clearance yielded from the fill of the street a coin of Gratian, a small fragment of a large draped marble statue (p. 198, No. 26), and a small fragment of the Price Edict of Diocletian (p. 215, No. 47*A*). Since easy access to the building was denied, a bridge was thrown across the Street of the Monuments from the north, leading at porch level directly into the frigidarium (Room 6) of the bath. When subsequently it proved impossible to penetrate farther into the building on this line a second bridge was constructed farther to the east. To accommodate the tracks of this bridge at porch level a north-south trench had to be dug through a deep deposit of almost solid ashes in the area east of the bath (see Plans XX–XXI). No floors or walls were encountered in this trench (see p. 170, n. 25). On the surface a small piece of marble sculpture (p. 198, No. 21) came to light and in the fill near the porch another fragment of the Price Edict of Diocletian (p. 215, No. 47*B*). The ap-proach from the east provided access, as it turned out, only to the tepidarium (Room 9) of the bath. The caldarium (Room 13) remained inaccessible from north, east, and west and was not cleared. It has to be approached from the south.

The City Bath as revealed by the excavations (Plan XX and Fig. 56) was approached in anti-quity by staircases leading up from the footpath along the Street of the Monuments to the level of the raised porch (see p. 79). From the porch, entrance to the building was effected through two rectangular vestibules (Rooms 1 and 2) at opposite ends of the north façade. They were of unequal size, that to the west (Room 1), near the street intersection, being the larger, but its entrance was

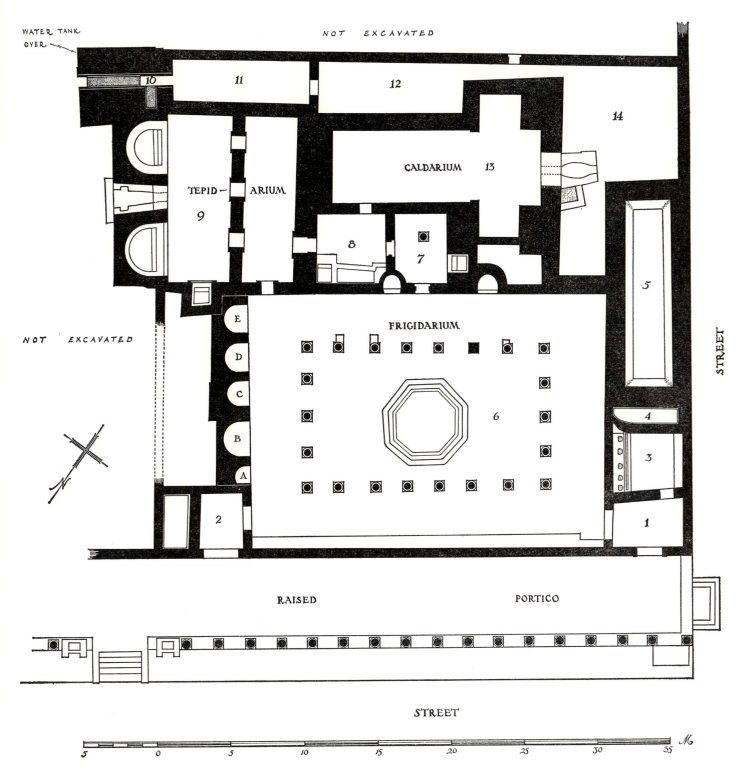

WATER TANK
OVER

NOT EXCAVATED

10   11   12   14

'TEPID — ARIUM
9

CALDARIUM 13

NOT EXCAVATED

8   7

E
D
C
B
A

FRIGIDARIUM

6

5

4

3

2

1

RAISED   PORTICO

STREET

STREET

5   0   5   10   15   20   25   30   35   M

Fig. 56.—Diagrammatic Plan of City Bath. *G.R.H. Wright*

narrower (1.60 m.) than that of Room 2 (2.40 m.). Two coins of Phocas were found, virtually at floor level, in the debris that filled Room 2. A narrow doorway in the south wall of Room 1 gave access to an inner chamber (Room 3), of equal width but of greater depth, that served as the latrine of the bath (Pl. XXXIII *B*). Five toilets were ranged against its east wall. A limestone column base with part of the shaft attached and part of a shaft of a column of lesser diameter, found set against its north wall, may have helped to support the roof. The water for the latrine was supplied from a separate tank (4.45 × 1.15 m. and 1.20 m. deep) immediately to the south (Room 4). The tank was heavily built and tapered at its east end to provide access to a drain underneath it. From the tank the water passed through a small aperture into a channel running northward immediately in front of the toilet seats. Here it was available for use in washing hands and feet. At the north end of Room 3 the channel turned back, running under the toilet seats to the south wall, whence the sewage was channeled westward in the drain under the tank. It emerged from the west wall of the bath about 30 cm. above street level and was guided across the street in a covered conduit (1.20 m. high) that emptied into the building area of the next insula westward. Our partial clearance of the street had revealed that it was closed off by a wall running on the line of the rear (south) wall of the bath (see Plan XX) and inclosing a portico visible in the next insula. The fact that the conduit and its masonry substructure closed the street to traffic implies that the blocking farther to the south had already taken place.

Southward of Room 4, at the west side of the bath, was a much larger reservoir (12.30 × 3.20 m.) built of carefully but not elegantly dressed blocks, accurately fitted and laid in double thickness (Room 5). The stonework was the most solid in the entire structure. Inside the reservoir were found many large identically cut stones, with their inner faces arcuated and their outer faces carved with shallow fluting. They may be the voussoirs of its vaulted roofing. The floor of the reservoir was high above the base of its retaining walls and had a heavy quarter-round molding of concrete along its edges to guard against leakage. How water reached the reservoir was not evident, and what is known about its distribution is noted in appropriate contexts below. A coin of Aulus Pupius Rufus came to light in the fill.

The two vestibules (Rooms 1–2) led at right angles and through doorways of approximately equal width into the large rectangular open court (*ca.* 24.30 × 16.70 m.) that formed the frigidarium of the bath (Pl. XXXIV). In the center of the court (Room 6) was a large sunken octagonal pool 80 cm. deep. It had an inclosing frame rising 40 cm. above the paving of the court. This provided a back rest for people seated around the pool, while a ledge 25 cm. wide and 25 cm. above the floor of the pool provided a footrest. The maximum diameter of the pool was 4.45 m. Water to fill it came in from the west under the paving of the court. The drain for emptying it ran out through a pipe in a northeasterly direction. A lion-headed waterspout (p. 193, No. 6) was found at the bottom of the tub. Colonnaded porticoes surrounded the court on all four sides. The spirally fluted blue marble columns, twenty-two in all, were footed on square plinths and had white marble bases and white Corinthian capitals (Pl. XXXVI *D* and Fig. 57). Neither the columns nor the capitals were of uniform dimensions. No architrave or frieze blocks came to light in the excavations. Behind the east portico were ranged five niches. Doorways led to the interior of the bath from the south portico.

The courtyard with its porticoes, its pool, and its niches must originally have been elegant. There were remains of marble incrustations on its south

Fig. 57.—Column of Frigidarium
(Room 6) of City Bath.
G. R. H. Wright

wall, and it was possible to see and to trace, particularly at the east, the patterns of an inlaid marble paving (Fig. 58). Reused pedestals set in front of the second and third columns (from north) of the east colonnade once bore life-size marble statues (Pls. XLVI and XXXVIII) which were found as they had fallen. They have been identified as Roman copies of Hellenistic statues of Aeschines

statues came to light: from the east portico a fragment of a draped female figure (p. 195, No. 11) and the toes of a sandaled foot on a filleted base (No. 19); from the south portico an odd pierlike object with human legs in relief (No. 14); from the west portico remains of an Eros on a sea monster (No. 13), a knee and shin with part of an animal attached (No. 15), and a booted or unfinished foot

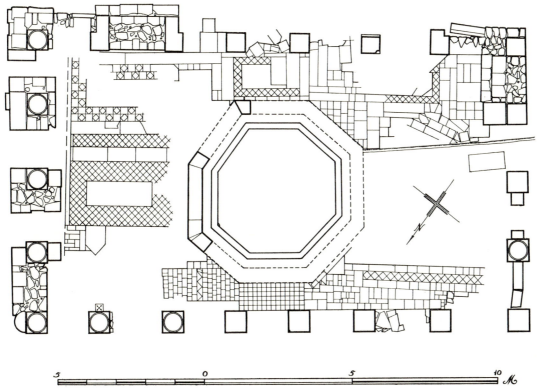

Fig. 58.—Diagram of Remains of Marble Paving in Frigidarium of City Bath. *J. E. Knudstad*

(p. 195, No. 10) and Cleopatra I (p. 188, No. 9). The pedestal in front of the second column bears (upside down) an inscription (p. 214, No. 36). A large capital shorn of its ornament but with a section of shaft attached was set into the floor in front of the fourth column, but no statue was found in front of it. The torso of a nude female figure (Pl. XLI) from a group of the Three Graces was found on the floor behind the plinth of the second column (from south) of the west colonnade (see pp. 194–95, No. 8). There might have been room for such a group, a typical bath ornament, on a pedestal of small stones that fills the first inter-columniation (from south) of the west colonnade (see Plan XX). In the debris that filled the court and particularly in the porticoes fragments of a number of other life-size or even larger marble

on a base (No. 16); from the southwest corner of the porticoes a bare right foot (No. 17) and a booted calf (No. 20); and from the open court the toes of a foot on a base (No. 18) and a fragment of a buttock and thigh (No. 23). Whether or not all the statues that these pieces represent were part of the embellishment of the bath, it is clear that the area where they were found served also as a place of transit for sculpture brought in from outside. This was indicated by the discovery around the court and particularly in the east portico of several basketfuls of sizable marble chips (59 pieces by actual count) without identifiable surface features, and it was subsequently verified by evidence of lime burning in Rooms 7 and 14.

The original elegance of the frigidarium, many of its elements taken from earlier structures, was

11*

only dimly visible in the remains. The floor had sunk irregularly in various areas. The marble paving had in large part been looted or relaid without reference to patterning. Cement patches were obvious everywhere. Intrusive benches and water channels were visible on all sides. Only the plinths of the columns seemed to have maintained their original alignment and level. Part of the miserable condition of the court was clearly the result of long and hard usage. Part of it, however, was clearly the result of a change in building levels in the double insula. To obtain in this part of the bath the higher floor level required by the raised porch the builders had to introduce fill. They covered the fill with slabs, examples of which are visible in the south portico near its east end, and over the slabs they spread the bedding for the inlaid marble paving. The fill was either imperfectly packed or had subsided in connection with drainage both from the surface of the court and from its water-supply system. It was impossible to ascertain what was under the courtyard without wholesale destruction of the Byzantine remains. Clearly, however, the Byzantine builders either found available or provided a solid footing for the plinths of their columns, since these remained in such relatively excellent alignment. The first alternative would imply that the Roman predecessor of the Byzantine structure also had an interior peristyle.

In the north portico, between the two vestibules, the only feature to be noted is a single continuous row of small stones about 20 cm. high set at a distance of about 90 cm. from the outer wall of the court and marking, probably, the emplacement of a bench. The stones could have formed the lower part of the bench or its footrest.

On the east the court was inclosed by five niches (*A–E* on Fig. 56), the interstices between their arcs being filled with rubble. A heavy structural wall running east and west between Niches *B* and *C* (see Plan **XX**) had no continuation in the trench 5 meters eastward through which the rail line was run at porch level to the southern part of the bath. The entire niche area had undergone much change and repair, and how far one should go in postulating an original uniformity and suggesting an original purpose is debatable. The series now begins at the north with a seminiche (*A*) that seems to be either an afterthought or a remainder, and ends at the south with a niche (*E*) that has all but lost its form. Niches *C* and *D* are of about the same size, while

Niche *B* is wider and Niche *E* deeper than the others. In all but *A* the masonry that shaped the niches consisted of well cut stones laid in regular courses ending with square facing blocks. These could have carried the arches that must have completed their semidomes. The niches showed signs of plastering and, if Niche *C* is any criterion, originally had stone flooring only some 25 cm. above the floor level of the court. At this level they could have served as the setting for masonry tubs, as traces of a layer of cement on the flooring of *C* suggests, but there are no indications of retaining walls for tubs. Niches *A*, *B*, *D*, and *E* were filled with masonry to about 50 cm. above the floor level of the court and at least Niche *B* had been heavily cemented at this level, though again indications of a retaining wall that would have transformed the cemented area into a tub are missing.

In the course of their history the niches had an irregular wall 60 cm. high set in front of them and projecting about 70 cm. into the east portico. Between the outer stones of this wall and the faces of the niches a space about 20–30 cm. wide was left open and in it was imbedded an inclosed water channel about 15 cm. wide and 5 cm. high. This channel emerged behind the south jamb of the doorway leading from the east vestibule (Room 2) into the east portico (see Plan **XX**) and continued along the south and east sides of the vestibule, connecting with a conduit that ran under the paving of the porch and eventually along its edge to the fountains adorning the porch (see p. 79). It was not clear how the water channel was brought around a large orthostat that now is set in front of Niche *D*, nor is the original course of the channel in the area of Niche *E* certain. As found, the channel extends up across the raised floor of Niche *E* in a southeasterly direction to the northwest corner of a recess in the north wall of the tepidarium (Room 9), where it received water vertically along the line of a channel cut in the wall of the recess (see Plan **XX**), probably from a tank set on top of the recess. How the water may have reached such a tank is unknown. After the channel was constructed through Niche *E*, the niche no longer served whatever its original purpose may have been. That the entire arrangement had anything to do with the emplacement of tubs in any of the niches is by no means evident. Rather it seems to have been intended to serve the fountains adorning the porch. If the niches were walled in along the portico side to provide tubs at their raised floor level, the water could have run off from them through the channel, but bath water perhaps would not have been deemed suitable for use in the fountains. In Niche *D* and at niche level in the fill directly in front of it were found the base and two large fragments of a marble statue of Herakles (p. 196, No. 12) dedicated to the city by Marcus Ulpius Cominius. On the filled-in surface of Niche *E* a coin of Heraclius came to light and in the water channel running across it a coin of Phocas. At floor level in front of Niche *E* there was a coin of Justin II.

The south wall of the frigidarium was pierced by two doorways, one (85 cm. wide) about 95 cm. from its east end and the other (90 cm. wide) directly opposite the octagonal pool. Excavation of the tepidarium (Room 9) revealed that the first of these had an earlier sill 33 cm. below the level of the frigidarium, which indicated a rise in level in the interior of the establishment. This doorway was found blocked up with oddments of masonry and with one sculptured marble slab. Though severely damaged, the slab (see p. 193, No. 5) revealed traces of a head tossed high, of flowing tresses, and of a wreath of ivy leaves around the neck of the figure, all indicating that it is the missing part of the relief of the dancing maenads found by the Italian archeologists in their clearance of the south side of the Street of the Monuments (see p. 81).

Rows of unmatched irregularly laid stones were set in front of the south wall of the frigidarium along most of its course (see Pl. XXXIV *A* and Plan XX). Some of these no doubt served as benches, but some served other purposes. Directly behind the second intercolumniation of the south colonnade, counting from the east, the lowest row of stones was overlaid with a curved facing of cement that may at one time have been painted red; the top of a second, inner row had a marble-slab surfacing. In front of this area the floor of the south portico was solidly cemented. Whether the cement provided the emplacement for a water basin or pool secondarily set into the portico or whether it was connected with the podium (see p. 166) erected between the adjacent columns is difficult to say. Farther westward, flanking the central doorway asymmetrically, the intrusive masonry serves as the facings for and forms the steps of two semicircular tubs that were cut through the south wall

of the frigidarium (see Plan XX). Both tubs are clearly secondary features, but how far along in the history of the establishment they should be placed is not easy to determine.

In the southwest corner of the frigidarium intrusive masonry set along the walls served as the emplacement for a channel which received water from two lion-headed waterpouts. One spout was found in the south portico and the other in the octagonal pool, but their original positions are marked by shallow depressions at the tops of the south and west walls as preserved. It may thus be inferred that the stone footing of these walls did not extend above their present tops and that their superstructures were of mud brick. Certainly there were no remains of fallen masonry in the area. The spout in the west wall was on a line with the northeast corner of the reservoir (Room 5), whence it received water. Its level, however, was nearly that of the top of the reservoir as preserved. The spout in the south wall had behind it, in a mass of masonry filling, water channels running respectively to it, to the more westerly of the semicircular tubs set into the south wall, and to a tub in an alcove in Room 7. The water must have come to these channels from the reservoir (Room 5), but the traces of the connections were dim. The spout in the west wall also fed the octagonal pool in the center of the court, by means of a channel leading from it under the paving of the court (see Fig. 58 and Plan XX). The two spouts and the channel running along the walls at the southwest corner of the frigidarium became the source of supply for a succession of installations in this corner. The latest of these was a crude basin formed by a quarter-circle of stones in the angle of the masonry supporting the water channel (see Plan XX). It was set upon a deposit of hardened lime that reached a depth of about 30 cm. along the south side of the south portico and extended out into the open court. Perhaps this basin was nothing more than a trough for mixing mortar with the lime supplied by installations in Rooms 7 and 14. When some of the hardened lime was hacked away there appeared fragments of an elaborate mosaic pavement that extended the length of the last intercolumniations of the west and south colonnades. It contained representations of fish, dolphins, and at least one water fowl and had a wide border decorated with a loose vine scroll (see p. 253). The border extended on the south under the rows of stones supporting the water channel that was fed by the lion-headed spouts and may therefore be said to belong to a relatively early phase of the frigidarium. Why in this area alone mosaic instead of marble slabs should have been used to pave the courtyard is not clear. There were indications at the edges of the mosaic paving that it was once contained within marble slabs rising vertically from the floor. Perhaps the mosaic formed the bottom of an L-shaped plunge contrived under the shelter of the porticoes to provide for the warmer months of the year a cooler bath than the octagonal pool in the center of the open court. It should be noted in this connection that the plinth of the next to the last column of the south colonnade was provided at the time of its emplacement with a projection in a recess of which (see Fig. 58) was found imbedded a part of the vertical marble slabbing that inclosed the plunge, thus indicating that it was part of the original Byzantine construction. Vertical plaster bedding for more such slabbing ran westward to the corner pier of the peristyle. It is possible that the waterspout in the south wall of the frigidarium originally supplied the plunge and that the channel that carried water from both spouts was a secondary feature.

At the end of the masonry supporting the water channel an outlet for surplus rain water from the paved surface of the frigidarium was crudely cut into its west wall, connecting with the drain from the latrine (Room 3). Just north of this point the stumps of crude walls made of reused stones inclose an area that has the depth of the west portico and the width of two intercolumniations (see Plan XX). These walls must have been raised to ceiling height with mud bricks, thus forming an intrusive room which has all the earmarks of a watchman's lodge. The inclosure had openings to the east and north, the latter providing a clear view of all who came into the bath through the west vestibule (Room 1), and a stone platform (*ca.* 3.00 × 0.60 m.) with a footrest on the west side. The platform rises about 60 cm. from the floor of the court.

Around the peristyle there are other intrusive materials that testify to the long usage and gradual disintegration of the structure. The two intercolumniations at the southwest corner are shut off by masonry. This represents part of the inclosure that provided for the emplacement of the L-shaped plunge described above and perhaps provided also

for the mounting of the Three Graces (see p. 163). On the east side the plinths of the third, fourth, and fifth columns (from the north) have crude masses of masonry set about them, while the plinths of the first and second columns are joined with a similar mass of stones (see Fig. 58 and Plan XX). These masses, which contain architectural members, are not benches and had nothing to do with the water-supply system. Perhaps they served to strengthen the columns or, if the columns had fallen, held wooden supports for the roof of the portico to replace the columns. A coin of Justin II was found in the dirt filling of the mass around the third column.

In the south colonnade the second intercolumniation from the east is entirely closed up with what appears to be a podium (see Fig. 58 and Plan XX). The stones along the north, that is, toward the interior of the court, are set back from the faces of the plinths. The fill extends southward for a distance of about 1.15 m., maintaining a level equal to the height of the plinths. Access to the platform thus created is provided at the south along its entire length by a continuous step with a rise of 20 cm. and a tread of 35 cm. (see Pl. XXXIV *A*). This feature was apparently part of the original construction of the Byzantine bath, for the plinths were cut with southward projections that flank and contain the sides of the podium. Conceivably it was a bema, used by officials for the transaction of business that required public hearings, so that in effect the City Bath served as the *ekklesiasterion* or the *dikasterion* of the Byzantine city, replacing the separate structures provided for these puposes in the well developed democratic cities of Hellenistic and Roman times. It is interesting to note in this connection the organization of the marble paving near and directly in front of the podium (see Fig. 58). Plain fields framed by geometrically segmented borders (see p. 254) may mark the places where people appearing before the magistrate or official stood in accordance with the protocol of Byzantine court procedure. A water channel runs northward under the floor from the region of the bema, where a small section of the paving had caved in, toward a sump in the northeast corner of the court. In the channel was found a coin of Gordian III. When the entire floor of the frigidarium was swept in the final cleaning, coins of Anastasius and Maurice Tiberius were found in the south portico and east of the octagonal pool, respectively, and a third coin of the fifth century came to light in a chink between paving stones. Other coins, found higher in the fill over the courtyard, include single pieces of the fifth century, of Anastasius, of Justinian, of Justin II, and of Heraclius.

A word must be said in this connection about the walls that inclosed the frigidarium and carried the roofs of the porticoes. The north wall, which was of course also the exterior wall of the building, had the regular thickness of a single row of stones. At the east no regular wall came to light, this side being inclosed by the five niches. These were built without relation to a wall, the interstices between their arcs being filled irregularly with rubble. The whole system of niches may thus have been a Byzantine device to cut off the eastern end of what in a Roman structure was a larger space unit. On the west there was a solid wall, the stretch separating the frigidarium from Rooms 1 and 3 having the thickness (*ca.* 55 cm.) of a single row of stones and that inclosing the reservoir (Room 5) being of double thickness. The west wall, in the two courses observable, was not bonded to the south wall and had short stones not more than 20 cm. long pieced in along its course, particularly toward the north (see Plan XX). The south wall has a variety of structural forms, not clearly observable throughout. At the east it is a very solid mass, two stones and all of 90 cm. thick. This construction comes to an end 1.80 m. west of the doorway leading into the tepidarium (Room 9), where there is still visible in the second course from the top a corner that lines up with the east face of the middle row of stones in the east wall of Room 8 (see p. 168). From this point the south wall of the frigidarium proceeds westward (as can be seen from the interior of Rooms 7 and 8) with a regular thickness of 60–65 cm. and is surmounted, strangely enough, by a badly mutilated cornice 45 cm. thick (Fig. 59). This construction continues (save for individual stones of an upper tier and interruption of the cornice near the doorway to Room 7) to the point where the south wall abuts the inner row of stones of the reservoir wall.[22] The cornice is awkwardly placed just above and behind the rows of intrusive stones that were set against the south wall (see p. 165). A water channel had been cut in its upper surface. Toward Rooms 7 and 8 the thickness of the well built wall that it

[22] The west wall of the frigidarium in turn abuts it.

crowns was reduced at cornice level, as though for the lodgement of beams. One might therefore imagine that the wall was part of a Roman structure and had been incorporated in the Byzantine bath. The only difficulty is that the cornice level is only 2.20 m. above that of the Street of the Monuments. If this piece of masonry is not Roman, there is nothing in the frigidarium (save perhaps the plinths of the columns) that can be associated with the earlier period.

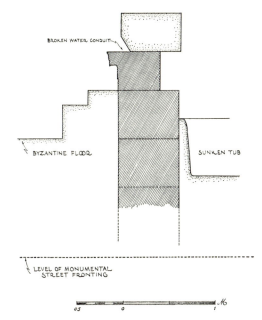

Fig. 59.—Section of Cornice-Crowned Wall along South Side of Frigidarium of City Bath.
G.R.H.Wright

The two courses of the south wall that rise above the level of the cornice-crowned section and the west wall of the frigidarium contained reused stones that are carved with portions of commemorative inscriptions. The same type of inscription occurs on stones built into the exterior west wall of the building and in walls of Rooms 5, 7, 14, and 15. Stones with similar texts were also found unattached in the frigidarium. The place of origin of these stones (pp. 212–14, Nos. 20–35, 39–40, 42–46) is of importance for the dating of the Byzantine City Bath (see p. 174). A fragment of a framed marble panel found loose in the fill at the south side of the frigidarium bears parts of two texts of a different type (see p. 214, No. 41).

From the frigidarium (Room 6) entrance was provided to the interior of the bath primarily through the doorway leading into Room 7. The doorframe, with its heavy monolithic jambs, maintained the thickness of the cornice-crowned section of the south wall of the frigidarium, but the coarseness of its moldings contrasts sharply with the refinement of the cornice. Thus the jambs are a feature of the Byzantine construction and not of the wall, which is presumed to be Roman (see above). In Rooms 7 and 8 there were heavy masses of fallen rubble vaulting which indicated how the rooms had been roofed and which, when removed, revealed a heavy deposit of lime and ashes particularly in Room 7. The lime, together with obvious indications of firing, proved that a great deal of marble, probably both sculptured and slabbed, had been reduced to a more useful commodity here.

Room 7 was originally quite regular in shape, measuring 3.50 m. in width and 4.60 m. in depth. At the west, in an alcove about 1.25 m. square, was set a simple tub that was fed by one of the channels running eastward from the reservoir (Room 5). The walls of the room were constructed of large well laid blocks save at the northeast corner, where a rough mass of masonry had been introduced to support the semicircular tub that was let into the south wall of the frigidarium. At the southeast a section of the inclosing wall had been pushed into the area of Room 13 when the rubble vaulting fell. Some of the original marble pavement (*opus segmentatum*) survived just inside the doorway. Near the center of the room was a marble column base that may have been on its way to be burned or, more likely, may have carried a vertical support for the rubble ceiling after it had cracked and was threatening to fall. Similar installations have been noted in Room 3 (see p. 145) and in Room 18 of the Roman Villa (see p. 120), but neither presupposes a vaulted ceiling.

A doorway with monolithic unmolded jambs led eastward from Room 7 to Room 8 (Pl. XXXIII *C*), which was also paved with small square marble slabs. The room is square (4.60 × 4.60 m.), but its shape was obscured somewhat by the introduction of two tubs at the north, one a long rectangular affair (0.90 × 2.45 m.), the other about 1.10 m. square (see Plan XX). The water for these tubs and for the adjacent semicircular tub let into the south wall of the frigidarium came from the channel carved in the top of the cornice of that wall (see Fig. 59). The duct which conducted the water through the wall to the tubs in Room 8 was still

visible. From the tubs the water was led off in a southerly direction. The intake procedure implies, of course, that during the period in which these tubs were in use the doorway connecting the frigidarium (Room 6) and the tepidarium (Room 9) directly was blocked up (as found), because the ultimate source of supply must have been east of the doorway, presumably the tank which also fed water down through Niche *E* to the channel along the east side of the frigidarium (see p. 164).

The walls of Room 8 are of interest in connection with the circulation through the bath and in connection with the history of the establishment. At the northwest corner they shared the fate of the walls at the northeast corner of Room 7. The south wall is exceptionally well preserved and shows regular coursing of large stones and a pair of heavy unmolded orthostats that form the jambs of the doorway leading into the caldarium (Room 13). On the north there is visible the back of the cornice-crowned south wall of the frigidarium. The east wall, which separates Room 8 from Room 9, has a thickness of three rows of stones (1.60 m.). The two inner rows were hacked through to provide an opening into Room 9, while the outermost row has a pair of doorjambs set into it. The east face of the middle row falls into line with the east end of the cornice-crowned wall along the south side of the frigidarium. We have here, therefore, another possible indication of an earlier building on the site, but so far as can be seen the rows are not bonded into either the frigidarium wall at the north or the north wall of Room 13 at the south.

The doorway leading eastward from Room 8 gave upon the tepidarium (Room 9), a large slightly irregularly shaped chamber (10.90–11.95 × 5.40–5.60 m.). Its most important feature is a pair of large semicircular basins contained in apses (*ca.* 3.50 m. in diameter) symmetrically placed in the east wall (see Pl. XXXV *A* and Plan XX). At the north there was a rectangular recess (1.40 × 1.65 m.) containing a tub (Pl. XXXV *B*). The floor of the room was constructed in hypocaust fashion, being supported on piers of baked bricks. The roof was of rubble vaulting, as were the semidomes of the semicircular basins in the east wall. The rubble had fallen in large sections, but portions of the semidome of the southern basin were still in position.

How the heavy rubble vaulting was carried across the room is explained in part by the existence below the floor of a severely burned wall (*ca.* 90 cm. thick) running north and south approximately through the middle of the chamber (3.50 m. from the west wall and 4.50 m. from the east wall). At hypocaust level it has three openings (see Fig. 56) that permitted the circulation of the heated air under the floor. The openings were capped by sill-like stones so that at floor level a continuous surface was provided. Two spirally fluted columns of blue marble, sections of which were found in the debris, probably stood on the solid sections of the wall between the openings. Also discovered in the debris were heavy stone blocks that are longer than the typical building stones and square in section instead of rectangular. These probably served as beams or unmolded architraves that stretched from column to column and from columns to terminal walls to carry the heavy vaulting. In the western half of the room a single low barrel vault is indicated, but in the eastern half the builders no doubt took advantage of the semidomes over the large basins to use cross-vaulting.

The tepidarium was presumably originally paved with marble slabs, which would have been removed by looters before the building fell into ruins, for no traces survived. The typical tile bedding for the floor had been broken into fragments and depressed by the fall of the rubble vaulting and its massive stone supports. Save at the northwest corner of the room the piers upon which the *suspensura* rested were therefore not reached by excavation until well below the level of the north-south wall that ran below the floor. The piers were excavated to their bedding only in the northern third of the room (see Pl. XXXVI *A*). Elsewhere excavation was halted at the level to which the floor had been depressed and to which the piers were preserved intact (see Pl. XXXV *A*). They were about 40 cm. square when freestanding, but of various sizes along the sides of the room, and were built of square and rectangular baked bricks cross-bonded to give the piers maximum strength.[23] A few circular bricks were used in the northwest corner of the room. The piers were spaced typically at intervals of about 40 cm.

At the northwest corner of the room, where the fallen vaulting had not depressed the floor and its

[23] The bricks were uniformly 4.5 cm thick. The square bricks were of two sizes, 32 cm. and 22 cm. on sides respectively.

supports, the piers of the *suspensura* rose to a height of almost 2 meters above their bedding (Pl. XXXV *C*). Supported by piers of this height throughout, the floor would have been at the level of the doorway leading into the tepidarium from Room 8, and calcification and blackening of the walls by heat and smoke are actually visible, particularly at the north and west, to approximately that level. The two semicircular basins in the east wall and the smaller rectangular tub in the north wall would thus have been entered by stepping down from the floor. But piers 2 meters high were really not necessary for good draft, and a close inspection of the masonry raised the question whether originally the floor was at a lower level. At the west and north there is a 4-cm. offset in the walls about 40 cm. below the top of the sill of the doorway leading to Room 8. The best explanation of this offset is that it was intended to receive the ends of tiles that rested upon the piers of the *suspensura*, which would imply a lower floor only about 1.50 m. above the bedding of the piers. The piers would then have been about 1.40 m. high. The level of their bedding is very close to that of the Street of the Monuments. Several other details of construction suggest an earlier floor in the tepidarium. The filling by means of which the small rectangular recess in the north wall was converted into a tub was carried down the equivalent of four courses (*ca.* 1.70 m.), though the tub itself is only 65 cm. deep (see Pl. XXXV *B*). The top four courses of the north wall, moreover, seem to be of different construction from the lower courses. In the east wall it is possible to trace inside the northern semicircular basin, two courses down from its rim, the 4-cm. offset that was noted in the north and west walls. Below the line of the offset the projecting ends of the piers framing the basin were constructed of stones 65 cm. across the face, while above this line the stones measure only 45 cm. across the face. Such details could not be observed in connection with the southern basin because the original construction had been obscured by a secondary inner facing of stone.

Certain other structural features of the tepidarium likewise have bearing on the matter of the earlier floor. In the space between the two semicircular basins in the east wall excavation revealed an irregularly shaped plastered tub whose bottom was flush with the upper floor of the room. A wall to contain the tub at the east had been built against the masonry inclosing the semicircular basins (see Plan **XX**). Immediately inside this applied shoring, at the south, were found remains of a corbeled connection between the masonry masses of the two semicircular basins. Removal of the tub revealed the reason for the corbeled opening, for below the tub was the brick furnace which supplied the heat for the tepidarium. The heated air passed from the furnace into the hypocaust and out through two corbeled openings in the south wall of the tepidarium (see Pl. **XXXV** *D*) into Room 11. The two openings are of different heights, that to the west rising almost to the level of the higher floor, that to the east only to the level of the lower floor (see Section *BB* on Plan **XXI**). The south wall of the tepidarium was of irregular construction and in all likelihood had been rebuilt in connection with the changes in the interior of the chamber. Like that to the west it was a facing wall. Set against the north wall of Room 11, it was poorly constructed, irregularly coursed, and in precarious condition when excavated. It was divided into two parts by the north-south wall that ran down the middle of the tepidarium under the floor and that here emerged as a pier, being bonded into the north wall of Room 11. Evidence of rebuilding was extensive on the east and south sides of the tepidarium. The introduction of the plastered tub required the addition of supporting masonry at its sides as well as at the back (to the east). At the south a large well-like opening was left in this masonry, connecting with the area of the *suspensura* and showing there a corbeled opening through which heated air was conducted from the furnace to the area under the semicircular basins and thence upward by large vertical ducts (19 × 15 cm.) in the walls inclosing the basins. Presumably the well-like opening served as the emplacement for a metal cauldron in which water could be heated to provide steam for the room.

The last indication of the use of Room 9 represents the period when lime burners were busily at work in Rooms 7 and 14 and is provided by three marble heads found in the fill in the northwest quarter of the room. They represent Cleopatra I, Asklepios, and a mythological figure. The head of Cleopatra goes with the female statue found in the frigidarium (see pp. 163 and 188–90), but no traces of statues associated with the other two heads (see pp. 191, No. 2, and 192, No. 4) were found. Presumably the heads were hidden here by the lime burners, perhaps with the idea that they might later be disposed of more profitably as sculptures than as lime.[24] Thus it would seem that the room was already out of service as a tepidarium and relatively inaccessible, perhaps because the rubble vaulting had caved in over most of its area.

To fix any upper or lower date for the disintegration of the room and its use by the lime burners is manifestly impossible. The earlier stages in its history it will be well to consider after a brief survey of the remaining portions of the bath because of their strategic importance for the knowledge of the history of the building. Here we need merely record the additional fact that only three coins were found in Room 9, issues of Gallienus, Maxentius, and Justinian. All three came from the fill and thus show merely that the abandonment of the room did not precede the reign of Justinian[25].

Of the rooms along the south side of the bath only imperfect knowledge could be obtained because of their relative inaccessibility. Room 11 (2.70 × 9.20 m.) was choked with heavy masonry blocks deriving in large part, it would seem, from its south wall, which had caved in and had been

---

[24] A similar inference can be drawn for the portrait head found in the courtyard (Room 8) of the Public Building (see p. 157).

[25] A word may be added here about the area to the east, through which we cut a trench so that the dump cars could be brought into the vicinity of Room 9. Since the tracks were brought across the Street of the Monuments at the level of the raised porch along the north side of the double insula and through a break in its façade where a water channel led under the pavement to the fountains that adorned the porch (see p. 164), it was anticipated that a floor would be encountered beyond the porch. In spite of repeated soundings no floor was found. Nor was the way blocked by transverse walls save for a crude piece of construction set against the northeast corner of the masonry framing the northern semicircular basin of Room 9. To receive the tracks of the railway the fill was trenched to a maximum depth of 1.90 m. It sloped downward toward the northeast and revealed at first occasional field stones, broken bricks, and fragments of mortar. After a few meters' penetration toward the south nothing was found save a massive and continuous deposit of ashes, originating no doubt from the furnace which heated Room 9. Thus it would seem not only that the furnace was in long use but also that in the Byzantine period the section of the double insula between the City Bath and the apsidal hall partially cleared by the Italian archeologists (see p. 79) was not structurally developed, in spite of the porch and the porticoes along the Street of the Monuments (see Fig. 18).

rebuilt in part with smaller stones, perhaps in connection with the use of the area south of the bath. Save for these blocks and a single coin of Justinian found virtually at the level of its earthen floor, Room 11 yielded only earth fill resting on a deposit of soot and ashes that became progressively deeper toward the east. The ashes derived, of course, from the corbeled openings in its north wall, through which the heated air from the furnace was exhausted after it passed under the *suspensura* of the tepidarium (Room 9). The north wall of Room 11 was more heavily constructed than the south wall of Room 9, which was set against it. An unexpected feature of its construction was the emplacement of an arch with a span of 2.79 m. on the line of the lower, more easterly flue opening. The arch appeared to be a secondary feature of the wall, which continues structurally the masonry shell of the adjacent semicircular basin but is not bonded to the wall inclosing the caldarium (Room 13) at the west.

At the east Room 11 leads through a narrow vertical opening into Room 10, a hollow well constructed cube of heavy masonry (*ca.* 5.20 × 6.30 m.). The vertical opening has a counterpart toward the east, which was not further explored. The cube was capped by a flat rubble mass still firmly in place. Clearance of the interior of the cube revealed a continuous stratified deposit of black soot in the main chamber and in a blind alcove running northward from it toward the adjacent semicircular basin in Room 9. This installation bears all the earmarks of a chimney to exhaust the heated air and smoke from the hypocaust under the tepidarium. Room 11, therefore, must have served no other purpose than to provide the ducts through which the heated air and smoke moved toward the chimney. The masonry cube may, of course, also have supported a container in which water was heated to supply the basins in the tepidarium. How Room 11 was roofed was not apparent. Its west wall was in ruinous condition but showed that there was an opening into the irregularly shaped area designated as Room 12 (see Fig. 56 and Plan XX). This area (*ca.* 3.30 × 9.70 m.) could not be excavated completely. It appeared to be closed at its western end by a row of stones channeled at the top as if to conduct water in the direction of the caldarium. Room 12 can scarcely have served any purpose other than to conduct the heated air and smoke out from under the *suspensura* of the

caldarium to join in Room 11 with the exhaust from the tepidarium.

Room 13, at the very heart of the bath, gave every evidence of being the most solidly constructed chamber of the entire establishment. It is 14.20 m. long and 4.70 m. wide, with bays at the west end that give it a cruciform ground plan. The north and south bays measure 2.80 × 2.50 m., and the terminal (west) bay is 5 meters wide and 1.50 m. deep. Vertical flue channels cut in the walls of the bays show that they contained basins. The room could not be cleared because of its inaccessibility to earth-moving equipment, but it was clearly the caldarium of the bath. Its surface is still strewn with large sections of its fallen rubble vaulting, which clearly show that the bays were vaulted separately and therefore that the room was cross-vaulted at its western end. Around the mass of fallen rubble strong double walls of heavy blocks are clearly visible save at the southeast and the north. At the north the thrust of the vaulting over Rooms 7 and 8 had pushed the upper courses of the wall inclosing Room 13 down into its interior, and at the south, where there must have been a corbeled flue opening to conduct the smoke and heated air out into Room 12, calcification of the limestone by heat probably weakened the masonry and caused it to fall.

In the terminal bay there was an opening (*ca.* 2.15 m. wide) which was found partially exposed. A sounding just inside this opening revealed a solid bedding of baked bricks 3.90 m. below the top of the walls. Further penetration into the room would no doubt have revealed the remains of a hypocaust floor crushed and depressed by the weight of the masses of stone and rubble with which the room is choked. Even if due allowance is made for the height of the *suspensura*, floor level must have been at least one step below the level of the doorway through which the caldarium was entered from Room 8.

How the caldarium was heated was revealed by partial clearance of the irregularly shaped area designated as Room 14, whose major dimensions are 7.80 m. from east to west and 7.50 m. from north to south. This large space was by no means functionally adapted to the purpose it was found to have served. The room had lost the regularity of its shape by the intrusion of the well built reservoir (Room 5) at the west. At the north it was delimited by an almost equally solid wall set against the south wall of the frigidarium (Room 6) and used to convey a water channel from the reservoir eastward across the area of Room 15 to tubs in the frigidarium and Room 7. Along the east it was bounded by the massive terminal wall of the caldarium (Room 13). The south and west walls had the thickness of a single stone and were bonded at the southwest corner. The west wall had remains of a rough plaster facing. The regularity of the stonework of the south wall was interrupted near its eastern end, but the break is less likely to have been structural than the result of a cave-in.

The entire room was filled to within about a meter of the surface and for a depth of about 1.50 m. with a deposit of earth, field stones, and chips mixed apparently with lime and hence of exceptional solidity, so that it had literally to be chopped away with a pick. A floor level was reached along the east side of the room about 2.40 m. below the top of the caldarium wall. The floor had been laid against a rough wall emerging from the opening in the terminal bay of the caldarium. When the area in front of this opening was penetrated to greater depth a similar wall was revealed on its north side. Between the two walls was the brickwork of a furnace and of flues leading through the opening into the caldarium (see Plan XX). This, then, was the furnace room (Pl. XXXVI *B*) for the caldarium. Excavation north of the furnace showed among other things a heavy deposit of ash beginning 2 meters down from the top of the caldarium wall. Excavation of the bed of the furnace and of the area west of it produced quantities of powdered lime. It will be recalled in this connection that there was a heavy deposit of lime in the adjacent corner of the frigidarium also (see p. 165). The furnace, therefore, had been transformed into a limekiln which, to judge by the quantity of the unused product, had been in operation no little time.

Another feature appropriate to the use of Room 14 as the furnace room of the caldarium was a well lined trapezoidal shaft immediately north of the furnace. It was excavated to a depth of 2.50 m. below floor level. Recesses providing foot- and handholes in its north and south walls indicated beyond doubt that the shaft gave access to a driven well, a concomitant of the heating arrangement for the caldarium. Two details brought to light in the excavation of the shaft were puzzling. Its east wall encroached on the area of the caldarium

wall (see Plan XX), which was corbeled across the shaft (Pl. XXXVI *C*), and thus indicated that the shaft must have existed before the caldarium was constructed. It may in fact be one of the earliest features of the entire development of the area. The second puzzling detail was a layer of plain white mosaic paving slightly above the level of the corbeling that carried the caldarium wall across the shaft (Fig. 60). Some few traces of this

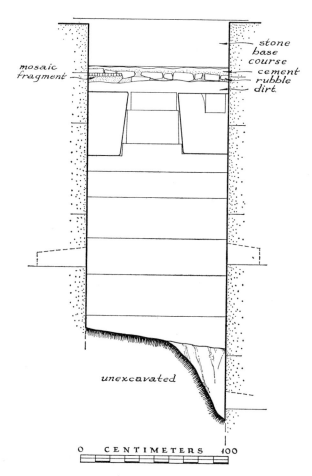

Fig. 60.—Section of Well Shaft in Room 14 of City Bath. *J. E. Knudstad*

paving were found also north of the well shaft, but not outside the context of the caldarium wall. It can thus be inferred that the corbeling originally served another purpose than that of carrying the outer course of the caldarium wall across the shaft, that the area of Room 14 once had a function other than that of furnace room, and that during the period when Room 14 or any part of it was set out with mosaic pavement such walls as may have inclosed the area of the caldarium ran on a line east of the well shaft. The present east wall of Room 14 (see

Pl. XXXVI *C*) contains blocks with commemorative inscriptions (p. 214, Nos. 44 and 46) such as were found also in the walls of the frigidarium.

It may be doubted that Room 14 was roofed during its period of use as a furnace room. But it was protected by inclosing walls and provided with an entrance through a narrow passage that extended eastward between the outer wall of the bath and the southern bay of the caldarium (see Fig. 56). The doorframe was elaborate but no doubt constructed of reused material. The connecting passage was so narrow that it provided scant room for the movement of people, and fuel for the furnace could have been brought in through it only with some difficulty.

The area designated as Room 15, the only remaining unit of the bath, had been cut into by one of the semicircular tubs set into the south wall of the frigidarium and was crossed at the level of the walls of the frigidarium by cemented water channels leading to this tub, to its neighbor in Room 7, and to the north bay of the caldarium. Excavation of the remainder of Room 15 yielded nothing but fill and undressed masonry, suggesting that the space was not otherwise used in the building as we know it.

It is evident that the history of the part of the double insula occupied in Byzantine times by the City Bath is long and complicated and that it cannot be fully clarified until excavation has laid bare the remainder of the block, particularly the area to the south of the bath. Yet there are at least some clues to portions of that history, and these it is important to set down for the record. The available evidence consists of (1) the indications of lime burning in Rooms 7 and 14, (2) the sculptures found in the frigidarium (Room 6) and the tepidarium (Room 9) and the incidental installations in the former, (3) the coins, (4) the inscribed blocks reused in some of the walls, (5) the structural changes in several parts of the bath and the functional changes implied by some of them, and (6) the interrelation of certain of the structural features of the complex. These factors must be considered in their relation to one another and to the rehabilitation of the Street of the Monuments if what can at present be said about the history of the area is to be clarified.

From the coins we can infer with absolute safety that the City Bath continued in use at least in some parts (especially the frigidarium) to the very end of the Byzantine period and that its history as we know it cannot go back before the late Roman period, probably not before the beginning of the fourth century of our era. Lime burning in Rooms 7 and 14 may have continued into Arabic times, particularly in Room 7, but the installation in Room 14 is the earlier, judged by its efficiency and the extent of its residue. The sculptures installed on pedestals and in such places as Niche *D* in the frigidarium represent the more brilliant imperial Roman phase of the history of the city and show by their preservation here that the structure had some pretensions in the fourth and fifth centuries as a center of civic life. It was set out with them in token of its importance as the hearth of the city's continuing cultural aspirations. The podium in the southeast corner of the frigidarium would, if it is correctly interpreted as a bema, point in the same direction and suggest that the peristyle court of the frigidarium was used for such administrative and judicial business as continued to be transacted in public in Byzantine times.

To determine the chronological implications of what is known about the structural changes in the building, it is important to consider the raising of the floor level in the tepidarium (Room 9). When the floor was raised, it will be recalled, rough masses of masonry were introduced in the area between the two semicircular basins in the east wall to support a new high-level tub and at the same time to provide a vertical channel through which heated air was conducted almost directly upward from the furnace to an opening which presumably served as the emplacement for a metal cauldron. The raising of the floor may have been required by an accumulation of soot and ashes in the hypocaust, but the new installations imply that the tepidarium was at the same time being transformed into a steam room, that is, into a caldarium. If this implication is correct the original caldarium (Room 13) must have been out of commission, whether because of the weakening of its walls, the cracking or fall of its vaulting, or merely lack of the means of keeping it in operation. That the function of Room 9 (the original tepidarium) was changed is indicated by the introduction of makeshift tubs in Rooms 8 and 7. In the bath as originally planned these rooms were probably apodyteria. With the introduction of the tubs, whose water was provided presumably by a tank over the tub in the north wall of Room 9 (the later caldarium), they assumed the function of a tepidarium. That the original caldarium (Room 13) went out of use at a relatively early date is suggested by the extensive indications of the use of its furnace for lime burning. Keeping in mind also what has been learned about the calcification of the walls of Room 9 (the original tepidarium) and about the irregular construction of its south wall, we can develop the following succession of events in the life of the buiding.

1. The building was erected and placed in service with all rooms serving their intended functions.
2. The caldarium (Room 13) went out of use and even the tepidarium (Room 9) fell into disrepair, its south wall weakened and the hypocaust choked with soot and ashes.
3. The tepidarium (Room 9) was renovated and placed in service as a caldarium, Rooms 8 and 7 serving henceforth as a tepidarium.

Of the period to which the first of these events (the erection of the building) should be assigned we have several indications. One is the absence from the coin yield of anything like a fair proportion of issues of even the third century of our era. The few early pieces are almost certainly "strays." A second is the use of the fragment inscribed with the Price Edict of Diocletian in the lower paving of the raised porch (see p. 81), implying, of course, that the edict was no longer in force. A third is the use in the frigidarium (Room 6) and in the original tepidarium (Room 9) of spirally fluted blue marble columns with white marble bases and capitals like those used in the Triumphal Arch of the Constantinian period (see p. 77) and in the rebuilt oecus of the dwelling connected with the Public Building on the Street of the Monuments (see p. 158). The fourth and probably the most important is the reuse in various parts of the bath (see p. 167) of blocks inscribed with portions of commemorative inscriptions and thus obviously taken from some other civic structure. The fact that such texts appear on the Tauchira Gate at Ptolemais and on the standing curtains of the city wall of Tauchira itself (see p. 61) suggests that these blocks came from the city wall of Ptolemais and presupposes its abandonment as an instrument of defense. Elsewhere it is argued that the spoliation of the city wall and the abandonment of perimeter defense was an accepted fact and normative for the character of new buildings erected in the first half of the fifth century (see p. 26). We would therefore

be inclined to infer on the basis of the evidence currently available that the City Bath as we know it belonged to the rehabilitation of the Street of the Monuments that is associated epigraphically with the period between Constantine and Arcadius and Honorius. The date implied by the architrave inscription honoring Arcadius and Honorius that is assigned to the portico of the City Bath (see p. 81) is thus the logical one for the construction of the building. The renovation of the bath as exemplified by the changes in the tepidarium could well be assigned to the period of Justinian, who is known from the literary sources to have restored the city's water-supply system (see p. 28), upon which the operation of such an institution as the City Bath naturally depended. The partial disintegration and temporary disuse of the building may thus represent the end of the fifth or the very beginning of the sixth century.

That only a few major events in the history of the City Bath have been covered is obvious from the multiple changes in the frigidarium. But to place these changes in a chronological sequence there is not sufficient evidence. Insufficient also is the evidence for a clear understanding of the use of the site in the Roman period. The solid cornice-crowned masonry that forms part of the south wall of the frigidarium looks definitely like a survival, but, as we have seen, the level of the cornice is very low even in relation to that of the Street of the Monuments. Moreover, of the three rows of masonry that separate Room 8 from Room 9 the two westernmost rows (a double wall) form a corner with the end of the cornice-crowned wall. And, finally, the original sill of the doorway leading directly from the frigidarium to the tepidarium (Room 9) is level with the *earlier* floor of the tepidarium and is actually some 33 cm. below the floor of the frigidarium. This doorway was blocked up and not in use when frigidarium and tepidarium had floors in the same plane, no doubt because the tepidarium was then serving as caldarium. To explain the lower level of the doorway in question must we assume that the floor level of the frigidarium had also been raised? Or can we assume that the doorway goes with the adjacent cornice-crowned wall of supposedly Roman vintage and that the Byzantine builders preserved it and contrived some sort of transition from the higher level of the frigidarium to the lower level of the tepidarium which disappeared when the floor of the latter was raised ? As things stand there seems to be no way to settle the question. Thus the only intelligible indication of Roman construction that we have on the premises is the well shaft that came to light below floor level in Room 14, with a bit of mosaic pavement directly above it. This shaft, as we have seen, was not in alignment with the walls of the Byzantine building.

While, therefore, the earlier building remains quite unknown, it is clear that the site was occupied in Roman times. The chances are that a city bath stood on approximately the same site, for it lies directly north of and at a level below the great water reservoirs that appear as Buildings 10, 11, and 12 on Plan XXII. It is not obvious how the City Bath was supplied with water because the area to the south of it has not been explored. Such exploration will most likely reveal traces of water conduits connecting it with the reservoirs to the south. The Beecheys saw remains of an aqueduct leading from the Square of the Cisterns "through the centre of the town" (see p. 71) and incorporated it on their plan (Fig. 4). To the history of the bath as a public institution the City Bath of Ptolemais has little to add that is unusual or important. It is one more example of an utterly familiar type of structure developed along thoroughly commonplace lines. This more than anything else suggests that if the site was actually occupied in Roman times by a city bath, the earlier and later buildings were in all probability not greatly dissimilar.

FINDS OF THE EXCAVATIONS

SCULPTURE

By D. M. Brinkerhoff

THE SIGNIFICANCE OF THE SCULPTURAL FINDS

THE Libyan settlement which pseudo-Scylax calls the "harbor at Barca" must have been in existence as early as the fifth century, but it became a city and received the name Ptolemais only in the third century before Christ. It rose to some prominence during the reigns of the Hellenistic kings Ptolemy III and IV, after the former reunited Cyrenaica and Egypt through his marriage to Berenice of Cyrene. In 96 B.C., sixty odd years after Rome was asked to arbitrate a Ptolemaic family dispute, Cyrenaica became a Roman province. Nearly all the sculpture found at Ptolemais appears to have been created subsequent to the Romanization of the area and prior to the official acceptance of Christianity, which marked the end of the classical era, but much of it illustrates the persistence of Greek, Hellenistic, and Egyptian traditions. This artistic record shows clearly the impressively successful balance between cosmopolitan unity and local variety that distinguished Eastern Roman civilization. In Ptolemais the regional vitality of plastic art found a multifaceted expression, while viewed as a whole its character may be said to be homogeneous.

This essay endeavors to assess the statuary by paying particular attention to the most outstanding and unusual discoveries, which deserve more discussion than an inventory permits. In the inventory (pp. 188–207) each work is listed and described, with appropriate references. The collection can be logically divided into three parts, as suggested by the content and technique of the finds themselves. The first part is Egyptian in nature, the second comprises works assignable to the centuries immediately before and after Christ up to the Hadrianic age, and the third includes sculpture of the later imperial epoch.

THE EGYPTIAN GROUP

The subject matter of the first works to be considered demonstrates clearly that one of the artistic traditions at Ptolemais was closely related to Egypt. They are distinct in character from the monuments discussed in the second and third parts of this essay. Most of them, however, date from the second century after Christ and hence are contemporary with the bulk of the sculpture at the city.

There is abundant evidence elsewhere to show that Egypt's exotic lure was especially prominent during the late Republican and Augustan periods and during the Hadrianic–Antonine age. In earlier Egyptianizing work, such as the Nilotic mosaic at Palestrina and similar decoration at Pompeii, it is the novel or even the quaint, often with a humorous aspect, that appeals. The second phase, beginning with the so-called Hadrianic revival, included many works of Egyptian derivation. Since the intent was serious, the manner was sober. Yet, from the Hellenistic period on, successful attempts actually to blend Greek and Egyptian styles in sculpture were very few. The Egyptian temple reliefs and statues of the Ptolemies are as peculiar as the figure of Hadrian's favorite, Antinoüs, in the pose of a pharaoh, naturalistically carved in Greek marble.

The various approaches embodied in the later imperial stage are seen in various examples found during the excavations of the city of Ptolemais.

Some pieces prove that the Egyptianizing vogue there was not essentially different from that of other parts of the Roman world, yet local preferences were responsible for some extremely interesting choices. A goat(?) and a ram (Inv. Nos.59–60) and an Egyptian shrine of Greek marble (Inv. No. 14) are hybrids behind which there probably existed Hellenistic examples of such syncretistic art. A Ptolemaic queen, Cleopatra I (Inv. Nos. 1 and 9), illustrates the Greek rather than the native tradition in Egypt. When such subjects and styles as those in this group are found so near their source, one suspects that something more than mere fashion is involved. The people of Ptolemais, a city which was essentially a Hellenistic foundation, in a district which had furnished soldiers for the Ptolemaic armies, had ample reasons for a particular fondness for works of art of Egyptian inspiration. The statues they selected recalled their past, and through them the art of Hellenistic Egypt becomes better known.

The discovery of the statue of Cleopatra I (193–173 B.C.), an Antonine copy of a Hellenistic original, was one of the major achievements of the excavations (Pls. XXXVII *B–D* and XXXVIII). The queen's coiffure is adorned with the skin of an Indian elephant, once complete with tusks and trunk. The comparatively small ears of the animal, as opposed to the African species, display the characteristic roll of flesh corresponding to life and also to the antique manner of representation. The helmet extended in a triangular shape onto the back at shoulder height. The massing of the heavily draped body with its complicated folds produces a heroic effect associated with Hellenistic sculpture at its best. The stylish *déhanchement* of the pose, so like the swinging twist of a late Gothic madonna holding the Christ child, is partly due to the fact that the earthly queen once cradled a cornucopia in her left arm, from which cornstalks protruded. In her outstretched right hand would have been a sacrificial patera. This explains the roll of drapery across the waist; tucked up under the left arm, it freed both hands. The motif was a favorite one during the third century before Christ, witness the sacrificing maiden known as the "Girl from Anzio."

A close correspondence to the drapery arrangement of the Ptolemais statue is seen in a version of Athena, also known through a Roman copy, found in the neighboring city of Cyrene and now in the British Museum. The goddess wears an aegis instead of a plain baldric. The original of the type has been dated to the third quarter of the third century B.C., partly because of the style of the surfaces and rhythm and partly because the form of the costume was borrowed to represent the divinized Ptolemaic queens. Statues of a few such queens are known from inscribed fayence jugs on which they appear in relief. An unlabeled fragment of one, found by the Ernst von Sieglin expedition to Alexandria, depicts another queen. Her appearance is so close to the Ptolemais figure that she may now be identified as Cleopatra I also.

The figures known from the jugs reflect the cult images of the goddess-queens. The Ptolemais statue does too, as does a very similar marble statue of a queen deified as Isis, from the same city. The latter wears a uraeus on a bovine helmet complete with horns, which associates her also with priestesses of the goddess Hathor, who was equated with Aphrodite. Such syncretism, characteristic of Ptolemaic policy, really began with Ptolemy II and the deification of his queen Arsinoë II in various guises, including that of a Tyche holding a double cornucopia symbolic of the wealth of the kingdom.[1] Arsinoë II has been suggested as the subject of the other statue at Ptolemais. Her husband commenced the series of royal temple tombs in Alexandria, where the official images stood. The same royal pair may appear in two bronze statuettes from Egypt; the queen is bareheaded and holds a double cornucopia, while the king wears an elephant skin like that on the Ptolemais statue of Cleopatra I. Under Ptolemy II this type of helmet, previously shown only on the divine Alexander the Great, apparently was adopted by a living god-king. A queen with an elephant helmet first appears on coins of Ptolemy V Epiphanes, sometime before his marriage to the Syrian princess Cleopatra I in 193 B.C., which are inscribed ΒΑΣΙΛΙΣΣΑΣ ΚΛΕΟΠΑΤΡΑΣ. This coinage means that the Ptolemais statue may be identified as a copy of a statue of the first Cleopatra which also portrays her, from the evidence of the cornucopia, as a Tyche.

The figure probably was valued as a symbol of Alexandria or Egypt or, with less likelihood, Africa. To explain why requires a brief account of the history of the elephant skin. Ptolemy I paid homage to the power and wisdom of Alexander the

[1] Athenaeus *Deipnosophistae* xi 497 *b–c*.

Great by depicting him in an elephant helmet, rather than in the lion skin of Herakles, on tetradrachms minted shortly after 318 B.C., which were soon imitated in Syria by Seleucus. To the west, Agathocles of Syracuse issued a similar coin, depicting either himself or Africa, after 310 B.C., while he was warring against Carthage. This coin has sometimes been held to represent the first use of the image to represent Africa, and Agathocles did have some control over Libya between 310 and 307 B.C., but all the other personifications of the continent are female while this is an unlabeled male head. The iconography of the elephant helmet over a female face first appeared with the title Africa on the coins of Pompey in the first century B.C., followed by several issues of the Roman senate and also of the native rulers of Mauretania. From Tripolitania westward this personification became the meaning of the symbol during the imperial age, and its representation in various media acquired the larger ears of the African elephant, thus differentiating it from the personification at Ptolemais, which does not, therefore, stand for Africa.

The symbol continued in use in Egypt. Cleopatra VII, wearing the elephant helmet, appears on the emblema of a patera of early imperial date from Boscoreale, now in the Louvre, amid adornments suggesting the richness of the whole kingdom. It seems that the original creation identifying the queen of Egypt may have been intended to symbolize the realm rather than the city. A Roman coin of M. Aemilius Lepidus, about 65 B.C., supports this hypothesis, for on it appears a standard Tyche head, wearing jewels and turreted crown, called Alexandria. Its reverse deals with the period in which the personification under discussion was created, for it shows the ancestor of Aemilius, who was one of three Romans sent to Ptolemy V in 201 B.C., crowning the boy king with a wreath. Had the distinctive elephant-helmet symbol meant Alexandria, there is every reason to suppose it would have been used.

After the Ptolemaic empire became a thing of the past, the imperial mint at the Egyptian capital continued to produce the image of the female head or bust with elephant skin during the reigns of eight emperors from Nero to Antoninus Pius. On one of the dies of a coin of Galba, A.D. 68–69, apparently re-issued under Otho, on which the headdress is reduced to a small cap and the elephant ears are omitted entirely, the subject wears a military costume and is called Alexandria, but all the other issues are unlabeled. Hence one cannot be certain of the identity when the representation is of Roman date, especially after the variety introduced into the subject of personifications by Hadrian. But on his coins which continue the conventional series the elephant-capped figures of Alexandria look very different from the statue at Ptolemais. The face and helmet on the latest issue are closest in their appearance to those of the Ptolemais statue and assist in dating it to the middle of the second century after Christ. The large bronze coins of the subject, almost medallions, issued at Alexandria by Antoninus Pius in A.D. 158–59, are really much more similar to the example of the Ptolemais statue in their details and sense of scale than they are to the other smaller, earlier imperial coins. The numismatic resemblance is perhaps closest to those Hellenistic issues labeled ΒΑΣΙΛΙΣΣΑΣ ΚΛΕΟΠΑΤΡΑΣ.

What is striking and significant here is the evident desire to revive a bygone age. The marked antiquarianism of this whole period, seen in literature for example in the attitude of Pausanias as he toured ancient Greece, is apparent in the statue found at Ptolemais, a beautiful recreation of a Hellenistic original. This is supported further by the correspondence of its finish to that of the late Hadrianic or early Antonine statue of Apollo from Cyrene, now in London. The center-parted hair of the latter is also carved in a regular succession of strands, and the volumes of the cheeks are defined by the same curves. The head of another Ptolemaic queen, Berenice II, also found at Cyrene and of Hadrianic date in all likelihood, reproduces the wide eyes and long eyelids of the Ptolemais figure. It becomes apparent that there was something approaching a revival in Cyrenaica of types recalling the heritage of the past during a good part of the second century of our era.

In spite of the Ptolemaic subject of the statue of Cleopatra, circumstantial evidence points to the probability that it or its artist came from Greece. The material, as is true of nearly all the sculpture in our inventory, possesses the characteristic fine grain and golden hue of Pentelic marble. In fact, the bulk of the sculpture found in Cyrenaica, which had no marble of its own, seems associated with Attic workshops. A Herakles (Inv. No. 12) in the Ptolemais group was signed "Asklepiades of Athens."

And a larger than life-size signed example of the type of Cleopatra I exists. Its stance is reversed, so that the drapery arrangement is different from the knees down, but the large overfold is the same, and a piece of the cornucopia is preserved. The inscription on the plinth reads "Eisodotos the Athenian made it." This statue, however, was found in Crete, and its suggested date of A.D. 150–200 is comparable to that of the only other major figure now known, the new discovery at Ptolemais. It does not prove that the latter was likewise an Athenian product, but the implication is very clear, for it shows that the type was a familiar one during the heyday of the Attic workshops.

Additional discoveries illustrate even more clearly the Eastern character of some of the sculpture of Ptolemais. A small black granite base with hawk's feet (Inv. No. 58, Pl. XLII B) must represent the Egyptian god Horus, whom the Greeks equated with Apollo. The goat(?) and the ram (Inv. Nos. 59–60, Pl. XXXIX A–B) are matched by two rams at Cyrene and another at Alexandria. All are alike in that they were supported by an anthropomorphic head, a herm, or a double herm beneath the stomach. The only remains on the underside of the Ptolemais examples are traces of hair from a herm head and a curved indentation in the stone; the heads may have had the features of an Isis or a personification of Libya, identified by twisted locks. One of the rams at Cyrene is supported by a double herm with heads of Zeus-Amon and either Libya or Isis. In the example now in the Greco-Roman Museum of Alexandria the small beast (only 40 cm. long) lies upon the head of a Bes, similar to the Greek Hermes, who, however, preferred to use his shoulders. That these marbles were zodiacal signs is possible, but the animals also figure in the worship of Amon, Mendes, and Khnum and are generally more lively when they appear in the zodiac.

Another example recalling the native tradition of Egypt is a shrine or altar whose upper part is missing (Inv. No. 14, Pl. XXXIX C). In the front of the rectangular block there is a small niche, big enough to hold a diminutive cult image such as a Horus. On the rear corners of the sides can be distinguished human feet and elongated legs carved in a kind of "pneumatic" style, looking like nothing so much as rubber tubes. A cloak of skin is carved on the back.

Precisely similar pieces are extremely rare, but one rather specific parallel does exist in the Cairo Museum (see p. 197, n. 81). It depicts a priest holding a shrine a little narrower than himself and standing on a base of an architectural form similar to the one at Ptolemais and whose frontal niche contains a figure of Osiris. The entire object depicts a sacred presentation in the Egyptian fashion. The bearer might represent a group whose duty was to honor a particular god or pharaoh. In Hellenistic Egypt these religious units, which the Greeks called "phyles" after their own tradition, revered Alexander and his Ptolemaic successors.

There is considerable significance, then, in the fact that Egyptian sculpture of the Saite period was found by the Italian archeologists in the "Palazzo" at Ptolemais (see p. 9), brought there apparently in Hellenistic or early Roman times. The context in which its presence is to be understood is suggested by a piece seen by Alan Rowe (see p. 198, n. 87) in the museum at Cyrene and connected by its inscription, as he reads it, with the fifth phyle of the festival of the "Two Benefactor-Gods." The unit was established by the Canopic Decree of 237 B.C. and served to honor Berenice III, deceased daughter of the divine king and queen. Similar honors were no doubt bestowed on the royal family of Egypt at Ptolemais after the death of Arsinoë II, as local inscriptions testify, so that the discovery there of a *naophoros* is in line with the tradition of the city (see pp. 8–9). The material used in the piece and the awkwardness of the execution imply that the tradition was inherited by, rather than directly familiar to, the sculptor, who approached his subject in the antiquarian spirit of the second century of our era. Some of the Egyptianizing examples from Hadrian's villa in Tivoli are comparable with it in spirit, although nothing like it in form has been found in the Roman West. The shrine seems rather to be another subject of Egyptian character that was thought to be desirable and appropriate by the population of Ptolemais during the Roman age and whose presence demonstrates further the mixed character of the city.

LATE HELLENISTIC AND EARLY IMPERIAL WORKS

The classical art of the first centuries before and after Christ was distinguished by an increased demand for Greek and Hellenistic sculpture, not only for originals and adaptations but also for copies, made possible by the development of the pointing process of exact reproduction around 100 B.C. The works attributable to this period commence in the century of Augustus and culminate with the reign of Hadrian, which marks the end of the early imperial epoch. Like the Egyptian group this division is for analytical purposes essentially typological rather than chronological. The two groups are alike in that each work illustrates the continuing vitality of some aspect of the inheritance of the Hellenistic age in the East. The frame of reference here is broader than Egypt, but this group does not include sculpture whose tradition primarily recalls Attica, which will be dealt with in the following section. The marbles presently to be examined include a female portrait head and nude and draped subjects illustrative of the continued popularity of the *sfumato* technique. The quality for the most part is excellent.

A female portrait can be dated stylistically in the second half of the first century B.C. This head of an elderly lady (Inv. No. 3, Pl. XL) is certainly equal in importance to any of the other sculptures recovered and surpasses many of them in quality and in interest of subject. Furthermore, it is the only piece that was retrieved from any sort of context, for it was found at the Roman level in the Public Building on the Street of the Monuments (see p. 157). The modeling is deceptively naturalistic, not only on all parts of the face but in the way the wrinkles in the neck are carved. Yet it is too generalized to represent the maplike Roman portraiture tradition that is labeled "verism." And the features are not sufficiently abstracted to be close to contemporary Egyptian work. Rather the work is primarily the result of the Hellenistic development of naturalistic and sometimes ethnic studies, particularly of older people, such as the famous head of Euthydemos I of Bactria (*ca.* 200 B.C.). Such portraits were generally limited to effigies of kings or philosophers and other well known figures. The average Greek was represented only upon his tombstone; the typical Egyptian wished he could afford a portrait to survive him, but it was the Roman who spread abroad the custom of depicting the features of more ordinary mortals. The individual portrayed at ancient Ptolemais was no typical citizen, however. One cannot say the fillet around her head implies royalty, but a small knot above the center part matches a larger protuberance above the diadem in the Vatican portrait of the last Cleopatra to rule Egypt (see p. 192, n. 37). Coins of the queen show a like coiffure, as do several of Roman origin, for example those of Octavian's sister, wife, and daughter. One suspects that the Ptolemais head depicts the wife of the local representative of Roman authority or a priestess.

In late Hellenistic sculpture, before exact copying began, many works combined several known motifs and thus capitalized upon a subject whose popularity was already assured. Nowhere is this more evident than in the many figures of the female nude, mostly variations on the theme of Aphrodite bathing or adorning herself. To increase their appeal such works were often given a very soft, highly polished surface. A beautiful female torso exemplifies a number of these characteristics (Inv. No. 8, Pl. XLI) and heads a group whose similar technique makes an attribution to the imperial era a reasonable conclusion. At first glance the figure appears to be a fine Aphrodite of the Capitoline type, who covered her nakedness with one arm before her bust while the other extended down so that her fingers, whose imprint is still visible, touched her right thigh. However, she also matches perfectly one of the Three Graces, with whom she is more properly identified. If she is compared with one of the several examples of the group in the Cyrene Museum (see p. 194, n. 58), it becomes clear that she is like the figure facing front at the spectator's right. "Nudae ... conexae ... una aversa pingitur, duae nos respicientes," wrote Servius of their appearance in a painting.[2] No Aphrodite of the Medici, or of the Capitoline, or of any other type in which the arms crossed before the body had a dowel hole below the right breast, but in the Three Graces a dowel supported the center figure's right arm. Comparable works from Cyrene, such as the other examples of the Three Graces and the famous Aphrodite now in Rome, at once so cool and so voluptuous, typify a later, perhaps Antonine, continuation of the style.

The manner in which the Grace was conceived, carved, and finished is an example of the *sfumato* technique, or *morbidezza*, popular from the fourth century B.C. and developed by Praxiteles among others. Early in the Hellenistic age it was refined and spread abroad by his sons and followers at Cos, Alexandria, and elsewhere. It was particularly

---

[2] *Commentarii in Aen.* i. 720 (ed. E. K. Rand *et. al.* [Lancaster, 1946] p. 294).

distinctive when used in portraiture and was a perennial favorite in Egypt and the coastal islands off Asia Minor. The Grace reveals how the technique was applied to figure sculpture. Together with comparable material from Ptolemais it illustrates the development of this distinctive style.

How the vogue for a *sfumato* effect became a taste for an elaborate softness can be amply demonstrated by a marble statue of Harpocrates (Inv. No. 66, Pl. XLIX *A*). An Egyptian subject, the child of Horus (cf. Inv. No. 58), whose silencing finger warned initiates to keep the secret of his mysteries, enjoyed wide popularity. His soapy finish contrasts most sharply with the Grace's. Centers specializing in such slick surfaces also existed at Cos and Rhodes, both of which, from at least 150 B.C., supplied the export market and met local demand. Production in the same tradition appears to have continued until the middle of the second century of our era. Thus there is no certainty about when the Harpocrates was made, but his glistening surfaces are surely comparable to another fine example of the same subject from a temple of Roman date at Ras el-Soda, between Alexandria and Abuqir, in Egypt.

To the group composed of the Grace, showing a connection with Cyrene, and the Harpocrates, whose identity and technique recall Egypt, may be added a figure depicting Dionysos (Inv. No. 65, Pl. XLIX *B*). The god is draped, yet the smooth softness of the carving seems to indicate that the artist was trained to produce the *morbidezza* displayed by the two statues of nude figures. The impression of three-dimensional movement is such that one suspects an original of the Hellenistic age was the first expression of the conception, although no other examples of the type are known. It apparently depicts Dionysos at Naxos appearing to the sleeping Ariadne, for it was found with a fragment probably representing her. The pose of the god and even his costume recall figures of Artemis. The base of such a statue, to judge by a booted foot and a dog's forepaws preserved on it, was found by the Oriental Instute expedition (Inv. No. 49, Pl. XLIII *D*). The missing figure could not have been the same as the Artemis Rospigliosi, an example of which is at Ptolemais.[3] Maybe it was a late Hellenistic development of the Rospigliosi type called the Lateran variant, but

the exact form of the base of this version is not known. In both versions the goddess was walking swiftly to her right, while the Dionysos shown here moved toward his left. In subject matter the closest parallel to the Dionysos is in another medium, for a similar depiction of the god occurs in a Pompeiian fresco, as has been pointed out by Pesce.[4] The Dionysos, then, also illustrates the fluidity of motifs in ancient art. It was said to have been found by its Italian excavators in a pre-Hadrianic context. At any rate it represents a later stage of the *sfumato* technique at Ptolemais, which apparently continued throughout the eastern Mediterranean until the end of the second century of our era. Its style merged with others which, originating earlier in the classical age, were combined by copyists of the imperial era. An example is furnished by a fountain nymph from the frigidarium of the "Palazzo", one of two identical figures whose attitude and "wet" drapery reproduce the Venus Genetrix type (Inv. No. 67, Pl. XLIX *C*). In her left hand she holds a jar through which water was piped. The finish again is distinguished by a *morbidezza*, here applied to carving in the manner of the fifth century B.C.

Several pieces prove that the art of the provincial city was quite comparable to that of other centers. From the Villa came a small herm of Dionysos which conforms to no particular archetype (Inv. No. 27, Pl. XLII *D*). Its waving hair, unlike the tightly curled ringlets of archaizing herms derived from an original attributed to Alkamenes, indicates that its inspiration should be sought in the art of the later fourth century B.C. or the Hellenistic age. The eyes and the angular cut of the lower eyelids would have been filled in with paste when complete; one even wonders from the carving whether this was a finished work. This very observation, however, offers a clue to its function, for it would have been perfectly usable as architectural decoration. The mass of stone over the head and at the back becomes meaningful in the light of such a hypothesis. A similar head found at Cyrene[5] has the same haziness of feature, and a like piece of marble above and behind the coiffure was probably used in the same way.

That the architectural decoration of the city

---

[3] See Pesce, *Il "Palazzo delle Colonne,"* pp. 80–81 and Fig. 100.

[4] *Ibid.* p. 85 and Fig. 102.

[5] See Enrico Paribeni, *Catalogo delle sculture di Cirene* ("Monografie di archeologia libica" V [Roma, 1959]) No. 371.

was not only typical but also continued to maintain a high standard is revealed by the two lion-headed waterspouts from the City Bath (Inv. Nos. 6–7). One (Pl. XLII *A*) was cut from the lowest drum of a column. Comparable waterspouts formed part of the original decoration of the "Palazzo."[6] The mechanical regularity of the carving of whiskers and manes suggests a date in the imperial period.

Some idea of the general aspect of Ptolemais as a typical Hellenistic and Roman Mediterranean city becomes evident from the fragments just cited, in addition to the traces on the site of street colonnades and buildings defining its form. Its sculptural decoration can be imagined a bit more precisely from a fragment found in the City Bath (Inv. No. 13, Pl. XLII *C*). It apparently was part of the decorative embellishment of a Tyche's throne. All that survives is the rear end of a sea creature with the feet of a diminutive standing figure, probably an Eros, on its back. The clue as to the use to which the marine animal was put is that the front of the fragment ends in a vertical plane.

The idea of personifying the fortune of a city received fresh impetus at the beginning of the Hellenistic age with the creation of the distinctive Tyche of Antioch by Eutychides.[7] It is a group composition whose second and subsidiary figure represents the geographical location of the city on the Orontes River. The whole composition which the Ptolemais fragment represents is suggested by an enthroned Tyche with a small Triton at her left, now in Rome (see p. 197, n. 76). What seaport the monument in Rome personified is not yet known. The Ptolemais fragment probably stood for the city where it was found, and, like the group in Rome, the work is a Roman copy of a Hellenistic subject, popular in various forms (cf. Inv. Nos. 1 and 9). Unfortunately the provenience of a head of the Tyche of Ptolemais (Inv. No. 61, Pl. XXXVII *A*) is unknown, and no connection can be established between it and the fragment of the sea creature.

The appearance of various Tyches at the provincial city may testify to an exaggerated dependence upon Fortuna. It is more likely that they helped give the center a sense of identity. What seems most significant is that the iconography of their personifications was so purely Hellenistic during the Roman era.

[6] See Pesce, *op. cit.* Pl. VIII *B*.
[7] Pausanias vi. 2. 7.

WORKS OF THE LATER IMPERIAL AGE

By the beginning of the second century after Christ the free and wandering eclecticism in the sculpture of the previous epoch had made familiar most of the styles, types, motifs, and many of the single works created in the past. An attitude occasionally verging on reverence toward the art of bygone ages had been made vastly easier to express in plastic form by the pointing process of copying. The method was widely, but not universally, employed in the later imperial era. A variety of subjects continued to be copied after the first century of our era, but many of the copies possessed a rather dry, mechanical, and commemorative air. Sometimes the front would be a careful replica, but the back would be finished arbitrarily. This does not mean that fine statues were not produced, especially during the reigns of Trajan and Hadrian.

A figure of Herakles is represented by three fragments found in the City Bath, the inscribed base, part of the calf of one leg, and the right buttock and thigh (Inv. No. 12, Pl. XLV A–B). The latter two pieces indicate only a standing male nude; it is the base which is most revealing. Across the front of the pedestal one can distinguish the inscription "M. Ulpius Cominius, with his own means, for his native city." Since Ulpius suggests Trajan, who bore the same name, a date in the earlier part of the second century is likely for the creation of the statue. On the base appear the feet of Herakles, firmly planted, and on a support by the left foot is part of the customary lion skin. There is no trace of the club, but it may have rested on the copyist's tree trunk. The latter feature is of considerable interest, for on it appears the signature "Asklepiades of Athens." No other signed statue was found. With the Herakles may be grouped another work on the strength of its inscription, for Ulpius Cominius also dedicated an Athena found by the Italian archeologists (Inv. No. 64, Pl. XLIX *D*). A very fine copy, although the expression of the Medusa on the aegis leaves something to be desired, it lacks only the head and arms. The marble used for these pieces is Pentelic, so that both the sculptor and his material were Attic. One wonders whether the statue was carved at Ptolemais. The answer to this question remains obscure, for at present we know only that some statues were transported, that some artists traveled about, and that Attica continued to serve as one of the principal sources for marble and for finished works of sculpture. It is useless to claim that because no sculptor's shop has been found at Ptolemais none was there, but one can point out that in the absence of the original a statue cannot be reproduced without a model, a sketch, or a cast. Hence any Libyan centers which featured equipment for turning out such work were more likely to have been in larger cities such as Cyrene, which is also a possible place of origin for some of the sculpture found at Ptolemais. However, a stonecutter must have been present in Ptolemais to carve the inscription. To the eventual solution of this tantalizing problem these two pieces furnish additional evidence.

A third impressive replica of a well known type completes this group of deities or mythological figures. It is an example of the Artemis Colonna (Inv. No. 68, Pl. L *A*), whose original was created around the middle of the fourth century B.C. It was found by the Department of Antiquities and is still *in situ* decorating the "Odeon." Its impressive scale and quality recall the foregoing remarks concerning the importation of finished sculpture. The esteem in which this kind of statuary was held was so great that similar types were adapted for use as portraits and were supplied without heads but with sockets for their insertion. The heads, carved separately and roughly finished, could be completed and made into recognizable likenesses by the individual who cut the inscription or by a specialist in portraiture. The details of such local operations, like those of the precise movement of sculptors and sculpture, are still unknown.

At Ptolemais several labeled but headless statues depicting familiar types, with sockets to receive portraits of local worthies, illustrate the practice just referred to. Slight variations in technique suggest that they do not all date from the same period but may have been commissioned at different times during the second and perhaps the early third century of our era. Thus their presence implies that the provincial center shared in the general prosperity of this so-called golden age, and their apparent cessation would indicate that the city did not escape the subsequent economic decline occurring in the course of the third century, although Africa fared better in this respect than did other parts of the Empire.

A female figure (Inv. No. 62, Pl. L *B*) of the type of the larger of the so-called "Herculaneum women," originally representing Demeter in the Hellenistic

archetype of the third century B.C., can be added to some dozen portrait statues of this kind already recorded. A pedestal bearing the name Claudia Eupomane and located in front of the City Bath on the Street of the Monuments probably indicates the lady's identity, for the statue was found near it. It is interesting to note how closely the manner of carving of the drapery at ankle level resembles that of the Athena (cf. Pl. XLIX *D*), ably executed in both cases with clearly delineated folds. The portrait of Claudia was set up by M. Antonius Flavianus according to the inscription. An effigy of Marcus Aurelius Flavianus (Inv. No. 63, Pl. L *C*) also stood near the City Bath on the Street of the Monuments. Since he bore the same name as the donor of the Claudia, one may suppose that these two figures depicted members of the same family, though they were not necessarily contemporary. The male statue does not appear to have been so carefully executed. The type was derived in the second century B.C. from a creation of the fourth century representing the orator Aeschines. Here the long and relatively undifferentiated folds in which the body was swathed, particularly the rather summarily carved ends of the himation hanging from the left forearm, typify this variety of statue, designed to support the head of a dignitary of the provincial city. This one must have performed such a function rather well, for the drapery lines lead upward to the chest where a roughly circular series of interrupted folds was designed to enframe the neck and individualized head. The right hand provided an additional visual accent beneath the face, while the left, to show the cultured character of the person represented, may have held a scroll.

An Aeschines type, from which No. 63 was derived, enhanced the aura of dignity of the portrait statues at Ptolemais (Inv. No. 10, Pl. XLVI). The orator did not stand on the Street of the Monuments but was placed before a column in the frigidarium of the City Bath, near the Cleopatra (Inv. No. 9), whose base was in front of an adjacent column. Since the Aeschines figure was often adopted for use as a contemporary portrait, one cannot say that the famous speaker was represented. A statue of this kind from Cyrene, now in the British Museum, bears the likeness of Hadrian (see p. 195). Although both were derived from the same type, the appearance of the himation differs considerably, proving that exact duplication was not always the rule in the production of these replicas. Indeed, the sculptor of the Ptolemais statue showed notable ingenuity in his use of the running drill to vary the drapery interest, especially around the waist at the level of the left hand. Beneath this hand the grooved marble folds descend to a case for scrolls, a capsa, whose carrying strap is clearly shown. The other hand is held close to the chest in the traditional manner proper to a public speaker in ancient Greece. Since the carving appears to be of an earlier date than that of No. 63, it seems that the presence of the Aeschines, with either the head of the orator or that of a local citizen, encouraged M. Aurelius Flavianus to select a type of similar derivation at some time in the late Antonine or the early Severan age. His statue at present is set up in the Street of the Monuments, and the Aeschines is now the Oriental Institute Museum.

Another form of memorial favored during the imperial age was the carved sarcophagus. To indicate that this aspect of human existence was also represented at Ptolemais, two interesting fragments from earlier excavations are included here. Their dates are not far from A.D. 200. A sarcophagus lid depicts husband and wife, both reclining on their left elbows, supported by pillows (Inv. No. 70, Pl. LI *A*). It is the better preserved of two covers of the same sort and provenience. Although the type is known well enough, it is more common in the Greek East than in the West. The grooves in the drapery girdling the lady's hips recall those on the shoulders of the magistrate (cf. Pl. L *C*). She held a wreath in her right hand, and her husband, whose right arm rested tenderly on his wife's shoulders, clasped a scroll in his left. The other fragment is mythological in content (Inv. No. 69, Pl. LI *B*). In relief along the surviving end appears an Amazon. To the left one of her two Greek adversaries is partly preserved. Herakles herms were represented at the corners. The lower half of this sarcophagus is missing, but its cornice survives at the top. The beautiful moldings, especially the egg-and-dart and bead-and-reel motifs, are carved so deeply that the high-lighted surfaces are interspersed with deep pockets of shadow, recalling the phrase "the black and white style" often used to designate this manner of cutting typical of the late Antonine and early Severan ages but derived in some respects from the Flavian epoch of the first century after Christ. These details are very close

to the Severan architectural decoration of Leptis Magna and Sabratha, traceable in their technique to western Asia Minor and the so-called "school of Aphrodisias." Such work was more widespread, however, and the iconography is probably more indicative of the source. Both the style of the couple and the battle scene constituted standard items in Attic workshops. Indeed, the market in Cyrenaica appears to have been an Athenian monopoly, to judge from the sarcophagi found at Cyrene.

It is interesting to note that the two sepulchral monuments discussed above were found at Ptolemais in a tomb together with another sarcophagus and a second lid like No. 70, making two complete, though fragmentary, works. Ghislanzoni did not believe that the Amazon sarcophagus and either of the unfinished lids, in spite of their provenience, could have matched "a cagione dello stile e dell'epoca diversa de' due monumenti."[8] A number of the Cyrene examples exhibit these apparent discrepancies, but the various units do go together nevertheless. Since the discovery at Ptolemais, subsequent research has demonstrated that sarcophagi were usually shipped in an unfinished state, lacking the final touches, especially those which would transform the heads into portraits. Thus the sides could be touched up as soon as received, but, if there was a sudden request for a sarcophagus, its lid was used in the condition in which it had arrived. The Ptolemais lid discussed above (Inv. No. 70) lacks the ultimate refinements, for the stripes shown on the mattress should be "embroidered" with incised lines and the barren zones between them would normally be carved with mythological vignettes in low relief. And, finally, it is quite possible that the folds and wrinkles in the man's himation would have been made crisper to match his wife's costume. Thus Ghislanzoni's accurate observations, when studied in a new light, lead to a different evaluation.

Since it has been demonstrated that one of these covers was fitted above the Amazon sarcophagus (Inv. No. 69), it is reasonable to assume that the second lid matched the other sarcophagus. This is an Erotes sarcophagus, also an Attic type, and its architectural moldings are close to those of No. 69. Both sarcophagi were apparently decorated on all four sides, but, whereas the Amazonomachia extended all the way around, the back of the

[8] *Notiziario archeologico* I 121.

Erotes sarcophagus had garlands upon it. It is this feature that defines the precise origin of all the fragments.

A sarcophagus from Salonica, now in the Louvre, has the Amazonomachia on the front and sides and garlands on the rear (see p. 207). Not only do its sides show elements found on both of the Ptolemais sarcophagi, but its cover shows a reclining couple like the pair on both of the Ptolemais lids. Another Amazon sarcophagus at Salonica has an unfinished couple on its lid. There was a workshop there, closely linked to the more prominent one in Athens, whose local specialty was garland sarcophagi similar to those made at the home of this type in the island of Proconnesus. Thus Salonica is the logical source for the two fragmentary funerary monuments at Ptolemais. The weathered Pentelic marble used for these pieces shows blue-gray veins, just the type used for such commissions, where "second-grade" marble was perfectly acceptable.

Just as the citizens of the Roman Empire have left a record of a strongly developed feeling of personal identity in individual monuments, so also did they exhibit a sense of civic consciousness with respect to the centers in which they lived. The Tyche of Ptolemais (Inv. No. 61, Pl. XXXVII *A*) shows that this city was no exception. It resembles a personification of Cyrene in the way the hair was drilled in long waves over the temples, but the Ptolemais Tyche's crown, in the usual form of a city wall, has its stones more carefully indicated.[9] The idea of the personification of a city was not new, for it was first given plastic expression in the Hellenistic period. From the age of Hadrian onward the concept was a familiar one in Roman sculpture and numismatics. The date of this representation of Ptolemais in the time of the Antonines, for such appears to be its period, is most appropriate, since it falls precisely in the middle of the age when ancient Africa was at the height of its prosperity. With respect to Ptolemais this observation is supported by the presence of the statues whose significance was assessed above and confirmed by works of a different character which are about to be discussed. Together they indicate the scope and variety of the sculpture of the city at the zenith of its civic development.

In the course of the excavations, the Oriental Institute expedition discovered a relief on a

[9] See Paribeni, *Catalogo delle sculture di Cirene*, No. 427.

marble slab that had been used in the blocking of a doorway in the City Bath (see p. 165). The subject is a bacchante, still visible in spite of the weathered state of the slab, although only her head, thrown back and looking up to the left, and parts of her hair and drapery are easily discernible (Inv. No. 5, Pl. XLVIII *B*). Italian excavators had found other reliefs depicting dancing maenads on the Street of the Monuments in 1935, which they assembled in their original form, adorning a circular base, to reconstruct a copy of a famous relief whose first creation has been attributed to Callimachus in the fifth century B.C. The new fragment complements these reliefs in scale, style, and technique and is undoubtedly part of the same group, for it represents the eighth bacchante, matching the same figure on plaques in Madrid and elsewhere. It is possible, however, that as first conceived the series showed six dancers in ecstatic poses of joy rather than eight and that the latest piece found may be a subsequent addition, since the composition was put to varied uses. The idea of a circular relief may represent one such adaptation. The other fragments from Ptolemais have been dated in the Antonine period, a conclusion reinforced by the rather flat style of carving of the whole group.

A very different kind of head (Inv. No. 2, Pl. XLVII *A*), from the City Bath, suggests the variety of sculpture that was visible in the city. It is a well preserved example of an Asklepios type related to the Zeus of Otricoli, the best known surviving example of the Capitoline Jupiter. Since Pliny (*Natural History* xxxiv. 79) lists a "Thundering Zeus" by Leochares as being on the Capitoline, it has been suggested that it, although made in the fourth century B.C., inspired features of the canonical image. A supposed replica at Cyrene was signed by Zenion, who was, so far as we know, a local sculptor. Our head is probably also a local product, but it is interesting that it resembles so closely a generic type distributed over a wide area At Sabratha, where a temple of Zeus-Serapis was erected in the Antonine period, there was recovered an impressive colossal bust of Jupiter, made of marble from Luni and probably imported from Italy. The features are obviously derived from the Capitoline Jupiter but are not identical. Another modification of the hair to include five locks across the brow and the addition of a modius would have produced a Serapis. An example of one, also of Italian marble, turned up in a temple of Mithras unearthed in London in 1954 and is now in the Guildhall Museum. A Poseidon retrieved from the bay off Baiae is like the Zeus version, except for a dolphin in place of an eagle to the right of the feet. Yet the closest surviving prototype of the Ptolemais head seems to be not a Zeus, nor a Serapis, nor a Poseidon but an Asklepios head of about 300 B.C. from Melos (see p. 191). In both cases the eyes are large and pensive-looking and the lips are parted in a relaxed expression. One cannot absolutely exclude any of the other possible identifications. Serapis seems least likely, for, although the flat spot on the top of the Ptolemais head could have supported the modius or grain measure worn by the Ptolemaic god, there are no traces of such. Recent studies of the development of the Serapis type have shown that there was quite a lot of variation over the centuries, but only a few examples, also without modius, offer reasonably close parallels.

Positive identification seems less significant than the fact that heads of deities whose typological features were no longer sharply differentiated were being produced by the late second century of our era. Perhaps this Ptolemais head was made as a piece adaptable to different needs, capable of mutation, and serviceable as the local sculptor's standard item for a variety of different orders, though such an ingenious artifice seems somehow more sophisticated than is consonant with the workmanship. The style, a provincial counterpart of the luxuriant, light-catching technique called Antonine baroque, hardly extends beyond the hair framing the face, for the rest is much more summarily carved. The drillwork, limited to the facial area, has produced curly shapes within the locks, whose larger curves often follow the smaller drilled ones.

The value of this head, with its distinctive technique as evidence of local work, becomes more apparent when another male head found in the same room of the City Bath is contrasted to it (Inv. No. 4, Pl. XLVII *B*). The second reveals what had happened in the development of sculpture at Ptolemais by the beginning of the third century after Christ. That it represents work executed in Libya no later than this time can be proved by precisely comparable heads at Leptis, made in connection with the building program culminating under Septimius Severus. Characteristic heads there display the same technique of carving hair in long grooves interrupted by ridges. The Ptolemais head, identifiable only as a mythological figure, is also related to the Asklepios discussed above, and the two types demonstrate successive stages in the development of the representation of different parts of the head. Together they illustrate an increased use of the drill, a growing lack of concern for the appearance of the back of the head, which received even more cursory attention in the later example, and a tendency to depict larger eyes farther forward and thus less deeply recessed in their sockets beneath the brow. In them one sees the first stirrings of elements of the late classical style in incipient form. Since the work at Leptis Magna was the product of sculptors from western Asia Minor who worked in the African city, we can now show that artists of the Aphrodisias school came also to Ptolemais.

A final group of monuments demonstrates that the continuity of art and culture in Ptolemais endured until well into the late classical age, preserving traditions established in the now remote past. The first is a grave stele of a Samnite gladiator named Hippomedes found during the period of Italian occupation (Inv. No. 71, Pl. L *D*). At the top appear nine palms of victory, indicating the number of his triumphs. An amphitheater in which he may have performed existed in the city. Until a few decades ago it was generally assumed that the population of the eastern part of the Empire was not addicted to watching gladiatorial contests, but a sizable number of inscribed monuments and literary sources have indicated the contrary. One can recall the intensity with which the Greens and Blues opposed each other in Constantinople during the Byzantine age. Evidence can also be cited from the pugilistic contests of the Olympic games, to mention another example of a brutal display of competitive spirit. This aspect of classical civilization was firmly established as an integral part of the ancient scene. The armor worn by Hippomedes fits a description of the Samnite warriors.[10] The plume decorating the crest of the helmet and part of the right arm, whose hand held a short stout sword, are missing. The thick greave on the left leg is clearly evident, and apparently the rows of triangles around the torso depict the protective sponges mentioned by Livy (*spongia pectori tegumentum*). The carving of the figure and of the inscription indicates a third-century date.

[10] Livy *History* ix. 40. 2–3.

At the Villa quite a number of fragmentary bits and pieces of figurative sculpture were found, such as a less than life-size male head now in Chicago (Inv. No. 28, Pl. XLVIII *C*). Its quality may appear indifferent, but it is important because it furnishes evidence for artistic activity during the third century of our era. The marble is Pentelic, but the technique seems more local than Attic in inspiration. For example, the eyelids appear heavy and irregular, a feature seen also in the herm head from the Villa (Inv. No. 27, Pl. XLII *D*). The consistently heavy-handed treatment of the hair, mustache, and beard produced a decidedly asymmetrical appearance. The bone structure above and below the eye sockets is pronounced, creating a vivid impression of the man represented. The hair, bound with a fillet, is modeled in large locks. This portrait head has a stylistic air suggestive of the middle of the third century of our era. Aemilianus, prefect of Egypt in A.D. 257 and a little later a pretender to the imperial crown, is thought to have minted coins at Alexandria depicting himself. On these he appears to have similarly modeled hair and to have worn a like beard. The comparison is an exceedingly tentative one, however. The angular cut of the lower eyelid visible on the coin and on the Ptolemais head recalls a similar idiosyncrasy on the herm head.

Other fragmentary marbles from the fill over the Villa show that the dwellings in the area were well supplied with conventional pieces such as statuettes of the female nude, identifiable with equal validity as nymphs or as Aphrodite (Inv. Nos. 37–41, Pl. XLIII *C*). One fragment does not fall in such a category, for it was less common as a subject, being in fact a Tyche (Inv. No. 36, Pl. XLVIII *D*). With it, the collection at Ptolemais is seen to have included a work of the fourth century of our era. The small seated figure has lost its head, right forearm, and left hand and is broken off below the navel, just where a broad roll of drapery surrounding the hips dipped down to the lap. Part of a cornucopia survives beside the left shoulder; its broken lower portion was held in the now missing left hand. The simple garment is clearly but schematically indicated by roughly carved folds and held in by a rather high-waisted belt. The identity of this personification can be precisely determined.

In 1793 four silver-gilt statuettes were discovered on the Esquiline Hill in Rome. One of them, whose cornucopia and drapery agree with those of the Ptolemais fragment, represents Constantinople (see p. 200). Both examples of the personification match a numismatic image of a seated Tyche appearing on a silver multiple issued at the new capital to commemorate its founding in A.D. 330. A probable *terminus ante quem* exists also, for on coins of Constantius II Constantinople is personified differently—equipped with the Nike of Rome and a spear, in an altered pose, and with no cornucopia. The presence of a Tyche of Constantinople at Ptolemais complements what is known about the city from some of its later architectural remains, namely that it continued to be important during the early Byzantine period. But its acquisition of sculpture of the type discussed here apparently ceased as the Christian age succeeded the classical.

Seen as a whole, the sculpture of Ptolemais provides a partial revelation of the tremendous sweep of ancient culture. Incomplete and subject to vagaries and vicissitudes of time, the finds nevertheless illuminate several periods within that era with great clarity. Aspects of the relative unity and diversity of Mediterranean art are clearly indicated, and most of the characteristic developments in Roman imperial sculpture reached Ptolemais, which also has revealed that many of the area's artistic traditions were founded solidly upon the Greek, Hellenistic, and Egyptian past. Rather than continuing steadily, sculptural activity seems to have been concentrated in various periods of vigorous change or of spiritual rededication to life. During such phases in the collective self-consciousness of classical civilization, it fell to the plastic arts to give to existence that heightened sense of identity which it is their mission to impart.

INVENTORY

EXPEDITION FINDS

Life-Size and Over

Nos. 1 and 9. Portrait statue of Cleopatra I as a Tyche of Egypt or Alexandria (Pls. XXXVII *B–D*, XXXVIII). Head (No. 1): height 35 cm., width 25.5 cm.; body (No. 9): height including base 1.55 m., girth at waist 1.40 m. Found in City Bath: head in fill in Room 9; body in Room 6, fallen from pedestal in front of third column (from north) of east portico. Head in local museum; body in Oriental Institute Museum (A 30922).

The face is sweet and youthful. The cheeks, forehead, and chin are circumscribed by a delicate oval, within which the features are indicated in a rather abstract, generalized manner. The nose is broken, and the surface of the chin is abraded. The hair is parted in the center and laid in finely rippled strands to the sides, covering the ears except for the lobes. Curling locks extend onto the shoulders at the front. The skin of an Indian elephant head is worn as a helmet and covers the figure's crown, the back of the head, and the neck. Breaks at the ears indicate that the helmet originally extended a little farther forward. At top center may be seen the base of the elephant trunk; lower and to the sides are the stumps of the two tusks. No other life-size marble head of Hellenistic type exactly like this one seems to be known,[11] but there are some small bronze versions.[12]

[11] The closest parallels are the following: (1) Head with elephant skin and reed crown (*EA* 4857; Adolf Michaelis, *Ancient Marbles in Great Britain*, tr. from the German by C. A. M. Fennell [Cambridge, 1882] p. 222, No. 19). (2) Portrait head of Roman lady with elephant skin (Walther Amelung, *Die Sculpturen des Vaticanischen Museums* II [Berlin, 1908] 494, No. 296, Pl. 68). (3) Head with elephant skin and corkscrew Isis locks (Frederik Poulsen, *Catalogue of Ancient Sculpture in the Ny Carlsberg Glyptotek* [Copenhagen, 1951] No. 278 [second-century dates given should be A. D., as originally published in *Katalog over antike skulpturen* in 1940, not B. C.]; *EA* 4401). (4) Head with elephant skin, Isis locks, cow horns, and modius (*EA* 3622; C. L. Visconti, *Monuments de sculpture antique du Musée Torlonia reproduiti* [Roma, 1884] pp. 193–94, No. 267, Pl. 67; cf. Otto Brendel in *MDAIR* L [1935] 245).

[12] (1–2) C. C. Edgar, *Greek Bronzes* (*CC* XIX [1904]) Nos. 27843–44, Pl. XVII, and *Greek Moulds* (*CC* VIII [1903]) No. 32047, Pl. VII. (3) Paul Perdrizet, *Bronzes grecs d'Égypte de la collection Fouquet* (Paris, 1911) pp. 39–40, Pl. 34. (4) A. Ruesch (ed.), *Guida illustrata del Museo nazionale di Napoli* (1908) p. 374, No. 1671; A. Petro Bienkowski, *De simulacris barbararum gentium apud Romanos: Corporis barbarorum prodomus* (Cracow, 1900) p. 38, Fig. 18. (5) *Ibid.* pp. 94–96, Fig. 95; Luigi Milani, *Il R. Museo archeologico di Firenze* (Firenze, 1912) I 169–70, No. 2337. (6–7) *Sammlung Ernst von Sieglin* I A, pp. 71–72, Pl. *XXIX* 1, 3. (8) H. B. Walters, *Catalogue of the Bronzes, Greek, Roman, and Etruscan, in the Department of Greek and Roman Antiquities, British Museum* (London, 1899) p. 248, No. 1524; Bienkowski, *op. cit.* No. 63, Fig. 96. All are examples of bosses, emblemata, or weights. No. 4, once called a boss, is now exhibited as a weight (cf. Marvin C. Ross in *AJA* L [1946] 368–69). No. 8 is typologically the farthest removed.

Bienkowski, *op. cit.*, lists others (see his No. 62, Fig. 97, and *b* and *c*), none of which can be classified as bronze versions of our Inv. No. 1. They represent Roman Africa and either depict a non-Greek ethnic type or have an African elephant headdress, or both. Bayet,

The body is clothed in a chiton of heavy material, which falls in deep vertical folds around the right leg. A mantle hangs down the back, and one end comes forward over the left shoulder. The main part of the mantle is wrapped around the right hip with a large overfold, whose upper part becomes a thick roll and whose lower edge goes diagonally over the main part and ends above the left knee with a tassel. A strap, visible only in front, runs diagonally across the chest from the left shoulder; there is no belt, and the feet are clad in sandals. Stylistically the type follows the Cyrene Athena and fits a date shortly after 200 B.C., but the drapery is not exaggerated like that of another Ptolemais Tyche, which has a transparent overfold.[13]

A careful examination of the figure's neck and shoulders has shown that head and body were carved from one piece of marble.[14] The elephant helmet, adorned on top with cow or bull horns (now broken stumps), extended to an area between the shoulders, like the bovine helmet of a comparable figure from Ptolemais.[15] This explains the rough unpolished sur-

among others, has made an excellent study of such figures (see n. 21 below).

[13] For Athena see Arthur Hamilton Smith, *A Catalogue of Sculpture in the Department of Greek and Roman Antiquities, British Museum* II (London, 1900) No. 1479; Rudolf Horn, *Stehende weibliche Gewandstatuen in der hellenistischen Plastik* (*MDAIR* "Ergänzungsheft" II [1931]) p. 42, Pl. 11:1. For Tyche see Giacomo Caputo in *RAL* IX (1954) 458–66, Fig. 3, and see p. 460, n. 1, for a Tyche from Apollonia (for Ghislanzoni reference "*op. cit.*, p. 96, fig. 48" read "*Notiziario archeologico* I [1915] 162, Fig. 48"). The style begins with Arsinoë III and culminates with a figure in Paris (Margarete Bieber, *Sculpture of the Hellenistic Age* [New York, 1955] pp. 93, 131 and Figs. 357–59, 519). Cf. unidentified figure of queen from Cyrene, now in London (Smith, *op. cit.* No. 1403), which looks like Arsinoë III, now analyzed astutely in Gustavo Traversari, *Statue iconiche femminile cirenaiche* (Roma, 1960) pp. 27, 28, 33–38, No. 3, Pls. II, XXV 1, XXVI 1.

[14] Figures of this type and scale made from one block, exclusive of the arms and attributes, are rarely found in Cyrenaica. Of the forty–five collected by Traversari, *op. cit.* pp. 21–87, only the early Antonine No. 18 (pp. 54–56, Pl. XIV 1) appears identical in technique.

[15] S. Ferri, "L'Iside Basilissa de Tolmetta," *Libya* III (1927) 38–49, Figs. 1–14. The cow skin has a uraeus superimposed upon it, so that it resembles an elephant helmet. The origin of such multiple combinations goes back to the late fourth century B. C.; cf. a head of Alexander with elephant crown and ram horns (Danish National Museum, *Oriental and Classical Antiquity* [Copenhagen, 1950] p. 82, Room 8, No. 6). Hence the now broken projections on our statue are not to be identified as supra-orbital margins of an elephant skull. On classical knowledge of elephants see Salomon Reinach in Daremberg and Saglio, *Dictionnaire des antiéquits grecques et romaines,*

face of the upper back, where the stone has broken around a fault. Attached to the left arm at the height of the armpit appear a nubbin toward the rear and a jointed section of a stalk toward the front; these are remains of the cornstalks that projected from the cornucopia which was held by the missing left hand and forearm. The position of the cornucopia would have been similar to that seen on a fayence jug depicting Cleopatra's predecessor Arsinoë III and would have corresponded closely to that on an unlabeled fragment of another figured Ptolemaic jug.[16] The marble of the Ptolemais figure is abraded around what seems to be a dowel hole in the drapery where the upper part of the cornucopia was attached; the lower tip of the cornucopia may well have reached the break in the crest of the drapery ridge above the left knee. The texture of the stone is different along a clearly marked line on the front of the left thigh and reveals the exact location of the cornucopia.

Ptolemaic coinage depicting a female head clad in an elephant helmet was once identified as that of Cleopatra II or III,[17] but later the identity was changed to the first queen so named.[18] She married Ptolemy V in 193/192 B.C. and, after he died in 180 B.C., served as regent for Ptolemy VI until her own death in 173 B.C. The type continued during the rule of Ptolemy VIII[19] and was adapted, on the Boscoreale patera, to Cleopatra VII.[20]

The origin and significance of the elephant helmet as a symbol associated with Alexander the Great and its Roman usage on personifications of Africa, Egypt, and Alexandria have been repeatedly studied.[21] The Ptolemais figure complements the few similarly helmeted statues which recall Hellenistic originals.[22] As a Roman copy it may depict Alexandria,[23] but, since the representation is now seen clearly to be the portrait of a queen of Egypt, the country should be preferred. Numismatic and sculptural parallels show that it was reproduced in the Antonine age, probably by an Athenian sculptor, as the foregoing essay attempts to demonstrate (pp. 179–80)[24]. Since the Oriental

s.v. "Elephas" and note Fig. 2620, showing the small-eared Indian variety. Cleopatra I was identified with Isis, Hathor, and others (Julien L. Tondriau, "Princesses ptolémaïques comparées ou identifiées à des déesses," *BSRAA* XXXVII [1948] 12–33).

[16] Horn, *op. cit.* pp. 36–40, Pl. 11:2 (from *Sammlung Ernst von Sieglin* III, Fig. 129*A*).

[17] Reginald Stuart Poole, *A Catalogue of the Greek Coins in the British Museum: The Ptolemies* ... (London, 1883) pp. lxxii, 96, 98 and Pl. XXIII 3, 10.

[18] J. Svoronos (I. Sboronos), *Die Münzen der Ptolemaer* (4 vols.; Athens, 1904–8) II 202–3, III, Pl. 40:13 and 16–17, II 225 and 227, III, Pl. 47:13–14. This dating is adhered to by Carl Watzinger (*Sammlung Ernst von Sieglin* I B, p. 22) and Walther Giesecke (*Das Ptolemäergeld* [Leipzig und Berlin, 1930] p. 90).

[19] Svoronos, *op. cit.* Vols. II 246 and III, Pl. 51:13, 15. On the first, the features are coarse and heavy; the second recalls the earlier youthful face. The eighth Ptolemy was the immediate successor to the sixth; see T. C. Skeat, *The Reigns of the Ptolemies* ("Münchener Beiträge zur Papyrusforschung und antiken Rechtsgeschichte" XXXIX [1954]) pp. 6, 13–15.

[20] Matteo della Corte, *Cleopatra, M. Antonio e Ottaviano nelle allegorie storico-umoristiche dell'argenterie del tesoro di Boscoreale* ("Pompeii rivive" I [Pompei, 1951]) pp. 33–43, Fig. 3; cf. Jean Charbonneaux, "Un portrait de Cléopâtre VII au Musée de Cherchel," *Libyca* II (1954) 6, 49–63, Figs. 1–10. The patera may be a Roman copy (see Gisela M. A. Richter, *A Handbook of Greek Art* [London, 1959] pp. 211–13; cf. n. 12 above).

[21] See Agnes Baldwin Brett, *Catalogue of Greek Coins* (Boston, 1955) p. 298, No. 2248 (cf. No. 2237, Pls. 106 and 115); M. Troussel, "Le dieu Ammon et la déesse Africa," *Actes du 79ᵉ Congrès des Sociétés savants, Alger ... 1954, Section d'archéologie* (Paris, 1957) pp. 123–61, Figs. 1–3; Jocelyn M. C. Toynbee, *The Hadrianic School* (Cambridge, 1934) pp. 34–38, Pls. X 5–25, XX 3, XXII 4, XXIII 1–3, XXX 1; Jean Bayet, "Un bas-relief de Sour-Djouab et l'iconographie des provinces romains sous l'Empire," *Mélanges d'archéologie et d'histoire de l'École française de Rome* XLVIII (1931) 40–74, Pl. 1; Ernest Babelon, "Alexandre ou l'Afrique," *Aréthuse* I (1923–24) 95–107, Pls. 18–19. Cf. Salvatore Aurigemma, "L'Elefante de Leptis Magna," *Africa italiana* VII (1940) 67–86, Figs. 1–19; Maxime Collignon, "L'Afrique personnifiée," *MP* XXII (1916) 163–73, Pl. XVI.

[22] Danish National Museum, *loc. cit.*; C. C. Edgar, "Two bronze portraits from Egypt," *JHS* XXVI (1906) 281–82, Pl. 18.

[23] The imperial representations of the city are listed by J. G. Milne, *Catalogue of Alexandrian Coins* (Oxford, 1933) p. 133. A few labeled billon issues show a female head with a cap topped by tusks and trunk, best illustrated in George MacDonald, *Catalogue of Greek Coins in the Hunterian Collection, University of Glasgow* II (Glasgow, 1905) Pl. 85; Reginald Stuart Poole, *Catalogue of the Coins of Alexandria and the Nomes* (London, 1892) Pl. XXIV 212. Toynbee (*op. cit.* p. 46) suggests that the figure may wear a uraeus and notes a Roman example with mural crown (*ibid.* Pl. XI 12–13; cf. E. A. Sydenham, *Roman Republican Coinage* [London, 1952] p. 137, Nos. 831–32, Pl. 24.

[24] See coin of Antoninus Pius (Poole, *Catalogue of the coins of Alexandria*, Pl. XXIV 1170; better in Giovanni Dattari, *Monete imperiali greche: Numi Augg. Alexandrini catalogo* [Cairo, 1901] Pl. 8:2454) dated A.D. 158/159 by Joseph Vogt, *Die Alexandrinischen Münzen* (Stuttgart, 1924) II 87–88. See similar statue (Luigi Savignoni in *MDAIR* V [1890] 147–49, Fig. 2) suggesting authorship. Cf. Athenian signatures in Egypt (Paul Graindor, *Bustes et statues-portraits d'Égypte romaine* [Le Caire, 1936] p. 28). Comparable heads from Cyrene represent Berenice II (Jean Charbonneaux in *MP* XLVII [1953] 125; Bieber, *op. cit.* p. 92, Figs. 346–47) and Apollo (*ibid.* p. 160, Figs. 678–79; Fritz Muthmann, *Statuenstützen und dekoratives Beiwerk an griechischen und*

Institute excavations, the Department of Antiquities of Cyrenaica has discovered another draped female statue, complete with head, which seems also to represent a Ptolemaic queen.[25]

No. 2. Head of Asklepios (Pl. XLVII *A*). Height 40 cm., width 27 cm. From City Bath, Room 9, fill. In local museum.

The broad face of the god is accentuated by a low brow, strongly marked eyebrows, and large eyes set well apart; the eyelids are clearly indicated. The nose is broken from bridge to tip, and a piece of the beard is lacking below the chin. The entire face is surrounded by short, thick locks of curling hair which extend onto the cheeks on either side of the mustache. The hair on the rest of the head, including the flattened crown, is far more summarily carved. The locks are indicated by masses cut in S-shaped curves in which extensive drilling is visible, and their arrangement on both sides of the face is almost symmetrical. From this hirsute frame the open eyes gaze into the distance, and the benevolent expression is enhanced by the slightly parted lips. A regular circular cut at the base of the neck is ancient and would have fitted neatly into the shoulders of the torso.

An Asklepios head of the late fourth century B.C. from Melos (now in the British Museum) indicates the prototype.[26] It is comparable to a Zeus from Mylasa, Caria (now in Boston).[27] The Ptolemais Asklepios diverges from imperial Roman Zeus types known in Cyrenaica, such as one signed "Zenion, son of Zenion" and dated A.D. 138.[28] An attempt to place Zenion in the school of Aphrodisias in Caria

has been countered by the suggestion that he was a local sculptor.[29] That the Ptolemais head was the work of a local sculptor seems a logical proposal also. It recalls more accurately the head of a figure of Asklepios from the Baths at Leptis.[30] The latter is of marble from Luni but has been labeled local work of the Severan age. The greater clarity of cutting evident in the Ptolemais example indicates a prior date at the end of the Antonine period. The indebtedness to Aphrodisias for the appearance in Leptis of the technique of drilled grooves, seen frequently in Antonine and Severan work, has already been established.[31] The wide range of provenience for this manner of representing bearded heads suggests the export alike of art and of artists who continued the tradition where they settled.[32] There is often little difference among the various standardized types.[33]

The flat spot on the crown of the Ptolemais Asklepios reveals that it could have easily become a Serapis, but no trace of the attachment of a modius is visible. These two gods were sometimes associated in Egypt.[34] Although the Hellenistic Serapis often lacks a modius, post-Hadrianic examples generally include it and also show the characteristic five locks across the brow.[35]

römischen Bildwerken: Ein Beitrag zur Geschichte der römischen Kopistentätigkeit (Heidelberger Akademie der Wissenschaften, philos.-hist. Klasse, "Abhandlungen," 1950, No. 3 [Heidelberg, 1951]) pp. 71 and 76, Pl. 14, Fig. 31).

[25] Height 1.78 m., of which 6 cm. is the attached base. Found in 1959 by the Department of Antiquities, during the clearance of the east cardo, beside an outer wall of the *triconchos* (Building 16 on Plan XXII). In local museum. Evidently it was not *in situ*, and its original position may have been near that of Cleopatra I. This figure leans on a herm at her left. It is of Pentelic marble.

[26] A. H. Smith, *Catalogue of Sculpture in the Department of Greek and Roman Antiquities, British Museum* I (London, 1892) No. 550; E. Thiemann, *Hellenistische Vatergottheiten* ("Orbis antiquus" XIV [Münster in Westfalen, 1959]) pp. 22–25, 131–32.

[27] L. D. Caskey, *Catalogue of Greek and Roman Sculpture* (Cambridge, Mass., 1925) No. 25.

[28] Paribeni, *Catalogo delle sculture di Cirene*, No. 185, Pl. 106. Cf. Sabratha Antonine Jupiter (Renato Bartoccini in *Rivista della Tripolitania* I [1924/25] 284, 286, Fig. 3; Bartoccini, *Guida di Sabratha* [Roma-Milano, 1927] pp. 53–54, Fig. 19).

[29] See Maria Squarciapino, *La scuola di Afrodisias* ("Studi e materiali del Museo dell'Impero Romano" III [Roma, 1943]) pp. 35–37, Pls. *G* and IX, countered by François Chamoux in *BCH* LXX (1946) 77, Pl. 4, and LXXI (1947) 371–72. The Cyrene Zeus may reproduce the Thundering Zeus of Leochares (see Guy Donnay in *Gazette des beaux-arts*, VIe période, LIII [1959] 14, Fig. 9; Karl Schefold in *MDAIR* LVII [1942] 254–56).

[30] Renato Bartoccini, "Le terme di Lepcis," *Africa italiana* IV (1929) 127, No. 4, Fig. 127.

[31] Renato Bartoccini in *Africa italiana* I (1927) 74; Squarciapino, *op. cit.* pp. 80–96; J. B. Ward Perkins in *Proceedings of the British Academy* XXXVII (1951) 280 and references there cited, Pls. 6–7.

[32] Gisela M. A. Richter, *Three Critical Periods in Greek Sculpture* (Oxford, 1951) pp. 41, 52, Figs. 91–96; Jocelyn M. C. Toynbee, *Some Notes on Artists in the Roman World* ("Collection Latomus" VI [Brussels, 1951]) pp. 29–33.

[33] See Poulsen, *Catalogue of Ancient Sculpture in the Ny Carlsberg Glyptotek*, Nos. 521–27. Compare No. 521 (Zeus) and No. 524 (Poseidon) with a Poseidon from Baiae (Heinrich Fuhrmann in *ADAI*, 1941, pp. 614–15, Fig. 120, and Amedeo Maiuri, *I campi Flegrèi* ["Itinerari dei musei e monumenti d'Italia" XXXII (3d ed.; Roma, 1958)] pp. 42, Fig. 20, and 72), with the Cyrene Zeus cited in n. 28 above, and with a Poseidon from Corinth (Squarciapino, *op. cit.* p. 34, Pls. *G b* and VIII).

[34] A. D. Nock, *Conversion* (Oxford, 1933) p. 86.

[35] Luigi Castiglione, "La statue de culte hellénistique du Sarapieion d'Alexandrie," *Bulletin du Musée hongrois des beaux-arts* VII (Budapest, 1958) 17–39, Figs. 1–23. Standardization and export of the contemporary Serapis

No. 3. Portrait head of an elderly lady (Pl. XL). Height 28 cm., width 17 cm. From Public Building, Room 8. In Oriental Institute Museum (A 30930).

The lady would have been 60–70 years old when represented. She has a clever face, marred by an expression of dissatisfaction around the mouth with its corners drawn down. The center-parted hair lies in shallow waves and is bound with a fillet. The fillet is flat on the crown and the rear, and its ends are lifted to a small knot at the nape of the neck.[36] Where it crosses the part there is a small bump.[37] The bridge of the nose and the tip of the chin are broken. The surface on the left side is marred by small scars over the eyebrow, beyond the eye, on the cheek, and at the outer edges of the ear. The rear right quarter of the head is lacking. The marble is unquestionably Greek and probably Pentelic.

The naturalism evident in the irregular modeling of the nose and the wrinkles around the eyes recalls comparable features on the head of a priest in Athens.[38] Since the lady, like the priest, wears a fillet, she may have been a priestess or the wife of the local political leader. Similarities to several Egyptian heads exist but are not very close.[39] Rather, the style is a good example of the technique common to the Mediterranean area,[40] as in heads of Julius Caesar and others.[41]

The provenience, in a building of the Roman Republican period, supports a date on stylistic grounds in the second half of the first century B.C.

No. 4. Male head from peopled-scroll pilaster (Pl. XLVII *B*). Height 27 cm., width 28 cm. From City Bath, Room 9, fill. In local museum.

This fragmentary head consists of two pieces; the upper part, comprising the right eye, brow, and crown, is lacking. The hair flutters back and down in waves carved in a distinctive grooved style. The face is round and puffy in appearance. The mouth is indicated by a straight line. The tip of the chin is missing, and the surface of the face is scratched and pitted. The remaining eye is wide open, its lower lid only summarily represented, producing a rather vapid effect. The streaked white marble, very like Proconnesian, is typical of Asia Minor.

A number of factors help to identify this head. It is squat, with a distinctive square chin. The back is flattened and unfinished. There is no neck. In all these respects it narrowly resembles a head at the top of a peopled-scroll pilaster in the Severan basilica at Leptis Magna.[42] The outline of the Leptis face, when seen in front view, shows a contour along the jaw which is close enough to that of the Ptolemais head to be interchangeable with it. The technique of grooving the hair and leaving bridgelike struts joining the locks duplicates precisely carving methods visible on other heads which decorate the Severan architectural complex at Leptis.[43] The same style appears on a head found in the forum at Smyrna.[44] A provenience

---

type, whose brow, nose, and mustache are close to the Asklepios, are illustrated by an Italian marble head found in the Walbrook district of London (*ILN*, Oct. 16, 1954, pp. 636–37) and another replica, in plaster, from the Aventine in Rome (*ILN*, Jan. 8, 1955, pp. 60–61, Figs. 14–15).

[36] Cf. coiffure of Octavia and Cleopatra VII (Sydenham, *Roman Republican Coinage*, pp. 193–94, Nos. 1200 and 1210, Pl. 29; cf. J. J. Bernoulli, *Römische Ikonographie* I [Stuttgart, 1882] Münztafel IV 92–96 and II 1 [1886] Pl. XXXII 9, 12–15). The style endures until coins of Julia (see H. A. Grueber, *Coins of the Roman Republic in the British Museum* [London, 1910] II 96, No. 4651, and III, Pl. LXXI 6).

[37] Cf. the protuberance on top of a head of Cleopatra VII (Georg Lippold, *Die Sculpturen des Vaticanischen Museums* III 1 [Berlin, 1936] pp. 170–71, No. 567, Pl. 62).

[38] E. B. Harrison, *Portrait Sculpture* (American School of Classical Studies at Athens, "The Athenian Agora" I [Princeton, 1953]) pp. 12–14, No. 3, Pl. 3; Ernst Buschor, *Das hellenistische Bildnis* (München, 1949) pp. 49, 55, Fig. 44.

[39] Graindor, *Bustes et statues-portraits d'Égypte romain*, pp. 20–22, No. 61, Pl. 54; cf. Frederik Poulsen in *From the Collections of the Ny Carlsberg Glyptothek 1938* II (Copenhagen, 1939) 31–32, Figs. 32–34.

[40] The idea that Egypt was the principal source of the veristic strain in Roman and other strongly naturalistic portraits of the last century B.C. is under attack. See Gisela M. A. Richter, "The origin of verism in Roman portraits," *JRS* XLV (1955) 39–46. Cf. B. v. Bothmer,

"La tête égyptienne d'Auxerre," *Revue des arts* IX (1959) 99–108, Figs. 1–7; Pierre Montet, "Un chef-d'oeuvre de l'art gréco-égyptien: La statue de Panemerit," *MP* L (1958) 1–10, Pls. I–V, Figs. 1–4.

[41] François Chamoux, "Un portrait de Thasos: Jules César," *MP* XLVII 131–47, Pl. XII, Figs. 1–9. Cf. a head from Minturnae (Achille Adriani in *Notizie degli scavi di antichità*, 6th series, XIV [1938] 195–96, Fig. 24). Vagn Poulsen kindly informed me of a female head from Italy, close to Ptolemais Inv. No. 3, now published in Arvid Andrén, "Greek and Roman heads in the Malström collection," *Opuscula Romana* II ("Skrifter utgivna av Svenska Institutet i Rom," 4°, XX [Lund, 1960]) 21, No. 7, Pls. XII–XIII.

[42] Squarciapino, *La scuola di Afrodisias*, Pl. *V* (facing p. 85).

[43] Ward Perkins in *Proceedings of the British Academy* XXXVII 269–304, Figs. 1–2, Pls. 1–15, and *JRS* XXXVIII (1948) 73–74, Pl. IX 4.

[44] Rudolf Naumann and Kantar Selâhattin, "Die Agora von Smyrna," *Istanbuler Forschungen* XVII (1950) 104, No. 30, Pl. 41 *d*. The Hellenistic beginnings of the style are evident in a relief head from Cyzicus (Arnold Schober, *Die Kunst von Pergamon* [Wien, 1951] p. 120, Fig. 103).

within the orbit of the Aphrodisias school, already established for sculptors active at Leptis, applies to the Ptolemais head and the carved pilaster to which it belonged.[45]

Peopled-scroll pilasters, well documented with respect to their origin and manufacture, were widely used in Africa and the East.[46] Their influence extended beyond the imperial frontiers.[47] The pilaster from which the Ptolemais head came has not yet been found. It would have a decorated vine pattern arranged in circular loops, one of which would surround the face. The monument must have arrived unfinished from its Asia Minor workshop, no doubt as part of a supervised shipment of building material, late in the second century after Christ, to be completed on the site.

No. 5. Head of maenad in relief (Pl. XLVIII *B*). Height of slab 65 cm., width 60 cm. Used to close opening between Rooms 6 and 9 of City Bath. *In situ.*

In the area to the right center on this battered relief appears the upturned head in left profile. Its top now merges into the pitted surface, but the outlines grow clearer from the brow downward. Eye socket, nose, mouth, chin, and neck show the angle of the head. The best preserved details are a channeled drapery fold in front of the neck and an equally regularly carved section behind the head which shows two locks of hair and a leafy twig that may be part of the thyrsus. The marble is Pentelic.

The outline is precise enough to identify the fragment as part of the group of dancing maenads previously found at Ptolemais. When the group was published it was realized that there should be another figure to fill the circular base around which the figures danced, and this maenad, known from other copies, fits easily into its pre-assigned niche.[48] Its poor condition is due not only to its later use but

also to the fact that the whole group probably adorned a fountain.[49] A copy in Madrid best preserves the pose of this maenad, whose date falls in the Antonine age.[50]

Callimachus in Athens has generally been named as the artist of the original, but the masters of the Nike Temple parapet, active in the last quarter of the fifth century B.C., have recently been suggested.[51] A Dionysos statue apparently stood on top of the drum. Because of the wealth of associations of the Ptolemies with Dionysos it is probable that an early free copy of the original base stood in Egypt around 200 B.C. and was topped by the figure of Ptolemy IV as Neos Dionysos in place of the god.[52] That this could account for the presence of the copy at Ptolemais, especially in view of the Egyptian nature of much of the other sculpture found there, seems likely.

Nos. 6–7. Two lion-headed waterspouts. Diameter of faces *ca.* 35 cm. One (Pl. XLII *A*) cut from lowest drum of a column. Originally in south and west walls of Room 6 of City Bath but found in octagonal pool (No. 6) and south portico (No. 7) of that room (see p. 165). In local museum.

These architectural features continue a standard functional and decorative scheme seen at Ptolemais as well as elsewhere in the ancient eastern Mediter-

[45] Many sculptors are known to have come from Aphrodisias (see Toynbee, *Some Notes on Artists in the Roman World*, pp. 27–31). It is not probable, however, that this inland city was also the only source of the steady and sizable volume of architectural components traceable to western Asia Minor. Cf. Charles Picard in *Revue des études latines* XXXII (1954) 329 and n. 4. A coastal center such as Smyrna or Cyzicus is another likely possibility. Did the island of Proconnesus, whose products blanketed the East, ship its stone direct? See Inv. Nos. 69–70, esp. p. 207 and n. 170.

[46] J. M. C. Toynbee and J. B. Ward Perkins, "Peopled scrolls: A Hellenistic motif in imperial art," *PBSR* XVIII (1950) 1–43, Pls. I–XXVI.

[47] Benjamin Rowland, Jr., "The vine-scroll in Gandhāra," *Artibus Asiae* XIX (1956) 353–61, Figs. 1–5.

[48] Caputo, *Lo scultore del grande bassorilievo con la Danza delle Menadi in Tolemaide di Cirenaica* ("Monografie di archeologia libica" I [Roma, 1948]) p. 17, Pl. 14 left.

[49] Rudolf Horn in *ADAI*, 1936, p. 549, Fig. 40.

[50] *EA* 1683; see also Werner Fuchs, *Die Vorbilder der neuattischen Reliefs* (*JDAI* "Ergänzungsheft" XX [1959]) p. 77, n. 11, and type 28 on pp. 80–81, which corresponds to the Ptolemais fragment. Fuchs' type numbers are those of Friedrich Hauser, *Die neu-attischen Reliefs* (Stuttgart, 1889); see pp. 99–100 and Pl. 2 for type 28. Cf. Caputo, *Danza delle Menadi*, pp. 18–19, 24; G. Gullini in *Archeologia classica* V (1953) 159.

[51] By Rhys Carpenter, according to C. C. Vermeule in a review of Ernest Will's *Le relief cultuel gréco-romain* (Paris, 1955) in *Gnomon* XXIX (1957) 373; cf. Gullini, *op. cit.* p. 162, n. 1.

[52] Suggested by Caputo (*Danza delle Menadi*, pp. 18–19, 24), who, however, calls the monument an original of the early second century B.C., and rejected by Fuchs (*op. cit.* p. 77, n. 11), who, in proving its Antonine date, seems to deny a connection with any Ptolemy. But a number of fundamental studies involving Ptolemaic symbolism are very convincing in this regard: Julien L. Tondriau, "Les thiases dionysiaques royaux de la cour ptolémaïque," *Chronique d'Égypte* XXI (1946) 149–71, and "Un thiase dionysiaque à Péluse sous Ptolémée IV Philopator," *BSRAA* XXXVII 3–11; Friedrich Matz "Der Gott auf dem Elefantenwagen," Akademie der Wissenschaften und der Literatur (Mainz), *Abhandlungen der geistes- und sozialwissenschaftlichen Klasse*, 1952, No. 10, and *Ein römisches Meisterwerk: Der Jahreszeitensarkophag Badminton–New York* (*JDAI* "Ergänzungsheft" XIX [1958]) p. 121 (cf. pp. 90–92). A head presumed to depict Ptolemy IV was found at Ptolemais (see Caputo in *RAL* IX 461).

ranean.[53] The face is framed by the mane, carved in a series of regular locks. Above the open mouth the whiskers and nose reveal the same symmetrical regularity. The heavy brows curve forward over the eyes and continue up the center of the forehead to the mane. No other lion heads produce quite the same effect of static ferocity, but their tradition is Greek and their ancestor is a lion spout from Epidauros.[54] The rendition of the brows is more formal than on a vaguely similar lion on a Pergamum frieze, and a spout from Corinth, made in the first century after Christ, is closer.[55] The relative simplification of the Ptolemais spouts, plus the reuse of a column drum for one of them, shows that they are local work of the first half of the second century after Christ. Later examples differ from them in various ways.[56] The fact that they resemble earlier Corinthian work, rather than Aphrodisian, further suggests the predominance of Attic influence (cf. Inv. Nos. 1, 9, and 12) until the later part of the century (cf. Inv. Nos. 2 and 4).[57] Their material is low-grade local sandstone. Quite possibly they were made as emergency replacements after the widespread destruction which occurred during the Jewish revolt.

No. 8. Torso of one of the Three Graces (Pl. XLI). Height 98 cm., girth: bust 1.05 m., waist 83 cm., hips 1.10 m. From City Bath, Room 6, west portico. In local museum.

The torso itself is complete, but head, arms, legs, and support are lacking. The Grace stood with her weight on her left leg and the other leg thrust slightly forward. The firm yet sensuous modeling depicts a youthful form. The deeply recessed navel below the line of the rib cage and the fullness of the abdomen above the round volumes of the thighs create a remarkably voluptuous impression. Long tresses of hair fell onto the left shoulder and down over the collarbone on the right, covering part of the necklace, which, like the hair, was probably painted in antiquity. The stone is a gray-veined dead white marble with medium crystals, probably Proconnesian but in any

case from Asia Minor or one of its adjacent islands. A few small chips have been knocked out of the surface of the legs and trunk. The other, larger scars on the torso were not originally visible, as is evident from a conjectural restoration.

This was the facing figure seen on the right in a group of three intertwined Graces. The composition from which it came is preserved more completely in one of the four replicas known at Cyrene.[58] The corresponding figure preserves the head, which is turned to the left. The dowel hole and traces of attachment below the right breast of the Ptolemais torso supported the outstretched right arm of the center Grace, which crossed the body of our torso. The right hand of the center Grace rested on the left arm of the Ptolemais figure. This arm extended downward to the left hip, and the hand crossed the body to touch the opposite thigh with the fingers. The abraded and indented surfaces of the Ptolemais torso correspond exactly to such a restoration. Thus the left arm was arranged in the *pudica* gesture, a detail which is seen in the same Cyrene example also. The other arm was bent, with the elbow lowered and the hand raised to rest on the near shoulder of the center Grace, as the Cyrene group demonstrates. The latter also possessed supports at either end in the form of vases covered by drapery, but only the support at the right end survives. The Ptolemais torso apparently had a like support at the lower part of the left thigh, according to the present condition of the marble. The corresponding area on the outside of the other thigh also shows a roughened surface. At this point the body of the Grace was pressed against the right hip of the center figure of the group, as in one of the other copies in Cyrene.[59]

The surface of our fragment is in fair condition and once was highly polished. In its soft *sfumato* finish—a technique first practiced during the Hellenistic age, when it was particularly popular in Alexandria and the islands off Asia Minor—it recalls the crouching Aphrodite of Rhodes.[60] That statue combines a kneeling pose with the Anadyomene motif. The Grace is another example of such dual combinations, for her *pudica* gesture is borrowed from an Aphrodite type.[61] Al-

[53] See Pesce, *Il "Palazzo delle Colonne,"* p. 25, Pl. VIII *B*; Anton Hekler, *Die Sammlung antiker Skulpturen* ("Budapester Sammlungen" I [Wien, 1929]) p. 67, No. 53 (cf. pp. 103–4, No. 94, and 146, No. 142); Giulio Jacopi, "Il tempio e il teatro di Apollo Eretimio," *Clara Rhodos* II (1932) 93–97, Figs. 16–20.

[54] Franz Willemsen, *Die Löwenkopf-Wasserspeier vom Dach des Zeustempels* ("Olympische Forschungen" IV [Berlin, 1959]) p. 53, Pl. 62.

[55] *Ibid.* pp. 68 and 101, Pls. 71 and 97.

[56] *Ibid.* p. 108, Pl. 108.

[57] See Giulio Jacopi in *Monumenti antichi dell'Accademia nazionale dei Lincei* XXXVIII (Milano, 1939–40) 82, Pl. XLII *a, c.*

[58] Paribeni, *Catalogo delle sculture di Cirene,* No. 302, Pl. 144 (cf. Nos. 301, 303–4, Pls. 144–45).

[59] *Ibid.* No. 301.

[60] Bieber, *Sculpture of the Hellenistic Age,* p. 83, Figs. 294–95; B. M. Felletti-Maj in *Archeologia classica* III (1951) 45 and n. 4.

[61] Felletti-Maj, *op. cit.* pp. 149–50. The priority of statue *vs.* painting cannot be argued here. Recent research confirms the fact that the second century B.C. was a likely source not for the origin of the statuary composition but rather for its reworking, and Callimachus proves it was known previously in some form, substan-

though the origin of the composition of the Three Graces is to be sought in the third century before Christ, this adaptation should date from the second, as does the Rhodian Aphrodite.[62]

The actual date of the Ptolemais torso is Roman. In contrast to the Aphrodite of Cyrene, a superbly finished, somewhat academic masterpiece, now dated to the middle of the second century after Christ,[63] the Ptolemais work seems warmer and more alive and hence closer in time and spirit to its original. Yet the same relative fullness in the abdomen and thighs characterizes the modeling in both cases. Their supports were of approximately equal height. The same fullness characterizes the modeling of the Grace in the group from Cyrene which the Ptolemais torso most nearly resembles. She and her sisters have been dated in the first century after Christ because of their style and, through an examination of their supports, in the second.[64] Here, however, the exact form of the support is not known, and the richness of style and superior modeling permit a date any time between the Flavian and the early Antonine age. The later choice appears more probable.

No. 9. See Inv. No. 1 (pp. 188–90).

No. 10. Headless figure of Aeschines type (Pl. XLVI). Height including base 1.82 m., girth at waist 1.45 m. Found in City Bath, Room 6, fallen from its pedestal in front of second column (from north) of east portico. In Oriental Institute Museum (A 30921), base and right foot partly restored.

This statue and Inv. Nos. 6–8, 11–20, and 23 all formed part of the sculptural decoration of the frigidarium of the City Bath. The figure of Aeschines type is executed in a somewhat coarser and darker stone, which gives it a heavy appearance. Perhaps the marble is Pentelic. The torso is tightly swathed in a Greek himation reaching to the ankles. After inclosing

the right arm, which is held across the chest with only the hand free, the himation is thrown up over the left shoulder and falls down to the capsa at the figure's left. The diagonal folds of the costume emphasize the pose in which the famous orator was first represented. He stands on his left leg, and the gently bent right knee pushes against the himation. The right arm pulls the end of the himation down from the throat and presses firmly against the drapery around the body. Yet the himation, which ordinarily hangs loosely, is drawn tight by the left arm, and the composition thus resembles the letter K seen in reverse, for the man represented has stretched it by placing his left forearm behind his back. The resulting folds and darts converging at the left hip create a tense and dramatic effect. There are cracks at the left part of the chest, down the center of the torso, where a number of chips are missing, and along the right leg and thigh. Pieces of the skirt have been reassembled along the bottom edge in front and at the left knee. The drapery end hanging down the back is damaged below the left elbow and behind the left knee.

The original conception of Aeschines has been attributed to the Attic sculptor Leochares[65] and has been variously dated between 340 and 314 B.C., before and after Aeschines was exiled from Athens in 330.[66] A replica in Naples from Herculaneum preserves the head. There are a number of portrait adaptations of the Hellenistic and Roman periods, the most relevant of which is from Cyrene (now in London) and may depict Hadrian.[67] The Ptolemais statue, however, has many more folds in the himation, which is arranged more tautly. The person represented is probably not Aeschines but either an emperor or a prominent local citizen of the second or third quarter of the second century after Christ.

No. 11. Athena fragment of Farnese type (Pl. XLIV *A*). Height *ca.* 35 cm., width 55 cm. From City Bath, Room 6, east portico. In local museum.

tiating Picard's attractive suggestion that the group was known in Cyrene before 200 B.C. See Gisela M. A. Richter in *JRS* XLVIII (1958) 12; C. A. Trypanis, *Callimachus* ("The Loeb Classical Library" [Cambridge, Mass., 1958]) p. 239 and notes thereto; Charles Picard, *La sculpture antique* (2d. ed.; Paris, 1926) p. 510.

[62] Cf. the conclusions of Achille Adriani, "L'Afrodite al bagno'di Rodi e l'Afrodite di Doedalsas," *Annales du Service des antiquités de l'Égypte* XLIV (1944) 37–70, and in *BSRAA* XXXIX (1951) 144; Georg Lippold, *Handbuch der Archäologie* III 1 ("Handbuch der Altertumswissenschaft" VI 3 [Munich, 1950]) p. 346; Gisela M. A. Richter, *Catalogue of Greek Sculptures in the Metropolitan Museum of Art* (Cambridge, Mass., 1954) No. 159.

[63] Muthmann, *Statuenstützen*, pp. 94, 125, 219, Pl. 17a–b.

[64] Paribeni, *op. cit.* No. 302; Muthmann, *op. cit.* p. 107 and n. 24.

[65] See Donnay in *Gazette des beaux-arts*, VIe période, LIII 12–15.

[66] Bieber, *Sculpture of the Hellenistic Age*, p. 62, Figs. 194–97; Horn, *Stehende weibliche Gewandstatuen*, pp. 21–22, 60; Luciano Laurenzi, *Ritratti greci* ("Quaderni per lo studio dell'archeologia" III–V [Firenze, 1941]) pp. 108–9, No. 46, and Pls. 17, 48; Karl Schefold, *Die Bildnisse der antiken Dichter, Redner und Denker* (Basel, 1943) pp. 102–3.

[67] Buschor, *Das hellenistische Bildnis*, p. 45, Fig. 10; A. H. Smith, *Catalogue of Sculpture in the Department of Greek and Roman Antiquities, British Museum* II, No. 1381; Margarete Bieber, "Roman men in Greek himation," *Proceedings of the American Philosophical Society* CIII (1959) 375–417, Figs. 1–62 (for Hadrian see p. 399, Fig. 38).

The view shown is from the rear. The fragment consists of the right shoulder and includes the locks of hair which hung down below the back of the neck in ropelike curls. The curls are indicated rather schematically, and similar treatment of the drapery suggests that the statue stood against a wall. The snake which adorned the right shoulder is missing, but its original position is clearly indicated by a serpentine line carved in relief. The weathered marble appears to be Pentelic.

The front of the fragment is severely battered. Half of an enormous socket for the head survives, as does most of a socket for the right arm. It is likely that Inv. No. 19 (Pl. XLIV *B*, second from left) is from one of the statue's sandaled feet. An unlabeled colossal left hand holding a staff[68] is probably another fragment of the statue.

The statue must have been about one and a half times life-size. The shoulder with its tresses and the other two fragments mentioned above conform to the Athena known as the Farnese type.[69] This statue brings the total number of figures of the goddess at Ptolemais, excavated from a very limited part of the extensive site, to four.[70] Athena was quite popular at Cyrene also.[71] A preference for a colossal scale was particularly evident in the region from the Hadrianic age onward.[72] The date of this Farnese replica at Ptolemais in all probability falls in the Antonine age, which witnessed such a peak of artistic production for the cities of the Libyan Pentapolis.

No. 12. Three fragments of statue of Herakles by Asklepiades of Athens. Base (Pl. XLV *A*): length 1.10 m., maximum depth 60 cm., height 15 cm., height of tree stump at figure's right *ca.* 35 cm., height of pier at his left *ca.* 50 cm. Found in City Bath, Room 6, Niche *D*. *In situ.* Calf fragment: length *ca.* 33 cm., girth *ca.* 58 cm. Found between Niches *C* and *D*. In local museum. Right thigh and buttock (Pl. XLV *B*): length 70 cm., girth below buttock 90 cm. Found in front of Niche *D*. In local museum.

The base is one of four sculptural fragments found

at Ptolemais to date which bear the Greek inscription (p. 214, No. 37) "M. Ulpius Cominius, with his own means, for his native city."[73] It is the only one which carries a signature: "Asklepiades of Athens," located on the tree trunk (see pp. 179 and 214, No. 38). The artist is otherwise unknown. The material is Pentelic marble.

The paws of the customary lion skin are visible at the base of the pier. Since there is no trace of the club, it may have rested on the same support. The statue of the hero would then have matched one found in the Roman baths at Argos.[74] The finely carved fragment which preserves the right thigh and buttock has a break in its polished surface on the outside of the right hip. If the comparison with the Argos example is acceptable, the break marks the spot where Herakles placed his right hand.[75]

The principal significance of the fragments is that they demonstrate an artistic connection with the copyists of Athens. The second century after Christ, according to the style of the lettering, seems to be the date. The donor's name, Ulpius, relates him to Trajan.

No. 13. Fragment of sea creature (Pl. XLII *C*). Maximum height 65 cm., width 50 cm., depth 40 cm. Found in City Bath, Room 6, west portico. *In situ.*

The fragment depicts the rear part of a sea creature with the feet of a cupid(?) on its back. The cupid's left foot stands on the beast's tail, which ended in a double fin or flipper, visible on the back and left side. Between the extant fin and the surviving tailpiece must have been a tapering semicircular coil joining them, for the flipper faces forward. Below is a large fin, matching one on the other side. A small fin appears to the right of the cupid's right foot. Above it, the tapering body bears no sign of being partly human, and thus there is no possibility that it may have represented a Triton. The material is Pentelic marble.

The figure's right side, which seems to be the back, is roughly carved, and the fin there runs straight up and down. In front of the forepart of the creature is a smoothly cut flat vertical surface, where this piece was attached to something else. One suspects that this may have been a throne, on which perhaps the Tyche of the port of Ptolemais reposed. The city

---

[68] Length 26 cm. Its width, corresponding to the width of the hand at the knuckles, is 11 cm. In local museum.

[69] A. Preyss, "Athena Hope und Pallas Albani-Farnese, *JDAI* XXVII (1912) 88–128, Pls. 9–11, Figs. 1–27 (esp. Fig. 7, a rear view of head and shoulders). A more recent appraisal of the type is in Domenico Mustilli, *Il Museo Mussolini* (Roma, 1939) pp. 136–37, No. 13, Pl. 85.

[70] Including Inv. No. 64 and two torsos in the local museum.

[71] A. H. Smith, *op. cit.* Vol. II, No. 1382; Paribeni, *op. cit.* Nos. 121–36, Pls. 76–80.

[72] See Goodchild, *Cyrene and Apollonia*, pp. 70–71.

[73] The other three are a statue of Athena (Inv. No. 64), a small fragment found before 1941, and the base of a group with two figures, perhaps Dionysos and a satyr, of which only the feet survive, found in 1955 by the Department of Antiquities in the "Odeon." All three are in the local museum.

[74] Jean Marcadé in *BCH* LXXXI (1957) 408–13, Figs. 1*a*, 2–5.

[75] *Ibid.* Fig. 3.

served as the seaport of Barca. The scale of the fragment is such that the supposed Tyche would have been larger than life-size, the head as big as the Tyche head found at Ptolemais (Inv. No. 61).

The whole composition which our fragment represents could well have been similar to that of an enthroned Tyche found in Rome.[76] In that example a Triton faces forward by the left of the throne. The smooth surface of the cut at the end of the Ptolemais fragment shows that it was placed at right angles to whatever it abutted. If it was located to the left of a throne, the Eros(?) would have faced the same way as the Triton in the Rome example.

No. 14. Lower part of priest holding *naiskos* (Pl. XXXIX C). Height including base 1.15 m., width of base 67 cm., depth of base 58 cm. Found in City Bath, Room 6, in front of sixth column (from west) of south portico. *In situ.*

In its present state, this fragmentary monument comprises a rectangular Pentelic marble block on an attached base. Two long human legs run vertically along the rear edges; the feet extend along the sides, standing on the base. The base may have had low relief carving on its front, for on the right part is what might once have been a small human figure. Above the front of the base is a shallow square *naiskos* for a statuette or offerings. On the back of the block a carved flattish element tapers downward to an ancient break, just above which are several small circles. It seems to be part of a cloak, made from the skin of a lion or a panther, whose tuft at the end of the tail is now missing.[77] Above are two large dowel holes which may have supported the upper part of the body of the priest. Below, the base is badly weathered and abraded. The block ends at its top in an irregular, roughly horizontal break. The scale of the legs at the corners suggests that the total original height was more than two meters.

The monument was an adaptation of a type found in Egypt from the eighteenth dynasty onward.[78] An

example from the twenty-second dynasty shows a similar composition, but the *naiskos* is tall and narrow and the draped *naophoros* clearly stands to the rear, supported by the standard rectangular shaft behind his back.[79] His feet, however, are in the same relative position. On each side his hands clasp the block, at hip height, on a line directly above the feet. In the Saite period and after, the same general type enjoyed some popularity outside Egypt, as a statue holding a small *naiskos* demonstrates, for it was found in Smyrna.[80] Another comparable work of the same date, though smaller in scale, shows the bearer holding a *naiskos* atop a high pedestal which rises from between his feet, so that the top of the shrine is about at waist level.[81]

The sides of the Ptolemais block reveal no traces of supporting hands, but they may have been attached to the missing upper portion. Perhaps the hands were free to hold some cult object. Two examples from Hadrian's villa depict offering-bearers carrying trays.[82] Like the Ptolemais figure, they seem to have no precise counterparts within the Egyptian sculptural tradition. Such adaptations began during the Hellenistic period.[83] The use of Greek marble for such subjects, in conjunction with a relative misunderstanding of Egyptian artistic principles, is a known feature of Hadrianic Egyptianizing work, seen for example in figures of Antinoüs.[84] In view of the increasing popularity of Egyptian divinities and their festivals during the second century in Egypt, at Rome, and presumably in Cyrenaica too, a Hadrianic date is only a *terminus ante quem.*[85]

XXV; Ludwig Borchardt, *Statuen und Statuetten von Königen und Privatleuten* III (CC LXXXVIII [1930]) No. 742, Pl. CXXXVII.

[79] Borchardt, *op. cit.* Vol. IV (CC XCIV [1934]) No. 1212, Pl. CLXX.

[80] Giuseppe Botti and Pietro Romanelli, *Le sculture del Museo Gregoriano egizio* ("Monumenti vaticani di archeologia e d'arte" IX [Città del Vaticano, 1951]) pp. 32–40, 137, No. 40, Pls. 27–32.

[81] Borchardt, *op. cit.* Vol. III, No. 730, Pl. CXXXV.

[82] Botti and Romanelli, *op. cit.* Nos. 165–66, Pl. 74; Pierre Gusman, *La villa impériale de Tibur (Villa Hadriana)* (Paris, 1904) pp. 312, 315, Figs. 576 and 575 respectively. The trays are restorations but appear to be correct.

[83] Cf. Labib Habachi, "A strange monument of the Ptolemaic period from Crocodilopolis," *Journal of Egyptian Archaeology* XLI (1955) 106–11, Pl. XXI, Fig. 1.

[84] Botti and Romanelli, *op. cit.* No. 143, Pls. 67–72; Gusman, *op. cit.* pp. 282, 309–10, Figs. 559–60.

[85] See Harold I. Bell, *Cults and Creeds in Graeco-Roman Egypt* (Liverpool, 1953) pp. 64–70 and notes thereto; G. la Piana in *Harvard Theological Review* XX (1927) 287–303.

[76] B. M. Felletti-Maj, "La Tetide della Stazione Termini," *Archeologia classica* I (1949) 46–48, Pls. 13–16; Salvatore Aurigemma, *The Baths of Diocletian and the Museo Nazionale Romano* ("Guide-Books to the Museums and Monuments of Italy" LXXVIII [4th ed.; Roma, 1958]) pp. 113–14, No. 291, Pl. LIX.

[77] Cf. Ahmed Bey Kamal, *Stèles ptolémaiques et romaines* I–II (CC XX [1905] and XXI [1904]) No. 22183, Pl. LVII. For assistance in locating comparative Egyptian material I am indebted to Dr. Gilbert, Directeur de la Fondation égyptologique Reine Élisabeth, Brussels, and for helpful comments to Dr. W. S. Smith, Curator of Egyptian Art, Museum of Fine Arts, Boston.

[78] Cf. Georges Legrain, *Statues et statuettes de rois et de particuliers* II (CC XLIX [1909]) No. 42161, Pl.

The donor could have been an Egyptian priest of a phyle, as described in the foregoing essay (p. 180).[86] A conventional Egyptian statue of such a priest is reported from Cyrene by Rowe.[87] In the eastern Mediterranean area some phyles continued from the Hellenistic age at least through the Hadrianic age, as illustrated by the Pergamene political heritage in Asia Minor.[88] In religious practices connected with the worship of Isis, the members of the priesthood were Egyptians who preserved the Hellenistic organization of the cult throughout the imperial era.[89]

No. 15. Left knee and shin with attached fragment of animal (Pl. XLV *C*). Height of shin 45 cm., width of piece *ca.* 35 cm., depth *ca.* 30 cm. From City Bath, Room 6, west portico. In local museum.

This fragment is one of a number which may well be all that remains of a life-size copy or adaptation of the little Herakles Epitrapezios by Lysippos.[90] The hero was conceived as seated, knees bent, upon a rock covered by his lion skin as in this piece. Inv. No. 16, left foot and base, also seems to come from such a statue. In a replica from Nineveh,[91] the right foot is drawn back so that the heel is off the ground (as in Inv. No. 17). That copy shows the hero wearing a type of greave on each leg (cf. Inv. No. 20). A more complete version in Naples[92] illustrates how, in this adaptation, he held his club in his clenched left hand (cf. Inv. No 21). The same statue preserves his drinking cup with its ring-shaped handles, which he held in his outstretched right hand (cf. Inv. No. 22) as he sat, originally in heroic nudity, but in miniature, on a banqueting table (cf. Inv. No. 23). Except for Inv. No. 22, all the fragments were found within or near Room 6 of the City Bath. Considering the confused condition of the site, the hypothesis that these fragments from the most vulnerable parts of a statue

once formed part of a popular subject is an engaging archeological supposition.

No. 16. Booted left foot and adjoining support on fragment of base (Pl. XLIV *B*, right end). Total height 41 cm., width 21 cm., depth 42 cm., height of base 6 cm. From City Bath, Room 6, west portico. In local museum. See Inv. No. 15.

No. 17. Bare right foot with raised heel on base (Pl. XLIV *B*, center). Total height 26 cm., width 22 cm., depth of base *ca.* 40 cm. From City Bath, Room 6, southwest corner of porticoes. In local museum. See Inv. No. 15.

No. 18. Toes on base (Pl. XLIV *B*, left end). Total height 22 cm., width 17 cm., height of base 16 cm. From City Bath, Room 6, fill. In local museum.

No. 19. Toes of sandaled foot on base (Pl. XLIV *B*, second from left). Total height *ca.* 22 cm., width *ca.* 8 cm., depth 25 cm. From City Bath, Room 6, east portico, in front of Niche *B*. In local museum. See Inv. No. 11 (p. 196).

No. 20. Booted calf (Pl. XLIV *B*, second from right). Height 40 cm., maximum girth 48 cm. From City Bath, Room 6, southwest corner of porticoes In local museum. See Inv. No. 15.

No. 21. Back of clenched hand. Length 13 cm., width 12.5 cm. From surface east of City Bath. In local museum. See Inv. No. 15.

No. 22. Fingertip attached to ring-shaped holder. Length of fragment 8 cm., width 6 cm. From court of Villa. In local museum. See Inv. No. 15.

No. 23. Fragment of buttock and thigh. Height 12 cm., diameter 25 cm. From City Bath, Room 6. In local museum. See Inv. No. 15.

No. 24. Fragment of draped shoulders. Height *ca.* 28 cm., width *ca.* 20 cm. From City Bath, Room 9. In local museum.

No. 25. Fragment of draped shoulder with tresses. Height 15 cm., width 9 cm. From Public Building. In local museum.

No. 26. Fragment of drapery. Height 31 cm., width 22 cm. From street west of City Bath. In local museum.

[86] See Edwyn Bevan, *A History of Egypt under the Ptolemaic Dynasty* (London, 1927) pp. 208–14, who translates "phyle" in the Canopic Decree as "tribe." See also Kamal, *op. cit.* No. 22186, Pls. LIX–LXI.

[87] See *Bulletin of the John Rylands Library* XXXVI (Manchester, 1953/54) 495–96, No. 4. The date may be not Ptolemaic, as Rowe claims, but Roman imperial. See also Inv. No. 58 (p. 202 below).

[88] See E. Bosch, "Ankara: Die Phylen," *Jahrbuch für kleinasiatische Forschung* III (1955) 57–67, esp. p. 62.

[89] See La Piana, *op. cit.* pp. 304–5. For a portrait see C. C. Vermeule, "Oberlin's head of an Isis priest of the second century A.D.," *Allen Memorial Art Museum Bulletin* XVII 1 (Oberlin, Ohio, 1959) pp. 7–13, Figs. 1–2.

[90] Bieber, *Sculpture of the Hellenistic Age*, pp. 36, 162 and references there given, Figs. 80, 81, 690.

[91] *Ibid.* Fig. 80.

[92] *Ibid.* Fig. 81. If Inv. No. 21 is the piece this writer believes it to be, then the hand holds the end of an object like the handle of a club.

Smaller Sculptures and Statuettes

No. 27. Herm head (Pl. XLII *D*). Height 15 cm., width 10.9 cm. From court of Villa. In Oriental Institute Museum (A 30919).

This male head is carved with regular features gently indicated except for the angular cut of the lower eyelids, which dip down in a peculiar fashion. The center-parted hair flows back in undulating strands under a ribbon to disappear beneath a mass of stone with a flat top extending over the crown of the head and down the back to the shoulders. There are three short locks of hair in front of and a single long strand behind each ear. The mustache and flowing beard are softly carved, their locks ending in little curls. The lips of the small mouth are slightly parted. The summary treatment throughout and the marble incasing the head are in keeping with a function as a supporting architectural element. Similar examples adorn the Naples Museum.[93] Although the marble is Pentelic, the only other relevant example of the type was found in Asia Minor.[94] Their mutual ancestor appears to be a herm found at Pergamum.[95] The correspondence is not close, however; in fact, this piece appears to be a variation from the second century after Christ, perhaps local, of the standard types.[96] The softness of feature is echoed by a Dionysos bust from Cyrene.[97] An architectural herm at Cos[98] is even more comparable.

No. 28. Head of bearded man wearing fillet (Pl. XLVIII *C*). Height 11 cm., width 7 cm. From fill over court of Villa. In Oriental Institute Museum (A 31076).

This severely weathered head now has an indistinctness of feature which does not detract from a certain rugged charm. Around a rather lean face the hair and beard formed regular locks. The left half of the mustache and much of the nose have disappeared. There remain a well marked bridge between prominent brows and heavy-lidded eyes to give the face an expression of dignified reserve. Part of the neck survives, and several folds of a mantle seem to be represented on the left side, now interrupted by a break whose surface slopes upward to the back of the head. These features suggest that the original bust or statue may have been carved in one piece.[99] The golden Pentelic marble shows its crystals where it has been hit or scratched around the nearly obliterated ears and on the smooth cap of hair above the fillet.

The combination of Attic marble and *strophion* suggest comparison with portraits of priests found in Athens. An Antonine head shows the fillet placed closer to the brow.[100] That of a boy made in the third quarter of the third century after Christ has the wreath in the same relative position as the Ptolemais head.[101] The lad's locks are also regular, of course on a smaller scale, and the hair inside the circle of the fillet likewise forms a smooth sketchily indicated cap. More significant, however, are the sharply cut angles at the outer edges of the eye sockets, which both heads possess. A third-century date for the Ptolemais head is most apparent on the basis of a comparison of its irregularities around the eyes and its expressive qualities. These come closest to the same features on a head made in Athens before A.D. 267 whose right eye gives a similar illusion of being wider open and farther forward than the left.[102] Their present effect of asymmetrical sobriety must have originally been somewhat less marked.

No. 29. Alabaster head of woman. Height 11 cm., width 7 cm. From fill over court of Villa. In local museum.

No. 30. Calcified head of woman. Height 8 cm., width 5 cm. From fill over court of Villa. In local museum.

---

[93] These are such minor works that they are not listed by Ruesch or others, but a new guide to the museum is forthcoming. A pertinent example is No. 112, Sala I, Corridoio dei tirannicidi.

[94] Gustave Mendel, "Catalogue des monuments grecs, romains et byzantins du Musée Imperial Ottoman de Brousse," *BCH* XXXIII (1909) 254–56, No. 2, Figs. 1–3.

[95] Albert Ippel in *MDAIA* XXXVII (1912) 312, Pl. 23.

[96] Ludwig Curtius, *Zeus und Hermes* (*MDAIR* "Ergänzungsheft" I [1931]) pp. 48–78, Figs. 1–33.

[97] A. H. Smith, *Catalogue of Sculptures in the Department of Greek and Roman Antiquities, British Museum* II, No. 1441. Cf. Marcadé in *BCH* LXXVII (1953) 500–510, No. A 4118, Figs. 5–8; Fuhrmann in *ADAI*, 1941, pp. 400–402, Fig. 31.

[98] Luciano Laurenzi, "Monumenti di scultura ... dell'Antiquarium di Coo," *Clara Rhodos* IX (1938) 36–39, Fig. 21. Cyrene has busts of Hermes and Herakles on a portico (Goodchild, *Cyrene and Apollonia*, p. 43, Item 11), but their style is harder and more precise.

[99] A good discussion of the various ways marble was used for portraits in the East during the imperial age is to be found in Harrison, *Portrait Sculpture*, pp. 4–5.

[100] *Ibid.* No. 29, Pl. 18.

[101] *Ibid.* No. 46, Pl. 29.

[102] *Ibid.* No. 49, Pl. 31 (cf. Pl. 46 *d–e*). Traces of the use of the drill to delineate the pupils of the eyes are sometimes effaced in heads better preserved than the Ptolemais work, as in an example in Aquileia which has the same vertical lines carved between the brows and equally clear eyelids; Frederik Poulsen, *Porträtstudien in norditalienischen Provinzmuseen* (Det Kgl. Danske videnskabernes Selskab, "Historisk-filosofiske Meddelelser" XV 4 [København, 1928]) p. 14, No. 12, Pl. XVII.

No. 31. Left arm holding lyre (Pl. XLIII *A*). Height 19 cm., width 17 cm. From fill over court of Villa. In local museum.

The soundboard of the lyre has a tortoise-shell pattern engraved upon its convex surface and a series of diamond-shaped motifs on its concave surface. Within each of the latter appears a smaller diamond or lozenge. At the bottom of the inner side was fastened the tailpiece, to which the strings of the lyre were anchored, but it no longer exists. The strings were then stretched over a bridge, which does survive and is represented as a rectangular box-shaped projection. At the top of the body of the lyre, in the center, there is now a hole. Probably it is a socket into which was thrust a bracket holding the strings, for these would have been represented by slim metal rods running from the tailpiece to the crossbar between the arms. From the body of the lyre the two arms, spiraling like goat horns, which they were clearly intended to be, extended upward. The arm next to the youth's body is more complete; the other is now little more than a stump. Seen from the rear, the upper part of the body of the lyre between the arms has a profile which tapers to a point like the bottom section of a heart. The fragment is of Pentelic marble.

The most interesting feature of this piece is the accuracy with which it conforms to the lyre described in Homer's *Hymn to Hermes* (verses 20–51). The god was said to have invented it, using a tortoise shell and goat horns, on the first day of his existence. The right hand of this statuette would have held the plectron. Lyres are represented more commonly in antiquity on vases than in statuary.[103] A partly restored instrument of the same type is held by a statue of the muse Terpsichore.[104] The Ptolemais fragment, however, from the heaviness of the undraped arm, more likely formed part of a statue of a poet, like that of Alkaios(?) in the Louvre.[105] It is probably not a replica of the latter, however, for there are no traces of drapery. Could it represent Hermes himself? The date is undoubtedly Roman.

No. 32. Fragment of male torso (Pl. XLIII *B*). Height 9.5 cm., width 9.5 cm. From fill over court of Villa. In local museum.

The crudity of this piece indicates that it is unfinished. Hence it and Inv. No. 35 may both testify to the existence of local sculptural activity.

No. 33. Man wearing collar. Fragment. Height 19 cm., width 14.5 cm. From fill over Villa. In local museum.

No. 34. Draped male figure. Fragment. Height 13 cm., width 7 cm. From fill over Villa. In local museum.

No. 35. Fragment of boy with water jar (Pl. XLVIII *A*). Height 25 cm., width 22 cm. From fill over south portico of Villa. In local museum.

Apparently this is unfinished work (cf. Inv. No. 32). The back is semicircular.

No. 36. Fragment of personification of Constantinople (Pl. XLVIII *D*). Height 10.5 cm., width 10 cm. From fill over Villa. In local museum.

When complete, this marble statuette of a seated female figure would have been about a foot (*ca.* 30 cm.) high. There now survives only the section from the neck to just below the navel. The figure wears a chiton with long sleeves, a high belt, and a mantle on the left shoulder and around the hips. The right arm is broken at the elbow; the right hand probably held a patera. The left arm, complete to the beginning of the wrist, cradled a cornucopia whose upper end with its fruits of plenty still rests against the figure's shoulder. Long tresses of hair fell down about the neck.

The nearest parallel is a complete silver-gilt figure representing Constantinople (5.4 inches high) which once decorated a chair in Rome.[106] Personifications of Rome, Antioch, and Alexandria were found with it,[107] but only the new Rome carried a cornucopia. Coin images illustrating the eastern capital furnish a date between A.D. 330 and the reign of Constantius II.[108] The arrangement of the rather roughly carved drapery on the Ptolemais fragment is consistent with such a dating and with the handling of the similar but more richly decorated tunic and cloak of the silver-gilt figurine. The schematic drapery on the two figures, arbitrarily separated around the visible

---

[103] The subject is admirably discussed by Max Wegner, *Das Musikleben der Griechen* (Berlin, 1949) pp. 37–42, Fig. 4, Pls. 16*a*, 19, 22, who gives a list of representations (pp. 215–20) and sketches (Figs. 20–21) showing the development of the lyre.

[104] Lippold, *Sculpturen des Vaticanischen Museums* III 1, pp. 65–70, No. 517, Pls. 7, 9.

[105] Schefold, *Die Bildnisse der antiken Dichter, Redner und Denker*, pp. 66–67. A better photo in Étienne Michon, *La sculpture grecque au Musée du Louvre* (Paris, 1934) at left on 13th plate, shows restorations; cf. Michon, *Catalogue sommaire des marbres antiques* (Paris, 1922) p. 5, No. 588, Pl. 3.

[106] O. M. Dalton, *Catalogue of Early Christian Antiquities ... of the British Museum* (London, 1901) No. 333, Pl. 20.

[107] *Ibid.* Nos. 332, 334–35, Pl. 20.

[108] Jocelyn M. C. Toynbee, "Roma and Constantinopolis in late-antique art from 312 to 365," *JRS* XXXVII (1947) 135–44.

navel, is as similar as one can expect it to be.[109] A find of such late date as compared with the other objects recovered accords with our knowledge of Ptolemais as an active center from the late third to the sixth century.[110]

No. 37. Aphrodite fragment (Pl. XLIII *C*, right). Height 18 cm., width 10 cm. From fill over court of Villa. In local museum.

The body is preserved from waist to knees. The abraded surface at the right groin, where the right forearm was attached, proves that the figure was a *pudica* type.

No. 38. Aphrodite fragment (Pl. XLIII *C*, left). Height 16 cm., width 9 cm. From fill over court of Villa. In local museum.

This fragment includes the area from the waist to the lower part of the thighs. Perhaps the figure was like No. 37.

No. 39. Aphrodite fragment. Height 12.5 cm., width 7 cm. From fill over court of Villa. In local museum.

No. 40. Aphrodite fragment. Height 11 cm., width 7.5 cm. From fill over court of Villa. In local museum.

No. 41. Aphrodite(?) fragment. Height 8 cm., width 7.5 cm. From fill over Villa. In local museum.

No. 42. Bent arm with armband. Length 17 cm., width 4 cm. From fill over Villa. In local museum.

No. 43. Hand and arm bent at wrist. Length 10 cm. From fill over Villa. In local museum.

No. 44. Right hand holding cantharus. From a Dionysos(?) statuette. Height 7 cm., width 11 cm. From fill over Villa. In local museum.

No. 45. Hand holding roll of cloth. Length 8 cm., height 3.5 cm. From fill over Villa. In local museum.

No. 46. Hand holding drapery. Length 12 cm., height 8 cm. From fill over Villa. In local museum.

No. 47. Hand with raised knuckles. Length 5.5 cm., width 3.5 cm. From fill over Villa. In local museum.

No. 48. Elongated finger. Length 6.5 cm., height 1 cm. From fill over Villa. In local museum.

No. 49. Fragment of statue of Artemis (Pl. XLIII *D*). Base: height 5 cm., width 34 cm., depth 22 cm.; statue leg: height 25 cm. From fill over Public Building. In local museum.

On the irregularly shaped base can be seen the left foot of the goddess and her right foot and leg to just above the knee. The latter owes its preservation to the abutting support.

The feet are clad in hunting boots, which permit the identification of Artemis. One of her dogs sat beside her, for his front paws are visible to her right. The location of the dog's body and rump behind the support is apparent from the rough surface of the stone and from a depression in the base. The now golden marble is evidently Pentelic.

Artemis was often depicted walking or running through the forest, as in the well known Rospigliosi type. Her hound generally trots or leaps beside her. Our fragment apparently matched a version of Artemis called the Lateran variant of the Rospigliosi type.[111] Only the torso survives, but a more complete replica[112] has a slightly modified pose and other details which seem to go perfectly with the Ptolemais fragment. The right leg of the goddess touches the stump support, to whose other side the dog, whose limbs are missing, was attached. This comparable piece unfortunately lacks its base, but the torso shows the top of one boot, the short chiton, and the mantle which made up the hunting costume of Artemis. According to a very ingenious and credible hypothesis its original formed part of the Attalid dedication on the Athenian acropolis,[113] which would thus be the prototype of the Ptolemais statue also. Its marble is also Pentelic, and its date in the second century after Christ provides further correspondence to our fragment.

No. 50. Man with Vase. Base: height 2.5 cm., depth 5 cm.; figure: height 9 cm. From fill over Villa. In local museum.

No. 51. Draped legs. Height 12 cm., width 9 cm. From fill over Villa. In local museum.

[109] This arrangement was, however, something of a convention, as both earlier and later Tyches show. See Marcadé in *BCH* LXXVII 558–63, Figs. 48–49; Walters Art Gallery, *Early Christian and Byzantine Art* (Baltimore, 1947) No. 104, Pl. 15.

[110] See Christian Lacombrade, *Synésios de Cyrène, Hellène et Chrétien* (Paris, 1951) p. 207 and n. 38; Caputo and Goodchild, *"Diocletian's Price-Edict at Ptolemais,"* *JRS* XLV 106–15; Michon, *Catalogue sommaire des marbres antiques*, p. 92, No. 1786.

[111] See L. Beschi, "Nuove repliche dell'Artemide tipo Rospigliosi," in L. Polacco *et al.*, *Sculture greche e romane di Cirene* (Università di Padova, "Pubblicazioni della Facoltà di lettere e filosofia" XXXIII [1959]) p. 266, Fig. 90.

[112] *Ibid.* pp. 265–66, 269, 271–72, 274, Figs. 91–92.

[113] *Ibid.* pp. 289–95.

No. 52. Thigh. Height 9.5 cm., width 3.5 cm. From fill over Villa. In local museum.

No. 53. Thigh, knee, and calf. Height 9 cm., width 8 cm. From fill over Villa. In local museum.

No. 54. Knee and calf. Height 9 cm., width 4 cm. From fill over Villa. In local museum.

No. 55. Calf. Height 11.5 cm., width 4.3 cm. From fill over Villa. In local museum.

No. 56. Calf. Height 10 cm., width 4 cm. From fill over Villa. In local museum.

No. 57. Calf. Height 4.5 cm., width 3 cm. From fill over Villa. In local museum.

No. 58. Black granite Horus(?) fragment (Pl. XLII *B*). Base: height 3 cm., width 12 cm., depth 9 cm.; statuette leg: height 8.5 cm. From fill over Public Building. In local museum.

This small fragment of a hawk was probably intended to represent the Egyptian god Horus, who wore a double crown. Only base, clawed talons, left leg, and part of the stone between the legs survive. The thickness of the leg as compared to the size of the claws establishes this as an Egyptianizing statuette. These heavy proportions approach those of a hawk in the Vatican collection, surely the most earnest and comical bird of antiquity.[114] A black basalt Horus in the same museum has slimmer legs and illustrates the more authentic proportions.[115] Evidence for the worship of Horus in Cyrenaica during the Hellenistic period is scanty indeed.[116] Our fragment shows that there was an interest in Egypt during the Roman age at Ptolemais, but it is another example of the Egyptianizing style represented by Inv. No. 14.[117]

No. 59. Goat(?) torso (Pl. XXXIX *A*). Height 17.8 cm., length 39.9 cm. From fill over court of Villa. In Oriental Institute Museum (A 30920).

See Inv. No. 60.

[114] Botti and Romanelli, *Le sculture del Museo Gregoriano egizio*, No. 182, Pl. 78.

[115] *Ibid.* No. 53, Pl. 42.

[116] See Vitali, *Fonti per la storia della religione Cyrenaica*, pp. 89, No. 229, and 149.

[117] Some Egyptian sculpture from the fill of the peristyle in the "Palazzo" at Ptolemais seems to have been an art collection of the Roman age, like Hadrian's at Tivoli. See excellent discussion by Klaus Parlasca in review of Pesce's *Il "Palazzo delle Colonne"* in *OLZ* LIV (1959) 12–15 and references there given. Cf. Pierre Montet in *Comptes rendus de l'Académie des inscriptions et belles-letters*, 1955, p. 330; Luciano Laurenzi in *Annuario della Scuola archeologica di Atene* XXXIII–XXXIV (1955–56) 129–30, Nos. 152–55; Evaristo Breccia in *Monuments de l'Égypte gréco-romaine* I (Bergamo, 1926) 67, Nos. 56–59, Pl. XXXI 1–4.

No. 60. Head and body of ram (Pl. XXXIX *B*). Height 18 cm., length 20 cm. From fill over court of Villa. In local museum.

The first of these fragmentary animals (Inv. No. 59) lacks the head, all four legs, and the tail. There is nothing distinctive about it beyond the shape and the way in which the coat is indicated. The form is unlike that of any dog,[118] and the sculptor clearly has not shown the curly fleece of a ram, by which Inv. No. 60 is identified. Instead the body is covered with broad leaflike curves, with a line carved in the center of each, which suggest tufts of long shaggy hair. The animal corresponds to descriptions of goats, especially the Syrian variety found in Lower Egypt.[119] Because goats and rams of some species are difficult to distinguish from each other, both were connected with the worship of deities such as Zeus-Amon or Mendes, a goat god, whose hieroglyph was that of a ram.[120] A ram appears with Amon in the fourth century B.C. on a gold stater of Cyrene.[121] It is interesting that one of the issues of the Roman mint at Cyrene[122] seems to show a beast like the long-haired animal from Ptolemais.

The ram statuette (Inv. No. 60) includes the rear half of the head, with the horns, and the upper part of a foreleg but is broken off just in front of the hind legs. The left side is incomplete and shows that the figure was to be used against a wall. The ram was apparently the object of a local cult at Ptolemais and Barca.[123]

The belly of each animal has a depression for the mounting. On the evidence of a ram at Cyrene[124] the support was a herm, and the Ptolemais ram has traces of hair from a herm head on its underside. Apparently it had a single herm, whereas the work at Cyrene has heads of Zeus-Amon and either Libya or Isis. The spiraling "Libyan" locks of the latter are characteristic of a Hellenistic and Roman coiffure which was popular in Alexandria.[125] In the

[118] See the dog of Artemis (Beschi, *op. cit.* Figs. 89, 91–92).

[119] See R. Lydekker, *Encylopedia Britannica* (11th ed.; 1911) *s.v.* "Goats."

[120] See Dorothy Burr Thompson in *AJA* LIX (1955) 201; Perdrizet, *Bronzes grecs d'Égypte de la collection Fouquet*, p. 48, No. 81, Pl. 21.

[121] BMC, *Cyrenaica*, p. 25, No. 106, Pl. XIII 3.

[122] *Ibid.* p. 118, No. 33, Pl. XLIII 4 (cf. No. 34, Pl. XLIII 5, and p. 120, No. 42, Pl. XLIII 9).

[123] *Ibid.* pp. clxii, clxiii, clxxix, No. 46c, and 105, No. 47, Pl. XXXVII 16–17; cf. Pesce, *Il "Palazzo delle Colonne,"* p. 34, Fig. 39.

[124] Paribeni, *Catalogo delle sculture di Cirene*, No. 416, Pl. 181.

[125] See Bieber, *Sculpture of the Hellenistic Age*, pp. 89–90, Figs. 328–33; Klaus Parlasca's review of Achille Adriani, *Sculture monumentali del Museo greco-romano di Alessandria* and *Testimonianze e monumenti di scultura*

museum there another ram (from Maryut) may be seen, perched on a bust of Bes.[126] Such iconography, known only in Egypt and Cyrenaica and foreign to the native Egyptian tradition, appears again to be Egyptianizing (cf. Inv. Nos. 14, 58).[127] The date of both our statuettes should fall in the second century after Christ, for their workmanship and Pentelic marble are consistent with the Hadrianic and Antonine sculpture discovered to date at Ptolemais.

FINDS FROM EARLIER EXCAVATIONS

No. 61. Head of Tyche of Ptolemais (Pl. XXXVII *A*). Height 32 cm., width 22.5 cm. From the Italian(?) excavations. In local museum.

Most of the left side of this twice life-size head is broken away. The roughly vertical break runs from the mural crown through the hair, which was parted in the center, and down through the drilled eyeball and right cheek. The right side is well preserved and is notable for the precise delineation of the individual stones of the crown, which represents the walls of the city and one of the projecting bastions. The hair is pulled to the rear in horizontal strands, indicated by deep drilling, and reveals the lower half of the ear. Delicate modeling, considering the large scale, characterizes the line of the jaw and cheek. The neck is smoothly cylindrical. The Pentelic marble has weathered to a golden brown.

This Tyche is comparable to one of the five examples at Cyrene[128] in its modeling and drillwork, but none of them indicates more than the bastions in the crown. A coin of Ptolemais issued under Crassus shows a conventional Tyche head.[129] The quality of cutting

and the distinctive drilling of our head are Antonine hallmarks and date the personification to the Roman period in which Ptolemais enjoyed an assured if modest pre-eminence.[130]

No. 62. Statue of a lady, perhaps Claudia Eupomane (Pl. L *B*). Found in front of City Bath, during Italian excavations of the Street of the Monuments. *In situ*.

This headless portrait statue was found near an inscribed base which probably identifies the lady. The head was set into a conventional type of body derived from the statue of the larger of the two Herculaneum women, originally representing Demeter and of post-Praxitelean date.[131] The neck survives in the socket which was made for it. The arrangement of the hands and the tightly pulled himation over the chiton recall the pose of the statue of Aeschines type (Inv. No. 10), from which Inv. No. 63 was derived in the second century B.C. The statue of Demeter became a common model for portrait use about a century later and continued so until the late Roman period, according to the thirteen portrait statues counted at the last listing.[132] The Ptolemais example is a good one and well preserved except for the missing head and left hand. The lady stands with her weight on the right leg; the left leg is bent so that the knee establishes an attractive play of folds in the himation. Below appears the end of the chiton, whose carving is close to that of the Athena (Inv. No. 64). The gathered portion of the himation ends in a zigzag below the end of the left arm, from which a strong diagonal runs up to the right hand. This hand tugs at the drapery, in turn, to produce a diagonal across the chest to the left shoulder. The back of the statue is executed in the customary summary style. The marble is Pentelic.

This type of figure, sometimes with that derived from Demeter's daughter and companion Persephone, the other Herculaneum woman, and the male figure represented by Inv. No. 63 occur together in relief on some Attic tombs.[133] It seems likely that Inv.

---

allessandrina ("Documenti e ricerche d'arte alessandrina") I and II [Roma, 1946 and 1948]) in *OLZ* LIV 27–28 and references there given.

[126] No. 20265. See Musée gréco-romain, *Rapport sur la marche du service du Musée pendant les années 1910–1911* (Municipality of Alexandria, 1912) p. 17, Pl. VII 21, which gives the dimensions as 30 cm. high and 40 cm. long. The animal, of yellow limestone, is complete but battered. The curls of its coat are small and regular. The feathered headdress of Bes beneath the animal's stomach is clearly shown in the photograph.

[127] The ram couchant as a guard animal is known in Hellenistic Egypt, where it is derived from earlier examples. See W. M. Flinders Petrie, *Naucratis* I ("Third Memoir of the Egypt Exploration Fund" [London, 1886]) pp. 26–27; F. W. von Bissing in *BSRAA* XXXIX 61; Jean Capart, *L'Art égyptien, deuxième partie: Choix de documents*. II. *La statuaire* (nouv. ed.; Brussels, 1948) Pls. 320–21. The more usual lion was also still used (see Breccia in *Monuments de l'Égypte gréco-romaine* I, 98–100, Pl. LII).

[128] Paribeni, *Catalogo delle sculture di Cirene*, Nos. 425–29, Pls. 184–85, esp. No. 427.

[129] BMC, *Cyrenaica*, p. ccvi, No. 25 *bis a*, Pl. XLII 10.

[130] See C. Coster, "The economic position of Cyrenaica in classical times" in *Studies ... in Honor of Allan Chester Johnson* (Princeton, 1951) pp. 24–25.

[131] See Paul Herrmann, *Verzeichnis der antiken Originalbildwerke der Skulpturensammlung zu Dresden* (2d. ed.; Berlin, 1925) Nos. 326–27; Bieber, *Sculpture of the Hellenistic Age*, pp. 22–23.

[132] Franklin P. Johnson, *Lysippos* (Durham, N. C., 1927) pp. 154–57, 162, Pl. 26. In spite of attributions to Lysippos and Praxiteles (see *EA* 1292; Brunn-Bruckmann's *Denkmäler* 310), only the stylistically ascertained date is known.

[133] See Alexander Conze, *Die attischen Grabreliefs* (4 vols. in 6; Berlin, 1893–1922) IV, Nos. 1894–1917, Pls. 405–10; Alice Muehsam, "Attic grave reliefs from the Roman period," *Berytus* X (1950–52) Pl. XXI (cf. Pl. XX 1).

Nos. 12 and 62–64 were all Athenian works. The date of the Claudia should be Antonine, sometime before that of her husband (Inv. No. 63).

No. 63. Statue of a man, perhaps Marcus Aurelius Flavianus (Pl. L *C*). Height 1.40 m. Found near City Bath during Italian excavations of the Street of the Monuments. *In situ.*

The identification occurs on a pedestal found with the statue. There is a socket for the portrait head, which has not been found. As an Antonius Flavianus set up the statue of Claudia (Inv. No. 62) and Valeria Marciana put up this effigy of her son Marcus Aurelius Flavianus, apparently the two statues were erected by members of the same family. Aurelius is wrapped in a large himation (pallium) and stands in an attitude derived in the later Hellenistic period from the effigy of Aeschines (cf. Inv. No. 10). The main differences are that here the right hand grasps some folds coming from the left shoulder and the left arm hangs down instead of being held at the waist with the hand toward the back. Sometimes the left hand holds a scroll. Here the left hand is missing, but a small attachment below the stump of the arm indicates that this may have been the case. The proportions are more slender here than in the Aeschines type, and there is nothing to interrupt the long folds of the himation, which do not define the body too clearly. The marble is Pentelic.

The costume seems to have been worn first by a boy from Eretria, whose statue is now in Athens,[134] and by Dioskurides, a magistrate in Delos in 138/137 B.C.[135] It occurs on Roman Republican statues and tombstones[136] and on Attic grave reliefs of the second and third centuries after Christ.[137] The unusually deeply drilled narrow folds and grooves in the drapery on the shoulders and right arm, especially immediately above the stump of the wrist, correspond very closely to those of the six torsos of the same type found in

the Agora at Athens.[138] The pronounced drillwork suggests a date for the effigy of Aurelius in the late Antonine or early Severan age.

No. 64. Statue of Athena (Pl. XLIX *D*). Total height 1.85 m. From the Italian excavations at the "Odeon." In local museum.

This handsome Pentelic marble statue of the goddess was dedicated by M. Ulpius Cominius, who was also the donor of the Herakles by Asklepiades of Athens (Inv. No. 12) and two other works (see p. 196, n. 73). It is included here for comparative purposes with respect to the other inscribed material and to point up the fact that there were at least two monumental statues of Athena at Ptolemais, both of the Farnese type. The other is represented by a shoulder fragment (Inv. No. 11) and probably a foot (Inv. No. 19) and a hand (see p. 196). This one, though lacking head and arms, yet exudes an impression of grandeur typical of the better work at Ptolemais. Only the aegis seems a little odd. This statue has been cited as characteristic of the sculpture one might reasonably expect to have been exported from Athens, not only because it may be a reproduction of an Athenian original but also because of its quality.[139] It has already been published by Caputo,[140] who states that it came from the theater which be believes served as the Roman *bouleuterion* and *curia* and who on epigraphic grounds dates it no later than the Hadrianic age. Goodchild argues against Caputo's interpretation of the function of the "Odeon" (see pp. 92–93).

No. 65. Statue of Dionysos (Pl. XLIX *B*). Height with base 86 cm. From the Italian excavations. In local museum.

The god walks with left foot forward and right foot turned outward at a right angle. The right arm is extended somewhat forward, while the left is close to the side and partly concealed beneath a mantle. The overfold of the cloak surrounds the hips and thighs, covering the right knee; its end crosses the left leg and is caught up by the left forearm. The body of the god is clad in a short-sleeved tunic, over which is worn a distinctive animal skin, perhaps that of a panther, whose legs form a high belt knotted in front. On the feet are hunting boots like those of Artemis (Inv. No. 49). On the base is a support

---

[134] Brunn-Bruckmann's *Denkmäler* 519; *EA* 624; Bieber in *Proceedings of the American Philosophical Society* CIII 379–80, Fig. 4.

[135] Buschor, *Das hellenistische Bildnis*, pp. 36, 38, Fig. 9. His reference there given should be Joseph Chamonard, *Exploration archéologique de Délos.* VIII. *Le Quartier du Théatre* (Paris, 1922–24) pp. 39–40, Fig. 14.

[136] Bieber in *Proceedings of the American Philosophical Society* CIII 385, Figs. 11–12; Olof Vessberg, *Studien zur Kunstgeschichte der römischen Republik* ("Skrifter utgivna av Svenska institutet i Rom" VIII [Lund- Leipzig, 1941]) pp. 185–96 and 240, Pls. XXVII, XXIX 2–3, XXXII 2–4, XXXIV 3, XXXVI 2, LVIII 1, and LXXXV.

[137] Muehsam in *Berytus* X, Pls. XXI, XXIV = Conze, *Attischen Grabreliefs* IV, Pls. 464, 458.

[138] Illustrated together by Bieber in *Proceedings of the American Philosophical Society* CIII 399–404, Figs. 41–46, who says "the folds on the fronts agree with each other." There seem to be minor differences due to the final touches, so that one (*ibid.* Fig. 42) agrees more closely than the others with our Inv. No. 63.

[139] See Alan J. B. Wace in *BSRAA* XXXVI (1946) 96–97.

[140] In *RAL* IX 458–66, Figs. 1–3.

on the figure's left in the shape of a tree trunk. The fine white Parian marble is scarcely weathered and has a good *sfumato* finish.

Two publications by Pesce show the statue before the head and right hand fell victim to vandalism during World War II;[141] the other hand had not been found. The interesting pose is that of Dionysos as he appeared at Naxos to the sleeping Ariadne, a fragmentary figure of whom was found with the statue of the god.[142] The identification of Ariadne, made on the basis of a Pompeian painting,[143] receives added support from the detailed publication of a sarcophagus from Alexandria which illustrates the same scene.[144] The date of the sarcophagus falls between the end of the first and the middle of the second century after Christ. Since Pesce gives a pre-Hadrianic but Roman context,[145] the Ptolemais representation may be approximately contemporary.

No. 66. Statuette of Harpocrates (Pl. XLIX *A*). Height 1.10 m. From the Italian excavations. In local museum.

This nearly complete nude statuette shows clearly the *morbidezza* which commenced in the post-Praxitelean period, was popular in Alexandria and the islands (see p. 194, n. 60), and is seen at Ptolemais in the statues of Dionysos (Inv. No. 65) and the Grace (Inv. No. 8). The god appears as a young man standing in a relaxed Praxitelean, almost indolent, pose, the weight on the right leg and the left leg advanced. The drapery thrown over the left arm and reaching to the feet serves also as the support. The head is turned toward the left, and the right arm,

which has been pieced together from fragments, is raised so that the hand is beside the chin. A silencing finger would be visible before the mouth if all the fingers on both hands were not gone. A socket at the top of the head once held the symbolic crown. Other sockets, at the back, in the center, and at the right shoulder, indicate that the figure was attached to a wall. The narrow base was not meant to hold the statue but must have been set into the floor of a temple. The marble, now grayish white, is certainly eastern Aegean and, like Naxian marble, has large crystals.

Pesce describes the work in detail, going beyond the summary account rendered here, but does not seem to know its provenience in the city.[146] The discovery of a nearly identical statuette of Harpocrates in a sanctuary near Alexandria establishes once again the eastern connections of Ptolemais.[147] The Alexandria example is slightly larger, of similar marble, and has the same holes in the upper left arm and drapery which, according to other images of the god, were to hold a figurine of Horus[148] rather than a cornucopia, as Pesce supposed on the basis of a statue, of marble from Luni, from Hadrian's villa. The *puntelli* marks on the Alexandria example show how these statues were reproduced after a Hellenistic original in that city (cf. Inv. Nos. 1, 9). The Harpocrates at Ptolemais is Roman. In spite of the fact that the finish of the body is close to the prototype, the flat unarticulated style of the face betrays a post-Hadrianic date, so that on the whole the statue illustrates the remarkably strong feeling for the Hellenistic tradition in the East during the Antonine age.

No. 67. Venus Genetrix as a fountain figure (Pl. XLIX *C*). Height 68 cm. From the Italian excavations. One of two in local museum.

The well preserved but headless figure holds a jug in the left hand, bored to serve as a fountain. The clinging drapery reveals a body of the standard

[141] *BSRAA* XXXIV (1941) 43–47, Pl. III, and *Il "Palazzo delle Colonne,"* pp. 84–85, Fig. 102.

[142] Pesce in *BSRAA* XXXIV 44, Fig. 2; Pesce replaced this identification by the designation "nymph" in *Il "Palazzo delle Colonne,"* p. 85, Fig. 107, where he also abandoned the earlier definitions of the marble as Pentelic for Dionysos and Parian for the female figure, labeling both as fine-grained white marble. In the present writer's opinion both are Parian. There is no directional grain, no mica is in evidence, and the soft white finish contrasts with the warmer ivory or golden effect produced by the different mineral content of the Pentelic pieces such as Inv. No. 64. My thanks are due Prof. J. B. Ward Perkins, Director of the British School at Rome, for generous assistance in this matter.

[143] See Olga Elia, *Le pitture della "Casa del Citarista"* ("Monumenti della pittura antica scoperti in Italia," sezione 3, "La pittura elenistico-romana: Pompei," fasc. 1 [Roma, 1937]) pp. 19–22, Pls. *B*, *C*, and VII (Museo nazionale di Napoli No. 9286).

[144] Adriani, "Epifania di Dioniso a Nasso," *BSRAA* XXXIX 5–29.

[145] In *BSRAA* XXXIV 47. Traces of fire damage on the left side may have been incurred during the Jewish revolt of A. D. 115–16.

[146] *BSRAA* XXXIV 40–43, Pl. II, and *Il "Palazzo delle Colonne,"* pp. 86–87, Figs. 112–13. Surely there was an Iseum at Ptolemais, but the changes in the city were such that perhaps none of the statues were found where they were first installed. An Isis temple would have been appropriate for several of the sculptures found by the Oriental Institute (Inv. Nos. 1 and 9, 2, 8, 14[?], 58–60[?]). A comparison with Cyrene gives an idea of what must still lie buried at the site (see E. Ghislanzoni, "Il Santuario delle divinità alessandrina," *Notiziario archeologico* IV [1927] 147–206, Figs. 1–22, Pls. 18–31).

[147] Adriani, *Annuaire du Musée gréco-romain* (1935–1939) (Alexandrie, 1940) pp. 136–38, 140–42, 147 and Pls. *I* 1, LVI, LVII.

[148] See Henry Stuart Jones (ed.), *A Catalogue of the Ancient Sculptures Preserved in the Municipal Collections of Rome. I. The Sculptures of the Museo Capitolino* (Oxford, 1912) pp. 292–93, No. 28, Pl. 71.

genetrix type, standing with the weight resting on the left leg. The chiton dips below the left breast, and a himation held up and behind the figure by the right hand forms a backdrop for the whole body. The end of the himation is wrapped around the left arm. The very white, close-grained marble with minute crystals is Parian, according to Pesce, who gives the provenience as a frigidarium.[149]

The title comes from an inscription on a coin of Sabina which depicts this figure without the jug.[150] The original has therefore been traced to Arcesilaus, who made the cult image for Caesar's temple of Venus Genetrix in the Forum (Pliny *Natural History* 155–56). The style recalls the fifth century B.C. so clearly that the first creation has been attributed to Callimachus, among others.[151]

During the imperial period the genetrix type became a fountain figure in Athens and elsewhere.[152] The crouching Aphrodite type was also so adapted in Antioch.[153] Cyrene has two miniature replicas of the original genetrix version.[154] On a larger scale, and with covered breast, the goddess was adapted to portray mortal ladies.[155] The pair at Ptolemais testifies to the connections of the city with Athens and probably to the latter's export trade in such works during the second century after Christ.

No. 68. Artemis Colonna (Pl. L A). Height without base 1.50 m. From Department of Antiquities excavations at the "Odeon." *In situ.*

The statue depicts the goddess walking gracefully forward, clad in a woollen peplos with an overfold reaching to her hips. The figure lacks the head, the arms, and most of the left foot. The hair was parted in the center and gathered at the back, where it hung over the quiver, whose baldric is visible on the left shoulder and breast as it encircles the torso. The arms came down close to the body, then bent so that the forearms projected forward. Artemis clasped her bow in her left hand. The right hand, which held an arrow, was inclined across the chest and supported by a *puntello*, visible below the right breast. The left foot is advanced, so that the leg is outlined against the peplos. A long shallow gouge from the knee downward, at the end of a cut running diagonally down from the right hip, and the absence of most of the left foot, which projected beyond the base, give the figure a more static appearance than it once possessed. The Pentelic marble is now a gleaming ivory.

The namesake of the type is a statue of Artemis found on the estate of the *principe* Colonna near Rocca di Papa and now in Berlin, where there is also an example of the head.[156] The Palazzo Corsini in Florence has another replica with the head.[157] The type was popular in Athens during the imperial age,[158] and at Miletus an example was found in the nymphaeum.[159] It descends from an original of the mid-fourth century B.C. Clarity of cutting to produce a fine balance in the surface interest and a sense of volume distinguish the Ptolemais replica and argue for a date in the first half of the second century after Christ.

No. 69. Fragment of Amazon sarcophagus (Pl. LI B). Height 60 cm., length 1.20 m. From the Italian excavations. In local museum.

See Inv. No. 70.

No. 70. Fragment of unfinished sarcophagus lid with married couple reclining on a mattress (Pl. LI A). Length *ca.* 2.60 m., width *ca.* 1.00 m., height at shoulders 75 cm. From the Italian excavations. In local museum.

These examples of Attic-type funerary sculpture have been published before,[160] so that a description

---

[149] Il "*Palazzo delle Colonne*," p. 81, Fig. 101.

[150] Harold Mattingly, *Coins of the Roman Empire in the British Museum* III (London, 1936) 360, Nos. 944–49 (Pl. LXV 19–20) and 538, Nos. 1883–84 (Pl. XCIX 4).

[151] Charles Picard, *Manuel d'archéologie grecque: La sculpture.* II. *Période classique, Ve siècle* (Paris, 1939) pp. 615–23, Figs. 247–49; Hans Schrader, *Phidias* (Frankfurt am Main, 1924) pp. 311–21, Figs. 283, 285, 287, 299, 311, 317. Ernst Langlotz, "Aphrodite in den Garten," *Sitzungsberichte der Heidelberger Akademie der Wissenschaften*, philos.-hist. Klasse, 1953/54, 2. Abh., p. 15, has proved that the first creation cannot have been by Alkamenes.

[152] Homer A. Thompson in *Hesperia* XXII (1953) 53–54, Pl. 19 a–b. The Athens statue (No. S 1654) will be published in the forthcoming volume on the Agora sculpture by E. B. Harrison.

[153] Richard Stillwell (ed.), *Antioch-on-the-Orontes* II (Princeton, 1938) 172, No. 132, Pl. 5. The list in Reinhard Lullies, *Die kauernde Aphrodite* (Munich-Pasing, 1954) pp. 10–17, indicates that Antioch No. 21 was the only one so used.

[154] Paribeni, *Catalogo delle sculture di Cirene*, Nos. 239–40.

[155] Gisela M. A. Richter in *Proceedings of the American Philosophical Society* XCV (1951) 189, Figs. 39–42.

[156] Carl Blümel, *Römische Kopien griechischer Skulpturen des vierten Jahrhunderts v. Chr.* (Staatliche Museen zu Berlin, "Katalog der Sammlung antiker Skulpturen" V [Berlin, 1938]) Nos. K 243 and K 250, Pls. 59–61.

[157] *EA* 337. Other replicas are listed by Wilhelm Klein, *Praxiteles* (Leipzig, 1898) pp. 310–11, n. 2, and by Ernst Pfuhl in *JDAI* XLIII (1928) 11, n. 1, Fig. 4.

[158] S. P. Karusu, "ΑΓΑΛΜΑ ΑΡΤΕΜΙΔΟΣ ΕΞ ΑΙΤΩΛΙΚΟΥ," ΑΡΧΑΙΟΛΟΓΙΚΗ ΕΦΗΜΕΡΙΣ, 1953–1954, Part I, pp. 63–80, Figs. 1–4, Pls. I–III. E. B. Harrison will publish a new replica from the Agora (No. S 1239).

[159] Julius Hülsen, *Das Nymphaeum* (Staatliche Museen zu Berlin, *Milet* I 5 [Berlin, 1919]) pp. 58–60, Figs. 6, 6a, 6b.

[160] See A. L. Pietrogra. de, "Sarcofagi decorati della Cirenaica," *Africa italiana* III (1930) 108–40, Figs. 1–2 (Inv. No. 69) and 6 (Inv. No. 70).

here is unnecessary. As the foregoing essay explains (p. 185), it was once thought that the sarcophagus and the lid did not go together, although they came from the same tomb in the local necropolis and this tomb contained a second sarcophagus and another unfinished lid like Inv. No. 70.[161] There is no way of knowing how they matched, but it now seems clear that the four pieces, the two better preserved of which are listed here, represented two sarcophagi.[162] Their weathered marble is Pentelic shot through with streaks of bluish gray.[163]

The presence at Cyrene of an unfinished lid, whose reclining couple is only roughed out,[164] demonstrates that the practice of shipping unfinished sarcophagi was known in the area. A lid comparable with it and with the two at Ptolemais occurs at Salonica on a sarcophagus whose front and sides depict battling Greeks and Amazons[165] as on Inv. No. 69. A second like monument from Salonica, now in the Louvre, has a completed couple on the lid and an Amazonomachia on three sides of the sarcophagus.[166] The back has two garlands carved upon it. A variant of the Proconnesian garland sarcophagus was popular in Salonica, a local Attic workshop.[167] The back of the second sarcophagus at Ptolemais shows two garlands, and its sides (the front is no longer extant) indicate that it was of the Attic Erotes type.[168] Added to the other motifs, its motifs help to relate the Ptolemais monuments to Salonica, which must have been their source.

The presence of an Amazon and an Erotes sarcophagus in the same tomb recalls a parallel discovery in a mausoleum at Xanthos, where there were two sarcophagi whose typological home was Asia Minor.[169] A monopolistic connection with Greece alone, however, is indicated by the sarcophagi found in Cyrenaica,[170]

where the Amazonomachia appears at Cyrene and Benghazi also.[171] The popularity of the subject in later classical times dates from the second century B.C.[172] The better preserved pieces at Ptolemais may be comparatively dated to the late Antonine age.[173]

No. 71. Stele of the gladiator Hippomedes (Pl. L D). Height 1.20 m., width 60 cm. Found by soldiers during Italian occupation. One of two similar works in local museum.

Hippomedes stands in right profile, ready for attack, inside a deep niche framed by pilasters and an arch. The figure is carved in exceptionally high relief and is in good condition except for the missing forearm. The full complement of armor is very carefully represented: helmet, chain mail over the arms, large oblong shield, and short sword. The representation of the sponges worn by Samnites seems to be unique.[174] A stout greave on the left leg completes the costume. The material of this stele and of its mate, which depicts a Thracian, seems to be a local sandstone.

This monument has been published in Louis Robert's study of the type.[175] Evidence for gladiatorial combats at Cyrene comes from a stele and a tomb painting found there.[176] The provenience given by the excavation report for the Ptolemais stele is the necropolis, where it was reused in late antiquity as a wall face.[177] The date suggested by the lettering is the third century after Christ.

---

[161] See Ghislanzoni in *Notiziario archeologico* I 117–22, Figs. 25–26.

[162] Gerhart Rodenwaldt in *JHS* LIII (1933) 182, n. 8.

[163] On the use of such marble, see J. B. Ward Perkins in *JRS* XLVI (1956) 10–11.

[164] *Ibid.* p. 12, Pl. 3:1, 2, 5.

[165] *Ibid.* p. 12, Pl. 3:6.

[166] Carl Robert, *Die Antiken Sarkophag-Reliefs* II (Berlin, 1890) No. 69, Pls. 28–29; *Encyclopédie photographique de l'art* III (Paris, 1938) 313 A.

[167] Ward Perkins in *JRS* XLVI 15.

[168] Pietrogrande, *op. cit.* pp. 109–11, Figs. 3–5. On this type, see Rodenwaldt, in *JHS* LIII 188 (cf. Fig. 2) and *JDAI* XLV (1930) 143 and n. 2, Figs. 22–23. The modeling of the Erotes and the garlands is far flatter on the Ptolemais sarcophagus than on the Metropolitan Museum example of Hadrianic-Antonine date.

[169] See Rodenwaldt in *JHS* LIII 181–213, Figs. 1–17, Pls. 10–15.

[170] This is the view held by Ward Perkins in "Four Roman garland sarcophagi in America," *Archaeology* XI

(1958) 98–104, where the distribution patterns of Attic and Proconnesian sarcophagi are defined (p. 104), and in *JRS* XLVI 15. It is significant that almost none of the latter type, recognizable by their material and garland motif, have been found in Cyrenaica but that they were frequent in Egypt. Thus this is one of the few instances in which the two regions differ artistically. Cf. conclusions of Pietrogrande, *op. cit.* pp. 138–40.

[171] Carl Robert, *op. cit.* No. 131, Pl. 48; Vermeule in *AJA* LXIII (1959) 335, Pl. 84, Fig. 35.

[172] See Bernhard Schweitzer, "Späthellenistische Reitergruppen," *JDAI* LI (1936) 158–74, Figs. 1–9.

[173] Roman Redlich, *Amazonensarkophage des 2. und 3. Jahrhunderts n. Chr.* ("Schriften zur Kunst des Altertums" IV [Berlin, 1942]) pp. 112–13. The same style of cover continued into the third century (see Henry Stuart Jones, *op. cit.* pp. 77–81, No. 1, Pl. 16).

[174] See F. Drexel in Ludwig Friedlaender, *Darstellungen aus der Sittengeschichte Roms* IV (9th and 10th ed.; Leipzig, 1921) 262–63 and references there given. Cf. August Mau, *Pompeji in Leben und Kunst* (2d ed.; Leipzig, 1908) pp. 228, Fig. 112, and 438, Fig. 258.

[175] *Les Gladiateurs dans l'Orient grec* ("Bibliothèque de l'École des hautes études ... Sciences historiques et philologiques," fasc. 278 [Paris, 1940]) p. 124, No. 68. (Second stele from site is No. 67.)

[176] *Ibid.* pp. 124–25, Nos. 69–70.

[177] Ghislanzoni in *Notiziario archeologica* I 122–24, Fig. 27b. (See Fig. 27a for second stele from site.)

INSCRIPTIONS

The inscriptions of Ptolemais so far as we know them today cannot rival those of Cyrene in either the importance or the variety of the materials. What was exposed above ground was noted by the Beecheys in 1821–22 and was copied by their immediate successor Pacho.[178] What Pacho copied was incorporated in the *CIG*, but save for the better understanding of the Edict of Anastasius occasioned by the bodily transfer of the inscription to France (see p. 30) nothing was done to improve or extend the knowledge of the materials until the period of the Italian occupation and the Italian excavations. Interestingly enough it was D. M. Robinson who first used the change of circumstances to review the evidence, but it remained for Oliverio to put us all in his debt by his careful scrutiny of the older material and his publication of the new Italian finds.[179] Since the Comtroller of the Department of Antiquities had already asked Miss Joyce Reynolds of Newham College, Oxford, to deal with the material in the projected corpus of inscriptions of Cyrenaica, the Oriental Institute expedition did not concern itself programmatically with the inscriptions of Ptolemais as a whole and is content to refer to them in the publication of Oliverio, while lamenting the absence for all of Cyrenaica of comparative tables of letter forms used in the datable texts from each of the several periods.[180] What is presented here, therefore, is only an annotated list of the new texts brought to light by the work of the expedition. The new material has been made available to Miss Reynolds, and her comments upon it are herewith gratefully acknowledged.

The inscriptions discovered during the Oriental Institute excavations are neither numerous nor important. They number 48 and are mostly fragmentary. Only three (Nos. 1, 2, 14) were in their original intended location. All the others were either found loose in the accumulation of debris covering the three sites excavated or were inscribed on blocks reused in the construction of the buildings on those sites. There had been some hope that the excavation of the City Bath might produce important additions to the Latin text of Diocletian's Price Edict, which the Italian archeologists had found near the site on the Street of the Monuments.[181] Two additional pieces (No. 47 *A* and *B*) did actually come to light outside the building, but they are trivial and cannot be assigned to a particular part of the text. Of dedications to Roman emperors there are only three, to the *divi augusti*, to Septimius Severus, and to Gratian (Nos. 1, 15, and 17 respectively), the last two being fragmentary. Men of consular rank appear twice or perhaps three times (Nos. 3, 11, 14 below), but only the name of the Byzantine *consularis* Paul is completely preserved, and he is not further identifiable. One text (No. 5) provides information about the continuance of the offices of ephebarch and strategos, but otherwise the material is relatively sterile.

The excavation of the City Bath brought to light a considerable number of texts which, while fragmentary and unimportant in themselves, require brief comment here. They consist typically of the names of persons recorded in close proximity to one another on large building stones that were reused in the construction of the City Bath in Byzantine times. The appearance of several such texts on the towers of the Tauchira Gate at Ptolemais and of a great many of them on the extant curtains of the city wall of Tauchira itself suggests that the blocks reused in the City Bath were taken from the curtains of Ptolemais' city wall, where, following Oliverio's suggestion about similar texts,[182] they served to record the names of soldiers on guard there in the defense of the city. What this implies about the respective dates for the abandonment of the city's perimeter defenses and the construction of the City Bath has been considered above (p. 174). What invites comment here is the

---

[178] See Beechey, *Proceedings*, pp. 357–58, and Pacho, *Rélation d'un voyage dans... la Cyrénaique ...*, pp. 397–403.

[179] See Robinson, "Inscriptions from the Cyrenaica," *AJA* XVII (1913) 185–87 (Nos. 75–90), and Oliverio, *Documenti antichi* I 1 (1932) pp. 42 and 68–69 (Nos. 2–5), II 2 (1936) pp. 139–63 and 243–58 (Nos. 139 and 482–537). Oliverio's material has been incorporated in *SEG* IX 70–75.

[180] An excellent example of the nature and the importance of such comparative tables for the proper placing of new dateless texts will be found in the section by C. B. Welles on the inscriptions of Gerasa in Kraeling, *Gerasa*, Figs. 9–16.

[181] See Caputo and Goodchild, "Diocletian's Price-Edict at Ptolemais" *JRS* XLV 106–15, esp. pp. 106–7.

[182] *Op. cit.* Vol. II 2, p. 247.

fact that the inscriptions (Nos. 20–35, 39–40, 42–46) introduce the names with a date formula consisting of the *siglum* Ⳑ and the number of the year. The question is what era was used? The appearance of year numbers as high as 304 and possibly 310 in similar texts at Tauchira and a synchronism between "year 254" and "year 3" of Alexander Severus in an inscription at Cyrene indicate that at Cyrene certainly and at Tauchira very probably the Actian era was used.[183] The same era must be thought to have been used also at Ptolemais.

TEXTS FROM THE VILLA

1. Cippus standing in street at north side of main entrance, that is, outside Room 18 (see Fig. 43). Complete in one line; letters 7.5 cm. *In situ.* Pl. LII *B.*

    ΘΕΟΙΣ ΣΕΒΑΣΣΤΟΙΣ (*sic*)

    The form of the stone and the use of the dative case in the inscription suggest that it is an altar and as such a testimony to the imperial cult at Ptolemais. On the use of the dative case in such contexts see most recently, A. Benjamin and A.E. Raubitschek, "Arae Augusti," *Hesperia* XXVIII (1959) 67–68, where the literature is cited. For immediate parallels to the text see especially Motella: Διὶ Σωτῆρι καὶ Θεο[ῖ]ς Σεβαστοῖς καὶ τῷ δήμῳ (*MAMA* IV [1933] No. 309, A.D. 136/137); Pergamum: Θεοῖς Σεβαστοῖς καὶ Ἑρμεῖ κεῖ καὶ Ἡρακλεῖ *IGRR* IV [1927] 128 No. 318, no date but see H. Schrader "Die Arbeiten zu Pergamon 1902–1903: Die Inschriften," *MDAIA* XXIX [1904] 167–68, No. 8); Pednelissus: Θεοῖς Σεβαστοῖς καὶ τῇ γλυκυτάτῃ πατρίδι (*SEG* II [1925] 131, No. 724, no date); and Tire: Θεοῖς Π[ατρώ]οις καὶ Θεοῖς Σεβαστοῖς (L. Robert, *Études anatoliennes* [1937] p. 65, third century). The question of possible date is difficult, and at present paleography provides no help. Theoretically the *terminus a quo* would be Livia's designation as *augusta.* But suggestions to the effect that she was included with Augustus in dedications mentioning οἱ Σεβαστοί (so Schrader, *op cit.* and M. Fränkel, *Die Inschriften von Pergamon* VIII 2 [Berlin, 1895]

[183] For the two pertinent texts from Tauchira see Oliverio, *op. cit.* Vol. II 2, pp. 174, No. 175, and 190, No. 261; *SEG* IX 78, No. 446, and 82, No. 521. For the text from Cyrene see Oliverio, *op. cit.* Vol. I 2, pp. 177–80, No. 53.

p. 269, No. 374*c*) because of the Apollonia monument (*MAMA* IV 49–56) are without foundation because the ᾿Ιουλία Σεβαστῇ (line 2) is supplied and the restoration τοὺς...ἰδίους] Σεβαστούς (line 1) has a more limited significance. The earliest datable instance of collective usage would seem to be from Akmonia: τοῦ σύνπαντος τῶν [Θ]εῶν Σεβαστῶν [οἴ]κου (*MAMA* VI [1939] No. 263). It is attributed to the period of Nero, with which it is possible to connect also the paeanists τῶν Σεβαστῶν of *Inscriptiones Graecae* XIV (1890) No. 1084, if it is assumed that the "order" goes back to the Neronian period (Suetonius *Nero* 20). See J. H. Oliver "Paeanistae," *TAPA* LXXI (1940) 312–13. The general tenor of the immediate parallels to the Ptolemais text suggests that the Θεοὶ Σεβαστοί represent the imperial cult in a relatively advanced stage, with a succession of *augusti* or the οἶκος involved (so C. B. Welles in personal communication). See also in general A. D. Nock in *CAH* X (1934) 481–503 and on the use of Σεβαστός his articles "Studies in the Graeco-Roman beliefs of the Empire *"JHS* XLV (1925) 84–101, esp. pp. 92–93, and "Notes on the ruler cult," *JHS* XLVIII (1928) 41–42.

2. Standing column in Room *B* of house adjoining Villa at south. Complete in two lines, letters 7 cm. (line 1) and 4 cm. (line 2), covered with plaster. *In situ.* Pl. XXIV *B.*

    1.   Ⳑ ΙϚ ΖΩΙΛΟΣ
    2.   ΚΟΣΜΟΥ

    17/16 B.C. On the use of the Actian era, see above. There are no traces of letters before Κ and after Υ in line 2.

3. Five fragments of a limestone slab (16.2 × 13.8 cm.) from fill. Parts of three lines, letters 3.5 cm. In local museum.

    1.   ]ΘΥΠΑ[
    2.   ]ΠΑΤΕ[
    3.   Π]ΡΕϹΒΕ[

    Line 1 apparently involves a reference to a *legatus.*

4. Fragment of limestone slab (11 × 6 cm.) from fill. Parts of three lines, letters 3.5 cm. In local museum.

    1.   ]ΙΝ[
    2.   ]ΕΡΓ.[
    3.   ]ΟΥΤ[

5. Fragment of marble slab (9 × 9 cm.) from fill. Parts of four lines. letters 1.5 cm. In local museum. Pl. LIII *A*.
   1.   ]ΑϹΘΕΙϹ Υ[
   2.   Ε]ΦΗΒΑΡΧΟΥ[
   3.   ]ϹΤΙΟΥ ϹΤΡΑ[ΤΗΓΟΥ
   4.   ]ΟϹ ΠΑΤΗΡ ΤΟ[

For the late survival of the offices of ephebarch and strategos at Cyrene see Oliverio, *Documenti antichi* I 2, pp. 177–80, No. 53.

6. Fragment of marble slab (*ca.* 11 × 5 cm.) from fill. Parts of two lines, letters 4 cm. In local museum. Pl. LII *C*, middle row at right.
   1.   ]Ο̣[
   2.   ]Ϲ̣Π̣[

7. Fragment of marble slab (13 × 7 cm.) from fill. Parts of three lines, letters 4 cm. In local museum. Pl. LII *C*, top right.
   1.   ]··[
   2.   ]ΗϹ[
   3.   ]ѠΝ[

8. Fragment of marble slab (7 × 8 cm.) from fill. Parts of three lines, letters 2 cm. In local museum. Pl. LII *C*, middle row in center.
   1.   ].[
   2.   ]ΑΙ Γ̄· Ι̣Ο̣[
   3.   ]Τ[

9. Two fragments of marble slab (maximum width 22 cm.) from fill. Parts of five lines, complete at left and at bottom, letters 12–14 cm. In local museum.
   1.   ΠΟΤΑ[
   2.   Φ[
   3.   ΦΙΛΟΙ̣ ΠΑ̣[
   4.   ΑΜΑΧΟΙ Δ[ΙΑ
   5.   ΒΙΟΥ
             (wreath)

G. Klaffenbach, through C. B. Welles, kindly points out the funerary character of the inscription as indicated by the use of the wreath (see Ganszyniec in *R.-E.* XI [1922] col. 1598, *s. v.* "Kranz") and suggests restoration as an epitaph of two men, possibly brothers, with additional lines at top of texts.

10. Fragment of marble slab (17 × 17 cm.), inscribed on both sides, from fill. In local museum. Recto: parts of three lines, letters 55 cm.
   1.   ].ΟϹΔΑ̣[
   2.   ]ΤΟ Ε̄ [
   3.   ]ΦΑΙΔ··[

Verso: Parts of four lines, letters 3 cm. Pl. LII *C*, top left.
   1.   ].N··[
   2.   ]·P·LACV[
   3.   ]CVRAN[TE
   4.   P[O SVIT

11. Two fragments of marble slab (24 × 12 cm.) from fill. Parts of four lines, complete at right; possibly two different texts, letters 2 cm. (line 1), 3 cm. (line 2), and 2.5 cm. (lines 3–4). In local museum. Pl. LII *D*.
   1.   ]ANO COS
   2.   P]ROCOS
   3.   ]ADHIBI
   4.   OP]IBVS SVIS

The scripts of the first line and the last three lines are similar but not identical, that of line 1 being the coarser and hence perhaps a later addition. The name of the consul (or perhaps rather *consularis*) is not identifiable, and that of the proconsular legate unfortunately is not preserved.
In line 4 perhaps *iussit* should be restored before *opibus suis*.

12. Fragment of marble slab (11 × 12 cm.) from fill. Parts of three lines, letters 7 cm. In local museum. Pl. LII *C*, bottom.
   1.   ].[
   2.   ]VR.[
   3.   ]··[

13. Two nonadjacent fragments of marble slab from fill. In local museum.
   A. Fragment (11 × 7 cm.) with part of one line, letters 2.8 cm.
           ]X NVṂ[
   B. Fragment (12 × 11 cm.) with parts of four lines, letters 2.8 cm. (line 2) and 2.3 cm. (line 3). Pl. LII *C*, middle row at left.
   1.   ]··[
   2.   ].AETḬ[
   3.   ].PTOLEMẠ[
   4.   ]···[

Line 3 of *B* presumably refers to the city of Ptolemais itself.

TEXTS FROM THE PUBLIC BUILDING

14. Paving stone of porch (Room 1; see Fig. 51).
Complete in four lines, letters about 3.5 cm.
In situ. Pl. LIII *B*.

1.   ΕΥΤΥΧѠC ΕΠΙ ΤΟΥ
2.   ΜΕΓΑΛΟΠΡΕΠΕCΤΑΤΟΥ
3.   ΠΑΥΛΟΥ ΥΠΑΤΙΚΟΥ ΕΓΕ
4.   ΝΕΤΟ ΤΟ ΕΡΓΟΝ ΤΟΥΤΟ

The Paul of this inscription is apparently not yet otherwise known. As an ὑπατικός (*consularis*) who, by virtue of the archeological context of the inscription, can be said to have been creating an official residence for himself at Ptolemais, he must be thought to have served as civil governor of the province of Libya Pentapolis. This seems to fix his term of office in the period between Diocletian, who created the province and made Ptolemais its capital, and Anastasius, under whom the capital was moved to Apollonia (see p. 27). The application to Paul of the title μεγαλοπρεπέστατος (*magnificentissimus*) is unexpected and somewhat difficult. In the reign of Anastasius the title of the *dux* of Libya was still περίβλεπτος (i.e., *spectabilis*), while Paul with the title *magnificentissimus* belonged necessarily to the higher order of the *illustres*. On the *dux* see the Edict of Anastasius from Ptolemais (Oliverio, *Documenti antichi* II 2, pp. 135–63, No. 140, line 3; *SEG* IX 67–70, No 356); on the correlation of order and title see P. Koch, *Die byzantinischen Beamtentitel* (Diss.; Jena, 1903) pp. 10–45. Moreover, epigraphic evidence for the use of the title μεγαλο-πρεπέστατος, for example from the province of Arabia (see R. E. Brünnow and A. von Doma-szewski, *Die Provincia Arabia* III [1909] 281–84, and Welles in Kraeling, *Gerasa*, pp. 470–71, Nos. 279–80), has been taken to imply that civil governors did not receive it until the reign of Justinian and then only as a sequel to the advancement of the military governors from the order of the *spectabiles* to that of the *illustres*. The evidence from the *Corpus iuris civilis* does not contradict this conclusion but gives a more complete picture of the development of titulature in the Byzantine period. It indicates on the one hand that μεγαλοπρεπέστατος came to be applied in the first half of the fifth century to the highest government officials, the *praefectus praetorio*,

the *praefectus urbi*, the *magistri peditum* and *equitum* (see Koch, *op. cit.* pp. 36–37), and thus properly also for instance to the consul and prefect of A.D. 431: ᾿Αντιόχῳ μεγαλοπρεπεστάτῳ ἐπάρχῳ καὶ ὑπάτῳ (*Codex Iustinianus* i. 12. 3 [*Corpus iuris civilis*, ed. P. Krueger, II (6th stereo. ed.; Berlin, 1895) 65]) in an edict having to do with the religious affairs of Constantinople. On the other hand it also shows that at about the same time, in connection with the Councils of A.D. 431 and 451, the new even higher title ἐνδοξότατος (i.e, *gloriosissimus*) was already being applied to those holding these offices (Koch, *op. cit.* p. 68) and that senators were already being spoken of as *illustres* (rather than merely as *clarissimi*) as early as A.D. 389 (see Koch, *op. cit.* p. 38). More important, perhaps, than the element of fluidity which this adds to the development of titulature and rank in the fifth century is the fact that there is recorded an instance in which a certain Acacius as governor of the province of Armenia in the reign of Justinian already had the title μεγαλοπρεπέστατος in advance of the edict by which incumbency in that office conferred upon the incumbent the rank of *spectabilis* (see *Novellae* xxi. 3, xxxi. 1; *Corpus iuris civilis* III 142, 235–36; cf. Koch, *op. cit.* p. 54). In the absence of further epigraphic evidence for the use of μεγαλοπρεπέστατος especially from Libya, perhaps the best explanation of the titulature used in the inscription under discussion here is that Paul did not obtain the title because it came with his office as civil governor of Libya Pentapolis but had previously acquired the right to use it, whether by virtue of a special act of the emperor, or by virtue of having actually served as senator (instead of having obtained senatorial rank *ex officio*), or by virtue of having previously held some higher office. Whether the order of the words in the inscription (with the title appearing before the name Paul rather than in connection with the indication of his rank) reflects this possibility is not clear (see Koch, *op. cit.* p. 48). It should be noted, moreover, that, while there is a lacuna in the text of the *Notitia dignitatum* where the detailed list of the civil officials of Libya should be given, the general list for the *dioecesis Orientis* rates the governors of the two Libyas as *praesides* not as *consulares* (see O. Seeck,

Notitia dignitatum [1876] p. 3). This would seem to underline the suggestion that there was something unusual about the appointment of Paul.

15. Stone block (43 × 54 cm.) from Room 2, reused as impost for the arcaded portico between Rooms 2 and 1. Parts of five lines, letters about 5.5 cm. In local museum. Pl. LIII *C*.

1.   ].·[
2.   ]ΑΔΙΑΒΗΝΙΚΟ[Ν
3.   ]ΙΟΥΛΙΟΣ ΧΡΥ[Σ
4.   ]ΣΑΝ ΤΑΣ ΟΣΠ[
5.   ]ΟΡΤΟΥ ΦΙ.[

In line 2 H and N are in ligature.
In line 4 N and T are in ligature; the last letter, partially preserved, could be I or Π.
In line 5 the Y is inclosed in the O.

This text is a dedication to Septimius Severus from the period after his Parthian campaign and thus from the first years of the third century. The Julius Chrys..., who, with one other person, dedicates whatever it was that they "made" (restoring ἐποίη]σαν) or "restored" (restoring ἀποκατέστη]σαν) in line 4, is not otherwise identifiable.

16. Fragment of marble (6 × 6 cm.) found in fill. Parts of two lines, letters 1 cm. In local museum.

1.   ⌞ΙΒ Τ[
2.   ΑΣΤ[

17. Plastered block (35 × 90 cm.) reused in base of Byzantine west wall of Room 8 near its southern end. The inscription is cut in the plaster and rubricated; part of one line, letters about 25 cm. *In situ.*

Γ]ΡΑΤΙΑΝ[ΟΥ

18. Fillet of spirally fluted blue marble column found in oecus of dwelling attached to Public Building. Complete in one line, letters about 2.5–3 cm. *In situ.*

ΙΟΥΛΙΟΥ ΣΙΛΒΑΝΟΥ

19. Two fragments of porous limestone block found in fill over Public Building. Parts of 4 lines possibly complete at the right, letters 5 cm., rubicated. Pl. LIII *D*.

1.   ].ΒΑΙΟ[
2.   ]ΒΑΙ ΚΑΙ ΟΣΙ[
3.   ]ΗΣ ΜΟΝΟΣ[
4.   ]ΕΤΩΝ ΑΠΑ[

This is possibly a funerary inscription. It is tempting to complete the]ΗΣ of line 3 as ΖΗΣ]ΗΣ.

Texts from the City Bath

20. Stone (120 × 40 cm.) reused upside down in exterior west wall. Three texts, the first being complete. *In situ.*

A. Top left. Four lines, letters 4 cm.

1.   ⌞Γ ΓΑΒ
2.   ΙΔΙΟΣ
3.   ΣΕΒΗ
4.   ΡΟΣ

29/28 B.C.
Lines 3–4 have Σεβῆρος for *Severus*.

B. Bottom left. End of one line, letters 6 cm.

]ΙΑΛΜΙΟΣ

C. Bottom right. Beginning of one line, letters 6 cm.

⌞Α ΔΑΧΙΣ

31/30 B.C.
A series of small letters appears between and above the text as rendered. Miss Reynolds calls my attention to the Cyrenaican practice of inserting the patronymic in this way and reads the insertion as ΔΑΧΙΟΣ.

21. Stone (70 × 40 cm.) reused in exterior west wall. Parts of two lines, letters 15 cm. (line 1) and 13 cm. (line 2). *In situ.*

1.   ΚΛΩΔΙΟ[
2.   ]ΕΝΙΟΣ[

22. Stone (120 × 40 cm.) reused upside down in exterior west wall. Parts of three texts. *In situ.*

A. Top left. Part of one line, letters 5 cm.

⌞ΙΗ ΜΙΔΙ[

13/12 B.C. or, if the H belongs to the name, 21/20 B.C.
A further letter, Δ, appears below the letter that is dotted in the transcription.

B. Top right. Part of one line, letters 10 cm.

⌞ΙΡ ΑΠΟΛΛ[

A.D. 69/70.
It has been noted that in the date formula of this type of text units, tens, and hundreds follow one another in various orders.

C. Bottom right. Parts of two lines, letters 4 cm.

1.   ⌞Ε ΣΕΡΗΝΟΣ Φ[
2.   ΟΣ ΠΛΟΚΑΜΟ[

27/26 B.C.

23. Stone (87 × 28 cm.) reused in east wall of vaulted reservoir (Room 5; see Fig. 56). Part of one line, letters 20 cm. *In situ.*

]ΟΥ ΚΑΙ ΛΟ[

24. Stone (110 × 27 cm.) reused in east wall of vaulted reservoir (Room 5). Part of one line, letters 20 cm. *In situ.*

]ΑΝΙΚΟ[

25. Stone (80 × 40 cm.) reused in vaulted reservoir (Room 5). Part of one line, letters 20 cm. *In situ.*

⌊ΙΗ ΛΥ[

14/13 B.C.

26. Stone (100 × 38 cm.) reused upside down in west wall of frigidarium (Room 6). Parts of two texts. *In situ.*

A. Upper left. Part of one line, letters 10 cm.

ΔΙΟ[

B. Center. Parts of two lines, letters 6 cm.

1. ⌊ΙΗ ΝΥΜΦ[ΙΟΣ
2. ΑΡΙΣΤΟΥ̣

14/13 B.C.

27. Stone (23 × 40 cm.) reused in west wall of frigidarium (Room 6). Parts of four texts. *In situ.*

A. Top. Letters 4.5 cm.

1. ⌊ΙΒ ΚΛΑ[
2.]....[

20/19 B.C.

B. Middle. Letters 5 cm.

⌊Α [

31/30 B.C.

C. Lower right. Letters 3.5 cm.

⌊ΙΒ Π[

20/19 B.C.

D. Bottom. Letters 7 cm.

⌊ΙΑ Α[

21/20 B.C.

28. Stone (120 × 60 cm.) reused in southwest corner of frigidarium (Room 6). Parts of two texts. *In situ.*

A. Top right. Parts of two lines, letters 8 cm.

1. Κ]Λ̣ΑΥΔΙΟ[
2.]ΙΟΣ ΚΟ[

B. Bottom left. Parts of two lines, letters 4.5 and 4 cm.

1.]Α̣ΘΑΜΑΣ
2.]ΠΛ

29. Stone (65 × 65 cm.) reused in southwest corner of frigidarium (Room 6). Parts of three texts. *In situ.*

A. Upper left. Parts of two lines, letters 9 cm.

1.]Ν̣ΚΙΟΣ
2.]Κ̣ΙΟΥ

B. Upper right. Parts of two lines, letters 6 cm.

1. ΚΟΥ[
2. ⌊Α

31/30 B.C.

C. Bottom. Letters 12 cm.

]ΑΡΧΟΣ[

30. Stone (120 × 39 cm.) reused in south wall of frigidarium (Room 6). Parts of four texts. *In situ.*

A. Upper left. Parts of two lines, letters 8.5 cm. (line 1) and 17 cm. (line 2).

1.]ΓΑ
2.]Σ

B. Center, in box. Two lines, letters 10 cm.

1. ⌊Γ ΛΥΚΟϹ
2. ΛΥΚΟΥ

29/28 B.C.

In line 1 the C is inset in the O.

C. Right. Letters 19 cm.

⌊ΙΕ ΦΙΛ̣[

17/16 B.C.

D. Bottom right. Letters 6 cm.

ΑΓΑΘΕΙ[

31. Stone (100 × 37 cm.) reused in south wall of frigidarium (Room 6). Letters 4 cm. *In situ.*

]ΟϹΚΟϹ[......]. ΙѠΝΟϹ

32. Stone (120 × 37 cm.) reused in south wall of frigidarium (Room 6). Parts of 3 lines, letters 5.5 cm. *In situ.*

1.].Ι ΚΛΑ̣Υ̣Δ̣Ι̣ΟΣ
2.]Ι.Ο̣ΝΙΟΣ
3.]ΟΥΤΙΟΣ

Another, illegible, text is at the lower right.

33. Stone (120 × 40 cm.) reused in south wall of frigidarium (Room 6). Two texts. *In situ.* Pl. LIV C.

A. Along top. Letters 4–6 cm.

⌊ΙΕ ΛΥΚΟΣ ΝΙΚΑΣΙѠΝΟΣ

17/16 B.C.

B. In middle. Letters 6–9 cm.

⌊ΙΗ ΕΡѠΣ ΕΡѠΤΟΥΣ

14/13 B.C.

The final Σ is in the lower right corner.

34. Stone (60 × 40 cm.) reused in south wall of frigidarium (Room 6). Parts of two(?) texts. *In situ.*
   A. Top. Letters 10 cm.
      └ZK AP![or   └Z KAP![
   24/23 or 4/3 B.C.
   B. Lower right. Parts of two lines, letters 6 cm.
   1.   └Z ΔHM[
   2.   ]IAṖI[
   24/23 B.C.

35. Stone (115 × 45 cm.) reused atop east wall of frigidarium (Room 6). Letters 17 cm. *In situ.*
       └I ΑΠΟΛΛ[
   22/21 B.C.

36. Pedestal reused upside down in front of second column (from north) of east portico of frigidarium (Room 6). Complete in two lines, the first of which is illegible, letters 4 cm. *In situ.* Pl. LIV *D.*
   1. . . . .
   2. ḲṚITΩN MṆḤMHΣ XAPIN

37. Base of statue of Herakles (p. 196, No. 12) found in Niche *D* of frigidarium (Room 6). Complete in two lines, letters 3.5 cm. *In situ.* Pl. XLV *A.*
   1. M. OYΛΠIOC KOMINIOC
   2. EK TΩN IΔIΩN TH ΠATPIΔI
   The same dedicant appears on a statue of Athena and on two other fragments in the local museum (see p. 196, with n. 73).

38. Same statue base, on tree stump at left of Herakles, complete in two lines, letters 1.5 cm. *In situ.*
   1. AΣKΛEΠIAΔHC
   2. AΘHN[AI]OC EΠOIE
   The sculptor is otherwise unknown.

39. Fragment of reused stone (12 × 30 cm.) from fill at north side of frigidarium (Room 6). Parts of two lines, letters 6 cm. *In situ.*
   1. └IE .[
   2.]ĖPṖ[
   17/16 B.C.

40. Two fragments of reused stone from fill at north side of frigidarium (Room 6). Perhaps parts of No. 39. *In situ.*
   A. Fragment (15 × 23 cm.) with part of one line, letters 8 cm.
       ]E![

B. Fragment (15 × 15 cm.) with part of one line, letters 8 cm.
       ]ANT[

41. Fragment of framed marble panel (25 × 5 × 5 cm.) from fill at south side of frigidarium (Room 6). Beginnings of fourteen lines of two texts, letters 1 cm. In local museum.
   A.
   1.   .[
   2.   Ḅ[
   3.   Ṭ[
   4.   .[
   5.   E[
   6.   N[
   7.   E[
   (4.5 cm. space)
   B.
   8.   BAṬ[
   9.   ḲĖ[
   10. AP[
   11. Π[
   12. PE[
   13. AΠ[
   14. K[
   Perhaps the panel recorded the names of city magistrates or of the priests of a cult.

42. Stone reused in entry wall of tub in Room 7. Parts of three lines, letters about 5 cm. *In situ.*
   1.]...A.X[
   2.]KAPNIΣ[
   3.]AΛMANT[

43. Stone reused upside down in south wall of Room 15. Letters 18–19 cm. *In situ.*
       ]AIANT[

44. Stone reused in east wall of Room 14, above well shaft. Parts of two or three texts, letters 26 and 13 cm. *In situ.* Pl. XXXVI *C.*
     ]OY └IH MAPKO[C
   14/13 B.C.

45. Stone reused in south wall of furnace in Room 14. Parts of several lines largely illegible, letters 8 cm. *In situ.*
       Φ[
       └IH ṆE[
   14/13 B.C.

46. Stone reused in east wall of Room 14, south of furnace. Letters 7 cm. *In situ.*
       └IZ O[
   15/14 B.C.

47. Fragments of Price Edict of Diocletian.

  A. Fragment of marble slab (13 × 15 cm.) from fill in street west of City Bath. Parts of 4 lines, letters 1.5 cm. In local museum. Pl. LV *B*.

     1.   ].✳VIGINTI
     2.   D]ECIM
     3.   D]VODECIM
     4.   ]TO

  B. Fragment of marble slab (9 × 10 cm.) from fill in trench east of City Bath. Parts of three lines, letters 1.5 cm. In local museum. Pl. LV *C*.

     1.   DE]CIM[
     2.   ]I SIN PV[
     3.   ]V NVM ✳[

These two new fragments of the Price Edict of Diocletian were found in the immediate vicinity of the remainder of the text (see p. 81).

Texts on Façade of the Tomb of the Kartilioi

48. Above doorway (see pp. 111–12 and Fig. 38). Complete in two lines, letters 10 cm. *In situ.* (*CIG* III 5211; Pacho, *Rélation d'un voyage dans ... la Cyrénaique...*, p. 403, Pl. LXXVIII)

     1.   ΑΥΛΟΥ ΚΑΡΤΙΛΙΟΥ
     2.   ΚΑ (*leaf*) ΠΙΤωΝΟC

The ivy leaf was introduced to make less noticeable a fissure in the surface of the stone.

49. At right of doorway. Complete in three lines, letters 7 cm. *In situ.* (*CIG* III 5210; Pacho, *op. cit.* Pl. LXXVIII)

     1.   ⌊ ΙΕ ΧΟΙ[Α]Κ Ζ
     2.   ΚΑΡΤΙΛ[Ι]Α ΠΕ
     3.   ΤΡωΝΙΑ

17/16 or 20/19 B.C.

For line 1 Pacho read ΙΒΧΟΙ ΛΚΣ, which *CIG* renders ⌊ ΙΒ Χοι[ὰ]κ Ē. There was no opportunity to compare the earlier reading in the field.

For line 2 Pacho read ΚΑΡΤΙΛ ΛΤC, which *CIG* properly renders as above.

50. At left of doorway. Complete in three lines, letters 5–6 cm. *In situ.* (*CIG* III 5209; Pacho, *op. cit.* Pl. LXXVIII)

     1.   ]Ẹ ΠΑ[ ]Ν Ζ ΚΑΡ
     2.   ΤΙΛΙΑ ΜΥ.
     3.   .ω ⌊ ΙΔ

17/16 B.C.

For line 1 Pacho read L[ΠΑ ΛΥΣΕΑΡ, which *CIG* renders ⌊ Ē Πα[υνὶ Ē Κ]αρ-.

For line 2 Pacho read ΤΙΛΙΑΛΛΥ, which *CIG* renders -τιλία Μυ-.

For line 3 Pacho read as above, which *CIG* completes with -ρτ]ω ⌊ Ī δ.

51. At left of doorway, below No. 50. Complete in three lines, letters 5–6 cm. *In situ.*

     1.   ]Λ[..]ṚΥΝΙ Ε
     2.   C[]ΡΑ ΚΑΡΤΙ
     3.   ΛΙΟΥ ⌊ Ι

The year and the name of the month are obscure in line 1.

If C[ ]ΡΑ of line 2 is to be read CAPA and interpreted as the Hebrew name Sarah, it would provide further testimony to the existence of persons of Jewish descent at Ptolemais.

CONSTRUCTION AND ARCHITECTURAL ORNAMENT IN THE VILLA

By G. R. H. Wright

On excavation the building designated No. 5 on Plan XXII quickly revealed its essential character. The parallels with the "Palazzo" (Building 13) eight blocks to the east on the same street are manifold. Indeed, most of the circumstances adduced in designating the latter a "casa d'abitazione signorile"[184] are equally applicable here—a peristyle, a cryptoporticus, halls characterized by their mosaic pavement as triclinia, an oecus, a bathing

[184] See Pesce, *Il "Palazzo delle Colonne,"* p. 92.

establishment too small to have been public, and tabernae, which at Pompeii and Herculaneum are found only in domestic and never in public buildings. There is thus nothing to suggest that the building was other than a notable dwelling.

The type of dwelling represented here has been placed in its proper historical setting above (pp. 83–89), and on this point little additional comment is required here. That the type is not Roman is insured by the persistence of the orientation of Cyrenaica toward Egypt and the Greek East. In this respect the general position has been clearly stated by D. S. Robertson: "Houses of the Eastern and African provinces were usually Greek in plan."[185] Pesce has already noted in connection with the "Palazzo" the absence of the typical Roman axial planning and the precedence which the peristyle takes over the atrium.[186] Its antecedents lie in the palatial Alexandrine house of which the chambers of rock-cut tombs at Sidi Gaber and Anfushy preserve at least a reminiscence. Plommer[187] has appositely noted also the effect of the traditional Egyptian "pavilion" as manifested in the pseudoporticus of the "Palazzo." But for all its possession of elements in common, the dwelling under discussion here conveys an impression quite other than that suggested by its line of descent. The absence of sophistication and the simple spreading lines emphasize a solid horizontality that is more properly suggestive of a country than of a town house. It is only logical, therefore, that we have come to speak of it as the Villa and that comparison has been made with such dwellings of the wealthier North African settlers as have come to light for instance at Uthina (see p. 87). The present context invites closer attention to the materials and methods of construction and the architectural decor employed in the erection of the structure.

The basic fabric of the Villa is comparable with that of the "Palazzo," and the remarks of Pesce in this connection deserve to be quoted. "In the Hellenistic tradition is the construction in (dry-jointed) dressed masonry which dominates in this as in almost all ancient building in North Africa and Syria even during the Roman period."[188] As for the material likewise for the method: "The general structural principle consisting of the pre-dominance of the straight line over the curved, of the architrave over the arch, is typically Greek and opposed to the other principle which animates

the curvilinear architecture of Rome."[189] Naturally in a villa this distinction has little force, but it is worth noting that the only examples of arcuation are the vaulted caldarium (sanctioned by Hellenistic tradition) and the colonnaded entrance to Room 14.

Ashlar masonry, however, although the basis of the construction, was by no means the sole medium employed. Extensive use was made of mud brick in the upper portions of the walls (see p. 119). This, of course, is not exceptional[190] and would be worthy of little notice were it not for the tardiness with which the general use of mud brick in the domestic building of the classical world has been accepted, owing no doubt to the accidents (or inefficiencies) of earlier excavation. At Euesperides, on the outskirts of modern Benghazi, the only other site in Cyrenaica where domestic buildings have been largely excavated, walls of mud brick resting on footings of undressed stone in the traditional fashion were the rule in the poorer structures.[191]

In the southern portions of the Villa mud-brick walls were preserved in places to a height of some 2 meters. The bricks are square in plan and of a dimension conforming to the thickness of the walls (*ca.* 43–45 cm.). The courses are about 5 cm. deep, and the bricks were laid in a bed of earth mortar 1 cm. deep. In some places it appeared as though a type of construction midway between mud bricks proper and *terre pisé* had been adopted, in which a complete course of earth was laid and rammed, topped with a mortar bed, and followed by a succeeding course of earth. The composition of the mud is coarse and irregular throughout with an aggregate of pebbles unlike that generally encountered. Such construction was naturally concealed by the universal plaster finish given to the walls—stone and mud brick alike—which in turn bore painted decoration.

In the stilted apse of the caldarium (Room 1) an interesting form of wall construction is observable that will receive further attention below in connection with the interpretation of the Villa's wall decoration (see p. 235). What we have here are piers of squared stone rising from the stone socle and joined together at the top by a single masonry

[185] *Handbook of Greek and Roman Architecture* (1943) p. 306. See also H. S. Jones, *Companion to Roman History* (1912) p. 164: "In the provinces of the Empire we find several types of houses which depart from the Italian model under the influence of local conditions. In Africa the prevailing scheme in houses of moderate size is that of a single court surrounded by colonnades about which the rooms are grouped."

[186] *Il "Palazzo delle Colonne,"* p. 95.

[187] *Ancient and Classical Architecture*, p. 242.

[188] *Il "Palazzo delle Colonne,"* p. 99.

[189] *Ibid.* p. 98.

[190] See Ashby, *The Architecture of Ancient Rome*, p. 27.

[191] The Ashmolean excavations at Euesperides (1952–54) are not as yet published.

course. The spaces between the piers were filled with masses of rubble laid in mortar. This form of construction is a happy medium between over-all stone construction and mud-brick construction, the extra strength it provided being necessary in this instance to carry the weight of the semidome crowning the apse. It belongs to the general category of "Versteifungen," which Delbrueck treats in connection with his discussion of the origins of rubble and mortar vaulting.[192] There are various other types, from the "Gerüst fester Steinmauern" to the "Fachwerk aus Steinbalken," all set into the cores of walls. More closely related to the type in the Villa are the "pillars of large squared blocks" set into walls of *opus incertum* which are known from construction of the fourth century B.C. at Motya in Sicily and from the Roman Capitol at Dougga in North Africa.[193] Still closer, perhaps, is the type of reinforcing shown in sections of the Temple of Fortuna at Praeneste.[194] The technique is, of course, equally applicable to the strengthening of rubble and mud-brick walls. Its antiquity is not in dispute, and whether it originated in areas once under Phoenician influence, as has been suggested, does not concern us here.

Evidence for the roofing of the Villa is almost entirely lacking. The caldarium was manifestly vaulted, but the structure elsewhere can only be surmised. Since tegulae were almost entirely lacking in the fill, it can probably be assumed that a considerable portion of the building was covered with flat roofs of poles, brush, and mud in the style universal in the Near East during all ages.[195] The flooring was variously of mosaic, *opus sectile*, or beaten earth.

Nothing could better demonstrate the fundamental difference between the Villa and the "Palazzo" as revealed by the excavations than the ornamental elements of the architecture. In the "Palazzo" there was found a wealth of material, while from the Villa we have scarcely enough elements to be absolutely certain about the main order. This melancholy state of affairs is, of course,

[192] R. Delbrueck, *Hellenistische Bauten in Latium* II (Strassburg, 1912) pp. 88 and 99.

[193] See Ashby, *op. cit.* p. 29 and Pl. XV.

[194] See Delbrueck's description of the construction of the northeast corner of the "Apsidensaal" of the Temple of Fortuna (*op. cit.* p. 85 and Fig. 81).

[195] The same lack of evidence and the same general assumption apply to the "Palazzo" (see Pesce, *Il "Palazzo delle Colonne,"* p. 19.

due in large measure to destruction and looting, but it testifies also indirectly to the relative plainness of the Villa. All of the surviving pieces are of the same local limestone that was used in the walls of the building.

By far the largest body of information relates to the order of the peristyle. It was of the type Vitruvius terms Rhodian, where one end is of larger columns, those at the angles being equipped with brackets to take the architraves from the columns of lesser height. Usually the larger columns are at the north, but in the Villa, because of the incidence of the *ghibli*, they were at the south. They were laid out in the form of an arc, which gave a very shallow segmental exedra to the court. The somewhat makeshift way in which the south stylobate accords with its neighbors, the difference in the masonry of the east stylobate (blocks set transversely), and the variations in detail of the bases and entablature of the east colonnade as compared with the south and west colonnades inevitably raise the question whether the builders adapted earlier remains or whether their successors made reconstructions. But there is not sufficient evidence available to render productive the pursuit of such lines of speculation.

The order consisted of unfluted Ionic columns plastered and painted (see p. 225), small Ionic capitals of simple design, an entablature with architrave and Doric frieze cut in one block, and a simple cornice with lion-head waterspouts (see Fig. 46). For the purpose of describing the order the east, west, and north colonnades may be taken together, since the slight differences in detail did not materially affect the elements nor the proportions.

As noted above (p. 126), the column base and the lower portion of the shaft were cut in the same block. The height of these blocks varies from 24 cm. to 43 cm., but the norm is clearly about 30 cm. Then, as preserved *in situ*, follow a maximum of two drums which in two extreme instances are 0.94 and 1.465 m. high but show a clear norm of about 1.20 m. These drums are each scored medially to simulate two drums each about 60 cm. high. Finally, the one capital that was found was cut in the same block with the upper portion of the shaft, with a height of 35 cm. Thus the first problem is to assess the total height of the columns. The inference is obvious. They consisted of a base block about 30 cm. high, three double drums of about 1.20 m. each, and a capital block about 30 cm. high, giving a total normal height of about 4.20 m., with the actual figure almost certainly slightly in excess. However, a difficulty arises in connection with the capital block (Pl. XXVI *D*). It is hardly possible to doubt that it is proper to the order, and the lateral recesses cut to receive awning poles, exactly matching those of the bases, would seem to render discussion on this point needless. But this block gives the upper diameter of the shaft as 52 cm., whereas the lower diameter is 57 cm., and there is no regular diminution generally observable in the columns as preserved, that is, to the height of the second double drum, save at the southern end of the east colonnade. Thus, if the foregoing inference as to the total height is correct, some columns would necessarily have diminished 5 cm. in the upper third or else some of the divergence would have been taken up in the plastering. One or the other of these alternatives must have been the case unless the capital blocks varied in size. A total height of something over 4.20 m. would be about seven and a half times the lower diameter, a very proper ratio. In Delian houses the Doric columns can be over eight lower diameters high. Moreover, the "Palazzo" provides a useful analogy. The Corinthian columns with figured capitals that form the porticoes to its Rooms 7 and 12 have striking similarities in dimensions with our order, and the lower diameter of the shaft is virtually the same (56.5 cm.)[196] The total height of these columns is 4.33–4.37 m., a satisfying corroboration. There is a possibility of direct partial reconstruction at the Villa. A double drum 1.41 m. high was found lying in the vicinity of the southern columns of the east colonnade. If applied to one of the adjacent columns as preserved it would give a height of about 4.20 m. With allowance of about 30 cm. for the capital block, a total height of about 4.50 m. would be obtained. There is, however, no certainty that the drum had not been moved; and there is, moreover, the difficulty of diminution, for it is precisely these columns which give some evidence of diminution in the second double drum.

The base of the order has a lower diameter of 77 cm., an upper diameter of about 58 cm., and a height of 19 cm. It is composed of a heavy torus molding below, a scotia, and a lighter type of

torus above; these principal moldings are separated by pairs of fillets or half rounds of varying forms (see Pl. XXIII *A*). Note in this connection the slight differences between the bases of the west (Plans XIV 4 and XV 2) and the east (Plans XIV 5 and XV 3) colonnades. The upper torus is surmounted by a half-round or the like, and a fillet with an apophyge leads into the shaft. As already noted, the evidence for diminution of the unfluted shaft is very unsatisfactory. Those columns of the west colonnade which are manifestly preserved to over one-half of their original height do not appear to show any, whereas at the south end of the east colonnade two columns appear to diminish from 57 to 54 cm. in the second double drum.

The Ionic capital is of simple, one might almost say atrophied, design (Pl. XXVI *D* and Plan XIV 3). In the absence of an apophyge two small fillets separate the neck of the shaft from the appallingly flattened, protrusive echinus. The *canalis* is bounded by straight lines, and the abacus (62 cm. wide) had a simple cavetto and fillet; the total height of these three members (5 cm. each) is a mere 15 cm. in comparison with the 57-cm. lower diameter of the shaft. This mean type of capital is highly characteristic of the Ionic order at Ptolemais, appearing on the small engaged columns from the Villa (Plan XIV 14) and the Public Building (Plan XVIII 1), in the façade of the pseudoporticus of the "Palazzo,"[197] and on a monumental scale in the columns of the podium in the Square of the Cisterns (Pl. XX *C*). In the surviving capital of the Villa the volutes are plain and the ornament must have been in plaster, as with the capitals of the pseudoporticus of the "Palazzo." Of the various fragments of volutes found in the fill over the Villa, however, some are plain and others have the spirals carved in the stone. The latter differ slightly in detail among themselves—another instance of minor divergence. The ornament of the echinus likewise must have been rendered in plaster (that shown in Fig. 46 being purely conventional), again as with the capitals of the pseudoporticus of the "Palazzo." The *pulvini* were recessed to lodge awning poles, as mentioned above.

The following, then, are the principal dimensions of the column:

[196] See Pesce, *Il "Palazzo delle Colonne,"* pp. 31–32.

[197] *Ibid.* Fig. 6 and Pl. II *A*.

ELEVATION

Height of base	19 cm.
Height of capital	15 cm.
Possible total height	*ca.* 4.20–4.50 m.

PLAN

Lower diameter of base	77 cm.
Lower diameter of shaft	57 cm.
Upper diameter of shaft	52 cm.
Width of abacus	62 cm.

The entablature, as has been stated, consists of the architrave and frieze cut in a single block and surmounted by a cornice. Each of these three members is approximately 30 cm. high, so that the height of the entablature as a whole is close to one-fifth of the height of the columns. Nowhere are variations in the same element greater than in the case of the architrave-frieze blocks. The one constant feature is the depth (48 cm.). Three blocks were found, two from the north end of the west colonnade and one from the south end of the east colonnade. The variation in interaxial spacing made it possible to determine exactly their original positions. Indeed, the variation in length of the architrave-frieze blocks was quite probably a predetermining factor in much of the design of the peristyle. It seems to have governed the column spacing and, since the frieze was designed to show one triglyph over each column and four triglyphs over each intercolumniation in the west portico and presumably three over each intercolumniation in the east portico, the dimensions of the triglyphs and metopes had to be accommodated to the lengths of the blocks—truly a surprising phenomenon.

The two blocks from the west colonnade (e.g. Pl. XXVI *B*) contain the same elements, so that a single description will suffice, but it must be noted that the dimensions of the elements (independent of those affected by the lengths of the blocks) vary considerably, in some instances by as much as 1.5 cm. The total height of the block drawn (Plan XIV 1) is 54.6 cm., as opposed to the 60.5 cm. of the block from the east colonnade (Plan XIV 2). In the former the architrave comprises 22.8 cm. and the frieze 31.8 cm., whereas the two elements are nearly equal in the block from the east colonnade. Again, unlike that of the block from the east colonnade, the architrave consists of two fasciae, the upper 14.4 cm. and the lower 5.2 cm. Another fascia would bring the dimensions into line with those of the east colonnade, but such a separate

block would of course be structurally impossible. What is the reason for this salient divergence? To compensate for columns of different heights? Making do with blocks supplied by indifferent quarrymen? Reuse of earlier material? Different building periods? There is no obvious answer.

The frieze of the west colonnade is surmounted by a 5-cm. taenia. Below this is another continuous band crowning both triglyphs and metopes, 4.4 cm. high over the triglyphs but only 1.5 cm. over the metopes. The metopes, however, have in compensation, immediately below, another crowning molding in the form of a bold *cyma reversa* 5.8 cm. high. The grooves of the triglyphs are stopped at the top by chamfers without any trace of curvature. The regulae (9 mm. high) support guttae 1.9 cm. high, and the line of the regulae is continued across the *viae* by a shallow fillet molding. So far the description is straightforward, but words fail to describe the spacing of the triglyphs and the metopes. On the block that is drawn (2.315 m. long) the system of four complete triglyphs over each intercolumniation and one triglyph over each column does, indeed, permit fairly regular dimensions. At the left extremity of the block there is a third of a triglyph (*ca.* 7 cm.) and at the right two-thirds (*ca.* 13 cm.), allowing the triglyphs to be approximately 22 cm. wide (with a variation of less than 5 cm.). Accordingly the metopes have a width of about 25 cm., which accords well with their height of 25.3 cm. (including the *cyma reversa* molding). On the companion block, however, with a length of only 2.10 m., the dimensions necessarily change, since the number of elements remains constant. Here the triglyphs vary between 19.5 and 20 cm., while the metopes are either 22 or 23 cm. wide, thus becoming upright rectangles if the crowning *cyma* of 4.5 cm. is reckoned in their height (26.5 cm.). Otherwise, they remain reasonably square.

As to the architrave-frieze block from the east colonnade (Plan XIV 2), the salient differences of the architrave have already been noted. It is taller, and it is plain. The differences in the details of the triglyph frieze are manifold. Primarily the scheme differs in having only three triglyphs over each intercolumniation. Even on a block only 2.125 m. long this scheme allows more massive triglyphs than those of the west colonnade. The triglyphs and the metopes are of the same width (26 cm.). Thus the metopes are almost exactly square, for their height is 26.5 cm. including the simple cavetto crown molding that here replaces the *cyma reversa* of the west colonnade. The heavy triglyphs are more boldly blocked. The grooves are bisected by a narrow fillet rather than by a medial arris. They are stopped at the top by a straight chamfer, above which the glyphs merge into the taenia without any separating line. This fashion was frequently observed in the fragments lying about at Ptolemais.

Two complete cornice blocks were recovered and substantial parts of several others, mostly from the vicinity of the east portico. They seem to have been approximately half as long as the architrave-frieze blocks. They are of simple form (Plan XV 1) and completely unrelated to the otherwise Doric entablature, so that the triglyphs are devoid of mutules. Neither do the blocks bear dentils or modillions or other Ionic ornament. The sole elaboration is a lion-head waterspout which survives in fairly recognizable form (Pl. XXVI *C*). The cornice blocks were cut completely through to lodge the beams, which thus rested on the upper surface of the architrave-frieze blocks (see Fig. 46). It was this factor which incontrovertibly showed that they belonged to the entablature of the east colonnade, for slight depressions on the upper surface of its architrave-frieze block exactly match the cuttings in the cornice. These imply the use of wooden beams about 18 cm. wide, set approximately 35 cm. apart, for all the examples found near the east portico. The uppermost band of the sima has been beveled away (see Fig. 46), but on a block from the north end of the court it remains and gives a completely horizontal upper surface to the cornice. There is no reason to suppose that this cornice did not extend beyond the east colonnade, since there is no positive evidence to the contrary.

Of the south colonnade, with its two bracket-bearing columns that made the connection with the southern ends of the east and west colonnades, there is little to tell. Only the bases and the lower portions of the shafts survive, and nowhere was any fragment discovered that could be associated with the upper portions of the columns or with the entablature. Here the lower diameter of the shaft is, or rather was meant to be, almost exactly 10 cm. greater than that in the other colonnades, and the moldings of the base are those of the west and north colonnades as opposed in their slight differences to those of the east colonnade. The height of the base

proper is about 22 cm., as compared with 19 cm. for the smaller columns. From the surviving drums it can be postulated that the larger columns were constructed somewhat along the lines of the smaller ones and that they consisted of a lower block containing the base and the lower portion of the shaft, a single drum followed by three double drums, and an upper block containing the neck of the shaft and the capital. This would make the larger columns taller by something slightly more than the height of the extra single drum. The following dimensions would be norms corresponding to those for the smaller columns:

Height of base block	0.38 m.
Height of single drum	0.50 m.
Height of 3 double drums	3.81 m.
(1.27 m. each)	
Height of capital block	0.38 m.
Total height	5.07 m.

The true height would almost certainly be slightly in excess of this figure, again giving a ratio of approximately seven and a half times the lower diameter, and would suggest for the height of the ceiling over the south portico something approximating 6 meters as compared with 5 meters for the other three porticoes.

In spite of the paucity of remains and the surprising divergences which they reveal but leave unexplained, the impression given by the main order of the building is clear. It unquestionably represents the end of the Hellenistic era, when the later evolution of the orders was complete and in elevation all of them had much the same appearance, so that elements of each could be and were readily combined.

Following a discussion of the peristyle it is fitting that some mention be made of the formal entrance to it, that is, the doorway which leads from the vestibule (Room 18) into the east portico, for this is the one feature which can be completely reconstructed with certainty (see Figs. 44–45). The monolithic jambs stand intact (Pl. XXI *B*), and the lintel which they supported was found relatively undamaged nearby (Plate XXVI *A*). The lintel gave headroom of 2.50 m. It was apparently backed by an orthostat much thinner in relation to its height, but such a block was not recovered. The practice of spanning doorways with more than one orthostat was general at Ptolemais, and indeed it was in this connection that the Greeks most vigorously apprehended the principle that "strength in a beam depends on depth."[198] The jambs are 30 cm. wide at the base and 34 cm. at the top, so that the doorway narrowed upward, but the external margins of the jambs are vertical. The difference is taken up by two diverging moldings which extend onto the lintel block. An identical arrangement is to be seen on a pair of jambs which still stand on the north side of the Square of the Cisterns. The 8-cm. band outside the molding on each jamb was stepped back and obviously faded into the plastered surface of the wall. The purpose of the moldings was to break up the single frontal plane so as to give the impression of a converging, inward-inclined frame. The lintel block is 40 cm. high and slightly over 2 meters long. The depth of its soffit is 33 cm., which allows a depth of about 23 cm. for a backing block. The soffit was not cut square to the faces, and its angle matches a slight rake to the upper surfaces of the jambs. That is, the soffit was inclined slightly downward to the line of vision of one approaching the doorway (see Fig. 45)—a device which occurs also in the Temple of Demeter at Cyrene. The lintel displayed a salient corona, which ran on to the ends of the block and so appeared to project over the extremities of the jambs that were plastered into the wall. Below this were small dentils with short returns following the slope of the corona. Below these, in turn, were two retreating moldings above a narrow taenia which supported five regulae, each with six guttae set against a plain architrave band 18 cm. high. The regulae and the guttae were beveled in a symetrically opposed fashion, and the nature of this exquisite detailing can be understood only by reference to the drawing (Fig. 45). However, the virtuosity whereby one edge of the jamb moldings appears to run up into the foreground of the lintel and one into the background, although in point of fact they are both in the same plane, can barely be shown in any drawing. These features, coupled with the inclination of the lateral dentils, are indeed sophisticated.

The only other significant architectural ornament discovered *in situ* was associated with the residential suite of the Villa (Rooms 9–14). The bases of two of the columns at the angles of the impluvium in Room 11 were found still in place, as were several elements of the colonnaded entrance

to Room 14. Common to both these features was the use of octagonal plinths for the columns.[199] In Room 11 the bases were cut in one block with the lower portions of the column shafts (44 cm. in diameter). The bases are Ionic, somewhat resembling in detail those of the east portico, and the shafts are unfluted (Pl. XXIII *D* and Plan XIV 11). A fragment of a Doric capital (Plan XV 6) resembling those of the "Small Peristyle" of the "Palazzo" was discovered in this vicinity, but any association would be entirely hypothetical.

Fortunately the remains of the arched entrance to Room 14 permitted a reconstruction (Fig. 48) in which only the columns are entirely conjectural. Discovered *in situ* were the plinths and bases which supported two attached pillars and two central columns. The lateral passages were trabeated, and the central opening was surmounted by an arch; one of the beams and one voussoir of the arch were recovered in the fill nearby.

The four base elements exhibit the same decorative treatment, each having a low panel recessed into the bottom portion of each face. The plinth and the base proper are cut in one block. The plinths for the two columns are octagonal (Plan XIV 10), whereas the plinths for the pillars are rectangular. The pillar plinths abut the walls, so that the bases proper, which reproduce exactly the moldings of the column bases, are attached to the walls by a few centimeters of plastered filling. On the west side it could be noticed that the wall had been plastered before the base was put in position. Manifestly, rectangular pillars were superimposed on these elements, but what to call them is somewhat problematical. They would resemble jambs, and, indeed, the base elements are almost identical with the larger ornamental bases for the doorjambs of Room 16 (see Pl. XXIII *B*). How the pillars were capped to accord with the columns would be interesting to know. Or were they perhaps treated as antae? The columns and capitals shown in Figure 48 are, of course, entirely imaginary and merely to be regarded as formal.

The surviving beam (1.54 m. long and 36 cm. high) spanned the western aperture if its more ornate face was designed to be seen as one entered the room. The decoration of this face is noteworthy (Pl. XXVII *A*). At the bottom a plain fascia (3.5 cm. high) gives the impression of a vestigial

---

[198] See Plommer, *Ancient and Classical Architecture*, p. 142.

[199] For octagonal plinths in the "Palazzo" see Pesce, *Il "Palazzo delle Colonne*," pp. 31–32.

architrave. Then, separated by a projecting taenia, follows an exquisite "frieze" of upright palm leaves separated by spines, the cores of the leaves being alternately convex and concave. Above this is a row of dentils and then a projecting cornice. One end of the block was left plain to be built into the side wall. The other end provided the impost for the arch. This function is emphasized in several ways, primarily by an apparent projection of the cornice an additional 15 cm. or so at the rear face, but only for about 60 cm. While the moldings are carried around to the rear face with the cornice to this extent, the other ornament is not, and beyond them the rear face is plain and the cornice vestigial. The function of impost for the arch is further emphasized by diagonal incisions in the ornate face that set mock limits in the fascia and in the cornice of the beam at the appropriate places (see Pl. **XXVII** *A*). These have the same purpose as the beveled moldings on the jambs of the doorway to the east portico, that is, to break up a single plane. They simulate the *versurae procurrentes* of Vitruvius, which seem to have come to Rome by way of the Hellenistic theater at the end of the first century B.C., where they gained great favor in imperial architecture. The arch was constructed of voussoirs 31 cm. high that echoed the ornament of the beam and showed one ornate face (Pl. **XXVII** *C*) and one plain face. Extensive remains of color on the one block preserved (see p. 226) show that the colonnade was brilliantly painted. The extrados of the voussoir is unworked. The upper surface of the beam demonstrates some slight smoothing in the impost section, but elsewhere, except for a curious band 8 cm. wide and 6 cm. from the edge of the ornate side, it was left rough. It would seem, then, that except for a possible light screen erected on this side, the entablature was entirely ornamental and stood free of superincumbent walling.

In addition to the material of known provenience described above, a number of random fragments that were found in the fill are worthy of comment. Most important are two groups of cornice blocks. The first group, comprising cornices with cuttings to lodge beams, consists of half a dozen blocks with an average length of about a meter and identical in treatment. Of these, two complete blocks and a fragment show an outward return of the moldings (Plans XIV 9 and XV 8). The beam lodgments were not cut completely through as in the cornice of the

peristyle. They are about 30 cm. apart and about 10 cm. wide. The ornament was well cut and severe— simple modillions with a rosette in the angle coffer. It would seem from their number and distribution about the peristyle that these blocks formed the *epikranitis* of the rear wall of the south portico or else were from the entablature of the upper story behind the south portico. The blocks of the second group were manifestly decorative, and in almost every instance the inward return of the moldings shows them to be terminal elements. Two crisply cut blocks (e.g. Plans XIV 6 and XV 4) with clean heavy modillions perhaps formed a single unit of decoration with a total length of about 2.50 m. The other blocks vary slightly in detail but are alike in showing violent use of the drill (Plans XIV 7–8 and XV 5, 7). One of these (Plan XIV 8) closely resembles a block found at the "Palazzo" which Pesce assigns to the upper order of the Grand Peristyle.[200]

There were a large number of fragments of ornamental plaster cornice moldings in the fill of most of the rooms. There were also several fragments of door lintels, one showing two terminal consoles (Pl. **XXVII** *B*). Although simpler, they are of the same general type as the lintel of the doorway to the east portico. Several pieces of a small ornamental archivolt were well cut, plastered, and painted red (Plan XV 9). Two incomplete examples (Plan XIV 14) were discovered of an element which occurs also in the dwelling attached to the Public Building on the Street of the Monuments (Plan XVIII 1). In form it is a small pier with an engaged half-column of the Ionic order. A projecting tongue at the rear demonstrates that it was designed to be built into a wall (see p. 128).

From the architectural ornament it is possible to draw some chronological conclusions regarding the Villa. A building of the Greek East ornamented in the mode of the end of the Hellenistic era, it could in principle be dated from the second century B.C. to as late as that tradition is likely to have survived essentially intact in this area. For lack of analogous evidence the upper limit is problematical.

The order of the peristyle provides the clearest and most unmistakable associations with this epoch. "By the second century," says Plommer,[201] "it was everywhere the custom to give a colonnade, whether of Ionic or Doric columns, a Doric archi-

[200] *Ibid.* Pl. VIII *C*.

[201] *Ancient and Classical Architecture*, p. 259.

trave and frieze and an Ionic cornice, usually with dentils. Pompeian peristyles, Pergamene stoas, the Bouleuterion at Miletus ... all show this form of entablature. It was made easier by the increasing approximation of Doric and Ionic columns." For, as Lawrence says: "All the Orders, in fact, now gave much the same effect in elevation. And in all three a greater range of variation was allowed in decoration."[202] The continual shrinkage in scale and significance of the capital, both Doric and Ionic, is one of the most noticeable features of this change of outlook and, as has been noted above, such mean-looking capitals are highly characteristic of the Ionic order at Ptolemais. The inner rectangle and the middle pairs of Ionic columns in the Hypostyle Hall at Delos provide a most striking analogy to these "extraordinarily simple"[203] capitals. Nearer at hand are the large numbers of Ionic columns imported by Juba II, when in 25 b.c. he began to build his capital at Cherchel in Algeria. The tomb attributed to him "is surrounded by an array of completely unfluted shafts with tiny capitals characteristic of the latest Hellenistic Ionic."[204] These are, however, of different design from those at Ptolemais. At Ptolemais the engaged order of the pseudoporticus of the "Palazzo" displays all the comparable elements, which are commented on by Pesce as follows: "... sormontato da capitello ionico, dove la decorazione dei girali sui dischi frontali delle volute e delle foglioline d'edera con gambo al raccordo fra echino e volute era plasmata a stucco..."[205] and "a questo pseudocolonnato ionico era imposta una trabeazione di ordine dorico ...."[206]

The entrance to the east portico of the Villa is the one feature that is preserved almost intact and, although it reproduces the customary appearance of Greek doorways, one aspect deserves comment. The type preserves the scheme first exhibited on a monumental scale in the great Mycenaean tholoi and originally derived from Egypt.[207] "The lintels are uniformly longer, overlapping the sides of the dromos," and in the "grandest of all tholos tombs" the sides of the doorway "slant towards one another

as they rise, and the whole doorway is inclined inwards, in imitation of the Egyptian pylon."[208] Interesting, however, are the methods whereby these effects were obtained in the Villa. They can only be described as illusionistic. Thus, although the outer margins of the jambs were cut square to eliminate the necessity of specially trimming the adjacent courses of the walls, they were masked by plaster and the diverging moldings give the impression of parallel-sided jambs slanting toward each other with a lintel which seems to overlap the sides. The inward inclination was simulated by canting the lintel so that the soffit was visible at an angle. This impression is also sustained by the expert detailing of the ornament. The lateral return of the dentils follows the same inclination as the corona—surely an exercise in false perspective suggestive of the tendency that in wall painting found expression in the so-called "Second Pompeian Style."

The entrance to Room 14 is the one other striking architectural feature of the Villa to survive in large part. The bold exhibitionist use of the arch would be noteworthy in any context. The ornamental arches at Priene dating from the latter half of the second century b.c. provide a definite *terminus post quem* for such a feature, and one of them, namely that in the Lower Gymnasium, establishes all the elements of the scheme in the Villa. For, although at Priene the order is a "blind" one, there is a central arch springing independently from lateral lintels as at Ptolemais.[209] The popular application of this idea, however, proved to be in the porches of temples and propylaea, and in this connection the combination of the arch with the orders became "common in Asia in Roman Imperial times."[210] Two methods were employed—either "the horizontal entablature was carried unbroken round the curve of the arch" or "the horizontal entablature

[202] A. W. Lawrence, *Greek Architecture* (1957) p. 201.

[203] *Ibid.* p. 272 and Fig. 160.

[204] *Ibid.* p. 224.

[205] *Il "Palazzo delle Colonne,"* p. 13.

[206] *Ibid.* p. 14; see also Pls. IIA (reproduced in Plommer, *op. cit.* Fig. 76) and VIIA.

[207] Plommer (*op. cit.* p. 153) appears to deny the continuity.

[208] Lawrence, *op. cit.* p. 59. Vitruvius *De architectura* iv. 6. 1 gives detailed rules for obtaining the proportions of doorways incorporating such diminution and inward inclination.

[209] Plommer, *op. cit.* p. 262, Fig. 86.

[210] See Robertson, *Handbook of Greek and Roman Architecture*; in addition to the representative examples cited *ibid.* p. 227 (the Temple of Dushara at Si' in the Hauran, the Propylaea at Baalbek, and a temple at Termessus in Pisidia), there are the Propylaea at Damascus and the Temple at Atil in the Hauran (see Ashby, *The Architecture of Ancient Rome*, p. 62, Fig. 12, Pl. XXXIV, and S. B. Murray, *Hellenistic Architecture in Syria* [1917] p. 14). The earliest example in this list (Si') is Augustan.

was broken and spanned by an independent arch of narrower border."[211] The second method, which concerns us here and of which examples are less common, can be illustrated by the porch of a temple at Termessus in Pisidia, which is of the second century of our era,[212] and at a much earlier date in the wall decoration of Cubiculum 16 of the Villa dei Misteri at Pompeii.[213] In the former instance the congruence of similar features is particularly striking, for the columns stand on octagonal plinths and the entablature is ornamented with a register of "palm leaves."[214] The latter motif (of Egyptian origin) had long been in the classical repertory, one of the most striking early examples being in the curious "double-bell" capitals of the Messalian Treasury at Delphi, dating from the second half of the sixth century B.C.[215] Then, approaching the period under discussion here, we have the capitals of the inner columns of the upper story of the Stoa of Attalus at Athens.[216] However, it reached the height of its popularity in the first century of our era, when it adorned the cornices of a series of great Roman temples.[217] It may be of some importance to note that when it was first introduced in Rome at the beginning of the first century of our era, the palm-leaf decoration was assigned to the cornice, whereas at Ptolemais and Termessus it belongs to the frieze-and-architrave section of the entablature. It appears in this position, in its fully developed form, for instance on the wall of the pronaos of the large temple at Kom Ombo in Egypt.[218]

[211] Robertson, *loc. cit.*

[212] *Ibid.* p. 227 and Fig. 98.

[213] H. G. Beyen, *Die pompejanische Wanddekoration* I (1938) Plates, Fig. 18.

[214] Pesce (*Il "Palazzo delle Colonne,"* p. 97) gives a full analysis of the occurrence of the feature e.g. at Termessus, Ephesus, Miletus, Leptis Magna (Severan Basilica), and Kom el-Shuqafah.

[215] Robertson, *op. cit.* Fig. 46.

[216] See Lawrence, *op. cit.* Fig. 154, Pl. 146 *A*.

[217] E.g. the Temple of Castor, rebuilt in A.D. 6 (Ashby, *op. cit.* Pl. XXVI), the Temple of Concord, rebuilt in A.D. 10 (Robertson, *op. cit.* Pl. XIIa), the Temple of Vespasian, completed by Domitian (*ibid.* Pl. XIIb).

[218] Gustave Jéquier, *L'Architecture et la décoration dans l'ancienne Égypte: Les temples ptolemaïques et romains* (Paris, 1924) Pl. 37. The palm-leaf design is, of course, basically connected in Egypt with the capital. It was apparently transferred from capitals to flat surfaces as a continuous design and may perhaps be said to be more appropriate to vertical surfaces such as friezes than to inclined members such as cornices.

There is perhaps one other feature from the Villa which may have chronological connotations. Each of the cornice fragments (Plan XIV 6–9) other than those of the peristyle is furnished with brackets of one description or another beneath the corona. In no instance are they solid supports of the conventional Roman style, but their design is undoubtedly that of modillions. The antecedents and introduction of this feature have not been closely studied. In the publication of the "Palazzo," where similar modillions occur, little attention is given to them. However, it seems that toward "the end of the Republic"[219] this feature made its appearance, "but whether first in the Greek or Roman world it would be rash to decide."[220]

There remains only the task of bringing together the suggestions made above about the historical and geographical associations of the architectural features of the Villa and to apply them to what can on this score be said about its date. We begin necessarily with the observation that the Villa is a peristyle house of the eastern Mediterranean, relatively untouched by Western influences. To this we may add that, though the one is a highly concentrated structure and the other spready and diffuse, the "Palazzo" and the Villa have much in common, especially in the handling of detail, and can be said to belong generally to one epoch and one tradition. Judging by the order of the Villa's peristyle we have here a tradition that begins early in the Hellenistic period and is carried along presumably without interruption until the tradition of the Antonine and Severan ages replaces it. How far along in the continuing line of the earlier tradition the construction of the Villa should be placed is the all-important question. The answer depends upon the proper valuation and correlation of three factors. The first factor is the irregularity and incongruity of detail in the development of the order of the peristyle. Whatever may be said about the lack of suitable materials and skilled workmen in the region, it still remains true that those who had the means to erect dwellings of this kind were satisfied with less than the best. This does not augur too early a date. The second factor is the violent drillwork characterizing certain cornice blocks. For these the late second century would not be too early. In fact they could be Severan. Over against these factors stands the third factor—

[219] Ashby, *op. cit.* p. 47.

[220] Plommer, *op. cit.* p. 278.

the refined and highly sophisticated work of the formal extrance to the peristyle and of the arched entrance to Room 14.

It becomes a matter, then, of balancing these three factors and what they imply. Most out of line and therefore most readily disposed of are the obviously late cornice blocks with drillwork. If they were part of the Villa, they belonged to a separate element of the structure that was later than its main body, and the *naiskos* in the northwest corner of the court (see p. 126) may provide a solution to the problem they pose. These pieces, it will be recalled, have an inward return of the moldings and are therefore simultaneously unsuitable as elements of an *epikranitis* crowning the walls behind the porticoes and suitable as embellishment of a freestanding structure such as the *naiskos* or its portico. What really counts, then, is to balance properly the irregularities of the order of the peristyle against the niceties of architectural detail, especially of the entrance to the east

portico. On this score and because of the relation between Villa and "Palazzo" it may not be amiss to associate the Villa with the Roman rather than with the Hellenistic period of the history of Ptolemais. The impression created by the Villa is not one of association with the architectural pretentiousness of the Antonine period, nor is it likely that the period of Trajan, which had such lasting ill effects on Cyrenaica by reason of the Jewish insurrection, provides a proper setting for such a construction enterprise. We are therefore in all probability thrown back for historical reasons upon the first century of our era, and if we are correct in eliminating as atypical and as later additions the drilled cornices there is nothing in the architecture that would conflict with an assignment of the Villa to the first century. To give a more precise date requires naturally the consideration of other types of evidence along the lines developed on pages 137–38.

WALL DECORATION IN THE VILLA

By C. H. Kraeling *and* L. Mowry

The Villa provides a welcome opportunity to observe further the nature and use of wall decoration at Ptolemais, supplementing what has been shown on this score by the Italian work at the "Palazzo."[221] The information concerning the decoration of the Villa comes from a variety of places—from the columns and walls of the porticoes surrounding the peristyle court, from the chambers along the south and west, and from the debris with which the rooms were filled.

Evidence that the columns of the great peristyle were once coated with plaster survived on most of those found standing, and where by chance plaster was absent the natural cavities and irregularities of the stone were such as to have demanded its application, if the normal effect of elegance was to be achieved. In most instances the plaster on the columns has a yellowish tinge, but the four columns at the west end of the north portico give clear indication of the use of brighter colors, at least directly above the bases. Beginning at the

[221] See Pesce, *Il "Palazzo delle Colonne,"* pp. 39–41, 103–4.

west end, the lowest drums of these four columns were painted alternately a solid Pompeian red and a deep green. It was evident, however, that these colors were superimposed upon a yellow undercoating, and it would seem that the green and red were applied to a zone running only part of the way up the columns, the upper part remaining yellow. One might assume that the red and green decorative bands alternated around the entire peristyle, as the even number (34) of the columns would permit, were it not for a red tinge in the plaster about a meter above the base of the easternmost column on the curving stylobate of the south colonnade. Perhaps only the nine columns of the south portico and the seven of the north portico were given the additional decoration, with the sequence of colors reversed at the south, while the columns of the east and west porticoes were solidly and simply yellow. The base and drum now mounted at the southeast corner of the peristyle (see Pl. XXII *A*) were found separately in the fill and erected there to fill a gap. The traces of red that appear on the drum are, therefore, without bearing upon the question of the alternation of colors around the peristyle.

There is also evidence that color was applied to the colonnaded entrance from the diwan (Room 12) to the dining room (Room 14) of the private apartment in the southwest corner of the building. On the one voussoir from the arched central opening of the colonnade (Pl. XXVII *C*) the colors were still particularly bright. The upright convex and concave palm leaves of its frieze were (from left to right) yellow, green, pink, and green, and the spines between them were tan. The same tan was applied to the dentils above the frieze and to the fillets at the base of the cornice. Dark brown lines ran across the face of the dentils and along the lower face of the upper fillet. Below the frieze the taenia showed traces of tan, and the fascia of the simple architrave had clear indications of pink. The cornice seems not to have been painted.

As for the walls inclosing the porticoes, the evidence for their decoration is limited, perhaps by accident, to the south portico. Here sufficient plaster remained on the east, south, and west walls to show that they were uniformly decorated. From the mosaic floor upward for a distance of about 52 cm. a pink plinth, heavily streaked with red, ran around this entire area (Fig. 61). The plinth, in this case alone so far as our knowledge of the building goes, was divided into structural units about 1.35 m. long by vertical stripes about 2 cm. wide. The red streaks upon the pink surface were therefore quite in order, imitating the veining of marble blocks. Above the plinth ran a continuous green band about 4 cm. high, bordered at the bottom by white and dark (originally blue or black) stripes that were respectively about 5 mm. and about 1 cm. high. There was evidence along the western part of the south wall that the area above this border was paneled—red and yellow panels alternating—but it was not possible to determine the width and the height of the panels. The red panels were outlined by pink stripes about 1 mm. wide, and the yellow panels had a red stripe about 5 mm. wide inscribed about 8 cm. inside the edge of the field.

The evidence for wall decoration in other parts of the Villa was found in Rooms 5, 6, 10, 12, 14, 15, 16, and 17. For the most part it was limited to the remains of colored plaster still adhering to the stone footings of the walls, but in the rooms at the south, where the mud-brick upper portions of the

walls were by good fortune preserved (see p. 119), it was possible on occasion to trace the decoration to a height of about 1.60 m. above floor level.

Rooms 15, 16, and 17 belonged to the more formal part of the Villa and were decorated in becoming fashion. In Room 15 only a small fragment of the decoration remained *in situ*, but in a strategic location, while in Room 16 a good third of the painted plaster was still in position and in Room 17 perhaps a fourth. Because the paving had been removed before the rooms were filled in with debris it is difficult to determine accurately the height of their painted plinths.

Room 17 (see Fig. 61) had a white plinth (*ca.* 37 cm. high) upon which was executed in a dark color (probably green) a schematized floral design consisting of a vertical dart-shaped element with simple scrolls projecting to the right and left (Pl. LVI *A*). The design was repeated around the room, individual examples occupying 60–80 cm. of the length of the field. Above the plinth was a contiuous yellow band (*ca.* 10 cm. high) framed at the bottom by a dark (black or blue) stripe and at the top by a white stripe, each about 1 cm. high. From this band upward the walls were painted a solid Pompeian red with no paneling or figure representation. This can be stated with confidence because of the height (*ca.* 1.50 m.) to which and the size of the area over which the plaster was preserved.

In Room 16 the wall decoration was better attested than in any other part of the Villa, the plaster on most of the south wall and on large sections of the east and west walls being preserved intact (see Pl. XXIII *B*). But execution did not match the standards maintained elsewhere in the building. In some measure this may be the fault of the plasterer, who left a surface heavily scored with the marks of his trowel. The poor plastering, however, raises the question whether the room was at one time replastered and then redecorated, so that inferiority of workmanship in both regards may represent a period late in the life of the building. In parts of the building where replastering and redecoration had obviously occured, the earlier layers of plaster remain on the walls and are merely covered by the later. There may have been special circumstances to recommend the removal of the original plaster in Room 16, circumstances having to do with the blocking of the doorway to Room 17. Even so, the pattern is substantially the same as that used throughout the

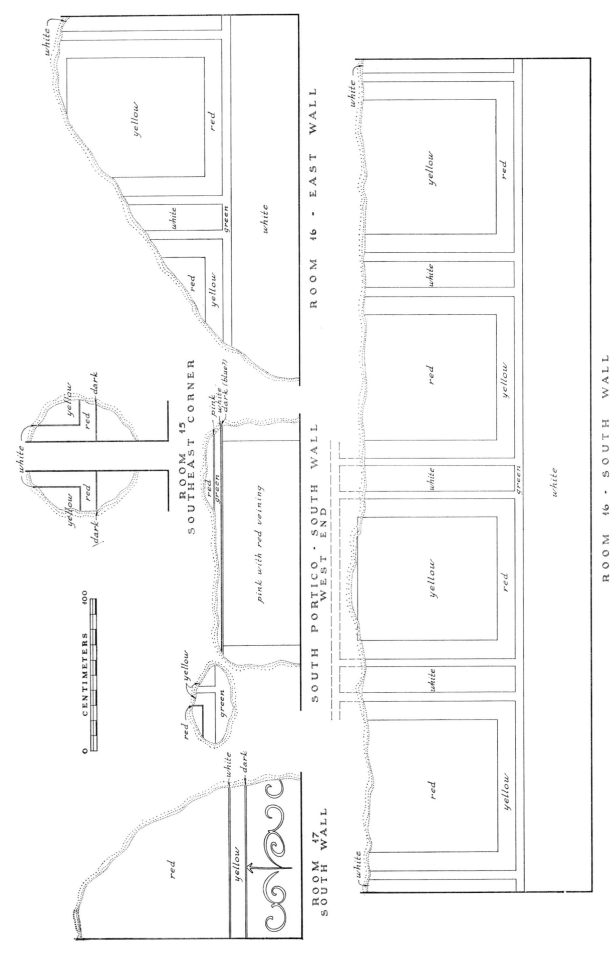

ROOM 46 · EAST WALL

ROOM 46 · SOUTH WALL

ROOM 15 SOUTHEAST CORNER

SOUTH PORTICO · SOUTH WALL WEST END

ROOM 47 SOUTH WALL

CENTIMETERS

0   400

Fig. 61.—Designs of Wall Decoration in Villa. J. E. Knudstad

rest of the Villa. The white plinth here (*ca.* 46 m. high) was surmounted by a green band (*ca.* 6 cm. high) outlined above and below with red stripes. At regular intervals the band extended vertically and divided the upper wall surfaces into panels (see Fig. 61). The east and west walls each had three large rectangular panels and the south four; on the north wall there was room for one panel on each side of the doorway. The panels were alternately red and yellow around the entire room. They varied in width between about 79 and 89 cm. because of the differences in the length of the walls, but they must have been of uniform height. This height it was possible to fix on both the south and the east wall at about 95 cm. Each panel was framed by a band about 12 cm. wide, red panels being framed in yellow and yellow panels in red. Between the framed panels on each wall and in the corners of the room were narrow rectangular white fields, set off from the panels by vertical extensions of the green band that ran at the bottom of the whole design. The white fields were about 17 cm. wide between panels, and in the corners about 9 cm. was allowed on each wall, the adjacent sections masking inaccuracies in the turn of the corner. How the uppermost part of the decorative scheme was handled and whether it had a crowning feature are matters for speculation. Clearly the frames of the panels must have inclosed them above as well as below and at the sides, and clearly the narrow green border must have been carried around the top of the paneled zone to match the bottom. Above this there may have been a painted or a plaster cornice or a simple crown molding or even a blank white space to match the plinth. That plaster moldings were used in the Villa was indicated by fragments found in the fill of most of the rooms.

Room 15 had a similar decorative scheme, only more simple in keeping with its character as a subsidiary chamber that was entered and received its light only from Room 16. A small section of colored plaster adhering to the wall in the southeast corner of the room shows a white plinth (*ca.* 48 cm. high) and above it a red border (*ca.* 10 cm. wide) which turned from the horizontal to the vertical at least at the ends of the walls (see Fig. 61) and thus framed fields. But how large these fields may have been it is not possible to tell; we know only that the adjacent fields on the east and south walls were both done in yellow.

Rooms 9–14 constituted an apartment devoted and especially adapted to the purposes of comfortable and by no means inelegant private life (see pp. 128–30). The mural decoration was in keeping with the character of the apartment, and some care was taken to maintain its excellence, as evidence of redecoration particularly in Rooms 10 and 14 indicates. The dining room of the suite (Room 14) was decorated no less than four times during the life of the building.

Entered from both the west and south porticoes, the intimate peristyle court (Room 11), with its shallow pool in the middle, provided the foyer of the apartment. Since it was open to the sky in the center and hence continually exposed to the light, all traces of color have disappeared from the plaster on its walls. But that it was appropriately decorated can be inferred from the yellow tinge in the plaster on one of its column bases that was found buried in the fill of the south portico.

In what we venture to call the "diwan" of the apartment (Room 12) sections of painted plaster were found *in situ* on the east wall at either side of the entrance. These showed that the room had been plastered and decorated three times. The first and second of the schemes of decoration were closely related to and typical of what we found elsewhere in the Villa, but the third scheme, about which unfortunately we know the least, suggested a variation upon the traditional theme (Fig. 62). The decoration applied to the first plastering consisted of a white plinth (only *ca.* 31 cm. high) surmounted by a green band (*ca.* 8.5 cm. high) set off at the bottom by a dark (blue or black) stripe (*ca.* 5 mm.) and at the top by a red stripe (*ca.* 2 cm.) contained within white stripes (each *ca.* 5 mm.). Above this decorative border there was on either side of the door a yellow field, but no indications of vertical subdivision of the field survived either on the wall or on the loose fragments found in the fill. The decoration applied to the second plastering was much the same. The plinth was a bit lower (*ca.* 30 cm.); the border separating the plinth from the field was a little higher (*ca.* 12.5 cm.) and a bit more ornate. An additional white stripe was used to set off the dark stripe at the bottom of the green band, and a dark color was used in place of red along the top. The field above the border was again yellow at either side of the door; inside this field a white stripe was noticeable about 5 cm. in from the edge, but again there was no indication

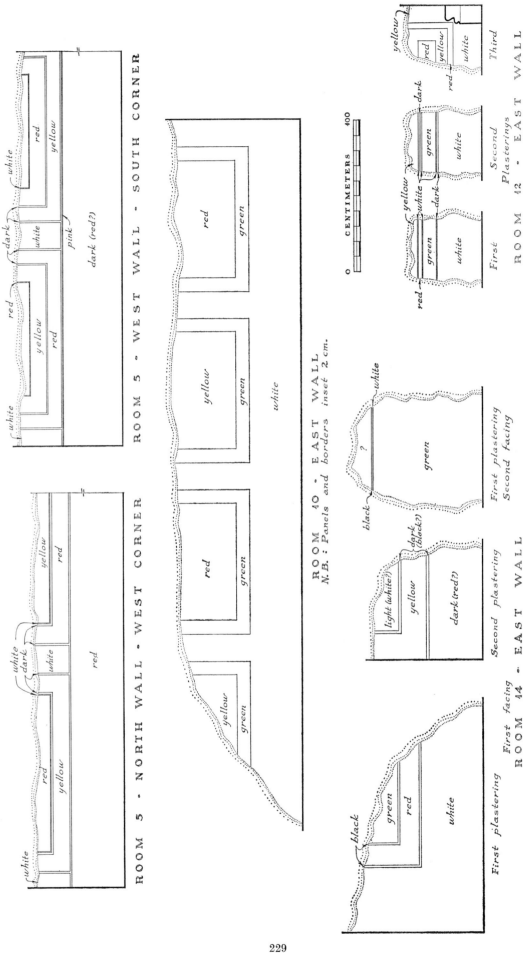

ROOM 5 · WEST WALL · SOUTH CORNER

ROOM 5 · NORTH WALL · WEST CORNER

ROOM 10 · EAST WALL
N.B. : Panels and borders inset 2 cm.

ROOM 44 · EAST WALL

ROOM 42 · EAST WALL

Fig. 62.—Designs of Wall Decoration in Villa. *J. E. Knudstad*

of vertical subdivision of the field. The decoration on the third plastering is known only from a single fragment at the south end of the east wall, and the colors are quite indistinct. The plinth here was only about 19 cm. high. It was bordered by a red band not more than about 4 cm. high which turned up at right angles to the floor about 11 cm. short of the end of the wall. Between the vertical extension of the border and the end of the wall the surface was painted yellow. Inside the angle made by the band the surface was again yellow. One would by analogy expect here a large yellow panel, but such was apparently not the case. Inside the field and at a distance of about 8 cm. above and to the left of the bordering red band there was inset a horizontal red element of which only the vertical dimension of about 12 cm. could be determined. It could have been either a square or a long horizontal bar, but its appearance inside a bordered field is unusual.

The decoration of the bedroom of the suite (Room 10) is also known from its east wall, and the remains show that it was plastered and decorated twice. The first painting (see Fig. 62) was applied to a plaster surface especially prepared for it, a surface into which five panels had been carefully recessed to a depth of about 2 cm. from the face of the wall. This was the only instance in the entire Villa in which the wall paneling was more than two dimensional. Of course the recessing of the panels must have been carried around all four walls of the chamber. The area below the panels constituted the plinth (*ca.* 35 m. high) and was left white. The panels were each 95 cm. wide on the east wall and were spaced at intervals of 18 cm., but their height could not be ascertained. They were alternately red and yellow save for a green border (*ca.* 9 cm. wide) around the inner edge of each of the recessed fields. The strips of plaster between the panels were left white, continuing decoratively their structural relation to the plinth. There was surprisingly little irregularity in the dimensions of the arrangement, both painted and structural, the workmanship being of the highest quality throughout. The depth of the room (5.80 m.) provides almost exactly for five recessed panels of 95 cm. each and for six separating bands of 18 cm. each. Sometime after the first decoration the plaster surface of the recessed panels was purposely hacked, the resulting holes providing anchorage for a layer of plaster that filled the recesses and leveled the surface of

the entire wall. The new surface was decorated, but not enough is known of the new decoration to permit its description.

It has been noted above (p. 130) that the east wall of the dining room (Room 14) of the apartment was at some point in its history increased in thickness by about 20 cm. In each of its two phases the wall was plastered and painted twice. The replasterings extended around the entire room, so that four layers could be distinguished even where the thickness of the walls had remained constant. The original decoration of the room (see Fig. 62) included a white plinth (*ca.* 43 cm. high), which was carried up vertically at the north end of the east wall and therefore probably also at the north end of the west wall (see Fig. 43 for plan of room). The vertical extension of the plinth was here given additional width (*ca.* 43 cm.) to set off the wall decoration from the colonnaded entrance to the room. It is not likely that the vertical white strips in the southeast and southwest corners of the room were equally wide. The plinth, with its vertical extension, was bordered by a red band (*ca.* 13 m. wide) edged on each side with a dark (black?) stripe about 1.5 cm. wide. This border inclosed one or more green fields of undetermined height and length. On the second plastering a dark (red?) plinth about 37 cm. high was developed around the entire room. This was bordered by a yellow band (*ca.* 17 cm. high) edged with dark (black or blue) stripes about 2 cm high. This border turned up at the north end of the east wall (see Fig. 62) and hence presumably also at both ends of each wall. At the north end of the east wall it framed a light-colored (white or yellow) field whose height and length are unknown. When the east wall received its second facing and was first plastered, a zone reaching to about 75 cm. above floor level was painted green (see Fig. 62). This high green plinth was bordered at the top by a white stripe and a black stripe, each only about 5 mm. high. Above them was a monochrome field, but its color was indistinct and there was no positive or negative evidence of vertical subdivision. The same green plinth appeared also on the corresponding layer of plaster on the west wall at heights up to about 83 cm. above floor level and extended to the very end of the wall at the south, leaving no room for a vertical framing element. From what remained of the second plastering of the thickened wall all except vague traces of color had disappeared, so that the final phase of the decoration is completely unknown.

The Villa boasted of at least two other well decorated chambers, namely the two formal dining rooms on the west side of the building (Rooms 5–6). Room 6, the large state dining room, showed remains of four thicknesses of plaster, so that it may have been redecorated at least three times, and in fact large quantities of fragments of painted plaster were found in the fill of the room. But, save at the west, the walls of the room had been destroyed and robbed even of their stone footings, and the plaster remaining *in situ* was either within the height of a normal white plinth or devoid of all traces of color. Hence the decorative patterns are unknown.

In Room 5, the smaller of the formal dining rooms, conditions would have been somewhat similar save for one circumstance. The walls had at one time been covered with a coating of mortar as much as about 10 cm. thick, a coating preserved in the southwest corner to a height of about 1.10 m. Behind this protective barrier the remains of two successive decorative treatments (and plasterings) are preserved at the north, the west, and the south, though not always in an equally intelligible manner. The first decorative treatment (see Fig. 62) involved a colored plinth—red with light or dark veins— between about 36 and 40 cm. high and bordered by a pink stripe (*ca.* 5 mm.). Above this was a dark stripe not more than 1 cm. high separating the lower zone from a paneled area above. On the north and south walls this area was laid out in seven panels, on the west wall in five. The panels were alternately red with a yellow border and yellow with a red border. Between them were narrow vertical fields about 17 cm. wide. In order to obtain the predetermined division of the wall space, it was necessary to vary the width of the panels, those on the west wall being about 97 cm. wide and those on the north wall as much as 1.03 m. A narrow red stripe was superimposed upon the yellow panels about 11 cm. in from their edges, a white stripe on the red panels. The borders of the panels remained constant at 11 cm. as we should expect. They terminated in dark stripes set off on either side by white stripes, but the distribution of the white stripes is not uniform around the room. Of the decoration on the second plastering not enough is visible to permit its reconstruction.

To what has been said about the decoration that survives on the walls of the Villa a word must be added about the plaster fragments found loose in the debris with which the premises were filled. Bushels of such fragments came to light and were carefully inspected. They were instructive in various ways. The plaster fragments found in Rooms 13, 13a, 9, 8, and 7, like those from the entire northern end of the Villa, were normally white, showing that these were service or servants' rooms and were never decorated. The plaster fragments from the rooms whose decoration has been described above gave supplementary testimony in two particulars. They gave a more vivid impression of the brightness of the colors and showed that the range of colors noted on the walls was really that of the decoration as a whole. Black, a deep and a bright green, red, pink, yellow, and white apparently constituted the decorators' pallette. If the dull gray that we have repeatedly referred to as "dark" was actually originally the expensive and more fugitive blue, it was used sparingly in stripes and never in fields or borders. The painted fragments also testify to the absence of figured representation, such as one might have expected, for instance, in the middle of the large monochrome fields. Not a single fragment came to our attention with other than rectilinear or angular decorative elements.

It is in order, now, to correlate the evidence for the wall decoration of the Villa with what is known about wall decoration generally in the Hellenistic and Roman periods. To the body of information already available on this general subject from Attica, Macedonia, South Russia, Greek Anatolia, the Greek islands, Alexandria, and Italy the first material from Cyrenaica, presented by Pesce, was a welcome addition, particularly because it represented an area not previously accounted for. The new evidence from the Villa supplements what the Italian archeologists discovered and may even permit some slight adjustment of the perspective in which the Cyrenaican material has been seen. At the same time, it opens the door to speculation about the ways in which at least the earlier phases of the general development of ancient decorative wall painting are to be interpreted.[222]

[222] From the enormous literature interpreting the material and from among the works that treat especially the earlier "styles," we cite the following as particularly valuable: A. Mau, *Geschichte der decorativen Wandmalerei in Pompeji* (1882); M. Bulard, "Peintures murales et

About the wall decoration of the Villa two things will be apparent at once. The first and most important is that it is homogeneous throughout, a matter to which proper attention will be paid in due course. The second is that it differs in all the more salient features from the elaborate products of Campanian and Roman wall painting that we associate with the fully developed forms of the Second, Third, and Fourth Pompeian Styles. There is here no break-through into depth of space, no figured and pictorial representation, and no riot of pretended architectural construction. Nor does it lend itself to comparison with examples of Roman wall painting of the post-Pompeian period.[223] It is therefore within the framework of the earlier phases of wall painting in the Hellenistic and Roman periods that a proper place for the wall decoration of the Villa must be found.

We begin here naturally with what Mau originally called the "incrustation style" and what Rostovtzeff further defined as the "structural style." Delos, Olynthos, the tombs on the outskirts of Alexandria, and the atrium of the House of Sallust provide the classic examples of this style that every textbook reproduces. With this type of wall decoration the material from the Villa is not in immediate accord. In the "structural style" the emphasis is invariably upon the horizontal, the walls being so treated as to develop a series of ascending zones—typically plinth, frieze, and cornice with intermediate areas—within which again the horizontal factor is dominant. There was a noticeable tendency in this earliest form of decoration to work as much with plaster as with paint, adding to the thickness of the wall to produce molded friezes and cornices and grooving or incising the plaster to represent the drafting and coursing of stone masonry. The function of the painter in this context was primarily to complete the impression of the structural reality that was simulated, but

eventually, by varying the colors of the structural elements, he was able to impart to the imitation of structure the additional decorative qualities that the term "bunter Quaderstil" seeks to express.[224]

Clearly these are not the dominant characteristics of the decoration of the Villa at Ptolemais or, for that matter, of the "Palazzo." In the Villa there are, it is true, zones beginning with a plinth at the bottom, and in the south portico the plinth is so decorated as to indicate individual blocks of veined marble. Also there are traces of molding of the wall surface, in the recessing of the panels in Room 10 and in the copious loose fragments of applied plaster moldings. But the zonal division, so far as we can know it, gives the impression of simplification over against the ornate threefold form of the "structural style," and there are no indications of painted masonry blocks laid in courses. Above all, the emphasis of the panels is invariably on the vertical, and the impression which they actually convey in their regular alternation of color, their frames, and their surcharged stripes is that of a form of surface adornment, in other words of wall sheathing rather than of wall construction. This impression does not in our judgment preclude the possibility that what presents itself in the Villa as a form of surface adornment was at the outset also tectonic in character. Nor does it mean that precisely in relation to the use of color in rhythmic interchange the decorators of the Villa sought other effects than those that tended to give the "structural style" the qualities expressed by the term "bunt." It does mean, however, that if the wall decoration of the Villa has its ultimate origin in a structural form, that form is other than the one underlying the well known "structural style" and that in the search for color effects we have comparable and analogous developments rather than indications of a direct relation to the "structural style."

If it is clear, then, that the wall decoration of the Villa is not of the "structural style" it should be equally clear that its closest counterparts will be found in the earliest examples of the Second Pompeian Style, which Beyen has studied with great care and regards as transitional in some sense between the First and the Second Style.[225] The period to which these early examples belong is that which begins with the founding of the Roman

---

mosaïques de Délos," *MP* XIV (1908) 2–205; R. Delbrueck, *Hellenistische Bauten in Latium* II (1912) 128–40; M. I. Rostovtzeff, "Ancient decorative wall painting," *JHS* XXXIX (1919) 144–63; E. Pfuhl, *Malerei und Zeichnung der Griechen* (1923); A. M. G. Little, "The decoration of the Hellenistic peristyle house in South Italy," *AJA* XXXIX (1935) 360–71; H. G. Beyen *Die pompejanische Wanddekoration* I (1938) *Text* and *Tafeln*.

[223] For the latter see F. Wirth, *Römische Wandmalerei vom Untergang Pompejis bis ans Ende des dritten Jahrhunderts* (1934).

[224] See O. Deubner, "Expolitio," *MDAIR* LIII (1938) 19.

[225] *Die pompejanische Wanddekoration* I 37–52.

colony of Pompeii in about 80 B.C.[226] It is the period, therefore, that follows the destruction of Delos, that marks the low ebb in the fortunes of the mercantile cities of the eastern Mediterranean and in part on this account has yielded few contemporary examples of wall decoration from this entire region. For the counterparts of the wall decoration of the Villa we have therefore to go with Beyen to Italy and the West, more particularly to Pompeii (cella of the Temple of Jupiter, fauces of the Casa del Fauno), to Sicily (Soluntum), and to Rome (Rooms 2, 3, and 4 of the Casa dei Grifi).[227] In the particular type of decoration used in these instances the surface is devoid of subdivision by painted or actual pilasters or columns that are set in front of the plinth and that reach from the floor to an architrave just below ceiling level. It is devoid also of all attempts to create depth perspective either by molding the representation of architectural members or by providing vistas into open space. It lacks, finally, even the occasional figured representation added as an enrichment of the unbroken surface. In other words the wall is still decoratively a solid entity. None the less in all the examples of "Übergangsformen" that Beyen has analyzed there is already visible the simplification of zonal pattern which later becomes canonical and in which a central zone set between plinth and upper zone begins to receive the major emphasis.

So far as the Villa is concerned we have already noted the importance of the plinth and the zone containing the carefully arranged and balanced panels and the fact that the treatment of the uppermost part of the walls is necessarily conjectural. Here certain factors determining such conjecture have to be given proper attention. Most important in this connection is the height to which the wall decoration can be known with certainty. In Room 16 we were fortunately able to determine the height of the panels forming the second zone of the decoration. Allowing for the plinth (46 cm.), the panels (95 cm.), the upper and lower panel frames (12 cm. each), and the upper and lower bands (6 cm. each) inclosing the framed panels, we can determine the nature of the wall decoration to a height of 1.77 m. above floor level. Since there was a second story above Rooms 15, 16, and 17 and since the rooms at ground level cannot have been much more

than 3 meters high (see p. 127), there would not in these rooms have been much space for the development of a third zone of decoration. There would have been even less space if allowance had to be made for a plaster molding above the paneled area and for the height of the joists supporting the upper floor. In these rooms, therefore, the panel zone was presumably the dominant and, in a sense, the all-sufficient decorative element. In Room 10 and Room 5 the situation is somewhat different. The height of the panels in these rooms is unknown, but they must have been higher than those of Room 16 since they were wider.[228] Observing the relation of height to width in Room 16 and applying the same proportion we can safely infer that the panels of Rooms 10 and 5 might have had a height of 1.25 m. or even 1.50 m., but scarcely more. If we allow for the maximum, the development of the wall to the top of the properly framed and inclosed panel zone would cover only about 2.15 m.[229] Assuming the typical height of the rooms of the Villa to be that of the west, north, and east porticoes, whose ceiling height has been established at about 5 meters (see p. 124), we have to allow for an upper zone equal to that of the plinth and the panel zone combined. Certainly a zone of such height would not have been left blank. In Rooms 10 and 5, then, the Villa must have had precisely the tripartite system of decoration that is presupposed in the development of the Second Style.

While in the examples of the transition to the Second Style in Italy and Sicily the plinth is normally more elaborately developed than in the Villa at Ptolemais, the treatment of the second or main zone is closely analogous. In the fauces of the Casa del Fauno and the cella of the Jupiter Temple at Pompeii as well as in Room 3 of the Casa dei Grifi at Rome there are series of vertical monochrome panels.[230] In the example at Soluntum in Sicily similar panels are overlaid with decorative garlands from which ribbons and masks are suspended.[231] The panels are recessed and framed, quite as in Room

[226] *Ibid.* p. 21.
[227] *Ibid.* pp. 39–52, Figs. 4–9.

[228] The panels of Room 16, it will be recalled, were from about 79 to 89 cm. wide, while those of Room 10 were 95 cm. wide and those of Room 5 ranged from 97 to 103 cm.
[229] The figure represents an allowance of 40 cm. for the plinth, 1.50 m. for the panels, 22 cm. for the upper and lower panel frames, and 3 cm. for the upper and lower borders inclosing the framed panels.
[230] See Beyen, *op. cit.* Figs. 4, 5, and 9.
[231] *Ibid.* Figs. 6a–c.

10 of the Villa, but there is not in the Western examples the same rhythmic alternation of basic panel and frame colors. Instead the panels have the same color throughout, a less striking but certainly more elegant and tasteful treatment and one that was more appropriate in the context of a more elaborate plinth and a richly developed upper decorative zone.

Of particular importance for the close relation between the decoration of the Villa at Ptolemais and these earliest examples of the Second Style in the West is the appearance in both of narrow strips or fields between the panels. Indeed, this element is taken by Beyen to be one of the most important features of wall decoration of the Second to Fourth Styles.[232] In this connection it is noted that the narrow vertical fields or strips are usually lighter in color, especially in the earlier examples. It is also noted that, while the earliest examples of such three-zone panel decoration in the West belong to the first century B.C., their decorative forms tend to reappear after the main course of development has brought new modes to predominance.[233] By itself the form is not therefore an absolute criterion of date, save so far as the *terminus a quo* is concerned, and something more is required to place the decoration of the Villa in the proper chronological frame of reference. Perhaps a closer study of two features will be helpful in this connection.

Attention is directed first to the narrow fields that separate the panels. In the Western examples they are in all cases actual panels separately framed and having apparently no other function than to break up the monotony in the parataxis of the wider panels. They are therefore quite unrelated either to the plinth or to the development of the third or uppermost zone of the decoration. At Ptolemais in the Villa, for instance in Room 16 (see Fig. 61), the narrow vertical elements are similarly completely contained in the intermediate decorative zone, and only their light color (white) makes one hesitate to place them entirely on a par with the wide panels. In Rooms 10 and 5 and on the first plastering of the first facing of the east wall in Room 14 (see Fig. 62), however, the situation is quite different. In Rooms 10 and 14 the narrow vertical elements between panels and at the ends

of series of panels rise directly out of and continue the white color of the plinth, while in Room 5 they are based directly on the plinth, quite as the wide panels are but not caught up in an over-all framework with them.

This difference is worthy of note because of its relevance to the question of what this whole paneled type of wall decoration represents. It would seem natural at first glance to seek its antecedents in the rows of orthostats that are occasionally represented directly above the plinth in the "structural style."[234] One serious obstacle to this interpretation, quite aside from the difference in shape, is that the panels are typically represented as recessed into the wall or are actually so recessed, as we have seen above, and thus are typically shown inclosed with frames. Beyen[235] is therefore correct in speaking of the panels as "Platten," that is, as representing slabs set into the wall. The fact that they are frequently elaborately veined, as in familiar examples in the Casa dei Grifi, indicates that they represent marble slabs. We are thrown back therefore, in some sense, to the context of incrustation work properly so-called to understand what is represented in the second zone of the decoration of the Villa at Ptolemais and of the examples that reflect the early form of the Second Style in the West. It should be obvious that the way in which the panels are framed in the Villa—with wide strips in contrasting colors—corresponds more closely to actual examples of marble sheathing and marble floor inlay than do the examples of painted paneling at Rome, Pompeii, and Sicily.[236] In this respect, then, the decoration of the Villa is more primitive than that of the comparable buildings in the West.

It will be recalled that the narrow vertical fields that separate the panels are sometimes seen not to form an element of the paneling but to rise from the plinth and to extend it in a vertical direction. This arrangement, together with the white color in which they are rendered, suggests that their con-

---

[232] *Ibid.* p. 39. Examples from the period of the First Style are given *ibid.* pp. 40–41.

[233] *Ibid.* p. 52.

[234] See e.g. J. Chamonard, *Exploration archéologique de Délos.* VIII. *Le Quartier du Théatre* (Paris, 1922–24) pp. 358–91, esp. Figs. 225 (House of the Trident), 227 (House II *E*), 228 (House VI *H*), 230 (House of Dionysos), 235 (House IV *B*).

[235] *Op. cit.* e.g. pp. 39–40.

[236] For such examples at Ptolemais see Pesce, *Il "Palazzo delle Colonne,"* pp. 29–30 and 68, and the frame of the *opus sectile* panels in the floor of Room 6 of the Villa (Fig. 69 below).

notation is tectonic rather than appliqué, and this suggestion can be verified in the construction of the Villa itself. It has been pointed out above (pp. 216–17) that in the caldarium (Room 1) the apse wall was constructed of stone piers rising from a stone socle and joined together at the top by a single course of masonry. The rectangular spaces between the piers were filled with rubble (see Pl. XXV *A*). This type of construction provided the extra strength required to carry the weight of the semidome of the apse. It is precisely such wall construction of optimum strength that the painted decoration of Rooms 10 and 14 of the Villa represent in the relation between the plinth and the narrow white fields between the wide framed panels. The narrow white fields are a painted echo of the piers that rise from the plinth or socle and divide the wall into rectangular compartments. The panels imitate the slabs of marble that could have been and probably were set against the masses of rubble with which the compartments between the piers were filled. As imitated in Room 10, these slabs were recessed into the wall.

It is in the context of this connection between decoration and wall construction that the wall paintings of the Villa at Ptolemais can be said to have more than casual interest and importance, and it is in this connection also that some general conclusions about their date and origin can be hazarded. There are three questions of general interest upon which the material from Ptolemais may have some bearing. The first is the question of the origins of the basic elements that went into the formation of the Second Style—the elements that were there before the break-through into open space. Beyen has indicated that in his judgment the regular interchange of narrow and wide vertical panels is of more fundamental importance for the basic examples of the Second Style than the over-all division of walls by the representation of pilasters or columns.[237] If the decoration of the Villa at Ptolemais suggests a tectonic basis for this arrangement of narrow and wide vertical panels, shall we say that the earliest examples of the Second Style also presuppose a structural form, but

a form other than that of the "structural style"? And if so, what is the provenience of this other structural form? Is it in areas or in types of buildings in which ceilings were lower and in which construction by the use of regularly coursed masonry blocks was a comparative luxury?

The second question of general interest upon which the decoration of the Villa may bear is that of the use of marble incrustation. For the interpretation of the history and development of marble wall incrustation the basic requirement is a proper correlation of the literary evidence (particularly the passage in Vitruvius *De architectura* vii. 5. 1) with the evidence provided by the monuments. The decline that set in in the economic life of the eastern Mediterranean with the first century B.C. and the ease with which valuable marble slabs could be removed from walls may well have deprived us of much important evidence for the use of marble incrustation elsewhere than in the West. The evidence for actual marble incrustation in the "Palazzo" and for painted representation of marble incrustation in the Villa at Ptolemais suggests that it may be well not to fix too narrowly the geographical and chronological limits of the context within which such incrustation may have been used.[238]

The third question of general interest upon which the decoration of the Villa may bear is that of the general history of wall decoration outside the narrower confines of Latium and the Campania. In this connection it should be noted that the decorative forms applied when the Villa was

---

[237] *Op. cit.* p. 41: "Von Wänden mit Pilastern oder Säulen ist mir keine bekannt, an der wechselnd schmale und breite Rechtecke gereiht wären, was noch stärker darauf hinweist, daß die allerältesten kanonischen Wände des zweiten Stils nicht von Wänden mit Pilastern oder Säulen abzuleiten sind."

[238] At issue here, of course, is what Deubner sets forth in his articles "Expolitio" (in *MDAIR* LIII) and "Inkrustation" (*R.-E.* Supplementband VII 285–93), where it is concluded that incrustation properly so-called did not come into use until between 50 B.C. and A.D. 50 and was in fact a Roman invention. I am inclined to believe that Deubner's interpretation does scant justice to Vitruvius' use of the word *antiqui* when the latter speaks of those *qui initia expolitionibus instituerunt* and to both the statement of Pliny about the palace of Mausolus (*Natural History* xxxvi. 47) and the actual evidence for incrustation in Asia. On the latter see Dörpfeld, "Die Arbeiten zu Pergamon, 1902–1903," *MDAIA* XXIX (1904) 116–20, esp. p. 119, where he suggests that in the original Greek form of the dwelling adjacent to the agora in the lower city marble paneling may have been used in at least a few rooms. This does not mean to say that marble incrustation did not, as Pliny suggests, become particularly popular in the early days of the Empire at Rome, supplanting wall painting.

erected were repeated, essentially unchanged, through the successive plasterings. Since the Villa remained in use at least through the period of Gordian III, as the coins indicate, these plasterings represent a process of upkeep covering a century or more. What, then, shall we say about the repetition of a single decorative form during so long a time in such a locality? Does it suggest either a continuous or an original dependence upon wall decoration as practiced in Italy and the West? And if not, shall we say that in areas more properly Greek than Roman in their cultural orientation the earliest decorative forms, also known in the West, continued in use where they were basic or had their origin?

To attempt to answer fully the questions raised is scarcely necessary or appropriate to the purpose of this report, but one word of comment is definitely in order here. The system of wall decoration with narrow vertical strips between rectangular vertical panels that Beyen has interpreted as marking the transition from the First to the Second Style seems to have existed also apart from the development of the recognized "styles." This is suggested by its continuation into the period of the Second and later styles, as for instance in the background of the initiation scenes of the Hall of the Mysteries in the Villa dei Misteri at Pompeii,[239] and by the ubiquity of its appearance at the beginning of the Roman period at Priene, Athens, Corinth, and Ostia.[240] The latest of the examples at Ostia provides an analogy also to its continuation virtually unchanged down into the third century of our era as in the Villa at Ptolemais.

If, as this body of evidence suggests, the wall

[239] Beyen, *op. cit.* Fig. 21.

[240] See Wiegand and Schrader, *Priene*, p. 318 and Fig. 362; H. A. Thompson, "Excavations in the Athenian Agora," *Hesperia* XVIII (1949) 217 and Pl. 40:2; R. L. Scranton, *Corinth.* I 3. *Monuments in the Lower Agora and North of the Archaic Temple* (Princeton, 1951) p. 114 and Pl. 53; Wirth, *Römische Wandmalerei*, Figs. 29, 61, and 64.

decoration of the Villa represents a *koiné* of usage that stands apart from or, perhaps better, alongside the high-flown "styles" of the Campanian development, then the date at which the system impinges upon the sequence of styles at Pompeii can serve as a provisional *terminus a quo* for its appearance also in Cyrenaica. Judged by the pattern of its wall decoration, the Villa at Ptolemais could therefore have been built as early as the first half of the first century B.C.

That the actual date of the Villa is somewhat later than such a *terminus a quo* is suggested by certain other considerations. The first of these is that as it was executed the decoration of the Villa was intended to impress not so much by reason of its form but rather through the richness and boldness in the rhythmic interchange of its reds, yellows, green, and white. This was probably an expression of the same growing delight in color effects that is attested also in the Villa's repertoire of mosaic design. A second consideration is that in Room 17, the plinth was turned into a field for the application of a simple floral design. This suggests that the tectonic character of the decoration, so clearly indicated in Room 10, was on occasion lost sight of, if not denied.

How far into the period of the Roman Empire one should go in seeking a *terminus ante quem* for the original decoration of the Villa is a question that cannot be answered with assurance. We have but one clue, namely the fact that some rooms saw four successive plasterings and paintings before the building was abandoned after the period of Gordian III. While there is no reliable basis upon which one can calculate the lapse of time between the first and the fourth decoration and between the last redecoration and the abandonment of the building, it is perhaps safe to say that 150–200 years can well have elapsed in the entire interval. A date around the middle of the first century of our era is therefore entirely possible for the first decoration.

MOSAICS AND MARBLE PAVING

By L. Mowry *and* C. H. Kraeling

The preservation of remains of wall decoration in the Villa was in a sense a stroke of good fortune, but the recovery of floor decoration there, in the dwelling attached to the Public Building on the Street of the Monuments, and in the City Bath was well within the range of what could be expected. The floor decoration consists of mosaics and marble inlay (both *opus sectile* and *opus tesselatum*), quite as in the "Palazzo," and provides a welcome addition to what can today be known about such pavements in the domestic establishments of Cyrenaica at Ptolemais and in the House of Jason Magnus at Cyrene.[241] The discussion of the new material consists of a description of its several elements followed by a brief attempt at its interpretation.

MOSAICS IN THE VILLA AND ADJACENT DWELLING

In the Villa mosaic pavements were uncovered in Rooms 1, 5, 6, 11, 12, 14, and 20 and in the north, west, and south porticoes (see Fig. 43 for locations). It is possible that the east portico also was originally paved with mosaics, but it had been so completely looted of its structural elements in antiquity that not a scrap of paving remained. The use of mosaics in the rooms indicated, and only in these, follows an intelligible pattern. That is, the areas of common use—the porticoes around the court, the two formal dining rooms (Rooms 5–6), the rooms of the bath (Rooms 1 and 20), the more formal rooms of the residential suite (Rooms 11, 12, and 14)—were dignified by their use. On the contrary, bedrooms (such as Room 10) and service rooms and areas (such as Rooms 8, 9, 13, 13*a*, 19) were not set out with mosaic pavements

[241] On the mosaics of the "Palazzo," see Pesce, *Il "Palazzo delle Colonne,"* pp. 101–2, Figs. 10, 20, 22, 24, 29–35, 42–44, and 49–52, Pls. XV and XVII. What is said here about floor decoration of the House of Jason Magnus represents merely the results of casual personal observation. The publication of an accurate account of this material can now be expected. The importance of the mosaic pavements of the churches of Cyrenaica is currently being brought to light by the work of Goodchild at Cyrene, Apollonia, and Qasr Lebia (for the last see *ILN*, December 14, 1957).

and, except for Room 10, were not supplied with mural decoration (see p. 226). Hence it is probable that the mosaics uncovered exhibit the full range of the Villa's original use of this type of floor decoration.

Preservation of the mosaics was, of course, by no means perfect. Virtually all the floors had suffered damage, some more than others. Imperfections due to wear appeared throughout. Wholesale destruction was limited to the east portico, by hypothesis, and to the north end of Room 20. In the caldarium of the bath (Room 1) one section of the mosaic had disappeared so completely and the line of breakage coincided so neatly with the borders of that section that in all likelihood an emblema was removed from it before the room was completely buried. In any case, there were no instances of the kind of disfigurement that at other sites reflects the Arab conquest.

There are interesting indications of the limitations under which the mosaicists of the Villa worked and of the procedures they adopted to cope with some of its structural peculiarities. They made no effort to undertake major pictorial compositions nor to develop a great scenic program, contenting themselves instead with geometric patterns and occasional emblemata. This may reflect a tradition to which they adhered, or it may represent the limits of their technical competence. They restricted themselves in the bulk of their geometric work to two colors, blue and white, departing from this standard only in the rooms of the bath (Rooms 1 and 20), in the smaller of the two formal dining rooms (Room 5), and in the multiple guilloche of Room 11, that is, in contexts where emblemata were projected and where special purposes were served. The emblemata, of course, show a much greater variety of colors, but there was no indication that these were separate compositions done elsewhere and then inserted in the paving as units. Nor is it clear that the restraint shown in the use of colors in the geometric work was imposed by strictures of a financial nature. The red and yellow tesserae added to the dominant blue and white in Rooms 1, 5, 11, and 20 are so soft and chalky and hence so poorly preserved that they could not have been used in areas such as the porticoes, where they would have been exposed to much wear. Finally, it is to be noted that in none of the emblemata do we find work of the quality and character of *opus vermiculatum* and that only in the areas immediately surrounding pictorial compositions are the tesserae of the geometric designs smaller than the typical dimension of 7.5 mm. to 1 cm.

As to procedure, it can be seen in the emblema at the entrance to the smaller formal dining room (Room 5) that there were at least two mosaicists at work, presumably a master and an apprentice whose tigress is of inferior workmanship (see p. 250). To cope with the irregularities in the shapes of the individual rooms and the courses of the individual walls, the mosaicists purposely treated as a plain white field a zone around the four sides of the rooms, beginning their design in a square or rectangle especially established by them for their own purposes. In effect, therefore, the designs cut sections from or were inscribed in sections of the floor, being set in carefully constructed frames, as in so much of the oldest mosaic work of the Hellenistic period.[242] In the Villa the frames themselves became standardized. Ranging in width from 12 to 15 cm., they consist typically of three elements—an outer border of three rows of blue tesserae and an inner border of two rows of blue tesserae, the two separated by three, four, five, or even six rows of white tesserae.

GEOMETRIC FORMS AND DESIGNS

The north and west porticoes (and perhaps the east portico) of the peristyle court were by nature suited to and paved with designs in long strips, suggesting the type of carpets known as "runners." The entire course of the north portico was laid out as a single field (15.055 × 1.09 m. including borders) with a pattern in which pairs of octagons separated by a square alternated continuously with pairs of squares separated by an octagon (Fig. 63, Pl. LVII *A*). Both figures were outlined with double rows of blue tesserae. Each octagon had at its center a diamond of blue tesserae inclosing a white crosslet. The octagons had a standard internal diameter of 39 cm.; the squares measured 12.5 cm. inside the borders. The entire field had twenty-seven octagons

[242] See Bulard, "Peintures murales et mosaïques de Délos," *MP* XIV 188–89.

in line and naturally one less square. This was shown by a few blue tesserae set across the portico on a line with the west face of the large square block marking the northeast corner of the stylobate around the court. They fixed the terminus of the design.

In the west portico, with its continuous strip of paving 31.31 m. long, the field was laid out in three different patterns. At the north end for a distance of 7.42 m. the pattern consists of groups of intersecting circles forming trefoils and quatrefoils (Fig. 63, Pl. LVI *B*). Groups of three intersecting circles are set along the sides and at the ends of the design, while groups of four occupy the interior. The outer half of each circle is so inscribed as to form a pelta. Single rows of white tesserae keep the elements of the quatrefoils distinct at their point of junction, and blue diamonds inclosing a single white tessera adorn the spaces between the elements of the design.

The second design of the west portico is broken off at its southern end, so that its length is not actually apparent, but this can be calculated from the location of its northern end. As the second design was arranged by the mosaicists, its northern end was on a line with the right-hand door socket of the northerly of the two doorways giving on the large dining room (Room 6). Since the first design, as a proper carpet feature, covered the section of the portico in front of Room 5, it is logical and in strict conformity with the "runner" idea that the second design should extend the entire length of Room 6, ending at the left-hand door socket of its southerly doorway. This would give it a total length of about 10.50 m. The second design corresponded in elegance to its position in front of the great formal dining room. In contrast to the first it presented within its frame a continuous or overall pattern whose basic elements were rows of four squares that overlapped one another and those of the next row (Fig. 63, Pl. LVI *C*). The overlaps produced rectangles along the sides of the squares, and the interlock between the rows cut small squares from the ends of the rectangles. At the same time the combination of overlap and interlock created squares of intermediate size inside the larger squares, and these were inscribed within circles. The arcs which the circles cut from the rectangles and the outlines of the squares were done in blue. Diamonds of blue tesserae inclosing a white crosslet ornamented the centers of the

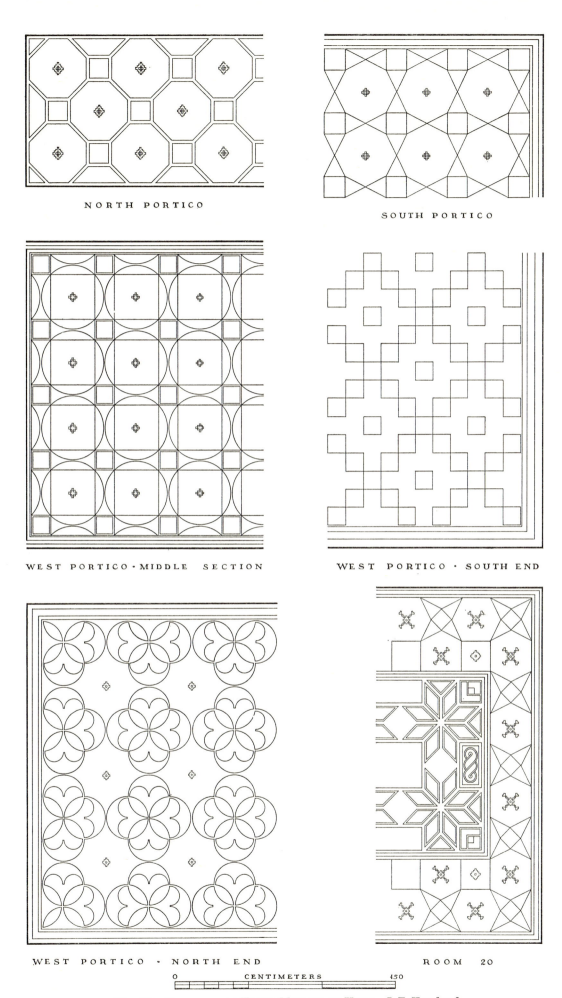

NORTH PORTICO

SOUTH PORTICO

WEST PORTICO·MIDDLE SECTION

WEST PORTICO·SOUTH END

WEST PORTICO·NORTH END

ROOM 20

0   CENTIMETERS   450

Fig. 63.—Patterns of Floor Mosaics in Villa. *J. E. Knudstad*

circles. The large squares were 54 cm. on each side, the intermediate 29 cm., the small 12.5 cm., and the rectangles 12.5 by 29 cm., including in each instance the framing borders. The diameter of the circles was 38–39 cm. There was room for twenty-six rows of squares in the section of the portico in front of Room 6.

respectively (Fig. 64). At the south the steps leading down from the oecus (Room 16) projected about 90 cm. into the area (see Pl. XXIII *B*), and along the north the curve of the colonnade reduced the depth in excess of 2.50 m. Clearly the field required an over-all pattern, and for this a combination of octagons and four-pointed stars was chosen (Fig .63,

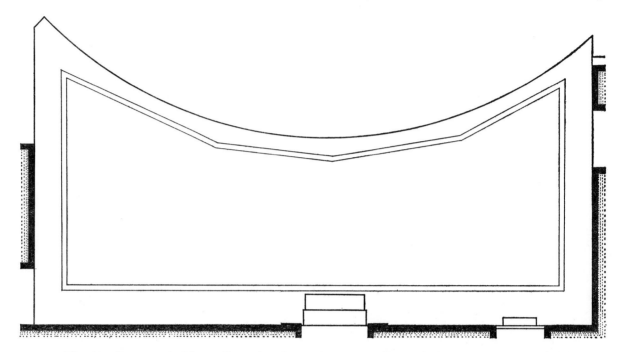

Fig. 64.—Diagram of Mosaic Paving in South Portico of Villa. Scale, 1:100. *J.E.Knudstad*

The third design of the west portico must have run a distance of about 11.50 m., ending some 52 cm. inside the terminal southern wall of the portico. It was an over-all diaper pattern of blue squares (13 cm. to a side) arranged in diagonal rows running from one side of the field to the other (Fig. 63, Pl. LVI *D*). The diagonal rows intersected at every fourth square, and the centers of the fields thus formed were occupied by single unattached blue squares. The design may have recommended itself for use at this point because it permitted ready extension into the short ell created at the southern end of the west portico by its westward extension to the arc of the curved colonnade framing the south portico. The field of the mosaic was here widened to 3.62 m. over an area 2.06 m. long.

In paving the south portico the mosaicists faced a different kind of problem. Here they had to cope with an area that was 15.15 m. long and 7.70 and 7.90 m. deep at its eastern and western ends

Pl. LVII *B*). Set tip to tip the four-pointed stars were done in blue, framing the octagons entirely, and had at the center a white square. The octagons measured about 43 cm. in diameter, the squares 15 cm. on a side. Each octagon had at its center the familiar diamond of blue tesserae inclosing a white crosslet. The curve of the portico must have bothered the workmen, for instead of following it exactly they constructed the northern border of the field by running four straight lines at obtuse angles to one another (see Fig. 64). Thus the width of the blank white area outside the design varied between 50 and 75 cm. at the north. At the south the border ran 90 cm. from the north wall of the oecus to clear the steps, while to the east and west it was set back 75 cm. from the inclosing walls.

The description of the pavements in the residential suite must begin with the small peristyle court (Room 11). Its intrinsic importance and the charm lent by its peristyle marked it as worthy of special attention by the mosaicists. The natural thing was to run a continuous, well bordered pattern around all four sides of the pool in the center. This the mosaicists did in the usual blue, using their openest and lightest pattern, that of simple quatrefoils touching at their tips and set in diagonal lines across the field (see Fig. 68 and Pl. XXIII *D*). A diamond inclosing a single white tessera decorated the field formed by each group of four quatrefoils. Single white tesserae formed the centers from which the petals of the quatrefoils radiated. From tip to tip the quatrefoils measured only 20 cm. Because the builders had laid out the pool and the small peristyle as squares, while the court itself was about a meter shorter from north to south than from east to west (7.20 × 8.15 m.), it was impossible to develop the mosaic design equally on all four sides (Fig. 65). But the blank white areas maintained widths of about 30 cm. next to the stylobate and 40 cm. along the inclosing walls, except in the northeast corner, where the border had to be set out 90 cm. from the inclosing wall to carry around the puteal giving access to the cistern. Along the north and south sides of the court the decorated fields within the borders were only 68 and 64 cm. wide.

The nature of the court apparently suggested to the mosaicists the propriety of introducing emblemata into the over-all design, but the irregular development of the design, the asymmetrical emplacement of the doorways, and the puteal imposed difficulties. Only at the west did they come up with a satisfactory solution, by creating, off-axis but in front of the doorway to Room 12, a separately framed panel filled with a multiple guilloche and inset with an emblema that shows a lion attacking an onager (Pl. LVIII *A*). The bands of the guilloche, five and eight in number, are made up of four strands represented by lines of blue, red, yellow, and white tesserae. By chance this emblema (see p. 249) was relatively well preserved. At the south and east, in sections cut off from the field but not separately framed, larger emblemata (see p. 249) were introduced and set closer to the axes of the pool. These, preserved only in part, represented a gazelle in flight and a garlanded bull respectively (Pl. LVIII *B–C*). Whether there was an emblema on the north side of the court is unknown because here the paving has suffered severe damage. The asymmetrical position of the doorway leading to the west portico would have made appropriate emplacement a problem.

In Room 12, to which the small peristyle court (Room 11) gave access, the mosaics were arranged in an unusual way that suggests both a particular type of use and provision for the emplacement of particular movable furnishings. The blank area adjacent to the inner (west) wall is unusually deep (70 cm.), the whole framed central field being pushed eastward toward the door, as it were (Fig. 66). Even at the north and south the field begins some 57 cm. from the walls, which is slightly more than normal, but at the east the distance is only 25 cm., which is unusual. Moreover, the field

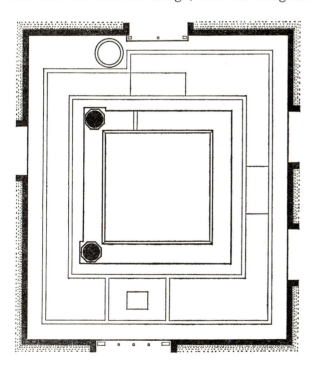

Fig. 65.—Diagram of Mosaic Paving in Room 11 of Villa. Scale, 1:100. *J. E. Knudstad*

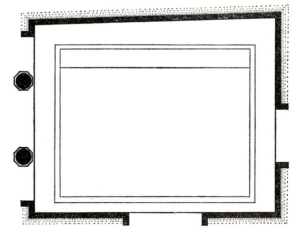

Fig. 66.—Diagram of Mosaic Paving in Room 12 of Villa. Scale, 1:100. *J. E. Knudstad*

inclosed by the typical border was divided into two unequal parts. The larger part, a rectangle 5.16 by 3.34 m., was set out with an over-all diaper pattern composed of diagonal rows of blue squares intersecting at every fourth square (see Fig. 68). The centers of the fields formed by the diagonals were occupied by single unattached squares. The same pattern was used at the south end of the west portico, but in Room 12 the squares are only 5 cm. on a side and create a much finer impression. The smaller part of the field, a strip 5.16 m. long but only 49 cm. wide, was set out with octagons framed by portions of blue four-pointed stars, each star inscribed with a white square (Pl. LIX D). The octagons measured about 35 cm. in diameter; the individual triangles were about 12.5 cm. high and had as their bases the squares, which measured about 12 cm. on a side. There were fourteen octagons in the series. This pattern is familar from the south portico, but in Room 12 the normal diamond was not used in the centers of the octagons.

The unusual emplacement and arrangement of the mosaic design in Room 12 calls for an explanation. We suggest that the extra wide blank area along the west wall was occupied by a low bench or a long bolster and that the strip in front of it, containing the octagons, was intended to set off the bench or bolster and perhaps also to provide a setting for small tables and cushions. The room is on this account to be regarded more properly as the diwan rather than the oecus of the suite, thus representing an Oriental installation in a Mediterranean establishment, but as such not inappropriate to the region to which Cyrenaica belongs.

The only other chamber of the residential suite paved with mosaics was Room 14. In this room, with its elegant colonnaded entrance, we have the first of three of the Villa's chambers in which the arrangement of the mosaic paving is similar in spite of differences in the designs. The other two are Rooms 5 and 6, opening directly off the west portico. In all three the principle of organization involves rectangular fields contained one within another, but the sides are not equidistant from one another as they would be if the rectangles were organized about a point in the center of the room. Instead, either the common base line is the entrance wall of the room or the rectangles have one side closer to the entrance wall than to the other three walls (see Figs. 67, 69, 70). This arrangement has

the effect of giving the room a focal area off its geometric center and of creating sigma-shaped fields one inside another along the three inner walls. The focal area, in the innermost rectangle and nearest to the entrance wall, is given a specially brilliant decorative treatment, while the fields of the outer rectangles are developed with simpler geometric designs of different kinds. The arrangement is a variant of the combination of T-form and sigmate paving that is commonly found in triclinia and must be interpreted as such.[243]

Room 14, nicely proportioned (ca. 4.88 × ca. 4.68 m.), well sheltered, and open along its entire north side to the diwan (Room 12) by virtue of its ornate colonnaded entrance (see p. 129 and Fig. 48), was the dining room of the residential suite. In the paving a zone of white tesserae ran around all three inner walls, 69 cm. wide at the south, about 63 cm. at the east, and about 60 cm. at the west (Fig. 67).

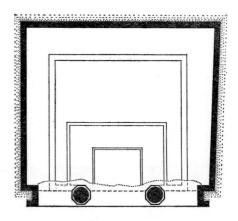

Fig. 67.—DIAGRAM OF MOSAIC PAVING IN ROOM 14 OF VILLA. Scale, 1:100.
J.E.Knudstad

This outer zone provided the emplacement for the couches of the triclinium. It ended against a typical border of blue and white lines of tesserae, which seems to have run all the way to the stylobate of the colonnade on the north side of the room, returning against the column bases. The field was set out with the design of intersecting circles forming quatrefoils and trefoils with the outer half of each circle so inscribed as to form a pelta, the design used at the north end of the west portico (see Pl. LVI B). From east to

[243] At Ptolemais the more typical combination is illustrated in Rooms 10 and 11 of the "Palazzo"; see Pesce, Il "Palazzo delle Colonne," Pl. XV.

ROOM 5   ROOM 6

0   CENTIMETERS   300

ROOM 11

ROOM 12

ROOM 14   ROOM A

0   CENTIMETERS   150

Fig. 68.—Patterns of Floor Mosaics in Villa and Room A of Adjoining Dwelling. *J. E. Knudstad*

west the field (*ca.* 3.34 m.) contained one trefoil, five quatrefoils, and one half-circle. Along the east side of the field there were first one and a half circles at the southeast corner, then two trefoils followed by three pairs of two circles, and at the end probably a half-circle. Adding the 1 cm. between circles we would get a north-south dimension of 3.28 m., which, with the 15 cm. required for the return of the border, would carry the design to the diagonal faces of the octagonal bases at the north side of the room. The return of the inner edge of the border would in this event be in line with the inner, southern faces of the octagonal bases, where the end of a row of blue tesserae has by good fortune been preserved, verifying the suggested arrangement.

Pl. LIX *C*). The meander inclosed on three sides the focal area developed as an emblema and set directly inside the entrance to the room. With its frame of one row of blue tesserae this measured about 126 by 63 cm. The emblema (see p. 250) showed two leopards drinking from a krater (Pl. LIX *C*). It must have been set directly against the return of at least the outer element of the outer border and was approximately on the axis of the arched central element of the colonnaded entrance.

The public banquet hall, Room 6, was the largest chamber in the entire Villa. Its paving was set out in the same fashion as that of Room 14, the sigma-shaped fields running along the three inner sides of the room and framing a focal area paved with *opus sectile* (see pp. 255–56). In a pavement of the

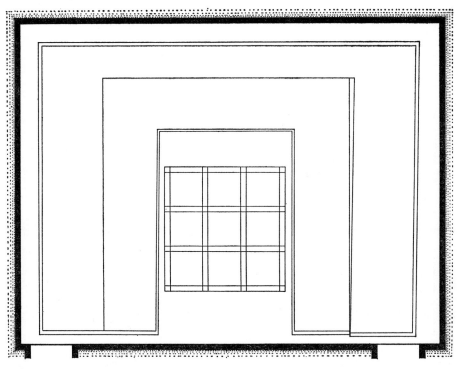

Fig. 69.—Diagram of Mosaic Paving and *Opus Sectile* in Room 6 of Villa.
Scale, 1:100. *J.E.Knudstad*

Inset into the field at the north was a smaller rectangle framed by a separate border (9.5 cm. wide) that consisted of two and three rows of blue tesserae with three rows of white tesserae between them. It measured 2.46 m. from east to west and about 1.53 m. from north to south, beginning at the inner faces of the column bases. Three sides of this area were developed with a meander pattern in which triple lines of blue tesserae traced an intricate course around dotted blue boxes (Fig. 68,

size required here any small inaccuracies in the development of the designs, such as could readily be taken up in narrower confines, would tend to become increasingly noticeable in their effects. The existence of asymmetrical features in the paving of Room 6 is actually quite noticeable. The workmen first set out a border of the usual type, framing a field about 10.20 m. long and 7.50 deep (Fig. 69). Along the entrance wall the border was supposed to run in a straight line some 27 cm.

inside the wall, but because of inequalities in the development of the design along the northern side of the field its return at the northeast corner was only 20 cm. from the wall, causing a very noticeable jog that was left uncorrected. Along the south, west, and north walls the blank white area outside the border varies in width from 53 to 63 cm., taking up the irregularities in the course of the inclosing walls. The large rectangular field thus formed was inscribed with a smaller one measuring 6.65 m. from north to south and 6.00–6.15 m. from east to west. A double row of blue tesserae formed the inner edge of the design in the outer field and at the same time framed the second field. But infelicity in the development of the design in the outer field at its northwest corner required the inset of a wedge-shaped strip of tesserae between the inner and the outer fields that tapered from a width of 12 cm. at the west to 4 cm. at the east. The inner field was separated by a solid border (8 cm. wide) of blue tesserae from the focal area set out with *opus sectile*.

The outer field was set out with the simple design of octagons and squares familiar from the north portico. Each octagon was decorated in the center with a diamond composed of alternate blue and white tesserae. The octagons measure 40–42 cm. in diameter, the squares 10–12 cm. on a side, not counting outlines. All outlines consist of double rows of blue tesserae. For the inner field the mosaicists used a design composed of hexagons framed by opposing squares and opposing four-pointed stars (Fig. 68, Pl. LIX A). The rendering of the points of the stars in outline instead of in solid blue lightens the pattern effectively. The pattern, with its several elements simply outlined by double lines of blue tesserae, can also be interpreted as large interlocking polyhedrons separated by squares. The hexagons and squares are ornamented at their centers by diamonds composed of alternate blue and white tesserae. The hexagons measure about 52 cm. in diameter and the squares 22–24 cm. across. Including their outlines the 16-sided polyhedrons measure about 1.35 m.

The organization of the paving in Room 6 reflects the arrangement of the movable furnishings and the circulation. The outer of the two sigma-shaped fields provided for the emplacement of the couches on which the diners reclined. The blank strip between this field and the walls formed a passageway (53–63 cm. wide) that allowed access to the couches and from the couches to the doors. From the doors there was also access to the inner of the two sigma-shaped fields which permitted the servants to offer the viands to the guests. The focal area, paved with *opus sectile*, must have served as a locus either for the display of the viands or for the performances of the entertainers, or for both in succession.

Room 5, the smaller of the two public dining rooms, was the more exquisite in its appointments to judge by its mosaics. Its wide entrance, with a total opening of 3.90 m., suggests that it was intended for summer use (see Plan XII and p. 133). Here, as in Room 14, where because of the smaller number of guests to be accomodated circulation was not a problem, the couches were evidently set directly against the walls. Their location is indicated by a zone of plain white mosaic paving about 95 cm. wide around three sides of the room.[244] On the fourth side, in front of the step leading down to the room from the west portico, the white zone is only 10 cm. wide. The area surrounded by this zone was laid out as a rectangular field (4.66 × 6.85 m.) by a typical border 18 cm. wide (Fig. 70). The field was decorated with simple blue quatrefoils set tip to tip, as in the small peristyle court (Room 11). Diamonds of blue tesserae containing single white tesserae ornamented the centers of the spaces marked out by the design. Terminated toward the interior by a border that consisted merely of a double line of blue tesserae and that at the north was carried around a cistern head, this field contained within it, asymmetrically placed, a smaller rectangular field (4.03 × 3.28 m.). If the outer field, providing the area within which those who served the viands moved, was on this account decorated with a simple pattern, the inner field was especially richly adorned in keeping with the special purposes that it served. Together with this richer development went the use of smaller tesserae (*ca.* 5–7.5 mm.) and better worksmanship.

The inner field was inclosed by a double border, rows of blue triangles with two segmentary sides set tip to base for the outer border and a single guilloche whose bands were made up of successive rows of blue, red, yellow, white, and blue tesserae

[244] At the west the white zone was reduced to 78–87 cm. by the application to the wall of a heavy layer of mortar. This represents the period when the shops encroached on the Villa (see p. 133). The mosaics continue underneath it at floor level.

for the inner border. The double border has outside it three lines of white tesserae, which taken together with the two lines of blue tesserae terminating the outer field give an outer frame 11 cm. wide. The guilloche was carried not only around the field as a whole but across it near its east end, thus setting off a rectangular panel (70 cm. × 2.71 m.) directly inside the doorway. This panel was set out with an emblema showing two tigresses approaching a krater (see p. 250 and Pl. LX *A*), the design used also at the entrance to the dining room of the residential suite (Room 14) but here adapted to a long narrow field. The emblema in Room 5 was so placed as to face the guests as they entered the chamber.

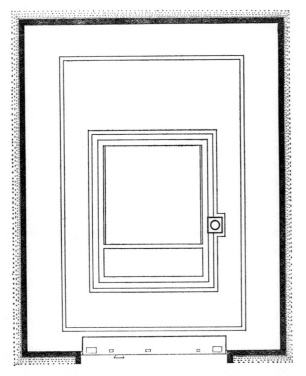

Fig. 70.—Diagram of Mosaic Paving in Room 5 of Villa. Scale, 1:100. *J. E. Knudstad*

The larger of the two rectangles inclosed by the guilloche was set off and reduced to a square 2.65 m. on each side by the interposition of lines of white tesserae, two at the east and west and five at the north and south. This field was so developed that at its precise center there was an eight-pointed star composed of eight separately defined lozenges (Fig. 68, Pl. LX *A*). Half-stars were set against the middle of each side of the field and quarter-stars into the corners. Squares were introduced between the projecting points of the stars, and these, because of the arrangement of the stars, inclosed and thus defined four octagonal areas symmetrically placed on the diagonals of the field. It required only the introduction of four lozenges set transversely into the heart of the field and of pairs of isosceles triangles along each side to develop the whole combination of stars, half- and quarter-stars, squares, lozenges, and triangles into an elaborate over-all design. Stars, lozenges, squares, and triangles were all inscribed inside their blue outline with successive rows of white, red, and yellow tesserae and were reduced thereby to blue cores. The blue cores of the squares provided a setting for Solomon's knots, whose bands repeated the color sequence of the guilloche. The symmetrically placed octagons created by the squares were reduced to circles by a filling of white tesserae and inscribed with the guilloche of the border. The medallions thus created contain emblemata representing the Four Seasons (see Pl. LXI and pp. 250–51). Winter and Spring, occupying the northeast and the southeast position respectively, face Summer and Fall, occupying the northwest and southwest positions. Each emblema, set in its own border consisting of a single line of blue tesserae, has a diameter of 42 cm. The square field in the middle of the decorative paving thus provides the focal point of the entire design.

Leaving these dining rooms with their own particular type of appointments, we come next to two other chambers that served special purposes, those connected with the private bath on the north side of the Villa. Of these the more important is Room 1, which formed the caldarium (see Fig. 43). Here the paving was in a ruinous condition due to the breakage of the tile piers supporting the floor of the *suspensura*. It was developed in two parts, namely the large rectangular section toward the east and the smaller apsidal extension toward the west (Fig. 71). The latter was inscribed with a border of three lines of blue tesserae running uniformly about the apse 53 cm. from the face of its curving wall. It was set out with the simple quatrefoil design of the open type, with diamonds decorating the fields (see Fig. 68), already familiar from the small peristyle court (Room 11) and the smaller public dining room (Room 5). This design ended on the line of the piers that framed the outer ends of the apse and abutted the border (15 cm. wide) that ran around the large rectangular section of the room. The border consisted of three and two rows of blue tesserae inclosing five lines of white. It ran 40–50 cm. from the faces of the walls to the north, east, and south, continuing to the west faces of the piers terminating the apse. To pass the piers it was set back about

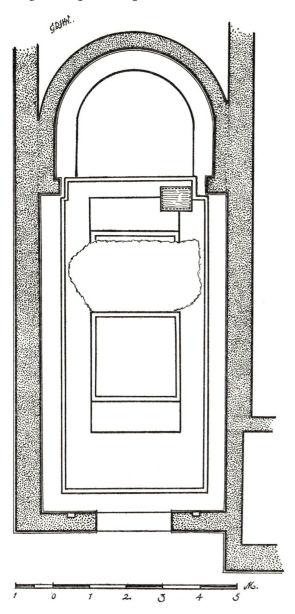

Fig. 71.—DIAGRAM OF MOSAIC PAVING IN ROOM 1 OF VILLA. *G. R. H. Wright*

5 cm. from the south pier and about 17 cm. from the north pier. The field inside this border was developed with an over-all design of intersecting circles (each *ca.* 30 cm. in diameter) forming interlocking quatrefoils (Pl. LVII *C*), the most compact and continuous of the several patterns involving quatrefoils. The field was only about 42 cm. wide

at the west but widened to 75 cm. at the north and south and 1.50 m. at the east. Within this field an area about 6.20 m. long and about 2.45 m. wide was set off by a double row of blue tesserae. At the east and west it contained rectangular terminal sections (2.45 m. × *ca.* 85 cm.) given over entirely to parallel rows of tesserae forming a herringbone design in black, blue, red, yellow, and white, which might be thought to represent the fringe of a carpet. At the northwest corner the field and its inset were interrupted by a cistern head. A single line of blue tesserae was run around this area (*ca.* 62 × 85 cm.), containing no doubt a squared slab in which a circular cover was seated. The remainder of the area was developed into two adjacent fields with black-and white crowstep borders. For the herringbone design and the crowstep borders smaller tesserae were used, indicating that the two central fields once contained emblemata. In the area of the smaller central field, to the west, the pavement was entirely ruinous. In the area of the larger central field, to the east, the bedding of the mosaic was found intact because it formed the top of a solid masonry pier in the middle of the *suspensura*. Here a few scant remains of lines of blue and white tesserae came to light, belonging perhaps to a border, but otherwise the bedding was bare of all traces of its mosaic coverage, suggesting that at least the emblema in this field had been removed or destroyed before the room was abandoned.

The last of the mosaic-paved rooms of the Villa is Room 20. The fact that it was adjacent to the caldarium (see Fig. 43) and the fact that as in the caldarium the central area of its mosaic design contained tesserae of more than two colors and of the smaller size suggest that it was part of the bath and that it was decorated with emblemata. It served perhaps for the emplacement of movable tubs used for cold baths (see p. 134). Of the mosaic paving only about 1.30 m. of its southern end, containing a design 2.34 m. wide, was preserved (Pl. LVII *D*). This sufficed, however, to reveal the nature of the design. Inside a typical border of lines of blue and white tesserae there was developed an outer rectangular field devoted to hexagons separated by four-pointed stars (see Fig. 63). The hexagons (32 cm. in diameter) were ornamented in the middle with blue diamonds framing a single white tessera and supplemented by sprigs projecting from the center of each face. The stars were composed of blue tesserae and contained at their centers white squares. Along the east and west sides of the design the outer field was widened to 49 cm. by the introduction of blue squares between the tips of the four-pointed stars and the frame of the inner field. These were inscribed with white diamonds inclosing a single white tessera.

The outer field was terminated by a somewhat narrower border of rows of blue and white tesserae which framed an inner field 1.10 m. wide and of indeterminate length. The design of the inner field, constructed with smaller tesserae (5–7.5 mm.), consisted of eight-pointed stars arranged in pairs down the length of the field (see Fig. 63). Between the projecting points of the stars there were thus formed along the width of the field squares, triangles, and a rectangle. Lengthways of the field the same geometric forms appeared, except that the number of rectangles and triangles was increased in proportion to the number of repetitions of the star design. On the axes of the field diamonds filled the intervals between stars at points of contact. Each four stars created in a line along the center of the field a succession of squares 30 cm. on a side. Triangles, rectangles, and the lozenges of which the stars were composed were inscribed inside their blue outlines with successive rows of white and red tesserae, being reduced thereby to blue cores. The blue cores of the rectangles provided a setting for three loops of a red, white, and blue guilloche that returned upon itself. The squares in the corners of the design were done in red and were inset with still smaller red squares, both being outlined in white. Toward the interior the smaller red squares contained groups of blue tesserae forming yet smaller squares. How the diamonds set between the stars were treated is not known. Nor is the treatment of the squares along the center of the field known, but the size of the tesserae implies that they were filled with emblemata.

Clearances made south of Rooms 15, 13, and 13a of the Villa uncovered portions of two rooms of an adjoining house (see Fig. 50 and p. 131), each with remains of mosaic paving. In Room *A* the design was executed in blue and white tesserae of the larger size and comprised two elements (Fig. 68, Pl. LX *B*). The first was a blue lozenge with circular and lanceolate insets in white, the circle being inscribed with a blue diamond containing a single white tessera. Adjacent to the lozenge were the remains of a rectangular field (1.00 × 1.93 m.)

that contained two eight-pointed stars set lengthwise of the field. The design was basically that of Room 20 of the Villa, but in Room *A* there was a single line of eight-pointed stars running down the center of the panel rather than two lines set side by side. Since the stars did not fill the width of the field completely, quarter- and half-sections of adjoining stars were included in the corners and along the sides at appropriate intervals down the length of the field. Squares ornamented with blue diamonds set around single white tesserae filled the intervals between stars at points of contact. Along the sides and at the ends of the field the triangular areas not included in the star pattern were adorned with blue peltae. A regular development of the design requires at the center of the field a large diamond interposed between the two stars, but how it may have been treated is unknown. The design was executed in the simplest manner by the use of double lines of blue tesserae inside a simple border of three lines.

In Room *B* a section of mosaic paving (dimly visible in Pl. XXIV *B*) came to light east of the column that was found standing within it. The design of intersecting circles forming interlocking quatrefoils is identical in character to the one used in the outer field in the main part of the caldarium (Room 1) of the Villa (see Pl. LVII *C*).

The paving of the Villa included originally about fourteen or fifteen emblemata, five of which are preserved in their entirety and four partially. No one of the scenes approaches the refinement of *opus vermiculatum*, but special care was evidently given to their production. The smaller tesserae (5–7.5 mm.) were used, and these were cut into the unusual shapes required for the composition and shading of the figures represented. To the four colors (blue, white, red, and yellow) used in preparing the settings for the emblemata others were added in the pictures themselves. These included brown, tan, a light gray, pink, terracotta red, rose red, lavender, a deep purple, and a bright green. The subject matter of the known compositions is typical and traditional and provides a natural basis for their description under three heads.

The first group, comprising the three emblemata of Room 11, deals with animals that have hoofs (see p. 260). The first of this series, so placed that it faced those entering the small peristyle court from the east, is only partially preserved. In what we have of its right half a bull is represented (Pl. LVIII C).[245] His body is seen from the side, and the off legs are shown bearing his weight as he moves toward the left, that is, toward the center of the composition. The mass of his body is rendered in terra-cotta red with lighter high lights at the flanks, thighs, and shoulder. All parts that are supposed to be in shadow, namely the belly, the inner edges of the near legs, and both sides of the off hind leg, are outlined in black. Elsewhere the outlining is in rose red. Both hind legs are firmly planted on the ground, giving an awkward lag to the near hind leg and overextending the body lengthwise.[246] From the position of the bull's right horn it would seem that his head is turned to a frontal position. Around his body is a rose-red flower garland, suggesting that he appears here in a ceremonial context, prepared perhaps for sacrifice. Above him, filling the background of the panel, is a threefold flower garland. The garlands apparently represent the usual mesh bags filled with flower petals and are rendered in red, blue, and yellow (beginning at top). They are high-lighted with black or with complementary colors and end in the usual tie-strings attached, in this instance, to the border of the composition.[247] Since the length of the emblema probably matched the width (1.58 m.) of the doorway before which it was placed, the composition must have included other elements at the left, perhaps an animal moving toward the right and at the center a sacrificial altar.

Of the emblema on the south side of Room 11 parts of the border are preserved at each end, so that we know it was 1.25 m. long, but only the lower left corner of the field gives indications of its subject (Pl. LVIII B). Here we see short sections of the thin forelegs of an animal shown in the position typical of the "flying gallop." The legs are outlined in rose red, but the body color was terra cotta. The feet end in cloven hoofs, suggesting that

the animal was a gazelle. A lacuna high above the legs, having the shape of a curving pointed horn, gives weight to this suggestion. Since the point of the horn faces forward, we must assume that the animal had its head turned in flight and was looking backward, presumably at a carnivore attacking it from behind.

The emblema at the west side of Room 11, so placed that it faced those reclining in the diwan, is preserved in its entirety. It represents an onager attacked by a lion (Pl. LVIII A). The onager is not in flight but has been brought to earth. Its hind parts are seen in a three-quarter perspective, with the legs doubled under, while the fore part of the body is raised and seen in profile. The forelegs are extended and bent at the joints as the animal struggles to regain its feet and escape from its attacker. The lion is seen in profile crouching on its haunches, its tail firmly curved upward, its forepaws encircling the onager's chest, its jaws clamped on the victim's neck. While the lion's head is thus inclined downward, that of the onager is extended upward in the agony of the struggle, providing an excellent contrast. Both animals are skillfully delineated. The gray tesserae that give the basic color to the onager's body are carefully set in curving lines at the rear to emphasize the roundness of the hind quarters. Blue high lights outline the jaw, the nose, and the eye sockets and follow the course of the muscles down the extended neck. The animal is completely outlined in black. Carefully modeled also is the tawny body of the lion, where the lines of yellow tesserae emphasize the curvature of haunches and body and where high lights are added in a lighter color to indicate the under parts of the belly and to help mold the face. The outlines of the body are in rose red save for the underside of the tail and the neck, where black is used. Stripes of red, yellow, and black interchange to develop the bristling mane. The eye is dotted with white, and the claws are rose red. Red seems to drip from the area where the jaws of the lion are imbedded in the flesh of the onager.

To quite another category belong the emblemata placed at the entrances to two of the dining rooms, Rooms 14 and 5. Both are variations of the same subject, a subject chosen with particular reference to the rooms they embellished (see p. 261). In each case the emblema represents felines drinking from a wine-filled krater. The version in Room 14 is the more compact and stylized and at the same time

---

[245] The section preserved is only *ca.* 40 cm. long at the bottom and as much as 80 cm. at the top. The probable total length is 1.58 m.

[246] The photograph (Pl. LVIII C) does not adequately show that the near hind leg is planted on the ground because the upper part of the undulating ground line is executed with light gray tesserae.

[247] The light yellow color of the lowest garland does not register effectively on the photograph.

the more balanced (Pl. LIX C). Unfortunately the upper part of the composition including the heads of the animals is lost. The picture here was so placed as to be seen by those reclining within the room. In the center of the field stands a tall gray double-handled krater, its outlines and the fluting of its body done in black. It has a relatively small base with a double-knobbed stem. The top is represented as being viewed from a high perspective so that the red wine in its interior can be seen. At either side leopards stand on their hind legs in the heraldic position, their forepaws resting on the side and the rim of the vessel respectively, their heads inclined forward and downward toward the interior of the vessel. Their tails are drawn in and curled around their near hind legs. The tail of the animal at the left is outlined in black and is wrapped around the leg from the outside in, rather than from the inside out as at the right. The upper parts of the bodies and forelegs are outlined in black, as are the rear edges of the off hind legs. The lines of tesserae forming the bodies follow the natural contours of the body and are graded from deep red along the crown of the back to yellow and white toward the underside. Black and red tesserae distributed in rows represent the spots of the pelt. The krater and the animals stand on an undulating gray base line. From behind them slightly curving stems in gray and black mount firmly toward the top of the composition. They should be the stems of vines whose leaves and grape clusters filled the field at the right and left of the animals' heads.

In Room 5, where the emblema was so placed as to be seen by those entering the room, the composition takes on quite a different character (Pl. LX A). Here it has lost its vertical symmetry and is visibly extended to fill the long narrow panel prepared for it. There are inequalities in the workmanship between the left and the right parts of the composition. In the center there stands again the gray krater outlined in black. Its base is rather awkwardly triangular and the knob between it and the body looks more like a hinge than an ornament. The body is appropriately fluted but does not lead over so symmetrically into the neck as in the example in Room 14, and on the neck short projections replace the long carefully stylized handles. The animals approaching from either side are tigresses. The one on the left has three legs firmly set on the ground and reaches forward toward the krater with her near front paw.

Both her near hind leg and her tail are visibly extended to fill the panel. The tigress at the right has both hind legs on the ground and reaches toward the krater with both front paws, but these fall just short of finding support on the krater's rim. Her neck is particularly elongated to bring her extended tongue within drinking distance, and her tail is flung upward, leaving a good portion of the field blank at the right. In the rendering of the two animals there are noticeable differences. At the left alternate curving lines of rose red, black, and white are used to produce a regular design representing the tigress' stripes, and a careful organization of tesserae of the same colors helps to mold the contours of the head. At the right there is a visible lack of order in the arrangement, so that no symmetrical pattern emerges, and on the head modeling is replaced by high-lighting with random black tesserae. Krater and animals are again placed on a gray ground line, which at the left forms a continuous strip. At the right, however, the strip is found only under the tigress' rear paws, and between it and the krater two simple long-leaved plants are represented in gray. The vines were necessarily omitted.

The remaining four emblemata of the Villa are those representing the Four Seasons, set into the intricate geometric design in the center of Room 5 (Pl. LX A). All are so set as to face the middle of the field, with the heads of the figures slightly turned toward anyone viewing them from that position. The series begins with Winter in the northeast corner. Spring follows in the southeast corner, Summer in the northwest, and Fall in the southwest. Unfortunately Winter is severely damaged (Pl. LXI A). We see only the chest, neck, and chin of a figure heavily wrapped in a gray cloak with black fold lines. The cloak was evidently draped over the figure's head.

Spring (Pl. LXI B) holds in her right hand a shepherd's crook, the upper part of which reaches into the white field of the emblema. Over her left shoulder are draped what appear to be two garments, a gray cloak outlined in blue and over it something yellow dotted with red and black which we suggest is an animal pelt. Neck and shoulders are bare and done in tan with patches of a lighter grayish flesh tone that represents high lights. At the right the neck is done in solid lavender to indicate the shadow cast by the head. The chin is damaged, but the face seems to have been pointed rather than roundish. The nose is angular and outlined on the right in lavender. The tan that normally appears in the rendering of skin was sparingly used on the right side of the face from ear level upward and across the forehead. Elsewhere the lighter gray predominates. The eye sockets are deepened by the use of brown and end above in black eyebrows and eyelash lines. Eyeballs are white and pupils black. The mouth is represented by two lines of rose-red tesserae separated by a thin line of black. The hair is black highlighted in gray, providing a strong contrast to the aureole of red flowers with bright green leaves that surrounds the face.

Summer (Pl. LXI *C*) has a fuller face and seems to be nude. She holds in her right hand a sickle, the curving upper end of which, done in a single line of blue tesserae, is visible at her right shoulder. She also holds, perhaps in her left hand, a sheaf of ears of grain. These are rendered by diagonally projecting lines of red and yellow and come up across her chest in a line from left to right. Identical ears of grain project from and form a crown around her hair, which comes down to her shoulders and is done in blue and gray. Against the dark background of the hair the face is of a flesh tan with lines of terra-cotta red along the left to give outline to the cheek. The same red darkens the eye sockets, providing the setting for the black eyebrow and eyelash lines, the white eyeballs, and the black pupils. The right side of the face from the ear down has a shadow line in lavender which joins with a shadow mass on the right side of the neck. The left side of the neck and the chest are done in tan and high-lighted in a lighter flesh tone. The neck is inclined somewhat to the right, and the face is turned slightly to the left.

Fall (Pl. LXI *D*) has a blue and red garment draped over her left shoulder and, more importantly, a succession of red grape clusters high-lighted in gray and alternating with green vine leaves coming up across her breast. Similar clusters and leaves project from her hair at the top of her head to the right and left. The hair, of terra-cotta red with black shadows, falls from the top of the head toward the shoulders, where it is gathered in heavy rolls. The face is round and full and the neck relatively solid. The tesserae showing the lighter gray flesh tones and those in tan along the sides of the cheeks and on the forehead are set in lines following the contours of the face. Eyebrows

and eyelids are set out in black as usual, with the eyeballs in white and the pupils in black. The nose is prominent and outlined in lavender at the right. On the neck the lavender shadow area is at the left because of the way the head is turned. Elsewhere the neck, the shoulders, and the chest are done in tan with high lights in gray. The Four Seasons, represented here with such force and delight in vivid color, are discussed in their historical perspective below (pp. 261–63).

MOSAICS IN THE PUBLIC BUILDING

As reported above (pp. 140–60), the entire site of the Public Building had been reworked at various times and certain of the rooms had undergone a complete change of function. At levels assignable to the earliest phase of the structural development three rooms contained remains of mosaic paving, namely Rooms 15, 17, and 30. Rooms 15 and 17 belonged to the area in which bathing facilities were provided for the Public Building, while Room 30 was part of the attached dwelling (see Fig. 51). All three mosaic pavings were geometric in character, matching closely those of the Villa in the size and color of their tesserae, in the delineation of the fields by linear borders, and in the nature of the designs used.

The mosaic which came to light in the northwest and southeast corners of Room 15 was found blackened by fire and covered with ashes. The design (Fig. 72) consisted of simple blue quatrefoils set tip to tip. The same design was used in Rooms 11, 5, and 1 of the Villa. Here again diamonds of blue tesserae framing a single white tessera ornamented the centers of the spaces marked out by the design. The quatrefoils measured 37 cm. from tip to tip. The field was bordered by three lines of blue tesserae, four lines of white, and two lines of blue.

The mosaic found in Room 17 had the same design as that used in Room 6 (outer field) and the north portico of the Villa (see Pl. LVII *A*), consisting of alternate octagons and squares outlined in blue, but in this instance their centers were not ornamented with small diamonds (see Fig. 72). The octagons measured 45 cm. in diameter and the squares 15 cm. on a side. The fact that the field was framed with the same double line of blue tesserae by means of which in the north portico of the Villa the design was adapted to its location and made into a "runner" is one of our reasons for suggesting that Room 17 was a portico in the earliest phase of the Public Building (see p. 156 and Fig. 52).

MOSAICS IN THE CITY BATH

Marble served as paving for most of the City Bath, but traces of mosaic work came to light at one point, namely in the southwest corner of the frigidarium (Room 6). The mosaic was badly dam-

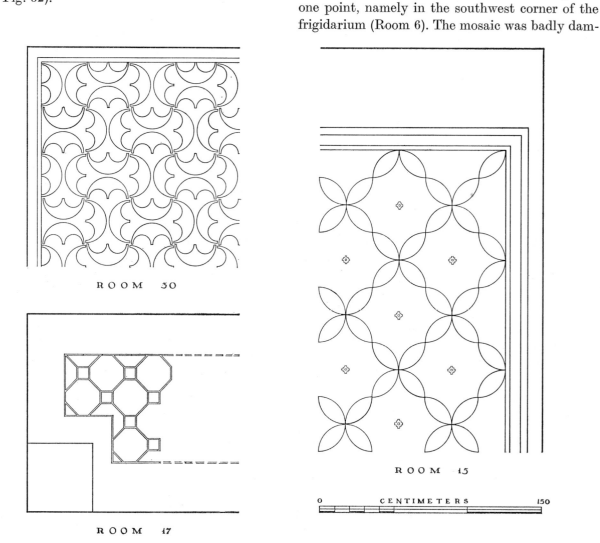

ROOM 30

ROOM 17

ROOM 15

0   CENTIMETERS   150

Fig. 72.—PATTERNS OF FLOOR MOSAICS IN PUBLIC BUILDING. *G. R. H. Wright*

In Room 30 a small section of mosaic paving remained in the southeast corner. The design was developed with the pelta, which was used occasionally in the "Palazzo"[248] and appears also in Room *A* of the residence adjoining the Villa (see Pl. LX *B*). Here, however, the peltae are arranged in interlocking groups of four radiating from and set symmetrically around a focal point (Fig. 72, Pl. LX *C*). They were constructed of blue tesserae like those that formed the simple linear border of the field.

[248] See Pesce, *Il "Palazzo delle Colonne,"* Figs. 20 and 29.

aged, and the few fragments surviving came to light under a deposit of hardened lime that had literally to be chipped away to reveal them.[249] It has been suggested above that the mosaic paved the bottom of an L-shaped plunge inclosed with marble slabs and contrived under the shelter of the porticoes (see p. 166). The arrangement for the anchoring of the slabs indicates that they were part of the original construction and hence a product of the period of Arcadius and Honorius.

[249] The lime was apparently produced in the furnace of the adjacent Room 14 (see Fig. 56), which originally served to heat the caldarium (Room 13).

What can be known about the design of the mosaic and about the nature and arrangement of its elements is little indeed. There was a wide outer border and an inner field. The border contained a loose vine scroll of no great elegance or complexity. Inside the field were depicted animals appropriate to an aquatic setting (Fig. 73). They included fish, dolphins, and at least one water fowl. In accordance with a tradition known to us from earlier and later examples and serving to emphasize the teeming

MARBLE PAVING

Marble was used for paving in all three of the buildings excavated by the Oriental Institute expedition and probably most copiously in the City Bath. The bath had, of course, been thoroughly looted before it was entirely abandoned, and marble paving slabs were among the things that could most readily be moved and put to use. The fact that heavy deposits of powdered lime were

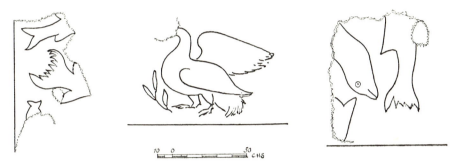

Fig. 73.—FIGURES OF FLOOR MOSAICS IN FRIGIDARIUM OF CITY BATH. *G. R. H. Wright*

complexity of marine life, the animals were distributed at random in the field as their shapes permitted.[250] Blue and orange tesserae predominated in the rendering of the animal forms, no one of which was completely preserved. The fish were remarkable for the contortion of their bodies and for the complexity of their tails, preserving in this regard and even at this late date a reminiscence of the fish-tailed monsters that first appeared in ancient art in the Hellenistic period.[251] The large full-breasted water fowl, seated on a branch, belongs, of course, to a quite different artistic tradition—that of the Nilotic landscape that remained a favorite down through late Byzantine times.[252] We have, then, in the mosaic in the City Bath a combination of pictorial clichés and traditions used in some confusion to give the semblance of elegance to a simple shallow pool.

found in Rooms 6, 7, and 14, (see Fig. 56), coming no doubt from the reuse of the furnace in Room 14 as a limekiln, suggests the ultimate fate of most of the paving. The quantity of marble paving actually found in the structure is therefore not to be taken as the measure of its use in the building. Quite on the contrary, the function of such rooms as the tepidarium (Room 9), the caldarium (Room 13), and the anterooms (Rooms 7–8) of the heated sections of the bath implies that they were originally paved with marble slabs just because no trace of any paving of any kind was found in them, except in one instance.[253] The one exception was Room 7, where a single gray marble slab (*ca.* 20 cm. square) was found in position immediately inside the doorway leading in from the frigidarium (Room 6). It suggests a reticulate paving of *opus segmentatum*.

Some elements of marble paving and a great deal of bedding marked with the outlines of the pieces originally set into it were found in the frigidarium (Room 6) of the bath. What remained of the actual paving and its bedding in the eastern

[250] For earlier examples see e.g. D. Levi, *Antioch Mosaic Pavements* II (1947) Pls. VI*b*, XXXI*c*, XXXIX*b*, LXII*a*; P. Gaukler, "Le domaine des Laberii à Uthina," *MP* III (1896) Fig. 5 (p. 198). For a later example (A.D. 539) see the mosaic from the church at Qasr Lebia in *ILN*, December 14, 1957.

[251] See K. Shepard, *The Fish-Tailed Monster in Greek and Etruscan Art* (1940).

[252] For a late example from the Church of St. John the Baptist at Gerasa see Kraeling, *Gerasa*, Pl. LXVIII*b*.

[253] The examination of the floor in Room 13 was limited to a section just inside the west wall of the room in the vicinity of the furnace opening. The absence of remains there may or may not be significant.

half of this great open court implies that the entire area framed by the four porticoes and containing the octagonal pool had at one time been set out with marble in some kind of design (see Fig. 58). The inchoate remains in the western half of the court seem at first glance to deny this implication, but in the absence of any visible dividing line between the two parts of the area it seems preferable to suppose that wear or the sinking of the floor had required repair of the paving at the west and that no attempt was made to reproduce the original pattern. In the northwest corner rectangular and triangular pieces of marble seem to have been relaid in a reticular pattern appropriate to their shapes but not along lines congruent with those in the eastern half of the court.

Remains and indications of regularly organized design begin at the north and south of the octagonal pool in the center of the court. At the north the space between the pool and the adjacent colonnade was developed as a rectangle by the use of marble squares set with their sides parallel to the sides of the rectangle. South of the pool a large rectangular marble slab was framed with small marble squares and triangles set in a reticular pattern. East of the pool this same design of plain field with geometrically segmented border was repeated with variations. On the axis of the court the large rectangular slab was again inclosed with marble squares and triangles set in a reticular pattern. In the southeast corner a corresponding slab was framed by squares and triangles in a combination of reticulate and imbricate patterns. The two fields and their borders were separated by marble strips between which the reticulate pattern composed of squares and triangles returned. There is nothing to show that this arrangement was continued in the northeast corner.

The general lack of correspondence in the development of the several parts of the paving in the court makes it interesting to speculate as to what the over-all design may originally have been and what it may have represented to those who conceived it. Even with maximum allowance for repeated repairs it would not seem as though we could count on a comprehensive pattern marked by balance and symmetry of elements similarly placed, such as one would naturally expect in the Roman period. The only alternative would seem to be an *ad hoc* development of certain parts of the courtyard in a specified manner and a thoroughly

casual treatment of all the rest. The nature of the designs used in the southern and southeastern parts of the area, each consisting of a plain field surrounded by an intricate border, suggests that they may have been intended to represent rugs spread on a floor. Point is given to this suggestion by the fact that the area so developed has its focus immediately in front of the podium contrived in the second intercolumniation of the south portico (see Fig. 58). If, as suggested above (p. 166), the podium was used by local magistrates or even the civil governor of the province for the transaction of community business, the emplacement of rug designs before and near the bema would have been entirely appropriate to decorate the area and to mark the spots where those who appeared before the authorities stood in presenting their cases or reports.

In the Public Building no remains of marble paving were found. Here again, as we have seen, a limekiln had been in operation. Since it represents the interval between the Roman and the Byzantine periods, the assumption must be that any marble used to decorate the Roman structure had been appropriated by the lime burners for their own purposes. In the dwelling attached to the Public Building marble paving came to light at one point, namely in the southeast corner of the large oecus (Rooms 27–28) that was axially placed south of the central courtyard (see Fig. 51). The paving consisted of gray marble slabs (*ca.* 20 cm. square) laid in a reticulate pattern without benefit of borders or other embellishments, so far as the available remains indicate. It is to be supposed that the paving was introduced in Byzantine times, perhaps in replacement of a much more elaborate marble flooring of the Roman period, at the same time that two spirally fluted blue marble columns were erected there.

In the excavation of the Villa fragments of strips of colored marble came to light with fair regularity in the fill. Some of them may have been brought in from the outside during the period of the growth of the fill. Others may represent the remains of marble baseboards set along the walls of the rooms and porticoes.[254] Marble was found *in situ* only in the paving of Room 6 (see Fig. 43), the larger of the two public dining rooms, whose floor mosaics are described above (pp. 244–45). Here

[254] In the "Palazzo" remains of such baseboards exist in position.

the innermost of the three zones of its paving, reserved as we have suggested for the entertainers or the display of viands, was laid out to contain a square (3.33 m. on a side) that was developed with the use of *opus sectile*. The square contained nine marble panels (91 cm. square) and was so organized that each panel and the entire group of nine were inclosed by marble strips 15 cm. wide (see Fig. 69). The framing strips were of grayish-blue marble save where they intersected. At the intersections red squares were introduced. Of the original nine panels four were preserved virtually intact and one in sufficient fragments to reveal its design (Pl. LIX B). The bedding of the four missing panels was still in place and was interesting to observe. It consisted of strips of baked clay set in the usual mixture of crushed bricks and mortar and so laid as to radiate from a central focal point. The clay strips were slightly concave and were marked with shallow transverse troughs, looking as though they had been cut from ordinary tile drain pipes.

the north side. This arrangement suggests that the ninth panel, in the center of the grid, brought either a recurrence of Pattern *A* or a separate Pattern *D* of which we have no knowledge.

All five of the known panels combine a lavish use of breccia marbles with others of solid color. Solid colors were used, naturally, to outline the elements of the design, while breccia appeared in the larger sections of the field set off by the outlines and particularly in the circular medallions placed at the center of each design. The panels were set off from the framing strips by reddish-purple borders (3.5 cm. wide) high-lighted on the inside by a white "rule" (1.5 cm. wide).

In Pattern *A* (Fig. 74 *A*) the part of the field adjacent to the border was set out with a mottled version of the reddish purple. The field was inscribed with two concentric circles, with diameters of 73 and 43.5 cm. Rings of yellow and green marble were used to delineate the outer circle, and a single ring of reddish purple served to outline

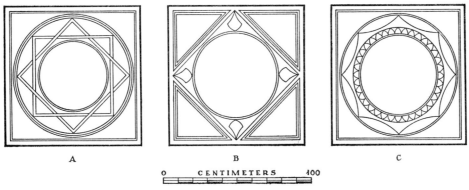

A   B   C

0   CENTIMETERS   100

Fig. 74.—DIAGRAM OF *Opus Sectile* PATTERNS IN ROOM 6 OF VILLA. *J. E. Knudstad*

Of the five panels of this *opus sectile* grid that are preserved in whole or in part, four are matching pairs. Together with the fifth panel they therefore illustrate three different patterns (Fig. 74). Their positions give a clue to the organization of the whole nine-panel group. Since Pattern *A* was found in position at the southeast and southwest corners of the square, it probably appeared also in the northeast and northwest corners. This probability is the more certain because Pattern *C* appeared in the intermediate position on both the east and the west side of the square. Judging by the correspondence between the intermediate panels of the east and west sides, we must infer that Pattern *B*, found in the intermediate position on the south side, was used also in the intermediate position on

the inner circle. The rings were each only 1.5 cm. wide. Into the area between the inner and outer circles were set strips of reddish-purple marble (2 cm. wide) outlining two intersecting squares that formed an eight-pointed star. Whitish breccia filled the areas between the intersecting squares and the outer circle, yellow breccia the areas contained within the star but outside the inner circle. The whitish breccia reappeared in the circular medallion in the center of the field.

Pattern *B* (Fig. 74 *B*) contained one square and one circle, the square being the setting for the circle. The square was set diagonally into the field and outlined by extensions of the reddish-purple strips that framed the panels. The white "rules" that high-lighted the border were continued along the sides of these extensions, forming triangles in the four corners of the field that were separately bordered in black. A vivid coarse-grained pinkish breccia was used to fill the triangles themselves. For that part of the square that was not occupied by the inset circle, the stonecutters chose a plain yellow marble, but this was inlaid at the corners with conventionalized leaves in green. The same green provided the narrow ring outlining the central medallion of mottled reddish purple. The rings and "rules" were of the same width (1.5 cm.) as those used in Pattern *A*, but the black borders of the corner triangles were only 1 cm. wide.

Pattern *C* (Fig. 74 *C*) was made up of circles and segments of circles. Concentric rings (1.5 cm. wide) of white and reddish purple set off overlapping circles with diameters 53.5 and 39.5 cm. The corners of the square field outside the outer ring were filled with grayish marble, while the medallion inside the inner ring contained a slab of breccia combining white and grayish tints. In the area between the two rings two designs were nicely adapted to each other. Outside the inner ring a zone only 3.5 cm. wide was inlaid with a wreath of thirty-six yellow leaves or petals, each about 4 cm. wide at the base, set in black. Circles whose hypothetical centers are outside the design cut eight segments from the area (7 cm. wide) that remained between the two concentric rings. These were filled with reddish-purple marble. The segmented eight-pointed star thus formed provided a yellow setting for the inscribed wreath.

That the Villa contained much additional marble paving is doubtful. Perhaps the water basin of the *naiskos* in the northwest corner of its large peristyle court was lined with marble, and perhaps marble was used in the important suite containing Rooms 15, 16, and 17, where no trace of paving was found. Otherwise all paving was done in mosaic, and wall covering was in painted imitation of marble sheathing. It is clear, therefore, that the Villa lagged well behind the "Palazzo" in quantity of imported floor and wall coating used by the builders, which is a measure naturally of the relative luxury of the two establishments.

INTERPRETATION

The study of pavements of the Hellenistic and Roman periods has taken on increasing significance during the immediate past not only because of the ever-growing body of information revealed by the excavations but also because of the light they shed on various aspects of ancient life and culture. Thus, for example, pictorial mosaics play an increasingly important role in the interpretation of ancient painting, in our understanding of the survival of classical mythology and literature throughout certain parts of the Christianized Byzantine world, and in the study of the iconography of Christian book illustrations. Similarly, mosaic pavements are proving useful in supplementing what is known about the form and decoration of ancient ceilings, about ancient symbolism, and even about the individual buildings and the plans of ancient cities. Above all, however, mosaic pavements now provide by virtue of the ubiquity of their preservation an important clue to the dating of private dwellings. In this connection we owe a great deal to publications on Olynthos, Corinth, Delos, Syrian Antioch, Palestine, provincial Africa, Gaul, Roman Italy, and especially Pompeii.[255] In the present context particular importance attaches naturally to the earlier mosaics of Tripolitania and Cyrenaica.[256] It is both proper and necessary that some attempt be made here to discuss the subject matter of the new mosaics uncovered at Ptolemais with a view toward their proper placement in the development of ancient mosaic pavements generally. Certain observations are a necessary preliminary

[255] See Robinson and Graham, *Excavations at Olynthos* VIII (1938); Scranton, *Corinth* I 3 (1951); Oscar Broneer, *Corinth*. I 4. *The South Stoa and Its Roman Successors* (1954); Broneer, *Corinth*. X. *The Odeum* (1932); Bulard, "Peintures murales et mosaïques de Délos," *MP* XIV 2–205; Levi, *Antioch Mosaic Pavements* (2 vols.; 1947); M. Avi-Yonah, "Mosaic pavements in Palestine," *QDAP* II (1933) 136–81 and III (1934) 26–73; *Inventaire des mosaïques de la Gaule et de l'Afrique* I–III, publié sous les auspices de l'Académie des inscriptions et belles-lettres (1909–25); Marion E. Blake "The Pavements of the Roman buildings of the Republic and early Empire," *Memoirs of the American Academy in Rome* VIII (1930) 7–159; E. Pernice, *Hellenistische Kunst in Pompeji*. VI. *Pavimente und figürliche Mosaiken* (1938). See also R. P. Hinks, *Catalogue of the Greek, Etruscan and Roman Paintings and Mosaics in the British Museum* (1933).

[256] See Aurigemma, *I Mosaici de Zliten* (1926); P. Romanelli, "Scavi e scoperte nella città di Tripoli," *Notiziario archeologico* II (1916) 340–52, and "Antichità della regione di Gurgi," *Notiziario archeologico* III (1922) 35–38; L. Alcock, "A seaside villa in Tripolitania," *PBSR* XVIII (1950) 92–100; Pesce, *Il "Palazzo delle Colonne,"* e.g. pp. 101–3.

to a detailed analysis of the decorative designs and the pictorial materials which they employ.

About the mosaics of the Villa, its neighbor, and the Public Building on the Street of the Monuments it can be said by way of introduction that, far from providing over-all figured treatments of floors, they define and organize them as fields, depending heavily therefore on the use of borders. Frequently, moreover, the typically rectangular fields thus outlined contain other fields similarly framed though not necessarily organized upon a focal point in the center of the room. This feature is recognized as characteristic of early mosaic construction, for instance at Delos.[257] Next it must be said that the new mosaics at Ptolemais, like those of the "Palazzo," contain none of the elaborate pictorial compositions familiar from the mosaics of Pompeii, provincial North Africa, and Antioch in Syria but show an array of geometric designs interlarded under special circumstances with pictorial emblemata. As in decorative wall painting, the limited use of the pictorial and its application only to areas especially set off from a larger whole reflect a restraining tendency corresponding either to the beginnings of the use of the pictorial or to a continuing or recurrent conservatism in the treatment of the surfaces. Finally, it will be evident from even a cursory inspection of the material that it lacks the ornateness of the polychrome mosaics of the second and third centuries of our era. The geometric designs are still elemental, linear, and devoid of the contrasts of light and shade that create an illusion of depth.

A sharper definition of the place of the new Ptolemais material in the development of mosaic work in general calls for an examination of the elements used in the designs, as listed below, and of the iconography and style of the emblemata.

Geometric Forms

1. Circles
   Intersecting
       Forming interlocking quatrefoils: Villa (Room 1) and adjoining dwelling (Room *B*)
       Forming quatrefoils and trefoils, outer half of each circle so inscribed as to produce a pelta: Villa (north end of west portico and Room 14)
       Inclosing Squares: Villa (west portico, center)

[257] See Bulard in *MP* XIV 188–89.

2. Quatrefoils in diagonal lines: Villa (Rooms 11, 5, and 1), Public Building (Room 15)
   Cf. Pesce, *Il "Palazzo delle Colonne,"* Fig. 30.

3. Peltae
   Groups of four radiating from a focal point: dwelling attached to Public Building (Room 30)
   Single space fillers: dwelling adjoining Villa (Room *A*)

4. Triangles
   Isosceles, with eight-pointed stars and squares: Villa (Room 5)
   With eight-pointed stars, squares, and rectangles: Villa (Room 20)
   Triangular areas in eight-pointed star design: dwelling adjoining Villa (Room *A*)
   Cf. *ibid.* pp. 37 (Room 10), 42 (Room 18).

5. Squares
   Overlapping rows of four overlapping squares: Villa (west portico, center)
   With octagons: Villa (north portico and Room 6), Public Building (Room 17)
   With hexagons and four-pointed stars: Villa (Rooms 6 and 20)
   With eight-pointed stars and pairs of isosceles triangles: Villa (Room 5)
   With eight-pointed stars, triangles, and rectangles: Villa (Room 20)
   Cf. *ibid.* pp. 36 (Rooms 7–8), 38 (Room 11).

6. Diaper pattern of squares in diagonal rows: Villa (south end of west portico and Room 12)

7. Diamonds interposed between tips of eight-pointed stars: Villa (Room 20) and adjoining dwelling (Room *A*)

8. Rectangles with eight-pointed stars, squares, and triangles: Villa (Room 20)

9. Lozenge: dwelling adjoining Villa (Room *A*)

10. Hexagons
    Framed by opposing squares and opposing four-pointed stars: Villa (Room 6)
    Separated by four-pointed stars: Villa (Room 20)
    Cf. *ibid.* Figs. 10, 34, 36, 52; see also pp. 29–30, 37.

11. Octagons
    With squares: Villa (north portico and Room 6), Public Building (Room 17)
    With four-pointed stars: Villa (south portico and Room 12)
    Created by surrounding squares: Villa (Room 5)
    Cf. *ibid.* Fig. 44; see also pp. 37 (Room 10), 45 (Room 19), 48 (Room 26).

12. Four-pointed stars
    With octagons: Villa (south portico and Room 12)
    With hexagons and squares: Villa (Rooms 6 and 20)
    Cf. *ibid.* Fig. 42 and p. 47 (Rooms 20–21).

13. Eight-pointed stars composed of lozenges
    At center of field: Villa (Room 5)

In parallel pairs, with squares, triangles, and rectangles: Villa (Room 20)

Two in series with quarter- and half-sections of stars, squares, and triangles: dwelling adjoining Villa (Room *A*)

Cf. *ibid*. Figs. 20, 24, 33, 43.

14. Herringbone: Villa (Room 1)

Decorative Space Fillers

1. Diamonds
   Inclosing white crosslet: Villa (porticoes)
   Inclosing single white tessera: Villa (west portico and Rooms 11, 5, and 20) and adjoining dwelling (Room *A*), Public Building (Room 15)
   Inclosing single white tessera and supplemented by sprigs: Villa (Room 20)
2. Squares: Villa (west and south porticoes, Rooms 12 and 20) and adjoining dwelling (Room *A*)
3. Peltae: dwelling adjoining Villa (Room *A*)
   Cf. *ibid*. Figs. 20, 29, 32, 35.
4. Circular inset: dwelling adjoining Villa (Room *A*)
5. Lanceolate inset: dwelling adjoining Villa (Room *A*)
6. Solomon's knots: Villa (Room 5)
7. Guilloche: Villa (Room 20)
8. Crosslets: Villa (porticoes)
   Cf. *ibid*. Fig. 34 and pp. 29–30 (Room 5), 42 (Room 18), 47 (Rooms 20–21).

Borders

1. Simple lines of tesserae: Villa (porticoes and all rooms) and adjoining dwelling (Rooms *A* and *B*), Public Building and attached dwelling (Rooms 15, 17, and 30)
2. Guilloche
   Multiple: Villa (Room 11)
   Single: Villa (Room 5)
3. Meander with squares: Villa (Room 14)
   Cf. *ibid*. Fig. 35.
4. Triangles set tip to base: Villa (Room 5)
5. Crowstep: Villa (Room 1)
   Cf. *ibid*. Fig. 20.

The list of geometric forms, decorative space fillers, and borders used in the new Ptolemais material contains nothing unusual. Indeed, the repertoire which the mosaicists who produced it had at their disposal was elementary and provided only the most commonplace items. Being essentially so commonplace they are of long established usage both separately and in the various combinations noted. The meander, for instance, appears in the pebble mosaics of the private houses of Olynthos, dated 425–350 B.C., and continues in use well into Byzantine times.[258] Under such circumstances it is not possible to give all the items of the inventory equal importance in any attempt to assign the Ptolemais mosaics to a specific period. For that purpose it is more important to note differences between earlier and later repertoires and particularly to capitalize upon what is currently known about the appearence, the period of greatest popularity, and the disappearance of certain specific forms.

The repertoire of forms characteristic of the pebble mosaics is now quite well known from the earliest pavements of houses at Pompeii, Delos, Olynthos, and elsewhere.[259] It includes—besides the meander with squares—the circles, the quatrefoil, the guilloche, and the crowstep of our inventory. However, several forms and designs typical of pebble mosaic are missing in our inventory. Among the latter are particularly the rows of dots intersecting at right angles, the diagonal lines forming diamonds (a simple diaper design), the overlapping leaf or scale design, the egg and dart, and the wave crest. Their absence indicates, no doubt, that the material under discussion here is removed in time from the earlier centuries of the Hellenistic period. It should be noted, however, that some of these forms and designs appear in the "Palazzo" at Ptolemais, for instance the rows of dots, the wave crest, and the overlapping leaf or scale design.[260] They were not unknown, therefore, at Ptolemais, but they do not of themselves imply that the mosaics of the main part of the "Palazzo" are earlier in date than those of the Villa (though this may indeed be the case), for it is obvious that the mosaicists of the "Palazzo" were more skilled than those of the Villa, as can be seen from the higher technical quality of their work and from their ability to produce *opus vermiculatum*, a type of mosaic of which the Villa contains not a single example. Be that as it may, it is also true that the "Palazzo" and the Villa contain no examples of the acanthus rinceau, which became increasingly

[258] See Robinson and Graham, *Excavations at Olynthos* VIII, Pls. 16, 17:1, and Kraeling, *Gerasa*, Pl. LXXXII*a* (Church of Procopius, A.D. 526/527).

[259] See Pernice, *op. cit.* Pls. 11–12; Bulard in *MP* XIV 188–89; Robinson and Graham, *loc. cit.* See also H. Goldman, *Excavations at Gözlü Kule, Tarsus* I (1950) 10 and Figs. 12–13 (pebble mosaics assigned to second century B.C.).

[260] See Pesce, *Il "Palazzo delle Colonne,"* Figs. 22, 42, 43, 44.

popular as an element of mosaic design beginning with the second century of our era.[261] Similarly, no examples are found among the known dwellings at Ptolemais of the three-strand guilloche nor of the twisted ribbon, whose use seems to begin in the second half of the first century of our era and which quickly became part of the universal repertoire of design.[262] These considerations would seem to suggest as the general chronological frame of reference for the mosaics under discussion here the period extending from the beginning of the first century B.C. to sometime before the end of the first century of our era. This can be narrowed down by the consideration of other forms of the repertory. Thus, for instance, the Solomon's knot,[263] the four-pointed star,[264] the eight-pointed star,[265] the border composed of triangles set tip to base,[266] and the guilloche used as a space filler instead of as a border are all associated in their origins with the first century of our era, and among these the rather awkward four-pointed star appears to go out of use beginning with the second century.

These impressions of a first-century association of the basic geometric forms of our inventory are by no means out of harmony with its range of incidental embellishments and borders. There is apparently no special study of motifs used as space fillers for geometric forms—particularly the diamonds with insets of contrasting color (single tessera, crosslet, alternate tesserae)—but a general survey of the material creates the impression that by the second century of our era the spaces contained within individual geometric forms were either filled with more complicated motifs or were used to create the illusion of depth.[267] Similarly,

the borders consisting of simple rows of contrasting tesserae and even of two-strand guilloches quickly gave way to ribbons, rinceaus, multiple guilloches, and architectural motifs.

For the date of the new mosaics at Ptolemais it is important next to turn from the consideration of geometric shapes, space embellishment, and borders to the designs combining them and from the larger environment of the Hellenistic and Roman world to North Africa. Here we are fortunate to have Aurigemma's careful study of the mosaics of the villa of Dar Buc Amméra at Zliten, near and east of Leptis Magna in Tripolitania. In the repertoire of geometric design at Zliten there is a good proportion of correspondence with the material from Ptolemais. Among the correspondences are the intersecting circles forming simple quatrefoils, the intersecting circles whose outer halves are so inscribed as to form peltae, the diaper design of squares set in diagonal lines, the lozenge framed with peltae and inset with a circle, and the four-pointed star.[268] To this documentation of the Ptolemais repertory at Zliten can be added from neighboring Carthage the eight-pointed star made up of lozenges[269] and from Tripolitania again the design of peltae set in groups of four around a focal point.[270] That the documentation of the Ptolemais repertory in North Africa fails to include such universal favorites as the combination of octagons and squares, the simple quatrefoils set tip to tip, the meander with squares, the crowstep, and the triangles set tip to base is probably quite fortuitous.[271]

What can today be known about the repertoire of geometric design used at Ptolemais, in Tripoli-

[261] For the differences between the first-century and the second-century repertoire of forms compare Marion E. Blake, "The pavements of the Roman buildings of the Republic and early Empire," *Memoirs of the American Academy in Rome* VIII 7–159, and "Roman mosaics of the second century in Italy," *Memoirs of the American Academy in Rome* XIII (1936) 67–214, and for the acanthus rinceau in particular see pp. 201–5 of the latter.

[262] See Levi, *Antioch Mosaic Pavements* I 376–77.

[263] See Blake in *Memoirs of the American Academy in Rome* VIII 103; Levi, *op. cit.* Vol. I 376.

[264] See Blake, *loc. cit.*; Levi, *op. cit.* Vol. I 374.

[265] See Avi-Yonah in *QDAP* III 29, n. 1; Blake, *op. cit.* pp. 60, 64, 120; Levi, *op. cit.* Vol. I 374, 379, 407–11.

[266] See Levi, *op. cit.* Vol. I 373, 376; Hinks, *op. cit.* p. lvii.

[267] See Avi-Yonah in *QDAP* II 138–41 for a valuable inventory of diagrams of such fillers.

[268] See Aurigemma, *I mosaici de Zliten*, Figs. 25–28. Most of the comparable designs appear in Room *N* of the Zliten villa. Among the borders found in the Villa at Ptolemais both the simple border and the guilloche occur at Zliten.

[269] See Hinks, *op. cit.* Fig. 77. The design is, of course, common elsewhere, e.g. at Pompeii (Pernice, *op. cit.* Pls. 25:5, 41:4), at Antioch in Syria (Levi, *op. cit.* Vol. I 379), and at Ptolemais in the "Palazzo" (Pesce, *Il "Palazzo delle Colonne,"* Figs. 20, 43).

[270] See *PBSR* XVIII, Pl. XXXI 1. For an example from Carthage see Hinks, *op. cit.* pp. 72–73 and Fig. 79 (No. 11), and for one from Verona see T. Campanile, "Negrar di Valpolicella," *Notizie degli scavi di antichità,* 5th series XIX (1922) Fig. 6 (p. 354).

[271] So also is the appearance of the design of intersecting and interlocking squares inscribed with circles in a church on the island of Rhodes (see *Clara Rhodos* VI–VII [1932–33] 555, Fig. 2).

tania, and in North Africa generally should for comparative purposes be supplemented with a thorough study of the mosaics of Cyrene, particularly those of the House of Jason Magnus. Courtesy suggests that the presentation of the Cyrenean material be reserved for the Italian archeologists who are now engaged in preparing it for publication. At least it can be said here, however, that the range of geometric design and figured representation in the Villa at Ptolemais finds close parallels in the House of Jason Magnus but that in execution and in the richness of the effects sought for the material in the House of Jason Magnus seems to be more advanced and later than the corresponding material in the Villa.[272] Perhaps when the full range of the material from Cyrene becomes available it will be possible to put in an orderly chronological progression the geometric mosaics of Libya as a whole and to make still more precise the suggestion that those of the Villa at Ptolemais belong to the first century of our era.

What has been said about the geometric mosaics needs to be supplemented by a consideration of the emblemata associated with them. Emblemata appeared among the new mosaics of Ptolemais only in the Villa. They fall into three groups, the animal scenes in the small peristyle court (Room 11), the scenes representing felines approaching a wine-filled krater in the triclinia (Rooms 14 and 5), and the Four Seasons (Room 5).

Imperfect preservation is a distinct handicap in the interpretation of the animal scenes in the small peristyle court. It is to mere chance that we owe the possibility of making any sense at all out of the emblema on the south side of the court. The identification of the scene as one showing a gazelle(?) fleeing from a pursuer provides for some association between it and the scene of the onager attacked by a lion on the west side of the court and suggests that the scheme of decoration as a whole placed some emphasis upon the representation of wild animals. If we could be sure that the north side also had an emblema and knew what it was,

we could be much more confident about the extent and the nature of that emphasis. As things stand, with the representation of the garlanded bull at the east side, it must remain questionable whether, how, and to what purpose wild and domesticated animals were balanced in the over-all scheme and whether the fact that the victims in all three scenes have hoofs is significant.

For the antecedents of the emblema showing the garlanded bull we have actually to go to the long series of cult scenes that stretches from at least the suovetaurilia on the rostrum of the Forum Romanum to the Dura Synagogue.[273] The scene showing the horned animal (gazelle?) in flight represents quite another tradition. Bounding cervids are familiar from the hunting scenes of North African and Syrian mosaics, but it is questionable whether the scene depicted in the Villa can be associated with this particular aspect of the tradition.[274] Rather, because of the use of the "flying gallop" and because of the fact that the animal has its head turned to look back, we are inclined to associate it with the scenes in which wild animals are shown attacking one another.[275] This is the aspect of the tradition which the excellent emblema of the lion attacking the onager also represents. For the latter immediate parallels are apparently not readily available, but cervids

---

[272] Examples in a single room of the House of Jason Magnus include the eight-pointed stars made up of lozenges and set in parallel rows, the square containing the Solomon's knot, the rectangle containing a guilloche returning upon itself, the herringbone, and the octagon with diamonds. The important differences are illustrated by the dentilated outlines of fields and inscribed elements that suppress linearity and add a nervous baroque touch to the combination of designs.

[273] Analogous to the former and almost equally well known is a relief from Venice in the Louvre. For the garlanded bullocks in the cult scenes of the Dura paintings see *The Excavations at Dura-Europos*. Final Report VIII, Part I. *The Synagogue*, by C. H. Kraeling (1956) Pls. LX–LXII. For local analogies to the garlands suspended at the top of the composition and interpreted as mesh bags containing flower petals see e.g. the funerary mosaic from Henchir-Thina (ancient Thenae) in P. Gauckler, *Inventaire des mosaïques de la Gaule et de l'Afrique* II, No. 23.

[274] For North African hunting scenes it is possible to refer simply to Aurigemma *I mosaici di Zliten*, pp. 131–201. The mosaics represent *venationes* in the amphitheater, but the iconography is borrowed from the hunt in the open, as the presence of the dogs that were used to raise and chase the quarry in the field clearly shows. For hunting scenes in Syria see e.g. Levi, *op. cit.* Vol. II, Pls. LVI, LVII, LXXVII, LXXVIII, LXXXVI a, XC a–b.

[275] For an example from neighboring Tunisia see Gauckler, "Le domaine des Laberii à Uthina," *MP* III, Figs. 3–5 (pp. 195, 198). Perhaps the closest analogy to the Ptolemais scene is a second-century emblema from Saltara that shows a wild goat attacked by a wolf (see Blake in *Memoirs of the American Academy in Rome* XIII, Pl. 35:4).

in precipitate flight are familiar from the Oriental tradition of the Hellenistic and Roman periods.[276]

The second group of emblemata is that showing animals approaching a krater filled with wine. This scene was used, as we have seen, at the entrances to two of the three triclinia. It was seen by those entering from without (Room 5) or by those reclining within (Room 14) and lent itself readily to both compact vertical and extended horizontal development. The animals were subject to variation (leopards in Room 14 and tigresses in Room 5) and the krater could be modified freely in its form, but the fact that the krater was filled with wine and as such was attractive to large felines is of basic importance for the composition and its symbolism and therefore also for the interpretation of the scene as appropriate to a triclinium.

Beginning in Hellenistic times animals in association with vessels, particularly vessels containing food and drink, are familiar elements of genre painting, mosaics, and even sculpture.[277] The obvious association in this instance, however, is with the Dionysiac ideology and more particularly with the body of legend that, beginning in Hellenistic times, refashioned the epiphany of the god in terms of the career and conquests of Alexander the Great. Of this body of legend we have only a fragmentary knowledge, through classical authors from Megasthenes to Nonnus, and thus we are somewhat handicapped in attempting to interpret its elements as they appear in pictorial compositions. Important for present purposes are mosaics representing the triumphal procession of Dionysos in India. An example at el-Djem in Tunisia not only shows felines in the main scene, drawing the chariot in which Dionysos rides in triumph, but also at the sides, where one approaches a krater filled with wine.[278] The special significance of this detail of the picture is apparently not known, but it is clear that the stylized and balanced scene in the Villa's triclinia is related to it.[279]

Representations of the Four Seasons are appropriate to villas, where indeed many of the Hellenistic and Roman examples occur, and particularly to the dining rooms, where the fruits of the seasons are enjoyed. In Cyrenaica, the home of Callimachus, they may have seemed particularly appropriate to the stratum of society which was familiar with his *Hymn to Apollo*. It is not strange, therefore, to find them in the Villa at Ptolemais, in the House of Jason Magnus at Cyrene, and in the villa of Dar Buc Amméra at Zliten,[280] that is, in three out of four of the better known domestic establishments in Libya. The interpretation of representations of the seasons has in recent years been materially advanced by Doro Levi's study of the mosaics of Antioch and especially by George Hanfmann's study of the Barberini Sarcophagus.[281] It is difficult, however, to keep pace with the new examples continually coming to light and to separate the types and subtypes of the late Hellenistic, the Roman, and the late Roman periods, the periods of their greatest proliferation. Of decisive importance for widespread usage of the imagery in these periods, as Hanfmann has correctly seen, was the standardization of the concept of seasonal change under the influence of scientific astronomy and the incorporation of the representation of the seasons into the repertoire of Dionysiac symbolism. The typical "Alexandrine" delight in the personification of abstracts may have been of contributing significance.[282]

Set into circular medallions, the Four Seasons of the Villa at Ptolemais are appropriately represented by busts only. All are females and all lack not only the late Roman hats but also and more particularly the wings that appear as early as the second half of the first century of our era and that are typical of much of the later iconography. Their attributes are the simple traditional ones: flowers

---

[276] For examples on the ceiling tiles of the Dura Synagogue see *Excavations at Dura-Europos*, Final Report VIII, Part I, Pl. XI 1 and p. 44. On the earlier history of this type of scene see M. I. Rostovtzeff, "Dura and the problem of Parthian art," *Yale Classical Studies* V (1935) 266–72.

[277] See e.g. S. Reinach, *Répertoire de peintures* (1922) pp. 363–68.

[278] A. Merlin, *Inventaire des mosaïques de la Gaule et de l'Afrique* II Supplément, No. 67.

[279] The proposition suggested by such scenes may well be that if even the wild animals accept Dionysos' epiphany and are tamed by the juice of the grape, so much more human beings.

[280] Aurigemma, *I mosaici di Zliten*, pp. 101–27.

[281] Levi, *op. cit.* Vol. I 161–62, 532–33, etc.; Hanfmann, *The Season Sarcophagus in Dumbarton Oaks* (2 vols.; 1951).

[282] Important in this connection is the description by Callixenus of Rhodes of the pageant at Alexandria in the reign of Ptolemy II, which Hanfmann (*op. cit.* Vol. I 112) has culled from Athenaeus *Deipnosophistae* v. 198 *A* and *N*. In the Dionysiac section of the pentaeteric pageant the Four Seasons were represented by persons gaily dressed and each carrying appropriate fruits.

and the shepherd's staff for Spring, ears of grain and the sickle for Summer, clusters of grapes for Fall, and the cloak drawn over and around the head for Winter.[283] Perhaps the sickle that goes with Summer was neglected or misunderstood by the mosaicist of Ptolemais, but his work shows none of the secondary elaboration of the symbolism illustrated for example by the addition to the representative of Spring of milk containers and young animals or the milking of animals. In regard to the symbolism the Zliten mosaics are more advanced than those of Ptolemais, since they include the milk containers in the representation of Spring and sprouting grain in that of Winter.[284] Of the masses of floating drapery which the Pompeian artists may well have introduced into the iconography in their rendering of the dancing or flying seasons, there is not a trace in any of the Libyan examples. Instead they show a simplified and slightly emended treatment of the more typically Hellenistic iconography. Spring and Fall wear the simple chiton that is tied with strings over the left shoulder and passes under the right arm pit, permitting the right breast to be shown bare if desired, while Winter wears, no doubt over the chiton, the heavy himation draped over her head. Summer is shown with the upper part of her body entirely nude, quite in keeping with the rendering in the Domus Aurea at Rome, on the Monument of Clodia at Roccagiovanne, and at Pompeii in the houses of Cn. Habitus and L. Tiburtinus.[285] In the Villa at Ptolemais Spring departs from the simpler rendering by the addition over the chiton of a second garment (see p. 250). The same detail appears in the representation of Spring in the House of Jason Magnus at Cyrene but not in the villa at Zliten in Tripolitania nor, to my knowledge, elsewhere. It may point to a local Cyrenaican variant in the iconography, and if it does represent an animal skin, as suggested above, the variant would indeed have meaning locally. It would suggest that in her capacity as shepherd Spring has protected the young of the flocks against the attacks of the wild animals of the jebel and wears the pelt of a slain raider in token thereof.

[283] It is impossible to say whether Winter had by her left shoulder the hydria found in certain of the early representations; see e.g. Hanfmann, *op. cit.* Vol. II, Fig. 96 (wall painting in the House of the Ancient Hunt at Pompeii).

[284] See Aurigemma, *I mosaici di Zliten*, Fig. 63.

[285] See Hanfmann, *op. cit.* Vol. II, Figs. 82, 84, 91, 92.

As to style, the Four Seasons of Ptolemais can be said to be buxom and full-bodied but not at all stolid or sober. They differ radically in this particular from the seasons of the Zliten villa, which probably represent Hanfmann's "powerful majestic" type most adequately.[286] The basis for the difference is not hard to define. The seasons of Zliten are lugubrious, monumental, and stolid in appearance because of the combination of elongated oval face, diminutive compressed lips, heavily shaded nose and neck, and faraway look. Fall at Ptolemais has perhaps an equally heavy neck, but her face is rounder, the shadow lines are not so strongly emphasized, the lips are fuller, and the pupil is not set so high in the eyeball, so that her gaze is within the immediate environment. Summer at Ptolemais might even be called "coy" rather than "majestic," thanks to the inclination of her neck, the slight turn given to her face, the sharper definition of her chin, and the more sympathetic look in her eyes.[287]

The Four Seasons in the House of Jason Magnus are set into the corners of a square inscribed with a circle, and the field in which they are developed thus allowed much more freedom for the representation of the associated symbols, for instance the sickle of Summer. But it is important to note, precisely in the case of Summer, how slender is the body, how elongated the neck, and how pointed the face. Everything tends to emphasize the vertical dimension, including the sheaves of grain that rise high above the crown of the head instead of encircling the face. But for all the vertical development, appropriate to the shape of the field, Summer at Cyrene is more closely related to Summer at Ptolemais than to the heavy-faced counterpart at Zliten.

Unfortunately we do not as yet have from Egypt, the crown land of Hellenism, a single representation of the Four Seasons. As in so many other instances, this lack provides a serious obstacle to the interpretation of the development and interrelation of the several iconographic and stylistic types known from other areas and later periods. What importance the consistency of the known examples from Cyrenaica may have is therefore at

[286] For his categories see Hanfmann, *op. cit.* Vol I 128.

[287] The dislocation and improper replacement of some of the tesserae in the figure of Spring give her a severe look in the photograph (Pl. LXI *B*) out of harmony with the original intent of the mosaicist.

present uncertain. All that can be said is that they have virtually nothing in common with the examples from Pompeii and that, while they are certainly related to the examples from the more westerly regions of North Africa, they are earlier or more faithful stylistically to a common prototype or both.

The new mosaics from Ptolemais cannot be said to rank with those of the villas and estates of provincial Africa in respect to either sustained pictorial effort or intricacy of design. Nor does the execution of detail match the excellence visible in the *opus vermiculatum* found in Tripolitania or, for that matter, in the "Palazzo" at Ptolemais itself. Even in the geometric range they are pedestrian and less refined in both definition and design as compared to those of the "Palazzo." But in one respect we believe they are more important than those of the "Palazzo," namely in that they represent a range of design more normative for the later development of geometric mosaic work in both Cyrenaica and Tripolitania. In spite of analogies between the mosaics of the "Palazzo" and the Villa, it seems that more of what was to follow regionally can be seen in historical perspective from the angle of the Villa than from that of the "Palazzo." That execution sometimes lagged, doing less than full justice to the quality of the models the mosaicists of the Villa were following, for instance in some of the emblemata, is a circumstance rather than a criterion of the importance and date of their work.

COINS

During the three seasons in which the Oriental Institute expedition was active at the site of Ptolemais coins were obtained in two different ways— by excavation and by purchase from residents of modern Tolmeita and vicinity, children and adults, who offered them for sale or as bakshish. The two categories were held strictly apart by the expedition and also, be it said, by the workmen. Surface finds are readily distinguishable from coins recently excavated, and all those offered for sale had the aridity, the loss of the oxidized outer layer, and the smoothness derived from handling that characterize the surface find. Purchase was not promoted nor announced as an expedition program. Rather it was indulged in to provide an impression of the potential yield of the site as a whole, in supplement to the yield from the specific buildings excavated. In the case of the surface finds it was, of course, impossible to ascertain from what parts of the ancient city they had come or even whether they were found within the city walls, but the distance separating modern Tolmeita from other antiquities sites is such as to make it quite certain that all coins purchased do reflect the yield of Ptolemais and its immediate vicinity.

The excavations yielded a total of 265 coins, all of which are in the custody of the Department of Antiquities of Cyrenaica at Shahat, and 173 coins were purchased. As might readily be expected, gold coins played no part in either category. Fourteen of the purchased coins turned out to be silver, but not a single silver coin came to light in the excavations. Since care was taken to avoid the purchase of pieces that had obviously been reduced by wear to mere "blanks," the number of purchased coins that remained unidentifiable after cleaning amounted to no more than ten. Among the excavated coins 107 were unidentifiable, in spite of careful cleaning. The reason for this high proportion is to be found in the fact that large parts of the fill which yielded most of the coins, particularly in the Villa, consisted of disintegrated mud brick. This type of fill has a gummy quality that in depth preserves a great deal of moisture, and the coins were therefore sheathed in a heavy coating of oxidized metal the removal of which tended to leave a high proportion of blanks.

COINS FOUND IN THE VILLA

Of the 211 coins yielded by the excavation of the Villa, 87 are illegible and 124 legible. The group includes 23 Ptolemaic pieces, 93 Roman imperial, and 4 Byzantine. They were identified as indicated in the following list.

PTOLEMAIC (CYRENAICAN REGAL ISSUES)

1 Ptolemy I (Soter)
1 Ptolemy IV (Philopater and Arsinoë III)
2 Ptolemy V (Epiphanes)
3 Ptolemy VIII (Euergetes II)
2 Second century B.C. generally
3 Ptolemy X (Alexander I)
11 Ptolemaic generally

ROMAN IMPERIAL

 1 Tiberius
 1 Domitian ?
 3 Trajan
 1 Trajan ?
 1 Hadrian
 4 Antoninus Pius
 2 Antoninus Pius ?
 5 Marcus Aurelius
 1 Commodus
 1 Didius Julianus
 3 Second century of our era generally
 1 Julia Domna
 1 Septimius Severus
 1 Caracalla
 1 Diadumenianus ?
 6 Alexander Severus
 6 Julia Mamaea
 1 Maximinus Thrax
12 Gordian III
 3 M. Julius Philippus
 1 Trajan Decius
 1 Trebonius Gallus
 2 Gallienus
 1 Gallienus ?
 7 Claudius Gothicus
 1 Aurelian
 3 Probus
 2 Diocletian
 2 Maximianus
 8 Third century of our era generally
 2 Licinius
 2 Constantine and sons
 7 Constantius II
 1 Fourth century our era generally

BYZANTINE

1 Theodosius
1 Arcadius and Honorius
2 Heraclius

Like the architecture, the wall decoration, and the mosaics the coins found in the Villa provide evidence for establishing its dating. Their evidential value is not actually proportionate to the size of the yield because of the great fill that covered the site under the circumstances set forth above (p. 139). Out of the 124 identifiable coins yielded by the excavation of the Villa 89 were found in the fill at levels sufficiently high above floor level to preclude the probability of their association with the life and construction of the building. The fact that they were intrusive does not, however, deprive them of all importance, but their evidential value takes the form of testimony to the disuse and progressive abandonment of the site.

To interpret what the coins tell about the abandonment and later history of the Villa three facts require consideration. The first is the relatively small number of Byzantine coins yielded by the site as a whole, namely 4 out of a total of 124 identifiable pieces. This indicates that at the end of the fourth century of our era the currents of city life were definitely flowing around rather than through the Villa.[288] The second fact to be considered is the wide range of the coin yield from the intrusive fill. This yield includes 12 Ptolemaic pieces, 17 Roman imperial of the second century of our era, 44 of the third century, 14 of the fourth century, and 2 of the seventh century. The prolonged period of looting and dumping explains this spread in part, but it can hardly explain the fact that of the 23 Ptolemaic pieces found on the site 12 are from the fill. Some special circumstance clearly underlies this aspect of the spread. Since practially all the Ptolemaic pieces were found at the northern end of the site, it may be suggested that those in the fill came with earth taken from the surface of adjacent insulae and dumped on the site of the Villa in connection with the construction of the Byzantine building immediately to the west (Building 4) or in connection with the preparation of the low-level courtyard around the apsidal building (church ?) immediately to the north (Building 6). As for the rest of the coins from the fill, the heavy concentration of coins from the third century of our era (just about half of the total yield) suggests that by the latter half of this century the building as a whole was already abandoned and subject to looting and disintegration. This inference is particularly plausible because of the third fact to be considered here, namely that with six exceptions the coins from the fill include all those found on the site that belong to the period after Gordian III. The exceptions are a coin of the third century generally, one of Claudius II, two of the period of the Tetrarchy, and one each of Theodosius and Arcadius. All but the two of the Tetrarchy period came to light in Room 1. The reuse of this room, beginning in late Roman

---

[288] Separate allowances must be made on other grounds for the continued use of certain portions of the Villa by squatters and looters and the owners of the tabernae along its northern side (see pp. 138–39).

times, as the site of a smelting establishment (see p. 134) is sufficient to explain the presence there of the late issues. It would seem, therefore, that the period of the Tetrarchy marks the end of the effective life of the building. In fact, the relatively large proportion of the coins from the reign of Gordian III that were found in the fill (10 out of a total of 12) suggests that we would be wise to keep the entire second half of the third century open as the period during which the life of the Villa as a private residence came to an end.

We turn now to the much smaller number of identifiable coins (35) found at floor or court level or in the very lowest part of the fill.[289] Upon them depends whatever it may be that the coins can tell us about the construction and the continuing life of the Villa. The facts about these coins are listed below.

ISSUE	LOCUS
1. Ptolemy I (Soter)	Street east of Villa, immediately south of main entrance
2. Ptolemy IV (Philopater)	Southwest corner of court, bottom of fill
3. Ptolemy V (Epiphanes)	Room 1, near floor level
4. Ptolemy V (Epiphanes)	North end of court, near garden level
5. Ptolemy X (Alexander I)	West portico, north end, bottom of fill
6. Ptolemy X (Alexander I)	Room 2, bottom of fill
7. Ptolemaic	East portico, north end, on wall of drain, below floor level
8. Ptolemaic	Room 1, near floor level
9. Ptolemaic	Room 7, base of doorframe
10. Ptolemaic	South portico, west end, bottom of fill
11. Ptolemaic	East portico, in bedding of floor, below stylobate level
12. Tiberius	Room 1, bottom of fill
13. Domitian ?	Room 1, near floor level
14. Trajan	East portico, floor level
15. Trajan	East portico, north corner, stylobate level

16. Hadrian	Court, garden level
17. Antoninus Pius	Court, north end, garden level
18. Marcus Aurelius	Room 6, near floor level
19. Marcus Aurelius	Room 2, floor level
20. Diadumenianus ?	Room 6, floor level
21. Alexander Severus	Court, southeast corner, garden level
22. Alexander Severus	East portico, center, stylobate level
23. Julia Mamaea	Exterior east wall, street level
24. Julia Mamaea	East portico, center, stylobate level
25. Julia Mamaea	Court, southeast corner, garden level
26. Julia Mamaea	Court, southwest corner, garden level
27. Julia Mamaea	Room 18, floor level
28. Gordian III	Room 7, bottom of fill
29. Gordian III	Room 1, near floor level
30. Claudius II	Room 1, near floor level
31. Roman, third century	Room 1, bottom of fill
32. Roman, the Tetrarchy	North portico, floor level
33. Maximianus	East portico, floor level
34. Theodosius	Room 1, near floor level
35. Arcadius and Honorius	Room 1, bottom of fill

The foregoing list contains no mention of the oecus and adjacent chambers (Rooms 15–17), whose floors were probably removed in the period of looting (see p. 127), nor of any of the rooms of the residential apartment (Rooms 9–14), which presumably were kept well swept. Of the two formal dining rooms it mentions only the larger (Room 6), which may well have been the less frequently used. The loci from which the coins actually come are the porticoes (10 coins), the court (7 coins), the caldarium (Room 1) of the bath (9 coins), a supply room (Room 2), the kitchen (Room 7), and Room 6 (2 coins each), the vestibule (Room 18), an exterior wall, and a street (1 coin each). The inference to be drawn from the distribution is that in general the coins come from areas where their loss could properly have remained undetected and that the list may on this account be said to be representative and typical.

A second feature of the list is the general continuity of the series of coins, especially so far as Roman imperial issues are concerned. The Roman series begins somewhat hesitatingly with single pieces of Tiberius and possibly of Domitian, is well established at the end of the first century and the

---

[289] In certain parts of the Villa portions of the fill as high as 50 cm. above actual floor level consisted of debris from the walls, their plaster coating, and fragments of their marble baseboards. Coins found in such fill it seemed logical to regard as belonging potentially to the Villa.

beginning of the second by the coins of Trajan, and continues with no significant breaks through the Tetrarchy. The general continuity is undoubtedly a testinomy to continuous occupation over a period of several hundred years, analogous to the testimony of the multiple replasterings of some of the walls. The presence of the two coins of the Byzantine period is explained by the reuse of Room 1 as a smelting establishment beginning in late Roman times.

To appraise the bearing of the coins upon the probable date for the construction of the building requires consideration of two questions. First, is the appearance of the individual pieces of Tiberius and Domitian(?) at all significant and, second, what are we to make of the presence on the premises of no less than 11 Ptolemaic coins? As to the first question, it is of course obvious that the caldarium (Room 1) of a private bath is scarcely a place where one would expect coins to be lost, though lack of natural light might prevent any that were lost there from being detected subsequently. Moreover, the reuse of the room as a smelting establishment must have had something to do with the relatively high number (9) of early coins coming from this one area, as it did with those of a later date.

Examination of the find-spots of the Ptolemaic pieces suggests that under the severest scrutiny and with allowance for the remotest contingency the use of 8 of the 11 pieces as witnesses to the date of the construction of the Villa might be questioned. These include the piece found in the street east of the Villa, the two pieces found in Room 1, and the five found at the bottom of the fill or near garden level. The reason for querying the first three is obvious. The last five are queried because, though they were found in the part of the deposit in which coins of the period of occupation would be expected to occur, there is a chance that they came in at a much later date, in the course of the looting and dumping, and somehow found resting places at or near the bottom of the fill. We are left, however, with three coins from peculiarly significant loci, and what they tell us goes a long way toward preserving the evidential value of at least the last five of the eight pieces questioned. The coin from Room 7 (No. 9 in list) was scraped out from the exposed edge of the bedding into which the jambs of the doorway leading from the kitchen to the service passage (Room 8) had been set. Coin No. 11, from the east portico, lay under the heavy deposit of refuse that had accumulated in the area in later times, imbedded in a clean layer of what must be assumed to be the earth that was leveled off to receive the bedding of the mosaic floor. Hence it appeared below the level of the stylobate. Coin No. 7 was found on top of a vertical side member of the drain that ran eastward under the east portico and was presumably kept in place by the slabs that once covered the channel. The drain served to remove excess rain water from the court of the Villa and ran at a sharp gradient downward toward the large drain coming down the middle of the street east of the Villa. It was clearly a part of the original construction of the building. If, as seems likely, these three of the coins were lost while the building was being constructed, what do they imply as to the date of construction? That they mean construction in the Ptolemaic period is of course possible, but not likely on other grounds.

So far as the available evidence is concerned it would appear that the Romans did nothing to supply the area with coinage between 91 and 67 B.C., that between 67 and 31 B.C. there were joint provincial issues of bronze for Cyrenaica and Crete authorized by the governor, and that there were separate provincial issues for Cyrenaica between 23 and 12 B.C. and again between A.D. 19 and 23. The pre-Actian bronze issues are said never to have been "more than occasional," and the Augustan issues are said to have diminished quickly and to have died out before the end of the first century B.C. except for the isolated outburst under Tiberius.[290] Since the efforts made by the Romans to help supply the local need for currency between 67 B.C. and A.D. 23 were so sporadic, it is probable that much of the Ptolemaic bronze remained in continuous use during all that time.

If, then, the earliest of the coins associated with the life of the Villa show a large proportion of small Ptolemaic bronzes still in circulation, this can be taken to reflect a situation continuing right up to the end of the first century of our era. By the time of Trajan Roman bronze was in good supply, not to mention Roman silver that may have come in as soldier pay (see p. 17). The rather tentative appearance in the Villa of earlier Roman imperial bronzes (single coins of Tiberius and possibly of Domitian) corresponds to what we might expect after A.D. 23, when the issue of

[290] BMC, *Cyrenaica*, pp. ccviii–ccix.

Roman provincial coinage for Cyrenaica ceased and when Roman imperial currency was being introduced. So far as the evidence of the coin yield is concerned, therefore, a date from the second quarter to the end of the first century of our era would be entirely appropriate for the construction of the Villa.

Coins Found in the Public Building

Only 25 coins are available from the site of the Public Building on the Street of the Monuments. The coins discovered in the three weeks' work on the site in the spring of 1954 were taken to Cyrene by the representative of the local Department of Antiquities for cleaning and are undoubtedly still there, but they could not be located after his departure from Cyrenaica. Since the work of these three weeks involved only the clearance of the surface along the northern and eastern parts of the site and of Byzantine construction at the southwest, the missing coins would testify only to the latest phases in the use of the site. Of the 25 coins available, only 13 proved to be legible. These include 2 Ptolemaic coins, a Roman provincial issue of Palikanus, 4 Roman imperial pieces belonging to the period from Trajan to Probus, and 6 Byzantine pieces belonging to the period from Arcadius and Honorius to Phocas. The coin yield is in harmony, therefore, with what the archeology of the site demonstrates, namely that there were two major periods of structural development and that these were widely separated in time. The second and last is clearly Byzantine, the first presumably Roman. There is nothing in the find-spots of the Ptolemaic and Roman pieces that helps to clarify the picture further, nor would it be wise to press the evidence in view of the small number of pieces in hand. One of the Ptolemaic coins came to light at floor level in the oecus (Room 27) of the attached dwelling, the other in the fill at the bottom of the limekiln in the courtyard (Room 8). The Roman provincial issue, from the period of Augustus, was found in the fill, the coin of Trajan on the staircase in Room 30. A coin of Faustina was found in the intake flue of the limekiln, that of Probus at floor level in Room 20.

Coins Found in the City Bath

The excavation of the City Bath on the Street of the Monuments yielded only 29 coins, 21 of which were identifiable after cleaning. The facts about the identifiable pieces are listed below.

ISSUE	LOCUS
1. Aulus Pupius Rufus	Vaulted cistern (Room 5), in fill
2. Gordian III	Frigidarium (Room 6), in front of bema at southeast corner, in drainage channel under paving
3. Gallienus	Tepidarium (Room 9), in fill
4. Maxentius	Tepidarium (Room 9), in fill
5. Gratian	Street west of City Bath, in fill
6. Anastasius	Frigidarium (Room 6), in fill
7. Anastasius	Frigidarium (Room 6), south portico, on floor (found when floor was swept)
8. Fifth century of our era	Frigidarium (Room 6), in fill
9. Fifth century of our era	Frigidarium (Room 6), between paving stones
10. Justinian	Frigidarium (Room 6), in fill
11. Justinian	Tepidarium (Room 9), in fill of hypocaust
12. Justinian	Room 11, easterly duct in north wall, floor level
13. Justin II	Frigidarium (Room 6), in fill
14. Justin II	Frigidarium (Room 6) east portico, in front of Niche *E*, floor level
15. Justin II	Frigidarium (Room 6), east colonnade, in masonry surrounding third plinth from north
16. Maurice Tiberius	Frigidarium (Room 6), east of pool, on floor (found when floor was swept)
17. Phocas	Frigidarium (Room 6), east portico, in water channel running through Niche *E*
18. Phocas	East vestibule (Room 2), floor level
19. Phocas	East vestibule (Room 2), floor level

20. Heraclius	Frigidarium (Room 6), in fill	
21. Heraclius	Frigidarium (Room 6), east portico, on filled-in surface of Niche *E*	

It is obvious that nine of the coins in the above list have no contribution to make to our knowledge of the history of the City Bath, No. 5 (Gratian) because it came to light in the street west of the premises and Nos. 1, 3, 4, 8, 10, 11, 13, and 20 because they were in the fill. This disposes quite incidentally of the earlier coins in the series save for No. 2 (Gordian III), which was found in a drain under the paving of the frigidarium and presumably is a stray. From the balance of the coin yield it can be inferred only that the City Bath as we know it was in full operation at the end of the fifth century of our era and that it continued to be used in one way or another until the early years of the seventh century. This inference is in general accord with the archeological findings.

Purchased Coins

The 173 coins that were purchased at the site of Ptolemais to provide a check on the general yield of the site include 159 bronze coins and 14 silver. The silver coins were identified as follows:

Athens, fifth century B.C. (trihemiobol)	1
Aegium, Achaean League, third century B.C. (hemidrachm)	1
Nero (denarius)	1
Domitian (denarius)	3
Trajan (denarius)	7
Antoninus Pius (denarius)	1

The only fact of interest here is the large number of pieces of Trajan. Perhaps they reflect the campaign that Marcius Turbo undertook with large reinforcements against the Jewish insurrectionists in Cyrenaica for Trajan in A.D. 115–16. Should we, perhaps, assume that one of Turbo's detachments was stationed for some time at Ptolemais to keep order there?

Of the 159 bronze coins 10 were unidentifiable after cleaning. The remaining 149 include the following:

Ptolemaic (Cyrenaican regal issues)	58
Seleucid?	1
Jewish Maccabean	1

Roman provincial	3
Roman imperial	46
Byzantine	38
Turkish (nineteenth century)	2

Disregarding as irrelevant to our purposes the two Turkish pieces and as too uncertain the one possibly Seleucid coin, we note first the large number of Ptolemaic issues. These are interesting both in their distribution among the several Ptolemies and in their proportion to the rest of the bronze. Among the 58 Ptolemaic pieces there are issues of the following:

Ptolemy I	2
Magas in revolt	1
Ptolemy III (Euergetes I)	1
Ptolemy V (Epiphanes)	8
Ptolemy VIII (Euergetes II)	17
Ptolemy X (Alexander I)	14
Ptolemy XII (Auletes)	2

Distributionwise they are interesting because of the relatively late date of the bulk of the pieces. With the heaviest coverage extending through the reign of Ptolemy X (Alexander I), the list reflects properly the continued economic dependence of Cyrenaica upon Egypt even after the death of Ptolemy Apion and thus after the beginning of the Roman protectorate. Proportionwise the Ptolemaic representation is interesting when seen in contrast to the meager number of Roman provincial pieces and to the relatively late date of the earliest Roman imperial bronzes. It may serve to verify the suggestion made in connection with the coins from the Villa that Cyrenaica relied upon Ptolemaic bronzes well into the first century of our era.

The purchased coins include by chance a bronze quarter-shekel of the type issued by Simon Maccabaeus (139–135 B.C.), which gives the first clear indication of the presence of a Jewish element in the population of Ptolemais. Its appearance is, of course, not unexpected but in the present context particularly fitting as a possible corollary to the several silver denarii of Trajan.

The Roman imperial bronzes and the Byzantine pieces have less to suggest. Single pieces of a long succession of emperors beginning with Trajan and ending with Heraclius are thoroughly meaningless. Modest concentrations occur only in the case of Trajan (5 bronzes), the Constantinian period (12 bronzes of Constantine and his sons), the two Justins (9 bronzes), and Heraclius (9 bronzes).

The highly technical questions of ancient currency and economic life that cluster temptingly around the consideration of any body of numismatic material from a site previously not investigated with an eye to coin yield are the prerogative and require the special competence of the trained numismatist. But one question of this type should at least be mentioned here in conclusion, not because it is new but because it has already been raised and still remains unanswered. This is the question of the appearance in Cyrenaica of so large a number of coins, especially of Trajan, currently and generally ascribed to the mint of Caesarea in Cappadocia.[291] Of the 17 pieces of Trajan found and purchased at the site of ancient Ptolemais 12 belong to this particular type. The question of the proper attribution of the series and of the circumstances attending the passage of so many of its pieces to Cyrenaica therefore becomes by that much more acute.

MINOR FINDS

Movable finds of the excavations in categories other than those dealt with above were neither numerous nor of great importance. Neither the City Bath nor the Public Building on the Street of the Monuments could have been expected to produce much in the way of personal property, and the Villa of the Roman period, where such objects could legitimately be expected, had been thoroughly looted. For the most part what came to light there had been either brought in with the fill or left by the squatters who occupied certain parts of the building after it ceased to be maintained as a private dwelling (see pp. 138–39).

Baked Clay

Remains of pottery vessels were common in the excavations, though they bulked large only in special areas and were by no means as common as for example in excavations in Palestine, Jordan, and Syria, where sherds are omnipresent. On the surface and throughout the fill sherds of Greek black and red wares and of terra sigillata ware appeared, but the former usually only in minute fragments and the latter in pieces of only slightly larger size. The earliest pottery found *in situ* came to light in the bedding of the base course of the Public Building on the Street of the Monuments (see p. 146). Aside from tiny bits it consisted of fragments of a lamp, a bolsal, and a small plate, all typical of the late fourth century B.C., that is, of the beginning of the Hellenistic period. The lamp had a deep handleless body, grooved at the outer edge of the rim, and a high narrow base. It was inclosed at the top save for the filling hole.[292] The ware of the cup and its peculiar "silver-frost" glaze show it to be a local imitation of the Attic type which in the late fourth century B.C. began to rival the kotyle in popularity. The impressed decoration on the inside of the base and the fact that the underside of the base was completely glazed indicate that it belongs late in the development leading down from the fifth to the fourth century B.C. The rest of the ceramic finds range from the late Hellenistic to the Byzantine period.

Numerically the best represented are globular cooking pots with horizontal ribbing. Several of these were found intact in the Villa (Pl. LXII *A*), where they had been left by the squatters who kept house among its ruins in Byzantine times. They are thin-walled and normally show traces of much exposure to fire. The handles are small and attached high on the body. A somewhat earlier, presumably late Roman, type, with less pronounced rim and handles attached vertically or horizontally to the short neck, was also found (Pl. LXII *B*, top). Plain and ribbed water jars with high looped handles and straight neck rising from a rounded or an elongated body were also common (Pl. LXII *B*, bottom right and left). Plates and dishes were by no means common save in the kitchen dump in the area of the east portico of the Villa (see p. 124). They were all reduced, however, to small fragments. The vessel shown in the center of the bottom row on Plate LXII *B* is presumably an amphora stand of Roman common ware.

Among products of the potters' workshops were the flues, made in lengths of 20–30 cm., which

---

[291] See BMC, *Cyrenaica*, p. ccx.

[292] Cf. O. Broneer, *Corinth. IV 2. Terracotta Lamps* (1930) p. 47 and Pl. III: 120 (Type VIII).

conducted heated air from the hypocausts upward in the walls of the caldaria (Pl. LXII *C*). They are either oval or rectangular with rounded corners, and some have lateral vents that must have connected with outlets or branches of the heating system.

As always the clay lamps, found largely in the Villa and the Public Building, provide an interesting insight not only into the chronological range of occupation but also into the cultural context of the life of ordinary people. With the exception of the late fourth century B.C. lamp mentioned above, the lamps range generally from the second century B.C. to the Byzantine period, with the majority representing Roman imperial times. The earliest as to type (Pl. LXIII *A*, upper left, and *B*, upper left), with their unadorned rims, deep bowls, and infundibula, represent local variants of the Cnidus lamps.[293] One of these is handleless and had a blunt-ended nozzle. The handle on the other lamp suggests that it may be a late copy of the early type. The latest lamps as to type (Pl. LXII *D*, above and below at left), with their ovoid shape and with a ridge framing the eye-shaped discus open to the nozzle, belong to the class that Petrie has called "groove lamps" and that are generally Byzantine in date.[294] The others are largely small roundish or ovule lamps with a simple lug handle and the nozzle projecting slightly or crowding the rim and thus belong to the first and second centuries of our era.[295]

The range of decorative patterns is by no means unusual. On the rims dots and ovules predominate, though there is also one example of a vine meander (Pl. LXIII *B*, lower right). The discus of a lamp of the first century of our era, with a long nozzle set off by volutes (Pl. LXIII *A*, upper right), has something close to the rayed decoration so common on the bronze originals which it imitates.[296] Another example of the same general date shows a fully developed rosette (Pl. LXIII *A*, middle row at left). Among the pictorial representations that were

developed on lamps from this time on, those found at Ptolemais give further examples of familiar themes—the crescent (Pl. LXIII *A*, top center), the gorgoneum (Pl. LXIII *B*, lower left), the eagle (Pl. LXII *D*, above and below in center), a figure that may be the maenad (Pl. LXIII *B*, lower right), Orpheus charming the beasts (Pl. LXIII *A*, middle right), and gladiators (Pls. LXII *D*, upper right, and LXIII *B*, upper right).[297]

To this general list of ceramic products two items of particular interest need to be added. A typical head of a Tanagra figurine was found in the fill at the south end of the Villa, and an equally typical pilgrim flask from the shrine of St. Menas in Egypt was found in Shop IV at the north end of the Villa (see p. 135).

GLASS

Objects made of glass were not plentiful among the expedition's finds, but there is no reason why they should have been. Tombs, where such objects are most commonly found in good preservation, were not a major feature of the expedition's work. At the Villa fragments of glass occasionally came to light in the fill, and the bases of a number of wineglasses were found in the kitchen (Room 7), where the preparation of meals continued long after the Villa was abandoned. All the pieces from the Villa are of the fourth century of our era or later. The wineglasses (see Pl. LXIV *B*, top) are of a common type.[298] Other glass finds include the stems of three goblet-shaped lamps, one plain (Pl. LXIV *B*, top center) and two beaded,[299] and fragments of five small bottles with rounded bases that are sometimes called "tear bottles."[300] The necks of seven larger bottles came to light, three medium long flaring ones (Pl. LXIV *B*, lower left) and two short ones (Pl. LXIV *B*, lower right).[301]

[293] Cf. *ibid*. pp. 53–54 and e.g. Pl. V: 190 (Type XIII). See also H. B. Walters, *Greek and Roman Lamps* (1914) pp. 50–54.

[294] W. M. F. Petrie, *Roman Ehnasya* (The Egypt Exploration Fund, "Memoir" XXVI Supplement [London, 1905]) p. 9 and Pl. LXII; see also A. Osborne, *Lychnos et Lucerna* (Alexandria, 1924) p. 18 and Pl. I 107.

[295] Cf. Broneer, *Corinth* IV 2, pp. 78–102, Types XXIII–XXVII.

[296] Cf. *ibid*. pp. 76–78, Type XXII.

[297] Cf. *ibid*. Figs. 194:1309 (crescent), 139:703 (Orpheus charming the beasts), 122:644 and 123:645 (gladiators); Walters, *op. cit*. Figs. 240:1128 (gorgoneum) and 300:1335 (eagle), Pl. XIX 558, 663, 787, and 703 (gladiators); Osborne, *op. cit*. Pl. II 18 (maenad).

[298] See e.g. C. C. Edgar, *Graeco-Egyptian Glass* (*CC* XXII [1905]) Nos. 32499, 32501, 32504; D. B. Harden, *Roman Glass from Karanis* (Ann Arbor, 1936) Pl. VI 479, 482, 484 and pp. 167–73.

[299] Cf. P.V.C. Baur in Kraeling, *Gerasa*, p. 519, Nos. 368–69.

[300] Cf. Edgar, *op. cit*. Nos. 32682–83.

[301] Cf. Baur, *op. cit*. Figs. 29:66 and 94, 28:5 and 93; see also Edgar, *op. cit*. No. 32591.

Only two have rims, and none have the common thread decoration. Two other fragmentary bottles are of more unusual types. One has a short flaring neck and a ribbed shoulder, while in the other the neck rises from a ringlike depression in the body (Pl. LXIV *B*, bottom center). The depression below the neck appears on elongated bottles, some square and some round, found elsewhere,[302] but the ribbed shoulder seems to be exceptional. Otherwise the fill over the Villa yielded only fragments of two round handles and one strap handle, a ring, and a few tesserae.

BONE

The excavations at all three sites yielded bone pins. About fifty examples were intact or nearly so, while eighty odd were in small fragments. A representative collection of the better preserved pieces is shown on Plate LXIV *A*. The types are simple and by no means unusual. No examples with figured representation on the head were found.[303] Other bone objects include fragments of spoons, needles, and small ornaments.

The two most important pieces in this category, found in the fill over the Villa, are an ivory foot of a small casket, fashioned in the form of a griffon, and a fragmentary bone plaque carved in relief (Pl. LXIV *C*). The plaque fragment (6.8 × 11.5 cm.) is slightly warped, owing no doubt to its thinness (1.5 cm.). Though showing no traces of nail holes, it may have been prepared to adorn a casket. The right and bottom edges exhibit a carefully cut frame. A vertical incision at the left may mark the first molding of the frame at the left or merely a subdivision of the field. The figure set into the framed field is a dancing satyr, ithyphallic, with an animal pelt draped around his shoulders or arms as a robe. The carving is sharp, if simplefied, and the pose is light and graceful. Carved bone and ivory appliqués for furniture, chests, and caskets of various sorts were by no means uncommon in late antiquity, between the third and fifth centuries of our era, though in time the simpler process of repre-

senting in outline by the use of incised lines apparently became more widely used than the more difficult relief representation. It is surprising how much of the classical tradition survives in the better examples of *Kleinkunst*, both in the range of their subject matter and in style. The subjects include Aphrodites, personifications, putti, scenes of a Bacchic character, and satyrs pursuing nymphs.[304] The piece from Ptolemais is a good example of the survival of the classical manner in approximately the fourth century of our era.

To complete the record of this category it should be noted that a collection of jawbones with well developed tusks was found in the kitchen (Room 7) of the Villa (see p. 132). These were subsequently identified as bones of domestic pigs, a reminder that "roast pig" was served at the Villa in its later years.

METAL

Objects of metal were encountered occasionally at all three sites, but no well preserved piece of any importance came to light. No silver appeared, and gold was limited to an earring, a link from a thin necklace, and foil from the heads of two bone pins. Iron was represented by a small ring, used perhaps in a lamp holder, and by a fishhook which, however, may be of Italian vintage.

Bronze is the metal that was typically in use, but the finds include only one piece of special interest. This is the beam or lever of a balance to which a pair of hooks was attached at the bottom and a ring at the top. The weight that was moved along the beam to bring the objects suspended from the hooks into balance is missing. This scale, together with the chain by which it was suspended, was found tucked into a corner of Room 12 of the Villa adjacent to the arcuated entrance to Room 14. It had somehow escaped the eyes of those who looted the premises. Other finds of bronze, from all three excavated sites, include nineteen nail and clamp fragments, four awl or pin fragments, six rings from light chains, and the foot of a statuette.

The dearth of metal found *in situ* in the Villa was explained by the remains of a smelting establishment in the apse of the caldarium of its

---

[302] Cf. Edgar, *op. cit.* Nos. 32541 and 32545. Usually such vessels have handles.

[303] On such pins, which are normally assigned to the fourth and fifth centuries of our era, see e.g. Oskar Wulff, *Die altchristlichen und mittelalterlichen byzantinischen und italienischen Bildwerke* (Staatliche Museen zu Berlin, "Beschreibung der Bildwerke der christlichen Epochen" III [2d ed.; 1909]) I 123ff. and Pl. XXI.

[304] See Wulff, *op. cit.* pp. 106–23, Pls. XV–XVI 374–83 and 390–98; J. Strzygowski, *Hellenistische und koptische Kunst in Alexandria* (Vienna, 1902) esp. pp. 5–6.

bath (Room 1). These remains included not only the furnace built of tiles taken from the piers of the hypocaust but also, from the fill nearby, large lumps of slag from the crucibles in which metal objects had been melted down. The lumps were rounded at the bottom as they had hardened in the crucibles.[305] The smelting establishment at the Villa and the limekilns in the City Bath and the Public Building are indications of the thoroughness with which the ancient buildings were gone over by looters and of the economic decline in late Byzantine times of what had been founded in the Hellenistic period as a proud and ambitious urban establishment.

[305] Two samples were sent for future analysis by Mr. Rutherford J. Gettens to the laboratory of the Freer Gallery at Washington, D. C.

INDEX

Poseidon, statues of, 187, 191
pottery, 75, 132, 137, 139, 146, 156, 269–70
Poulsen, Frederik, 189, 191–92, 199
Poulsen, Vagn, 192
Praeneste, 217
Praxiteles, 181, 203, 205
Preger, Theodor, 78
Preyss, A., 69
Priene, 47, 60, 84, 85, 88, 93, 159, 223, 236
priest: head of, 199; holding *naiskos*, 178, 180, 197–98
priestess, portrait head of, 181, 192
Princeton University, vii
Pritchard, J. A., 85, 87
Probus, coins of, 264, 267
Procopius, 27, 28, 43
Proconnesian marble, 193–94
Proconnesus, 186, 195, 207
Psammetichus, statuette of, 9
pseudo-Scylax, 3–5, 177
Ptolemaic bronze coins, 137, 139, 263–66, 268
Ptolemaic queens, representations of, 9, 178–81, 188–91
Ptolemais (medieval Tolometa or Tolomieta; modern
    Tolmeita), 1 and *passim;* capital of Libya Pentapolis
    at —, 20, 36, 51, 73, 92, 159, 211; cultural orienta-
    tion of —, 15, 177–88, 215–16; earliest settlement
    ("Harbor at Barca") at —, 3–6, 8, 33, 39, 177; early
    European visitors to —, 30; founding of —, v, 4–6,
    41, 177; — in inscription, 210; organization of —, 7;
    soldiers recruited from —, 16; Tyche of —, 12, 18,
    118, 183, 186, 189, 196, 203
Ptolemais-Acce, 16, 48
Ptolemies, 5–7, 58, 177–78, 180; city planning of —,
    48; symbolism of —, 193
Ptolemy I Soter, 6, 116, 178; coins of —, 264–65,
    268
Ptolemy II Philadelphus, 6, 9, 178, 261
Ptolemy III Euergetes I, 6, 7, 9, 41, 177; coin of —, 268
Ptolemy IV Philopater, 177, 193; coin of —, 264–65
Ptolemy V Epiphanes, 178–79, 190; coins of —, 264–
    65, 268
Ptolemy VI Philometor, 7, 8, 10, 70, 113, 190
Ptolemy VIII Euergetes II (Physcon), 115, 190; coins
    of —, 148, 264, 268
Ptolemy X Alexander I, coins of, 264–65, 268
Ptolemy XII Auletes, coins of, 268
Ptolemy Apion, 7, 10, 11–13, 115, 268
Ptolemy "the brother," 10, 12; *see also* Ptolemy VIII
Ptolemy the geographer, 3, 19, 35, 36, 50
Ptolemy "the younger," 7; *see also* Ptolemy VIII
Public Building on the Street of the Monuments
    (Building 8 on Plan XXII), vi, 15, 18, 19, 26, 28, 68,
    140–60, 269–70; architectural decor in —, 157–58;
    coins found in —, 156, 267; dating of —, 157–60,
    267; inscriptions found in —, 211–12; marble paving
    in —, 254; mosaic paving in —, 251–52
puteal, 128

Qasr Beni-Gdem, 26, 102
Qasr el-Hamar, 99
Qasr el-Heneia, 21
Qasr el-Shahden, 26
Qasr el-Suq el-Oti, 99
Qasr Lebia, 237, 253
Qasr Taurguni, 14
Qayrawan, el-, 29
quarries and quarrying, 10, 13, 15, 24, 50–51, 57, 105,
    107–8, 115, 138
Quarry Gate, 39, 57–58, 61, 62
quatrefoil motif, 153, 238, 241–42, 245–48, 251, 257–59
Quirites, 18
Quirinius, P. Sulpicius, 13

rainfall at Ptolemais, annual, 2, 68, 72
ram statuette, 178, 180, 202–3
Ramses II, 9
Ramses III, 3
Rand, E. K., 181
Ras el-Soda, 182
Raubitschek, Antony E., 209
rayed decoration on lamps, 270
rectangle motif, 248, 257
Redlich, Roman, 207
Reinach, Salomon, 189, 261
Reinaud, Joseph T., 29
reliefs, 81, 164, 186, 193, 271
reservoirs, 20, 24, 28, 69–73; water capacity of —, 70
reticular pattern, 254
Reynolds, Joyce, 16, 208, 212
Rhodes, 8, 10, 182, 194, 259
Rhodian type peristyle, 89, 124, 137, 217
ribbon patterns, 259
Rice, D. Talbot, 78
Richter, Gisela M. A., 190–92, 195, 206
Riese, Alexander, 20
Rinaldis, R., 74
rinceau patterns, 137, 258–59
rings, 271
roads and road engineering, 14, 21, 29, 33–37, 57–58
Robert, Carl, 207
Robert, Louis, 209
Robertson, D. S., 84, 85, 87, 216, 223–24
Robinson, D. M., 30, 43, 84, 85, 88, 158, 208, 256, 258
Robinson, E. S. G., xvii
Rocca di Papa, 206
Roccagiovanne, 262
rock-cut tombs, *see* chamber tombs
Rodenwaldt, Gerhart, 207
Rohlfs, Gerhard, 30, 71, 151
Roman army units in Cyrenaica, 15–17, 24, 58, 268
Roman engineering, 35, 36
Roman period, v, vi, 1, 3, 11–22, 34–36, 42, 51, 53, 58,
    61, 62, 64, 66, 68–70, 73, 79, 84, 85, 87, 92, 93, 105,
    115–16, 120, 138–41, 145–49, 152–60, 167, 174–75,

PLATES

PLATE I

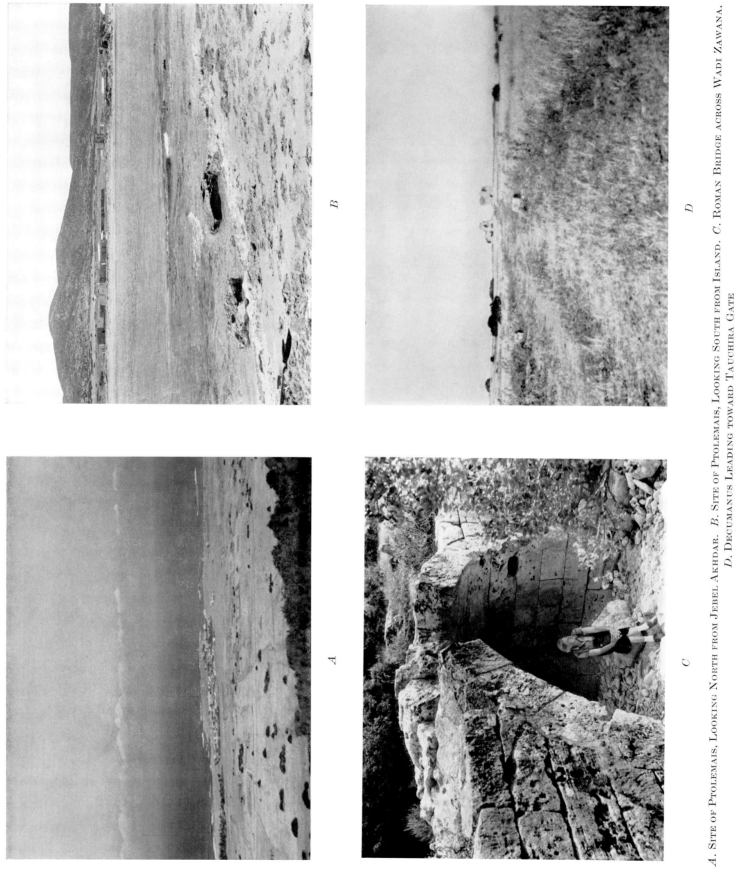

A. Site of Ptolemais, Looking North from Jebel Akhdar. B. Site of Ptolemais, Looking South from Island. C. Roman Bridge across Wadi Zawana. D. Decumanus Leading toward Tauchira Gate

PLATE II

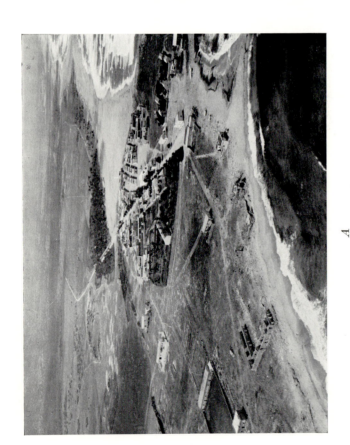

A. Air View across Promontory to Site of Harbor at West. *B.* Remains of Walls on East Side of Harbor. *C.* Base Course of West City Wall in Coastal Plain

PLATE III

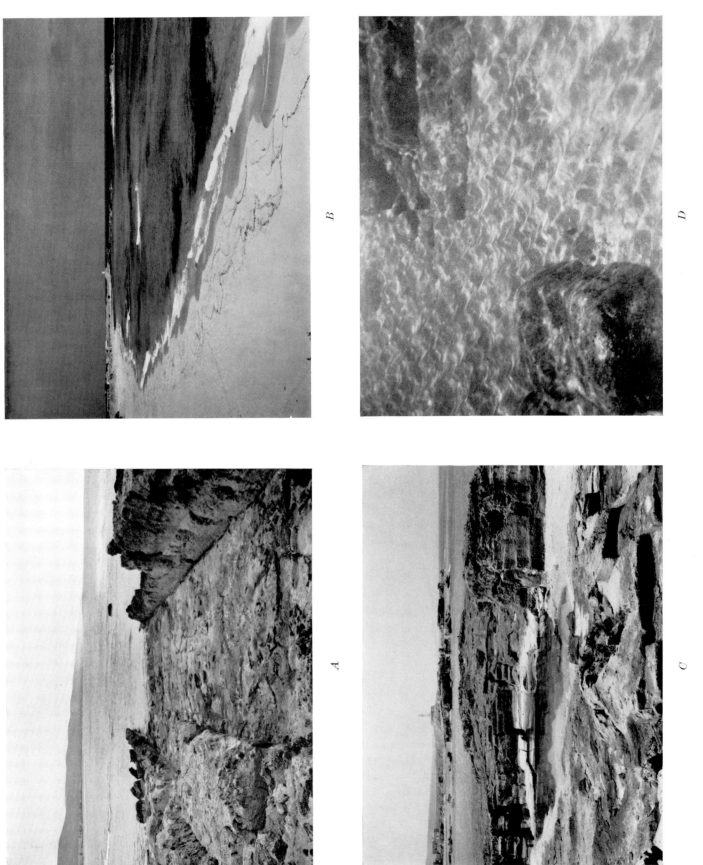

A. Possible Ship Pen at West Side of Promontory. *B.* Anchorage and Islands East of Promontory. *C.* Quarry on Island Sheltering Anchorage. *D.* Blocks of Breakwater Projecting from Island

PLATE IV

B

A

REMAINS OF CITY WALL. *A.* AT FOOT OF JEBEL AKHDAR. *B.* ON RIDGES OF JEBEL

PLATE V

A. Paved Roadway through Quarry Gate. B. Tower Protecting Quarry Gate. C. Paved Roadway through Barca Gate.
D. Harbor Gate at Apollonia

PLATE VI

A

B

C

TAUCHIRA GATE. *A.* AS SEEN FROM OUTSIDE THE CITY. *B.* JUNCTION WITH CITY WALL AT SOUTH.
C. NORTH SECTION OF PORTAL WALL

PLATE VII

TAUCHIRA GATE. *A.* WEST FACE OF NORTH TOWER. *B.* LOOKING NORTH FROM INSIDE. *C.* LOOKING SOUTH FROM INSIDE.
D. JUNCTION WITH CITY WALL AT NORTH

PLATE VIII

A. South Section of Portal Wall of Tauchira Gate.   B. Corner Pier of Doric Peristyle of Square of the Cisterns

PLATE IX

A

B

Square of the Cisterns. *A.* Looking North. *B.* Vaulted Chamber

PLATE X

A. Reservoir (Building 12), Looking Southeast. *B.* Reservoir (Building 11), Looking Southeast. *C.* Vaulted Cistern of Late Private House (Building 14), Looking North. *D.* Street of the Monuments, Looking East

PLATE XI

A. Triumphal Arch on Street of the Monuments. *B.* Peristyle and Oecus of "Palazzo." *C.* Bath of "Palazzo"

B

C

A

PLATE XII

A

B

"Odeon," Looking (*A*) Southwest and (*B*) Northwest

PLATE XIII

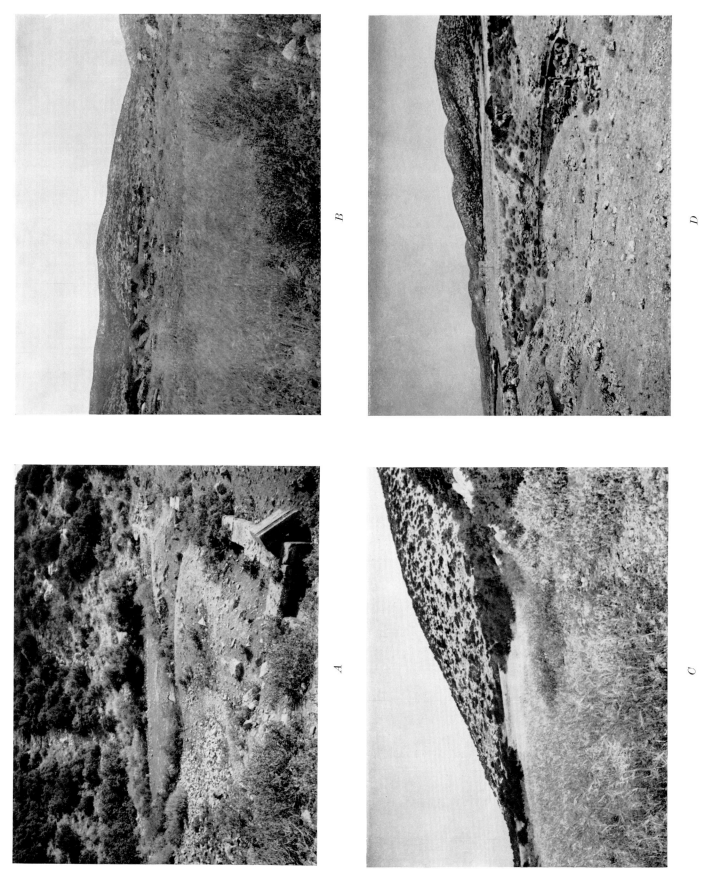

A. Upper Theater (Building 28), Looking South. B. Byzantine Theater (Building 7), Looking Southwest. C. Site of Hippodrome (Building 27), Looking East. D. Amphitheater (Building 1), from Northwest

PLATE XIV

A

B

A. Fortress Church (Building 2). *B.* Apse of Possible Church (Building 6)

PLATE XV

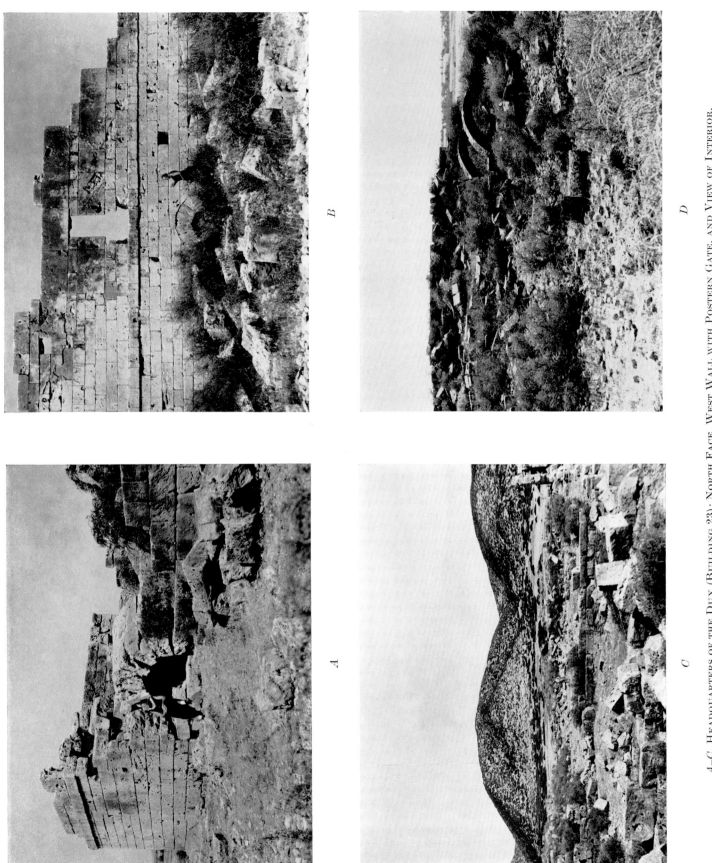

B

D

A

C

A–C. Headquarters of the Dux (Building 23): North Face, West Wall with Postern Gate, and View of Interior.
D. Interior of East Fortress (Building 24)

PLATE XVI

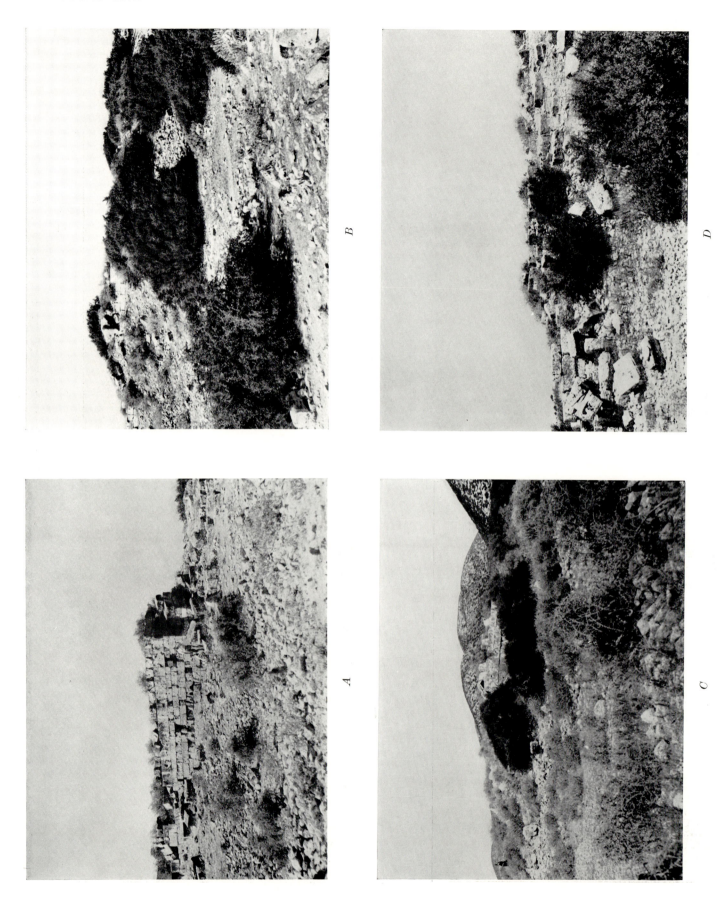

A. Northeast Corner of West Fortress (Building 4). B. Southwest Corner of Building 18. C. Northwest Corner of Building 20. D. Ruins of Building West of City

PLATE XVII

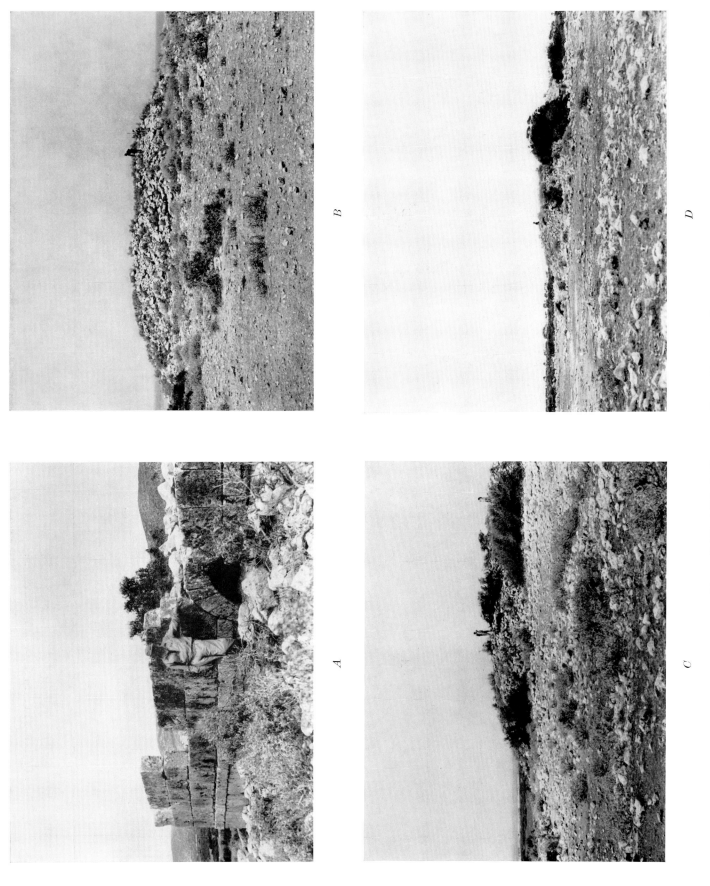

FORTS 2 (*A*), 4 (*B*), 5 (*C*), AND 6 (*D*) ON TAUCHIRA ROAD

PLATE XVIII

A. Capstones of Typical Cist Grave. B. Chamber Tombs Cut in Quarry Face. C. Interior of Typical Loculus Tomb. D. Niches in Walls of Chamber Tomb

PLATE XIX

A

B

A. Tower Tomb in Large West Quarry. *B*. Smaller West Quarry, with Tower Tomb in Background

PLATE XX

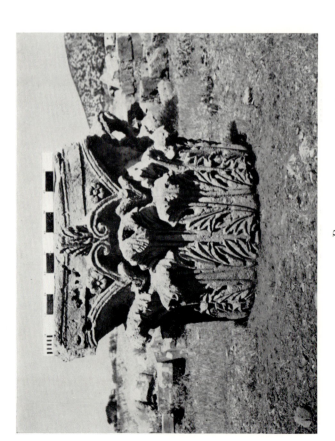

A. Doric Capital of Building 26. *B.* Corinthian Capital from Unknown Building. *C.* Column on Podium of Square of the Cisterns

PLATE XXI

C

A

B

Villa. *A.* Vestibule (Room 18), Looking from Vestibule into East Portico. *B.* Looking from Vestibule into East Portico. *C.* East Portico from North

PLATE XXII

A

B

VILLA. *A.* Peristyle Court, looking North. *B.* Ornamental Basin in Court

PLATE XXIII

B

D

A

C

Villa. *A.* West Portico, Looking North. *B.* Looking across South Portico into Room 16. *C.* Mud-Brick Wall Construction in Room 16. *D.* Room 11, Looking Southwest

PLATE XXIV

A. Room 11 of Villa, Looking South toward Adjoining Dwelling. B. Rooms B and A of Adjoining Dwelling, Looking East.
C. Looking from Room 11 of Villa Northwest to Rooms 9–10 and Beyond. D. Rooms 8, 7, 6, and 5 of Villa, Looking Northwest

PLATE XXV

Villa. *A.* Caldarium of Bath (Room 1), Looking West. *B.* Furnace Room of Bath (Room 24), Looking South. *C.* Rooms and Shops at North End, Looking West. *D.* Shops II, III, and IV, Looking West

PLATE XXVI

B

D

A

C

VILLA. *A.* LINTEL OF DOORWAY BETWEEN VESTIBULE (ROOM 18) AND EAST PORTICO. *B.* ARCHITRAVE-FRIEZE BLOCK OF MAIN ORDER.
C. CORNICE BLOCK OF MAIN ORDER, *D.* IONIC CAPITAL OF MAIN ORDER

C

A

D

B

Villa. *A.* Entablature Block of Colonnaded Entrance to Room 14. *B.* Lintel Found in North Portico.
C. Voussoir of Colonnaded Entrance to Room 14. *D.* Reeded Column Base Used to Plug Wellhead

Plate XXVII

C

A

D

B

Public Building. *A.* Site before Excavation. *B.* South Face Cleared. *C.* Room 3, Looking West. *D.* Room 5, Looking East

Plate XXVIII

C

A

D

B

Public Building. A. West Side of Courtyard (Room 8). B. Room 29, Looking North. C. Limekiln in Courtyard.
D. Staircase and Passage (Room 9)

PLATE XXIX

A

B

C

D

Public Building. A. Cold Plunge in Frigidarium (Room 10). Looking West. B. Sitz Bath in Northeast Corner of Frigidarium. C. Rooms 13 and 14, Looking East. D. Room 19, Looking West

PLATE XXX

PLATE XXXI

B

D

A

C

PUBLIC BUILDING. *A.* LOOKING NORTHEAST FROM SOUTH PORTICO (ROOM 26) OF ATTACHED DWELLING. *B.* OECUS (ROOMS 27–28) OF DWELLING, LOOKING SOUTH.
C. SOUTH PORTICO OF DWELLING, LOOKING WEST. *D.* ROOMS 20 and 21, LOOKING NORTHWEST

PLATE XXXII

A. Room 13 of Public Building, Seen through Furnace Opening in North Wall. *B.* Room 14 of Public Building, Seen through Furnace Alcove at North. *C.* Rooms 16 and 15 of Public Building, Looking South. *D.* Street West of City Bath

PLATE XXXIII

CITY BATH. *A.* SITE BEFORE EXCAVATION. *B.* LATRINE (ROOM 3), LOOKING NORTHWEST. *C.* ROOM 8, LOOKING WEST INTO ROOM 7.
D. WATER CHANNELS IN ROOM 15, LOOKING EAST

PLATE XXXIV

A

B

CITY BATH. *A*. FRIGIDARIUM (ROOM 6), LOOKING SOUTHWEST. *B*. LOOKING NORTH FROM CALDARIUM (ROOM 13) TO FRIGIDARIUM

PLATE XXXV

B

D

A

C

Tepidarium (Room 9) of City Bath. *A.* Looking East. *B.* Tub in North Wall. *C.* Northwest Corner. *D.* Southwest Corner

PLATE XXXVI

A

B

C

D

City Bath. *A.* Tepidarium (Room 9) with Hypocaust Excavated at Northeast. *B.* Furnace in Room 14. *C.* Well Shaft in Room 14. *D.* Column Re-erected in Frigidarium (Room 6)

PLATE XXXVII

A

B

C

D

A. HEAD OF TYCHE OF PTOLEMAIS (INV. 61). B–D. HEAD OF CLEOPATRA I (INV. 1)

PLATE XXXVIII

BODY OF CLEOPATRA I (INV. 9)

PLATE XXXIX

A

B

C

A. Goat(?) Torso (Inv. 59). *B*. Head and Body of Ram (Inv. 60). *C*. Lower Part of Priest Holding *Naiskos* (Inv. 14)

PLATE XL

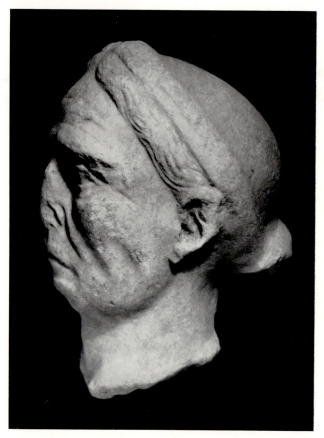

Portrait Head of Elderly Lady (Inv. 3)

PLATE XLI

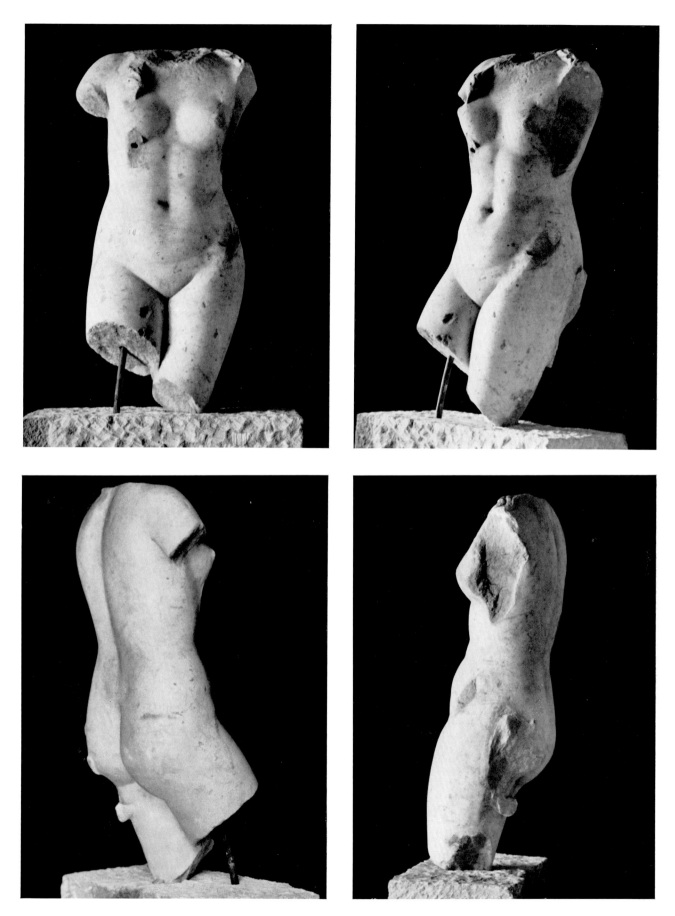

TORSO OF ONE OF THE THREE GRACES (INV. 8)

PLATE XLII

A

B

C

D

A. Lion-Headed Waterspout (Inv. 6). *B*. Fragment of Horus Statue (Inv. 58). *C*. Fragment of Sea Creature (Inv. 13). *D*. Head of Architectural Herm (Inv. 27)

PLATE XLIII

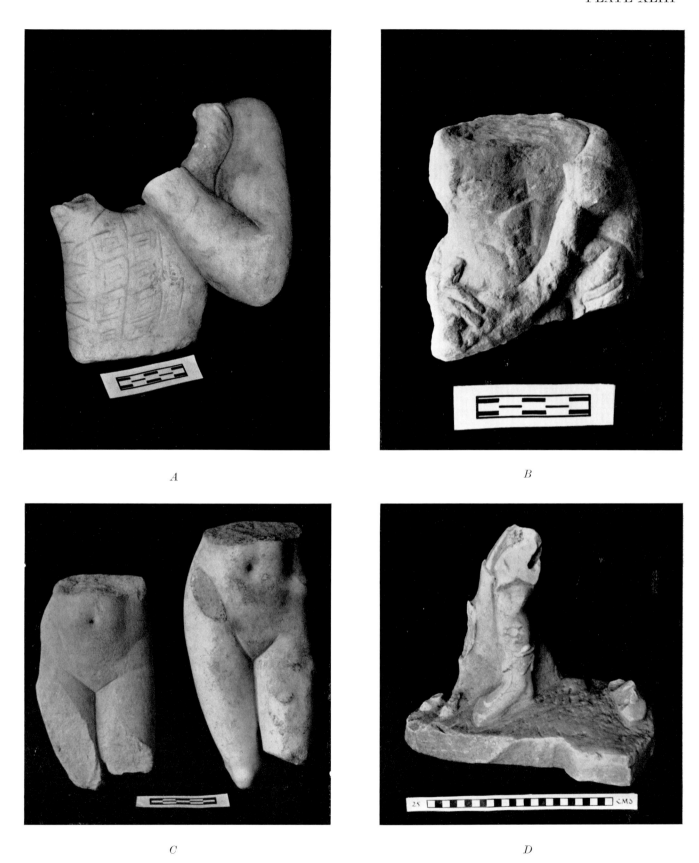

A. Fragment of Lyre Player (Inv. 31). *B.* Fragment of Male Torso (Inv. 32). *C.* Fragmentary Aphrodite Torsos (Inv. 37–38). *D.* Fragment of Statue of Artemis (Inv. 49)

PLATE XLIV

A

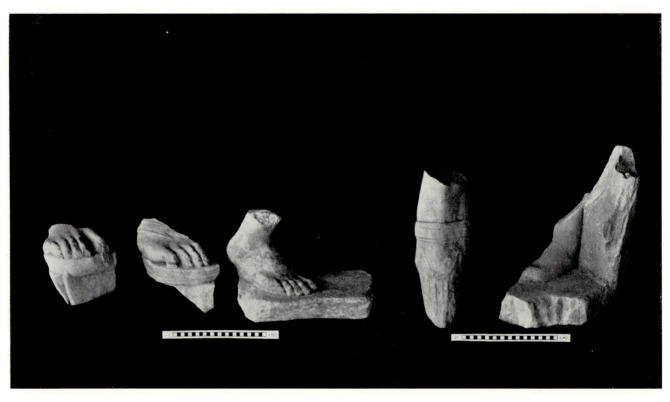

B

A. Fragment of Colossal Statue of Athena (Inv. 11). *B*. Fragments of Feet and Legs (Inv. 18, 19, 17, 20, 16)

PLATE XLV

A

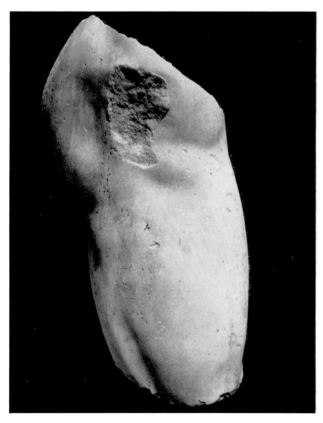

B

C

A–B. Fragments of Herakles by Asklepiades of Athens (Inv. 12). *C.* Left Knee and Shin with Attached Fragment of Animal (Inv. 15)

PLATE XLVI

HEADLESS FIGURE OF AESCHINES TYPE (INV. 10)

PLATE XLVII

A

B

A. Head of Asklepios (Inv. 2). *B*. Male Head from Peopled-Scroll Pilaster (Inv. 4)

PLATE XLVIII

A

B

C

D

A. FRAGMENT OF BOY WITH WATER JAR (INV. 35). *B*. HEAD OF MAENAD IN RELIEF (INV. 5). *C*. HEAD OF BEARDED MAN
WEARING FILLET (INV. 28). *D*. TORSO OF PERSONIFICATION OF CONSTANTINOPLE (INV. 36)

PLATE XLIX

A

B

C

D

A. HARPOCRATES (INV. 66).   *B*. DIONYSOS (INV. 65).   *C*. VENUS GENETRIX AS FOUNTAIN FIGURE (INV. 67).   *D*. ATHENA (INV. 64)

PLATE L

A

B

C

D

A. Artemis Colonna (Inv. 68). B. Statue of Claudia Eupomane? (Inv. 62). C. Statue of M. Aurelius
Flavianus? (Inv. 63) D. Stele of the Gladiator Hippomedes (Inv. 71)

PLATE LI

A

B

A. Sarcophagus Lid with Reclining Couple (Inv. 70). *B*. Fragment of Amazon Sarcophagus (Inv. 69)

PLATE LII

A

B

C

D

INSCRIPTIONS. BLOCK REUSED UPSIDE DOWN AS TRANSVERSE MEMBER IN CRADLE OF CITY WALL NORTH OF TAUCHIRA GATE (*A*) AND NOS. 1 (*B*), 10 VERSO, 7, 13*B*, 8, 6, AND 12 (*C*), 11 (*D*) FROM VILLA

PLATE LIII

B

D

A

C

Inscriptions. No. 5 (*A*) from Villa and Nos. 14 (*B*), 15 (*C*), 19 (*D*) from Public Building

PLATE LIV

A

B

C

D

Parts of Inscription Honoring Arcadius and Honorius (*A–B*) from Street of the Monuments and Inscriptions 33 (*C*) and 36 (*D*) from City Bath.

PLATE LV

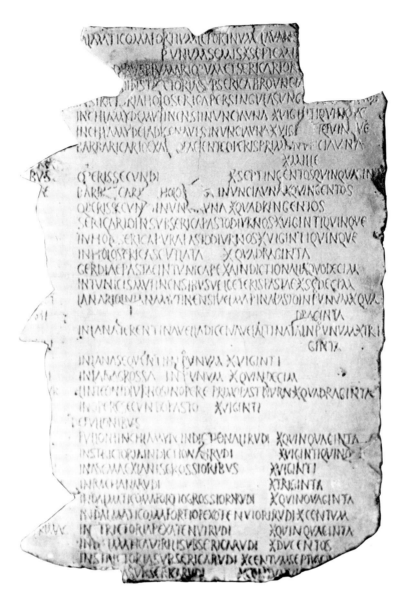

A

B

C

PRICE EDICT OF DIOCLETIAN. *A.* CAST OF SLAB FOUND IN FRAGMENTS ON SOUTH SIDE OF STREET OF THE MONUMENTS.
B–C. NEW FRAGMENTS FOUND OUTSIDE CITY BATH (INSCRIPTION 47)

PLATE LVI

VILLA. PAINTED PLINTH IN ROOM 17 (*A*) AND MOSAIC PAVING OF WEST PORTICO, NORTH END (*B*), MIDDLE (*C*), AND SOUTH END (*D*)

PLATE LVII

MOSAIC PAVING IN VILLA. A. NORTH PORTICO. B. SOUTH PORTICO. C. CALDARIUM (ROOM 1). D. ROOM 20

PLATE LVIII

A

B

C

REMAINS OF MOSAIC PANELS IN ROOM 11 OF VILLA. *A*. WEST SIDE. *B*. SOUTH SIDE. *C*. EAST SIDE

PLATE LIX

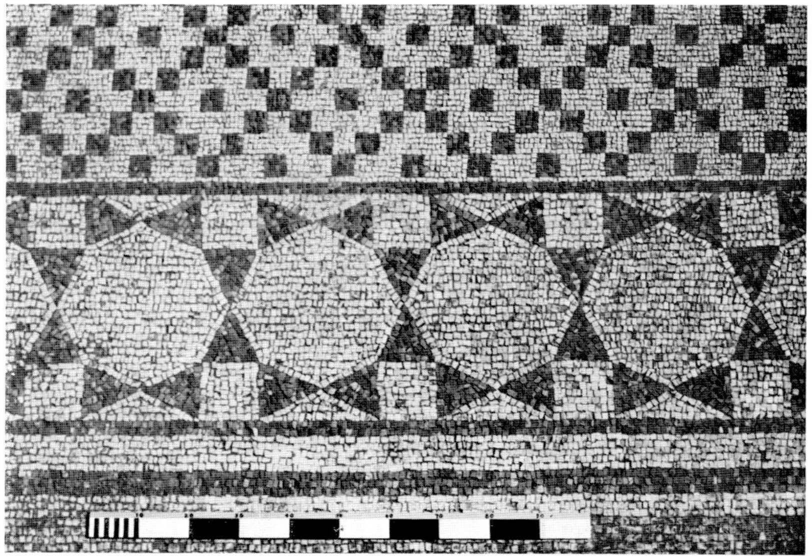

VILLA. MOSAIC BORDER (*A*) AND *OPUS SECTILE* (*B*) IN ROOM 6, FRAGMENT OF MOSAIC PANEL IN ROOM 14 (*C*), AND MOSAIC OF ROOM 12 (*D*)

PLATE LX

A

B

C

Mosaic Paving. *A*. Room 5 of Villa. *B*. Room *A* of Dwelling Adjoining Villa. *C*. Room 30 of Dwelling
Attached to Public Building

PLATE LXI

A   *B*

C   *D*

DETAILS OF MOSAIC IN ROOM 5 OF VILLA. *A*. WINTER. *B*. SPRING. *C*. SUMMER. *D*. FALL

PLATE LXII

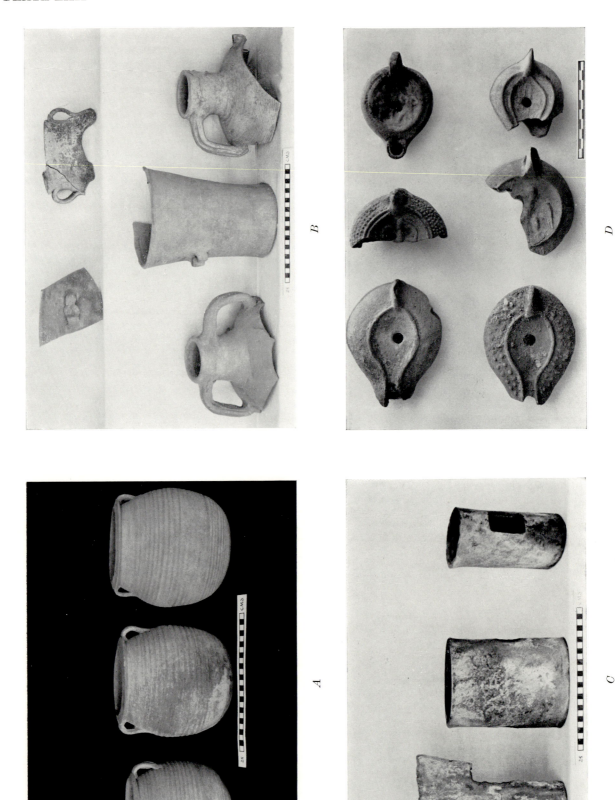

A. Byzantine Cooking Pots. B. Pottery Vessels. C. Tile Flue Sections from City Bath. D. Byzantine and Roman Lamps

PLATE LXIII

A

B

A. Hellenistic and Roman Lamps. *B*. Roman and Late Roman Lamps

PLATE LXIV

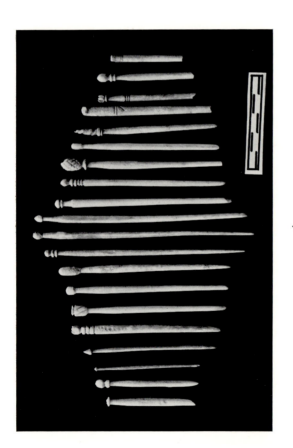

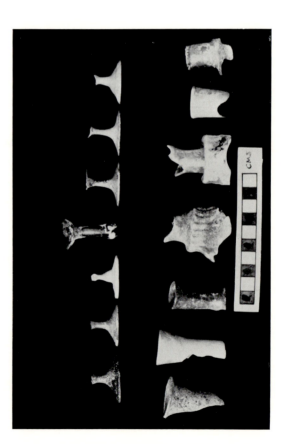

A. Bone Pins. *B.* Fragmentary Glass Vessels. *C.* Bone Plaque Fragment

PLANS

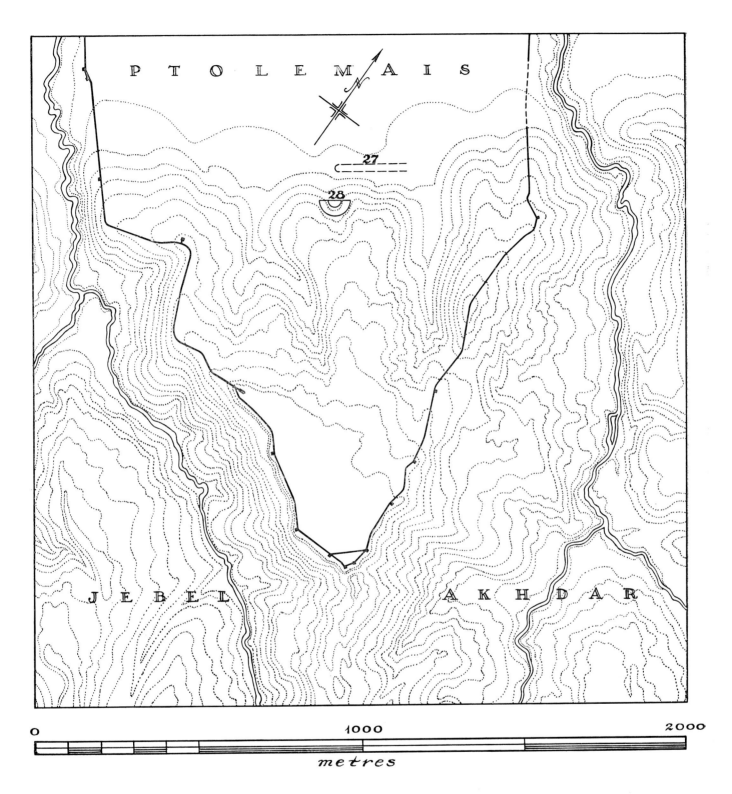

PTOLEMAIS

27

28

JEBEL AKHDAR

0   1000   2000

metres

Plan I.—City Fortifications on Jebel Akhdar

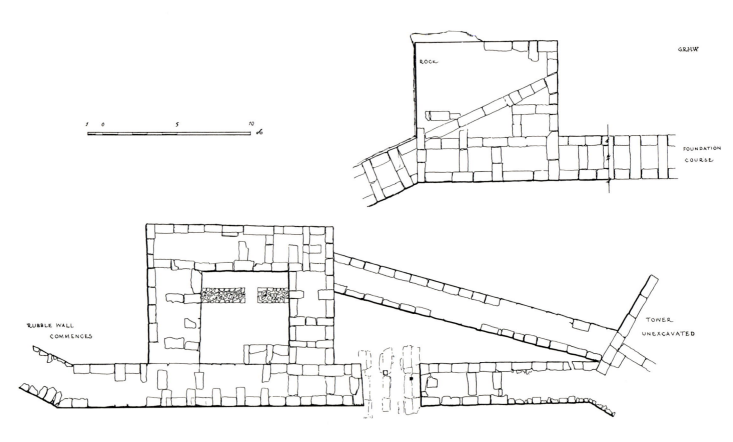

Plan II.—Barca Gate (*below*) and Tower in West City Wall

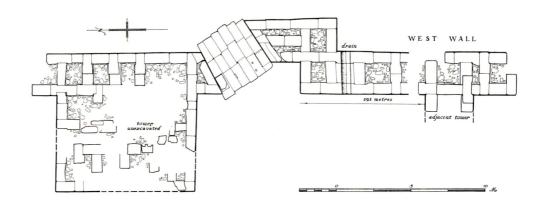

Plan III.—Quarry Gate

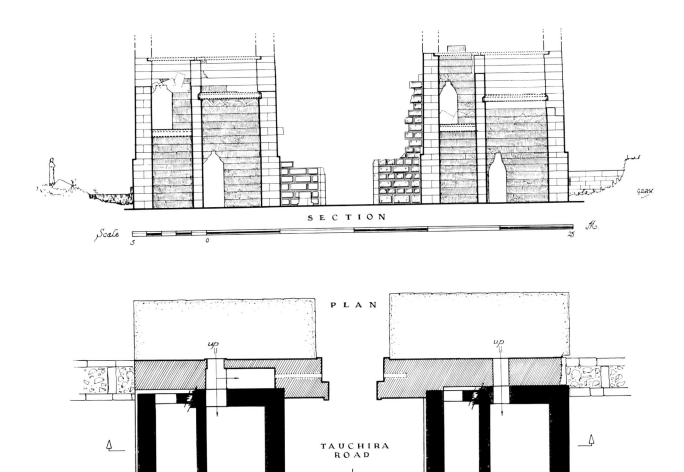

SECTION

Scale 5 0 25

PLAN

up up

TAUCHIRA ROAD

Plan IV.—Tauchira Gate

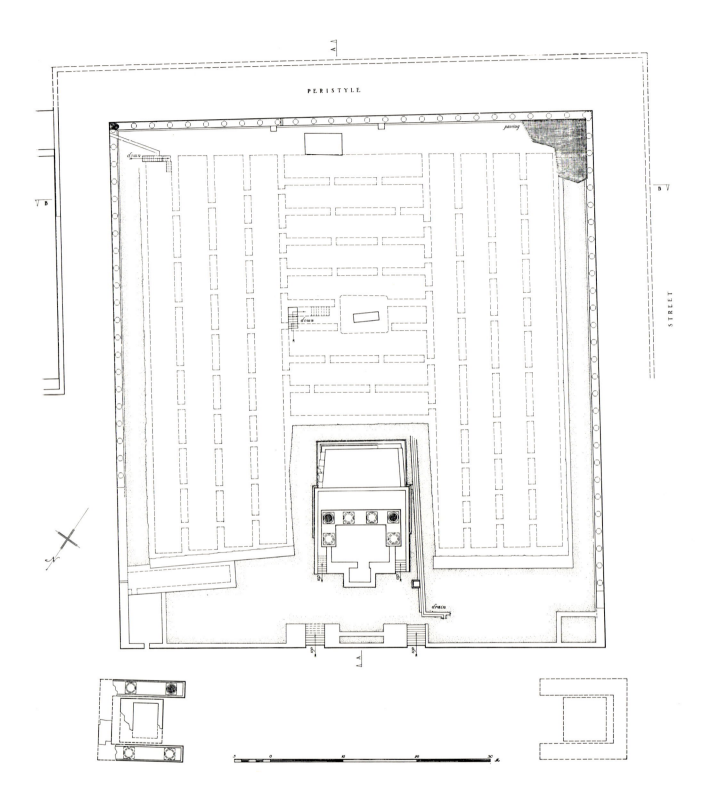

Plan V.—Square of the Cisterns

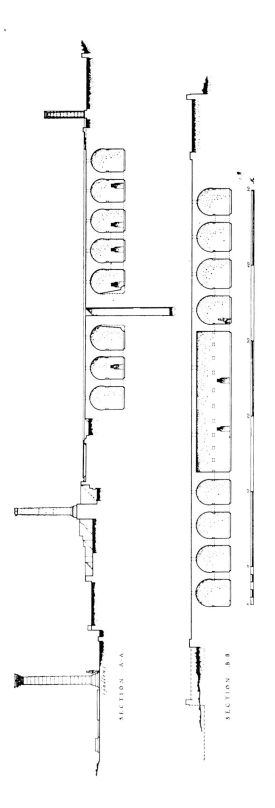

SECTION A·A

SECTION B·B

Plan VI.—Square of the Cisterns

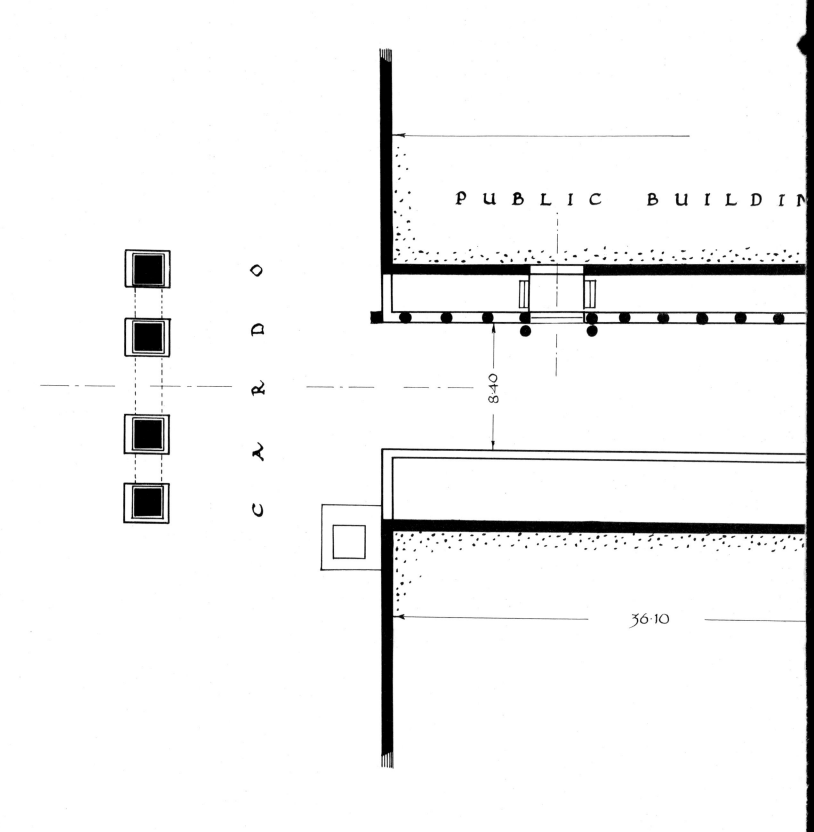

PUBLIC BUILDIN

CARDO

8·40

36·10

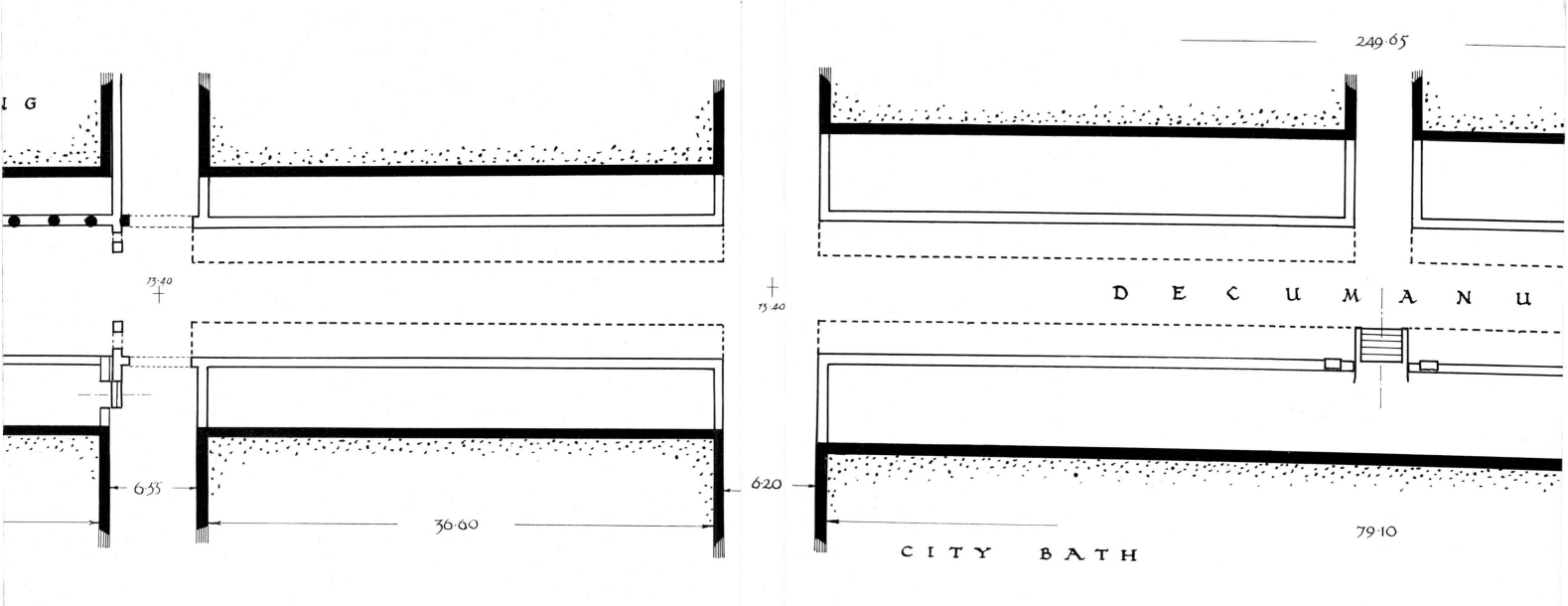

249·65

13·40

13·40

6·55

6·20

36·60

79·10

I G

D E C U M A N U

C I T Y   B A T H

Plan VII.—Street of the Monuments

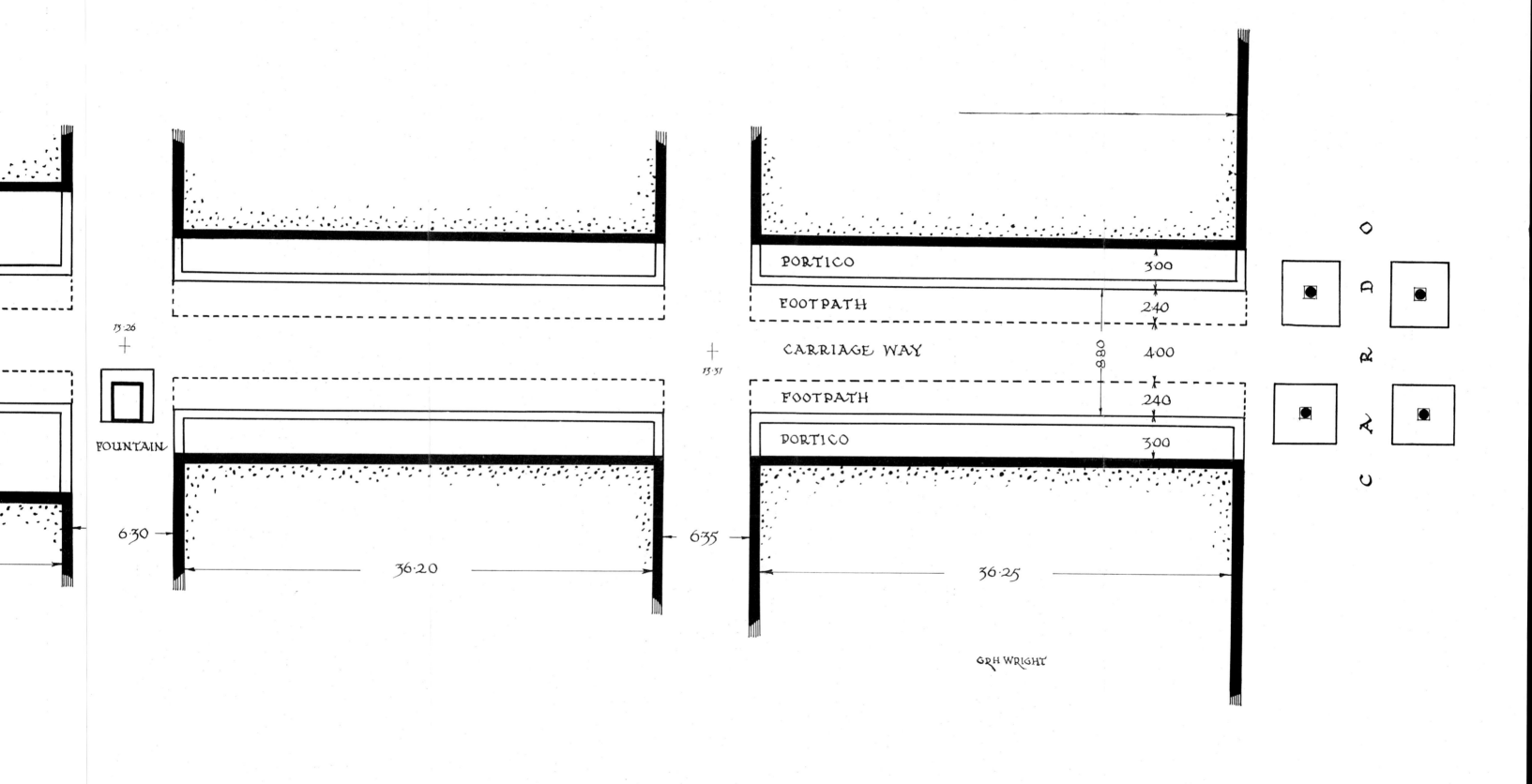

13·26

FOUNTAIN

PORTICO   3·00

FOOTPATH   2·40

CARRIAGE WAY   8·80   4·00

FOOTPATH   2·40

PORTICO   3·00

13·31

6·30   36·20   6·35   36·25

C   A   R   D   O

GRH WRIGHT

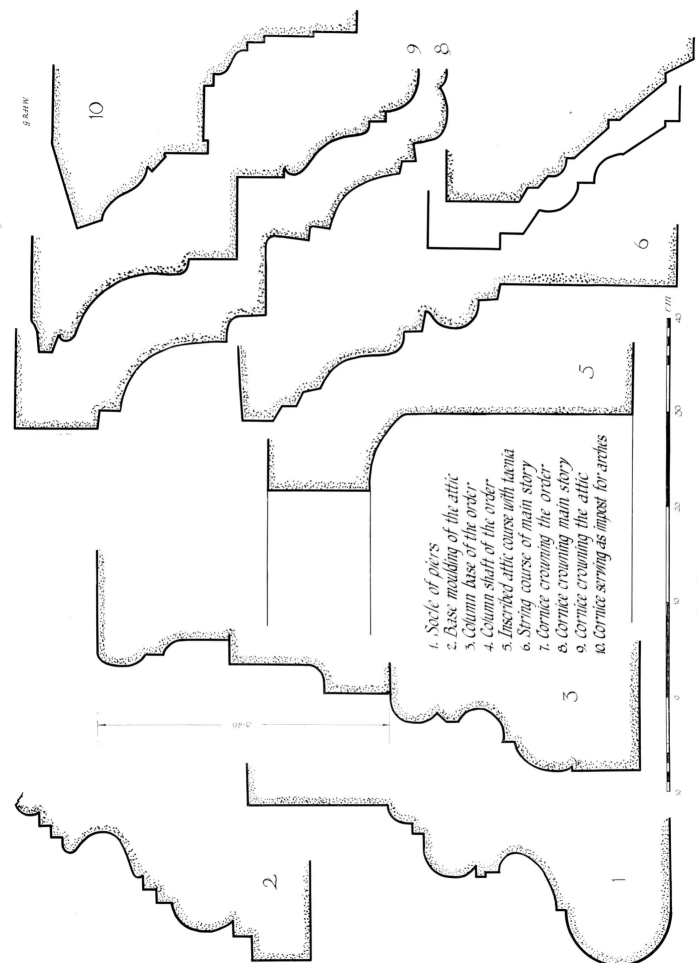

g.R.H.W.

1. Socle of piers
2. Base moulding of the attic
3. Column base of the order
4. Column shaft of the order
5. Inscribed attic course with taenia
6. String course of main story
7. Cornice crowning the order
8. Cornice crowning main story
9. Cornice crowning the attic
10. Cornice serving as impost for arches

Plan VIII.—Moldings of Triumphal Arch

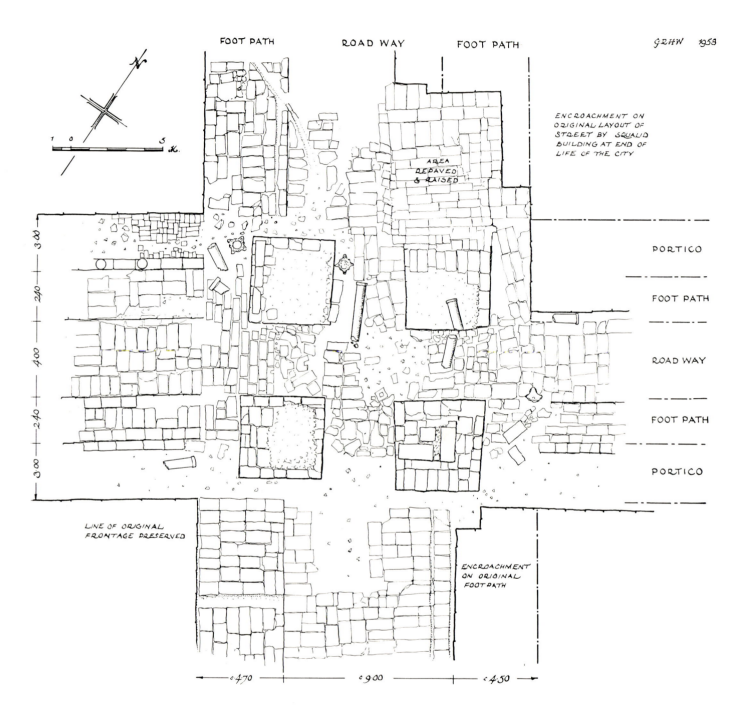

FOOT PATH   ROAD WAY   FOOT PATH   *G.R.H.W.* 1953

ENCROACHMENT ON
ORIGINAL LAYOUT OF
STREET BY SQUALID
BUILDING AT END OF
LIFE OF THE CITY

AREA
REPAVED
& RAISED

PORTICO

FOOT PATH

ROAD WAY

FOOT PATH

PORTICO

LINE OF ORIGINAL
FRONTAGE PRESERVED

ENCROACHMENT
ON ORIGINAL
FOOT PATH

c 470   c 900   c 450

Plan IX.—Tetrapylon

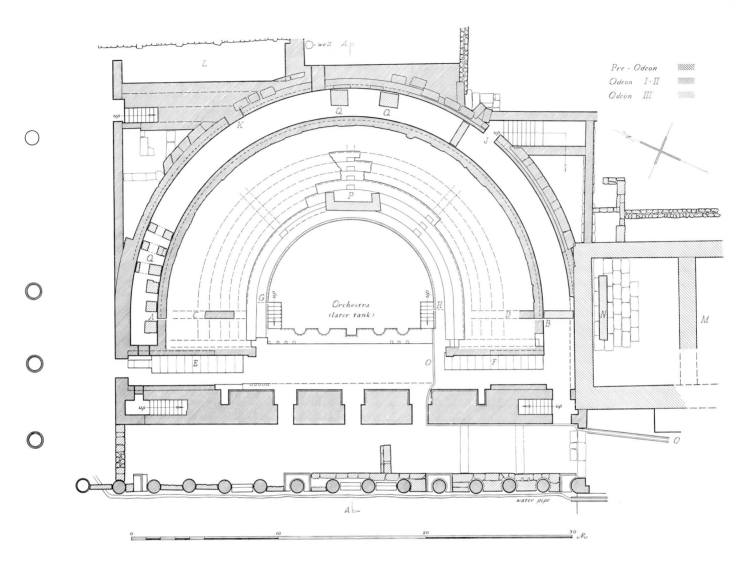

Plan X.—"Odeon"

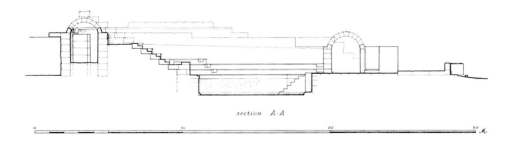

section A·A

Plan XI.—"Odeon"

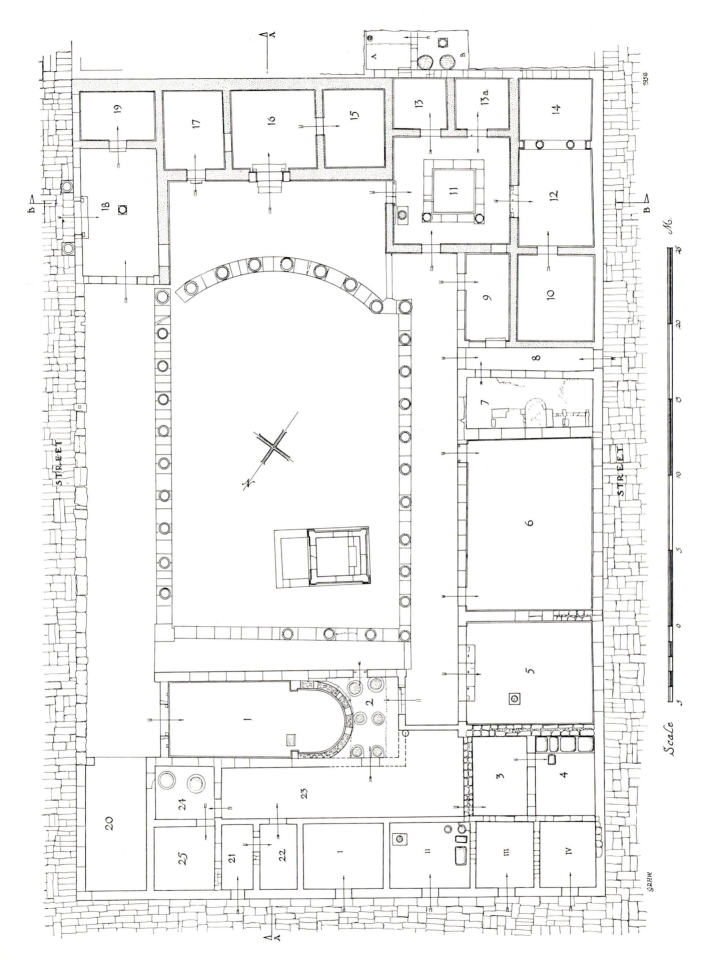

Plan XII.—VILLA OF THE ROMAN PERIOD

Scale

No.

STREET

STREET

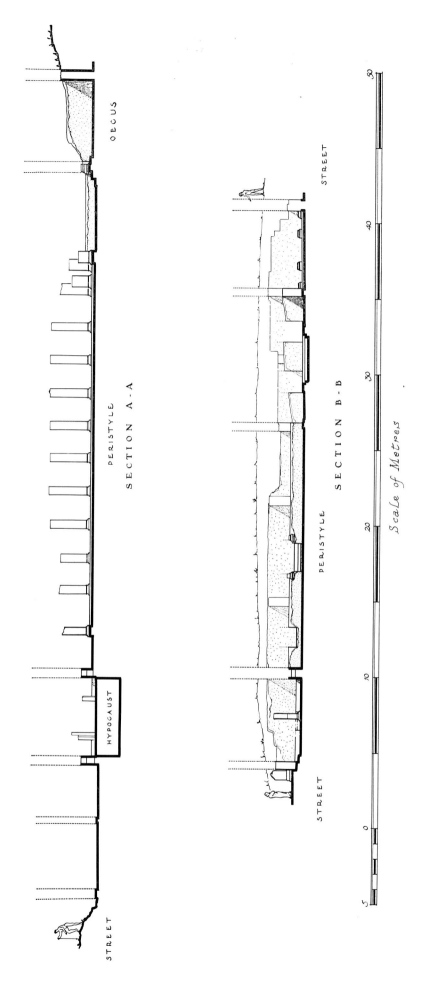

OECUS

PERISTYLE

SECTION A - A

HYPOCAUST

STREET

STREET

STREET

PERISTYLE

SECTION B - B

Scale of Metres

Plan XIII.—Villa of the Roman Period

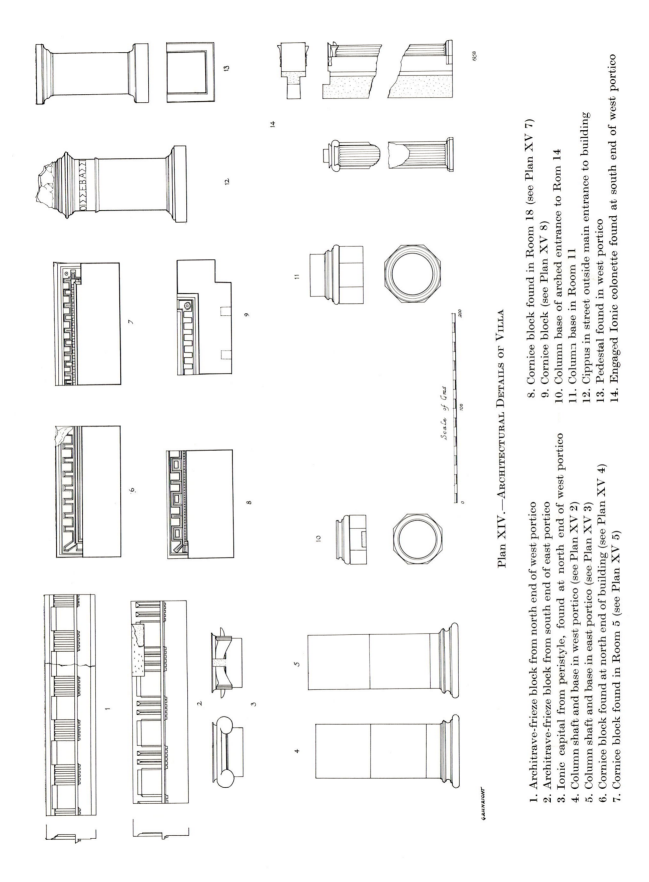

Plan XIV.—Architectural Details of Villa

1. Architrave-frieze block from north end of west portico
2. Architrave-frieze block from south end of east portico
3. Ionic capital from peristyle, found at north end of west portico
4. Column shaft and base in west portico (see Plan XV 2)
5. Column shaft and base in east portico (see Plan XV 3)
6. Cornice block found at north end of building (see Plan XV 4)
7. Cornice block found in Room 5 (see Plan XV 5)
8. Cornice block found in Room 18 (see Plan XV 7)
9. Cornice block (see Plan XV 8)
10. Column base of arched entrance to Rom 14
11. Column base in Room 11
12. Cippus in street outside main entrance to building
13. Pedestal found in west portico
14. Engaged Ionic colonette found at south end of west portico

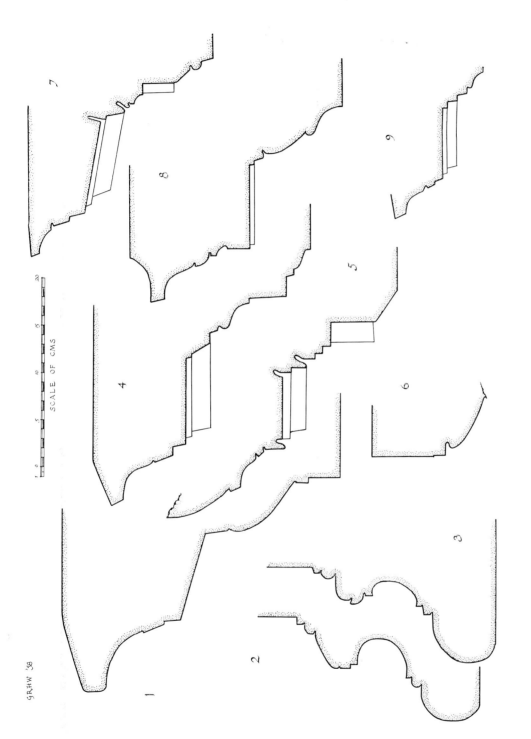

GRHW '38

SCALE OF CMS

Plan XV.—Moldings of Villa

1. Cornice block from east portico
2. Column base in west portico (see Plan XIV 4)
3. Column base in east portico (see Plan XIV 5)
4. Cornice block found at north end of building (see Plan XIV 6)
5. Cornice block found in Room 5 (see Plan XIV 7)
6. Small Doric capital
7. Cornice block found in Room 18 (see Plan XIV 8)
8. Cornice block (see Plan XIV 9)
9. Cornice fragment from ornamental archivolt, found in east portico

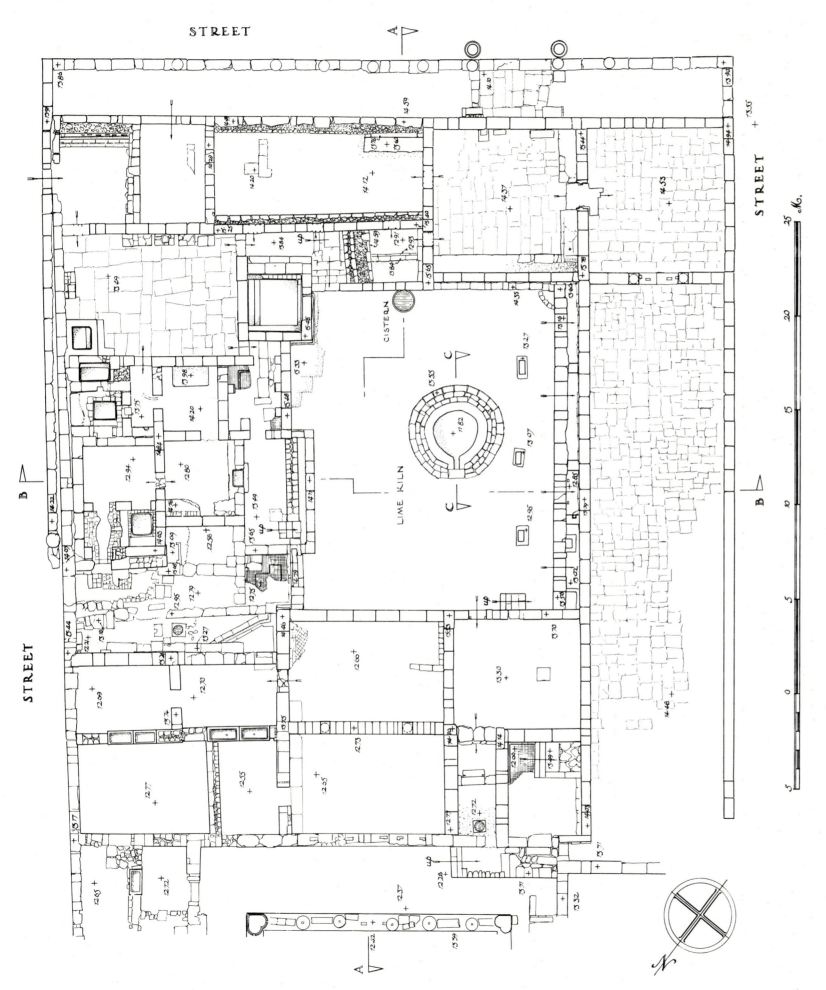

Plan XVI.—Public Building on the Street of the Monuments

STREET

STREET

STREET

CISTERN

LIME KILN

section A·A

section B·B

section C·C

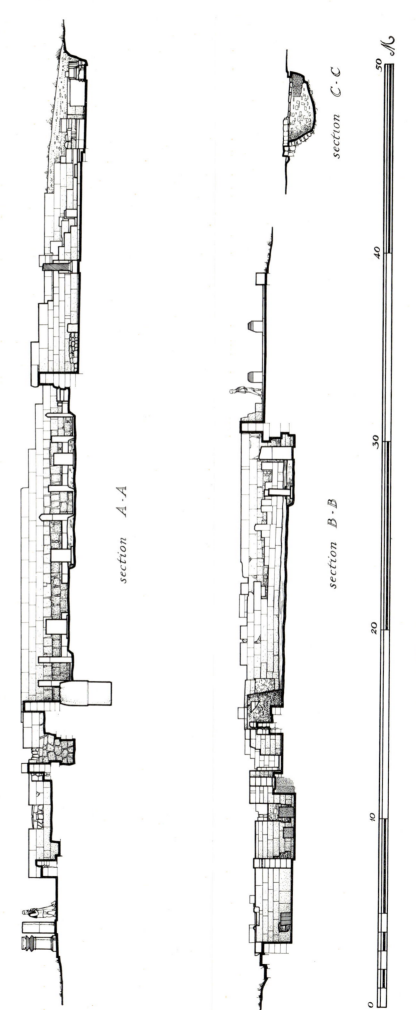

Plan XVII.—Public Building on the Street of the Monuments

Plan XVIII.—Architectural Details of Public Building

1. Engaged column from fill in Room 30
2. Fragment of small ornamental arch with false masonry scoring, from fill in Room 28
3. Doric capital from fill in Room 27 (see Plan XIX 5)
4. Large Doric capital with upper portion of fluted column shaft attached, from fill in Room 27
5. White marble pedestal with attached Ionic base, from fill in Room 3 (see Plan XIX 1)
6. Fragment of cornice block reused to block doorway between Rooms 2 and 3 (see Plan XIX 10)
7. Small Doric capital from fill in Room 26 (see Plan XIX 6)
8. Small column base with round plinth, from fill at north end of excavated area (see Plan XIX 3)
9. Small Corinthian capital from fill in Room 10
10. White marble Corinthian capital from fill in Room 19
11. Fragment of small ornamental pediment, found at south end of Room 8 at Roman level (see Plan XIX 8)
12. Cornice block of ornamental *epikranitis* with erased inscription, reused as riser in staircase at north end of Room 8 (see Plan XIX 12)
13. Angle pilaster at east end of Room 26 (see Plan XIX 2)

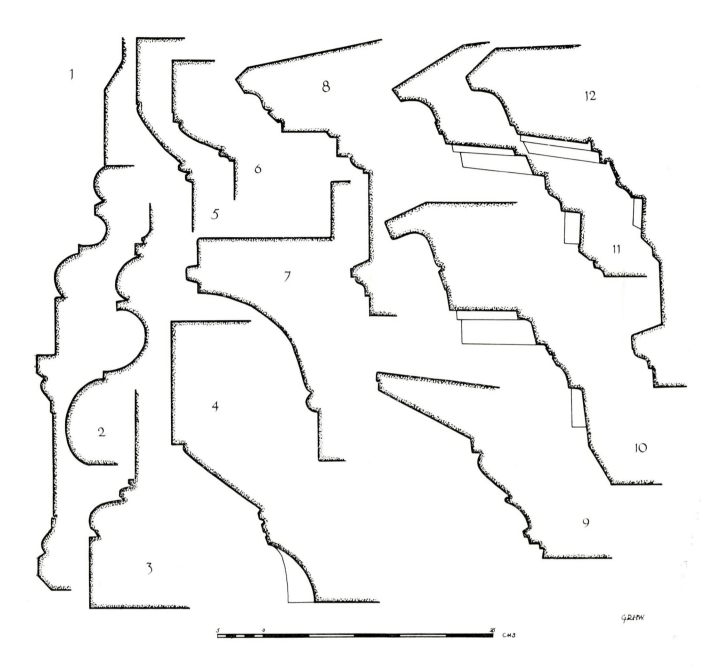

Plan XIX.—Moldings of Public Building

1. White marble pedestal with attached Ionic base (see Plan XVIII 5)
2. Angle pilaster at east end of Room 26 (see Plan XVIII 13)
3. Small column base with round plinth (see Plan XVIII 8)
4. Doric capital belonging to the order of original portico along Street of the Monuments, found in area of portico at south end of building
5. Doric capital from fill in Room 27 (see Plan XVIII 3)
6. Small Doric capital from fill in Room 26 (see Plan XVIII 7)
7. Terminal cornice block from fill at north end of Room 8
8. Fragment of small ornamental pediment (see Plan XVIII 11)
9. Fragment of cornice block from fill at north end of Room 8
10. Fragment of cornice block reused to block doorway between Rooms 2 and 3 (see Plan XVIII 6)
11. One of two cornice blocks with drill incisions, reused as risers in staircase at north end of Room 8
12. Cornice block of ornamental *epikranitis* (see Plan XVIII 12)

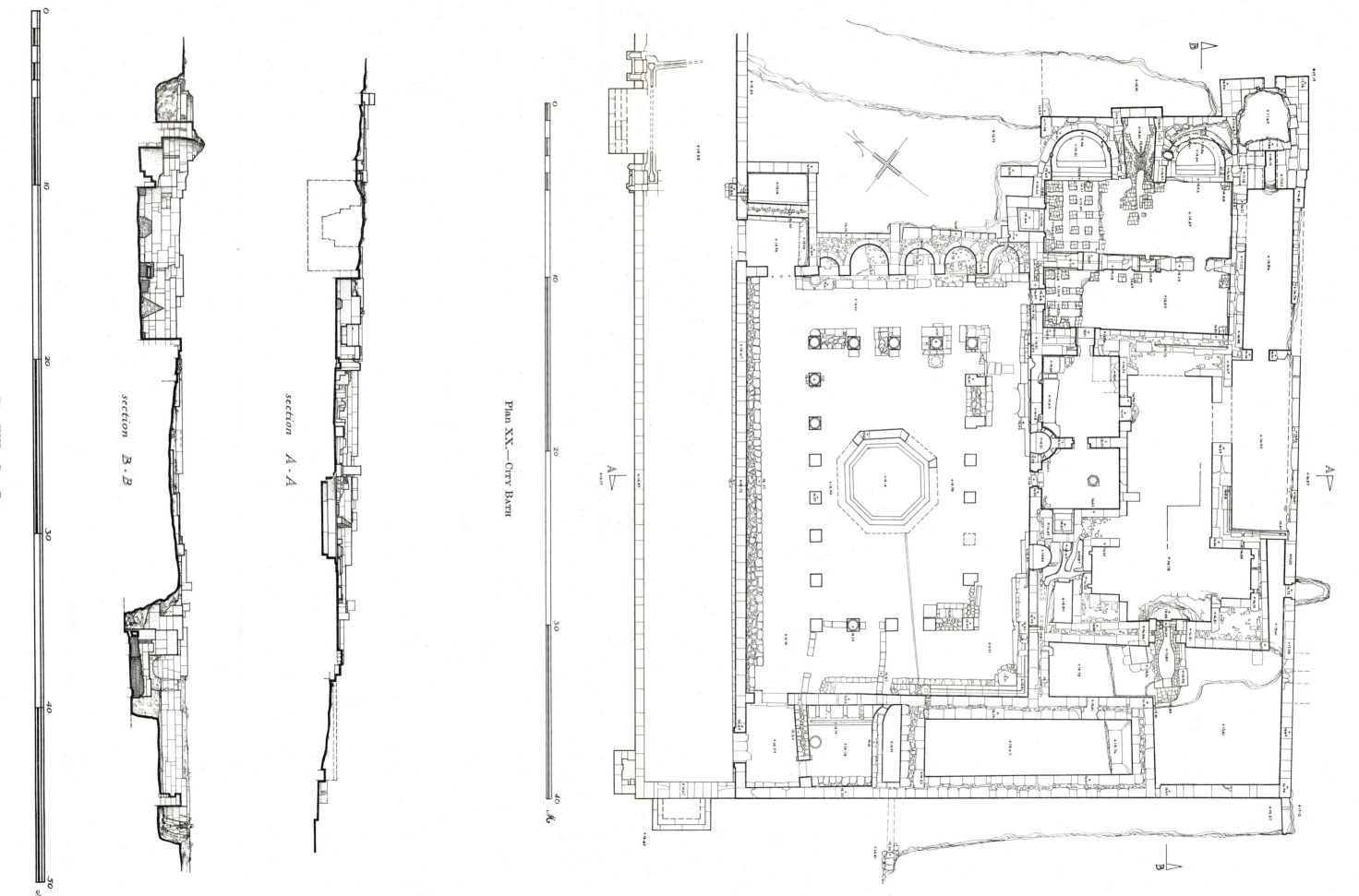

Plan XXI.—CITY BATH

section B·B

section A·A

Plan XX.—CITY BATH